SECOND EDITION

DRUGS
in society

CAUSES, CONCEPTS
AND CONTROL

Michael D. Lyman
Columbia College

Gary W. Potter
Eastern Kentucky University

 anderson publishing co.
p.o. box 1576
cincinnati, oh 45201-1576
(513) 421-4142

Drugs in Society: Causes, Concepts and Control, Second Edition

ISBN 0-87084-523-3
Library of Congress Catalog Number 95-76765

 The text of this book is printed on recycled paper.

Cover design by Edward Smith Design, Inc.   *Managing Editor* Kelly Grondin

Preface

In February 1995 President Clinton asked Congress for a record $13.2 billion to fight the drug war for the following year. Included in his request was a considerable increase in funds for national treatment initiatives. As Democrats hailed Clinton's anti-drug efforts, Republicans protested that today's war on drugs has all but faded into political obscurity. Although discussion about the nation's drug problem has waned considerably since the Clinton Administration took over the war on drugs in 1992, the problem of drug abuse has persisted. Despite widespread enforcement, interdiction, prevention, and treatment initiatives, it continues to flourish in each city, community, and neighborhood across the country. The extent of the problem has accelerated to the point that most of us now know someone or know of someone who is affected by substance abuse.

Of the many lessons to learn from studying America's drug problem is that change is an inevitable part of the drug abuse crisis. We cannot develop a sound drug control policy unless we first become students of history. Things are different today than they were in the mid-1980s when crack cocaine first appeared on the nation's drug scene. Things were different then than they were 10, 20, and even 50 years before that. Not only do the drugs of abuse themselves change, but patterns and trends of drug abuse also shift from one decade to the next. In addition, attitudes about drugs (both pro and con) often take on a different complexion from one decade to the next. Furthermore, people who traffic drugs are also keenly aware of the element of change in the drug business. When factors such as competition from rival criminal groups or effective law enforcement measures place pressures on criminal trafficking organizations, their methods of manufacturing, transportation, and marketing must also be modified. Many of today's drug trafficking organizations have become extremely resourceful in adjusting to political, economic, and social changes in the drug trade.

Indeed, domestic political agendas greatly affect the manner in which our government and society deal with the drug problem, and clearly such changes vary from one administration to another. One of the ironies of the drug problem is that, for the most part, people want the same things: safe neighborhoods and highways, drug-free workplaces, addiction-free babies, and so forth. It's just that individual politics and values often dictate different ways of achieving these goals. Political agendas affect the philosophies of dealing with both drug abuse and drug offenders, which in turn dictate which resources and how many resources will be made available to deal with the nation's drug problem. So with all of these variables at work, it is little wonder why finding a resolution to America's drug problem is so difficult. This brings us to the purpose of this book. *Drugs in Society: Causes, Concepts, and Control,* Second Edition deals with the three most pivotal areas of today's drug problem: drug abuse, drug trafficking and drug control policy. We should acknowledge that the preparation of any book is a considerable undertaking and this one is no exception. Furthermore, any text dealing with drug abuse necessitates periodic updating because drug abuse is a diverse subject that encompasses numerous disciplines such as sociology, politics, medicine, psychology, criminal justice, public policy, and law. Many social, political and public policy changes have set the stage for this text and this is precisely the premise for this second edition—change. It is a book about drugs, addictions, dealers, corrupt officials, the narcs, the courts, personal and public values, public policy, the laws, and the rising numbers of ruined communities and families throughout the country. Put simply, it is designed to give the reader insight into formulating possible solutions to America's drug dilemma.

Drug abuse is a sensitive public issue. Discussions typically generate the political volatility of other heated social issues such as abortion, gun control, and capital punishment. It is therefore one of our primary goals to address this subject in a realistic fashion with objective consideration given to both liberal and conservative social perspectives. The book, designed to offer a logical flow of information, is organized in three parts: Understanding the Problem, Gangs and Drugs and Fighting Back. Each contains chapters that focus on the many critical areas of America's drug problem and give the reader a foundation for critical thinking and rational decisionmaking within this complex, multidisciplinary field.

We would like to extend a sincere "thank you" to the many individuals who assisted in the preparation of this project. Specifically, thanks is most deserved to the many friends and associates in the drug enforcement profession, our colleagues in criminal justice and higher education, and the always helpful people at the National Institute of Justice, the National Center for Drugs and Crime Control, the Drug Enforcement Administration, and the Bureau of Justice Statistics. A special thanks is well deserved for Jenn Cover of Columbia College for assisting in research for the book, and Carolyn Goodman of East Mississippi Community College for her able editorial services and feedback. Special gratitude is also extended to Rita Walther, who provided many of the graphic illustrations used in this book. Finally, we would like to thank the good people at Anderson Publishing and their capable management and production staff. Their belief in our work helped to make the second edition of this book a reality.

Michael D. Lyman   Gary W. Potter
Columbia College   Eastern Kentucky University

Contents

Preface   iii
Introduction   xi

Part I
Understanding the Problem   **1**

Chapter 1
The History of Drug Abuse   **3**

History Repeats Itself   4
The Opium Menace of the 1800s   6
Late Nineteenth-Century Developments   7
The Twentieth Century   10
The Prohibition Era   13
Post-Prohibition Drug Abuse   15
The Postwar Era   20
The Turbulent 1960s   21
Late Twentieth-Century Developments   23
Looking Ahead   27
Summary   28

Chapter 2
Understanding Drugs of Abuse   **31**

Defining Drugs   31
Drugs and the Brain   32
Outcomes of Drug Abuse   33
Dependence versus Abuse   34
Drug Categories   35
Stimulants   35
Depressants   46
Hallucinogens   51
Narcotics   56
Cannabis   59
Inhalants   63
Summary   63

Chapter 3
The Nature of the Drug Problem   **65**

Consequences of Drug Abuse   66
Attitudes About Drugs   71
Why Do People Get High?   72
Drug Abuse Forums   74
Measuring Drug Abuse   77
Who Are the Drug Users?   78
Geographical Differences   79
Drug Abuse Trends   79
The Social Costs of Drug Abuse   80
Drug Consumerism   85
Theories of Drug Abuse and Crime   86
Summary   90

Chapter 4
The Illicit Drug Trade   **93**

The Business of Illegal Drugs   94
The Economics of Drug Trafficking   95
Merchandising and Distribution of Illegal Drugs   98
The International Perspective   103
Mexico   103
Colombia   108
Bolivia   113
Peru   115
Trafficking Trends in South America   117
Jamaica   119
The Golden Triangle   125
The Golden Crescent   130
Hong Kong   135
Summary   136

Chapter 5
Domestic Drug Production   **139**

The Pharmaceutical Drug Industry   140
Domestic Marijuana Cultivation   145
Clandestine Laboratories   151
Controlling Precursor Chemicals   155
Pharmaceutical Diversion   155
Summary   163

Chapter 6
Drugs and Crime   **167**

Drug Use and Predatory Crime   168
Police Corruption   171
Corruption in Foreign Countries   181
Money Laundering   186
Summary   199

Part II
Gangs And Drugs 201

Chapter 7
Organized Crime and the Drug Trade 203

The Nature of Drug Trafficking 204
Defining "Organized Crime" 206
The Alien Conspiracy Theory 209
The Mafia 210
Drug Gangs as Organized Crime 211
Summary 213

Chapter 8
Domestic Drug Trafficking Organizations 219

Traditional Organized Crime: The Mafia 219
Outlaw Motorcycle Gangs 230
Youth Gangs 239
Jamaican Posses 245
Prison Gangs 248
Ancillary Trafficking Organizations 253
Summary 254

Chapter 9
Foreign Drug Trafficking Organizations 257

Colombian Organized Crime 258
The Legacy of Medellin's Cartel 260
The Cali Cartel 270
The Bogota Cartel 274
The North Atlantic Coast Cartel 274
Mexican Drug Traffickers 275
Narco-terrorism 277
Cuban Drug Traffickers 287
Asian Organized Crime 288
Summary 291

Part III
Fighting Back 293

Chapter 10
The Drug Control Initiative 295

The Goals of Drug Control 296
Drug Laws 296
The History of Federal Drug Enforcement 298
Drug Interdiction 302
Coordination Organizations 312
Cannabis Eradication 320
Investigating Illicit Laboratories 320

Strategies for Street-Level Enforcement   321
Police-Community Drug Control Efforts   324
Summary   332

Chapter 11
Critical Issues in Drug Control   **335**

Drug Lord Abductions   336
Drug Courier Profiling   337
The Reverse Drug Sting   339
Zero Tolerance   341
Mandatory Minimum Sentencing   342
Electronic Surveillance   343
Drug Testing   345
Needle Exchange Programs   351
Forfeiture of Attorney's Fees   353
Drug Control and Sports   355
Other Public Policy Issues   358
Summary   362

Chapter 12
The Issue of Legalizing Drugs   **365**

The Pros: Arguments for Legalization   368
The Cons: Arguments against Legalization   374
Drugs in Amsterdam: The "Dutch Way"   381
The British Experiment   383
The Alaskan "Pot" Legalization Experience   384
A Proposed Solution   387
A Word from the Authors   389

Chapter 13
Understanding Drug Control Policy   **393**

Shared Responsibility   395
Development of Federal Drug Control Efforts   396
Policy-Related Factors   397
Private Sector Responses   397
The Role of the Military   398
Development of American Drug Policy   398
Strategies in National Drug Control   401
Drug Control in the Reagan-Bush Era   402
Drug Control and the Clinton Administration   406
Prohibition Then and Now   408
Legal Tools in Drug Control   410
The Witness Security Program   417
Summary   418

Chapter 14
Control through Treatment and Prevention   **421**

Understanding the Drug User   422
The Rise in Addiction   424
Treatment Programs   425
The Psychological Approach   429
Group Treatment   429
Does Drug Treatment Work?   433
Social Reintegration   434
The Cost of Drug Treatment   436
Drug Prevention   436
Project DARE   437
Project SPECDA   443
Summary   445

References   **447**

Index   **459**

Introduction

For many Americans, the drug problem is an abstract one involving other people and occurring somewhere else: heroin and crack are abused by the poor in outlying ghettos; cocaine and pharmaceuticals are used by the very rich; other drugs are consumed by fast-trackers in the entertainment industry. Even drug busts on local television feature characters from neighborhoods on the far side of town—certainly not where we live. However, as responsible people living in a modern society, we can no longer adopt an out-of-sight, out-of-mind mentality with regard to drug abuse. We must begin by being honest with ourselves about the realities of drug abuse. For example, most of us are too well acquainted with the most abused drug in the country: alcohol. Statistics show that the fatal consequences of alcohol abuse outweigh those associated with any other drug. In addition, the scores of people involved with the illicit drug trade, from members of organized crime groups to casual dealers, have little respect for our laws, legitimate forms of commerce, or a safe and prosperous society.

As the drug industry begins to command more loyalty from some parts of our population than does the Constitution, our own civil government and the principles of a truly free society slowly erode. Already in some South American countries the drug industry has, practically speaking, replaced civil government. In 1989, drug lords in Colombia, South America, retaliated against that government's drug crackdown by facilitating more than 50 bombings throughout the country. One such bombing resulted in the killing of 52 innocent people at the secret police headquarters in Colombia. Earlier that year traffickers claimed responsibility for the bombing of a Colombian airliner, tragically killing 107 people. Today, more than half a decade later, the drugs and violence there continue. *Drugs In Society: Causes, Concepts, and Control,* Second Edition addresses these and many other important issues associated with drug abuse in the United States.

Perhaps accepting the problem—that is, not assuming it is someone else's problem—is the first step in readying any workable solutions. This is the primary concern of Part I: Understanding the Problem. This section addresses the history of drug use and the development of drug control policy, drug pharmacology, theories of drug abuse, and the role of source countries in drug trafficking. Part I also focuses on drug-related crimes which support the illicit drug industry and are at the core of many senseless acts of violence in hundreds of neighborhoods around the country.

Organized gangs bankrolled by the lucrative drug trade are not only rooted in major U.S. cities but are now expanding to communities of all sizes. Not only are traditional organized crime groups like the Mafia involved in drug trafficking, but non-traditional youth gangs such as the violent Crips and the Bloods (which are imitated by other youth gangs on a more modest level) have also become reliant on the drug trade for fast money.

In many cities Jamaican posses strive for control of neighborhood sales of crack cocaine and use violence to maintain that control. Outlaw motorcycle gangs such as the Hell's Angels have long since added the drug trade to other criminal endeavors. These organizations and others are the focus of Part II of this book—Gangs and Drugs—which addresses the problem of organized crime involvement in the drug trade.

As Americans accept the reality of drug abuse, we are faced with many questions: How have things gotten so out of hand? What do we do now? Do solutions to the problem lie in the area of public health, culture, sociology, education, or criminal justice? While each of these areas offers some explanations, Part III: Fighting Back, considers what is being done and what can be done to best deal with the problem. In doing so, its chapters discuss the role of federal drug enforcement organizations, drug laws, and local drug enforcement initiatives. Additionally, critical issues such as drug courier profiles, covert police initiatives, needle exchange programs, drug testing in the workplace, legalizing drugs, and drug abuse in sports are all examined.

As an aid to our readers, we have prepared numerous critical thinking questions which are offered throughout each chapter. These are designed to stimulate thought and discussion about some of the more important dynamics of our national drug abuse problem. We have also endeavored to provide reading objectives at the beginning of each chapter along with important terms at each chapter's conclusion. All of these features are created to aid the student of drug abuse with the means to not only understand the problem but also to formulate realistic public policy solutions.

Today, drugs in our society perpetuate a myriad of social problems. They threaten our standard of living and the quality of our neighborhoods, ruin lives of drug users and scores of innocent people around them, and create a drain of precious public resources which could be put to work elsewhere. Society has responded by passing criminal and civil laws as well as implementing myriad social programs, each designed to deal with some aspect of the nation's drug abuse problem. Some of these initiatives have proven more successful than others, but limited as any initiative is, we can only hope that we can rise as a nation to meet the challenge.

Part I

Understanding the Problem

One of the assumptions of this book is that an educated society is better prepared to respond to the problem of drug abuse than one that is ill-informed. To that end, the first six chapters are designed to give the reader the essentials regarding the nation's drug abuse crisis. To begin, we offer an overview about how drugs of abuse emerged in modern society and what circumstances led to the gradual social control of them. Next, we discuss the social and health consequences of these drugs, followed by an in-depth review of the drugs most commonly abused in our schools and neighborhoods. We then offer an overview of the international and domestic drug trafficking problem, providing an understanding of the origins of illicit drugs. Finally, drug-related crime is discussed in the context of predatory, political, and white collar criminal behavior related to the drug trade. Each of these areas will prepare the reader for a discussion of organized criminal activity in the illicit drug trade, discussed in Part II.

The History of Drug Abuse

1

This chapter will enable you to:

- Understand the beginnings of the world's drug abuse problem.

- Realize the many social implications of drug abuse.

- Compare developments in drug control legislation during recent decades.

- Appreciate the development of our nation's national drug control policy.

Public perception of drugs and drug abuse has shifted dramatically over the past 200 years. Twice, Americans have accepted and then rejected drugs in our society. Understanding these striking historical swings, however, helps us understand our current reactions to drug use. America's recurrent enthusiasm for recreational drugs and the resulting campaigns for abstinence present resounding problems for public policy makers as well as for the public they serve. Because the peaks of these episodes are about a generation apart, citizens rarely have an accurate picture (much less recollection) of the latest wave of drug abuse. Criminologist David Musto suggests that fear and anger have been the primary causes of society's intolerance for drugs, and such emotions have distorted public memory so grotesquely that it becomes useless as a point of reference for policy formation (1991). The lack of knowledge concerning our earlier encounters with drugs impedes the task of establishing a workable public policy toward dealing with the problem.

Because of the notoriety of drug abuse during the 1960s, many people assume that this decade was most responsible for our nation's current drug problem. Indeed, as we will see, the 1960s played a significant role in the development and propagation of certain drugs of abuse, but the roots of the problem go back much further in history. In this chapter we have endeavored to condense the vast history of global drug abuse in an effort to understand both its earliest beginnings and its current role in modern society.

History Repeats Itself

Mankind's drug abuse legacy began thousands of years ago in such diverse areas as China, Egypt, India, the Middle East, and the Americas, where cannabis, ephedra, and opium were used for medicinal purposes and as general health tonics. In many cases, the medicinal use of these plants turned to recreational use, creating a pattern of use to abuse that has continued to the present. Seven thousand years ago the Sumerians left records of a "joy plant," presumably the highly addictive opium poppy (papaver somniferum). The euphoric effects of medicinal use of the plant led to recreational abuse of opium in Sumerian society.

The Chinese discovered alkaloid ephedrine (Ephedra sinica), an inhalant, as far back as 3000 B.C. and marijuana (cannabis sativa) by 2000 B.C. Chinese emperors in the third millennium B.C. ate or brewed cannabis in tea. Later on, the custom of drying and smoking cannabis was imported from India. Within a few centuries, alcohol abuse in Babylonia was significant enough to inspire legal controls. In 1700 B.C., the Code of Hammurabi included censure of public intoxication. Likewise, opium abuse in ancient Egypt increased to such an extent that by 1500 B.C. Egyptian scriptures had censured the practice. Again, opium use, which had medicinal origins as a pain reliever in surgery, had become opium abuse.

In South America, the Incas chewed the coca leaf, the plant from which cocaine is derived. By 1000 B.C., the Incas believed that the coca leaf (Erthroxylon coca) aided in the digestion of food and the suppression of their appetites. So highly valued was the coca leaf that it was used instead of gold or silver to barter for food and clothing. Coca chewing is even reflected in the art of that period. For example, a ceramic statue now housed in a museum in Ecuador portrays an Indian with the characteristic chewer's bulge in the cheek.

Greek literature in the first millennium B.C. records an awareness of both opium and alcohol. The hero of Homer's epic tale *The Odyssey* forbids his sailors from eating the lotus flowers when visiting the African land of the Lotus eaters. This imaginative tale about the lotus-eating dreamers suggests Homer's familiarity with opium use among North African cultures. Later, in 400 B.C., Hippocrates, the father of modern medicine for whom the Hippocratic Oath is named, recommended drinking the juice of the white poppy mixed with the seed of nettle. Yet another myth deals with Dionysus, god of wine, and drunkenness. Under the influence of alcohol, the followers of Dionysus ran amok, killing people and destroying property. So, while wine festivals were an important part of Greek culture, they were surrounded by legend which inspired laws that restricted the excessive use of alcohol.

In still another early culture, hallucinogens were commonly used. Around 100 B.C., the Aztec Indians of North America used dried peyote cactus buttons in religious ceremonies. Tribesmen believed that they would get closer to the gods and nature if they consumed this magical plant. Magic mushrooms (psilocybin) and morning glory seeds (ololiuqui) were other organic hallucinogens commonly used by the Indians.

Ancient cultures all around the world established customs of drug use quite independently. However, with improved ships, more extensive sea travel, and political and military expansion, one culture began to influence another. For instance, the Roman conquest of the eastern Mediterranean in the first century A.D. contributed to the spread of opium use. Whether the drugs were imported or indigenous to a culture, drug use continued to flourish.

Drug use was so established in India, both for recreational and commercial purposes, that the Susruta treatise of 400 A.D. catalogued with unprecedented detail various types of cannabis preferred by the Indians. For example, bhang, a strain generally considered weak in strength, was brewed into tea. Ganja, a more potent type of cannabis, was usually smoked. The high-grade charas, similar to hashish or sinsemilla, was commonly eaten by affluent Indians. Four hundred years later in the ninth century, Arab traders introduced opium to China. Within a few more centuries, opium smoking in China ("chasing the dragon") would become a major public health threat.

Drugs even entered military rituals in several parts of the world. Some eleventh-century Persian warriors smoked hashish to prepare for battle and for their fate as martyrs. Al-Hassan-ibn-al Sabbah (The Old Man of the Mountains) led such a band of Shiite Moslem warriors. Indeed, the word *assassin*, which later evolved through European use to mean the murderer of a political figure, comes from Hassan's name. On the other side of the world, Incan warriors commonly chewed coca leaves. Some historians partially attribute Pizarro's defeat of the Incan empire in 1532 to the fact that many Incan warriors were so inebriated that they were mentally and physically unable to fight.

As we also discuss in Chapter 2, in North America, Native American Indians have a long tradition of smoking tobacco, a custom which was eventually introduced to European sailors. Magellan took tobacco to parts of Africa while the Portuguese carried it to Polynesia. In the 1600s, Sir Walter Raleigh introduced pipe smoking to England. Jacques Nicot, who first took tobacco to France, claimed that tobacco had great medicinal properties. In fact, the stimulant that is the most dangerous chemical in tobacco, nicotine, is named after him. The popularity of tobacco spread so rapidly in many Asian and European countries that some governments began to censure it. Japan, for example, prohibited smoking in the mid-1650s, and at about the same time, in parts of Europe, smoking tobacco was punished by disfigurement or death.

The age of exploration contributed greatly to the spread of culture, colonialism, commerce—and drugs. Whether mildly stimulating or dangerously addictive, drugs and the drug trade flourished. Explorers introduced some African cultures to tobacco and borrowed other drugs from them. In 1621, the Ethiopian coffee bean was introduced in England, and by the 1650s, coffee houses were well established in London and elsewhere.

Figure 1.1

The History of Heroin

1874 Heroin is isolated from morphine.

1898 The Bayer Company of Germany commercially produces heroin, which is later found to be more potent than morphine.

1900 Heroin is determined to be highly addictive even though it was originally believed to be a cure for opium addiction.

1914 The Harrison Narcotics Act is passed, which restricts the manufacture, importation, and distribution of heroin.

1924 Heroin becomes readily available on the black market, as its manufacture is prohibited.

1930 The French Connection becomes the primary international supplier of heroin to the United States.

1964 The controversial methadone maintenance program is launched to treat opiate addicts.

1970 Heroin is classified as a Schedule I Narcotic by the Controlled Substances Act.

1985 U.S. government estimates that there are 500,000 to 750,000 heroin addicts in the United States.

1994 Heroin use and purity on the increase.

The Opium Menace of the 1800s

As we stated earlier, opium addiction had established itself as a major health threat in China. During the 1800s, the Manchu dynasty tried to restrict opium use through legislation focusing on trade. The main target of such legislation was the East India Company of Great Britain, which supplied China with opium from India, then a colony of the British Empire. In fact, the British forced their colonial subjects into a widespread system of opium production that gave the British a virtual monopoly on the opium trade. Today's opium cultivators in Southeast and Southwest Asia are the descendants of farmers that were forced to participate in the British opium trade. Despite legal controls, the opium problem in China became so great that hostilities broke out between Great Britain and China.

In the early 1800s, the Manchu government passed a standing order for its army to detain and search any British vessel suspected of carrying opium. This led to the first of two great **opium wars** between China and Britain (1839-1842). The first war resulted in the defeat of China. The victorious British quickly claimed that opium consumption was harmless, encouraged its use, and reaped the profits from its trade. Chinese officials continued their objections, and a second war (1856-1860) broke out. In this second opium war, also called the Anglo-French War, a joint offensive by Britain and France resulted in the second defeat of China. Presumably, profit from the opium trade was more important than the welfare of the Chinese people to those warring countries (France, Britain, Russia, and the United States) that imposed the Tientsin Treaty (1858) on China. China at first refused to ratify the treaty, but by 1860 the defeated nation was forced to agree to key provisions: the legalization of opium and the opening of eleven more ports to western ships.

Opium use had naturally spread to Britain and continental Europe where decades earlier the Romantic poet Coleridge had fought addiction to opium. Aiding in the perpetuation of the English addiction cycle was the manufacture of many opium-based over-the-counter preparations and tonics which included opium, morphine, and laudanum, each with harmless sounding names such as Mother Bailey's Quieting Syrup and Munn's Elixir. Other over-the-counter cures had cocaine as their only active ingredient. Such "cures" were typically sold by street-side peddlers, mail order houses, retail grocers, and pharmacists. At the time there also existed unrestricted access to opium in opium dens and to morphine through retailers.

Throughout the eighteenth and nineteenth centuries, derivatives from opium and new chemical preparations resulted from advances in chemistry. German chemists developed anodyne, a liquid form of ether, in 1730. The British chemist Joseph Priestly, best known for his discovery of oxygen, held laughing gas parties in his home after he invented nitrous oxide (N_2O) in 1776. During the early 1800s, chloroform gained popularity as an anesthetic. Meanwhile, a German pharmacist named F.W.A. Serturner developed the opium derivative morphine, which he named after Morpheus, the Greek god of dreams and sleep. Codeine, another opium derivative discovered in 1832, was used as a cough suppressant. Morphine use in surgery led to the invention of the hypodermic needle in 1853. Ironically, doctors at that time believed that patient addiction to morphine could be avoided if the drug were injected rather than swallowed.

During this time, because of a peculiarity of the U.S. Constitution, the powerful new forms of opium and cocaine were more readily available in America than in most nations (Musto, 1991). Under the Constitution, individual states assumed responsibility for health-related issues. This included the regulation of medical practice and the availability of pharmaceutical drugs. In actuality, America had as many laws regarding health professions as it had states. For much of the nineteenth century, many states chose to have no controls at all—lawmakers reacted to the free enterprise philosophy that gave physicians freedom to practice medicine virtually as they saw fit. In comparison, nations with a less restricted central government, such as Britain, had a single, all-encompassing pharmacy law controlling the availability of drugs that were considered dangerous. So, when we consider drug abuse in the nineteenth century, we are looking at a era of unbridled availability and limitless advertising of drugs.

Late Nineteenth-Century Developments

In the 1860s, the American Civil War literally triggered a drug epidemic, resulting in hundreds of thousands of morphine addicts, 400,000 in the Union Army alone (O'Brien and Cohen, 1984). The indiscriminate use of morphine and of commercially available opium-based drugs prevailed on the battlefields, in prisons, and even on the home front. Self-medication for grief and pain often resulted in high dosages and, eventually, addiction. Meanwhile, opium use increased on the West Coast, and many Americans quickly associated opium smoking with Chinese immigrants who were lured to California with the promise of work on the railroads. Chinese opium smoking was tolerated and even encouraged while the Chinese laborers worked for low wages, performing back-breaking tasks in jobs that few white Americans wanted. But when a series of economic depressions in the late 1800s made jobs, even low-paying ones, a scarce commodity, nativist white anger was turned loose on the Chinese and their practice of opium smoking. This drug abuse-cultural link was one of the earliest examples of a powerful theme in the American perception of drugs: an association with drugs and a feared or rejected group within society.

Similarly, cocaine would be linked with blacks and marijuana with Mexicans during the first third of the twentieth century. Opium dens were so commonplace in San Francisco that the city passed an ordinance in 1875 to ban opium smoking in opium dens. This was considered the first anti-drug law in the United States, and it resulted in a series of state and local legislative actions. (By 1912 nearly every state and many municipalities had regulations controlling the distribution of certain drugs.) However, the absence of any federal control over interstate commerce in habit-forming and other drugs, absence of uniformity among state laws, and a lack of effective drug enforcement had one important implication—the rising tide of legislation directed at opiates (and later cocaine) was more a reflection of changing public attitude toward these drugs than an effective strategy to reduce supplies to users (Musto, 1991). The reality is that the reduction of opiate use around 1900 was probably due more to a fear of addiction, particularly among physicians, than to any successful campaign to reduce drug abuse.

More newly discovered drugs contributed to the use-to-abuse pattern. Around 1870, Oscar Liebreich developed one of the first sedative hypnotics, chloral hydrate. In combination with alcohol, it was commonly abused as a recreational drug and for more nefarious purposes as the famous "Mickey Finn," a knockout cocktail used by muggers and robbers. Meanwhile, in 1878 cocaine was first isolated in an alkaloid form in an attempt to cure many of the postwar morphine addicts in the U.S. Early on, its retail price was exceedingly high (compared to industrial wages of the time), $5 to $10 per gram, but it soon fell to 25 cents a gram and stayed there until price inflation after World War I (Musto, 1991). Although problems with cocaine were apparent almost from the beginning, by the 1880s this "cure" was soon used recreationally on a widespread basis. This is partly because popular opinion and leading medical "experts" touted cocaine as being both a beneficial and benign stimulant. In fact, the crack cocaine epidemic that struck the U.S. during the mid-1980s was not the first, as the nation's original cocaine epidemic occurred within roughly a 35-year period from the mid-1880s to 1920. Contributing to the spread of cocaine use was the considerable support of its use by the European medical community and later by American medical professionals. In the absence of national legislation controlling the use of cocaine, its abuse spread. Initially, cocaine was offered as a cure for opiate addiction, an asthma remedy (the official remedy of the American Hay Fever Association), and an antidote for toothaches. In 1886, Atlanta-born John Styth Pemberton introduced the soft drink Coca Cola,® which for the next twenty years had a cocaine base. The soft drink was introduced as having the advantages of coca but lacking the dangers of alcohol.

Although cocaine failed as a cure for morphine addiction, it was erroneously hailed as a cure for other problems. One report in 1883 explained how Bavarian soldiers given cocaine experienced renewed energy for combat. Sigmund Freud, inspired by American and German medical literature, first used cocaine as an aid in therapy in the 1880s. He used the "magical substance" in the treatment of depression and believed it to be helpful with asthma and certain stomach disorders. Freud's professional use led to a secret habit that was known only to a few close friends and associates during the later years of his life.

As medicinal cocaine use spread throughout Europe, so did its commercial and recreational appeal. A popular European elixir called Vin Mariani (named after its inventor Angelo Mariani) surfaced in Paris and consisted of red wine and Peruvian coca leaf extracts. Historians believe that in the 1880s Vin Mariani was probably the most widely used medical prescription in the world, used even by Popes, kings, queens, and other rulers. At the same time, William A. Hammond, a prominent American neurologist, hailed cocaine as being no more habit forming than coffee or tea. After all, how could any substance that makes the user feel so good be so bad? Within one year of the discovery of cocaine, the Parke-Davis Company was marketing coca and cocaine in 15 different forms, including coca cigarettes, cocaine for injection, and cocaine for sniffing. Cocaine kits were also sold by Parke-Davis as well as by other companies. Cocaine kits even offered syringes for convenient injections. The company proudly announced that cocaine "can supply the place of food, make the coward brave, the silent eloquent and . . . render the sufferer insensitive to pain" (Musto, 1991). Musto further points out that several reports from the years before the Harrison Narcotics Act of 1914 suggest that both the profit margin and street price of cocaine were unaffected by the legal availability of cocaine from a physician. He suggests that "perhaps the formality of medical consultation and the growing antagonism among physicians and the public toward cocaine helped to sustain the illicit market."

As with other "cures" before it, cocaine had failed as a remedy for morphine addiction, so it was with great pride that the Bayer Company in Germany announced a "wonder drug" designed to cure morphine and cocaine addictions. The new drug, heroin, also a derivative of opium, was soon found to be at least three times as addictive as the morphine it was supposed to remedy. Cocaine abuse decreased considerably by the 1920s and then virtually disappeared from the American drug scene until the 1970s.

Meanwhile, the Aztec custom of using peyote had spread northward in the Americas. The Comanche Indians first incorporated peyote into their religious ceremonies in the 1870s. This religious practice continues and is protected by United States law. Less than twenty years later, the drug mescaline was isolated as the hallucinogenic ingredient in peyote. (Many decades later mescaline was thought by many to be a "risk-free" recreational drug.)

Although peyote use was confined primarily to religious ceremonies, at the turn of the century alcohol abuse was spreading throughout society to all social classes and racial groups. Epidemic alcohol addiction in the United States finally led to the controversial 18th Amendment and the era of Prohibition. Prohibition only limited the legal consumption of alcohol; illegal markets thrived. Alcohol, and even marijuana, which served as an inexpensive substitute for costly black market alcohol, were easily available, among other places, in underground bars called "speakeasies." Many famous jazz musicians performing in such speakeasies were also thought to be drug abusers as well.

The Twentieth Century

As the twentieth century unfolded, so did the introduction of many new drugs. In 1903, barbiturates were discovered in Germany, and in 1912 amphetamines were mass produced as an antidote for asthma. Benzedrine inhalers were introduced for the first time in 1932 for treatment of adverse respiratory conditions, and in 1938 the painkiller Demerol®, which is presently a highly prized substitute for heroin on the streets, was synthesized and placed on the market. As we see, drug abuse in the early twentieth century was nothing new or unusual. What was relatively new was the *variety* of drugs abused and the *extent* to which each decade since 1900 can be characterized by particular drug fads—particularly in the United States.

As early as 1887 and in the absence of federal laws, some states had begun regulatory procedures. Finally, because of growing concern over opiate addiction and the non-medical use of drugs at the turn of the century, several important federal legislative actions were taken. The first was a federal prohibition of the importation of opium by Chinese nationals in 1887 and a restriction of opium smoking in the Philippines in 1905. These actions were followed by the passing of the Federal Pure Food and Drug Act in 1906, which required over-the-counter medicines to correctly label the inclusion of certain drugs. However, the Act failed to restrict the use of these drugs. In the following seven years, the United States government participated in several international conventions designed to motivate other nations to pass domestic laws dealing with drug control. In 1909, the Shanghai Opium Convention strongly supported such controls, but its recommendation generated little actual legislation among the nations involved, including the United States.

Figure 1.2

The History of Marijuana ▐▐▐▐▐▐▐▐▐▐▐▐▐▐▐▐▐▐ | | |

c.2000 Reference to marijuana found in India.

1545 Hemp is introduced to Chile.

1611 Hemp is cultivated by early settlers in Virginia.

1856 Putnam's Magazine publishes an account of FitzHugh Ludlow's marijuana-consuming experiences.

1875 "Hashish houses" appear and are modeled after Chinese opium dens.

1920 Marijuana use for recreational purposes increases during Prohibition.

1937 The Marijuana Tax Act is passed and outlaws untaxed possession or distribution of marijuana.

1950-60 Recreational marijuana use spreads on college campuses and in high schools.

1970 The Controlled Substances Act lists marijuana as a Schedule I hallucinogen and defines penalties for possession and distribution.

1970-85 Marijuana use continues to spread to most segments of society. An estimated 57% of American youth have tried it.

1995 Marijuana use declines nationwide.

Resolutions Adopted by the Shanghai Convention

• Consider the desirability of reviewing each country's system of regulation of the use of opium in light of the discrepancies among the countries' regulatory systems;

• Adopt measures to prevent the exporting of opium and its derivatives to countries that prohibit the importation of such items, and;

• Take measures for the gradual suppression of opium smoking in each country's own territories and possessions.

By 1910, the president presented Congress with a State Department report stating that cocaine was more appalling in its effects than any other habit-forming drug in the United States. A year earlier, President Theodore Roosevelt had led the effort to ban drugs in the nation's capital when informed by local police of their suspicions that the use of cocaine predisposes the user to commit criminal acts. Failure to pass the proposed Foster Anti-narcotic Bill led to a debate at the famed 1911 International Conference at The Hague, which deliberated the issue of whether the U.S. would actually enact such legislation. Resulting from The Hague Conference, the Senate's ratification of the convention in 1913 committed the U.S. to enact laws to suppress the abuse of opium, morphine, and cocaine. The goal was a world in which narcotics were restricted to medicinal use. Both producing and consuming nations would have control over their own boundaries.

Returning from The Hague was the State Department's opium commissioner, Hamilton Wright, who began to structure a comprehensive federal anti-drug law. Blocking his efforts was the specter of states' rights. The major cause of addiction was thought to be indiscriminate prescribing of dangerous drugs by health professionals. Yet how could the federal government interfere with the prescribing practices of physicians or demand that pharmacists keep records? To Wright, the answer was obvious: the government's power to tax. After extensive negotiations with pharmaceutical, export, import, and other medical interests, the Harrison Narcotics Act was passed in December 1914 and became the hallmark of federal drug control policy for the next 65 years. Many persons viewed the Harrison Narcotics Act as a rational way to limit addiction and drug abuse through taxation and regulation. It was a regulatory device which, according to the American Opium Commission, "would bring the whole traffic and use of these drugs into the light of day and, therefore, create a public opinion against the use of them that would be more important, perhaps, than the act itself." The act was heralded as a method of drug abuse control and as a public awareness tool (OCDE Report 1983).

The success of the enforcement of the act was directly attributed to the chosen source of authority and constitutional power to collect taxes. Because it was basically a tax revenue measure, it required persons who prescribed or distributed certain drugs to register with the government and buy tax stamps. In addition, the law stipulated that possession of drugs by an unregistered person was unlawful unless prescribed by a physician in good faith. The responsibility of enforcement rested with the Department of the Treasury.

Because of so many ambiguities in the Harrison Act, conflict erupted between the medical community and law enforcement officials. From the beginning, the Treasury Department insisted that medical maintenance of opiate addicts (treatment through declining usage) was unlawful, but physicians opposed this belief. Lower courts of law initially upheld the practice of drug maintenance of addicts, but a series of Supreme Court decisions in the 1919 ruling in *Webb v. U.S.* stated that maintaining addicts on narcotic drugs, even by prescription, was illegal.

Early enforcement of the Harrison Narcotics Act resulted in mass arrests of physicians, pharmacists, and unregistered users. In fact, some 30,000 physicians were arrested during this period for dispensing narcotics, and some 3,000 actually served prison sentences. Consequently, doctors all but abandoned the treatment of addicts for nearly half a century in the United States. Furthermore, private sanatoriums that claimed to cure addiction had existed since the mid-1800s but were unable to serve all of the remaining addicts when physicians became wary of prescribing opiates for maintenance. To respond to this need, between 1919 and 1921, 44 cities opened municipal clinics to provide temporary maintenance for addicts. Such clinics soon found themselves aggressively targeted for investigation by agents of the Narcotics Division. By 1925, all these clinics had been closed. Despite popular criticism of the prohibition of narcotic drugs during this period, the Harrison Narcotics Act proved to

Provisions of the Harrison Narcotics Act

Section 1—This section required that any person who was in the business of dealing in the specified drugs pay a special annual tax of one dollar. In 1918 the Revenue Act increased the special annual tax on importers, manufactures, producers, and compounders to $24; on wholesalers to $12; on retailers to $6; and on practitioners to $3.

Section 2—This section prohibited the selling or giving away of any specified drugs except pursuant to the written order of the person to whom the drug was being given or sold. The written order was required to be on a special form issued by the Commissioner of Internal Revenue.

Section 4—It was unlawful for anyone who had not previously registered to engage in interstate trafficking of the specified drugs.

Section 8—The possession of any of the specified drugs was illegal with the exception of employees of registrants and patients of physicians.

Section 9—This section provided that the punishment for any violation of the act was to be not more than $2,000 or not more than 5 years in prison or both.

Section 10—This gave the Commissioner of Internal Revenue the responsibility for enforcing the act.

drastically reduce the consumption of narcotics in the United States. This conclusion is evident when observing the reduction of the number of addicts during a 25-year period: in 1920 there were an estimated 500,000 addicts, and in 1945, the addict population was roughly 40,000 to 50,000.

The Prohibition Era

Although moderate drinking was generally accepted during the eighteenth century, by the early nineteenth century some people began to perceive an increase in the abuse of alcohol. The American Temperance Society, founded in 1826, began gathering pledges of abstinence. Within three years, more than 200 anti-liquor organizations were active and by 1830, temperance reform "constituted a burgeoning national movement" (Lender and Martin, 1987). In the 1840s the Washington Temperance Societies conducted revival-style meetings to encourage similar pledges. These groups viewed the nation's growing cities, filled with the newly arriving Irish, Jewish, and Italian immigrants, as centers of deterioration and wickedness. The propensity of these people to drink heavily was viewed as the driving force behind their supposedly deviant lifestyle. As early as 1846, the state of Maine was persuaded to outlaw alcohol; similar attempts followed elsewhere. However, these efforts were hampered by the Civil War, and despite the passage of many liquor laws, the sale and use of alcohol remained widespread.

The National Prohibition movement, also known as the Noble Experiment, was spearheaded by Prohibitionists who felt that alcohol was a dangerous drug which destroyed lives, and disrupted families and communities. Consequently, they felt that it was the responsibility of the government to prohibit its sale. Between 1880 and 1890 a new wave of prohibition sentiment swept the evangelical Protestant churches. Organized by the Women's Christian Temperance Union (WCTU), the Anti-saloon League of America, and the National Prohibition Party, prohibitionists put pressure on their local politicians for an amendment to the Constitution.

In January 1919, **the 18th Amendment** was passed which outlawed the manufacture and sale of alcohol, except for industrial use. Prohibition marked a triumph of morality of middle and upper-class Americans over the threat posed to their culture by the "new Americans" (Gusfield, 1963). Nine months after the 18th Amendment was passed, it was followed by the passage of the Volstead Act which provided an enforcement mechanism. The law was sporadically enforced and met with considerable public opposition. In fact, Eric Goode writes that most Prohibitionists were extremely naive both about the feasibility of enforcing Prohibition and about the impact the Volstead Act would have on drinking and related problems (1993). Soon bootlegging, speakeasies, and smuggling flourished under the direction and dominance of local gangsters. It was estimated that Chicago had approximately 10,000 speakeasies in operation at any given time during the Prohibition era. Opponents of the law claimed that it was ineffective and that it represented an unnecessary restriction of personal choice. As a result, a massive campaign was mounted to repeal the amendment, which became a reality in 1933 with the ratifying of **the 21st Amendment**. Thereafter, the **Temperance Movement** faded. In Chapter 13 we discuss the policy lessons learned as a result of the Prohibition experience.

Prohibition created a virtual gold mine for crime which made millionaires out of petty thugs such as Meyer Lansky, Waxey Gordon, Owney Madden, Al Capone, Dutch Schultz, and many others. It affected the lives of many people throughout the country. It tainted politics and corrupted police officers. The stage was now set for one of the most lawless periods in the history of America—the **Roaring Twenties**. Despite the newly-passed law, no one would go thirsty during this period. There were flappers, bobbed hair, the Charleston, coonskin coats, the hip flask, and other memorabilia which gave this period its unique distinction.

It soon became clear to many entrepreneurial criminals that there was a need for an organized infrastructure to handle public demand for alcohol. Factories were needed to produce it; a transportation system was needed to deal with bulk shipments; and an importation system capable of dealing with large bulk shipments from England, Cuba, and Canada had to be constructed. This market demand for more complex organization combined with advances in electronic technology that would revolutionize communications—revolutionizing gambling and bringing what we now know as organized crime into the modern age.

The Roaring Twenties set the stage for clandestine abuse of alcohol and marijuana in the shadow of Prohibition. Interestingly, the opiate problem, in particular morphine and heroin, declined in the U.S. during the 1920s and 1930s until most of the problem was confined to individuals labeled by law enforcement and the powerful as social outcasts in urban areas. After World War I, America's international anti-drug efforts continued as both the British and U.S. governments proposed adding The Hague Convention to the Versailles Treaty. The result would mean the addition of domestic laws controlling narcotics. This incorporation resulted in the passing of the British Dangerous Drugs Act of 1920, a law often portrayed as a response to a bustling narcotics problem in Britain. During the 1940s, some Americans suggested that by adopting a medical model and supplying heroin to addicts (rather than relying on law enforcement efforts for drug control), the opiate problem in Britain had almost been eradicated. In fact, Britain had no such problem to begin with. This illustrates how the desperate need to solve the drug problem in the United States creates misperceptions about a foreign drug predicament.

In the 1930s, partly due to the popularity of marijuana and amphetamines, the Federal Bureau of Narcotics (FBN) was created within the Department of the Treasury. Under the direction of Commissioner Harry Anslinger, the FBN separated the enforcement of alcohol laws from those dealing with other drugs. Among other drug laws, the FBN was charged with enforcing the Harrison Narcotics Act, but the responsibility of interdiction remained with the Bureau of Customs. Although marijuana was not included in the Harrison Narcotics Act, the FBN did include an optional provision in the Uniform Narcotic Drug Act, which it extended to the states. During his tenure as bureau commissioner, Anslinger regularly issued reports and wrote books and articles which appeared in popular magazines, claiming that under the influence, marijuana users rob, kill, rape, and chop up their families in a drug induced frenzy (Goode, 1993). Consequently, concern about violent crime and the dangers of marijuana grew, and many states passed legislation prohibiting its use.

Post-Prohibition Drug Abuse

By the mid-1930s, national awareness about marijuana use resulted in its being placed on the FBN's enforcement agenda. Unlike opiates and cocaine, marijuana was introduced during a time of intolerance; consequently, it was not until the 1960s (40 years later) that it was widely used. Marijuana was not included in the 1914 Harrison legislation because, at the time, it was not considered a particularly dangerous drug.

The History of U.S. Drug Control

1909—*The Shanghai Opium Convention*—representatives of 13 nations meet to discuss ways of controlling illicit drug traffic.

1912—*The International Opium Convention*—the first binding international instrument governing the shipment of narcotic drugs was signed at The Hague, Netherlands.

1920—The First Assembly of the League of Nations established an *Advisory Committee on Traffic in Opium and Other Dangerous Drugs*. Under League auspices, three main drug conventions were developed over the next two decades.

1925—*The Second National Opium Convention*—established a system of import certificates and export authorizations for licit international trade in narcotics.

1931—*The Convention for Limiting the Manufacture and Regulating the Distribution of Narcotic Drugs*—introduced a compulsory estimation system aimed at limiting the amounts of drug manufacture to those needed for medical and scientific needs.

1936—*The Convention for the Suppression of the Illicit Traffic in Dangerous Drugs*—the first international instrument called for severe punishment for illegal traffickers.

1946—Drug control responsibilities formerly carried out by the League of Nations were transferred to the United Nations. *The Division of Narcotic Drugs* was also created to act as the secretariat for the commission and serve as the central repository of United Nations expertise in drug control.

1961—*The Single Convention on Narcotic Drugs*—codified all existing multilateral treaty laws. Placed under control was the cultivation of plants grown as raw material for narcotic drugs. Controls were continued on opium and its derivatives, and coca bush and cannabis were placed under international control, obliging governments to limit production of those drug to amounts needed for scientific and medical use.

1971—*The Convention on Psychotropic Substances*—until 1971 only narcotic drugs were subject to international control. This convention extended controls to include a broad range of man-made, mood-altering substances that could lead to harmful dependencies. These included: hallucinogens such as LSD and mescaline, stimulants such as amphetamines, and sedative-hypnotics such as barbiturates.

1981—*The International Drug Abuse Control Strategy* was formed and implemented a five-year program. The strategy included measures for the wider adherence to existing treaties coordinating efforts to ensure a balance between supply and demand of drugs for a legitimate use and steps to eradicate the illicit drug supply and reduce traffic.

1984—In its *Declaration on the Control of Drug Trafficking and Drug Abuse*, the U.N. General Assembly characterized drug traffic and abuse as "an international criminal activity" that constituted "a grave threat to the security and development of many countries and peoples. . . ."

1987—*The International Conference on Drug Abuse and Illicit Trafficking* focused on developing long term drug control strategies, policies, and activities to attack at the national, regional, and international levels drug abuse and trafficking.

The FBN, in an effort to avoid assuming additional responsibilities at the federal level, had minimized the dangers of marijuana use and failed to support federal marijuana control measures. Instead, in its 1932 annual report, it urged the states to adopt a Uniform State Narcotics Law, which was adopted in 1932. But by 1937, the FBN had changed its position. The desire to expand its power, budget, and personnel allocations led the FBN to engage in a scare campaign against marijuana and to support federal controls. Even scientific publications during the time fearfully described marijuana's alleged ominous side effects.

Due to public concern over its increasing popularity in recreational use during Prohibition, when marijuana was a cheap alternative to alcohol, states began passing legislation against its use or possession. Many of the early anti-marijuana laws were passed in the western states where marijuana was linked with Mexican laborers and was seen as part of the "Mexican problem." Like the earlier Chinese immigrants, Mexicans had been brought into the United States to work the farms and ranches of the Southwest in difficult, low-paying jobs the white majority did not want. In fact, as the Great Depression of the 1930s settled over America, immigrants became an unwelcome minority linked with violence and the smoking of marijuana. By 1931 "all but two states west of the Mississippi and several more in the east had enacted prohibitory legislation against it" (PCOC 1986). As a result of increasing public pressure, the FBN supported the Federal **Marijuana Tax Act** which was passed in 1937. This congressional measure was basically a nominal revenue measure patterned after the Harrison Narcotics Act. At the time, however, marijuana had some historic commercial use in the manufacture of rope, twine, veterinary medicines, and other products. In fact, at the time of its passage, it was estimated that there were more than 10,000 acres of marijuana being cultivated in the United States. Modeled after the provisions of the Harrison Narcotics Act, the Marijuana Tax Act required a substantial transfer tax for all marijuana transactions. The Act required that any person whose business related to marijuana pay a special tax. Additionally, the transference of marijuana had to be pursuant to a written order on a special form issued by the Secretary of the Treasury. The person transferring the marijuana was then required to pay a tax of $1 per ounce if registered and $100 per ounce if not registered.

Figure 1.3

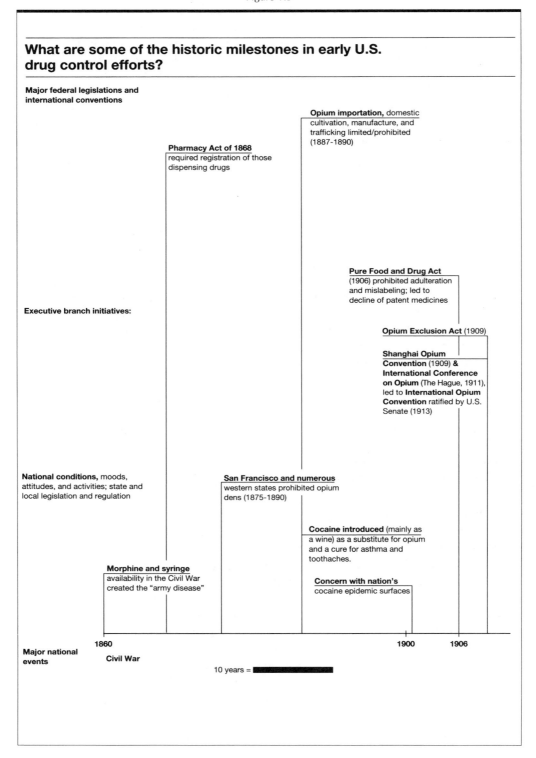

What are some of the historic milestones in early U.S. drug control efforts?

Major federal legislations and international conventions

Opium importation, domestic cultivation, manufacture, and trafficking limited/prohibited (1887-1890)

Pharmacy Act of 1868 required registration of those dispensing drugs

Pure Food and Drug Act (1906) prohibited adulteration and mislabeling; led to decline of patent medicines

Executive branch initiatives:

Opium Exclusion Act (1909)

Shanghai Opium Convention (1909) & **International Conference on Opium** (The Hague, 1911), led to **International Opium Convention** ratified by U.S. Senate (1913)

National conditions, moods, attitudes, and activities; state and local legislation and regulation

San Francisco and numerous western states prohibited opium dens (1875-1890)

Cocaine introduced (mainly as a wine) as a substitute for opium and a cure for asthma and toothaches.

Morphine and syringe availability in the Civil War created the "army disease"

Concern with nation's cocaine epidemic surfaces

1860

Major national events   Civil War

1900   1906

10 years =

Figure 1.3, *continued*

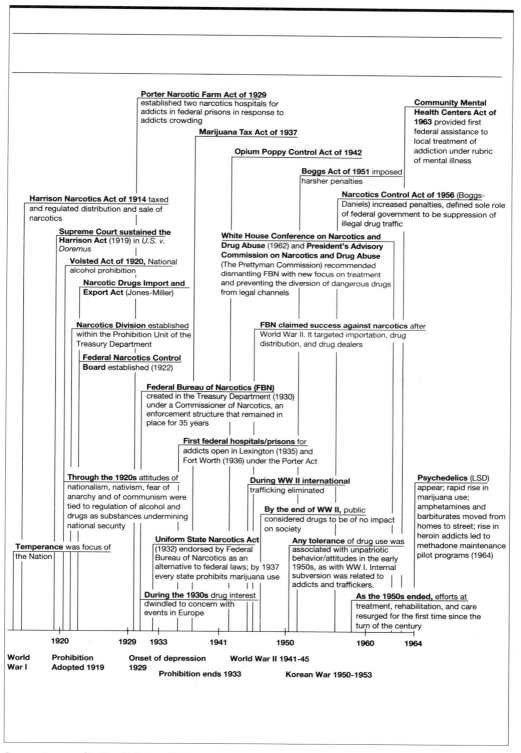

Source: Bureau of Justice Statistics, 1992.

The Postwar Era

In addition to marijuana, amphetamines, which were originally prescribed to curb obesity and depression, became popular among students, professionals, and even housewives who sought the euphoric effects of the drugs. The popularity of amphetamines continued through World War II, partly because they were so easily obtained with a doctor's prescription. As soon as the user market for amphetamines surpassed the legitimate sources of supply, an illicit market was created to meet the demand.

LSD (lysergic acid diethylamide) was popularized during the 1940s and 1950s in certain communities. It was initially discovered in 1938 by Drs. Albert Hoffman and W.A. Stoll, Swiss chemists who were experimenting with a parasitic fungus that grows on rye (ergot fungus). The use of LSD for mental disorders was widely researched in the 1940s and was praised by the psychiatric community in the 1950s. Soon, many members of the psychiatric community used LSD for both therapy and recreation. In 1962, Harvard professor Dr. Timothy Leary and his protege Richard Alpert began treating inmates at the Massachusetts Correctional Institute with LSD. One year later, under a cloud of scandal, they were relieved of their positions at Harvard. LSD was also tested by the Central Intelligence Agency (CIA) as part of its efforts to find the ultimate "truth serum" and then later in an attempt to find a "mind control" drug. In fact, the CIA administered LSD to unsuspecting, non-consenting victims, at least one of whom committed suicide.

Use of LSD through most of this time was restricted to a small part of the U.S. population. More common in the 1950s was the use of marijuana, tranquilizers, and various combinations of drugs. The coffee houses frequented by members of the 1950's "Beat Generation" often served as clearinghouses for these drugs as much as for coffee. Tranquilizers, ranging from the minor benzodiazepines to more dangerous barbiturates, can produce an intoxication similar to that produced by alcohol. Again, the easy availability of tranquilizers via prescriptions contributed to their abuse. (The two most widely abused depressants today are Valium and Librium.) Like many amphetamines, tranquilizers have been available through both legitimate and illicit markets. Mixed drug use, or **poly-drug** use, such as taking "uppers" in the morning for energy and "downers" at night to induce sleep, also became more commonplace during the 1950s and 1960s. Some adolescents at this time began experimenting with such drug trends as glue and paint sniffing, occasionally with lethal consequences.

During the 1950s, two major laws were passed: the Boggs Act of 1951 and the Narcotics Control Act of 1956. Essentially, these laws severely increased the penalties for violations of the import/export and internal revenue laws relating to marijuana and narcotics. These penalties included mandatory minimum prison sentences along with expanded fines for drug violations.

The Turbulent 1960s

The Age of Aquarius—the 1960s—is notorious for the celebration of drug abuse among youth and proved to be a watershed decade. The use of most illegal drugs was greeted with increased tolerance, as were a wide range of unconventional behaviors, including the growth of movements that stood in opposition to the war in Vietnam and to mainstream American culture, the coming into popularity of rock music and its related lifestyle, the creation of psychedelic art, and enormous media publicity devoted to drugs, drug users, and drug proselytizers. A vigorous drug subculture came into existence. During this time some social groups viewed drug use in positive terms, evaluated individuals on the basis of whether or not they used illegal drugs, and believed it a virtue to "turn on" someone who did not use drugs. This subculture proved to be a powerful force in recruiting young people into the use of illegal psychoactive drugs, and never before had drug abuse reached such a large youthful audience.

In Vietnam, U.S. soldiers became addicts by the thousands as had their counterparts in the Civil War. Heroin, marijuana, and hashish were widely available to servicemen, many of whom, once becoming addicted, turned to drug trafficking. Since the Vietnam War, recreational use of heroin has escalated in the U.S., especially in economically depressed inner cities. Consequently, as of 1989, the Drug Enforcement Administration estimates that there are roughly 500,000 to 750,000 heroin addicts in the United States. Controversial methadone clinics opened in 1964 to treat opiate addicts. Although methadone is effective, it is itself a highly addictive narcotic drug (see Chapter 14).

Soon there was a shifting of drugs of choice in the American drug scene. The use of psychedelic substances (such as LSD, MDA, and DMA), heroin, and marijuana began in the 1960s and continued through the early 1970s. By the early 1970s, cocaine was gaining impetus as a recreational drug but was only affordable to the affluent consumers. Despite the end of the Vietnam conflict in the early 1970s and the subsequent calming of the social and political waters, drug abuse failed to wane. The already popular use of PCP increased during this time along with the newly developed depressant Quaalude® (methaqualone). Cocaine was still growing in popularity to the point where small gold cocaine spoons on necklaces were the rage in some social circles. In fact, during the 1970s, New York's exclusive disco Studio 54 displayed a dance floor that was decorated by a huge coke spoon. Supposedly, preferred clientele were furnished free samples of the drug. By the end of the 1970s, use of cocaine and its close cousin, methamphetamine, was still gaining momentum. Methamphetamine and other domestic drugs—PCP (phencyclidine) and LSD—were illegally produced around the U.S. in an increasing number of clandestine laboratories.

Figure 1.4

The History of LSD

1938	LSD is first produced in Basel, Switzerland.	
1943	Dr. Albert Hoffman accidentally ingests a lysergic acid compound and experiences "fantastic visions." Hoffman later takes LSD purposely to study the effects.	
1949-53	LSD is researched for treatment in mental disorders, alcoholism, and epilepsy.	
1956	Recreational use of LSD by members of the psychiatric community is recorded.	
1962	Drs. Timothy Leary and Richard Alpert of the Harvard Center for Research in Human Personality use LSD on inmates at the Massachusetts Correctional Institute.	
1963	The federal government investigates Leary and Alpert, who are relieved of their positions at Harvard. The illicit	

market for LSD begins, and different types of LSD appear across the country.

1965 New York is the first state to outlaw LSD.

1967 LSD is reported to damage white blood cells in laboratory studies.

1968 Negative effects of LSD, such as flashbacks and "bad trips," are reported across the nation.

The popularity of LSD peaks and stabilizes in the late 1960s.

1970-1995 Different forms of LSD, such as blotter, micro-dot and window pane acid, appear on the illicit market.

Recreational use of LSD experiences phases of popularity and disinterest every 3 to 5 years.

Because of the growing epidemic of drug abuse across the nation, many drug laws were passed as an attempt to control the problem. In 1961, the United Nations adopted the Single Convention on Narcotics Drugs. The Single Convention established regulatory schedules for psychotropic substances and quotas limiting production and export of licit pharmaceuticals. In 1963, the President's Advisory Commission on Narcotics and Drug Abuse (also known as the Prettyman Commission) recommended a larger role by the federal government in treatment of drug addicts. Accordingly, the 1963 Community Mental Health Centers Act became law and provided for federal assistance to non-federal treatment centers.

Recommendations of the 1963 Prettyman Commission

- imposition of strict federal control for non-narcotic drugs

- transfer of the Treasury Department's enforcement and investigative responsibility to the Department of Justice

- transfer of the responsibilities for the regulation of legitimate drug trade from the Treasury Department to the Department of Health, Education, and Welfare

In 1965, the Drug Abuse Control Amendments were also passed. This federal action brought the manufacture and distribution of amphetamines and barbiturates under federal control and imposed criminal penalties for illegally manufacturing these drugs. In addition, it created the Bureau of Alcohol and Drug Abuse Control within the Department of Health, Education, and Welfare while enabling the Secretary of HEW to add substances to the controlled list (LSD was added the following year). Toward the end of the 1960s, the 1966 Narcotic Addict Rehabilitation Act created a federal compulsory treatment program and gave financial support to community-based treatment programs. Finally, in 1968, the FBN was transferred to the Justice Department and merged with the Bureau of Drug Abuse Control to form the Bureau of Narcotics and Dangerous Drugs (BNDD).

Late Twentieth-Century Developments

Although media attention to drugs and drug use declined between the late 1960s and late 1970s, the actual use of drugs did not. Numerous surveys point to a strong increase during this period. The late 1970s and early 1980s probably represent another turning point in the recreational use of marijuana, hallucinogens, sedatives, and amphetamines. However, recent studies show a considerable drop in the use of most drug types through the 1980s and the early 1990s.

The shift in drug control policy was finalized in 1970 with the passing of the Controlled Substances Act, which created a common standard of dangerousness to rank all drugs rather than concentrating on specific substances. It also allowed the scheduling of substances to be done administratively. 1970 continued to be an eventful year for drug control legislation with the passing of the federal Racketeer Influenced and Corrupt Organizations (RICO) and the Continuing Criminal Enterprise (CCE) laws, which were designed to focus on the leaders of large criminal organizations. As we will learn in greater detail in Chapter 11, this decade was the catalyst for many modern drug control policy issues and debates.

Thinking Critically #1

Project yourself 30 years into the future. Predict the incidence of drug use, both legal and illegal, in the United States. Discuss the type and availability of drug in the 2020s, any interdiction efforts, internal efforts to deal with the "drug problem" and the effects of drugs on future society. Base your prediction on past and current trends.

Finally, in 1972, the issue of decriminalization of marijuana as a policy option was debated by the Presidential Commission on Marijuana and Drug

Abuse. This sprang from the rising number of persons arrested on marijuana charges during the 1960s and 1970s. This, in conjunction with a growing scientific debate about the dangers of marijuana, generated pressure to reduce penalties for marijuana violations. In fact, not only did the Comprehensive Drug Abuse Prevention and Control Act of 1970 reduce federal penalties from marijuana violations, but the Carter Administration formally advocated legalizing marijuana in amounts up to one ounce. In addition, during the 1970s, 11 states decriminalized penalties for possession of marijuana although some small penalties were retained. The Gallup Poll on relaxation of laws against marijuana is instructive. In 1980, 53 percent of Americans favored legalization of small amounts of marijuana; by 1986 only 27 percent supported that view. At the same time those favoring penalties for marijuana rose from 43 percent to 67 percent. As a result, many states revised or "recriminalized" their laws relating to marijuana violations, indicating a newfound concern about the potential hazards of the drug, a trend that began in the late 1970s and continues today. One glaring example is the recriminalization of marijuana by popular vote in Alaska in 1990.

The Comprehensive Drug Abuse Prevention and Control Act (1970)

Although legal controls and public drug policy will be discussed in greater detail later in this text, the primary federal law addressing drug control will now be examined. The legal infrastructure to the federal drug control effort is the 1970 Comprehensive Drug Abuse Prevention and Control Act, Title II, which is also known as the **Controlled Substances Act** (CSA). This federal measure updated all previously existing drug laws and gave uniformity to federal drug control policy. Generally speaking, the CSA's four provisions consist of the following:

- mechanisms for reducing the availability of dangerous drugs;
- procedures for bringing a substance under control;
- criteria for determining control requirements;
- obligations incurred by international treaty arrangements

The CSA places all substances which were in some manner regulated under existing federal law into one of five schedules. The criteria by which drugs are placed in these schedules are theoretically based on the medical use of the substance, its potential for abuse, and safety or addiction (dependence) liability. These five schedules are listed below:

Schedule I
- The drug or other substance has a high potential for abuse.
- The drug or other substance has no currently accepted medical use in treatment in the United States.
- There is a lack of accepted safety for use of the drug or other substance under medical supervision.

Schedule II

- The drug or other substance has a high potential for abuse.
- The drug or other substance has a currently accepted medical use in treatment in the United states or a currently accepted medical use with severe restrictions.
- Abuse of the drug or other substance may lead to severe psychological or physical dependence.

Schedule III

- The drug or other substance has a potential for abuse less than the drugs or other substances in Schedules I and II.
- The drug or other substance has a currently accepted medical use in treatment in the United States.
- Abuse of the drug or other substance may lead to moderate or low physical dependence or high psychological dependence.

Schedule IV

- The drug or other substance has a low potential for abuse relative to the drugs or other substances in Schedule III.
- The drug or other substance has a currently accepted medical use in treatment in the United States.
- Abuse of the drug or other substance may lead to limited physical dependence or psychological dependence relative to the drugs or other substances in Schedule III.

Schedule V

- The drug or other substance has a low potential for abuse relative to the drugs or other substances in Schedule IV.
- The drug or other substance has a currently accepted medical use in treatment in the United States.
- Abuse of the drug or other substances may lead to limited physical dependence or psychological dependence relative to the drugs or other substances in Schedule IV.

In addition, the law imposes nine control mechanisms on the manufacturing, purchasing, and distribution of controlled substances.

Hallmarks of the drug abuse story in the 1980s include the synthesis of drugs and the lifestyles of some music and sports celebrities. Designer drugs are potentially deadly synthetic substances similar to opiates and hallucinogens. However, in some areas they are technically legal since they can be produced without certain illegal chemical analogs. Crack, a freebase form of cocaine, was developed about this time and provided a potent but cheap alternative to cocaine. The crack and methamphetamine markets of the 1980s spawned an upsurge in organized crime. Newcomers to the drug trade included such Los Angeles-based youth gangs as the Crips and Bloods as well as Jamaican gangs known as posses. Many cities across the United States are now terrorized by the drug-related violence of such gangs. This in turn provided a basis for much media and entertainment industry attention. One example is the 1988 film *Colors,* which portrays the violence of inner-city youth gangs involved in the drug trade.

Meanwhile, many top athletes were turning to anabolic steroids, a muscle builder, to maintain a competitive edge. Mass disqualifications of athletes dominated the coverage of the Pan Am games in Caracas, Venezuela, in 1983. In 1988, Ben Johnson gained notoriety but lost an Olympic gold medal due to his use of steroids. Other drugs ruined the lives of other celebrities. Comedian John Belushi died in 1983 as a result of respiratory complications from the use of cocaine mixed with heroin (an "upper" and a "downer"), called a "speedball." The deaths of two athletes in June 1985 helped bring home the tragedy of cocaine. Len Bias had been drafted by the Boston Celtics; he celebrated with cocaine and died of cardiac arrest as a result of the drug and a preexisting heart ailment. Football star Don Rogers also died that month from cocaine poisoning.

As drug use increased among American youth, so did drug education programs aimed at curbing the problem. Former First Lady Nancy Reagan's "Just Say No" campaign was subjected to ridicule by those who accused it of being simplistic and unrealistic, while supporters defended it as a common sense prevention strategy that focused on potential first-time users rather than hard-core street addicts. Despite lukewarm support for programs such as "Just Say No," the public became more intolerant of drug-related tragedies. This public outrage finally resulted in the controversial drug testing of air traffic controllers, train engineers, bus drivers, and other employees whose jobs were associated with public safety.

Figure 1.5

The History of PCP

1959	PCP was first developed as a dissociative anesthetic for use in surgery.
1960	Medical use of PCP on human patients was discontinued because of violent side effects.
	Veterinary medicine adopts the use of PCP as an animal tranquilizer.
1965	Recreational use of PCP spreads because of illicit production of the drug.

1965-70	PCP is sold as THC and cannabinol on the streets because people were beginning to associate the effects of PCP with negative experiences.
1978	President Carter enacts special legislation against PCP.
1980	Clandestine laboratory technology spreads in the manufacture of PCP.
1985	PCP use drastically declines with the advent of crack.

Additionally, the medical cover story of the decade—AIDS (Acquired Immune Deficiency Syndrome)—helped clarify the association between drug use and public safety. Those among the high risk groups for AIDS, a lethal, infectious disease for which there is no cure, are intravenous drug users such as heroin addicts. Because of the nature of heroin abuse and the illegality of heroin, activity commonly takes place in secluded settings, such as urban "shooting galleries," where the sharing of hypodermic syringes (also illegal in most jurisdictions) has become commonplace. American recreational drug use thrived in the 1980s, but not as a result of ignorance about the drugs themselves. Indeed, no society has been more aware of the tragic price paid for substance abuse.

Looking Ahead

It is difficult to speculate about the future of recreational drug use in our society because of the ever-changing social climate. As history has proven, the basis for social acceptance of some drugs and not others is not rational or consistent. Should certain drugs be authorized by law for recreational use? If lawfully sanctioned, under what circumstances should drug use be permitted? Given the high incidence of drug-related crime and drug-related health problems, can we responsibly consider the legalization of any dangerous substance? Or have the health problems associated with drug abuse and the ancillary crime associated with drug trafficking in the illicit market become so dangerous that a post-prohibition approach is required? It appears that the customary use of legal drugs such as coffee, tobacco, and certain over-the-counter drugs will continue throughout the 1990s. Alcohol use will undoubtedly continue despite initiatives on community, state, and national levels for curbing many of the dysfunctional aspects of alcohol abuse. Illicit consumption of substances such as marijuana and cocaine will most likely continue, but to what extent is questionable. Perhaps public education and prevention programs in the future will meet the challenge of informing drug users and prospective drug users of the dangers of these substances. In addition, it is likely that continued research will spread insight into the psychological and physiological effects of these drugs. Based on the advancements in chemical technology, clandestine drug manufacturers will probably conceive of new ways to increase the potency of drugs and to reduce the retail price.

Responsibility for combating the drug problem in the future rests with governmental functions such as law enforcement, treatment and prevention programs, and the court and correctional systems. Additionally, others who must share in this responsibility include parents, teachers, and community leaders. Only through this multidisciplinary approach can the incidence of drug abuse and drug-related crime be reduced and ultimately abolished.

Summary

Of all the social phenomena affecting public health and safety, it is clear that drug abuse has superseded all other forms of widespread social deviance. There is much agreement that drugs can cause severe social problems and that some drugs are less harmful than others. However, there is little agreement as to which drugs are less harmful and to what extent they should be tolerated.

Cannabis and the opium poppy have been generally accepted as the oldest mind-altering drugs of abuse, as historic records of their use date back some 7,000 years. Further, these two drugs have been associated with both medical treatment and recreational uses. The regional origins for these drugs include South America for the coca plant, North America for alcohol and peyote, and Mexico, Southeast Asia, Southwest Asia, and China for opium and cannabis.

Before the late 1800s drugs were, for the most part, legal and readily available. During and after the Civil War, morphine was widely used and abused as a pain killer. Toward the end of the nineteenth century "cures" for morphine addiction were developed. For example, cocaine (1878) and heroin (1898), both thought to be non-addicting antidotes for morphine addiction, were synthesized during the last quarter of the century. Other drugs such as barbiturates and amphetamines were also developed around the turn of the century and have proven to be some of the most widely abused drugs in history. Concern about the use of opiates at the turn of the century led to the passing of several pieces of federal legislation, such as the 1914 Harrison Narcotics Act. This comprehensive act exemplified national concern over the abuse of coca and opiate based drugs. The Harrison Act marked one of the first laws to break away from the era of legalized drugs into a period of regulation. The public perception of drugs grew increasingly negative, while drug abuse expanded during the early to mid-1900s, leading public policy into an attitude of prohibition. While Prohibition (1920-1933) was designed to reduce alcohol consumption, it inadvertently resulted in an increase of marijuana use. Along with this increase was an escalation in the clandestine abuse of other drugs, such as cocaine and heroin. Although alcohol prohibition failed to last, other drugs were becoming controlled more often as evidenced by the passing of the Marijuana Tax Act in 1937.

PCP was synthesized in the late 1950s. The drug ultimately proved to be harmful to human patients but was successful as a general anesthetic for animals. Shortly thereafter LSD, originally developed in 1938, was studied by Harvard Professor Timothy Leary and became one of the first widely used recreational "psychedelic" drugs. Much social and political unrest with civil rights protests, race riots, the women's liberation movement, and demonstrations against United States involvement in Vietnam marked the era of the 1960s. Abuse of drugs, including cocaine, marijuana, amphetamines, LSD, and PCP, also continued to flourish during this period, resulting in the passing of the 1970 Controlled Substances Act which specified all drugs that were to be considered unlawful. As the 1970s approached, however, the harmful effects of illicit drugs were downplayed by the media and entertainment industry as certain drugs like cocaine achieved an elevated status among drug users. To supply the growing numbers of drug users, many entrepreneurial drug chemists began to cook their own batches of drugs which included methamphetamine and PCP. By the early 1980s, there was a significant increase in clandestine laboratory technology, which in the 1990s continues to spread across the United States. Designer drugs such as "China White heroin" and "Ecstasy" are illicit drugs which were popularized during the 1980s. Each of these also represents innovative clandestine laboratory advances by domestic criminals entering the illicit drug market.

The drug using population of the 1980s also witnessed the genesis of crack, a potent, freebase form of cocaine. The popularity of crack created a great profit margin which lured many new organized crime groups into the drug trade. Competition over cities and neighborhoods as sales turf by street gangs and organized crime groups has become a primary concern of policy makers in the 1990s.

Do you recognize these terms?

Controlled Substances Act

18th Amendment

Harrison Narcotics Act

Marijuana Tax Act

opium wars

poly-drug use

Roaring Twenties

Temperance Movement

21st Amendment

Discussion Questions

1. Discuss China's role in global drug addiction and how that country attempted to deal with its own opium problem.

2. Discuss the early historical (both medical and recreational) use of cannabis.

3. How has the historical use of opium in China affected drug abuse in the United States today?

4. Discuss the Civil War's unique association with the drug morphine.

5. Discuss the first anti-drug law passed in the United States and the circumstances surrounding it.

6. Compare the drug abuse climate in the United States before and after the passing of Prohibition.

7. List the elements of the so-called "Age of Aquarius" that possibly accelerated drug use during the 1960s and early 1970s.

Understanding Drugs of Abuse   *2*

This chapter will enable you to:

- Understand the meaning of the term drug abuse

- Identify reasons why people take drugs

- Realize the various social forums in which drugs are taken

- Discover the pharmacology of popular drugs of abuse

- Learn the effects of drugs on the drug user

The literature on drug identification and pharmacology is rich with varying opinions, but not much is really known about their effects on the human physiology. For example, drugs like alcohol and cocaine often affect different users in different ways. Not only do the user's moods differ from one drug to another, but the development of tolerance and addiction differ from one user to the next as well. In this chapter, we will examine those drugs that are not only currently popular but potentially hazardous in society today. We will also study legal distinctions and categories of drugs as well as the effects those drugs have on those who use them.

Defining Drugs

It may seem somewhat absurd to attempt to define the word **drug** as it is such a commonly used word in our everyday lives. Today the word seems to serve as a catchall term for just about any medicinal or chemical substance. In fact, it refers to both dangerous substances, such as heroin or LSD, which are illegal to possess and have no medicinal use, as well as to more benign substances such as over-the-counter drugs like aspirin and certain non-prescription cold remedies. Webster attempts to define the word "drug" in a general sense as "a substance used by itself or a mixture in the treatment or diagnosis of disease." Although somewhat comprehensive, this definition still fails to recognize the use of drugs for applications other than the treatment of disease, such as recreational use. Therefore, at the risk of oversimplification, a more practical definition might be as follows: *A drug is any substance that causes or creates significant psychological and/or physiological changes in the body.*

It is here where we may first identify a primary misunderstanding about the word since the traditional definition fails to recognize *recreational* or nonmedical use of certain substances. Certainly most drug use in accord with a legitimate medical problem is not only lawful but appropriate, yet the word "drug" actually encompasses a much broader scope of definition. Webster's definition excludes consideration of the recreational category of drugs. Other "everyday" substances, such as sugar and caffeine, don't meet Webster's definition either, but they do alter the user's physical well-being and mental awareness and are, of course, perfectly lawful to possess. We should, therefore, recognize that a drug is actually any substance that alters the user's physiological and/or psychological state whether used for medicinal or nonmedical use.

Drug abuse is another term randomly discussed in substance abuse literature. Just exactly what does it mean? To some, drug abuse may refer to the taking of any illicit drug or the overuse of prescribed drugs. For others, drug abuse is illicit drug use which results in social, economic, psychological, or legal problems for the drug user. Stated plainly, the Bureau of Justice Statistics describe drug abuse as the use of prescription-type psychotherapeutic drugs for nonmedical purposes or the use of illegal drugs (1991).

Drugs and the Brain

We know generally how and in what way many drugs affect the user. However, the pharmacologic mechanisms through which various drugs exert their effects are only partially understood. Researchers have identified locations and substances in the brain that are closely associated with the effects of drugs and their reinforcement properties. Although the process is complex, the so-called neurotransmitter **dopamine** appears to play an important role in determining the effects of drugs like cocaine and heroin. For example, cocaine acts on the pleasure center of the brain to the extent that in some people, particularly those with personality disorders already in place, cocaine becomes more important and pleasurable than some of the most basic human needs such as food, sex, or exercise. Normally, dopamine is released by nerve centers and is then withdrawn. In the case of cocaine, dopamine continues to be transmitted, seriously raising the blood pressure and increasing the heart rate.

We also know that drug abuse may be a symptom of a larger problem. For example, people with certain psychiatric disorders may be prone to drug abuse. Drug and alcohol problems often occur along with other psychiatric disorders. Those with drug problems frequently have affective, anxiety, or personality disorders. Sometimes, however, the reverse is also true. One example of this is the self-medication hypothesis. In this case, a person who is depressed may use drugs to elevate his or her mood, or a person who is suffering severe anxiety may seek relief by the relaxing effects of certain drugs. In other cases, people who are addicted to one drug may seek to counter that drug's effects by taking another drug with opposite effects. This poly-drug use may result in an overdose or even the death of the user, depending on the mixture of drugs taken.

Problems of Side Effects

Adding to the dangers of substance abuse is the reality that drugs alter people's behavior. Psychoactive drugs alter people's moods, perceptions, attitudes, and emotions. As a result, concern is often expressed about the impact of drug use on work, family, and social relations. Another concern is that many drugs provide the user with unintended side effects. Although some of these side effects may be short-term and relatively harmless in nature, some have just the opposite effects. Heroin users, for example, take the drug initially for its euphoric effects, but they soon discover that euphoria is also accompanied by feelings of nausea, constricted pupils, and respiratory depression. Cannabis products such as marijuana and hashish can result in memory loss and disorientation. Users of hallucinogens such as LSD often complain of bad hallucinations and imagined flashbacks. Just exactly what constitutes the effects of any particular drug depends on a number of factors such as the mood of the user and how the drugs are taken. A good example is cocaine, a drug that usually elevates one's mood. In users who are depressed prior to drug consumption, however, a deeper depression may result. In addition, after the initial effects of the drug wear off, cocaine users experience anxiety, depression, fatigue, and an urge for more cocaine. Drug users will often look to drugs such as those in the stimulant family to enhance their intellectual or physical performance. Because these drugs increase one's alertness, there is a perception of improved performance, but in reality, the user experiences severe fatigue and a reduced capacity for learning which can offset any physical improvements caused by the drugs.

Outcomes of Drug Abuse

To best understand the many different drugs abused on our streets, we should first consider some clinical terms commonly associated with drug abuse. These terms define the predominant effects of drugs and are generally associated with the most dangerous drugs of abuse.

- **Physical dependence**. Physiological (or physical) dependence is characterized by a growing tolerance of a drug's effects so that increased amounts of the drug necessitate the continued presence of the drug in order to prevent withdrawal symptoms.

- **Psychological dependence**. Psychological dependence is a controversial term which generally means the craving for or compulsive need to use drugs, because they provide the user with a feeling of well-being and satisfaction. However, attempts to equate physical dependence or addiction with psychological dependence are highly questionable since psychological dependence may be developed for any activity from listening to rock music to enjoying sex.
- **Tolerance**. Tolerance is a situation in which the user continues regular use of a drug and must administer progressively larger doses to attain the desired effect, thereby reinforcing the compulsive behavior known as drug dependence.
- **The withdrawal syndrome**. Withdrawal is the physical reaction of bodily functions which, when deprived of an addictive drug, causes increased excitability of those same bodily functions that have been depressed by the drug's habitual use.

We should note that psychological dependence is subjective and difficult to define but is characterized by a person's compulsive need to use drugs. Furthermore, the extent to which drugs produce physical dependence will vary. Heroin, for instance, has an extremely high potential for physical dependence. In comparison, cocaine is not addictive in the same way as heroin, but its potential for psychological dependence is high in some people, particularly those with obsessive personality traits—especially when the cocaine used is in the form of crack. This variation in the potential for physical dependence is one reason for the scheduling of drugs under federal and state laws (see Chapter 11).

Dependence versus Abuse

When addressing the task of understanding the many different drugs that have been popularized on the street, perhaps we should first consider certain clinical terms and the definitions that are commonly associated with drugs and drug use. These terms define certain predominant effects of drugs and are generally associated with those drugs that are considered the most dangerous.

To begin, we should note that drug abuse can be described in many different ways. Generally, however, the pathological use of substances that affect the central nervous system falls into two main categories: substance dependence and substance abuse. Let's look closer at these two terms. *The Diagnostic and Statistical Manual* (DSM IV, 1994), endorsed by the American Psychiatric Association, outlines the criteria for substance dependence as the presence of three or more of the following symptoms occurring at any time in the same 12-month period:

(1) tolerance, as defined by either of the following:
 (a) a need for markedly increased amounts of the substance to achieve intoxication or desired effect

(b) markedly diminished effect with continued use of the same amount of the substance

(2) withdrawal, as manifested by either of the following:

(a) the characteristic withdrawal syndrome for the substance

(b) The same, or closely related substance is taken to relieve or avoid withdrawal symptoms

(3) the substance is often taken in larger amounts, or over a longer period than was intended

(4) There is a persistent desire or unsuccessful efforts to cut down or control substance use

(5) a great deal of time is spent in activities necessary to obtain the substance (e.g., visiting multiple doctors or driving long distances), use the substance (e.g., chain smoking), or recover from its effects

(6) important social, occupational or recreational activities are given up or reduced because of substance use

(7) the substance use is continued despite knowledge of having a persistent or recurrent physical or psychological problem that is likely to have been caused or exacerbated by the substance (e.g., current cocaine use despite recognition of cocaine-induced depression, or continued drinking despite recognition that an ulcer was made worse by alcohol consumption)

- *Physical dependence.* Physiological (or physical) dependence on a drug refers to an alteration of normal body functions that necessitates the continued presence of a drug in order to prevent the withdrawal (or abstinence) syndrome, characteristic of each class of addictive drug.

- *Psychological dependence.* Psychological dependence is a term that generally means the craving or continuation of the use of a drug because it provides the user with a feeling of well-being and satisfaction.

- *Tolerance.* Tolerance* is a situation in which the user continues regular use of a drug and must administer progressively larger doses to attain the desired effect, thereby reinforcing the compulsive behavior known as drug dependence.

- *The withdrawal syndrome.* Withdrawal* is the physical reaction of bodily functions that, when deprived of an addictive drug, causes increased excitability of those same bodily functions that have been depressed by the drug's habitual use.

Tolerance and *withdrawal* at one time were used to define the term *addiction,* implying that addiction was a physiological process rather than a psychological dependency. This distinction is not made clear by DSM III-R. In addition, addictions with obvious tolerance and withdrawal symptoms are not always disabling, as when a patient becomes addicted to prescribed pain medication.

Substance abuse is another term commonly used in both conversation and in the literature of drug abuse and has also been defined by the DSM IV. Substance abuse differs from substance dependence in that it is a less severe version of dependence. In short, "abuse" is diagnosed when the person's use of a substance is maladaptive but not severe enough to meet the diagnostic criteria for dependence. Understanding these terms helps us not only categorize drugs but recognize abnormal behavior which often accompanies drug use.

Drug Categories

To better understand the various types of drugs and their effects, a system of categories has been generally recognized. Each of these six categories (stimulants, depressants, hallucinogens, narcotics, cannabis, and inhalants) may contain both legal and controlled substances. Each substance possesses unique characteristics and will be discussed next.

Stimulants

Stimulants are a category of drugs that literally stimulate or excite the user's central nervous system. The two most common stimulants are nicotine from tobacco products and caffeine, commonly found in soft drinks, coffee, and tea. These substances are an accepted part of our culture and are, therefore, widely used. Generally speaking, these products are consumed not only for recreation, but when used in moderation, they may be taken to relieve minor fatigue.

Although health problems are commonly associated with the regular use of both nicotine and caffeine, other stimulants can produce a more powerful physical and psychological dependence. Stimulants are popular because they make the user feel stronger, more alert, and decisive. As we stated earlier, excessive use of stimulants ("uppers") may evolve into a pattern where they are taken regularly and countered in the evening with depressants ("downers").

Stimulants are used by an array of people including dieters; people involved in boring, routine, repetitive work; or by those working extra jobs and in need of additional energy for a longer period of time than the average workday. Accompanying a temporary sense of exhilaration is irritability and a loss of appetite. When the effects of the stimulant wear off, the body experiences a "crashing" or a sudden exhaustion. Depending on the stimulant in question, the "crash" is sometimes experienced in tandem with chest pains, headaches, and even bouts of paranoia.

Caffeine

Caffeine plays an important role in understanding drug abuse in many societies around the world. It is a bitter tasting, odorless chemical which can be either manufactured synthetically or derived from coffee beans, tea leaves, and cola nuts. It was first extracted from coffee in 1820 and from tea leaves in 1827 and is currently found in cola drinks, cocoa, and some diet pills. As a rule, it acts as a mild stimulant and is for the most part harmless to people, except for its addicting nature. In larger doses, caffeine is known for causing insomnia, restlessness, and anxiety in users. Physical effects of caffeine are also unique and include an increase in heart rate and possible irregularities in the heart. In fact, some researchers maintain that heavy coffee drinkers are more prone to develop coronary heart disease (Gilbert, 1984). Since caffeine is associated with insomnia, it has been used by many people to postpone fatigue. However, not all of the effects of caffeine have proven to be negative. For example, because caffeine decreases blood flow to the brain, it has been used in treating migraine headaches, and physicians have used it to treat poisoning caused by depressants such as alcohol and morphine. Furthermore, studies suggest that it somewhat increases the effectiveness of common analgesics such as aspirin as well as helping to relieve asthma attacks by widening bronchial airways (Gilbert, 1984). In any case, caffeine has probably become the most popular drug in the world and has etched a niche as a key factor in everyday American life.

Coffee

Of the caffeine drinks that have gained popularity over the centuries, coffee has become an American (and even a global) icon. The word coffee was derived from the Arabic word *gahweh* (pronounced "kehevh"). People drink it with virtually all meals: as a morning pick-me-up, as a midday break drink, and as a means to stay alert late at night. As a result of its popularity, the coffee industry represents one of the most profitable in the world. In fact, the coffee bean is thought to be the world's most valuable agricultural commodity. In the late 1980s, coffee imports into the United States alone cost more than $4 billion annually (Anderson, 1982).

Coffee, which is native to Ethiopia, has been cultivated and brewed in Arab countries for centuries. The drink was introduced into Europe in the mid-seventeenth century, and plantations in Indonesia, the West Indies, and Brazil soon made coffee cultivation an important element in colonial economies. Today, Latin America and Africa produce most of the world's coffee with the United States as the largest importer and consumer. Coffee's unique flavor is determined not only by the variety, but also by the length of time the green beans are roasted. After roasting, the beans are usually ground and vacuum-packed in cans. Since the flavor of coffee deteriorates rapidly after it is ground or after a sealed can is opened, many coffee drinkers buy whole roasted beans and grind them at home. Instant coffee, which makes up about one-fifth of all coffee sold, is prepared by forcing an atomized spray of very strong coffee extract, through a jet of hot air, evaporating the water in the extract and leaving dried coffee particles which are packaged as instant coffee. Another method of producing instant coffee is freeze-drying. Decaffeinated coffee is yet another popular form of coffee. To make decaffeinated coffee, the green bean is processed in a steam or chemical bath to remove the caffeine, the substance that produces coffee's stimulating effect.

Nicotine

As with caffeine, nicotine is another stimulant found in most societies around the world. Ever since colonial times, nicotine has maintained a large and prosperous tobacco industry and despite evidence of its ill effects on health, it is consumed almost as fast as it is produced. In the early 1900s, cigarettes were the most common form of taking nicotine. This occurred after a series of public health warnings about the dangers of chewing tobacco and its link to tuberculosis. Unaware of the high risks to the lungs, heart, blood, and nervous system, people switched to smoking cigarettes instead. In addition, the cigarette industry utilized automatic rolling machines for cigarette production, making them more affordable, and relied on extensive advertising campaigns for mass sales. In 1964, the first Surgeon General's report was issued, titled *Report of the Surgeon General's Advisory Committee on Smoking and Health*. It received mass media coverage and convinced many Americans of the dangers of smoking. In subsequent years, manufacturers produced low tar and filtered cigarettes, which were touted as being "safer." Finally during the mid-1990s, many anti-smoking campaigns have emerged, rallying support for increased number of no-smoking areas in public places. In many cities, smoking has been completely outlawed in stores and restaurants.

Thinking Critically #2

Assume you are an attorney whose client, a non-smoker dying of lung cancer, is suing the tobacco industry for damages inflicted from secondhand smoke. Submit your summation speech to the jury.

In addition to the discomfort experienced by nonsmokers, nicotine has been proven to be an addictive substance creating a physical dependence on the part of the smoker. Those who have developed a nicotine dependence often must seek specially designed programs to aid them in gradually cutting back on smoking. Nicotine, an extremely poisonous, colorless liquid alkaloid, turns brown on exposure to air, and as the most potent ingredient of the tobacco plant, *nicotiana tabacum* is found mainly in the leaves. Both nicotine and the tobacco plant are named after Jean Nicot, a French ambassador who sent tobacco from Portugal to Paris in 1560. Nicotine's effects on the human body after prolonged use can be devastating. It can affect the human nervous system, causing respiratory failure and general paralysis. It may also be absorbed through the skin. Interestingly, only two or three drops (which is less than 50 mg) of the pure alkaloid placed on the tongue is rapidly fatal to an adult (Hyman, 1986). A typical cigarette contains 15 to 20 mg of nicotine, but the actual amount that reaches the bloodstream and hence the brain through normal smoking is only about 1 mg. Nicotine is believed to be responsible for most of the short-term and many of the long-term effects of smoking and for the fact of tobacco smoking's addictive properties. Because of the popularity of filter-tipped cigarettes, nicotine yields have declined by about 70 percent since the 1950s. Nicotine is also produced in quantity from tobacco scraps and is used as a pesticide. Converted to nicotinic acid, a member of the vitamin B group, it is used as a food supplement.

Smoking

Smoking is a common practice in many societies and typically refers to the inhaling of tobacco smoke from a pipe, cigar, or cigarette. Although in the mid-1990s many public initiatives have focused on restricting smoking behavior, in 1993 it was estimated that approximately 46 million Americans still smoke (Levy, 1994). However, anti-smoking regulations in both public areas and work places are most likely contributing to a gradual decrease in this figure.

As we mentioned in our first chapter, the history of smoking as well as concerns about it are vast. American Indians smoked pipes, and European explorers had introduced the practice into the Old World by the early sixteenth century. Controversy over the health effects of smoking have stemmed from that time. Much of this concern is with good cause because cigarette smoke consists of more than 4,700 compounds, 43 of which are carcinogens, such as tar (Centers for Disease Control, 1992). Nicotine is considered the addicting agent that makes quitting smoking so difficult.

By the early 1960s, numerous clinical and laboratory studies on smoking and disease had been made. In 1964, a committee appointed by the surgeon general of the U.S. Public Health Service issued a report based on the critical review of previous studies on the effects of smoking. The report concluded that nearly all lung cancer deaths are caused by cigarette smoking, which was also held responsible for many deaths and much disability from various illnesses such as chronic bronchitis, emphysema, and cardiovascular disease. A more recent study estimated that about 400,000 Americans die each year from breathing their own smoke. A 1984 report by the service also suggested that passive inhalation of smoke by nonsmokers (secondhand smoke) could be harmful. Although considered controversial at the time, studies have since confirmed many of these charges. Some experts estimate that passive smoke kills as many as 50,000 Americans a year, and it is the third leading preventable cause of death, behind smoking and drinking. Studies have shown that children are particularly sensitive to passive smoke and that pregnant women who smoke may harm the fetus.

A Health Debate that Won't Die

The fact that puffing on a cigarette is an unhealthy activity is no longer seriously disputed, even by the tobacco industry. Much of the current medical debate has shifted to two related questions: Is nicotine addictive? And how dangerous is environmental tobacco smoke? Tobacco companies insist that nicotine, which is contained in varying amounts in all cigarettes, does not create a habit so powerful that it impairs a person's ability to quit. But the overwhelming consensus in the scientific community is that nicotine is an addictive substance. A Surgeon General's report has concluded it is as addictive as heroin or cocaine.

There is evidence that some cigarette company researchers have long known that it is the nicotine that appeals to smokers. A 1972 internal memo by a Philip Morris scientist contended that "no one has ever become a cigarette smoker by smoking cigarettes without nicotine." That was proved again a few years ago, when the company introduced the nearly nicotine-free Next. The public wasn't interested. The industry claims smokers turn away from such cigarettes because they lack "taste" or "flavor." But researchers maintain that these cigarettes taste no different; they lack the kick nicotine provides. A 1992 study found that people who puffed Next cigarettes didn't show the brain-wave changes that smokers ordinarily exhibit.

Tobacco companies have heavier artillery when it comes to challenging the EPA's 1993 report that labeled environmental tobacco smoke, or ETS, a carcinogen. They charge that the report—a review of 30 epidemiological, animal and laboratory studies conducted during the past two decades—is fundamentally flawed. The Congressional Research Service and some independent scientists have also criticized the report. The EPA found that fumes rising from the tips of lighted cigarettes (as opposed to the smoke that users exhale) is the most hazardous, with high concentrations of 17 carcinogens. The agency also concluded that environmental smoke produces serious respiratory illness in young children. Critics note, however, that the EPA didn't consider a threshold level for smoking damage. Scientists know cells have the ability to repair damage to their DNA. Can cells fix tobacco-induced changes, and at what level of pollution does the repair mechanism become overwhelmed? The agency regarded all smoke exposure as dangerous and the effects as cumulative. EPA scientists admit that the danger of getting a whiff of tobacco at the baseball stadium is generally not the same as driving in an enclosed car with a chain smoker. "I'd expect the ballpark risk to be minimal," concedes a researcher.

The agency also neglected the possibility that other factors besides ETS might have played the major role in inducing lung cancers and respiratory illness. Even if one accepts the agency's assessment, say critics, the risk of developing lung cancer from ETS is only about the same as the chance of dying in a bicycle accident. EPA supporters respond that several comprehensive reviews of ETS—by the Surgeon General, the National Academy of Sciences, and the National Institute for Occupational Safety and Health—support the report's conclusion. More corroborating studies have come since the report's release, including one that firmly links ETS to heart disease. The question, as always, is at what level the danger of exposure becomes a cause for action.

Source: Toufexis, Anastasia (1994). "A Health Debate that Won't Die." *Time.* April 18. p. 61. © 1994 Time Inc. Reprinted by permission.

Since 1964, health warnings have been mandated on tobacco advertising, and the use of such advertising has been restricted. Most states in the United States have also passed laws to control smoking in public places such as restaurants and workplaces, where nonsmoking areas may be required. Some U.S. airlines have prohibited smoking on flights lasting six hours or less, while others have prohibited smoking on all flights. Among the military, the U.S. Army has been particularly strict in imposing smoking restrictions. The tobacco industry and many smokers regard anti-smoking measures as harassment, whereas many nonsmokers defend the measures on the grounds that the government has a duty to discourage unhealthful practices, that public funds in one form or another become involved in treating diseases caused by smoking, and that smokers pollute the air for nonsmokers.

Smoking Facts

- 28 percent of men are regular smokers

- 23 percent of women are regular smokers

- 46 million Americans are former smokers

Source: Centers for Disease Control, 1993

Quitting is thought to be extremely difficult, especially for chronic smokers. In fact, in 1993 the Centers for Disease Control reported that 70 percent of regular smokers try to quit but only 8 percent succeed. In recent years, smoking-withdrawal clinics have become particularly popular, although most people who quit smoking are thought to do it on their own. Nicotine gum or the relatively new nicotine skin patches are useful tools for quitting the habit. Nicotine gum, which has been around for years, tends to lessen early withdrawal symptoms. Nicotine, patches, which are available by prescription, are yet another way to allow the smoker to deal with the behavioral aspects of quitting before confronting the physical effects of nicotine withdrawal.

Cocaine

From the 1960s era of the "flower children," cocaine has now advanced in popularity to become one of the most commonly abused drugs in the United States. Cocaine, considered the most potent natural stimulant, is extracted from the South American coca plant. In the late 1980s and early 1990s, cocaine has grown to be an illicit drug of great popularity on the streets and one that generates considerable wealth for criminal organizations in the United States and South America. In fact, cocaine and its freebase form, "crack," have grown into a multi-billion-dollar industry that sustains the emerging entrepreneurial drug gangs such as the Crips, the Bloods, and Jamaican posses, as well as a number of already well-established criminal organizations.

As discussed in Chapter 1, cocaine was hailed in the nineteenth century as a wonder drug for addiction and other ailments. Like the opiates, it was controlled by such legislation as the 1914 Harrison Narcotics Act. Now, because it is one of the most available and inexpensive drugs on the black market, there is an increasing demand for the drug. Cocaine, a white crystalline powder, is commonly diluted through the use of other white powders such as baking soda, lactose, mannitol, and even some local anesthetics like lidocaine. It traditionally has been snorted and then absorbed through the linings of the nose into the brain. Since the mid-1980s, smokeable "freebase" cocaine called "crack" has become popular in many U.S. cities.

Cocaine's limited but legitimate use is in nose and eye surgery. It is considered invaluable because of its ability to anesthetize tissue while simultaneously constricting blood vessels and limiting the amount of bleeding. Most other applications of cocaine have become obsolete due to the synthesis of other drugs that have similar characteristics.

For many years cocaine was thought to be relatively safe, unlike other drugs such as LSD and PCP. Studies have shown, however, that side effects from cocaine use are, indeed, common. They include anxiety, restlessness, extreme irritability, and paranoia. In the early 1970s, studies of cocaine-related deaths indicated that between 1971 and 1976 only 111 deaths had been reported. But with the advent of freebasing, those statistics increased markedly with the number of cocaine-related deaths quadrupling between 1979 and 1981. Current estimates are that only 10 percent of cocaine users inject or freebase the substance (as opposed to snorting it), but those who do inject or freebase account for 76 to 92 percent of all cocaine-related deaths. In any case, the risk of death prevails in the form of heart attack or stroke from excessive use, particularly from freebasing.

Because of its pleasurable effects, cocaine has the potential for dependence. In recent years it has been debated as to whether or not cocaine users can become physically addicted to the drug. Little doubt exists that cocaine has a strong potential for reinforcing compulsive use, but its use results in different symptoms than those resulting from heroin use. In fact, recent studies indicate that cocaine users clearly develop a strong psychological dependence but are not characterized by the physical dependence of heavy opiate use (BJS, 1991). Recurrent users may resort to larger doses at shorter intervals in order to maintain their highs. The danger of psychological dependence may be directly related to the amount and frequency of use. For years it appeared that the high cost of cocaine would serve to limit use and control many of the dysfunctional attributes of the drug. However, with the advent of crack cocaine, the drug has become more affordable and more commonly available. Despite its widespread availability, the danger of cocaine dependence is still limited, with the National Institute of Drug Abuse estimating that about 3 percent of all cocaine users will ever become "problem" cocaine abusers.

The cycle of cocaine use roughly approximates the following phases:

Phase 1 *Experimental*

Those that fall into this category do not use the drug consistently enough to become addicted but may easily fall into regular use due to peer pressure.

Phase 2 *Occasional*

The user in this phase maintains a consistency of cocaine use that falls short of compulsive (discussed next). Occasional use, however, tends to build tolerance.

Phase 3 *Compulsive*

The cocaine user in the compulsive phase will not pass up an opportunity to take cocaine. By the time he or she has reached this phase, a strong psychological dependence has taken effect.

Phase 4 *Dependent*

Once having reached this phase, the user has little control over choices to do the drug. He or she will experience severe states of depression and financial hardship and will commonly deal cocaine to friends in order to support his or her own habit.

The intensity of psychological effects of cocaine, as with many psychoactive drugs, depends on the rate of entry into the blood. Intravenous injection or freebasing produces an almost immediate and intense high. Conversion of cocaine hydrochloride into cocaine base yields a substance that becomes volatile when heated and produces crack, which is discussed below.

Excessive doses of cocaine may cause seizures and even death from respiratory failure, stroke, cerebral hemorrhage, or heart failure, most likely in individuals with pre-existing respiratory, circulatory, and heart ailments. There is no specific treatment for cocaine overdose. And because tolerance for the drug may not develop, users may never be able to gauge how much cocaine they can ingest safely. In fact, it is thought by some that repeated use lowers the dose at which toxicity occurs, so that there is no known *safe* dose. On the other hand, it is generally accepted that the lethal dose of cocaine is one and a half grams of pure cocaine hydrochloride. In terms of "street" cocaine, this means that ingesting about ten grams at a single sitting would be lethal. This is a very unlikely prospect for even the most robust cocaine users.

How Cocaine Works

The exact effects of cocaine on the human body are not quite clear. However, according to an article appearing in the January 1989 issue of *National Geographic*, the physical cyclical effects of cocaine are as follows:

> Upon ingestion, cocaine first enhances then later interferes with the transmission of the pleasure signals of the brain. A message is carried across the synapse between the axon of one nerve cell and the body of another by chemicals called **neurotransmitters**.
>
> Of the neurotransmitters released by cocaine, the most important is *dopamine*. Dopamine fills receptors on the body of the next cell and sparks a continuation of the message.
>
> Normally, pumps reclaim the dopamine but, according to a leading theory, cocaine blocks this process. Dopamine remains in the receptors, sending an enhanced message before breaking down. Prolonged cocaine use may also deplete dopamine, rendering the sensation of pleasure impossible for the user (White, 1989).

Crack

Since the mid-1980s, the practice of smoking, or *freebasing*, cocaine has become increasingly popular. Freebasing can be accomplished either through traditional methods or through the smoking of *crack* cocaine. Traditional freebasing, the method used before the advent of crack, is accomplished by mixing cocaine HCl with ether or some other volatile liquid, adding water, and then heating it. The fumes are then inhaled. The drug is then absorbed by the lining of the lungs and delivered within 15 seconds to the brain.

The method of smoking crack is less complicated than the traditional freebase method discussed above. It is also safer from a logistical point of view because crack is not a volatile material. All the user has to do is heat a chunk of crack with the use of a small glass pipe. The crack vaporizes, and the fumes are inhaled. The freebase high only lasts from 8 to 11 minutes, requiring the user to smoke more and more of the drug to prolong its effects. Crack is made from a cocaine hydrochloride solution that is heated in a pan together with baking soda. This yields a solid chunk of cocaine product, which is subsequently cut up into hundreds of tiny chunks resembling soap chips. The chips are then placed into small vials or plastic packets and sold anywhere from $5 to $50 per container.

Cocaine: How It Hurts

Daily or "binge" users characteristically undergo profound personality changes. They become "coked out." They are confused, anxious, and depressed. They are short-tempered and grow suspicious of friends, loved ones, and coworkers. Their thinking is impaired; they have difficulty concentrating and remembering things. Their work and other responsibilities fall into neglect. They lose interest in food and sex. Some become aggressive; some experience panic attacks. The more they use the drug, the more pronounced their symptoms become. Over time, cocaine exacts a toll on the user's mind and body.

Those that sniff the drug regularly experience a runny nose, sore throat, hoarseness, and sores on the nasal membranes (sometimes to the point of perforating the septum). Many experience shortness of breath, cold sweats, and uncontrollable tremors as their consumption increases. Long-term use may damage the liver.

Because cocaine kills the appetite, many habitual users suffer from malnutrition and lose significant amounts of weight. Poor diet results in nutritional deficiencies and a host of other problems, many of which are compounded by a lack of sleep and a deterioration of personal hygiene. Intravenous users risk hepatitis, AIDS, and other infections from contaminated needles. Freebase smokers risk harm to the lungs. Because adolescents are still growing and, therefore, more vulnerable to the effects of drugs, cocaine can be even more harmful.

Source: Bell, R. (1987). "Toward a Drug Free America." *Challenge Newsletter*. National Drug Policy Board (March).

Amphetamines

The amphetamine family of stimulants (dextroamphetamine, methamphetamine, and amphetamine, also referred to on the street as "speed") represents yet another popular but dangerous stimulant drug. Shortly after the introduction of amphetamine into the medical community, its prescribed uses increased. For example, the use of amphetamines in over-the-counter medicines, such as inhalers, was common for a while. Soon after, many dangerous side effects were documented, and the medical use of amphetamines was greatly reduced. Actually, medical use of amphetamines is strictly limited to conditions such as narcolepsy, attention deficit disorders in children, and some cases of obesity.

The illicit use of amphetamines closely parallels that of cocaine with regard to its short- and long-term effects. As such, amphetamines are often used as a cheaper substitute for costly cocaine. In many areas of the country, the clandestine manufacture of amphetamines is common as users desire the high but do not want to pay the higher price of cocaine. With this illicit production of the drug, organized crime groups, such as outlaw motorcycle gangs, provide an estimated 40 percent of the illicit amphetamine and methamphetamine consumed on the street.

Ice

The 1980s introduced the specter of a new drug epidemic. The new drug was a freebase form of methamphetamine known as *ice*. Primarily seen in Hawaii and along the West Coast, ice sells on the street for about $50 per gram. It was first developed by traffickers out of reconstructed methamphetamine, a popular recreational stimulant. Ice, whose popularity has impacted particularly hard in Japan, is also called *shabu* or *hiroppon* in the Orient. It consists of tiny ice-like crystals designed to be smoked (freebased) by the user. The expected high reported by the typical ice user is anywhere from eight to sixteen hours, compared to the eight- to ten-minute high offered by its close cousin crack, which is also a stimulant.

Side effects of ice include fatal lung and kidney disorders, in addition to long-lasting psychological damage. As mentioned, ice is not new but a converted drug, as crack was converted from cocaine. It has appealed to both recreational users as well as to those that desire a supercharged type of speed for alertness and physical steadfastness.

The emergence of ice in the United States is also distinguishable from the mid-1980s emergence of crack in that ice's host drug, methamphetamine, can easily be manufactured domestically. This is obviously an advantage for local traffickers who are proficient in the manufacturing and distribution of methamphetamine powder. The popularity of ice in the United States began in Hawaii in the mid-1980s. During a brief four-year period, police estimate that it surpassed the popularity of marijuana and cocaine there. The genesis of ice in Hawaii goes back to Korea, which, along with Taiwan, leads the world in manufacture and export of the drug. Koreans learned of the drug methamphetamine from the Japanese, who had developed it in 1873.

Depressants

Contrary to the effects of stimulants are the depressant category of drugs. Drugs falling into this category also have a potential for abuse due to their physical and psychological characteristics. Like many dangerous substances, if taken under the supervision of a physician, drugs in this category may be beneficial in treating conditions such as anxiety, irritability, tension, and insomnia. When abused, depressants produce a state of intoxication closely resembling that of alcohol.

As with stimulants, drugs falling in this category are not all controlled or unlawful. That is, even compounds that can be purchased over the counter can also have dangerous effects on the user. One such substance is alcohol, which, when taken in moderation, will produce a mild sedation. The name "depressant" does not literally mean that the user becomes depressed but refers to the depression of his or her central nervous system. Initially, in heavier doses some depressants may give the user an uplifting feeling similar to that produced by stimulants. After prolonged use, however, the user tends to become sluggish with impaired judgment, slurred speech, and a loss of motor coordination.

Tolerance to depressants (as with stimulants and narcotics) develops rapidly with regular use, which adds to the likelihood of an overdose or even death. Those that use depressants and fail to follow their physician's recommendations for use may find that their daily doses will increase 10 to 20 times the recommended therapeutic dose.

As we mentioned earlier, many stimulant users will frequently use a depressant to help them calm down at the end of the day. The level of danger rises, however, when the user chooses to mix depressants with alcohol, creating a *synergistic* effect. This occurs when two or more drugs are taken together and the combined action increases the normal effect of each drug. Because of this action, a drug that can normally be taken safely can have a devastating effect if taken with a drug that acts synergistically with it. Perhaps one of the most important dangers of depressant use is the abrupt cessation of high-dose depressant intake, which will result in the characteristic withdrawal syndrome (discussed above). Such a condition manifests itself by feelings of anxiety, vomiting, loss of appetite, increased heart rate, profuse sweating, and possibly convulsions similar to those occurring in grand mal epilepsy. The latter symptom will usually peak in approximately the third to seventh day of abstinence, depending on the type of depressant used, and is considered to be life threatening unless conducted under medical supervision.

Alcohol

Alcohol, one of the oldest drugs known, has been used as far back as records exist. In fact, legal codes limiting its consumption date as far back as 1700 B.C. As we have learned, growing concern about alcoholism and related social problems prompted Prohibition during the 1920s and early 1930s. As the moral approach to alcohol abuse was gradually abandoned, a more scientific approach was adopted referring to it as a disease. Recently, however, some experts have suggested that alcoholism is not as much a disease as a learned social behavior (Bower, 1988).

Although various types of alcohol exist, ethyl alcohol is the type consumed in drinking, and in its pure form it is a colorless, odorless substance. As a rule, people drink alcohol in three main kinds of beverages: *beers*, which are made from grain through brewing and fermentation and contain from 3 percent to 8 percent alcohol; *wines*, which are fermented from fruits such as grapes and contain from 8 percent to 12 percent alcohol naturally and up to 21 percent when fortified by adding alcohol; and distilled beverages (spirits) such as whiskey, gin, and vodka, which typically contain from 40 percent to 50 percent alcohol. If not kept in check, drinkers may become physically addicted to any of these beverages.

The effects of alcohol vary considerably from one person to another. Mild sedation results from low doses while higher doses, insofar as they tend to reduce anxiety, may produce a temporary state of well-being leading to more serious effects such as depression and apathy. Intoxicating doses typically result in impaired judgement, slurred speech, and loss of motor skills. In addition to the safety dangers associated with drinking and driving and related accidents, chronic users incur risks of long-term involvement with depressants. Tolerance to the intoxicating effects of alcohol develop quickly, leading to a progressive narrowing of the margin of safety between a dose that is intoxicating and one that is lethal.

Alcohol's effects depend on the amount in the blood known as **blood-alcohol concentration** or BAC, which varies with the rate of consumption and with the rate at which the drinker's physical system absorbs and metabolizes alcohol. The higher the alcohol content of the beverage consumed, the more alcohol will enter the bloodstream. The amount and type of food in the stomach also tends to affect the absorption rate. Studies have shown that drinking when the stomach is filled is less intoxicating than when it is empty; the foods in the stomach, which contain fat and protein, delay alcohol absorption. Body weight is also a factor; the heavier the person, the slower the absorption of alcohol. After alcohol passes through the stomach, it is rapidly absorbed through the walls of the intestines into the bloodstream and carried to the various organ systems of the body, where it is metabolized.

Thinking Critically #3

Predict the effects on society if Americans, attempting to reduce body fat and strokes, greatly increase their consumption of wine. How would this activity affect social behavior, health, and the "drug problem?"

Although small amounts of alcohol are processed by the kidneys and secreted in the urine and other small amounts are processed through the lungs and exhaled in the breath, most of the alcohol is metabolized by the liver. As the alcohol is metabolized, it gives off heat. The body metabolizes alcohol at about the rate of three-fourths of an ounce to one ounce of whiskey an hour. Technically, it is possible to drink at the same rate as the alcohol is being oxidized out of the body. Most people, however, drink faster than this, and so the concentration of alcohol in the bloodstream keeps rising. Alcohol begins to impair the brain's ability to function when the blood-alcohol concentration (BAC) reaches 0.05 percent, or 0.05 grams of alcohol per 100 cubic centimeters of blood. Most state traffic laws in the United States are based on the assumption that a driver with a BAC of 0.10 percent is intoxicated. With a concentration of 0.20 percent (a level obtained from drinking about 10 ounces of whiskey), a person has difficulty controlling the emotions and may cry or laugh excessively. The intoxicated person will experience a great deal of difficulty in attempting to walk and will want to lie down. When the blood-alcohol content reaches about 0.30 percent, which can be attained when a person rapidly drinks about a pint of whiskey, the

A Drink or Two a Day Cuts Heart Risk By Half

Being a moderate drinker appears to cut heart attack risk in half by increasing levels of HDL, or "good" cholesterol, a [recent] study suggests. The Harvard University study compared 340 first-time Boston heart attack patients—men and women less than 76 years old—with 340 other Bostonians and found:

- Those who drank one or more drinks daily cut heart attack risk by half. A drink was defined as 13.2 grams of ethanol, or a 12-ounce glass of beer.

- Moderate drinkers had a 35 percent lower heart disease risk.

- The drinkers had 10 to 20 percent higher levels of total high-density lipoprotein (HDL) and both kinds of HDL. Higher HDL decreases heart risks.

This study may finally explain why previous studies touted the benefits of moderate drinking but without knowing exactly why it worked. "We hope we've added a missing piece to the puzzle," says J. Michael Gaziano of Boston's Brigham and Women's Hospital and lead author of the report in today's *New England Journal of Medicine.* Even with this new evidence, drinking can have risks. Moderate drinking "can be desirable or undesirable, depending on individual characteristics," Gary Friedman and Arthur Klatsky of the Kaiser Permanente in Oakland, California, say in an editorial. Long-term alcohol abuse can cause cirrhosis, hypertension, cancers, and fetal damage. Other ways to raise HDL levels are exercise, and the replacement of saturated fat with monounsaturated fats when eating.

Source: Snider, Mike (1994). "A Drink or Two a Day Cuts Heart Risk by Half." *USA Today.* December 16. P. A-1. Copyright 1993, USA TODAY. Reprinted with permission.

drinker will have trouble comprehending and may become unconscious. At levels from 0.35 percent to 0.50 percent, the brain centers that control breathing and heart action are affected; concentrations above 0.50 percent may result in death although a person generally becomes unconscious before absorbing a lethal dosage.

Moderate or temperate use of alcohol is not harmful, but excessive or heavy drinking is associated with alcoholism and numerous other health problems. The effects of excessive drinking on major organ systems of the human body are cumulative and become evident after heavy, continuous drinking or after intermittent drinking over a period of time that may range from 5 to 30 years.

The parts of the body most affected by heavy drinking are the digestive and nervous systems. Digestive-system disorders that may be related to heavy drinking include cancer of the mouth, throat, and esophagus; gastritis; ulcers; cirrhosis of the liver; and inflammation of the pancreas. Disorders of the nervous system can include neuritis, lapse of memory (blackouts), hallucinations, and extreme tremors as found in delirium tremens. **Delirium tremens** ("the DTs") may occur when a person stops drinking after a period of heavy, continuous imbibing. Permanent damage to the brain and central nervous system may also result, including Korsakoff psychosis and Wernicke's disease. Recent evidence indicates that pregnant women who drink heavily may give birth to infants with fetal alcohol syndrome, which is characterized by face and body abnormalities and, in some cases, impaired intellectual facilities. Additionally, the combination of alcohol and drugs, such as commonly used sleeping pills, tranquilizers, antibiotics, and aspirin, can be fatal, even when both are taken in nonlethal doses.

Drinking habits in different societies vary considerably. Virtually every culture has its own general beliefs or sense of etiquette about the use and role of alcoholic beverages within its social structure. In some cultures drinking is either forbidden or frowned upon. The Koran contains prohibitions against drinking, and Muslims are forbidden to sell or serve alcoholic beverages. Hindus take a negative view of the use of alcohol; this is reflected in the constitution of India, which requires every state to work toward the prohibition of alcohol except for medicinal purposes. Abstinence from alcohol has also been the goal of large temperance movements in Europe and the United States. Some Christian religious groups strongly urge abstinence, including the Christian Scientists, Mormons, Seventh-Day Adventists, Pentecostalists, and most Baptists and Methodists. In some ambivalent cultures, such as the United States and Ireland, the values of those who believe in abstinence clash with the values of mainstream society who regard moderate drinking as a way of being hospitable and sociable. This accounts for the surplus of laws and regulations that restrict the buying of alcoholic beverages. Some psychologists say that this indecision in society makes it harder for some people to develop a consistent attitude toward drinking.

Some cultures have a permissive attitude toward drinking, including those of Spain, Portugal, Italy, Japan, and Israel. The proportion of Israelis and Italians who use alcohol is high, but the rates of alcoholism among them are lower than in Irish and Scandinavian groups. Some cultures may be said to look too favorably upon drinking, as do the French. In France the heavy consumption of alcohol has been related to the high number of people engaged in viticulture and in the production and distribution of alcoholic beverages. Various surveys indicate that subgroups within a society or culture do not all have the same attitudes toward alcoholic beverages or the same drinking patterns. Drinking behavior also differs significantly among groups of different age, sex, social class, racial status, ethnic background, occupational status, religious affiliation, and regional location.

Barbiturates

The most frequently prescribed depressants are barbiturates, which are commonly prescribed to induce sleep. About 15 derivatives of barbituric acid are currently in medical use. These are used to induce sleep or calm nervousness and usually take about one hour to take effect. Barbiturates are classified as ultra-short, short, intermediate, and long lasting, with the duration of effect lasting from 6 to 16 hours respectively. These include such drugs as hexobarbital (Sombulex), pentobarbital (Nembutal), secobarbital (Seconal), and phenobarbital (Luminal).

Quaaludes

A widely abused depressant of the late 1970s and early 1980s was the Quaalude®, or methaqualone. Although now outlawed, the quaalude (in counterfeit version) is still manufactured clandestinely in foreign markets, smuggled into the country, and sold on American streets. The quaalude is chemically unrelated to the barbiturate but has been responsible for many cases of poisoning and overdoses. It is sold in a tablet form, is ingested through the gastrointestinal tract, and is commonly stamped with the names "Lemon 714" or "Rorer 714." In large doses, it can cause coma and convulsions. Other than Quaalude, methaqualone has been marketed under other names such as Parest, Mequin, Optimil, Somnafac, and Sopor.

Hallucinogens

Although hallucinogens have been in existence in one form or another for hundreds of years, they first gained widespread, popular appeal during the 1960s. Hallucinogenic drugs are both natural (organic) and synthetic (manmade) and act on the central nervous system by distorting auditory, tactile, and visual perceptions of reality. Although the use of some hallucinogens has been

Figure 2.1

What are some of the effects of illegal drugs?

Drug type	Short-term effects Desired	Short-term effects Other	Duration of acute effects	DEA view of risk of dependence
Heroin	• euphoria • pain reduction	• respiratory depression • nausea • drowsiness	• 3 to 8 hours	• physical: high • psychological: high
Cocaine	• excitement • euphoria • increased alertness, wakefulness	• increased blood pressure • increased respiratory rate • nausea • cold sweats • twitching • headache	• 1 to 2 hours	• physical: possible • psychological: high
Crack cocaine	• same as cocaine • more rapid high than cocaine	• same as cocaine	• about 5 minutes	• same as cocaine
Marijuana	• euphoria • relaxation	• accelerated heartbeat • impairment of perception, judgment, fine motor skills, and memory	• 2 to 4 hours	• physical: unknown • psychological: moderate
Amphetamines	• euphoria • excitement • increased alertness, wakefulness	• increased blood pressure • increased pulse rate • insomnia • loss of appetite	• 2 to 4 hours	• physical: possible • psychological: high
LSD	• illusions and hallucinations • excitement • euphoria	• poor perception of time and distance • acute anxiety, restlessness, sleeplessness • sometimes depression	• 8 to 12 hours	• physical: none • psychological: unknown

Sources: NIDA, "Heroin," *NIDA Capsules,* August 1986: DEA, *Drugs of Abuse,* 1989; G.R. Gay, "Clinical Management of Acute and Chronic Cocaine Poisoning: Concepts, Components and Configuration," *Annals of Emergency Medicine,* (1982) 11(10): 562-572 as cited in NIDA, Dale D. Chitwood, "Patterns and Consequences of Cocaine Use," in *Cocaine Use in America: Epidemiologic and Clinical Perspectives,* Nicholas J. Kozel and Edgar H. Adams, eds., NIDA Research Monograph 61, 1985; NIDA, James A. Inciardi, "Crack-Cocaine in Miami," in *The Epidemiology of Cocaine Use and Abuse,* Susan Schober and Charles Schade, eds., NIDA Research Monograph, 110, 1991; and NIDA "Marijuana," *NIDA Capsules,* August 1986.

known to uplift the user's senses, some experiences with hallucinogens, particularly when "coming down," are of a negative and depressive nature. Tolerance is another trait of hallucinogen use. Users frequently find themselves requiring more and more of the drug to feel the original effects.

According to many, hallucinogen users experience the ability to "hear sights" and "see sounds." Colors are amplified into a kaleidoscopic prism within the mind. Occasionally, depression accompanies a negative or "bad trip" and may manifest itself in the form of suicidal tendencies in the user. Another negative side to the use of hallucinogens is the possibility of "flashbacks," which are fragmentary or recurring (probably imagined) hallucinations that may occur many months or even years after the last dose of the drug has been taken.

LSD

LSD (**LSD-25, lysergic acid diethylamide**) is produced from lysergic acid and is a clear, odorless liquid substance derived from the ergot fungus that grows on rye (see Chapter 1). Because of the extremely high potency of LSD and its structural relationship to a chemical already found in the human brain, its effects were originally studied as treatment for some types of mental illness. LSD is clandestinely manufactured and comes in several street forms:

- *Window Pane*. This form consists of thin squares of gelatin, each containing approximately one drop of LSD.
- *Blotter Acid*. This form of LSD is impregnated on paper, often with numerous miniature cartoons printed in rows. Each cartoon contains approximately one drop of LSD.
- *Micro Dot*. These are tiny multicolored tablets which are so small that they can be concealed under one's thumbnail. They are called such names as Purple Haze, Orange Barrels, and Strawberry Sunshine.

The average effective oral dose is from 30 to 50 micrograms, but the amount per dose varies greatly. The effects of higher doses will persist for 10 to 12 hours.

PCP (Phencyclidine)

PCP is a hallucinogen that was originally developed in 1959 as a general anesthetic. Because of negative side effects such as convulsions and delirium, its use for human patients was rapidly discontinued. In the 1960s, PCP became commercially available for use as a veterinary medicine under the trade name Sernylan. In 1978, PCP was transferred from a Schedule III to a Schedule II drug under the Controlled Substances Act. Because of this legislation, most (if not all) of the PCP encountered on the street is manufactured in clandestine laboratories rather than diverted from legal channels.

PCP has been sold under numerous other names that reflect its bizarre and unpredictable effects: Jet Fuel, Angel Dust, Supergrass, Rocket Fuel, or THC. Other names include Wac, Water, Shirms, Dips, and Shirm Sticks (names for liquid PCP or cigarettes dipped in liquid PCP). As indicated, PCP is available in two distinct forms: powder and liquid. The powdered form achieved most of its popularity during the early 1970s and through the mid-1980s but has been replaced in many areas with liquid PCP. The liquid form of the drug is yellowish-tan in color, much easier to manufacture than the powdered form, and able to retain a high volatility due to a higher concentration of ether present in its chemical makeup.

Phencyclidine or PCP

Physical and Psychological Damage

PCP affects motor and autonomic nervous system functions as well as sensory perceptions and behavior. Physical effects include stroke, brain hemorrhage, hyperthermia (with body temperatures as high as 108 degrees) increased heart rate, shortness of breath, sweating, increased salivation, increased secretions from the lungs, urinary retention, wheezing, and severe bronchial spasms. Bizarre movement disorders, such as tremors, writhing, and jerky movements, may occur, and grand mal convulsive seizures—prolonged seizures may follow high doses. Death can occur from respiratory depression, seizures, or cardiovascular collapse.

The psychological effects of PCP are unpredictable. Users report a range of effects, including a sense of euphoria and well-being, excitement, exhilaration, sedation, drunkenness, and slow or speeding thoughts. Outwardly, users may be disoriented and confused, and their speech may be slurred.

The most significant, observable change is in the personality of the user. Mood fluctuations, distortions in thinking, deterioration of attitudes, lack of personal responsibility, and impaired judgment regularly accompany PCP use.

Higher doses of PCP have produced violent psychosis with psychotic reactions that can last for weeks. These reactions include auditory and visual hallucinations, delusions, and paranoia. While these symptoms are most common in higher doses, they can occur at any level of use and may distort perceptions to the point that the user commits suicide or acts violently against others. The question of permanent brain damage from the use of PCP has not been settled.

Source: Miller, N. (1988). Toward a Drug Free America. The National Drug Policy Board (March).

Along with the rescheduling of the drug in 1978, the respective penalties for manufacture, sale, and possession were also increased to serve as a deterrent. Since the early 1980s, however, the proliferation of clandestine PCP laboratories has become evident in numerous states across the country.

Peyote and Mescaline

While PCP is a synthetic hallucinogen, the peyote cactus and its psychoactive ingredient mescaline are of an organic origin. This drug is derived from the so-called "buttons" of the peyote cactus. As mentioned in Chapter 1, the use of the peyote cactus by Indians in northern Mexico has been common since the earliest recorded history. The religious use of peyote by the Native American Church has been exempted from certain provisions of the 1970 Controlled Substances Act. Peyote is usually removed from the cactus, allowed to dry, ground up into a powder, and taken orally.

Psilocybin Mushrooms

Yet another organic hallucinogen is the psilocybin or "magic" mushroom (also called "shrooms"), which has seen some traditional use by Native Americans and is also relatively popular among recreational hallucinogen users. Mescaline affects the user much like LSD. As mentioned, the active ingredient is psilocybin, which can also be manufactured synthetically. When taken orally, psilocybin is one of the most rapidly acting hallucinogens. Its effects can usually be felt in 10 to 15 minutes, and reactions will last for about 90 minutes to four hours. Physical effects include dilated pupils, an increased heart rate, and a rise in the user's blood pressure. Psychological effects include difficulty in thinking, mental relaxation, detachment from surroundings, and feelings of anxiety. Tolerance to psilocybin has been well documented over the years.

MDMA

Adding to the list of popular hallucinogens is the relatively new drug MDMA (3,4 Methylenedioxymethamphetamine), which is also known on the street as Ecstasy, XTC, Eve, and Essence. This drug, which gained much popularity during the mid-1980s, had the misleading reputation of creating a strong euphoria for the user while being a relatively harmless drug. MDMA had its origin in 1914 when it was developed by the German pharmaceutical company Merck as a diet pill but was never commercially manufactured. Despite this fact, its possession or use was not prohibited until 1985. The popularity of the drug saw a brief upsurge during the 1970s as a substitute for the popular hallucinogen MDA, which was illegal. Nevertheless, its popularity was overshadowed by the prevalent recreational use of LSD.

As mentioned, MDMA was finally outlawed in 1985 and classified as a Schedule I drug. Strong opposition to this measure came from the psychiatric community, which claimed that the drug was beneficial in therapy. Just before that time, MDMA was especially popular in college towns and urban areas; it was thought by some to be an aphrodisiac. The popularity of MDMA during this period was fueled by many newspapers and television stations that carried stories about it. Even the popular comic strip *Doonesbury* featured the drug on occasion.

MDMA is taken orally and commonly packaged as a white powder contained within a gelatin capsule or as an off-white tablet. Street prices range from $8 to $20 per dosage unit throughout the country. Chemically, MDMA is similar to mescaline and possesses both hallucinogenic and stimulant properties. At low levels, it is mildly intoxicating, it rarely produces hallucinations commonly associated with other more common hallucinogens, and the effects last about 30 minutes.

Although much research is needed on MDMA, the National Institute of Drug Abuse (NIDA) reported in 1989 that MDMA can temporarily destroy brain-cell nerve endings in animals and may be capable of inflicting permanent brain damage in the long term. Because research findings have been inconclusive about MDMA's impact on humans and because there is some indication of therapeutic benefits, MDMA remains a controversial drug.

Narcotics

The term "narcotics" signifies a legal category of drugs that refers to opium and opium derivatives or their synthetic substitutes. Generally speaking, these drugs are painkillers that are indispensable in medical treatment but are also very potent and extremely addictive. The initial effects of the drugs may be unpleasant for the user and may include such side effects as nausea, vomiting, drowsiness, apathy, decreased physical activity, and constipation. Strong doses can lead to respiratory depression, loss of motor coordination, and slurred speech. Users that desire the brief euphoric effects of narcotic drugs may develop tolerance and increase their doses of the drug. Repeated use of narcotics will almost certainly manifest itself in both physical addiction and psychological dependence. Usually, narcotics are administered either orally or by injection. Intravenous drug users will commonly use one of two methods of injection:

1. *Skin popping*—injecting the drug just under the skin and into the muscle.
2. *Mainlining*—injecting the drug directly into the veins of the user.

In the event that the physically addicted user is deprived of the drug, the first withdrawal signs are usually noticed shortly before the time of the next desired dose, which is anywhere from 36 to 72 hours after the last dose. Other symptoms, however, such as watery eyes, runny nose, yawning, and perspiration will appear about 8 to 12 hours after the last dose. As the abstinence syndrome progresses, the user will experience loss of appetite, irritability, insomnia, "goose flesh," and tremors accompanied by severe sneezing. When the symptoms reach their peak, the user becomes weak and vomits while experiencing stomach cramps, diarrhea, and an increase in heart rate. These symptoms linger for five to seven days and then disappear.

Narcotics are of both natural and synthetic origins. Of the natural-origin narcotics, the most common are opium, heroin, and morphine. All of these drugs are derived from the opium poppy plant known as the papaver somniferum. This plant only grows in certain parts of the world and is most commonly found today in Southeast and Southwest Asia as well as in Mexico.

The opium poppy produces a seed pod that when unripe is traditionally lanced with a knife by farmers to obtain a milky liquid that oozes out of the incision. A more modern method, however, is the industrial poppy straw process of extracting alkaloids from the mature dried plant (see Chapter 4). Through this legal method of poppy harvesting, more than 400 tons of opium or its equivalent in poppy straw is imported annually into the United States.

The U.S. Drug Enforcement Administration estimates that at least 25 alkaloids can be extracted from raw opium. These fall into two categories:

1. The *phenanthrene alkaloids*, which principally produce morphine and codeine and are used as analgesics and cough suppressants.
2. The *isoquinoline alkaloids*, which are used in the production of intestinal relaxants and cough suppressants. (This category has no effect on the central nervous system and, therefore, is not regulated under the Controlled Substances Act.)

Heroin

Heroin (diacetylmorphine), a narcotic originally synthesized from morphine in 1874, was initially thought to be a cure for morphine addiction. It is a central nervous system depressant that will also relieve pain in the user.

Heroin was first controlled by the Harrison Narcotics Act of 1914, which was a law born out of international concerns about opium use and an increasing problem of addiction among middle-class women that used many over-the-counter remedies. Despite legal controls, it took some 20 years before existing stocks of heroin were ultimately removed from store shelves.

Today, heroin is considered the most widely abused drug in the narcotic family and is produced exclusively on a clandestine or illegal basis. In fact, it is considered a top choice of drugs to be trafficked by traditional Italian organized crime groups, as well as by African-American organized crime groups, international Chinese drug cartels, and more recently, Colombian cartels.

Pure Asian heroin is white (brown heroin comes from Mexico) and has a bitter taste. The differences in brown and white heroin are attributed to the methods of manufacturing, which make use of various refining methods, leaving different impurities. In fact, pure heroin is rarely sold on the street. Street heroin is usually only two to three percent pure and may be diluted with lactose, starch, quinine, or even strychnine, the latter of which accounts for many heroin overdoses (see Chapter 3).

As mentioned, heroin is usually administered through intravenous injection, but occasional users may choose to inject the drug under the skin or even smoke heroin on the tip of a cigarette. It has also been administered orally or by snorting. Because of the physically addictive nature of the drug, addicts may require several injections (or "fixes") daily.

Heroin depresses the central nervous system but also acts as a pain reliever. Because of the depressant nature of heroin, it tends to reduce severely the potential for aggressive behavior in users. Accompanying effects include a feeling of euphoria or "floating" and a sensation described as orgasmic. In addition, effects include constipation and suppression of the coughing reflex, followed by sleep or "nodding off."

"Black Tar" Heroin

A crude form of heroin that appeared on the drug scene during the early 1980s is "black tar" heroin. By most accounts, this type of heroin is thought to be manufactured by Mexican traffickers in the Sonora, Durango, Sinaloa, and Guerrero states of Mexico; smuggled to the United States by illegal aliens and migrant workers; and distributed through extended family connections in the United States. In 1987, according to DEA, law enforcement authorities found black tar in at least 27 states with most of the use concentrated in established Mexican-American communities.

Black tar is crudely processed heroin that may appear to be dark brown in color. It is either sticky like roofing tar or hard like coal. It is known by such street names as "tootsie roll" and "goma," and its growing acceptance in the street stems from its high purity, low price, and widespread availability. Black tar is typically smoked by the user, and its high level of purity may pose dangers for those who choose to inject it. The purity levels for black tar have been documented to be as high as 93 percent, with 60 to 70 percent considered common. Because of its high purity, a sharp increase in heroin-related injuries has been reported since its emergence in the early 1980s.

Hydromorphone

A commonly abused synthetic narcotic is Hydromorphone, which is also known as Dilaudid®. Marketed in both injectable and tablet form, it is faster acting and has a greater sedating effect than morphine, and its potency is anywhere from two to eight times as great. Dilaudid® is commonly obtained through theft in drug stores, fraudulent prescriptions, and diversion from legitimate manufacturers. The tablet form is normally a stronger form than liquid. The tablet is frequently dissolved and injected by the drug user.

Methadone

German scientists synthesized methadone during World War II because of a shortage of morphine. It is chemically unlike morphine but retains the same effects as morphine. The methadone maintenance program, introduced in 1964, was designed as a treatment for heroin addicts. Methadone is administered in both oral and injectable form and has a longer duration of effect than morphine or heroin. In fact, its effects may last up to 24 hours, thus making the drug a valuable aid in the treatment of heroin addiction (see Chapter 14).

"Designer" Drugs

"Designer" drugs have risen out of a new technology adopted by illicit drug manufacturers. That is, manufacturers produce potent drugs that are not yet covered by criminal codes and, therefore, are designed to be legally possessed. This process is attempted through resynthesizing already existing drugs to the point where they have the same basic effects on the user, but the chemical-molecular structure of the drugs has been altered so that they cannot be defined under the law as illegal. Most states today have adopted laws dealing with this problem; many of them have subsequently outlawed the analogs (basic chemicals) with which designer drugs are made.

One of the most dangerous of the designer drugs that emerged during the mid-1980s is "China white" heroin. Designer China white should not be confused with the China White that was common during the operation of the French Connection and which was actually an opiate derivative. Designer China white is a totally synthetic, white powder that has the same general characteristics of heroin but is estimated to be at least 1,000 times more potent.

Designer China white heroin is actually a compound known as fentanyl (3-methyl fentanyl or 3-alpha fentanyl). Users of this drug have reported dangerous side effects such as Parkinson's disease, which cripples part or all of the afflicted person's body.

Cannabis

Although indexed in this text as a substance in a category all its own, cannabis is classified by the Controlled Substances Act as a Schedule I drug—a mild hallucinogen. Cannabis sativa, or the hemp plant, grows wild throughout most areas of the world and has long been cultivated for its use in manufacturing rope, textile materials, certain feed mixtures, and as an ingredient in paint.

> ### Marijuana: A Profile
>
> When ingested, marijuana stays in the body for a long period of time. It is soluble in oil and fat but totally insoluble in water. The ratio is 600 to 1; hence once it gets inside the cell, it has difficulty getting back into the bloodstream the way that other drugs do. Alcohol, for example, is completely soluble in water and also in the bloodstream. So, as fast as it is consumed, it circulates in the bloodstream, is burned up, and leaves the body within 24 hours. Marijuana or its lipid-soluble cannabinoid molecules just stay in the body. A marijuana smoker, therefore, will usually smoke several joints just to get high and refortify his system before the existing marijuana has a chance to leave.
>
> Tests have revealed that marijuana is stored in the brain, which consists of about one third fat tissue. The impairment of brain cells disrupts primary chemical functions, resulting in the alteration of perception, memory, intelligence, and personality. Even long after the users feel high they may not realize it, but they are still under the influence of the drug as long it remains in their system.
>
> Marijuana is claimed to be nonaddictive because physical withdrawal symptoms are almost nonexistent. The reason for this absence, however, is because marijuana cannot be withdrawn rapidly. The body of the user has its own supply of the drug. It is estimated that it takes one week for the stored marijuana to drop to one half, two weeks to drop to one fourth, three weeks to drop to one eighth, etc.

Source: MacDonald, John B. et al. (1986). Addiction Research Foundation, Toronto, Canada.

Despite a lengthy history of both use and abuse, marijuana (also spelled marihuana) was outlawed by the 1937 Marijuana Tax Act (see Chapters 1 and 13), and by 1941 it had been deleted from the *U.S. Pharmacopoeia* and the *National Formulary*, the official compendium of drugs. Marijuana, both a domestic and a foreign money maker for drug traffickers, is produced in large quantities in countries such as Colombia, Mexico, Jamaica, and Panama, as well as in the states of Hawaii, Kentucky, Oregon, and California. Most commercial marijuana ranges from 3 to 4 percent THC content. Advances, however, in the chemistry and horticulture of marijuana cultivation have increased the potency of the plant over the years. Clandestine growers are constantly striving to increase the *THC* (*delta-9-tetrahydrocannabinol*) content of the plant, for it is the THC content that gives the user the desired high and reflects a corresponding market price for the drug. A rarer strain of marijuana, considered to be the most potent, is *sinsemilla* (a Spanish word meaning without seeds). Sinsemilla is a hybrid strain of marijuana that is prepared from the unpollinated female cannabis plant and may produce a yield of more than 12 percent THC content.

Summarizing Marijuana's Harmful Effects

1. Marijuana is fat soluble and is stored for months in the fatty tissues of the body. The lipid-soluble cannabinoid molecules (THC) become embedded in cell membranes and eventually saturate them. Once the cell membrane becomes saturated with THC, the vital nutrients can no longer be transported into and out of the cell, resulting in the loss of cell energy and ultimate cell death.

2. World renowned brain researcher Dr. Robert Heath of Tulane Medical School concluded from experiments on monkeys that the greatest damage occurs in the area of the brain that affects one's motivation.

3. Marijuana users claim that the drug is harmless because it is not physically addictive. The reason for this, however, is because it cannot be withdrawn rapidly. The body builds up its own supply. It takes one week for the stored marijuana to drop to one half, two weeks to drop to one fourth, three weeks to drop to one eighth, etc.

4. More than 8,000 scientific research studies were published in the book *Marijuana: An Annotated Bibliography* (University of Mississippi Research Institute). These studies concluded that marijuana is harmful to the mind and body alike.

Source: Committee on Substance Abuse and Habitual Behavior. Commission on Behavioral and Social Sciences and Education (1982). National Research Council, Washington D.C.

Cannabis products are usually smoked by the user. The high from the drug is felt in minutes and usually lasts for two to three hours. The effects of the drug vary from one user to the next but in mild doses generally include feelings of restlessness, well-being, relaxation, and a craving for sweets. Stronger doses will elicit stronger reactions, such as subtle alterations in thought formation, changes in perceptions, rapidly fluctuating emotions, an altered sense of self-identity, and impaired memory.

Research into the medicinal benefits of cannabis during the last 20 years has focused on the development of a cannabis product that will not produce negative side effects. Probably the most active research being performed on cannabis is for the treatment of nausea and vomiting caused by chemotherapeutic agents used in treating cancer patients. In addition, research continues on the use of marijuana in the treatment of glaucoma. Marijuana's potential dangers are subject to intense debate, and the issue is far from resolved, as can be seen from the two summaries which reach diametrically opposed conclusions.

Marijuana on Trial: Another View of its Dangers

Powerful support for fundamental revisions in our attitudes and policies toward marijuana was contained in an historic decision in September 1988 by Francis L. Young, the chief administrative law judge of the United States Drug Enforcement Administration. For the first time in history . . . there had been a full review of the evidence about marijuana in medicine before an impartial judicial tribunal. The federal government and reform organizations, including the Drug Policy Foundation, presented documents and expert witnesses on all sides of the issue over a period of many months . . . . There was vigorous cross-examination and the submission of extensive briefs. After presiding over this exhaustive inquiry, the DEA official recommended that marijuana be rescheduled so that it could be used by doctors in medicine.

In reaching that decision, Judge Young reviewed the massive body of evidence and came to conclusions that, while focusing on the issue 2 of medical use, destroy many of the fundamental ideas at the base of the drug war:

- "There is no record in the extensive medical literature describing a proven, documented cannabis-related fatality."

- "[T]he record on marijuana encompasses 5,000 years of human experience. . . . Yet, despite the long history of use and extraordinarily high number of social smokers, there are no credible medical reports to suggest that consuming marijuana has caused a single death."

- "In strict medical terms, marijuana is far safer than many foods we commonly consume."

- "Marijuana, in its natural form, is one of the safest therapeutically active substances known to man."

- "The evidence in this record clearly shows that marijuana has been accepted as capable of relieving the distress of great numbers of very ill people, and doing so with safety under medical supervision. It would be unreasonable, arbitrary, and capricious for DEA to continue to stand between those sufferers and the benefits of this substance in light of the evidence. . . ."

Source: Testimony of Arnold S. Trebach at the public hearing on drug control held before the Interior Committee of the Deutsche Bundestag, the Parliament of the Federal Republic of Germany, Bonn, March 13, 1989.

In addition to marijuana, another potent cannabis product is hashish or "hash." Most of the hashish encountered on American streets originates in the Middle East, where large plantations of the plant flourish. Basically, hashish (and its close cousin "hashish oil") is made by a boiling process in which all but the THC resins of the plant are extracted. Although usually smoked, hash can be eaten as well and contains about 20 percent THC content.

Inhalants

In the mid-1990s, a practice known as "huffing" has become popular among adolescents in many cities across the nation. Huffing is the inhaling of fumes which emanate from household products for their intoxicating effects. Inhalants include such common household products as aerosols, gasoline, glue, solvents, and butyl nitrates marketed as "room odorizers." Sniffing even moderate amounts of inhalants for even a short period of time can disturb vision, impair judgement, and reduce muscle and reflex control. Death from sniffing inhalants occurs suddenly and without warning as a result of suffocation, respiratory collapse, or heart failure. Substances falling in this category are widely available to drug abusers of all age groups. Because of this fact and because of their deadly side effects, inhalants are considered one of the most dangerous drugs available.

Summary

Perhaps one of the greatest reasons for drug abuse is a misunderstanding about the effects of drugs and their general pharmacology. Frequently, drug users listen to other drug users about the effects of a particular drug; such information is often incorrect. Drugs can be virtually anything that alters the user's physical or psychological makeup, and can be both legal or illegal to possess. Therefore, the word "drug" could rightfully refer to such compounds as heroin, LSD, and marijuana, along with sugar, salt, and caffeine.

All drugs, whether or not they are controlled, fall into one of six categories: stimulants, depressants, hallucinogens, narcotics, cannabis, and inhalants. Drugs in the stimulant category literally stimulate the central nervous system and make the user feel more alert. The most commonly abused illicit drugs in this category are cocaine (including crack), amphetamines, and methamphetamines. The depressant category represents drugs that have a different effect on the user. Although early stages of ingestion of depressants may create a feeling of exhilaration for the user, these drugs actually depress the central nervous system. Alcohol is a lawfully obtainable depressant, while depressants such as barbiturates and sedative hyponotics are usually physically addicting and pose the greatest physical dangers to the drug abuser.

Hallucinogens are a unique category of drug as they are not physically addicting and their use is not as common as other categories of drugs. Hallucinogens such as LSD, PCP, and MDMA (Ecstasy) are considered dangerous drugs for other reasons. For example, users of LSD encounter the possibility of "bad trips" or "flashbacks" resulting from the use of the drug. PCP users frequently become completely detached from reality while experiencing violent hallucinations. Those who use PCP can injure themselves (even breaking bones) unwittingly because PCP also acts as an anesthetic.

The narcotic category refers to drugs such as heroin, morphine, opium, and Dilaudid,® which are physically addicting and which emulate the effects of opium. All drugs within this category are controlled, and possession of lawfully manufactured narcotics is permitted only pursuant to a lawful prescription.

Marijuana or cannabis is discussed as an individual category of drug, but, according to the Drug Enforcement Administration, it is considered a mild hallucinogen. Although cannabis had a legitimate use during the early history of the United States, it is outlawed to one extent or another in all states. Its beneficial use in medicine is still under study, and some medical professionals claim that the THC content of the drug tends to aid in the remission of cancer of the iris.

Finally, the use of inhalants has become popular for many, especially adolescents because they are both readily available and legal to posses. Breathing the fumes of such household products as glue, paint, and gasoline, however, may pose more risk of physiological damage to the user's brain than other dangerous substances encountered on the street.

Do you recognize these terms?

blood-alcohol concentration	fetal alcohol syndrome
delirium tremens	natural high
dopamine	neurotransmitter
drug abuse	rush
drugs	tolerance
endogenous drugs	withdrawal

Discussion Questions

1. Discuss the reasons why people use drugs.

2. Define the terms psychological and physiological dependence.

3. Discuss the definition of the term "drug."

4. List and discuss the different categories of drugs, and give examples of each.

5. List and discuss some widely used synthetic narcotic drugs.

6. What are designer drugs and how do they effect the drug user?

The Nature of $\quad$ *3*
the Drug Problem

This chapter will enable you to:

- Learn the social and individual consequences of drug abuse
- Understand the reasons why people use drugs
- Realize the extent of the nation's drug abuse problem
- Consider the various theories and explanations of drug abuse

---

Despite decades of governmental efforts to thwart the use of illicit drugs in the United States, it is clear that throughout the remainder of the 1990s drug abuse will continue to be a major social problem. The varying reasons for this conclusion are the subject matter of this text, but one thing is increasingly clear: there will be no "quick fixes" or easy solutions to the problem. Dilemmas in searching out solutions to our country's drug problem are illustrated, in part, by arguments over which drugs are beneficial or harmful for the user. In addition, a considerable degree of debate exists over which drugs pose the greatest threat to public health and safety. Additionally, controversy centers on the issue of legalization of certain drugs that, according to some, are relatively harmless to the casual user and when controlled and legally proscribed (forbidden) create a series of different problems. The use of the term *drug abuse* illustrates, in part, the confusion surrounding the drug issue. To some people, any use of an *illicit* drug is drug abuse, while to others, using a drug to the extent that it compromises his or her physical or psychological well-being is a more accurate interpretation of the term. The latter definition implies that one can take drugs and use them responsibly (a premise that itself is controversial).

The current state of affairs involving drug use clearly indicates that pervasive use of dangerous substances is widespread. In 1988, for example, the White House Conference for a Drug Free America (WHCDFA) reported that approximately 37 million people used an illegal drug in the last year and that one in every 10 Americans used an illicit drug during the past month. Adding to the physical dangers of substance abuse is the reality that drugs alter a person's behavior. Psychoactive drugs alter a person's moods, perceptions, attitudes, and emotions. As a result, concern is often expressed about the impact of drug use on work and familial and social relations. In addition, there is growing concern about the relationship between mind- and mood-altering substances and violent crime in society at large.

Consequences of Drug Abuse

There can be no doubt that drug abusers account for a disproportionate amount of both violent and property crime. The question is why and to what extent do these types of crimes persist? Although the precise relationship between drugs and crime is still questionable, there are several manifestations of this relationship that deserve close attention. The first is the relationship between crime and addiction. Heroin addicts (as well as those addicted to other drugs) require money to maintain their habit. Addicts frequently find that the cost of their habit exceeds their ability to pay for the drugs, especially since illegal drugs are often priced at 40 to 50 times higher the clandestine cost of manufacturing them, If addicts cannot finance their habit, they will often turn to other sources of income, such as prostitution, burglary, and robbery, rather than seek treatment. The alternative, of course, is to become physically ill from the symptoms of withdrawal.

In addition to the problem of paying for a drug habit, drug users face additional difficulties in acquiring drugs in an underground marketplace, which brings them into contact with a wide variety of criminal actors. Although many addicts are accustomed to criminal lifestyles, those that are not are susceptible to victimization. Their habit brings them into contact with the criminal underworld, thereby creating opportunities for them to become involved in criminal activities that they might not ordinarily have considered—such as carrying a gun.

Finally, drugs are both a source of escape and a natural occupational recourse for many inner city youth. They provide a quick although illusory escape from the problems of poverty, unemployment and underemployment, poor education, and a myriad of other social problems faced by inner city youth. In addition, drugs provide a quick route to material success and accumulation of wealth for others, as discussed later in this chapter. It has become an attractive occupational alternative, that is, an "easy" way out. After all, the drug-using population is already out there, cash revenues are tax free, and the potential income can make millionaires out of young people barely in their twenties.

When we attempt to identify the antecedents of the "drug problem," we should realize that there is no single drug abuse problem, but rather a series of overlapping problems. For instance, because of chemical differences in each person's physical makeup, even the most common illicit drugs have very different effects on each user. These effects range from mild euphoria to deep depression, from relaxation to psychotic behavior, and from the "munchies" to drug-induced death by overdose. Likewise, there are many different types of users, from the "yuppie" professional that uses drugs "occasionally," to the physically addicted user in the poverty-stricken inner city. Those that traffic drugs also present a prism of different types, from the small-time freelancer in schools and on street corners to the leaders of vast international cartels.

Figure 3.1
Overview of the Drug Crisis

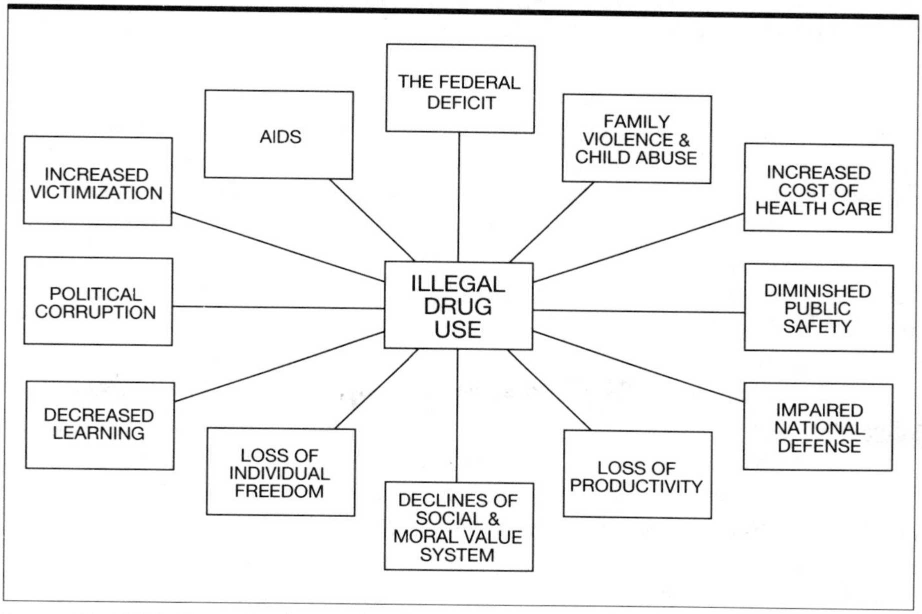

Source: The White House Conference for a Drug-Free America, 1988.

The social effects of drug trafficking are accentuated and reinforced by their direct and indirect economic impact. The sums spent on drugs represent resources lost to legitimate productive enterprises, and the money that is laundered by drug traffickers seems to corrupt all that come into contact with it. Consequently, drug traffickers who purchase legitimate businesses have learned that it is easy to integrate dealers into society. Drug traffickers who make use of existing legitimate businesses know that where such vast sums of money are involved, even respectable citizens can be induced to overlook the source of the money (see Chapter 6). In addition, the economic effect carries over into the workplace, where drug-using workers increase costs of production, raise levels of absenteeism, and raise the incidence of accidents on the job, all of which compel employers to implement expensive anti-drug abuse programs.

Severe health problems are also created when drug abuse prevails. These include drug overdoses and poisonings from "street" drugs as well as from improperly consumed pharmaceutical drugs. Even marijuana can have devastating long-term effects. Not only is marijuana the drug with which many users begin, but marijuana cigarettes have many times the tar and carcinogens that tobacco cigarettes have. Additional problems include addicted mothers who give birth to addicted babies and the spreading of diseases such as hepatitis and AIDS through the sharing of contaminated needles by drug users. The proliferation of the crack house has given rise to the spreading of the AIDS virus and in many crack houses, prostitution flourishes as sex-for-drugs is a common transaction.

Drug abuse also has the ability to affect society on a much greater level—national security. Many larger drug organizations, particularly the South American and Southeast Asian cartels, have already become so powerful that they wield as much power as many Latin and Central American governments. Drug money from these organizations has corrupted government officials, many of whom are charged themselves with the responsibility of drug control. In fact, the immense power and financial reserves of some of the largest drug trafficking organizations have made them attractive partners in intelligence operations (such as those conducted during the Vietnam War and in Central America), thereby rendering U.S. policy confused and contradictory at times. Other drug source countries that are hostile to the United States view drugs as a weapon to use against American society.

Drug production and abuse is clearly an international problem. Four known drug source countries, Afghanistan, Myanmar (formerly Burma), Iran, and Laos—all opium producers—have been decertified for United States assistance under the provisions of the Foreign Assistance Act. Two other countries, Panama and Syria, have been decertified for failure to control drug trafficking and money laundering. Colombia, the largest exporter of marijuana and cocaine to the United States, still receives U.S. assistance partly to encourage the Colombian government in its internal battle with the drug traffickers and insurgent groups.

Drugs and the Family

It is easy to see that the drug user can have a residual effect on the lives of family members. A portrait of the drug user is provided in Chapter 14, but experience has shown that the dependent drug abuser will lie and steal if necessary to support his or her habit. In many cases an occurrence called **"backstabbing"** takes place in families where a member uses drugs. Here, young and middle-aged drug users who have depleted their own resources will turn to family members for drug money. In some cases, the family is unaware of the seriousness of the situation and provides money to the user only to realize that more will be required soon. Many families cease to continue providing money while others continue in an effort to "help" their dependent family member. This phenomenon gradually depletes the family's financial and emotional resources to the point where family members lose faith in the drug user and begin to view him or her as troublesome, untrustworthy, or weak. In time, the person begins stealing items of value from the house so they can be sold for drug money.

Sadly, in many cases parents are part of the problem. Drug dealing children who come home with hundreds of dollars are sometimes not disciplined by parents because that money, although ill-gotten, is needed to pay bills and buy food. The parents tend to rationalize the behavior of their child in thinking that they will deal drugs anyway or that society has somehow failed to provide them with sufficient means to earn a legitimate income. When this occurs, the parents tend to take on a childlike-role, leaving the major decisions up to the primary bread winner—the drug dealing child. In other cases, parents who are drug users themselves will often fail to provide adequate attention, care, and financial support for their family, resulting in many children being taken in by grandparents, other relatives, or the state social service system.

Studies have also shown that unemployment and frequent drug use have been major contributors to the demise of the two-parent household while stable employment and low drug use are associated with high rates of forming a "traditional" two-parent family. Through the research we have learned that although drug abuse adversely affects all ethnic groups, the hardest hit are poor and minority families and those with female heads of households. Without help, mothers experience great difficulty in controlling the actions of their young ones who are constantly charmed by drug dealers and other forms of street-corner crimes. Of course, involvement in the drug culture also places youths in other forms of jeopardy, including arrest, street violence, drug overdose, incarceration, and truancy in school.

Drugs and Schools

In recent years, more than one third of those responding to Gallup polls cited drug abuse as one of the biggest problems in schools. Several reasons are given for this. For example, many students experience cognitive and behavioral difficulties which not only interfere with their studies but their classmates' schoolwork as well. Even non-drug using students and teachers are hampered by the actions of those who choose to use drugs. Both categories of people are at risk of victimization by drug-related crimes and drug users. The availability of drugs in schools has become a growing concern as well, for surveys have indicated that many students find that they can locate and purchase drugs without difficulty. In the 1989 Bureau of Justice Statistics School Crime Survey, 30 percent of students in grades 6 to 12 said that marijuana was easy to get at their schools with 11 percent claiming that cocaine was easy to obtain in school. Conversely, the survey reported that an estimated 43 percent of students found marijuana hard or impossible to obtain in school with 58 percent claiming the same about cocaine (BJS, 1992). Studies have also linked the availability of drugs with victimization and fear of victimization in schools. Those students who claimed that drugs were easy to obtain in schools also reported that they were likely to be victims of crime at school more so than those students who said that drugs were hard or impossible to find in school.

Health Complications

Many health-related complications associated with drug abuse are also evident in the nation's drug quandary. Users can die from overdose, medical reactions can result from taking certain types of drugs, users are exposed to HIV infections of the blood, hepatitis, tuberculosis, and other diseases; injuries result from accidents caused by intoxication; injuries can result from violence in obtaining drugs or associating with persons with violent criminal backgrounds, dependence can form with certain drugs, and chronic physical problems can develop in some drug users. Some of these effects, such as overdose, are directly related to drug use, while others are indirectly associated with drug-use behavior, like violence stemming from illegal drug transactions.

A brutal fact in the illicit drug industry is that some drugs sold on the streets are simply not what they are purported to be. This is sometimes due to increased purity of the drug over what the user has been accustomed, but another reason is that impurities are also commonly placed in drug solutions to either enhance or dilute the potency of the drug. Other times, drugs are sold as being something completely different than what they actually are. For example, during the late 1970s powdered PCP (phencyclidine), known as Angel Dust, acquired such a bad reputation on the street that dealers chose to rename it as THC or cannabinol. In actuality, THC is one of the active ingredients in marijuana, giving it its intoxicating effects, but it has no connection whatsoever with the hallucinogen PCP. Dealers simply believed that THC sounded better to potential drug buyers than angel dust.

Use of certain drugs can result in specific physical reactions. For example, cocaine use can result in convulsions or even cardiovascular failure because it creates changes in heart rate and blood pressure. The reaction often occurs quickly and under circumstances where medical treatment is not readily available. As we will see in the following chapter, the myth that cocaine is a harmless drug is now replaced with the realization that it may be more harmful than other so-called hard drugs, including heroin. In addition, the reinforcing properties of cocaine often lead to binge consumption, which in turn increases chances for dependence, overdose, withdrawal symptoms, or more serious cardiovascular complications including death. Residual physical problems for cocaine abusers can include a ruptured aorta, central nervous system problems, and intestinal and obstetrical problems.

Specific reactions to other drugs can also be noted. Heroin, for instance, is a central nervous system depressant which can leave the user with acute toxic reactions resulting from overdose. More often than not, this occurs because users may not be aware that the purity of the heroin they inject is higher than their systems can tolerate. Depressants and stimulants can also produce certain health complications, especially regarding drug-induced psychosis. Users lose contact with reality and experience a rapid pulse and elevated blood pressure.

Finally, health consequences are illustrated by the number of hospital emergency room admissions. During 1990, there were more than 635,000 mentions of drugs in the 371,208 emergency room episodes in DAWN (Drug Abuse Warning Network)-participating hospitals in 21 metropolitan areas in the United States (BJS, 1992). Nearly half of the episodes involved two or more drugs. The most commonly mentioned drugs were cocaine in 22 percent of episodes, alcohol in combination with other drugs in 31 percent of episodes, and heroin/morphine in 9 percent of reported episodes.

Attitudes About Drugs

Perhaps the varying attitudes people harbor about drug abuse and control create confusion about the issue. Many positions about substance abuse or control are no longer clear-cut. Some drug users and former drug users have spoken out forcefully against drugs while others have urged a reconsideration of prohibition policies. Many parents, while strongly anti-drug themselves, have ambivalent feelings about the drug laws when their sons or daughters are drug users. Drug use, which in the past has been more neatly confined to particular groups in society, now has taken root in all social strata. This means that virtually all of us either have friends, relatives, or associates who are or have been drug users.

Although drug control policy is discussed in Chapter 13, it might be helpful to review the basis of some attitudes behind drug use and control. From earliest recorded time, society has exhibited social conflict over such heated issues as religion and politics, the latter of which is afforded greater attention in this book. One's willingness to criticize or accept public consensus frequently hinges on one's political attitudes. Such attitudes will most likely lean toward the conservative (right) or the liberal (left) view. Those of the former persuasion tend to be more traditional and resistant to change while those holding liberal views tend to be more open-minded about change and willing to try the untried. Excesses in either of these convictions tend to foster unrealistic views and attitudes. The issues of drug use and control have blurred even these familiar political distinctions. While most conservatives, for example, favor tough laws, more police, and refined due process procedures for accused criminals, some leading conservatives are actually arguing for repeal of the drug laws. They base their positions on two fundamental conservative tenets: first, the belief that the free market is self-regulating and will reduce drug abuse if allowed to operate and second, the traditional conservative position put forward by John Stuart Mill that government should interfere as little as possible with individual freedoms. Liberals, on the other hand, have traditionally stressed due process rights, non-law enforcement approaches to crime, and the belief that crime is rooted in a myriad of social problems. Yet, in 1994 the leading liberal legislators, such as Representative Charles Rangel and Senator Edward Kennedy, were the strongest supporters of unyielding anti-drug efforts.

Why Do People Get High?

Almost everyone has seen someone use or knows someone who uses an addictive drug. Whether it be caffeine, nicotine, alcohol, or another drug, abuse is an everyday part of our lives. So, several essential questions about drug abuse can be asked. For example, why do people willingly engage in behavior that might be dangerous, illegal, or unhealthy? Furthermore, many drugs fail to have obvious effects on the user which makes us wonder why they are popular in the first place. For example, cigarette smokers generally don't appear to be in a state of euphoria when they smoke. The same is true for people when drinking a caffeine-based soft drink. How about harder drugs like heroin? We think we know why a heroin user uses the drug, and that is for the euphoric effect of it. In fact, the initial effects of many of today's popular drugs, like heroin, are downright unpleasant. Stated differently, if 100 people were selected from the population and administered heroin, they would probably get sick and never want to see the drug again. So what's the point of taking the drug in the first place? The same could be said for alcohol or cocaine. One's first drink of whiskey or first experience with crack cocaine is not always pleasant. Given this premise, perhaps it is true that the more pleasant effects a drug has on a user, the more attractive it is to them. If this is so, then why do people smoke without any noticeable effect from the nicotine? As you see, we have now come full circle in our quandary.

In the early 1980s, the National Institute of Drug Abuse published a lengthy monograph titled *Theories of Drug Abuse,* which described nearly 40 explanations of why people take drugs. Although numerous explanations have been offered on the subject, yet another glaring question still remains unanswered: is drug abuse representative of a universal human need? Some would argue that this is precisely the case, and that one of the great challenges of today is for society to develop a drug that is completely safe for recreational consumption. Although a controversial premise, it inspires thought. While some people are life-long abstainers, others use drugs on a more regular basis. Whether it be our daily fortification of coffee, tea, or cigarettes or a reliance on prescription pain killers or antidotes for minor ailments, some form of drug use is an everyday part of living for most Americans.

Explanations for drug abuse are in constant debate. For example, while some experts claim that there is a genetic basis for dependence and addiction, others argue that it stems from a learned behavior. However, if a genetic propensity for drug abuse does exist, then what created it? Alcohol abuse might be a good example. Experts suggest that an insensitivity to the effects of the drug results in excessive drinking. Therefore, the insensitivity of some drinkers causes them to feel only slightly drunk when they are actually very intoxicated. As a result, they tend to drink more than others do. Some have suggested that this hypothesis extends to drug use in general.

In opposition to the genetic theory of dependence, other experts such as Benjamin Stein (1988) have argued that a syndrome exists known as the "addictive personality." Under this theory, a drug user consumes drugs because they help organize an otherwise disordered life. The theory suggests that drug abusers are lonely, sad, and frightened people who possess a character flaw for which drugs offer a crutch. In comparison, other experts have suggested that drug abuse is simply learned behavior whereby the abuser fails to act responsibly with the drugs they abuse.

Thinking Critically #4

Create the "perfect" recreational drug for American society. (Remember, your creation must be free of harmful physiological or psychological effects). Describe its ingredients, methods of consumption, social applications, price, and method of distribution.

Social explanations stress the influence of society, culture, and peers in a person's life. Some drugs are more likely to be abused by certain classes of people while other types of drugs are more available in specific areas of a city and, therefore, are more widely abused. In addition, it has been argued that in many social circles it is more socially acceptable for men to drink more heavily than for women to. In some societies, drug consumption takes place in social, religious, or even family settings. In any case, social explanations should be considered along with others when searching for answers as to why people use drugs.

The "Usefulness" of Drugs

As we earlier suggested, to best deal with this perplexing issue it is important for us to abandon our stereotypes of drug use for its pleasurable effects. For the sake of discussion, let's accept the proposition that people do not use a drug necessarily for the pleasurable effects it supposedly has associated with it. Rather, let's assume that some drugs are used because people find them useful perhaps for less exotic reasons (Krogh, 1992). For example, hard-core heroin users don't use the drug for its euphoric effects but rather to help them get through the day, to survive. The same is also true for many smokers and coffee drinkers. So for many, drug use allows people to *function* on a day to day level. After all, being able to successfully perform on a job results in our receiving a regular paycheck—a powerful motivation.

In an attempt to better understand reasons for drug use, let's take a closer look at the reasons for wanting to alter one's physical or mental state. Research has shown that, as a rule, people take illicit drugs for the effects they produce. These may include mood change, pleasure, stimulation, sedation, or enhanced physical or psychological performance. In fact, more so than for their physical results, illicit drugs are taken for their mind-altering effects. As we will discuss in this chapter, drugs such as heroin have limited accepted medical use but may be taken for the relief of pain. Others like stimulants and sedatives have distinct medical applications but may be taken to produce excitement, alertness or feelings of relaxation. Given the many different variables about human nature—personal values, morals, beliefs, habits, lifestyles—it is logical to assume that different people use drugs for different reasons. As we will see some reasons are rational, and others are more enigmatic.

Drug Abuse Forums

Given our earlier discussions, it is probably safe to generalize that millions of people abuse drugs for a number of reasons. Young people in junior high and high school, career people, and even the elderly, from time to time, use drugs unwisely or illegally. Therefore, many different reasons exist to explain drug abuse behavior; accordingly, there are many circumstances under which drug abusers engage in their activity. Next we will consider some of the most common social forums of drug abuse.

The Natural High

The term "natural high" refers to a desired euphoric feeling naturally produced by the body. A multitude of studies by experts in social behavior suggest that people naturally desire to alter their state of consciousness at certain times throughout their lives. For example, children may help illustrate the innate desire to alter one's consciousness by the very manner in which they play. For all their innocence, they sometimes spin themselves into dizziness or desire to ride on the roller coaster at the local amusement park to achieve a thrill and the corresponding physical exhilaration. Many adults also enjoy riding the ferris wheel or other adrenaline-inducing rides for the mere excitement of the experience. Such an indulgence in and of itself may raise or distort perceptions of reality while generating endocrine drug reactions, such as the production of adrenaline and noradrenaline. These "highs" are particularly appealing as they are produced naturally without the interference of external chemical stimuli. However, the endocrine-producing glands in our bodies don't always produce "uppers" like adrenaline. In fact, the body also manufactures its own "downers," such as serotonin and gamma-aminobutyric acid butyric acid (GABA).

Chemicals like those mentioned are called **endogenous;** that is, they are produced in the body. Endogenous chemicals produced by the brain and various glands change our moods and actions and even resemble some drugs taken by people for recreational purposes. For example, a group of endogenous chemicals called **endorphins**, discovered in 1975, closely resemble heroin or morphine, but they are naturally produced by the human body and act to relieve pain. The release of endorphins has been well documented by runners with the so-called "runner's high," for example, who seem to generate these drugs to cope with pain and to provide energy while running.

Happy Hour

As with the term "natural high," the term "happy hour" does not refer to a reason why people become intoxicated but rather to a social forum where ritualistic recreational chemical use occurs in groups. Millions of people look forward to the traditional "happy hour" after a long day's or week's work. The altering of one's mental state or "attitude adjustment" through alcohol consumption is lawful, socially acceptable, and even commonplace. Such indulgence, however, is regulated through each state's criminal code because of the potential for accidents or criminal behavior if drinkers become intoxicated.

Although it is legal, alcohol can drastically change one's psychological and physiological condition. Because of this, most states have established limits for alcohol consumption in ways such as: 1) restricting where liquor can be purchased; 2) increasing penalties for driving while under the influence (alcohol and illicit drugs alike); 3) establishing special criminal provisions for crimes committed while intoxicated; 4) criminalizing the transportation of liquor out of bars in "gocups;" and 5) regulating open liquor containers in motor vehicles. More information about alcohol is available in the previous chapter on understanding drugs of abuse.

Medicinal Use

Ingesting "harder" and more dangerous drugs under certain circumstances is lawful if prescribed by a medical practitioner who has identified a physical or psychological requirement for such medication. Morphine, for example, is a dangerous and highly addictive narcotic drug, but when taken under a doctor's supervision, it can be an extremely effective pain killer both during surgery and recovery. The lawful distribution of dangerous drugs mandates the legal manufacturing of them by legitimate pharmaceutical companies. The highly controlled circumstances in the manufacturing, distribution, and storage of dangerous substances will be discussed in greater length later in this text.

Religious Use

Although some modern-day religions incorporate mind-altering substances such as wine in their ceremonies, few religions condone using enough of the substance for participants to become intoxicated. Exceptions to this, however, exist in certain cultures. For example, since the 1700s, North American Indian cultures have used peyote cactus, which produces a psychoactive drug, in religious ceremonies. Eating or smoking peyote was embraced in elaborate ancient ceremonies as a means to gain "oneness" with the spirits and with nature.

Today in most states, members of the Church of the Native American Indian are authorized to use peyote in their religious ceremonies. Use of the drug outside of a religious ceremony or by non-Indian participants, is prohibited under law. Ironically, those Indian cultures that embrace the use of peyote in their religious practices at the same time consider alcohol a curse. In a similar vein, followers of traditional Coptic Christianity, whose most recognizable U.S. denomination is the Rastafarians, use marijuana in their religious observations in much the same way other churches use wine (see Chapter 4).

To Alter Moods and Metabolism

When people are depressed, anxious, or bored, it is reasonable for them to desire a change in their mental state. Drugs are sometimes used both legally and illegally to create a shift in personalities, attitudes, and moods. Such measures might include the consumption of stimulants (uppers), depressants (downers), or even psychoactive drugs (hallucinogens that are either organic or clandestinely manufactured). In those cases in which the undesirable mood is due to a natural physiological chemical imbalance, certain drugs may be lawfully prescribed by physicians to help offset the body's chemical deficiencies. Excessive use of Valium® and Librium®, for example, was common in the 1950s to uplift depressed feelings. These drugs were commonly prescribed because most doctors believed that they were safe. In reality, not only can the drugs be dangerous by themselves, but they can be particularly dangerous if combined with other drugs. Today poly-drug use is common where many drug users ingest amphetamines in the morning as a "pick-me-up" and then take barbiturates in the evening to help "wind down." This, of course, creates a classic abuse cycle in which one type of drug is required to counteract another. Another common example of poly-drug use, particularly among those taking downers for medical purposes, is combining barbiturates and tranquilizers with alcohol, a combination that heightens inebriation and is potentially deadly.

To Inspire Creativity

Throughout the years, musicians, poets, and novelists have hailed the effects of certain drugs that supposedly promote creativity. Many artists have believed that drugs (often belonging to the hallucinogen family) can release inhibitions and unleash a creative thought process. These individuals include American short-story writer and poet Edgar Allen Poe (1809-1849), who had a weakness for laudanum (tincture of opium); British writer Aldous Huxley

(1894-1963), who experimented extensively with mescaline in the 1950s (and was quoted as stating "pharmacology antedated agriculture"); the nineteenth-century poet Oliver Wendell Holmes (1809-1894), who indulged in ether; and popular comedian Lenny Bruce (1926-1966), whose physical addiction to heroin ultimately cost him his life.

Measuring Drug Abuse

The current state of affairs involving drug use clearly indicates that pervasive use of dangerous substances is widespread. In 1992, a national report issued by the U.S. Bureau of Justice Statistics reported that more than 75 million persons in the nation have used illicit drugs. This estimate is based on self-reports from members of households 12 years and older, but as we will see, a number of methods are currently used to determine the extent of the drug problem, and results are often conflicting. Considerable information exists regarding the extent of drug abuse throughout the country. However, most methods focus on households, high school seniors, and arrestees and offenders and do not give any indication about other groups more difficult to reach. For instance, it is generally believed that many members of the homeless population are involved in some form of drug abuse. These persons are missed in the household surveys just like high school dropouts are not surveyed in high school senior surveys. Surveys have also revealed other aspects of the drug abuse problem. For example, an alarmingly high number of young adults have used illicit drugs, and the most commonly abused drug is marijuana. In addition, one third of the U.S. population knows someone who uses crack cocaine. Today most of what we know about drug abuse is derived from the following surveys:

1. *National Household Survey on Drug Abuse*: This survey has been periodically conducted since 1972 but is now an annual survey which randomly interviews people living in households and in specified group residences throughout the United States.

2. *High School Senior Survey*: Also referred to as Monitoring the Future, this survey has been conducted since 1975. In 1991 about 15,700 seniors were surveyed. College students and young adults are also surveyed. The survey has revealed that 44 percent of high school seniors have used illicit drugs while 50 percent of college students one to four years beyond high school have used drugs. 29 percent of seniors reported that they have used drugs in the past year.

3. *Worldwide Survey of Substance Abuse and Health Behaviors Among Military Personnel*: This survey has been conducted four times between 1980 and 1992. In 1988, 19,000 active duty military personnel were surveyed at military bases across the world.

4. *Survey of Jail Inmates*: This survey is comprised of interviews of local jail inmates who are awaiting trial or serving sentences in local jails. It was

conducted four times between 1978 and 1992. In 1989, for example, 5,675 inmates in 424 jails were surveyed.

5. *Survey of State Prison Inmates*: This survey is conducted every five to seven years. In 1986 an estimated 14,000 inmates were interviewed in 275 facilities.

The Results of Drug Abuse Surveys		
Survey	**Percent of Population who used Illicit Drugs**	
	Ever	**In the Past Month**
National Household Survey on Drug Abuse:	37%	6%
High School Senior Survey:	44%	16%
Worldwide Survey of Substance Abuse and Health Behaviors Among Military Personnel:	—	5%
Survey of Jail Inmates:	78%	44%
Survey of State Prison Inmates:	80%	52%

Who are the Drug Users?

The surveys have also provided information regarding who the drug users are. For example, the 1992 NIDA Household Survey on Drug Abuse reports several interesting findings about drug users:

*   males are more likely than females to use drugs;
*   people between the ages of 26 and 34 are the most likely to ever have used drugs;
*   people between the ages of 18 and 25 are more likely to have used illicit drugs in the past month, and;
*   whites and blacks are more likely than Hispanics to have ever used drugs.

Of course, as drug patterns and trends change over time, these statistics will also change. As people get older, drug use rates shift. For instance, in 1995 lifetime rates of use became the highest among those ages 31 through 39, reflecting the peak drug using years of the late 1970s.

David Musto, professor of psychiatry at Yale University, has written that we are quickly moving to a "two-tier system" of drug consumption, marked by declining use among middle-class whites and increasing use among poor minorities. In his book, *The American Disease: Origins of Narcotic Control*, he states that the American society is repeating an earlier cycle of drug use. Musto points out that at the turn of the century drugs were readily available and widely tolerated. As the incidences of abuse grew and people gained increased awareness, consumption dropped off and social attitudes became sterner. He further states that as the two-tier effect becomes more pronounced and minorities become more and more associated with drug abuse, public support for treatment might begin to wane. The result could be more public support for increased police, prisons, and harsher sentences, a reaction he feels will be futile. "My concern is that as drug use declines among middle-class Americans, they will refuse to invest in the long-term needs of the inner city, like education and jobs. A primary task facing the [country's] Office of National Drug Control Policy is harnessing the current anti-drug energy and making it productive" (Musto, 1973).

Geographical Differences

Trends of drug use in 20 major U.S. cities have been monitored by the Community Epidemiology Workgroup (1991), and findings reveal that drugs used in different cities differ. For the most part, availability and price of drugs determine the extent of use in most cities, but in most cases, cocaine has remained the major drug of abuse. Heroin use has declined in some cities but has shown an increased use in others. Stimulants, on the other hand, were most prevalent in western cities. Furthermore, the National Household Survey has shown that drug use varies across urban and rural areas with higher instances of use in the larger metropolitan areas. In contrast, High School Senior Surveys have shown that use of stimulants, inhalants, and sedatives were similar in both rural and non-rural areas with marijuana and cocaine being used more often in urban areas than rural.

Drug Abuse Trends

We know that drug use trends vary from year to year, and that many factors can be attributed to those trends. As we said earlier, drug prices and availability always play some role in the frequency of drug use. Other variables, however, should also be considered. What remains in question is just what those trends are. Although surveys have given some insight into long-term trends, their projections frequently differ. For example, trend data from the National Households survey report that current use of drugs increased during the 1970s but has since declined. Between 1988 and 1991, drug abuse declined and has remained stable. Trends for high school seniors are similar to those identified in the household surveys. Those surveys indicated that 1978 was the year of the highest frequency of drug abuse. Stimulants were the most widely used in the early 1980s with cocaine peaking in the mid-1980s. Encouraging news is that in 1990, for the first time in 16 years, the percentage of high school seniors who had ever used drugs declined to less than 50 percent, and the rates for current use were the lowest since the survey's inception in 1975.

It is true that while declining rates of drug use could indicate a reluctance to report use or that important segments of the population were missed, all surveys have indicated that overall drug abuse is down for most segments of the population. Exceptions, however, exist for some groups. For example, the number of people who use cocaine weekly or more frequently failed to decline. In addition, the number of college students who used cocaine or marijuana in the past 30 days was not significantly lower in 1991 than in 1990.

The Social Costs of Drug Abuse

As we have indicated, law enforcement initiatives against drug abuse and trafficking are a financially exhausting proposition. Drug abuse also costs society billions of dollars in many other ways. These explanations are seen in costs are for drug treatment and prevention programs, lost productivity on the job caused by impaired drug users, and the cost of other federal programs. For example, in 1988 the federal anti-drug budget was almost $5 billion, compared to President Clinton's 1995 proposed budget of $13.2 billion (see Chapter 13).

Besides the financial burden imposed on Americans by drug abuse, there is yet a greater price to pay—the effects of drugs on our youth. Studies have revealed that most drug users began to use drugs as adolescents or even as grade school children. The reasons commonly offered are peer pressure, few legitimate means of income, and broken homes, among others. Adolescent drug abuse also impairs the learning capabilities of children and, in some cases, can cause severe emotional problems.

Additionally, one should remember that drug abuse is an illegal activity, and when drugs are indiscriminately used around children, a message is sent to them that gives legitimacy to this activity, particularly when parents themselves are the drug users. The National Drug Policy Board reported in 1988: "In New York City an alarming number of child abuse incidents directly attributed to drug abuse were documented. Specifically, from 2,627 to 8,521 in two years."

The Violence

In August 1989, drug traffickers exploded a bomb alongside Secretary of State George Schultz's motorcade during his visit to Bolivia. The purpose of Schultz's visit was to deliver a speech supporting a Bolivian crackdown on the cocaine trade. This incident is not an unusual one for source countries like Bolivia as there have been many reports of Latin American traffickers that have offered large cash bounties for the assassinations of certain U.S. government officials that oppose the illicit drug trade.

The proliferation of drug-trafficking groups operating in the United States has also increased. For example, in October 1988 the Treasury's Bureau of Alcohol, Tobacco, and Firearms conducted what was dubbed as "Operation Rum Punch." In this operation, numerous members of cocaine- and crack-dealing Jamaican gang posses were arrested throughout the country. Authorities believe that violence exhibited by this group between 1987 and 1989 resulted in the murders of close to 1,400 people (Narcotics Control Technical Assistance Program, 1991).

With the propagation of drug gangs interested in their share of the drug pie, drug-related crime has also spread to ancillary areas where the profit motive outweighs the motivation of the addict to stay "well." Drug gangs such as the Los Angeles-based Crips and Bloods wage turf wars and calculated acts of revenge over the control of neighborhoods. These gangs also recruit members as young as eight years old to deal drugs or act as spotters in this vicious and violent business.

The pursuit of higher education and legitimate work is no longer considered by many of these individuals to be the best way to get ahead in life. The allure of gold chains, fast cars, status, and parties has stifled the growing process for many gang members. Indeed, drugs represent a set of already stifling environmental factors that create a social gauntlet between children and their education and legitimate employment. The violence associated with the drug problem poses one of the greatest social concerns. In numerous recent polls respondents consider drug trafficking as one of the greatest national concerns and in many caes a serious threat to national security.

Addicted Babies

Another recent health concern is the problem of drug-addicted babies. Studies have shown that drug use can affect the development of a child even before birth. Research has shown that marijuana and cocaine use during pregnancy is associated with substantial reductions in fetal growth. Infants exposed to drugs, especially heroin, are prone to exhibit withdrawal symptoms. Exposure to cocaine has been linked to various neurobehavioral and circulatory complications which include major congenital malformations. In 1989, the General Accounting Office (GAO) reported that of infants born at 10 mostly inner-city hospitals in five large cities, 1 percent to 18 percent had been exposed to one or more illicit drugs before birth. Of the babies born at the four hospitals where 10 percent or more of the newborns were identified as being drug-exposed, many had problems of low birth weight and premature birth. As indicated earlier in this chapter, health problems arising out of drug abuse are one of the principal concerns in drug control efforts. One such issue is the problem of cocaine-addicted babies.

In a 1988 study, Ira Chasnoff, president of the National Association for Parental Addiction Research and Education, estimated that 11 percent of all births, or 375,000 babies, are born to addicted mothers every year. This figure represents a threefold increase in such births since 1985. Detection of cocaine use by pregnant mothers can only be discovered within 24 to 48 hours after use, so even such a high estimate may be extremely conservative. Problems exist because the symptoms of a pregnant woman who suffers from cocaine addiction may not always be apparent to hospital officials. In many cases, pregnant addicts may not even visit hospitals until they are in labor.

Figure 3.2

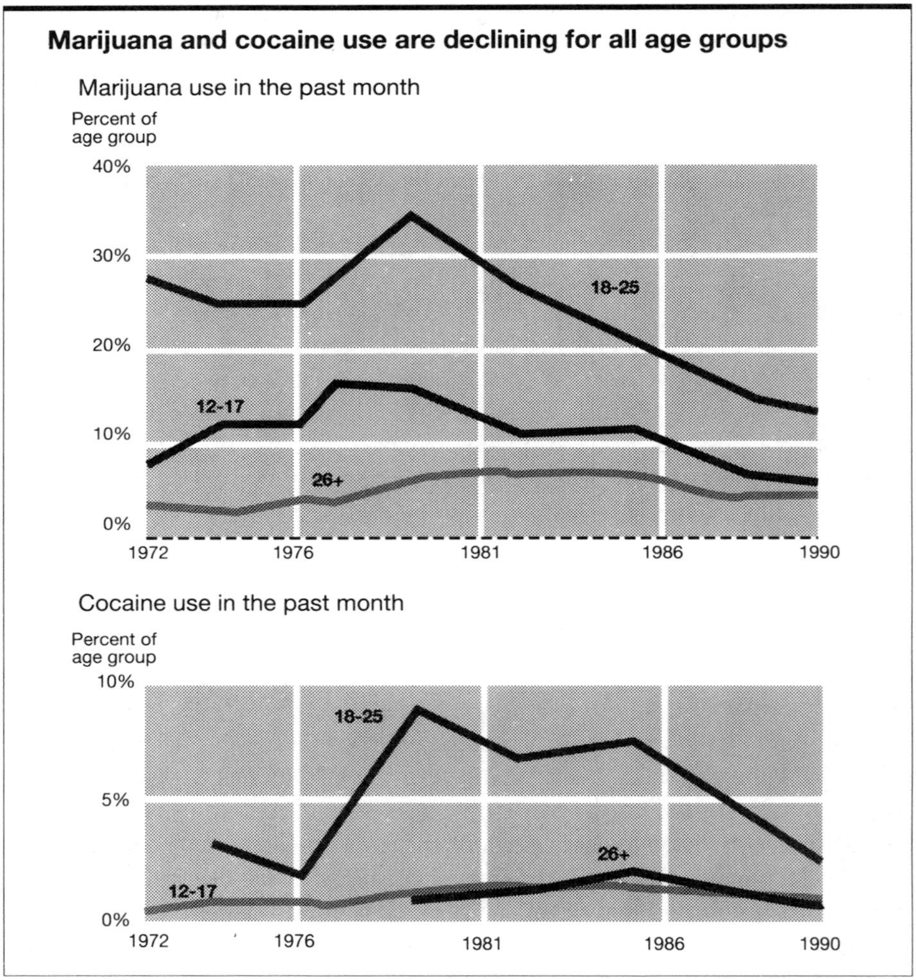
Marijuana and cocaine use are declining for all age groups
Marijuana use in the past month
Percent of age group
40%
30%
20%
10%
0%
18-25
12-17
26+
1972
1976
1981
1986
1990
Cocaine use in the past month
Percent of age group
10%
5%
0%
18-25
26+
12-17
1972
1976
1981
1986
1990

Note: These lines were constructed from interpolated data.
Source: NIDA, *National Household Survey on Drug Abuse, Population Estimates, 1991* (1991).

Much attention was focused on the issue of cocaine-addicted babies during the late 1980s because of the serious health-related risks facing unborn children. Such hazards include strokes while babies are still in the uterus, physical malformations, and increased risk of death during infancy. In addition, because of the earlier mentioned practice of "sex-for-crack" by some pregnant woman, many babies are born with ancillary health problems that include sexually transmitted diseases.

Dr. Gordon B. Avery of Children's National Medical Center in Washington, D.C. stated that it is typical for cocaine babies to be born prematurely. He added, "In addition to the medical complications facing otherwise normal premature babies, cocaine babies face special hardships such as hydrocephaly (water on the brain), poor brain growth, kidney problems, and apnea (an unforeseen stoppage of breathing)" (Kantrowitz, 1990). Confusion in this area of drug abuse partly exists because as recently as 1982 there were still medical textbooks on high-risk obstetrics being published which stated that cocaine had no harmful effects on the fetus. A fetus is particularly vulnerable to cocaine for several reasons:

- Although the placenta does shield the uterus from many large, complex molecules (particularly those that can't defuse across fatty cell membranes), it is an open door to cocaine. This occurs because cocaine is attracted to fatty compounds, and once the drug enters the blood and tissues of the fetus, it remains there longer than it does in an adult.
- The effects of cocaine on the mother-to-be also pose some threat to the fetus. That is, when a woman addicted to crack gets pregnant, the well-being of the fetus and of her own body are not her primary concerns.
- An estimated 40 to 50 percent of cocaine-addicted pregnant woman have been exposed to the AIDS virus.
- Among cocaine-addicted babies, the average birth weight is approximately 21 ounces lower than normal while the average head circumference is about three quarters of an inch smaller than the average among normal babies. These differences lead to future learning difficulties and an increased risk of infant mortality.

Demographically, the problem of cocaine-addicted babies extends beyond the inner city and across the national social spectrum. In many larger cities such as New York, hospitals report that their obstetric and pediatric wards are overburdened and that drug-related costs contribute greatly to the overall cost of health care (Revkin, 1989).

An emerging problem is children who were born to addicted to cocaine but survive for a few years. "They operate on an institutional level—they eat and sleep, and eat and sleep. Something has been left out" (Kantrowitz, 1990). Social workers and hospital professionals claim that these "cocaine children" may have difficulty playing or relating with other children as they display symptoms of paranoia and distrust toward others. It has become a sobering reality that even if drug abuse were halted today, society would be forced to deal with its effects in one way or another during future decades.

Drugs and HIV

One of the most recent dangers of drug abuse is the threat of contracting blood-borne viruses which can kill. AIDS and the HIV virus that causes AIDS are specific examples, and in 1990 about 12,000 of the 43,000 persons reported to have AIDS were IV drug users. Such viruses are very real threats to not just the IV drug user's health but to the health of others who associate with them as well. Recent statistics show that many heterosexual and pediatric AIDS cases in the nation can be traced directly to IV drug users. In 1992 the Center for Disease Control reported that almost 60 percent of children with AIDS under 13 years of age contracted the disease from mothers who were IV drug users. With the increase in popularity of cocaine in the 1980s and the more recent increase in the use of heroin in the 1990s, experts are predicting there is greater risk of HIV spreading throughout the drug-using community.

Lost Productivity

We have seen that drugs affect friends and families and logically the business workplace as well. Employees who use drugs may miss more work and be late for work more often than those who don't. In addition, illness, injury, encounters with the justice system, and related family problems also may result. It is common for drugs and alcohol to be used in combination, resulting in seriously affected coordination, concentration, risk taking, and other abilities. The extent of just how drugs affect the user depends largely on the user's dosage level, rate of consumption, and the person's experience in using the drug. The extent of the drug use problem in the workplace was illustrated in a study of 2,500 postal workers. It found that postal workers who had used marijuana were (Zwerling et al., 1990):

- 1.6 times as likely as nonusers to have quit their jobs or have been fired
- 1.5 times as likely to have had an accident and nearly twice as likely to have been injured
- 1.5 times as likely to have been disciplined by a supervisor
- 1.8 times as likely to be absent

Concerns about safety mainly concentrate on high-precision or high-risk occupations such as transportation (e.g., airline pilots, air traffic controllers, railroad engineers, truck drivers, etc.). Other concerns focus on production of shoddily manufactured products, bad business decisions, slow-moving business services, drug-related absenteeism, sickness, and employee turnover. Employee interaction can be negatively affected by mood changes by drug using employees. Sadly, many persons employed in the nation's public and private sectors are drug users. The 1985 National Household Survey on Drug Abuse found that 12 percent of adults employed full time reported current marijuana use during the past 30 days with 4 percent reporting cocaine use during the same time frame. The same report in 1990, surveying almost 7 million persons, found lower proportions of employed people using drugs: 6 percent of full- and part-time employees reported current marijuana use and 1 percent of full-time employees reported current cocaine use. Although the latter figure is somewhat encouraging, we must remember that drug trends fluctuate over time and that a resurgence of drug abuse in the workplace is always a distinct possibility.

Drug Consumerism

The clandestine methamphetamine/crack market has created a new type of consumerism (for lack of a better term) that accompanies trafficking ventures. The new consumerism can be viewed from two angles: the drug user consumerism and the drug dealer consumerism. Because of drug user consumerism, many supermarkets have noticed increased sales of items such as scouring pads, cough syrup, and inhalers of Primatene Mist®. The sales of these and similar items illustrate their greater worth in a clandestine market than in a legitimate market. Scouring pads and steel wool, for example, are used for cleaning drug pipes and holding crack at the bottom of the bowl. Grain alcohol is commonly used to ignite crack, and the inhalers give drug users an added euphoric feeling or "rush" while under the influence of stimulants.

Stolen goods are a common means for drug users to get money for drugs. Studies have shown that "T-tops" from the roofs of sport cars are commonly bartered or sold for drugs. Other favorites are virtually anything electronic, such as video cassette recorders, microwave ovens (also used to make crack), stereos, and video games. At the opposite end of the consumerism spectrum is the drug dealing side. Purchases of cellular phones, pagers, personalized license plates, jewelry, firearms, and automobiles for illegal purposes have actually boosted the legitimate market of these products. Cellular phones and pagers are commonly used to arrange drug transactions, deliver supplies, and arrange for money pickups. Personalized license plates have emerged as a type of status symbol. Variations of "boof" and "sling," for example, may refer to smoking and selling crack. Expensive rings and gold chains and watches are commonly used in bartering for drugs because such items are easily carried into crack houses and many dealers see them as status symbols.

Weapons such as the 9-millimeter semi-automatic have become popular with many drug dealers. The 9-millimeter, commonly referred to as a "muscle gun," is compact and has an intimidating appearance. Automobiles are also one of the most sought after of the drug dealer's status symbols. Vehicles such as Mercedes-Benzes and Rolls-Royces have been seized by law enforcement agents after the vehicles have been purchased with cash earned from illicit sources.

The buying trends discussed above pose serious ethical, moral, and legal dilemmas for retail merchants that may be suspicious of some customers but may not have firm grounds for refusing business from those customers. Problems arise when customers present merchants with large sums of cash in exchange for goods. Specifically, merchants should not morally judge persons because they possess large amounts of cash or because they are from a certain part of town. Still, merchants should realize that the money they receive from any transaction may ultimately be subject to forfeiture under federal law if the customer turns out to be a drug dealer.

Theories of Drug Abuse and Crime

The search for solutions for reducing drug abuse and crime has baffled law enforcement authorities, social scientists, and criminal justice academicians alike. Although many proposed solutions to the problem will be discussed throughout this book, several widely accepted social theories explain why people use drugs and under what circumstances they become lured into criminal lifestyles. Although these theories will be examined later in this chapter, perhaps it would be appropriate to first discuss the concepts of vice and of victimless crime, terms commonly associated with drug crimes and drug abuse.

Vice and the Victimless Crime

While "vice" in normal parlance refers to any bad habit or evil conduct, it specifically refers in legal jargon to the supplying of any illicit good or service. For example, smoking cigarettes may be a vice in the ordinary sense, but only activities that have been specifically outlawed are considered "vice crimes": drug trafficking, loansharking, gambling, and prostitution. Some vice crimes are actually legal under carefully regulated circumstances. Gambling, for instance, is legal in some states under some circumstances. Nonetheless, illegal gambling activity thrives on the skirts of controlled gambling institutions. Through uncontrolled illegal organizations, profits may exceed those that can be realized through legitimate channels.

Enforcement techniques, especially for vice crimes like drug trafficking, can be controversial because a police officer's professional code of conduct and the letter of the law with regard to criminal investigations are sometimes compromised in order to obtain information. Enforcement is particularly difficult in these cases because there is usually no complainant or victim as there is in more traditional criminal violations. Therefore, law enforcement officers must rely on a high degree of surreptitiousness and ingenuity to make arrests. This can be illustrated, for example, by the drug investigator that is tolerant of a certain amount of drug use on the part of his or her informant while other people are under investigation for drug use activity similar to that of the informer.

In a study of drug law enforcement, Peter K. Manning and Lawrence John Redlinger listed the questionable and corrupt practices that have been associated with narcotics agents. The list included taking bribes, using drugs, buying and selling drugs, arrogation of stolen property, illegal searches and seizures, protection of informants and their drug trafficking activities, and violence. In contrast, drug enforcement professionals, while willing to admit that there is a certain degree of corruption in all law enforcement agencies, defend their profession by pointing to several factors. First, because of the accessibility of federal grant money in the early 1990s, professional training is more readily available to drug enforcement officials than ever before. Second, the adoption of a field training officer program (FTO) for drug enforcement personnel in larger departments has helped weed out individuals during their probationary period that are not considered competent for the job. Third, because of an increase in drug testing programs within law enforcement agencies, administrators have a new tool to check officers for drug abuse.

As to the term "victimless crime," another distinction must be made. A crime is usually characterized by an act that hurts someone or something or by the potential for the act to hurt someone or something. An exception is in the case of drug abuse since the primary victims, the drug abusers themselves, are willing participants in the activity. In addition, there are generally no complainants in vice crimes, for the reasons previously discussed. So, when charges are filed in vice cases, the state (or government) is the complainant. Hence the term "victimless crime" came into use. This does not preclude the fact, of course, that innocent people are also commonly victimized by drug abuse. So why do people choose drug abuse as a social lifestyle? What fuels one's ambition to become involved in a criminal drug trafficking organization or in a behavior that is considered criminal? These questions will be addressed next in the context of sociological theories that attempt to explain the social nature of the drug problem.

Social Disorganization Theory

One popular explanation of drug abuse addresses the link with poverty, social disorganization, and a feeling of hopelessness. The correlation between drug abuse and young minority group members has often been tied to factors like racial prejudice, low socioeconomic status, lack of positive self-esteem and uncharitable urban surroundings. As a result, the link between drug use, poverty, and race has been associated with high levels of mistrust and defiance common to lower class urban areas (Winick, 1965). In spite of a strong suggestion that drug abuse is linked with social disorganization, the relationship between class status and crime in general remains unclear. In fact, a recent RAND research study shows that about one-third of drug-dealing youths arrested had legitimate jobs at the time they were arrested for drug violations (Reuter et al., 1990).

Cultural Transmission

Today, social disorganization theory is most closely associated with the work of Chicago sociologists Clifford Shaw and Henry McKay. Their study, first published in the early 1940s, developed the theory of *cultural transmission* and focused on crime within the context of a changing urban environment. Shaw and McKay examined criminality, particularly among young people, in Chicago during the 1920s and 1930s. They concluded that popular concepts of body build and IQ were no longer accurate predictors of criminality but that environmental factors in the cities themselves were. Shaw and McKay saw criminality as a product of decaying "transitional neighborhoods" that were changing from affluence to deterioration. The researchers examined certain neighborhoods that were consistently "high crime" neighborhoods over several decades. Specifically, research revealed that, although the ethnic composition of these neighborhoods changed over time, the level of criminality in these so-called *zones of transition* remained the same. As a result of this study, it has been suggested that the attitudes, values, and norms of these areas are not only conducive to crime but are transferred, over time, from one ethnic group to another. According to this theory, children become indoctrinated into a life of crime at an early age. This occurs particularly in males that associate regularly with criminals and drug dealers and look to them as role models.

Anomie

In 1938, Robert Merton introduced the concept of anomie to explain an individual's motive for involvement in deviant social behavior or crime. In his theory, Merton attempted to adapt the abstract concept of anomie to living conditions in American society. Earlier, French criminologist Emile Durkheim had applied the term to explain a feeling of "normlessness" that results in a breakdown of social rules and order. Merton later adapted the concept to fit living conditions in U.S. society. In this theory, Merton argued, the ends become more important than the means, and an individual will resort to deviant means if no legitimate means (such as education, employment opportunities, etc.) are available. Merton went on to emphasize that modern U.S. society is goal-oriented, with wealth and material goods being the most desired. The cultural goal of financial success, for example, is highly valued by the individual, but if that individual finds: (1) that less value is attached by society to how that success is achieved and (2) that legitimate routes to financial success are blocked, he or she may opt for illegal means to achieve that particular end. For example, owning a home is generally considered one of the "great American dreams," but for many low or fixed-income families, this dream cannot be obtained through legitimate means. As a result, people from these families often "become estranged from a society that promises them in principle what they are deprived of in reality" (Merton, 1964: 218).

To illustrate his theory, Merton cited a preoccupation with material success or *pathological materialism* endemic in American culture. A legitimate profit motive may be channeled through deviant means (drug dealing, for example) when social barriers preclude legitimate channels such as good schooling, good jobs, and higher income. The result may be the creation of a criminal, a person willing to break the law to reach his or her goals. Merton further explained that there are five modes of individual adaptation to the contradiction between promised goals and available means: conformity, ritualism, rebellion, retreatism, and innovation.

It is, of course, the first and third modes, conformity and rebellion, that may offer the most intelligible explanation of society's involvement in drug use. The fifth mode, innovation, creates one of the fundamental social infrastructures for involvement in organized crime. The crime phenomenon of the California youth gangs, for example, that spread to many major cities in the mid-1980s, suggests that Merton's philosophy has contemporary validity. Such gangs represent thousands of inner-city youth from the Los Angeles area that have become extremely organized and target large cities as the base from which hundreds of thousands of dollars of drug money is realized (See Chapter 8).

Opportunity Theory

Opportunity theory is another popular crime theory that parallels Merton's theory of anomie and one that attempts to explain that not only are legitimate social opportunities unequally distributed throughout society, but even some *illegitimate* criminal opportunities are blocked for some youths. Richard A. Cloward and Lloyd E. Ohlin (1960) wrote that many male adolescents experience extreme deprivation of opportunity. Therefore, many feel that their position within society is somewhat fixed and that there are few legitimate ladders to success. In fact, they argue that criminal opportunities are only available for youths who have grown up in areas where collusion exists between members of the underworld and the general society. In these areas, adult criminals have worked out arrangements (through corruption) between businesses, politicians, and the police leaving them all but immune from prosecution. Their criminal enterprises, drug trafficking, gambling, and so forth, offer a stable income and an alternative to legitimate economic success. Under the fostering of adult criminals, youths fit right into this model and create a criminal subculture, preparing to join adult crime organizations by first running with criminally active street gangs. Cloward and Ohlin have identified three types of delinquent subcultures: 1) the retreatist subculture (where drug use is the primary focus); 2) the conflict subculture (where gang activities are dedicated to destruction and violence as ways of gaining status); and 3) the criminal rackets subculture (where gang activity is devoted to utilitarian, or profit-motivated criminal pursuits).

Essentially, Cloward and Ohlin view crime as a function of different opportunities provided to youth to attain both *legitimate* and *illegitimate* goals. When avenues for legitimate goals are blocked, illegitimate avenues are then pursued.

Differential Association

Some researchers embrace learning theories in which differential association attempts to explain a person's involvement in criminal activity. This theory, first formulated by Edwin Sutherland in 1939, suggests that a principle part of learning criminal behavior occurs within intimate groups. This occurs in two ways. First, individuals, particularly those living in economically depressed areas, identify with the financially successful role models in their communities (drug dealers, pimps, and gamblers). Second, individuals are exposed to the lifestyle and techniques of criminal behavior in their communities. The specifics of what is learned is based on the frequency of contacts, intensity, and duration of each association. According to Sutherland, the individual learns specialized techniques, attitudes, justifications, and rationalizations. It is through the learning of these traits that a favorable predisposition to criminal lifestyles is developed. Sutherland offered nine basics of differential association:

Know at least Three

1. Criminal behavior is learned.
2. The fundamental basis of learning criminal behavior is formed in intimate personal groups (e.g., gangs).
3. Criminal behavior is acquired through interaction with other persons in the process of communication.
4. The learning process includes the techniques of committing the crime and specific rationalizations and attitudes for criminal activity.
5. General attitudes regarding respect (or lack of respect) for the law are reflected in attitudes toward criminal behavior.
6. A person becomes delinquent or criminal because of an excess of definitions favorable to violation of the law over definitions unfavorable to violation of the law.
7. Differential association may differ in duration, frequency, and intensity.
8. The processes for learning criminal behavior parallel those of any other type of learning.
9. Criminal behavior is an expression of general needs and values (as with noncriminal behavior), but it is not explained by those needs and values.

Summary  *Know*

Today's drug situation is a result of complex social interactions affecting many different people, places, and things. It is referred to in a number of different ways by public speakers, politicians, the media, and private citizens. Terms used to describe the situation include the drug crisis, the drug problem, the drug dilemma, the drug epidemic, and the "war on drugs." However people choose to refer to them, drugs have remolded the social fabric of communities, the work environment, the learning environment of schools, the criminal justice system, and the drug treatment industry, just to name a few. From all indications, drug abuse in one form or another is here to stay.

There is no single drug abuse problem. Drug problems are related to both health and public safety, and much controversy exists around the best solution for the problem. The existence of drugs in our communities poses a considerable financial burden for society. Costs include: the financial expense of street crimes such as robbery and burglary, criminal justice system costs, medical costs for victims, and the loss of productivity in the work place. Other hidden costs include the moral cost of corrupt public officials and family strife for drug users and their loved ones.

The very nature of the drug problem creates an element of criminality and the accompanying violence commonly associated with that element. New organized crime groups such as the Jamaican posses and the California-based Crips and Bloods have emerged since the "drug culture" materialized, and their presence has become well known in many communities throughout the nation. Long-established crime organizations have also flourished since the drug epidemic gained momentum.

Reasons why people take drugs are numerous. For example, some people desire a stimulation of the endocrine chemicals within the body. These internal chemicals tend to emulate the effects of morphine and give a feeling of euphoria. Other people use drugs to alter their moods in the traditional "happy hour" forum, and still others use certain drugs for treatment of physical or mental medical conditions.

Drug trafficking and related drug activity is referred to by many as a "vice" crime. Additionally, many tend to refer to this type of behavior as "victimless" because all participants are willing to engage in the act. Because of this observation, many feel that the enforcement of such crimes is the equivalent of government attempting to police morals and personal values, and that such crimes should not be considered crimes at all but should be regulated and taxed.

Explaining the criminal behavior that commonly accompanies drug abuse are several social theories. Included are theories of social disorganization, anomie, cultural transmission, differential association, and differential opportunity. Each of these theories adds to our understanding of drug abuse and criminality and can be applied to the study of modern-day criminal behavior.

Do you recognize these terms?

addictive personality	endorphins
anomie	pathological materialism
backstabbing	social disorganization
cultural transmission	vice crimes
differential association	victimless crime
differential opportunity	zone in transition
endogenous	

Discussion Questions

1. What is meant by the term "drug abuse."

2. Other than drug users themselves, who are the victims of drug abuse in our society?

3. Discuss some of the reasons why the drug problem is considered such a major social problem in the U.S.

4. Discuss some of the health-related problems inherent with drug abuse.

5. What are some social factors which contribute to a climate of drug abuse?

6. What are the distinctions between the terms vice and victimless crime?

7. List the ways that cocaine in addicted pregnant mothers affects their unborn.

8. What are endorphins, and how do they relate to drug abuse?

Class Project

1. Discuss with fellow classmates or friends their perception of the country's drug problem and what can be done to solve it.

The Illicit Drug Trade

4

This chapter will enable you to:

- Understand the various dynamics of the illegal drug business
- Comprehend the different facets of illicit drug marketing
- Understand the role of foreign drug source countries
- Discover the global magnitude of the world's drug problem

The criminal drug trade, by virtue of its illegal nature, is a covert enterprise where persons, business decisions, and transactions all occur outside the watchful eye of the public. Because of this secrecy, much misunderstanding exists about its inner workings. For example, many questions exist regarding the sellers, the buyers, business decisions, business logistics, and organizational dynamics. Addressing these areas is the purpose of this chapter. In 1927, bootlegger Al Capone told newspaper reporters that he was just a well-meaning businessman providing a public service that the government chose not to. Many of today's drug trafficking entrepreneurs might also perceive themselves as business persons who are also simply offering goods and services not legally available to the public. However, the realities of the drug trade are not as benevolent as this supposition suggests. The truth is that the illicit drug business is a money-driven, calculated undertaking giving no consideration to human anguish or social responsibility. Drug sellers and users alike demonstrate their contempt for law and order in their choice to participate and become involved with illegal drugs. In addition, compared to legitimate businesses espousing a "customer is always right" philosophy, the drug trade is anything but user-friendly. Allegiances are weak (or nonexistent) in virtually all levels of production, manufacturing, transportation, and sales. Sellers typically lie about the quality and purity of drugs being sold; users distort information about the "benefits" of drugs to potential users; arrested drug offenders regularly turn in longtime associates in lieu of going to prison; drug prices are inconsistent and unstable; and all players in the drug trade are often suspicious about their associates' relationship with rival organizations or paranoid about the presence of undercover agents in their operations. Indeed, trust, or the lack of it, is the hallmark of the illegal drug trade. So to understand public policy approaches to the illicit drug problem these premises must be understood.

Despite the many contemptible aspects to the drug business, the organizational dynamics of the illicit drug trade parallel those of legitimate industry in many ways, which helps to explain why this business has endured in America, in one form or another, for more than a century. Considerations such as personnel management, manufacturing costs, market acquisition, wholesale and retail sales, corporate security, and overhead are included in today's illicit cocaine, heroin, and marijuana businesses. Furthermore, these commercial aspects are found in both international and domestic trafficking organizations. An understanding of how these dynamics operate and interface is crucial in the formation of national drug policy as well as the development of criminal and constitutional law dealing with areas of drug control.

The Business of Illegal Drugs

Many estimates have been offered over the past decade or so to gauge the actual size of the drug trade. Law enforcement officials on federal, state, and local levels all perceive the size of the trade to be enormous, but there is little consensus as to how big it actually is. One estimate was offered in 1987 by the Select Committee on Narcotics Abuse and Control which estimated that Americans spend $140 billion annually on illegal drugs. In comparison, a more conservative estimate was provided by the Office of National Drug Control Policy in the April 1994, National Drug Control Strategy, which estimated that Americans are spending $49 billion annually on illegal drugs. In either case, the amount is too high to be ignored by policy makers and law enforcement personnel alike and is the focus of much of this book.

For the most part, marijuana, cocaine, and heroin make up the majority of drugs seized by authorities, and accordingly they provide the greatest financial incentive for traffickers. Estimates regarding the amount of those illicit drugs produced in the world comes from the 1991 International Narcotics Control Strategy Report, which estimated net metric tonnage worldwide at 23,000 for marijuana, 337,000 for coca products, and 3,400 for opium-based products. Of course, there are many other drugs available like LSD, PCP, and methamphetamine, which are illegally produced in secret laboratories throughout the nation.

The relative size of the illegal drug trade can be seen when it is compared to that of the legal pharmaceutical drug business. For example, in 1987 an estimated 172,000 workers were employed in the legal drug trade which produced shipments valued at $39 million. Accordingly, 32,000 employees who make up the tobacco industry produced more than $17 million in shipments annually. Because of growing conditions that are more favorable in other countries, only small amounts of cocaine and opium products originate in the United States. An estimated 18 percent of the marijuana supply was produced in the United States in 1990 with the rest originating in other source countries (BJS, 1992). In those countries, agriculture crops such as marijuana, cocaine, and opium are commonly grown. Most of these drugs are grown by independent peasant farmers who rely on them as their only source of income. In addition to the farmer, an infrastructure is also required to facilitate the rest of the drug business. For example, roads and bridges and clandestine landing strips are necessary to transport drugs to buyers.

The Economics of Drug Trafficking

With few exceptions, the drug trade attracts entrepreneurs who are profit motivated. As with any business, illicit or not, certain principles apply to the successful operation of the trafficking system. For example, drug traffickers in retail markets typically use a "just in time" business strategy. That is, in many cases only small amounts of drugs are supplied to street vendors, which minimizes their losses should the vendor be arrested by police or robbed by competitors. In many cities, the "just in time" strategy makes it possible for sellers to provide just enough drug for street vendors to sell in one day's time or for crack house operators to sell in, say, a week's time. Suppliers are aware that in addition to the type of drug seized, in some states the quantity of drug seized plays a role in the severity of the criminal charge. So, if the vendor is in possession of small amounts when arrested, not only will vendors possibly be looking at a lesser charge but the supplier's credit standing with their wholesaler will not be jeopardized for future sales. Any such losses can easily be compensated for with future sales. Obviously, with the drug trade being profit-driven, both wholesale and retail pricing plays an important role in realizing earnings. Let's now consider the role that price structure plays in the economics of drug trafficking.

Drug Prices

With profit the mainstay of the drug business, a number of variables can be attributed to the establishment, rise, and decline of drug prices. In addition to other factors, the laws of supply and demand play a major role in determining whether a certain drug's price increases, falls, or remains stable. For example, drug dealers are keenly aware that police investigations result in the arrest and imprisonment of persons associated with the drug trade. So to insulate themselves from police detection, trafficking managers hire lower level dealers to bear the risks of dealing on the street level. These sellers are often street corner minions trading in small quantities of drugs but they may also be couriers who have been entrusted with a greater amount of responsibility for transporting drug shipments. Occasionally, dealers are arrested and their stashes of drugs seized by police as well. For example, in 1990 more than 41 tons of cocaine were seized from private aircraft and vessels in the U.S., Bahamas, and other Southeast corridor trafficking routes. In addition to seizure by police, some drug shipments are also:

- stolen by rival criminal organizations
- thrown overboard vessels to avoid confiscation
- not picked up because of a fear of police surveillance
- flushed down toilets for fear of seizure by police
- abandoned after dealers are arrested by police

All of these circumstances result in the drug supply not arriving at the designated point of delivery, and consequently subsequent shipments of the same drug might be affected by an increase in the street price. This brings up another important business variable which parallels the drug trade with legitimate commerce: wholesale prices are much cheaper than retail prices. When cocaine, for example, is produced in South America, its wholesale price is often based on the amount that is purchased. So the larger the purchase, the better the price. After the drugs arrive in the U.S. for distribution, prices rise considerably. This is so not only because of the cost of production and transportation of the drugs, but also because of the risks undertaken by dealers and distributors. Here's an example: 10 kilograms of opium from Mexico is valued at $40,000. Once this opium is transformed into heroin of 40 percent to 70 percent purity, it will sell for $210,000 per kilogram in the United States at the *wholesale* level. Once the drugs reach the *mid-level stage* of distribution, heroin at 20 to 70 percent purity can be sold roughly for $500,000 per kilogram. Black tar heroin, of 20 to 60 percent purity, can sell for $850,000 per kilogram. In sum, the street price of this heroin is between 153 and 183 times the price it was at the time it was cultivated. Further complicating the price structure, the prices of drugs also depend on the country of origin or other geographical factors. This is evident when we consider that in 1990 the price of a gram of cocaine varied from $35 in Miami to $125 in Los Angeles.

Why Prices of Illicit Drugs Vary

- distances the drugs travel

- number of rungs on the distribution ladder before reaching retail levels

- shortages of drug supplies due to wholesale and retail losses

- changes in pricing at the export/import and subsequent levels

- buyer preferences for drugs from a particular nation and of certain varieties or grades of drugs

It is common for different grades of drugs to dictate the street price of that drug. For example, in the marijuana business, wholesale and retail prices of both commercial and sinsemilla grades were lowest in Houston, Texas. This is because the drugs were transported through Mexico to Houston, and the distribution chain was shorter than if the drugs were transported to Omaha, Nebraska, or Boston, Massachusetts.

The price of a drug may also affect how drug buyers conduct business. For example, higher prices for a drug may result in the potential buyer choosing not to purchase the drug until prices come down or until another dealer is located who is selling the drug for a cheaper price. Accordingly, the buyer may choose to cut back on the use of the drug because of the high price tag. Finally, buyers may opt to substitute a less expensive drug with similar effects for the expensive drug. In any case, it is clear that the more expensive the price of a drug, the less likely that it will sell as readily on the street. Knowledge of these business dynamics is the reason why police drug control efforts often attempt to raise the prices of drugs, thus making it too expensive for users to afford them. In addition, high drug prices are also thought to deter would-be users from beginning the use of that particular drug.

Demand Elasticity

The elasticity of demand refers to the relationship between the change in the use of an item and the price of that item. In legitimate business, if the price of a commodity rises, the total purchases of that commodity decrease. So, in the illicit drug trade, how much the total use of a drug decreases (due to high prices) depends on how sensitive the demand is to that rise in price. A close examination of retail drug prices tell us that demand elasticity hinges on the type of drug in question. For example, price elasticity is greater for heroin than it is for marijuana because heroin is a physically addictive drug while marijuana is not. So drug users are more willing to pay more for a drug they "need" than for a drug they may simply desire.

Financing Drug Deals

In the world of legitimate commerce, businesses are much less concerned with hiding profits than are their illegal business counterparts. Because of this, it is not uncommon for millions of dollars of capital to be borrowed from legitimate banking institutions. Once profits are realized, then regular deposits can be made into banks or other financial institutions for disbursement or reinvestment. As one might guess, the rules of the game are quite different for business transactions in the illicit drug trade.

Instead of borrowing money from a bank or other lending institution, drug dealers will often have a "revolving credit" arrangement with their suppliers whereby payment for the drugs is not required until the they have been sold. In such cases, payments are not made until the dealers take delivery on a subsequent drug shipment. In time, as the dealer's financial base grows, shell or front corporations are sometimes established which help disguise or "launder" drug profits.

The hiding of drug revenues is an essential component to the illicit drug trade, for profits are earned without paying taxes on those earnings. In legitimate business operations, businesses pay taxes on their profits in proportion to the amount of money changing hands. As a result, a large part of the profit realized by drug dealers is money that would otherwise be paid to the government. In the following chapter we will address the issue of money laundering.

Merchandising and Distribution of Illegal Drugs

The illicit drug trafficking chain refers to large shipments of drugs which are transported from their point of origin to their destination where they are broken down into much smaller quantities for street-level distribution. With each stage in the distribution cycle, the price of the drug increases. Accordingly, as the shipment of drugs gets closer to the street, along with an increase in price of the drug, the purity of the drug decreases. The distribution chain refers to the players along the trafficking route. For example, in a cocaine trafficking operation, the first level of players are the coca farmers who cultivate the coca plant and sell by the bushel to traffickers who then hire people to process the leaves into coca paste. Once the coca paste has been produced, it is sold to mid-level producers who will dry the paste on drying tables where it becomes cocaine hydrochloride or powder. Next, smugglers are hired to transport the cocaine to the United States to be delivered to wholesalers, who, in turn, sell quantities to retail salespeople. Finally, the retail salesperson sells small quantities to low-level street dealers, who bear more of the risk of arrest than any other player in the distribution chain.

At the retail level, the buying and selling of drugs often entails a complex exchange of schemes and roles. For instance, some people who are not necessarily involved in the actual sale of drugs may be used as **steerers,**" who locate potential customers for dealers. Others may act as guards or lookouts, charged with locating police vehicles spotted in the area of drug sales. In other cases, one player is assigned to sell the drugs while a different person takes the money from the sale. This represents the classic division of labor in the drug trade and illustrates how operatives can insulate themselves from detection because it may be more difficult for police investigators to observe transactions.

Figure 4.1

How do the roles and functions at various levels of the drug distribution business compare with those in legitimate industry?

Approximate role equivalents in legal markets	Roles by common names at various stages of the drug distribution business	Major functions accomplished at this level
Grower/producer	Coca farmer, opium farmer marijuana grower	Grow cocoa, opium, marijuana; the raw materials
Manufacturer	Collector, transporter, elaborator, chemist, drug lord	All stages for preparation of heroin, cocaine, marijuana as commonly sold
Traffickers		
Importer	Multikilo importer, mule, airplane pilot, smuggler, trafficker money launderer	Smuggling of large quantities of substances into the U.S.
Wholesale distributor	Major distributor, investor, "kilo connection"	Transportation and redistribution of multikilograms and single kilograms
Dealers		
Regional distributor	Pound and ounce men, weight dealers	Adulteration and sale of moderately expensive products
Retail store owner	House connections, suppliers, crack-house supplier	Adulteration and production of retail level dosage units (bags, vials, grams) in very large numbers
Assistant manager security chief, or accountant	"Lieutenant," "muscle men," transporter, crew boss, crack-house manager/proprietor	Supervises three or more sellers enforces informal contracts, collects money, distributes multiple dosage units to actual sellers
Sellers		
Store clerk, salesman (door-to-door and phone)	Street drug seller, runner, juggler	Makes actual direct sales to consumer; private seller responsible for both money and drugs
Low-level distributors		
Advertiser, security guard, leaflet distributor	Steerer, tout, cop man, look-out holder, runner, help friend, guard, go-between	Assists in making sales, advertises, protects seller from police and criminals, solicits customers, handles drugs or money but not both
Servant, temporary employee	Run shooting gallery, injector (of drugs), freebaser, taster, apartment cleaner, drug bagger, fence, launder money	Provides short-term services to drug users or sellers for money or drugs, not responsible for money or drugs

Source: Bruce D. Johnson, Terry Williams, Kojo A. Dir, and Harry Sanabria, "Drug Abuse in the Inner City: Impact on Hard-Drug Users and the Community," in *Drugs and Crime,* Michael Tonry and James Q. Wilson, eds., volume 13, *Crime and Justice* (Chicago: The University of Chicago Press, 1990), 19. © 1990 by The University of Chicago Press. All rights reserved.

Source: Bureau of Justice Statistics, 1992.

Marketing Illicit Drugs

It is common in the drug business for dealers to attempt to convince potential buyers of the purity or quality of their product. Typically this is done by offering a specific drug with an identifiable label. For instance: "Panama Red" or "Colombian Gold" marijuana. In other cases, the seller asks the buyer to trust his reputation as an honest local drug dealer. Still in other cases, drugs are sold based on the quantity offered. For instance, if a high price is being asked for a gram of cocaine, the seller may remind the buyer that there is actually a gram and a quarter available for the price of a single gram, giving the buyer the impression that he or she is getting more than his or her money's worth. Marketing is also apparent in the packaging of certain drugs. In Columbia, Missouri, for example, **blotter acid** (LSD) appeared on the street in the form of "Grateful Dead" album covers. Virtually every album ever produced by this rock group was available to buyers in blotter acid form. For the potential buyer to purchase the entire album, however, he or she had to purchase 12 individual dosage units of the drug, as the picture of the album was spread out over all 12 squares of paper, each containing the LSD. Heroin dealers also use marketing techniques to persuade buyers to purchase their heroin over that of another dealer. Techniques include marking bags with colored tape, symbols or pictures, or assigning a particular batch or dealer's heroin a brand name like "Red Lion" heroin. Brand names help users identify the heroin thought to be of a high quality. Interestingly, if an addict dies as a result of a drug overdose, other addicts will often seek out the specific drug used by the deceased, believing that the user failed to realize that it was of such a high quality.

As drug enforcement efforts become more successful and effective and as different drugs become more and more popular, drug dealers often shift their marketing strategies. These changes in drugs and drug use may result in the development of new drugs or analogs or the re-emergence of older drugs which have not been popular for awhile. In any event, it is always the desire of the drug dealer to increase the potency of the drug he or she sells. Once this can be accomplished, word will spread among drug buyers, who will seek out the new, more potent drug.

Distributing Illegal Drugs

Drug sales networks differ somewhat from one case to the next. For example, trafficking not only differs from rural to urban areas but also depends on the type of drug and the techniques of the group distributing it. Most large urban areas have sections of town which are known as drug distribution areas. These areas, sometimes called "**copping areas**," are typically well-known to drug users. Often these areas are nothing more than street corners or public parks where small amounts of drugs are sold. It is common for many different drug sales to take place in a short period of time. Buyers go to the copping area, pay cash for the drugs, and leave—all in a matter of seconds. Investigations have shown that dealers operating in copping areas often sell to known customers and strangers alike. As a rule, dealers in copping areas will employ lookouts and "steerers," who watch for both police and potential customers. Once dealers are tipped off as to the presence of police in the area, they can dispose of their drugs before being caught in possession of them.

Neighborhood bars, truck stops or homes in affluent areas of town are sometimes fixed locations for drug dealing. Studies in the habits of dealers and users have revealed that middle-class buyers will often make their purchases away from the typical urban copping area to avoid getting arrested. In some cases, drug deals are arranged by telephone, and a drop-off location is decided upon. Crack houses are yet another example of a fixed location for drug dealing. Such locations emerged during the mid-1980s and are often abandoned buildings or apartments in public housing projects located near copping areas. In the crack house are the necessary paraphernalia for taking cocaine. This equipment includes needles and syringes for injecting as well as pipes and heat sources for smoking crack. The Detroit Police Department identified two types of crack houses: 1) a "buy and get high party house," where drugs are consumed on the premises in conjunction with illicit sex acts and 2) a "hole in the wall" house where buyers would literally put cash into a hole in the wall at the front door of a house and receive crack cocaine from an unidentified seller.

Profit Margin

While it is true that wholesale and mid-level drug dealers make hundreds of thousands of dollars and escape detection, those operating on the lower rung of the trafficking chain, especially those who are considered heavy drug users, accumulate few riches. The Bureau of Justice Statistics cites several reasons for this (1992):

- Their profits often support their drug use.
- The drug business is a fragile enterprise subject to considerable disruption by police efforts, frequent absence of a reliable supply of drugs, and a high potential for loss by predatory competitors and disloyal employees.
- Their involvement in drug sales is often sporadic.
- Earnings tend to be spent ostentatiously for expensive cars, gold jewelry, and other consumer goods.
- Many dealers spend a substantial amount of their time in jail or prison.

These variables should be considered when estimating the annual income for drug buyers and sellers. In 1985, a study of the economics of drug dealing estimated the annual income from drug sales, purchases of drugs, theft of drugs, and avoided expenditures for substances at $6,357 (Johnson, et al., 1985).

Another recent study estimated a typical seller's gross income per year at $15,600 (Reuter, et al., 1990). The mystique of drug dealing is shadowed by an illusion that all drug dealers make a lot of money. Unquestionably, this is not always the case. Experts have also suggested that one reason for the small amount of money earned by low-level drug dealers is that they often deal drugs on a part-time basis. In fact, the RAND study concluded that the typical drug dealer netted between $25 and $2,500 per month from sales. Interviews during the study showed that in addition to drug dealing, 75 percent held jobs and that drug dealing only supplemented their income. The study also revealed that most small-time drug dealers were heavy drug users as well and spent an average of 25 percent of their earnings on drugs. In the case of marijuana dealers, profits were shown to be considerably smaller than for other types of drugs, and dealings were much more casual and sporadic than transactions involving other "harder" drugs (Reuter et al., 1990). The enormous profits to be realized in the American drug market have intrigued both domestic and foreign traffickers. Although many drugs such as methamphetamine, LSD, and phencyclidine (PCP) are produced domestically, and a rapidly increasing proportion of the marijuana consumed in the United States is grown domestically, foreign traffickers supply an estimated 80 percent of illicit substances consumed in the United States (DEA, 1988).

Cocaine is a primary example of a drug imported by foreign drug networks. America's cocaine supply originates almost exclusively in South America, but the coca plant is cultivated principally in Peru, Bolivia, Colombia, and Ecuador. Accordingly, processing laboratories have been seized in Colombia, Brazil, and Venezuela. In 1989, new markets in these foreign countries have emerged for *bauzco*, a form of crack cocaine. Other South American and Caribbean countries have also served as transshipment centers for drugs.

In 1994, the Office of National Drug Control Policy reported that in recent years the increase in the production of cocaine has resulted in a glut that has reduced its price and increased street purity. For example, in Miami, Florida, the price of a pound of cocaine in 1984 ranged from $18,000 to $23,000, but in 1989, the same quantity was selling for approximately $9,000. Accordingly, the purity of cocaine was about 35 percent in 1984, and in 1989 that figure was up to 70 percent (OCDETF, 1990).

Other drugs frequently smuggled into the United States from foreign countries are marijuana and hashish, both products of the hemp or cannabis plant. Mexico supplies an estimated 30 percent of cannabis to the United States while Colombia supplies an estimated 33 percent, although (as indicated above) these percentages have been consistently declining due to increases in domestic production in the United States. Other foreign countries contributing to the U.S. marijuana market are the Caribbean island of Jamaica and Belize in Central America.

The International Perspective

The U.S. Department of State's 1993 International Narcotics Control Strategy Report estimated the worldwide production of illicit drugs in 1992 at 1,165 metric tons, a 12 percent increase since 1988. Opium poppies, used to manufacture heroin, are predominantly grown in Iran, Pakistan, Afghanistan, Myanmar (formerly Burma), Thailand, Laos, and Mexico. The milk-like liquid is first dried, then processed into morphine, and later converted into heroin by a complicated conversion process. Once smuggled into the United States, heroin is diluted with substances such as milk, sugar, or baking soda, which enable the trafficker to have more product for sale, thus increasing profits. Essentially, the U.S. heroin market is dominated by high-purity heroin from Southeast Asia which is thought to have supplied an estimated 70 percent of the total worldwide production of heroin in 1992. Secondary sources of heroin include Southwest Asia and Latin America (ONDCP, 1994). Heroin on U.S. streets is considerably more pure than it was a decade ago, and, accordingly, prices have plummeted through the early 1990s. As of the preparation of this book, heroin prices seem to have stabilized.

Often, source countries create mutual alliances sharing resources to maximize their profits. This chapter will examine some of the most active drug source countries, the drugs that they produce, and methods of trafficking them. Due to the vast amount of money capable of being earned in the illicit drug trade, millions of people are thought to be involved in it as either users, buyers, sellers, manufacturers, or jobbers earning money by transporting drugs or hiding cash. Although arrest records in the United States indicate that thousands of people are employed in some capacity in the drug trade, it is widely believed that a larger number are employed in foreign countries. For example, in South America (Peru, Bolivia, and Colombia in particular), more than one million people are thought to be involved in the cocaine trade as farmers of the coca plant, laborers, processors, and exporters of refined cocaine product.

Mexico

Mexico's extensive involvement in the drug trade has proven to be one of the most serious impediments to domestic drug enforcement initiatives in the United States. According to the Drug Enforcement Administration, Mexico has supplied an estimated one-fourth of the heroin entering the United States in recent years. In addition, for decades Mexico has ranked second in the world in the production of high-potency marijuana. Today, marijuana cultivation occurs in virtually every state of Mexico with the heaviest concentration in the northern and western states of Sonora, Sinaloa, Chihuahua, Oaxaca, and Cuerra. Enforcement efforts have proven to be costly; between 1975 and 1985, more than $115 million of American money was spent in the cooperative efforts between the two countries. In previous years, Mexican president Miguel de la Madrid Hurtado had referred to the problem as a cancer in both our societies.

During the 1960s, the focus of American-Mexican drug enforcement efforts was the reduction of marijuana production and interdiction efforts along the entire 1,933-mile Mexican-American border. By 1975, the scope of drug enforcement in Mexico had widened to include opium poppies, which also grow in abundance throughout the country. Joint eradication initiatives between American and Mexican authorities ended in 1978 with the relinquishing of all such responsibilities to the Mexican government. Despite some successes, questions slowly emerged regarding suspected criminal involvement of Mexican officials in the illicit drug trade.

Many Mexicans still insist that if the demand for drugs in the United States were eliminated, the black market drug trade in Mexico would disappear. This proclamation, common to many drug source countries, addresses the historical and global dilemma of supply versus demand. It is becoming more clear, however, that drug trafficking in Mexico is no longer a problem for the United States only. Mexican drug abuse is soaring, particularly among youths. In 1985, the DEA reported that a survey of more than 11,000 Mexican students between the ages of 15 and 20 in 246 schools found that 15 percent of these young people reported that they had used drugs. The drug of choice was marijuana, but other drugs named were inhalants such as glue and paint. In the late 1980s, Mexican television stations aired special reports during prime time to illustrate the devastating effects of drugs on the youth of Mexico.

Mexican Drug Smuggling

Over the years, marijuana and heroin have been the most commonly exported drugs originating in Mexico. Law enforcement officials have observed that Mexican traffickers aid Colombian traffickers in the transshipping of cocaine through Mexico to the United States. With regard to Mexico, traffickers utilize overland smuggling methods as the most prevalent mode of moving illicit drugs from the Mexican interior to the United States. States most directly affected by Mexican traffickers are Texas, California, Arizona, and New Mexico, who share the Mexican border with seven ports of entry.

When we observe the Mexican border, it is immediately evident that there is no massive wall, fence, or barricade separating the two countries. Moreover, U.S. Border Patrol officers assigned to watch for illegal aliens and drug smugglers find themselves undermanned and lacking much of the necessary equipment and resources to do an effective job. The remoteness of much of the border area and the great distances to be covered make patrolling an almost insurmountable responsibility. In fact, drug smugglers literally walk over the Mexican border to meet fellow traffickers on the American side, often free of detection by Border Patrol agents. Ground smuggling techniques for marijuana and heroin have proven to be quite ingenious over the years. Such methods include drugs concealed in false gas tanks, and inside the backs of seats, dashboards and spare tires.

The movement of drugs through general aviation aircraft accounts for considerable drug smuggling activity from Mexico. Illegal shipments of marijuana and heroin are flown from Mexico during the late hours of the night and unloaded at predetermined locations by American confederates in the United States. According to the DEA, there have been more than 2,000 clandestine airstrips identified in Mexico, which are grouped into 10 different clusters. The number of these strips indicates the enormity of the air smuggling problem and illustrates Mexico's tenacious capacity for illicit drug production. It has been estimated that one-third of the airstrips are located around opium poppy growing regions while the remainder are used for marijuana smuggling. Almost any type of plane can utilize of these airstrips, ranging from small single-engine aircraft such as the Cessna 172 and 182, to larger transports. The proximity of the Yucatan Peninsula to the U.S. also makes an ideal transit point for drug smuggling flights, particularly those originating in the Guajira region of Colombia. In 1986, there were some 70 clandestine airstrips identified in the Yucatan Peninsula alone.

In a 1988 RAND Corporation Study, project director Peter Reuter asserted that the Mexican government, unlike governments in Colombia, Bolivia, and Peru, does not incur any major political threats by cracking down on the drug trade. In fact, there is increasing willingness on the part of the Mexican government to do just that. This is due in part to the large numbers of Mexican police that have died in drug enforcement efforts. Indeed, it is likely that more Mexican than American police have been killed while attempting to enforce U.S. drug policies.

Perhaps it is naive to hope that Mexican officials could eliminate all transshipment efforts by Mexican traffickers, but a closer working relationship between the two countries is desirable. For example, as of the preparation of this text, there is no Mexican-American provision for U.S. authorities to chase smugglers in "hot pursuit" across the border. Indeed, when U.S. chase planes approach the Mexican border, they are required under law to retreat.

Thinking Critically #5

Support or refute this statement: Interdiction officers of both nations should be allowed to cross the Mexican-American border in pursuit of drug smugglers. Predict outcomes if the current policy is changed.

The Mexican Heroin Trade

Mexico first emerged as a major heroin supplier during the early 1970s. This occurred just after the collapse of the "**French Connection**," a massive heroin trafficking operation between Marseilles and New York. Mexico experiences an opium harvest season between September and April. This includes two harvests, which peak in November and March. After the opium harvest, raw opium gum is transported from the growing fields to nearby villages by pack mules, pedestrian couriers, or vehicles. Because of the vast number of back roads and footpaths in Mexico, interdiction at this stage is almost impossible. The opium reaches the heroin processing laboratories by means of gatherers (acaparadors). Their job is to purchase designated amounts of opium gum from the cultivators and deliver it, usually by general aviation aircraft, back to the processors that placed the order.

The conversion process (raw opium to powdered heroin) takes about three days and yields brown heroin with a wholesale purity of 65 to 85 percent. In contrast, white powdered heroin manufactured in the Middle East (discussed next) yields an average purity of 85 to 99 percent, which allows a much greater profit margin for traffickers. Most conversion laboratories are located in remote regions of the country, but some have been discovered in large cities such as Mexico City, Nuevo Laredo, and Tiajuana.

Figure 4.2
Mexico
Opium Poppy and Marijuana Cultivation Areas

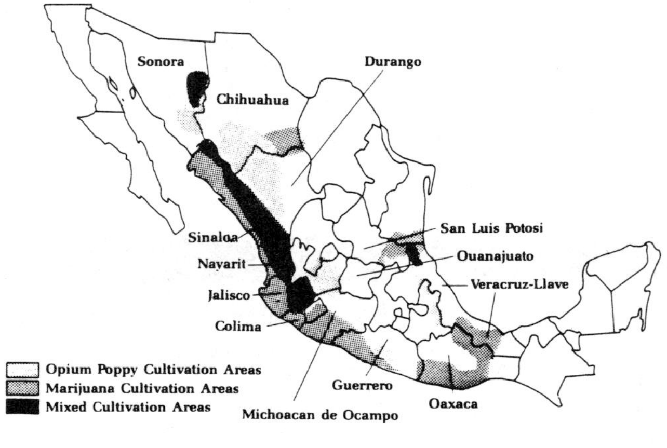

Source: Drug Enforcement Administration.

Once the complicated laboratory processing is completed by experienced chemists, the traffickers transport the heroin to principal population areas and prepare it for clandestine shipment to the United States. Once in the United States, the principal market areas for Mexican heroin are in the Southwest, contributing an estimated 80 to 90 percent of the market there and in the West, contributing about 50 percent of its market (DEA, 1988). While areas such as Chicago still account for a significant percentage of the market, Mexican heroin is virtually unavailable in the Northeast and Southeast United States.

Figure 4.3
Mexican Heroin
Selling Prices for the Equivalent of One Kilogram of Mexican Heroin
at Successive Stages of Trafficking (60-80% Purity)

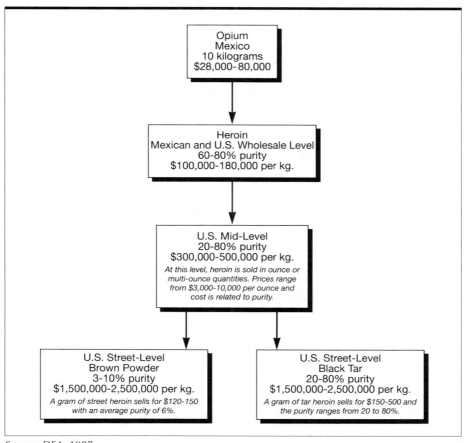

Source: DEA, 1987

Drug Enforcement in Mexico

The primary authority for drug enforcement in Mexico is vested in the nation's chief law enforcement officer, the Attorney General. It is the Attorney General that dictates who will be prosecuted and for what drug offense. The responsibility for apprehension of drug offenders rests with the Mexican Federal Judicial Police (MFJP), which investigates all federal crimes, including drug offenses. Drug regulatory functions are the responsibility of the Department of Narcotics under the Secretary of Health and Welfare and of the Director of Food, Beverages, and Drugs. The Department of Narcotics is responsible for enforcing drug violations in Mexico City and surrounding areas.

In her book *Desperados*, *Time* magazine correspondent Elaine Shannon exposes the circumstances surrounding the 1985 abduction and murder of DEA agent Enrique "Kiki" Camarena Salazar in Guadalajara (see Chapter 6). According to Shannon, certain Mexican officials not only helped to plan the abduction and murder but also created an elaborate coverup, one that continues as of the writing of this text. From Shannon's account, the Mexican government's involvement in narcotics is second only to that of the government in Panama (1988).

Events of the Camarena Murder

- *November, 1984.* Camarena assists in a raid on a huge Mexican marijuana plantation owned by drug lord Rafael Caro Quintero.

- *February, 1985.* Camarena is kidnapped in Guadalajara, tortured, and murdered.

- *December, 1989.* Caro Quintero and Ernesto Fonseca Carrillo, another drug kingpin, are convicted of the murder in Mexico City.

- *January, 1990.* A Los Angeles grand jury indicts six more Mexicans, including Humberto Alvarez Machain.

- *April, 1990.* Dr. Alvarez is abducted in Guadalajara and delivered to DEA agents in Texas.

Colombia

Colombia has the dubious distinction of being the world's most active illicit-drug-producing country. During the 1980s, an estimated 80 percent of the refined cocaine and more than 40 percent of the marijuana available in the U.S. market originated in Colombia (O'Brien & Cohen, 1984). As we will also discuss in Chapter 9, traffickers in Colombia have earned the reputation of being true entrepreneurs in the drug trade by becoming involved in virtually all aspects of the illicit drug business. Colombian traffickers have devised ways of financing drug plantations and laboratories as well as sophisticated smuggling and money laundering operations in the United States, Canada, and Europe.

Colombia is a country of contradictions. On one hand, it ranks as one of the most economically prosperous countries in Latin America. Its economy grew by 5.5 percent in 1987 and again by 4.5 percent in 1988. Despite a $15.7 billion foreign debt, Colombia has never fallen behind on debt service payments (Bagley, 1988). On the other hand, its enormous economic success is offset by the fact that it remains one of the most violent and corrupt countries in South America and, possibly, in the world. The Colombian involvement in U.S. cocaine trafficking can be traced back to the influx of Cuban refugees to South Florida in the 1960s after the Castro revolution. In Florida, many immigrant Cubans formed ethnic communities that served as the economic base of continued operation for the so-called "Cuban Mafia." The Cuban Mafia is a particularly pernicious organized crime group for two reasons. First, many of its leaders developed their illicit entrepreneurial skills under the tutelage of Meyer Lansky and Santo Trafficante when they ran massive gambling and drug smuggling operations in pre-revolutionary Cuba. Second, after the Cuban revolution, many of these future organized criminals were trained in the techniques of violence, smuggling, and other clandestine activities by the Central Intelligence Agency (CIA) as part of its efforts to raise and train an anti-Castro army. Once it was established in the United States, the Cuban Mafia became the major distribution organization for Colombian cocaine.

At first the south Florida Cuban Mafia organizations, in using their long-established Colombian cocaine connections, brought just enough cocaine to the United States for distribution in their own communities. But gradually they began to import larger and larger quantities of cocaine for expanding markets in the United States. By the mid-1960s, the Cuban networks expanded their distribution systems nationwide and relied on Colombian traffickers for nearly 100 percent of the cocaine distributed by the Cubans. The arrangement was simple: Colombians manufactured the drug, and the Cubans trafficked it in the United States.

Gradually, however, the Colombians came to want more control of the operation, and by the 1970s, they had expanded their own trafficking role in the United States. By 1978, the Colombians had severed most ties with the Cubans and assumed the dominant role that they now play in providing cocaine to the United States. It was also during the 1970s that the incidence of violence increased as a result of several localized cocaine-trafficking gang wars and gave rise to the Colombian trafficking cartel's notoriety (see Chapter 9). In 1981, an extradition treaty between Colombia and the United States was ratified, and for a time, traffickers were fearful of losing their immunity to U.S. criminal prosecution. If they were brought to the United States to face drug charges, they might not be able to bribe their way out, as they had done with relative ease in Colombia.

In 1982, Belisario Betancur Cuartas became president of Colombia. Although Betancur was strongly and openly opposed to drug trafficking, he also believed that the extradition treaty violated Colombia's sovereignty and said that he would not approve any extraditions during his four-year term. Rodrigo Lara Bonilla was then appointed as Minister of Justice by Betancur. In 1984 Bonilla organized a raid on Tranquilandia, the location of the Medellin

Cartel's largest cocaine laboratory, capable of producing more than three metric tons of cocaine a month. As a result of the raid, the police seized a total of 13.8 metric tons of cocaine worth an estimated $1.2 billion, along with firearms, aircraft, and chemicals necessary in the production of cocaine hydrochloride. During the month following the raid, Lara Bonilla was assassinated by an unknown gunman.

In November 1985, M-19 guerrillas (see Chapter 9) stormed Colombia's Palace of Justice, murdered 11 Supreme Court Justices, and destroyed the extradition files. The siege resulted in the murders of 95 persons. It is widely believed that the Medellin Cartel had hired the M19, as the destroyed extradition case files concerned Medellin Cartel members.

In June 1987, the Colombian Supreme Court overturned the **extradition** treaty with the United States. A total of 15 traffickers had been extradited since 1984. During the week of August 14, 1989, three more government officials were murdered. One of the victims was presidential contender Luis Carlos Galan, who was shot and killed by seven gunmen during a political rally near Bogota. The Galan murder prompted an enraged President Virgilio Barco Vargas to enact "summary extradition" for use in fighting the traffickers. This permits the extradition of drug criminals from Colombia to the United States while circumventing the Colombian court system.

When considering Colombia's extensive role as a source country, we should also consider the reasons that have enabled Colombia to maintain consistent control of the cocaine market and much of the marijuana market for such a long period of time. Three reasons can be cited for this:

1. Geographically, Colombia is well positioned to both receive coca from Peru and Bolivia and to export, by air or sea, processed cocaine to the United States.
2. The country's vast central forests are effective in concealing hidden processing laboratories and air strips.
3. Colombians have gained much experience over the years as early pioneers in the cocaine trade. Consequently, the drug organizations have progressed from small fragmented groups of criminals to sophisticated and professional criminal cartels that are quite proficient at their trade.

Colombia, despite its many problems, is one of Latin America's richer countries. Its economy grows by 3.5 percent a year, and its foreign debt is only $18 billion. Investors are attracted to Colombia by its coal and oil. The cocaine business endures in Colombia largely due to its high profitability and the excellent business practices initiated by the traffickers. Coca bushes grow best along the Andean mountain chain, mainly in Bolivia and Peru. Colombians import the semi-processed coca paste, run the laboratories that convert the paste into cocaine powder, and skillfully control the trade northward to the United States through Caribbean and Atlantic coast shipping routes.

The cocaine business incorporates more than one million people, from peasant growers in Peru and Bolivia, to the chemists and processors in Colombia, to the distributors on the streets of America (Filippone, 1994). Drug Enforcement Administration officials estimate that Colombian traffickers over the last ten years have increased tenfold the supply of cocaine to the United States. With the resultant market glut in the United States, traffickers are turning their attention to Europe by way of Spain, where cocaine brings four times the retail price that it does in Miami. In addition to cocaine, marijuana is also one of Colombia's primary illicit drug exports. According to the President's Commission on Organized Crime (1986), Colombia supplied 42 percent of the marijuana consumed in the United States in 1984. The major percentage of this traffic was controlled by large Colombian trafficking organizations.

Marijuana is cultivated in several regions throughout Colombia, but the largest of these is along the Guajira Peninsula. Members of large Colombian trafficking organizations purchase marijuana from growers and provide protection and financial incentives to them. Marijuana is harvested twice each year with the largest harvest occurring in the fall. The predictable harvest pattern closely parallels the level of availability of Colombian ("Colombo" or "Bo") marijuana in the United States.

The United States government estimates that almost 90 percent of cultivated Colombian marijuana is shipped to the United States by sea with the rest being shipped by air through the use of general aviation aircraft. The ships used are commonly referred to as "mother ships" and are usually large fishing vessels or freighters that can hold 50 tons for a 100-foot mother ship and 100 tons for a 400-foot mother ship.

Typically, these ships await their cargo while remaining at sea or stationed at selected Colombian ports. Once the shipment is ready for transportation to the United States, the ship travels to a selected beach site that is predetermined by the traffickers. An estimated 100 loading sites dot Colombia's north coast from Barranquilla to Portete, and all of these are linked by trails and airstrips to the major growing areas. When preparations are complete, the mother ship moves to a prearranged location about one-half to 3 miles off shore. Small boats then ferry loads of marijuana from the shore to the mother ship. This is usually done during the night to avoid detection.

Marijuana traffickers commonly use the same trafficking routes established by cocaine traffickers. These include the *Windward Passage* between Cuba and Haiti; the *Yucatan Channel* between Mexico and Cuba; and the *Mona Passage*, bordered by the Dominican Republic and Puerto Rico. It is from these routes that American ports along the Gulf of Mexico and the east coast are most accessible to smugglers. In May 1990, national elections were held to elect a new president of Colombia, as former president Virgilio Barco was prohibited by the Colombian constitution from seeking a second term. During the campaign, the drug issue overshadowed all other issues and resulted in the bloodiest election in the country's 180 years of independence (Post, 1990). Reminiscent of gangland-style voter intimidation of the 1930s, the violence during the nine months preceding the Colombian election included the assassinations of three presidential candidates, 262 police officers, 93 soldiers, three judges, 15 news media employees, and an estimated 1,700 Colombian civilians. During the two weeks before the election, nine bombs exploded at schools, churches, shopping centers, and supermarkets killing 320 persons. One bomb destroyed a Colombian airliner, killing all 107 persons aboard.

The office of president was sought by some 12 candidates. Of these 12, Cesar Gaviria, the Liberal Party's candidate, and Alvaro Gomez emerged as leading contenders. Gaviria's platform was basically the same as Barco's—he advocated a hard line against traffickers. Gomez, however, urged for the legalization of cocaine in the major drug-consuming countries and maintained that the only way to put the traffickers out of business was to deprive them of profits. Gaviria overwhelmingly won the election and assumed his duties on August 7, 1990.

Figure 4.4
Foreign Source Marijuana
Selling Prices for One Pound of Marijuana at Successive Levels of Trafficking.

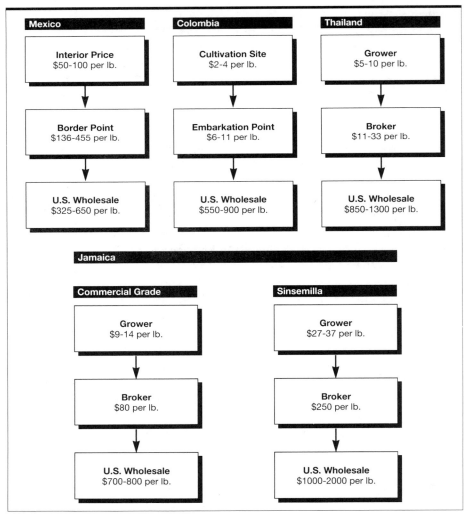

Source: DEA, 1987

Bolivia

Bolivia, a South American country that straddles the Central Andes Mountain range, encompasses an area roughly equivalent to the combined size of Arizona, Colorado, Utah, and New Mexico. Bolivia consists of three primary topographical regions known as the Altiplano. Bolivia exhibits wide variations in geography and climate. For example, the climate ranges from continuous humidity and heat of the Amazon basin to extreme cold and heavy snowfall of the upper Andes. Considered one of the poorest countries in South America, Bolivia has an estimated $570 annual per capita income (O'Brien and Cohen, 1984). Its notoriety as a drug source country is similar to Peru's as a coca leaf producing country for international traffickers. Although growing the coca leaf plant in Bolivia is perfectly legal, the processing of it into cocaine is against the law.

There are two principal areas of coca cultivation in Bolivia: the Chapare region in the department of Cochabamba and the Yungis in the department of La Paz. Bolivia's traditional role in international drug trafficking has revolved around the supplying of coca paste to traffickers in Colombia. Since the mid-1980s, however, Bolivia has been more and more involved in the conversion of coca paste to cocaine hydrochloride. Cocaine laboratories have been discovered in the departments of the Beni and Santa Cruz.

Ironically, the emergence of Santa Cruz as a cocaine processing center was intimately connected to the pro-United States military dictatorship of Garcia Luis Meza. It was under this regime that Roberto Suarez-Gomez, Sr., the head of Bolivia's premier cocaine trafficking family, consolidated his hold on the market with the assistance of Nazi war criminal Klaus Barbie, who helped reorganize both the security systems of the Suarez organization and Bolivia's internal security police. The Suarez family operation is one of the primary sources of cocaine paste in Bolivia. Under the leadership of Roberto Sr., also known as "little father," son Roberto Jr. and nephew Renato Roca Suarez produce an estimated 40,000 tons of coca paste per year and earn an estimated $600,000 per year. Roberto Sr. was forced to yield control of the organization in 1988 after his arrest.

A large portion of the Bolivian coca regions consist of flat, marshy lowlands that are virtually isolated from the outside world. Traffickers in Bolivia, therefore, primarily rely on general aviation aircraft for transporting drugs. Bolivia has averaged more than one government per year since 1825, so diplomatic efforts to establish eradication programs have been difficult (O'Brien and Cohen, 1984). Since the mid-1980s, however, the government of Bolivia has recognized the extent to which drug traffickers have used their tremendous financial resources to gain control over many political factions and financial institutions within the country. This has resulted in increased pressure from the government against traffickers.

In 1986, the Bolivian and United States governments joined forces in Operation Stop Prop to locate clandestine growing regions and manufacturing laboratories. To implement the operation, Attorney General Edwin Meese and

Secretary of Defense Casper Weinberger issued a joint emergency declaration under the provisions of the Posse Comitatus Act, allowing the use of United States military resources to assist United States law enforcement agencies. Under this plan, Blackhawk helicopters were used to transport United States agents and Bolivian police to remote cocaine laboratories in Bolivia.

Ninety-five police raids resulted in the seizure or destruction of 21 cocaine laboratories, 24 transshipment storage locations, and hundreds of pounds of refined and unrefined cocaine. Authorities estimated that the labs were capable of employing and housing up to 50 workers, who were able to produce 1,000 to 1,500 kilograms of powdered cocaine per week.

Figure 4.5
Cocaine
Selling Prices for the Equivalent of One Kilogram of Cocaine at Successive Stages of Trafficking.

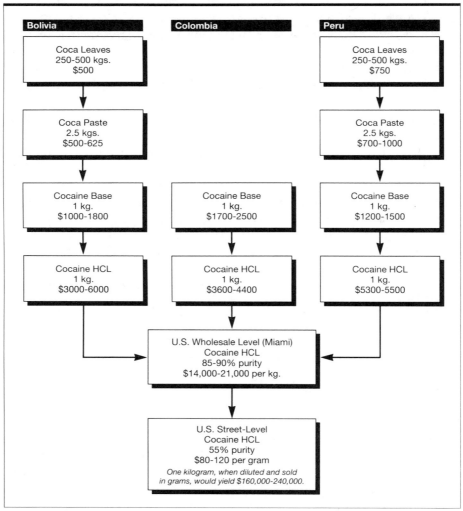

Source: DEA, 1987

Because of such crackdowns in Bolivia, many traffickers have abandoned their laboratories, leaving equipment and supplies intact. This resulted in a severe reduction in the demand for coca paste and a significant decline in the price of coca leaves. Between June and September 1986, the price of coca leaves fell from $125 per hundredweight to an all-time low of $15. Since then, however, the Bolivian government has reported that coca production was back up from 90,000 acres in 1986 to 119,000 acres in 1989 (DEA, 1987). After a 1989 summit between the heads of the main coca-producing countries in South America, the option of crop substitution was discussed as an alternative to the coca trade. Although it can be asserted that no legitimate crop will bring as high a financial yield as cocaine (an estimated $500 per acre), many experts believe that crop substitution combined with tougher law enforcement may place a considerable dent in coca production.

The cocaine business in Bolivia is less institutionalized than in Colombia and Peru, due to the organized crime influence of such groups as the Medellin Cartel and the "Sendero Luminoso"—the Shining Path—a guerilla group closely affiliated with peasant and farming interests (see Chapter 9). Indeed, much of the farming in Bolivia is done by out-of-work miners who left the highlands when tin markets collapsed in the early 1980s.

In 1988, Bolivia outlawed the growing of coca for export, and the government has initiated a plan in which loans are offered to the estimated 37,000 farmers that are willing to switch crops. In other initiatives, Bolivia has torched more than 9,000 acres of coca since 1987 and has reduced its five-digit inflation rate to about 10 percent, the lowest in Latin America. Still, experts estimate that a farmer working a typical 2.5-acre coca plot can earn as much as $5,000 a year, 10 times the average annual income.

Peru

For more than 2,000 years, Peruvians have chewed the leaves of the coca plant primarily to counteract the effects of high altitude and as an aid to digestion. A certain amount of coca is permitted under law for domestic use as well as pharmaceutical purposes. Although Peru is not considered a source country for cocaine, it is a primary contributor of coca leaves, which are cultivated and then sold to Colombian traffickers for processing. It has been estimated that Peru cultivates as much as 55 percent of the coca leaves used in world production of cocaine hydrochloride (Filippone, 1994).

Peru, like its neighboring country Bolivia, suffers from a weak economy, and the cocaine trade provides hundreds of millions of dollars in income that otherwise would not be realized. The coca leaf is the principal source of income for thousands of Peruvian farmers who find it far more profitable than coffee or other crops. In fact, a farmer who cultivates a little more than a hectare of coca leaf can earn the equivalent of several thousand dollars a year, at least 10 times more, and possible 100 times more, than they could earn from any legal crop (Filippone, 1994). In Peru, it is estimated that as many as 60,000 families depend on the coca growing business for their livelihood.

Figure 4.6

It is the runaway inflation experienced by Peru, as well as the internal political threat of the Shining Path, that most concern governmental leaders in Peru (see Chapter 9). To understand the conflict between the Peruvian government and members of the Shining Path, *Operation Snowcap* should be considered. Operation Snowcap, originating in 1987, began as an initiative to help residents of the beleaguered Andean nation with the drug problem. The operation originally consisted of 30 DEA agents assigned to a military-style firebase at Santa Lucia in the upper Huallaga Valley. The agents' function was to serve as a backup force to Peruvian police with a focus on attacking clandestine airstrips and laboratories operated by traffickers.

Thinking Critically #6

Considering the magnitude of the worldwide illicit drug trade and its impact on the United States, do you believe states should continue to criminalize drug use? Predict outcomes should current laws be either continued or abandoned.

In two incidents during April 1990, members of the Shining Path fired rocket-propelled grenades for more than two hours at the base and burned down the mission of an American priest, Father Mariono Gannon. The attacks came in the wake of an extended interdiction and eradication program by a joint Peruvian-United States team. As of the preparation of this book, the United States DEA has trained more than 600 Peruvian police in drug control tactics.

Trafficking Trends in South America

It is evident that Colombia is maintaining its status as the largest producer of cocaine hydrochloride in South America (and the rest of the world). While some coca leaf cultivation takes place there, the majority of coca leaves used in cocaine manufacturing come from neighboring countries Peru and Bolivia. The financial incentive for coca growers in these countries is augmented by the fact that the coca plant is a far easier crop to grow and harvest than other conventional crops. This is evident for three reasons:

1. Coca is a deep-rooted crop with a life span of about 30 years.
2. Income earned from growing the coca plant is many times the daily wage of growing a conventional crop. For example, farmers growing coffee will average $520 per acre annually, compared to $1,030 per acre for coca.
3. The coca plant can be harvested from three to six times a year and will grow in poor soil that is unable to support traditional crops.

The Colombian government's 1984 restrictions on the importation of ether and acetone, which are used in the cocaine conversion process, temporarily helped to disrupt cocaine production but has not accounted for a major decrease in its production. This is because laboratory operators found chemical substitutes for these solvents and have also devised ways to smuggle essential chemicals into the country.

Bolivia's involvement in the cocaine trade has remained somewhat consistent through the late 1980s. It is here that much of the required coca paste is manufactured for later production into cocaine. In addition, due to the tremendous profit margin, Bolivian traffickers are becoming more and more involved with the total conversion process of coca pasta into cocaine hydrochloride. According to a 1988 DEA report, this involvement does not yet rival that of the Colombians, although it is growing and certainly takes up the slack for any diminution in the Colombian trade.

Brazil's growing role in the South American drug trade is primarily that of a transshipment country, but it too may emerge as yet another source country for the finished cocaine hydrochloride product. This was evidenced by the 1987 seizures of six cocaine hydrochloride laboratories in various locations throughout the country. One of these laboratories, according to authorities, had been in operation for five months and was producing an estimated 2,000 kilograms per week.

Figure 4.7
Carribean Routes Used in Maritime Drug Trafficking

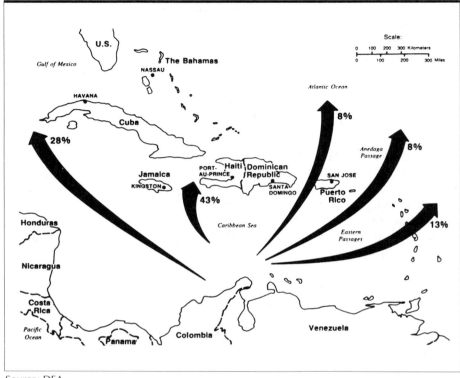

Source: DEA

One irony in the drug trade is that while many Americans claim drug abuse as the nation's number one priority, American chemical companies furnish an estimated 90 percent of the ethyl ether, acetone, and other processing agents required to make cocaine in South American jungle laboratories. Only in the late 1980s has there been any type of governmental focus on this problem. For example, the Federal Chemical Diversion and Trafficking Act was implemented to require chemical firms to maintain strict records on sales and equipment. Although this law is designed to deter criminal diversion of chemicals to traffickers, DEA reports that many phony "front" companies operating in the United States and Mexico have made tracking chemicals difficult. In addition, cocaine processors have successfully purchased precursor chemicals from German sources that either produced the chemicals themselves or purchased them from American companies.

There has been some evidence of cocaine trafficking in some of the other South American countries. This includes Ecuador, where some small cocaine labs have been seized; Paraguay, where traffickers have easy access to Bolivia and where there is evidence that cocaine processing was encouraged by General Stroessner's right-wing dictatorship; and in Uruguay, where some laboratory activity was detected in late 1988 and early 1989.

Jamaica

Smuggling and drug trafficking by Jamaican nationals is nothing new. However, it was only in 1985 that widespread media coverage of Jamaican gangs (or "**posses**") raised the public's awareness of the major role of Jamaican gangs in the global drug trade. While the presence of Jamaican posses in the United States will be discussed in greater detail in Chapter 8, this part of the text examines the larger role of the country of Jamaica and its contribution to international drug trafficking.

Jamaica and the Drug Trade

Jamaica's involvement in the international drug trade has always centered around two primary drug commodities: marijuana and cocaine. Although marijuana trafficking has a longer history than does cocaine trafficking, both drugs are a major financial contributor to Jamaica's organized crime element. High-grade marijuana has been cultivated in Jamaica for more than 100 years and is believed to have been introduced to Jamaica by laborers from India in the mid-1800s. Today, its use has spread to literally all segments of society, and it is estimated that between 60 and 70 percent of the island's population regularly consume marijuana (O'Brien and Cohen, 1984). Despite its years of cultivation, marijuana has been illegal since 1913. Indeed, marijuana is such big business in Jamaica and it is smoked with such frequency that the law cannot be adequately enforced.

In recent years, Jamaica's role in international drug trafficking has increased dramatically. Considered a consistent supplier of high-grade marijuana to the United States, Jamaican cultivators supply an estimated 17 to 20 percent of the American "pot" market. Although Jamaican traffickers cultivate marijuana, they do not grow coca leaves or manufacture cocaine hydrochloride. Indeed, their involvement with cocaine is that of retail distributor. Jamaican posses have reaped great profits through the sale of crack in the United States. More and more traffickers are considering the coastal areas of Jamaica as a stop-off point for loads of illicit drugs in transit from other source countries. Northern fishing ports such as Kingston are particularly popular for illicit drug transshipments.

Jamaica's Political History

Despite a turbulent history of political violence, in 1995 Jamaica's historically high crime rate was considerably lower than just 10 years earlier. Jamaica's Prime Minister, P.J. Patterson, has publically proclaimed that jobs and economic reform will continue through the 1990s. However, such good times were not always the case in Jamaica, a country whose volatile political climate has stemmed from long-time colonial control, poor economic conditions, and violent gangs. Once Jamaica gained complete independence from Britain in 1962, the government attempted to provide adequate housing and jobs for Jamaicans. During this period, the primary political parties in Jamaica were formed. The major labor unions dominating Jamaican industrial relations are the Bustamante Industrial Trade Union, the National Workers Union of Jamaica, and the Trades Union Congress of Jamaica.

For more than three decades the two dominant political parties in Jamaica were the socialist Peoples National Party (PNP), headed by Michael Manley, and the conservative Jamaican Labor Party (JLP), headed by Edward Seaga. These parties alternated in control of the country. In 1989, Michael Manley and the Peoples National Party once again gained political control of the Jamaican government through elections that year. The elections were considerably less violent than those in 1980 when extreme political differences between the two parties resulted in the deaths of an estimated 800 people and charges of CIA intervention on behalf of Seaga (who is known in Jamaica as "CIA-ga").

Neighborhoods in Jamaica are politically assigned, resulting in both political and geographic associations. Originating in the social and political unrest in Jamaica, violent subgroups known as posses soon emerged; their members adopted the word they had learned from American western movies. Some of the more violent gangs originate in the streets of Kingston, Jamaica's capital, and name themselves after the very neighborhoods from which they come.

Much of the turmoil in Jamaica can be traced to problems with public housing projects in the country. Probably the most significant event that precipitated drastic social changes began with the Tivoli Gardens housing project. Tivoli Gardens was the first public housing project built in Jamaica. Conceived in the 1960s, the project was an effort to provide jobs and housing to the Kingston ghetto of Trench Town. Edward Seaga, one of the leaders of the Jamaican Labor Party, provided Tivoli Gardens construction jobs and subsequent housing to JLP supporters. This created an atmosphere of "political affiliatory survival," in which one's political associations were directly related to his or her ability to secure good jobs or adequate housing.

Gangs in Jamaica existed for years before the current volatile political atmosphere existed, but with the building of the projects, the gangs have become politicized. Tivoli Gardens then became a power base and the home of one of the JLP's largest and most dangerous posses, the Shower Posse (nicknamed after a machine gun's "shower" of bullets).

The housing projects conceived by Seaga continued in operation even after 1972, when the socialist PNP came into power and Michael Manley became prime minister. Despite many sweeping social reforms, Manley was unable to undo the damage resulting from the housing scheme initiated by Seaga and the JLP. A sister program called Arnett Gardens was soon initiated by the PNP and patterned after Seaga's Tivoli Gardens. As with Seaga and the Tivoli Gardens project, Manley awarded his supporters with jobs and housing for the Arnett project, which soon became the power base for the Spangler Posse.

By the time of the 1977 election, most of the neighborhoods were politicized, and the posses had become so violent that Manley declared a state of emergency and placed the gang leaders and their top gunmen under arrest. This control effort failed to stop the wave of violence in Jamaica. Manley won the 1977 election, but the Jamaican economy failed to improve.

Just before the 1980 election, Seaga called on his JLP supporters in Miami to send hundreds of guns to Kingston. After winning that election, he made attempts to consolidate the posses that his own JLP party, in fact, had helped create. Some top gunmen were paid off and others were hired to assassinate rival gunmen. Seaga also sent other gunmen to the United States to engage in two traditional criminal practices of Jamaican posses: selling marijuana and selling cocaine.

The Rastafarians

Ganja, a term used to describe potent Jamaican marijuana, is particularly important to the Rastafarians and their way of life (also see Chapter 3). To understand the Rastafarian religion, which is not well documented, and its relationship to illicit drugs, it is necessary to look at its history. It was the objective of some Jamaicans, as well as other African descendants, to separate white and black cultures and revitalize their African heritage. In the 1930s, a black religious group appeared in Jamaica that recognized Haile Selassie (the emperor of Ethiopia) as their messiah. Before taking the name Haile Selassie, he had been known as Ras Tafari. Hence, his followers called themselves Rastafarians.

Orthodox followers commonly grow "dreadlocks," long locks of hair formed by washing the hair and allowing it to dry without being combed. Another religious practice is that of smoking ganja. It is considered a magical herb important to spiritual, mental, and physical health. Reggae singers, such as the late Bob Marley, sang of the effects of the "mystical herb" and brought worldwide attention to the Rastafarians.

It is important to note that although Rastafarians do recognize marijuana as an important characteristic of their religion, not all Rastafarians are criminals. Conversely, even though some Jamaican posse members may be members of the Rastafarian religion, the religion should not be arbitrarily associated with those Jamaicans that are involved with criminal activity.

As we will discuss later, the Jamaican youth posses strangely parallel youth gangs in the United States, especially the Los Angeles gangs. In both cases, a generation of youth have been exposed to much street violence and illegal drug trafficking.

Case Study: Operation Beacon

Mickie Munday and Jim Coley formed the core of the Beacon group. Now in their forties, they had been friends since high school. They got their start in the smuggling business in 1978. Their method then was unsophisticated. They made direct flights from Colombia in general aviation aircraft loaded, at first, with marijuana and, later, with cocaine. They would land on remote roads and canal banks in South Florida and unload their cargo. In December, 1981, Coley and a copilot flew across Cuba too high and too fast. The U.S. Air Force scrambled F-4s to intercept what they thought was a possible MiG and encountered Coley. Coley and his copilot dumped their load of cocaine, but they were met and questioned by U.S. Customs when they landed. Coley disappeared before charges were brought, but Harold Johns, the less cautious copilot, was arrested and convicted. Coley became a fugitive.

By October 1982, Coley and Munday were ready to resume smuggling. They joined with Phil Cardilli and Danny Simms to launch a combined boat/aircraft smuggling venture. Coley headed up air operations. Like other weekend vacationers, on Fridays he would fly a private plane from Boca Raton or Fort Lauderdale to Rum Cay or Long Island in the Bahamas. The plane would transport women passengers, referred to in the organization as "cover girls," and return to the United States with the passengers on Sunday or Monday. The intent was to avoid suspicion by appearing to be engaged in a vacationer's charter or a corporate outing. To this end, Coley and his copilot would wear "uniforms" of dark trousers, white shirt, dark tie, and epaulets.

Instead of spending the weekend in the Bahamas, Coley would fly to Colombia, pick up a load of cocaine, and fly to a group of uninhabited rocks in the Bahamas, named Scrub Cay, where the narcotics were dropped into two boats operated by Cardilli and Simms. Coley would return to Rum Cay or Long Island, where he would wipe down the aircraft, wash off the tires, and replace the remaining Colombian aviation gas with Bahamian gas to remove any physical connection between the aircraft and its secret intermediate stop. The aircraft would return to the United States with only the cover girls as cargo.

Cardilli and Simms would proceed from Scrub Cay to Nassau in two very different boats to wait for the organization's amphibian airplane to fly as cover for their return to the United States. They would clear Bahamian Customs and run across the Gulf Stream to Florida on a Sunday afternoon, where the boats were only two among hundreds of boats returning from the weekend. One of the boats was a classic narcotics smuggler's profile, a "gofast" that was all horsepower. The other boat was an open fisherman that was 40 feet long with no cabin to hide in and not enough power to run away. In fact, the open fisherman was built around a hidden drug compartment accessed by a complicated hydraulic system. If Bahamian or American Coast Guard patrols were encountered, the "gofast" would speed away as if attempting to escape and would draw law enforcement off the real target.

The open fisherman would enter the United States through Haulover Cut in northern Dade County and proceed up the intra-coastal waterway to a marina with dry storage in a warehouse structure, where it would be unloaded at a quieter time.

Munday's role was to monitor law enforcement. He operated out of a sophisticated radio room in his Miami residence. His monitors were linked to the aircraft, the boats, and to an observation post located in an 11th-floor apartment overlooking the ocean, the intra-coastal waterway, and Haulover Cut. Here Munday, Coley, or a confederate could watch the Cardilli/Simms boats return under the watchful eye of the amphibian as each million-dollar smuggling venture drew to a successful conclusion.

Munday had a falling out with Cardilli and Simms. In May 1985, Munday and Coley returned to their original mode, which was direct smuggling flights to the United States. Ironically, they had already been introduced, by Cardilli and Simms, to the informant that eventually did them in.

Before they resumed air operations, Munday and Coley flew many missions into the Florida Keys to test the effectiveness and range of the first aerostat radar balloon detection system deployed by law enforcement. Based on their studies, they decided to return from Colombia around the western side of Cuba and to approach Florida from the southwest. The aircraft would head for the Venice airport south of the Sarasota-Tampa metropolitan area in pre-dawn darkness, with lights and transponder off. They would approach the beachfront airport, flying 50 feet above the waves. Once over the runway, they would switch on lights and transponder, gain altitude, and immediately log on with Tampa air traffic control. The system accepted them as an aircraft that had just taken off from Venice, which had no tower to report arrivals or departures. They would fly to their ranch in Lakeland, Florida, and land on the strip there. The cocaine would be loaded in the trunk of a car, and the car would be hooked to a tow truck and towed to the delivery point in Miami. In the event of an encounter with law enforcement, the tow truck operator could plausibly deny knowledge of the contents of the trunk of the car.

Operation Beacon was begun in October 1984, as an Organized Crime Drug Enforcement Task Force (OCDETF) investigation led by Special Agents of U.S. Customs and the FBI with cooperation of the DEA and the Florida Joint Task Group. The probe was built around the cooperation of a citizen that had been used by Cardilli and Simms as a source of sophisticated electronics equipment. He had supplied the night vision goggles used by the group to electronically enhance night vision of boat and air crews, and also supplied forward-looking infrared radar (FLIR) of the type used by the military to see darkened targets in the night.

Ultimately, this citizen was asked to build a radio beacon (hence the operation's name) that would be activated by immersion and would signal the location of an airdropped narcotics load. Cardilli and Simms had introduced this person to Munday and Coley. The citizen, now cooperating with authorities, rose in the Munday/Coley ranks and was able to disclose, in advance, major narcotics shipments.

Other than that, Munday hadn't made a mistake. Even now, if alive, he is a wealthy fugitive unlike his lifelong pal, Coley, who is doing 20 years in federal prison.

It has been estimated that the Beacon group cleared more than $27 million in profits from the 20,000 pounds of cocaine that it was charged with smuggling. Real estate valued at $2.4 million was seized along with seven aircraft, 28 vessels, and 13 vehicles. Cash seizures included $106,000 found in Coley's home, $526,000 from the trunk of his Cadillac, and $1.4 million found buried in the ground at the Lakeland ranch.

Thanks to well-coordinated enforcement efforts, the Beacon group may have reimbursed the taxpayers for its own investigation. However, the social damage and human suffering inflicted by the Beacon producers can never be recouped.

Source: OCDETF, 1988.

The Golden Triangle

The opium poppy from which heroin comes thrives in the bright sun and cold nights of the Golden Triangle, a remote mountainous region in southeast Asia, consisting of parts of Myanmar, Laos, and Thailand. (Until 1989, Myanmar was known as Burma.) By 1976, the Golden Triangle supplied more than one-third of the heroin consumed in the United States. It continues to produce anywhere from four to five metric tons of opium annually. In fact, estimates are that heroin production in the Golden Triangle is increasing during the 1990s. For example, in 1991 it was estimated that traffickers from mainland China were selling 40 to 50 tons of more than 90 percent pure No. 4 heroin to the U.S. market, representing more than one-third of the Triangle's total yearly production (Schmetzer, 1991).

Although the opium trade in this region has been well documented since the 1930s, the Golden Triangle first gained widespread notoriety during the Vietnam war. It was here that drugs, especially opium and heroin, were readily available, cheap, and considerably purer than Mexican heroin. Today, poppy farmers in this region may realize anywhere from $50 to $500 U.S. dollars per day, depending on the size of their fields and the crop yield. The Golden Triangle today is responsible for much of the world's heroin supply. In fact, the DEA estimates that it furnishes approximately 50 percent of the heroin entering Canada and possibly 40 percent of that entering the U.S. market.

A kilogram of 90 percent pure heroin (referred to by traffickers as "Double Globe" and "Red Lion") is easily worth $6,000 in United States currency in growing areas such as northern Myanmar. The same kilogram, however, is worth between $175,000 and $225,000 after it arrives in the United States, and by the time it reaches the streets, it is only 2 to 5 percent pure, inflating the value of that same kilo to a street worth of $7 to $10 million.

To help illustrate the magnitude of opium production in the Golden Triangle, it was estimated that in 1983, the opium harvest in Myanmar produced 600 tons, Thailand 40 tons, and Laos 50 tons. In 1994, it was estimated that Myanmar produces 88 percent of southeast Asia's heroin and accounts for 60 percent of opium production worldwide (Lintner, 1994). With huge harvests and profits on the one hand, economic deprivation, persistent political instability, and military strife on the other, international efforts to control the southeast Asian drug traffic have not been successful.

The primitive technologies employed by drug traffickers in the Golden Triangle still result in massive opium production. Horse and donkey caravans haul the opium from Myanmar to numerous refineries in Laos and along the Thailand-Myanmar border. An estimated 80 to 85 percent of the finished heroin is transported over jungle trails and mountains into Thailand. The heroin crosses the border far away from Thai police inspectors. The remainder is smuggled to the United States through China, Hong Kong, and India.

Figure 4.8

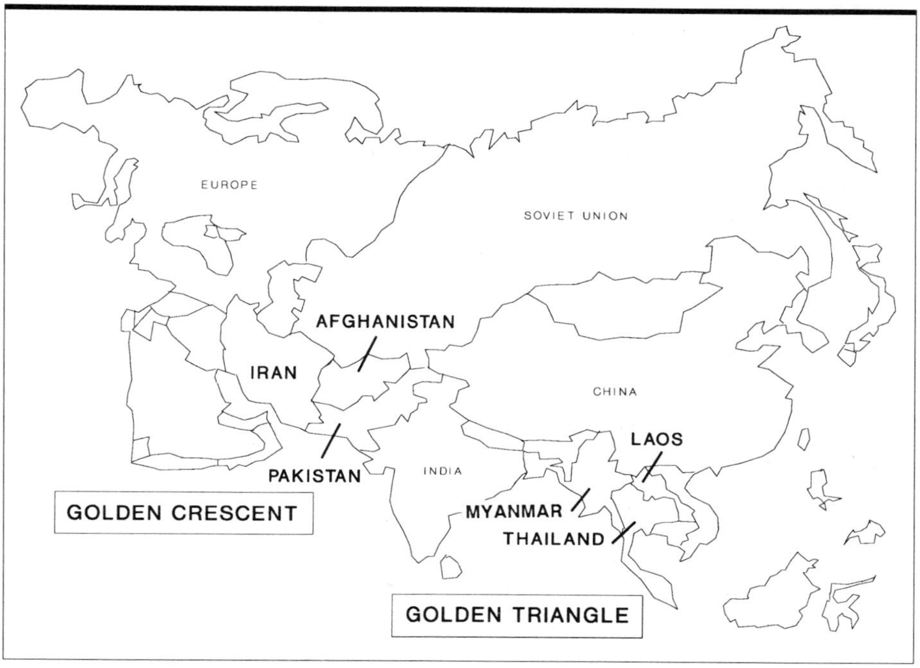

Figure 4.9
Drug Trafficking Routes: Southeast Asia

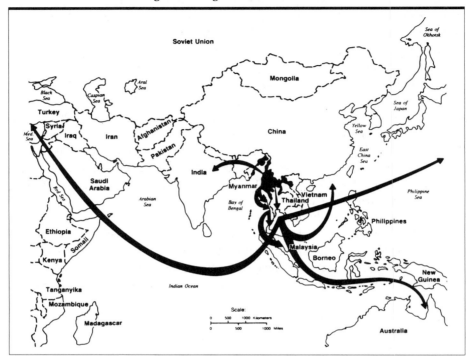

The Hill Tribes

Opium poppy cultivation in the Golden Triangle is conducted by a variety of ethnic minority groups commonly referred to as hill tribes. Living largely in inaccessible, economically underdeveloped areas, these tribal groups have sought to maintain their traditional cultures and to resist integration into the lowland political and economic systems that dominate southeast Asia. Hill tribe separateness has been reinforced by decades of neglect and discrimination on the part of the dominant lowland societies.

Hill tribe people are largely farmers, and for many of them, opium is an ideal agricultural cash crop because soil and climate are both well suited for opium poppy cultivation. Furthermore, opium resists spoilage, is compact, and has a high unit value, making it ideal for more primitive means of cultivation and transport. Middlemen are also readily available to make loans to tribesmen for future harvests or to purchase the opium crop with cash, a scarce highland commodity. Growing the opium poppy in this area is done through traditional methods of slash-and-burn farming without artificial fertilizer. Local laborers cultivate and harvest the crops. Unlike many legal crops that spoil easily, opium can easily endure primitive farming and marketing conditions.

To the hill tribes, opium poppy cultivation has been a socially acceptable pursuit since it was introduced by the British generations ago (see Chapter 1).

Unless the tribesmen are shown an attractive alternative, they have little reason to cease the activity. In the 300 opium-producing villages in Thailand, for example, five hill tribes have been uniquely associated with the cultivation of opium. Of these five, the Hmong and the Karen are the undisputed leaders. The Hmong left China more than 100 years ago and upon coming to Thailand, introduced their practice of growing the opium poppy. The Hmong are an independent people that live in the uppermost regions of the mountains of Thailand. So independent are the Hmong that governmental programs for health, farming, and education have failed miserably.

During the Vietnam war, the Hmong made up the bulk of a secret mercenary army fighting in Laos against North Vietnamese and Pathet Lao forces. They were provided with United States assistance, logistical support, and CIA advisers. Alfred McCoy in his book *The Politics of Heroin in Southeast Asia*, along with many others, contended that the CIA assisted various opium-producing client forces in Laos, Thailand, and the Shan States in transporting their opium during the war, thereby, at least indirectly, creating the massive infusion of heroin into American society during the late 1960s.

Officially, the government of Thailand realizes that the Hmong's involvement in the opium trade poses social problems for the entire country, but the hill tribes' opium trade is tolerated as an economic necessity. Opium produced by Hmong tribesmen is used to trade or barter for such necessities as clothing and food. The Karen add considerably to the volume of Hmong-produced opium. It was the Karen who were originally brought to the hills by the Hmong to assist them in their opium harvesting. Before long the Karen also realized the benefits of the opium crop and began cultivating their own. Many Karen soon became physically addicted to the opium.

In fact, the Karen used opium so freely for recreational purposes that the addiction rate in the tribe was alarming (an estimated 80 percent in 1985). Opium also served as the main pain killer for disease and other medical problems experienced by the tribe. Treatment for these addicts was therefore difficult. It has been estimated that there are approximately 35,000 addicts among the hill tribes in Thailand.

Thailand

Thailand is a southeast Asian country bordered on the west by Myanmar, on the east by Laos, on the southeast by Cambodia, and by Malaysia on the south. Much of the raw opium that is eventually converted to heroin and shipped to the United States is farmed by the people of northern Thailand's hill tribes.

The opium harvesting process in Thailand is basically as follows:

> In January, after a brief flowering of two or three days, the pod of the opium poppy stands exposed and is the sign of the beginning of another year's harvest. The opium harvest usually takes anywhere

from a few days to several weeks. Normally, field workers equip themselves with a small curved knife, which is used to lance the side of each pod, allowing the raw opium gum to seep through. The opium gum then remains on the pod for a few hours so that the warmth of the sun can dry it. The farmers then return to the fields to collect it by scraping it off of the pod and into a pail. It is then sold to traffickers, usually during the nighttime hours. Once the traffickers have purchased the opium gum, it is transported deep into the hills to hidden refineries for processing into heroin powder.

Ironically, the opium harvest poses some unique hardships for the hill tribes. Opium is a plant requiring a high altitude for a successful yield. The cultivation season begins during January, and temperatures in the mountains dur-

Figure 4.10
Southeast Asian Heroin
Selling Prices for the Equivalent of One Kilogram of Southeast Asian Heroin at Successive Stages of Trafficking (70-95% Purity)

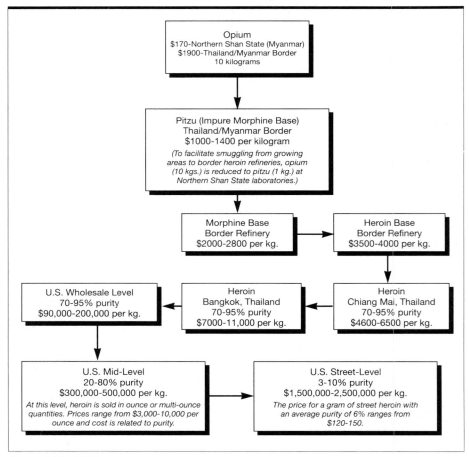

Opium
$170-Northern Shan State (Myanmar)
$1900-Thailand/Myanmar Border
10 kilograms

Pitzu (Impure Morphine Base)
Thailand/Myanmar Border
$1000-1400 per kilogram

(To facilitate smuggling from growing areas to border heroin refineries, opium (10 kgs.) is reduced to pitzu (1 kg.) at Northern Shan State laboratories.)

Morphine Base
Border Refinery
$2000-2800 per kg.

Heroin Base
Border Refinery
$3500-4000 per kg.

U.S. Wholesale Level
70-95% purity
$90,000-200,000 per kg.

Heroin
Bangkok, Thailand
70-95% purity
$7000-11,000 per kg.

Heroin
Chiang Mai, Thailand
70-95% purity
$4600-6500 per kg.

U.S. Mid-Level
20-80% purity
$300,000-500,000 per kg.

At this level, heroin is sold in ounce or multi-ounce quantities. Prices range from $3,000-10,000 per ounce and cost is related to purity.

U.S. Street-Level
3-10% purity
$1,500,000-2,500,000 per kg.

The price for a gram of street heroin with an average purity of 6% ranges from $120-150.

Source: DEA, 1987

ing this time sometimes drop to 5 degrees, making opium cultivation an even more difficult and unpleasant task.

Over the years, the Thai government has attempted crop substitution with crops such as coffee, kidney beans, and potatoes. These programs have met with only marginal success. This is because the inclement weather favorable for growing opium poses dramatically inferior growing conditions for other crops, killing the trees and rotting the beans before harvest.

In 1976, Thailand's Ministry of Public Health with the assistance of the World Health Organization established an opium treatment center near the city of Chiang Mai in the opium-growing regions of the Golden Triangle. Treatment begins with a balanced diet to build strength and includes immunizations and family planning. Because of the remoteness of the treatment center, many addicts were unable to take advantage of treatment. As a result, a "barefoot doctor" program was adopted to take medical help to the villages.

Considering the marginal success of the many programs that have been considered to deal with the opium-producing tribes in Thailand, four alternatives remain:

1. *Destroying the opium poppy crop.* Although theoretically considered an alternative, this has not been done for humanitarian reasons. Such an action might invite war or necessitate a major relief program.
2. *Move the tribes out of the hills.* This option would probably be unworkable because of the cultural differences between the hill tribes and the Thai people in the lowlands.
3. *Pre-emptive buying.* It has also been suggested that the opium could be bought by the government, but problems arise in this strategy due to the remoteness of the tribes and the fact that there would likely still be a lucrative black market for the drug.
4. *Crop substitution.* This has been generally considered the most logical alternative for destroying the opium production in Thailand, but it is one that would take an enormous amount of time and resources. Estimates of the time this would take range as high as 20 years.

Percent of Global Opium Production	
Golden Triangle (Myanmar, Laos, and Thailand)	73%
Golden Crescent (Afghanistan, Iran, and Pakistan)	24%
Mexico and Guatemala	2%
Lebanon	1%

Source: Bureau of International Narcotics Matters, March 1991.

The Golden Crescent

Following a decrease in illicit opium production in the 1970s in the Golden Triangle, three countries emerged as formidable producers of raw opium and heroin. These southwest Asian countries, Iran, Pakistan, and Afghanistan, have been dubbed the Golden Crescent because of the rich opium poppy growing regions in each country. "Southwestern Asia is responsible for an estimated 60 percent of the world's heroin" (DEA, 1986). Ironically, despite flagrant trafficking activities in this region, opium producers there have generally looked on the abuse of heroin as an "American problem." As of the preparation of this text, however, the heroin addicts in southwest Asia outnumber American addicts almost two to one.

Opium use in the Middle East dates back thousands of years. But it was not until a few decades ago that the Middle Eastern countries that make up the Golden Crescent became politically organized. While Iran was ruled by the Shah, the countries of southwest Asia formed an opium system that had little impact on the West. This was because much of the opium produced in the border regions of Afghanistan and Pakistan was smuggled to Iran to serve that country's immense addict population, which consists of one million addicts out of a total population of 40 million. There the opium was eaten or smoked by older, rural dwellers, although with Iranian modernization came an increasing number of heroin abusers among the urban middle classes.

In 1955, the Shah imposed a ban on domestic opium production in an attempt to suppress drug abuse. He did permit some legal production, however, to meet the requirements of registered addicts. As the Shah's dictatorship weakened and law and order in Iran became less prevalent, the farmers began to ignore the opium ban. Before the collapse of the Shah's regime in 1979, Iran served as a "sponge" for Afghan and Pakistani opium. After the fall of the royal family, Iran became a major producer of the drug for both its own domestic use and for exportation. Political chaos in Iran only aided traffickers in their operations.

Soon there was more than enough heroin in the Golden Crescent to supply European and North American markets. The role of Turkey as a heroin transshipment country also increased. Turkish traffickers, using the large population of Turkish guest workers in Germany as a cover, first flooded Germany, then the rest of Europe, with inexpensive southwest Asian heroin that frequently ranged into the 90 percent level in purity.

As evidence of Europe's heroin epidemic mounted, concerned United States officials suspected that it would spread to the United States. In October 1979, the Department of State convened a meeting in Berlin to discuss the problem. Attending the meeting were State Department representatives and DEA narcotics coordinators from United States embassies in Europe and southwest Asia.

Other international efforts were also considered in 1979, such as exploring crop eradication operations in Iran. With the untimely seizure of the United

States Embassy in Iran during November of that year, all possibilities for a constructive dialogue ceased. Additionally, the Soviet invasion of Afghanistan the following month also foreclosed close cooperation with that country. Another of the many ironies of the international drug trade is the fact that the Soviet invasion seriously disrupted heroin supplies from Afghanistan. The heroin pipelines resumed the flow of drugs, in much larger volumes than before, after aid to fundamentalist Moslem guerrillas, the Mujahedeen, began to flow from western nations. Only Pakistan (discussed later in this chapter) remained as a possible area for diplomatic endeavors in the area of drug control.

Figure 4.11
Southwest Asian Heroin
Selling Prices for the Equivalent of One Kilogram of Southwest Asian Heroin
at Successive Stages of Trafficking (50-95% Purity)

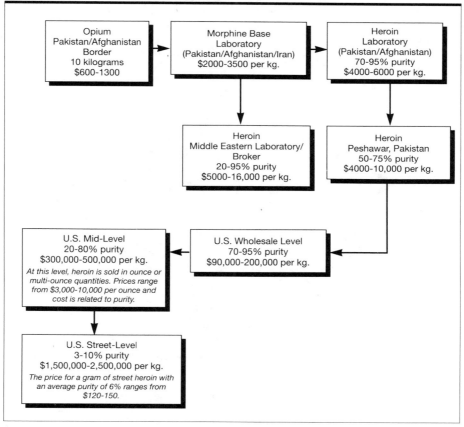

Source: DEA, 1987.

Pakistan

Pakistan is an extremely poor country. Indeed, it is one of the poorest in the world, and funds for narcotic suppression projects are extremely limited.

Nevertheless, Pakistani leaders are aware of the enormous impact on other countries of the opium produced within Pakistan's borders, as well as domestic problems that the opium trade and addiction have produced.

As an early response to the problem, the government of Pakistan issued an order banning cultivation and use of opium. This order was generally considered successful, and enforcement of it produced few problems despite the complicated tribal structure of the society in the growing regions. During the ban's first year, production fell from an estimated 650 metric tons in 1979 to less than 100 metric tons in 1980 (O'Brien and Cohen, 1984).

Figure 4.12
Heroin Trafficking Organization

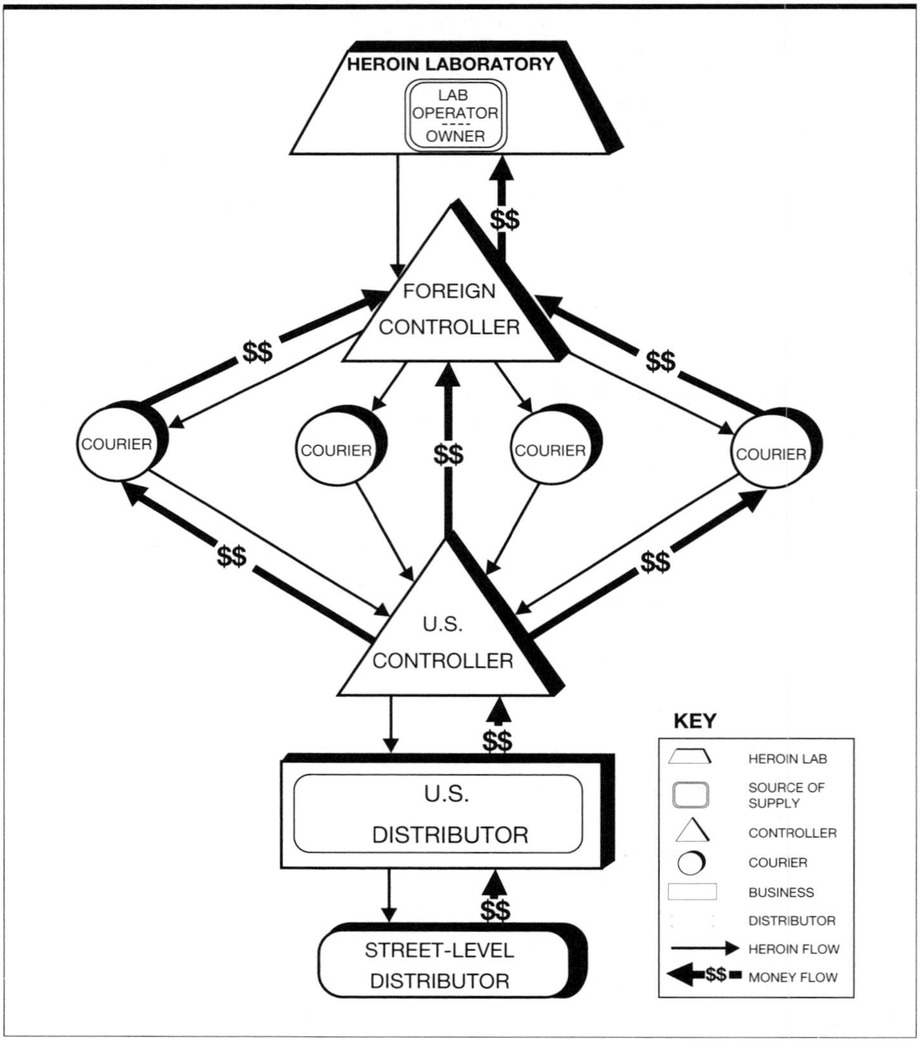

Source: DEA, 1984.

It soon became evident that United States assistance to Pakistan would be necessary to ensure that anti-drug laws would be maintained. The initial phase, which involved a crop eradication program, was the easiest. What remained, however, was the toughest challenge: to control the illicit production of opium in extremely impoverished areas where the farmers have few, if any, acceptable economic alternatives. To help Pakistan with difficult enforcement initiatives, the United States provided vehicles and communication gear to anti-narcotics units.

Since the mid-1970s, Pakistani traffickers have developed several unique but fairly unsophisticated networks for transporting drugs into the United States. Typically, the traffickers rely on family or Pakistani friends in the U.S. to distribute drugs. Additionally, they have also been known to make use of certain trusted black organizations in cities such as Los Angeles, Detroit, and New York. In addition, Pakistani traffickers have aligned with their Italian criminal counterparts in New York City.

Afghanistan

Afghanistan is the largest producer of opium in the Golden Crescent and one of the largest producers of opium in the world (second only to Myanmar). Although information about Afghanistan's role in drug production is scarce, with the 1988 withdrawal of Soviet military troops from the country after almost nine years of occupation, it is likely that opium production will increase.

Turkey

As a key country bordering Iran and the Golden Crescent, Turkey remains a major contributor to opium and heroin production in that region of the world. In 1987, the DEA estimated that six to seven tons of opiates, including refined heroin and morphine base, were smuggled into eastern Turkey from Iran.

Opium poppy farming has existed in Turkey for centuries and has represented a livelihood for thousands of Turkish farmers. For generations opium cultivation was conducted by private Turkish farmers, but in 1933, the Turkish government established an agency to buy the opium gum from the growers. The government then exported the opium gum to other countries, where opium alkaloids such as morphine and codeine were extracted for medicinal use. However, a considerable amount of gum was diverted and smuggled to the Middle East and France (the French Connection), where it was processed into heroin. Much of this heroin ultimately reached the United States. During the 1960s and early 1970s, an estimated 80 percent of the heroin on United States streets originated in Turkey.

In 1971, however, the Turkish government placed a ban on opium cultivation that became effective the following year. Because of trade losses after the 1971 ban, the Turkish government initiated the poppy straw program in 1974, in which legal opiates were produced. The poppy straw program operates under strict governmental control and allows for cultivation of the opium poppy on small licensed lots in seven provinces: Afyon (the Turkish word for opium), Isparta, Denizli, Usak, Burdur, Kutahya, and Konya.

Harvesting is done by hand after the opium has passed the green stage and has completely dried. Only the poppy heads and parts of the stalks are removed, and the result is the "poppy straw."

Between 1976 and 1980, Turkey exported an average of 8,800 tons of poppy straw per year. Today, much of the crop is purchased by the Dutch for processing in the Netherlands. India shares the market with the United States because of the "80-20 rule." This rule, supported by the United States, specifies that at least 80 percent of the raw narcotic material imported to the United States for legitimate use in medicine must originate either in Turkey or India. The remaining 20 percent can be imported from other countries.

One of the traditional opium producers in the region is the Pushtuns (also known as Pathans). This independent tribe, living on the border of Afghanistan and Pakistan, has produced great quantities of raw opium gum. The Kurds are yet another ethnic group in the Middle East that is heavily involved in traditional opium production.

The Kurds and Drug Trafficking

Because of the strict controls on opium cultivation, Turkey is not considered a primary source country. It does remain a major transshipment country for opiates that are produced in Afghanistan, Pakistan, and Iran (the Golden Crescent). Most of the drug dealing and trafficking in Turkey is controlled by criminal groups in Istanbul.

One such group that has a strong ethnic identity and that contributes significantly to Turkish organized crime is the Kurds. The Kurds speak Turkish and have a reputation for being fierce fighters, family oriented, independent, and devout Moslems. The Kurds have clans in both Turkey and Iran and do not recognize the border that separates the two countries. Because the Kurds frequently travel across the border, they have a convenient network for smuggling drugs.

Thinking Critically #7

Chapter 4 describes the torture and murder of DEA agent Enrique Camarena in 1985. In light of his tragic death, would you consider becoming a DEA agent? Explain your attitude in terms of both positive and negative aspects of this job.

Although many Kurdish areas lie between eastern and southern Turkey, trafficking by Kurds is by no means restricted to those areas. Many of the main heroin wholesalers in Istanbul are Kurds that first migrated from remote villages as unskilled laborers and later became wealthy in the narcotics trade. In addition to the Kurds, many Iranians also traffic large amounts of heroin from Turkey to their Iranian contacts in the United States and western Europe. An estimated 500,000 to 1.5 million Iranians reside in Istanbul alone. Using Istanbul as a main distribution point, the Iranian traffickers smuggle both legitimate and illegitimate goods (drugs and weapons alike) to western Europe and the United States.

Drug smuggling routes in Turkey lie primarily along the eastern and southeastern areas of the country. Heroin is generally smuggled from Iran to Turkey by Turkish Kurds that travel through the mountainous border area that is not heavily patrolled by either government. The DEA estimates that, because of the harsh winters in this region, most drug smuggling into Turkey is somewhat seasonal and therefore is concentrated between May and December of each year. Authorities believe that most drug payloads arrive in the Turkish provinces of Van and Hakkiri, although some morphine base has been smuggled into Syria and Lebanon.

As a rule, Turkey is not considered a source country for drugs but some refining of morphine base to heroin does occur there. In 1988, several Turkish heroin refineries were seized but were found to be somewhat primitive. These labs were set up to convert a specific amount of morphine base to heroin and were designed to be easily dismantled and moved to a different location.

As with heroin and morphine base, hashish (Turkey's biggest domestic consumer drug) is also commonly transported through Turkey from Lebanon. Other illicit commodities include firearms, which are often traded for drugs. In one specific case in 1987, the Bulgarian import/export agency Kintex was involved in a smuggling operation.

Hong Kong

Like the Golden Triangle and the Golden Crescent, Hong Kong also plays a significant role in international drug trafficking, particularly in money laundering and transportation. In recent years the Hong Kong Executive Council has considered new legislative proposals giving the courts more power to confiscate the assets of major traffickers.

New legal proposals would allow the court to infer that all property that the offender acquired during the six-year period prior to his or her arrest for a drug trafficking offense had been received as "payment or reward" for drug trafficking. The court would then levy a fine of an amount equivalent to the value of the property with a provision for imposing a prison term on a sliding scale up to 10 years upon default on payment of the fine.

Summary

The first half of this chapter illustrates the financial dynamics of the illicit drug trade in addition to how the drug trade parallels legitimate industry. Factors such as supply and demand, manufacturing, transportation, marketing, and security are all considerations for every illicit drug dealer. Understanding these organizational dynamics aids policy makers in anticipating the needs and weaknesses of illicit trafficking organizations.

The extent of global involvement in the illicit drug trade illustrates the magnitude of the problem, as many countries play a major role in furnishing the United States with dangerous drugs. Ironically, the U.S. is frequently blamed by these countries for providing a drug user market and nurturing an incentive for drug production in their countries.

The closest neighbor to the United States on the south is Mexico, a major producer of heroin and marijuana. Mexico's widespread involvement in the drug trade gained considerable momentum just after the collapse of the "French Connection" in the early 1970s. Efforts to thwart drug trafficking in Mexico (and some other foreign countries) have been hampered by widespread corruption within the government. Allegations of corruption among Mexico's Federal Judicial Police have been voiced for years but became more credible in 1985 with the abduction and murder of a federal DEA agent. Mexican police officers were ultimately charged with complicity in this crime.

In South America, the three Andean nations of Colombia, Peru, and Bolivia are the most active coca- and cocaine-producing countries in the world. In particular, Colombia, one of the most significant drug source countries, primarily produces cocaine hydrochloride from dried coca leaves but also produces high-grade marijuana. Drug trafficking cartels have expanded to the point where they now threaten the democratically elected government in Colombia. Much violence prevails as a result of this, but Colombian government officials, with aid furnished by the United States, are attempting to locate, arrest, and extradite members to the United States for prosecution.

The leaves used in the production of cocaine are primarily grown in Peru and Bolivia; Peru is the primary supplier. As in Colombia, trafficking organizations also have attempted to exert control over the governments in Peru and Bolivia.

Jamaica represents a marijuana source country that has generated dangerous gangs (known as posses) that share both political and profit motivations. Governmental unrest since the 1960s has created two opposing political parties that continually strive for governmental dominance. Jamaican gangs serve the political parties in Jamaica by rallying votes for them. In the United States, the posses occupy more than 18 cities and, in addition to dealing marijuana, distribute crack cocaine to generate profits that are then funnelled back to Jamaica.

The Golden Crescent is an opium-growing region in southwest Asia consisting of Afghanistan, Pakistan, and Iran. It is in this region that most raw opium is produced. Opium from this region is then funnelled to other trafficking groups, where it is processed into heroin and ultimately transported to the United States for distribution. The Golden Triangle refers to Laos, Myanmar, and Thailand in southeast Asia. This group of countries ranks second to the Golden Crescent in raw opium production and is instrumental in trafficking much of the world's opium and heroin.

Other drug source countries in Asia include Turkey, which serves as a transshipment country for Golden Crescent opium. Turkish Kurds have been responsible for much of the trafficking in this region of Asia.

Do you recognize these terms?

blotter acid	French Connection
copping areas	ganja
demand elasticity	posses
extradition	steerers

Discussion Questions

1. Explain the financial limitations of today's entrepreneurial drug trafficker.

2. Discuss to what extent the laws of supply and demand affect drug trafficking organizations.

3. To what extent do marketing and distribution practices affect the drug trade?

4. Which areas of the world are most active in the production of raw opium and in heroin refinement?

5. Discuss the political history of Jamaica and the illicit drugs produced there.

6. What contributions do Peru and Bolivia make to the world's illicit drug situation?

7. Explain the roles of both the Golden Crescent and Golden Triangle in global drug trafficking.

8. Discuss the volatile issue of extradition in Colombia.

9. Discuss the reasons why hill tribes in the Golden Triangle prefer opium as a cash crop over other legal crops.

Class Projects

1. Locate three recent articles from a newspaper or magazine that address the international drug problem. Discuss any trends in drug policy of foreign governments which you may observe.

2. Compare drug control initiatives in various foreign countries, and discuss similarities between them. Include in your discussion the strengths and weaknesses of the programs.

Domestic Drug Production   **5**

This chapter will enable you to:

- Learn the role that legitimate drug industry plays in the nation's drug abuse problem

- Understand the extent of the marijuana cultivation problem in the United States

- Realize the magnitude of the nation's clandestine laboratory problem

- Learn the consequences of pharmaceutical diversion in our country's drug problem

---

When we think of the nation's drug problem we tend to think of drugs such as cocaine and heroin which seem to dominate national media stories. We must, however, be cognizant of the contribution which legal manufacturers of drugs make to our modern "drug-reliant" society. After all, more often than not, a visit to the doctor's office results in a prescription for some sort of drug to treat almost any ailment—mental or physical. As we will learn in this chapter, the legal drug industry is more than just a benign wholesale and retail business. Rather, over the decades it has grown into a massive marketing machine catering to doctors and law makers, and often dictating to medical health professionals which and how often dangerous drugs should be prescribed.

As we discussed in the previous chapter, some illicit drugs, such as cocaine and heroin, are primarily produced in foreign countries. However, domestic drug producers and traffickers have also taken advantage of the opportunity to produce and cultivate illicit drugs. Marijuana, produced by both foreign and domestic traffickers, is used by some 19 million marijuana smokers in the United States (NIDA, 1988). Other drugs, such as methamphetamine, LSD, and PCP are also produced in clandestine laboratories in the United States and foster much criminal activity in the areas of drug manufacturing and trafficking. In addition to marijuana cultivation and clandestine laboratories, yet another source of drugs exists in the United States: pharmaceutical drug diversion.

Drugs that are legally manufactured for legitimate medical treatment are some-times diverted from the legal source of distribution and will also be discussed in this chapter.

The Pharmaceutical Drug Industry

We know that in addition to illicit drugs and the recreational use of them, legal drugs are manufactured which are intended to serve a legitimate medical purpose. After all, painkillers are essential at the scenes of automobile acci-dents, in the operating room, and in treating people who suffer from diseases such as arthritis and cancer. For sufferers of toothaches or migraine headaches, painkillers can literally make the difference between being able to face the day and being miserable and dysfunctional at home or on the job.

The term pharmaceuticals is a general one referring to a category of drugs which include capsules, pills, liquids, medicinal suppositories, lotions, and other preparations having a medical use. It is estimated by *Pharmacy Times*, a maga-zine publishing drug sales for the United States, that about 1.5 million prescrip-tions are written each year, half of which are new prescriptions and half are refills. The legal drug business (manufacturing and selling pharmaceuticals) is big business, comprising an estimated $30 billion dollar-a-year industry (Goode, 1993).

In recent years the pharmaceutical drug industry has been criticized for its aggressive marketing methods. Critics complain that profit margin, not the elimination of human suffering, is the primary motivator for drug manufactur-ing. Quite literally, drugs are manufactured for treatment of most illnesses and levels of mental and physical discomfort. The drug industry claims they have been taken hostage by soaring research and development costs which according to the Congressional Quarterly Researcher (1992) average an amazing $231 million for each new drug brought to market. Each year the drug industry spends millions of dollars on marketing and sales of drugs to physicians. Sadly, most of what many physicians know about a given drug they've learned from pharmaceutical sales representatives themselves whose sole job it is to make profits for the company for whom they work.

The Cost Crisis

In addition to the crisis of illicit drugs in America, another crisis is ongo-ing: the rising cost of prescription medications. In the 1990s, the lion's share of the blame for Americans paying the highest medication prices in the industrial-ized world rests squarely on the shoulders of the drug manufactures of this country (Pryor, 1994). In addition to being the beneficiary of considerable prof-its from drug sales, the drug industry also benefits from numerous tax breaks.

Chronology of Pharmaceutical Drug Control

1900s-1930s: *Outrageous claims of patient medications are exposed by muckrakers, prompting congressional action to regulate drugs.*

1906: The Pure Food and Drug Act is passed, which prohibits false and misleading claims.

1938: The Food, Drug, and Cosmetic Act (FDCA) is passed which increases federal oversight of prescription drugs, stating that they must be proven "safe" before they can be offered for sale.

1950s-1960s: *Congress begins to regulate drug prices.*

1959: Senator Estes Kefauver chairs Senate Judiciary subcommittee hearings on antitrust and monopoly, focusing on the drug industry.

1961: Senator Kefauver's committee concludes that drug prices are "unreasonable" and that some companies have unfair advantages due to the 17-year period of patent exclusivity. Legislation is introduced to shorten the period of patent exclusitivity to three years.

1962: The discovery that Thalidomide causes severe birth defects helps prompt amendments to the FDCA which include a requirement that drug companies provide the FDA information on adverse drug reactions.

1980s: *Drug-price increases outpace the rise in overall health spending, and expensive new drugs push the drug-inflation rate higher.*

1983: Congress passes the Orphan Drug Act, providing tax incentives to encourage the development of drugs to treat rare diseases.

1984: Congress passes legislation making it easier to market generic copies of drugs whose patents have expired.

1986: Sales of Tagamet®, a revolutionary anti-ulcer medication introduced by SmithKline in 1977, hits the $1 billion-a-year mark—the first to break that barrier.

1988: Congress passes the Medicare Catastrophic Coverage Act, providing for outpatient prescription drug coverage.

1989: Congress repeals the Catastrophic Coverage Act after recipients balk at being asked to help pay for the new benefits.

1990s: Several members of Congress introduce legislation to cope with high drug prices: some drugmakers pledge to limit price hikes, and the pharmaceutical industry mounts a public relations offensive.

1990: Sales of Glaxo's Zantac®, a drug similar to Tagamet® but with fewer risks of adverse reactions, reach $2.4 billion, a new record for a single drug in a single year.

1991: The Prescription Drug Cost Containment Act is introduced, which ties special tax breaks to a drug maker's willingness to link price hikes to the inflation rate.

—Medication Price Control Act is proposed, which denies research and development tax breaks to drug companies if their new products increase in price more than 2 percent above the consumer price index.

—At least five drug makers pledge to limit drug price hikes to the inflation rate.

—Two U.S. senators introduce a bill to eliminate provisions of the Orphan Drug Act giving companies a monopoly on marketing rights for drugs whose sales top $200 million.

Source: *Congressional Quarterly,* July 17, 1992.

These include receiving hundreds of millions of dollars in research and development tax credits, marketing and advertising deductions, and orphan drug tax credits. What's more, the drug industry benefits from the Internal Revenue Code 936 which permits pharmaceutical companies to move their operations to Puerto Rico where millions of dollars in taxes and sales can be legally avoided.

Senior citizens use the most prescription drugs of any age group (an estimated 30 percent of all prescription drugs sold annually) and as a result, a primary concern of today is their ability to afford necessary medications. In 1986, the American Association of Retired Persons (AARP), whose numbers are estimated at 33 million people, issued a report stating that prescription medications are the highest out-of-pocket expense for three out of four older Americans. A follow-up survey by the AARP revealed that the crisis is still escalating. For example:

• An estimated 8 million Americans over age 45 claimed that they were forced to cut back on necessary items such as food and fuel in order to pay for medications

• More than 18 million elderly Americans reported that they had trouble paying for their medications

- 23 million men and women over 55 have absolutely no prescription drug insurance coverage

Sadly, the majority of older Americans don't have private or public health insurance for prescription drugs with more than 65 percent of their medication costs being paid for out-of-pocket. In fact, Medicare, the government's health care program for the elderly and the disabled, fails to cover most outpatient prescription medications. For those senior citizens living on fixed incomes, the problem is compounded considerably. Granted, Medicaid's prescription drug program can act as a safety net in helping the poor obtain their medications, but this number only includes about 1.9 million people who are eligible. Stated differently, this means that 84 percent of the poor (or near poor) do not qualify (Pryor, 1994). In August 1992, another report addressing the high cost of prescription drugs was released by the General Accounting Office. The report addressed the responses of 29 manufacturers of widely used prescriptions. When explaining why costs were so high, the company gave the standard answer that price increases were necessary to fund research and development of new drugs. Pryor (1994) argues that the simple fact is that a manufacturer spending 15 percent of its sales on research and development would only have to increase prices by 1.5 percent each year to increase research and development by 10 percent. So it appears that all of the excess profits are flowing into marketing, advertising, and into the pockets of stockholders.

The drug price crisis can be illustrated in the cost of combating AIDS. Initially, the drug AZT, used to treat HIV, was outrageously high, costing users up to $10,000 a year when it went on the market in 1987. But AIDS activists protested, pointing out that the drug had actually been developed by government researchers at the National Institutes of Health, and asked that the manufacturer, Burroughs Wellcome Co., reduce the price. As a result, it was discovered that the drug works at half the original dose, which brought down the price to about $3,000 per year (Rovner, 1992). Of course, because most Americans' insurance fails to cover prescription drugs, even inexpensive medications can pose a considerable hardship.

Calls for reform of the pharmaceutical industry have become commonplace in newspapers, periodicals, and television commentaries. Although its not likely that sweeping reforms will take place soon, some fine-tuning of the industry is still realistic. Suggestions have included placing caps on prescription prices, creating mechanisms for making physicians more aware of the prices of the drugs they prescribe, increasing the use of less expensive generic drugs, and reducing marketing costs for drug companies.

The Drug Approval Dilemma

Under federal law, no new drug can be marketed in this country until the FDA approves it as safe and effective. This finding is made on the basis of the manufacturer's NDA (New Drug Application), which can contain thousands of pages of data from clinical tests which took from two to ten years to complete. During all this time, the drug is not available for use, except on a very limited basis as part of a clinical trial. Of course, the FDA is not the sole cause of clinical testing, as such tests would even be necessary in the absence of FDA regulations. But clearly, these regulations have caused significant delays in the availability of new pharmaceutical drugs for treatment of disease (not to mention the considerable expense). Studies have revealed that over the past three decades, the FDA's requirements have more than doubled the development costs for new drugs as well as substantially reduced the rate at which new drugs are introduced, resulting in a considerable lag in the availability of new drugs. Those who defend the FDA's current procedures inevitably refer to the event that led to present day practices—the thalidomide affair.

Thalidomide was first introduced in Germany in 1957 as a nontoxic sedative. It was sold in more than 40 countries before it was associated with severe birth defects. In the United States, approval for thalidomide was requested in 1960 but withheld by FDA reviewer Dr. Francis Kelsey while she investigated reports that the drug caused peripheral nerve injury. By 1961, news of the drug's fetal side effects was well known, and it was removed from the world market. Because of Dr. Kelsey's decision to withhold the drug pending investigation, it was never made available in this country, and essentially thousands of children throughout the United States were spared birth defects. As a result, Dr. Kelsey was awarded the President's Gold Medal for Distinguished Service.

Resulting from the thalidomide decision, the powers of the FDA were expanded in 1962 under the Kefauver-Harris Amendments to the Food, Drug, and Cosmetic Act. The earlier statute, enacted in 1938, had prohibited the marketing of new drugs until they were found to be "safe" by the FDA. However, the 1962 amendments added a new criteria: that the drug be proven to be both safe and *effective*. Ironically, the thalidomide scare was one addressing safety and not efficacy. After the 1962 amendments, the FDA's role shifted from that of an evaluator of evidence to an active participant in the research process. Between 1962 and 1967, the average review time for new drugs more than quadrupled, rising from seven to thirty months. Although in recent years the FDA has attempted to streamline this process, NDA review time has not improved. By the end of the 1980s, average NDA review time was 32 months (Kazman, 1991). In addition, the average development time for new drugs, which averaged between four to six years in the 1960s, has now doubled to ten years (Kazman, 1991).

The obvious policy question stemming from the thalidomide experience is this: how many lives are lost during the lengthy development and review process for new drugs? Let's consider two examples. Misoprostol, approved in 1988, was the first medication used to prevent gastric ulcers that result from aspirin and other anti-inflammatory drugs. Such drugs are commonly taken by arthritis suffers who often develop ulcers which are thought to cause 10,000 to 20,000 deaths each year through internal bleeding. Misoprostol is reported to produce a 15-fold reduction in such ulcers. By the time the drug was approved in the U.S., it was already available in 43 foreign countries. So, if the drug is 94 percent effective (as reported) and if the FDA's estimate that there are between 10,000 and 20,000 annual ulcer-related deaths, then Misoprostol could have saved between 8,000 and 15,000 lives during the FDA's nine-and-a-half-month review period.

Experts have debated the best way to deal with lengthy delays in the approval process of new drugs, but a consensus does not exist. Some have suggested that the FDA's veto power over new drugs be changed to a system of *certification*. Under this proposed system, new drugs which have not been approved could still be available by prescription but clearly labeled as unapproved. This system would enable critically ill persons to go beyond the circle of official approval but remain under the supervision of a physician. Regardless of what happens with the approval process, it is clear that the pharmaceutical drug business faces two critical issues in the upcoming years: The development time for new drugs and the built in expense of developing those drugs. Both are problems of such enormity that quick fix solutions are unlikely.

Domestic Marijuana Cultivation

Over the decades marijuana has consistently remained one of the economic staples in the illegal drug business. So far in this book we have discussed several foreign cannabis sources which focus on smuggling their products into the United States. The majority of foreign marijuana operations consist of peasant farmers who grow the crop as their primary source of cash. Because marijuana grows in almost all 50 states, domestic cultivation also contributes greatly to the nation's overall drug problem. Whether foreign or domestic enterprises are concerned, marijuana cultivation and trafficking has proven to be a relatively easy-entry illicit market. All that is required for a simple growing operation is seeds, a water source, land, and a willingness to enter into a criminal enterprise, which in some states can result in a prison term as long as 25 years.

In 1989, the Department of Justice indicated that domestic marijuana accounted for a conservative 25 percent of the country's retail marijuana market, although recent indications are that this percentage is growing rapidly. As of the preparation of this book, no single criminal organization is thought to control domestic marijuana production and trafficking, probably due to the easy-entry nature of the business and the difficulty such organizations would experience in attempting to monopolize it. Consequently, the domestic marijuana market has spawned a unique rural criminal who lives and operates in these scarcely populated agrarian areas. In addition to the protective rural environment, law enforcement in these areas is often diffused resulting in growers who can operate with impunity while their operations are cloaked by thick forests, lush vegetation, and inaccessible mountain slopes. These factors also help conceal marijuana growing operations from rival growers or "pot poachers" in the area. In recent years, because police use airplanes to spot growing fields, growers have scaled down the size of their marijuana patches to an average of about 100 plants per plot or less (DEA, 1984, 1989).

Thinking Critically #8

This section, titled "Domestic Marijuana Cultivation," discusses the results of increased law enforcement efforts by rural police officers. In light of these unfortunate results, do you agree or disagree that police should continue to vigorously enforce the law against marijuana cultivation in those areas?

To help hide their plants, growers are also disbursing them among corn, tomato plants, and along riverbeds and creeks. As we discuss later in this chapter, growers have even resorted to indoor growing operations to not only conceal their operations, but to provide them year-long harvesting opportunities. Over the years, police agents have also discovered deadly booby traps in and around marijuana patches which are difficult (if not impossible) to detect. Other safeguards have included hidden steel-jaw traps, guard dogs, and armed guards. These devices are designed to not only serve a deterrent for police and poachers, but as a signal to the nearby growers who are often heavily armed and potentially violent.

Business Considerations

Marijuana growers are a somewhat fragmented group of traffickers who rely on kinship or local ("good-ole-boy") networks. Operations are typically financed by either previous transactions or by "jobbers" furnishing special lighting, fertilizer, or other equipment in exchange for a percentage of the harvest. Police have documented cases, however, where large-scale cultivation operations are financially backed by business executives looking for alternate ways to invest their money. The packaging of marijuana remains somewhat universal throughout the country. After harvest, it is usually placed in large trash bags for transportation to its destination. For smaller retail sales of one-quarter pound or less, smaller zip-lock baggies are usually used.

Marijuana growers have learned that many police raids are a product of so-called "search and destroy" missions that are often based on informant information. Therefore many growing operations are now automated, allowing the grower to be absent in case of a police raid. This explains why such operations are often expensive, unproductive, and are rarely a top enforcement priority for police.

Figure 5.1
Domestic Marijuana
Selling Prices for one pound of Marijuana at Successive Levels of Trafficking

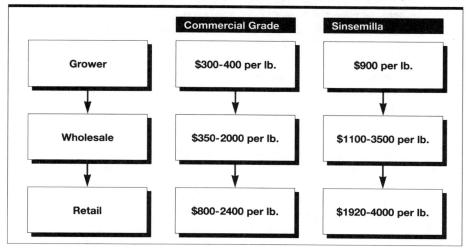

Source: DEA, 1987.

Let's now examine the types of marijuana or cannabis most commonly cultivated. As we discussed in Chapter 2, there are several types or grades of marijuana. It is becoming increasingly clear that the marijuana cultivation business is experiencing a horticultural revolution of sorts. That is, many growers are continuously experimenting with different techniques of producing more potent strains of marijuana for higher profits. Each cultivated grade represents different types of growing technology and results in differing degrees of potency (and prices) for the manicured retail marijuana plant. Although state and federal drug laws do not differentiate among the grades of marijuana (they only require a showing that the drug evidence is cannabis), the grower is very interested in producing the most potent plant for greater profit margins. The DEA has identified three basic types of marijuana that grow domestically: **Indian hemp**, **commercial**, and **sinsemilla**.

> *Indian Hemp.* Indian hemp (commonly referred to as ditchweed) is the most prevalent type of marijuana that grows in the United States. This is a wild growing marijuana that has little market value and typically grows in uncultivated areas such as fields, ditch banks, fence rows, and along railroad tracks. Indian hemp grows in many types of soil and reproduces itself each year by its own seeds from the previous year's crop. These seeds can lay dormant for up to seven years. Because Indian hemp is not cultivated from potent seeds, its THC content is quite low, averaging around 0.14 percent, as compared to other types. Because of its low potency, it will sometimes be mixed with other more potent marijuana as "filler."

Commercial Grade. Commercial grade marijuana is the most common type of marijuana sold on the street. It is produced from those cannabis plants that have been cultivated in a growing area where the male and female plants are permitted to grow in the same location and the female plants have been fertilized. As a rule, the entire marijuana plant (usually the female) is harvested, stripped of its leaves, and marketed. The growing season usually begins around mid-April with harvest season beginning sometime during August. At maturity, plants may reach heights of 15 feet and can be harvested up until the first frost (usually sometime in October). The THC content of the commercial marijuana plant ranges from 5 to 8 percent.

Sinsemilla Grade. Trends toward the production of higher and higher grades of marijuana have persisted since the mid-1960s. Sinsemilla, a Spanish word meaning "without seeds," is a cannabis plant that represents the most potent type of marijuana on the illicit market and the type that will bring the highest profit return for the trafficker. In the mid-1980s the DEA found that about one-fourth of domestic marijuana was sinsemilla. Sinsemilla is produced from unfertilized female cannabis plants in a growing area where the male cannabis plants are removed before pollination. Marijuana plants allowed to grow in this fashion produce more flowers and resin in an attempt to attract male pollen. It is the resin and flowers that contain the highest amounts of THC, usually averaging between 8 and 12 percent potency. Frequently, it is only the female **flower tops** (buds) that are harvested and marketed.

Many growers select seeds obtained from Afghanistan, Thailand and Mexico that can range in price from $1 to $5 each. One high-grade strain of sinsemilla grown in the United States is *cannabis indica*, imported from Afghanistan. This is popular because it grows into a short, squatty plant that produces 1 to 2 pounds of buds per plant. These buds are high in THC content and mature in 4 to 5 months.

Hashish is also produced from marijuana. This is accomplished by taking the drug-rich resinous secretions of the cannabis plant and drying and compressing them into a variety of forms such as balls or cookie-like sheets. Another form of cannabis, **hash oil**, is produced by repeated extraction of cannabis materials to yield a dark, tenacious liquid. The THC content of both hashish and hash oil is considerably higher than the plant itself.

Many marijuana growers have also perfected indoor growing techniques that enable them to harvest plants year-round. According to the DEA, a technique developed by Oregon pot growers is one called **cloning**. In this technique, growers cultivate hybrid marijuana and select the most superior plants. A "cut" is then taken from the mother plant and soaked in a root stimulant. After the cutting develops roots, it is planted in pots and aided by a halide lighting system.

Case in Point

An investigation in Wyoming revealed a case of two men who had indoor hydroponic marijuana operations near Henry, Nebraska and Guernsey, Wyoming. The two friends exchanged ideas and information on marijuana cultivation but maintained independent operations with independent customers. One of them developed an automatic watering and fertilization system, and the other developed an automatic, timed track-lighting system. In addition to sharing these ideas, they purchased their growing equipment together to reduce overall costs, producing high-grade sinsemilla. Each organization was capable of producing 100 plants at a time, and the two organizations could have produced more than 1,000 pounds per year, selling for as much as $1,000 per pound on the street.

Source: Drug Trafficking: A Report to the President of the United States (1989). U.S. Department of Justice.

Another technique, called **hydroponics**, is also used to grow marijuana in a greenhouse. Hydroponics is the science of growing plants in a soil-free, mineral-rich solution and is commonly used for indoor cultivation of tomatoes and cucumbers. Marijuana produced by the hydroponic method will typically produce a THC content at least twice that of marijuana produced by traditional methods. The DEA estimates that it takes only one square foot of space to grow a mature plant. Therefore, a facility with only 400 square feet of hydroponic growing area can, under optimal growing conditions, cultivate marijuana on a year-round basis and generate an estimated $5 million a year.

Marijuana cultivators and processors come from a wide range of backgrounds and operate in a variety of ways. For example, research by Ralph Weisheit has found that many West Coast growers cultivate the plant for their own use and for sales to friends but are not necessarily large traffickers. In fact, he has suggested that a considerable number of domestic cultivators are still operating within the context of a counterculture frame of reference. Weisheit's research in other areas, such as the Midwest, has generally shown marijuana cultivating and processing to be a disorganized, ancillary business often engaged in by otherwise law-abiding farmers. Research in Kentucky, however, has indicated that cultivation there is becoming more highly organized, with law enforcement officials warning of a "cartelization" of the trade.

In eastern Kentucky, in particular, where high-grade marijuana with THC content as high 18 percent is grown in small plots because of the rugged topography, there is increasing evidence of sophisticated organization in the marijuana market and of the creation of incipient organized crime groups. Ironically, one of the things that appears to have stimulated the change from small, ad hoc, disorganized growing to the creation of highly organized criminal groups is Kentucky's federally funded law enforcement campaign against the marijuana industry. Stepped-up enforcement seems to have resulted in the creation of a more efficient and more dangerous marijuana industry.

Close-Up: City Drugs Infiltrate Country Life

Every few months, the parcel truck would tool down the dusty road, carrying packages to the same house near the hamlet of Shellsburg, Iowa. Nothing seemed suspicious until authorities were tipped off about the contents. The goods were cocaine, an informant said. After nearly two years of watching and waiting, two men were arrested. The occupant of the house pleaded guilty to drug trafficking. A neighbor is expected to face trial this spring. Prosecutors say that in 15 months the two sold cocaine with a street value of $1.4 million.

The drug scourge is spreading to rural America. This incident is just one example. There are many. Cocaine, speed, and even crack are becoming more common in corn country. Drug labs and marijuana farms are reaping big profits in small towns, and rural police and prosecutors are seizing more dope and charging more dealers. "In small rural communities, you just don't expect to find top quality dangerous drugs available in large quantities, and that's what we're finding," said a Minnesota Bureau of Criminal Apprehension special agent. "We're making undercover purchases in towns with populations of 50." "It used to be safe in a small town," the agent said, and parents didn't have to worry because their children were far from dangerous drugs. "Now LSD, methamphetamines, or pure cocaine are available to anyone who really looks for it."

"You're seeing it all over the country, and it's finally coming to roost here," the agent added. "This is the end of the line." That not only concerns police but also lawmakers. Senator Charles Grassley of Iowa convened a hearing in 1989 to examine the growing problem.

"What we're finding is, given the extra money a dealer can make in the state, it really behooves them to make inroads—and they are," said a spokesman for the senator. Police say that they are constantly surprised by the magnitude of the problem. One narcotics agent said that he was shocked when an informant (who had also been a dealer) recently said that he had 50 cocaine customers in a small Minnesota town and that another dealer had 100.

Experts cite numerous reasons for drug dealing in small-town U.S.A.: a depressed rural economy, a ready market with less competition than in big cities, and an ideal environment—remote settings where neighbors may be miles away, police patrols are infrequent, and law enforcement agencies often are undermanned and inexperienced. A hog farmer near Strawberry Point, Iowa, was caught in 1987 trying to flee with "his overalls in one hand, a kilo of cocaine in another arm," said an assistant U.S. Attorney. The farmer was sleeping when authorities entered his house.

Sometimes, drug activity is concealed by transient populations in rural areas. In other instances, remote locales provide the perfect opportunity to avoid detection, particularly with methamphetamine labs, which emit a stench when producing a form of speed called "crank." Such labs, often run by biker gangs, have been found from Missouri to Oregon.

Authorities say that they have stepped up enforcement efforts in rural areas and have results to prove it. For example, in central Illinois, 83 persons in Peoria, Knox, and Tazewell counties were charged in 1988 in Operation Iron Eagle. Included were members of a biker group called the Satan Brothers, accused of dealing cocaine and methamphetamine. Almost all have pleaded guilty.

In South Dakota, drug sale cases rose 50 percent in 1988, said the director of the state Division of Criminal Investigation. He said that 11.3 pounds of cocaine were seized in 1987, about five times the annual amount in previous years.

In Iowa, 65 persons were indicted last October, and authorities seized 14.5 pounds of cocaine, more than 500 pounds of marijuana, and more than $300,000 in cash. Officials say that two-thirds of those indicted were Iowans. More than 55 of those charged have pleaded guilty or been convicted.

In West Virginia, 33 persons were convicted or pleaded guilty to running a crack ring out of a shopping mall in Charles Town, about 80 miles from Washington. U.S. Attorney William Kolibash said that the potent form of cocaine known as crack, supplied by Jamaican dealers, was blatantly sold until arrests in 1989. In Yakima, Washington, the Drug Enforcement Administration office, covering 11 largely rural counties, made 143 arrests during 1988.

Source: *The Kansas City Star,* August 3, 1990.

Clandestine Laboratories

As we have pointed out throughout this book, of the many different drugs that have become popular over the years, some are organic in nature and some are synthesized by chemists in illicit drug laboratories. It should be noted here that even though some drugs may be of an organic origin, a degree of chemical synthesis is necessary for the completion of the finished product. This is true, for example, with heroin and cocaine.

Many popular drugs that have emerged over the years are synthetic in nature and originate in the *clandestine* laboratory. These include:

*   Hallucinogens (LSD, PCP, MDMA)
*   Stimulants (methamphetamines and amphetamines).
*   Controlled substance analogs ("designer drugs")

Drugs such as LSD seem to be available almost everywhere in the country, but production of them appears to be regional. For example, for years LSD and PCP laboratories have been abundant in California, but much of the methamphetamine is produced in illegal laboratories in the West and Southwest. The size of most clandestine labs is relatively modest, as they generally produce one specific drug. Expertise to operate a lab is usually minimal, and much of the equipment and chemicals is readily available and inexpensive. This is true especially when considering the profits which can be realized. One of the most commonly produced illicit drugs in the United States is the stimulant methamphetamine. One of its immediate precursors, Phenyl-2-propanone (P2P), is easily synthesized into methamphetamine. Like many other drugs, the production of methamphetamine is fairly cheap and effortless. The actual setting up of a lab can cost as little as $2,000 and can be enormously profitable as one day's production can generate as much as $70,000 (BJS, 1992).

The spreading popularity of illicit labs is partly due to successes in federal drug interdiction efforts. Many traffickers feel safer making their own drugs domestically than they do risking detection and arrest as a result of dealing with foreign suppliers. As with the marijuana cultivator, the clandestine lab operator commonly seeks isolation in rural settings where his or her activities will go unnoticed. For example, the largest illicit methamphetamine laboratory ever discovered in the United States was located in the mountains of rural McCreary County, Kentucky, and involved participants from Kentucky, Florida, Illinois, and Tennessee. Often this desire for rural isolation is because of the distinctive odors emitted by "meth" and PCP labs. In an urban setting, these odors can reveal the existence of a lab.

Despite the numerous types of drugs produced by illicit laboratories, the manufacturing process can be broken down into three distinct categories:

- *Extraction labs.* The extraction lab produces illicit substances by removing elements from one substance and creating another. Both hashish and methamphetamines are manufactured by using the Benzedrine inhaler method of extraction.

- *Conversion labs.* This lab converts existing illicit drugs to a different form of the same drug. Crack is an example of a drug, cocaine, which is converted into a freebase form for street sale.

- *Synthesis labs.* A synthesis lab transforms one substance to another resulting in a different and more powerful drug. For example, the precursor P_2P is a dangerous drug that is used to manufacture methamphetamine powder. This process is different from the methamphetamine extraction method discussed above.

Investigating a clandestine lab is especially dangerous for police because of the explosive, corrosive, and hazardous materials usually associated with the drug manufacturing process and because many labs are fortified with deadly booby traps. In many cases, even a slight spark can create a chain reaction resulting in a massive explosion of the laboratory. In some instances, agents have fainted from fumes emitted from the laboratories. Because of this, investigators that raid the labs now wear protective plastic jumpsuits, rubber gloves, respirators, and air tanks. Portable showers contained in vans are sometimes used to allow agents that have become contaminated to wash off.

Close-Up: The Meth Lab

The briefing from the California drug agent was to-the-point: "We have word that the cooker could be all screwed up from smelling this stuff, and he could be violent." The plan for the raid was simple: run into the suspected methamphetamine lab located just east of here in a wooded and hilly area, "grab the guy and come out." It was a scenario increasingly played out in the piney woods in this part of the country. Methamphetamine labs are sprouting like mushrooms, and the illegal stimulant, also known as crank, crystal, and speed, is rivaling the popularity of cocaine for a growing army of users.

Twenty minutes after the briefing, the investigators, armed to the hilt, turned off a gravel road and drove up a secluded drive. The movement of the men seemed at odds with the gentle spring country afternoon. The warm sun filtered through a thick stand of trees and danced off a small farm pond. The day would have otherwise seemed languid. Not today. A half-dozen drug agents dressed like Ninja warriors in black chemically resistant, flame retardant hoods, shirts, and pants charged breakneck from a van. Their target: a faded gray ranch-style house like any other a tourist might pass if roaming these hollows and hills.

State troopers took positions at the sides of the house. Two drug agents rigidly aimed automatic pistols and shotguns into a window and door. Other agents stormed the house.

It was over in seconds. "The house is clear," a sweating federal drug agent yelled hoarsely. His chest was heaving. The agents led out a groggy man of 55 that had moved into the house the previous year.

The air inside the house was tested for toxic fumes, but none were detected. The lab in the back would easily rival any high school chemistry laboratory. The walls were covered with plastic sheets, and a long hose ran from a condenser to a ceiling exhaust fan where gasses were released to the air. Thousands of dollars of flasks, beakers, glass tubing, and large glass pots lined the walls. Two 12-liter pots containing methamphetamine oil were still cooking on two stoves under the watchful eye of a closed-circuit camera.

In cluttered rooms and hallways and in a shed outside, agents found more evidence: 25 gallons of hydrochloric acid, 25 barrels of freon, and containers of red phosphorus, a chemical that when overcooked can produce deadly phosphine gas, used in World War I. Finally, in a back bedroom the agents struck paydirt: 29 heat-sealed baggies of white methamphetamine powder.

Source: OCDETF, 1988.

Criminal drug lab operators have also been documented not only mixing toxic chemicals that are deadly, but also routinely dumping toxic waste down bathroom drains or in holes dug outside in the ground. These actions make some lab locations akin to hazardous waste sites.

Clandestine laboratories are also often operated by nonprofessionals—individuals with a limited knowledge of chemistry. Other labs are run by people that have learned various processing techniques through their peers in the criminal underworld. The methamphetamine market, for example, was dominated for many years by the Pagans Motorcycle Club. The skills utilized in drug processing and the safety procedures initiated by a group like the Pagans are highly suspect.

Figure 5.2

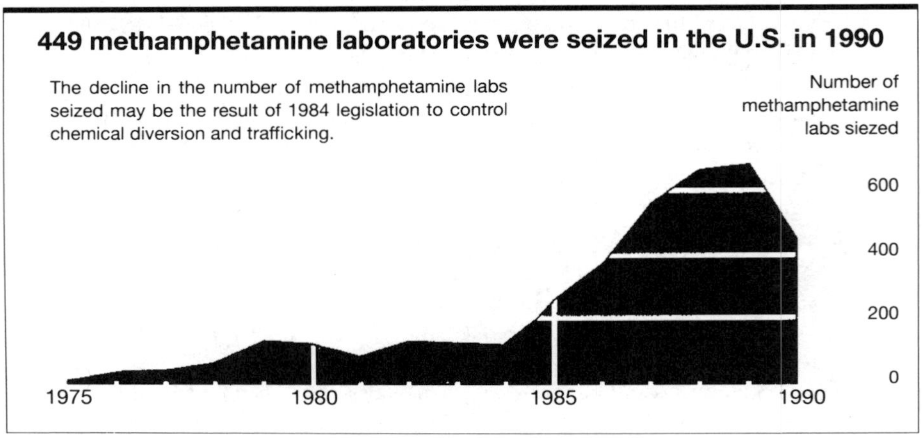

449 methamphetamine laboratories were seized in the U.S. in 1990
The decline in the number of methamphetamine labs seized may be the result of 1984 legislation to control chemical diversion and trafficking.
Number of methamphetamine labs siezed
600
400
200
0
1975
1980
1985
1990

Source: DEA as presented in BJS, *Sourcebook of Criminal Justice Statistics, 1990,* NCJ-130580, 1991, table 4.43.

Figure 5.3

How many clandestine laboratories has DEA seized?
Number of clandestine laboratories siezed
800
600
400
200
0
1975
1980
1985
1990

Source: DEA as presented in BJS, *Sourcebook of Criminal Justice Statistics, 1990,* NCJ-130580, 467.

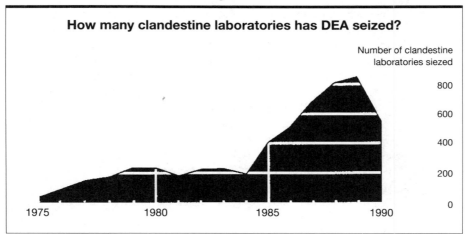

Controlling Precursor Chemicals

Legally obtained substances known as **precursors** are typically used by illicit lab operators to make their final product. In addition, essential chemicals called solvents are also needed to produce the final drug product but don't actually become part of the drug itself. In 1988, the Chemical Diversion and Trafficking Act was passed requiring detailed record keeping and reporting of transactions of all purchases over a designated quantity of each chemical and report all "suspicious" purchases sales to the DEA. In turn, the DEA has power to deny the sale of chemicals to any person or company they deem likely to use them for the making of an illegal drug.

In addition to the federal government, 37 state governments have also passed their own legislation regulating the sale of precursor chemicals (BJS, 1992). Several of these require companies that manufacture these chemicals to obtain a license with a state agency and to maintain records which are regularly supplied to that agency. Essentially, the controlling of precursors is yet another way in which manufacturers of illicit drugs can be identified for arrest or possibly deterred from drug trafficking activity.

Pharmaceutical Diversion

The DEA estimates that because of growing popularity on the street, more than 200 million dosage units of legally made drugs find their way from legitimate sources, such as hospitals and pharmacies, to the street drug abuser every year. Some are lost through drug store thefts and others through forged prescriptions. It is estimated that the greatest amount of these drugs are diverted by a handful of corrupt physicians, pharmacists, osteopaths, veterinarians, dentists, nurses, and other medical professionals.

As we have discussed in earlier chapters, society foots the bill for drug abuse in terms of shoplifting, street crime, and predatory criminal acts relating to drug abuse. Society also pays the bill for drugs diverted through Medicaid and prepaid prescription plans offered by some companies and unions.

Methods of Obtaining Drugs through Diversion

- Stealing from patients

- Stealing from hospital pharmacies or other doctors

- Writing prescriptions for family members' names

- Diluting drugs before administering them to patients and using the rest

- Siphoning off injectable drugs

The 1970 Controlled Substances Act authorized the DEA to regulate all aspects of the drug manufacturing and distribution process in the United States. For the more potent drugs, the DEA can even dictate the thickness of warehouse walls where they are stored (i.e., eight inches of concrete with steel rods). The DEA also controls the order form needed to purchase drugs (three carbon copies with one forwarded to DEA headquarters). Through these mechanisms, the DEA claims that much of the diversion from warehouses and factories has been controlled. The result has been increased diversion at the retail level, marked by a sharp rise in drugstore robberies and burglaries along with increased pressure on some doctors and druggists to cross the line from "professional" to "pusher."

Problems in drug diversion involve both medical professionals (discussed later) and people who attempt to acquire drugs through deceit and trickery. These persons are often called scammers.

The Scammer

To aid in understanding the problem of drug diversion, investigators should also look at the various scams used by street criminals to obtain pharmaceutical drugs. The word scam is defined by Webster as "to cheat or swindle, as in a confidence game." This is precisely what is happening within the medical care community. This criminal, known as the **scammer** or **"professional patient,"** acquires drugs through deceit and sells them on the street for profit.

Of all of the scammer's targets, the most likely is the physician. This is so because once a prescription has been successfully conned out of a physician, because it appears to be legitimate, the scammer will experience little trouble having it filled by the pharmacist. Pharmacists are the second-most-likely target of the scammer, especially in trying to pass forged or altered prescriptions. In addition to forgery and alterations of prescriptions, a pharmacist can be an unwitting partner to a scammer. Three methods are the most common: 1) either by filling prescriptions for the same drugs for the same patient from "different" physicians; 2) filling prescriptions for the same patient too frequently; 3) accepting refills for prescriptions when the scammer is calling in the prescription pretending to be the physician.

Literally hundreds of diversion schemes have been uncovered throughout the years. The following examples, however, will give some insight into the practices of "professional patients."

> *The Fat Lady Scam*
> This is a common deception which is usually perpetrated by several women who are severely overweight. The plan involves the women moving into a new community and developing a schedule requiring each member to visit a maximum number of physicians each day for a week or so. The scam unfolds as each woman tells the physician that she is chronically unhappy with her life because of

being overweight. Additionally, her husband is going to leave her and fight for custody of the children, and she is considering having her stomach stapled . . .etc. At this point the patient begins hinting about a particular drug, such as preludin, amphetamines, or another Schedule II drug. The physician will usually refuse to prescribe Schedule II drugs for this purpose but might be willing to prescribe Didrex®. After the patient is issued a prescription for this drug, the woman might request a prescription for Valium® to keep her from getting too edgy. So, instead of taking the prescribed drugs the women sell them for considerable profit on the street.

The Breast Cancer Scam

This scam is a fairly common one in many states and involves individuals who are actually experiencing a legitimate medical problem. For example, it was first documented in the St. Louis area and it involved a woman who suffered from breast cancer. The woman would simply appear at a physician's office and present her case for treatment. In this case Dilaudid® was the only drug which would give her relief, and physicians would usually agree to give her a prescription. The patient saw seven doctors on a regular basis in different surrounding towns and as with the previous scam, the prescription drugs obtained were sold on the street for a substantial profit.

The Toothache Scam

This scam is popular among narcotics addicts who are also experiencing a tooth decay problem. These scammers will try to obtain Schedule II narcotics from dentists and physicians at the same time. Sometimes scammers have attempted to obtain telephone prescriptions for the desired drug without even seeing the dentist. If the scammers choose to see the dentist, they will appear but with a concocted "legitimate" reason for having to be somewhere else, so the dentist will be pressured to issue a prescription for pain killers such as Demerol® or Dilaudid®. Once obtained, the drugs are sold on the illicit market.

The Altered "Scrip" Scam

Those prescribers who short cut the proper prescription writing practice, especially those who use Arabic-numerals for dose amounts (not reinforced by a written number), are easy targets for professional patients. By simply matching the ink color of the prescriber's pen or ball point, a prescription for 10 can be altered to 40, 5 can become 25, etc. A prudent prescription becomes excessive and proportionally more profitable to the professional patient.

Many other scams exist which are facilitated by con-artists who are elderly, handicapped, or simply clever or brazen enough to attempt such a fraud. All professionals within the medical community are obligated, however, to report any such attempts by criminals when they are first detected.

Doctors as Offenders

What is it that makes a professional registrant choose to become a law violator and a "white-collar" drug dealer? Below are some motivating factors.

1. *Greed*. Pharmacists and physicians have cheap and easy access to drugs that command top dollar on the street. For example, they pay only about $50 for 500 tablets of Knoll Pharmaceutical Company's Dilaudid,® a synthetic narcotic similar to morphine (see Chapter 2). On the street, Dilaudid,® will easily bring between $50 to $60 per tablet. Some corrupt professionals barter drugs or prescriptions for merchandise. Others make their living by operating "diet clincs," where they freely dispense or prescribe amphetamine tablets, even though the use of the drug for weight control is questionable.

2. *Sexual Favors*. Some investigations have revealed instances where some physicians and pharmacists give drugs or prescriptions in return for sexual favors. There have been cases of amphetamines being given to prostitutes to help them stay awake.

3. *Salvaging a Failing Medical Practice*. Drug diversion is a particular problem in cases of failing medical practices, whether caused by incompetence, impending retirement, or location problems. Illicit activity on the part of these physicians often results from having been accustomed to high incomes that have been reduced or from being deeply in debt. An unethical solution to the problem is to write illegal prescriptions or dispense pills for the easy income.

4. *Self-addiction*. The addiction to drugs is an "occupational disease" for some members of the health care community. Long hours and the easy availability of drugs make the medical professional susceptible to drug abuse. Those physicians that have become addicted may turn to diversion to finance their addiction.

5. *Senility*. Some senile doctors and pharmacists have unwittingly yielded to the demands of drug abusers. In other cases, a nurse, medical receptionist, or family member has "taken over" the practice of a senile professional and allowed dangerous drugs to be diverted.

6. *Rationalization*. Some professionals justify selling to abusers by rationalizing that they will get drugs anyway, perhaps through street crime or prostitution.

Some of the specific methods which physicians have commonly used include:

• Physicians writing prescriptions in a patient's or family member's name, picking up the drugs themselves, and then telling the pharmacist they will deliver them to the patient.

- Physicians sending patients to pharmacies to have prescriptions filled but requiring the patient to bring the drugs back to the doctor's office where only part of the drug is administered, with the physician keeping the rest.
- Physicians writing prescriptions in their own name at various pharmacies at the same time.
- Physicians (and nurses) self-administering injectable drugs taken from nurses' stations, hospital emergency rooms, or hospital pharmacies.
- Physicians ordering drugs from a number of pharmacies at the same time, using DEA official order forms while ordering the same drugs from one of the many mail order drug companies.
- Physicians obtaining drug samples and self-administering them.

Although medical care institutions have both a legal and moral obligation to their employees, many shun this responsibility to report a suspected diversion problem or simply look the other way rather than addressing the situation. Responsible hospitals, through their boards of directors, regulate their personnel and establish formal policies regarding impairment with strict enforcement (or treatment) provisions. In the case of addicted registrants, many state hospital boards have adopted a policy whereby a physician or nurse can voluntarily submit to treatment under an employee assistance program and remedy the problem before it results in the prosecution of the physician and embarrassment to the hospital.

In addition to diversion problems experienced with physicians, similar problems are observed with nurses working within the medical field. A distinction should be made here between diversion of drugs for resale and diversion because of personal addiction. Studies have shown that many of those nurses who are diverting drugs do so because of personal physical addictions to those drugs rather than a desire to profit off the sale of them.

Theft of Drugs

Most health-care institutions experience some degree of diversion, and generally it is the employees who are the culprits. As indicated, those employees most likely involved with drugs are those who have access to drugs, for example, physicians, nurses, pharmacists and other employees, and they will most commonly divert drugs such as Valium®, Morphine, Demerol®, Tylenol III w/Codeine®, Percodan®, Percocet®, and Ritalin®. The type of drug user and available opportunities will have a bearing on whether tablets, capsules, or injectable substances are preferred. Diversion may occur in many different areas of the health-care facility but may most commonly be at one of the following locations:

- the hospital pharmacy
- the nursing area
- the recovery floor

Substituting Drugs

In the event an outright theft of drugs is not considered safe by the diversion criminal, the substitution of a controlled drug for a noncontrolled substance might be considered. Substituting drugs may be accomplished, for instance, by appearing to inject a patient with the prescribed medication while, in fact, a worthless substance may be used in its place. This may cause the patient to suffer, believing the prescribed medication is not effective and could result in additional medical setbacks for the patient. Techniques for substitution vary but most commonly include 1) theft through charting (a technique for backdating), and 2) forging other nurses' names.

Addressing the Problem

Sadly, diversion persists, in part, because many facilities fail to discipline those involved. Compounding the problem is the fact that in many cases violators themselves have ways of avoiding punishment. For example, suspected users might quit their position and join another hospital. This might happen if drug users on the job are suspected by one or more employees, and in an effort to avoid being confronted they simply change jobs. So, when the diverter's new employer calls for an employee reference, incriminating information is not shared, thereby allowing the user to carry on with unlawful activities.

Thinking Critically #9

Assume you are a member of the board of directors for a major hospital. Suggest a policy for the control of prescription drugs. Include procedures for the prevention of diversion and enforcement of the policy.

In other cases, employees who are caught diverting drugs will be transferred rather than disciplined. Medical care professionals, like many other types of professionals, are somewhat "clannish" and reluctant to "snitch" on fellow workers. So, by transferring suspect employees, embarrassing publicity for the institution is avoided. Of course, these reactions offer no incentive for violators to discontinue their involvement in diversion activity.

Problems in Diversion Investigations

Even though pharmacists are required by law to account for every dose of dangerous drugs that they order, suspicious fires, robberies, and break-ins can destroy prescription files and cover shortages of pills. For these and many other reasons, evidence of diversion is difficult to acquire. For example, undercover agents investigating this type of criminal behavior may find that the suspect doctors claim that they were just "practicing medicine" and attempting to cure a patient by prescribing drugs for an illness. Other violations are more blatant, such as when physicians literally sell drugs to friends and associates or barter prescriptions for merchandise.

Other problems arise in the prosecution of diversion cases. For example, prosecutors are usually anxious to file charges against drug dealers from the street, but when the drug dealer happens to be a physician in the community, charges are sometimes difficult to bring, and prosecutors are often reluctant to try "respectable" citizens who have the resources to mount an active defense against the charges. There are other pressures on prosecutors. They may have a social or political relationship with the registrant. And if they are in a rural county where doctors' offices are few and far between, they know that any doctor forced out of business could leave some families without easy access to medical care. Furthermore, inconvenienced voters often have good memories when the prosecutor has to stand for re-election, creating a situation where the prosecutor may actually be punished by the very public he or she serves for attempting to apply diversion laws to physicians.

Even when charges are brought against physicians, prosecutors may have a difficult time convincing juries of the seriousness of the violation, or it may be difficult to explain the complexities of the diversion case to the jury. Because of these considerations, a conviction may not be forthcoming in the case.

Case Study: The Five Star Health Club

The Five Star Health Club in Fairmont, West Virginia, was in reality a gambling casino. Just three days prior to a police raid that closed it forever, the club was locked up by its owners. This was not the owners' only line of work. Three of the "five stars," the Spadafore brothers, Donnie, John, and Ralph, were drug dealers. The others were their attorney and an ex-cop that was a convicted gambler.

Over a period of years beginning in 1979, the Spadafore organization smuggled multi-kilo quantities of cocaine into Fairmont then broke it into smaller consignments for distribution in central West Virginia and in Erie, Pennsylvania. Among many other local endeavors, they owned a grocery where, on inquiry, the grocer would pour grams of cocaine from the middle Bisquick box on the shelf.

The gang originally made their wholesale purchases in Miami but soon tired of paying stateside prices and branched out into their own version of international drug smuggling. Donnie, the leader, brought in an Erie, Pennsylvania, organized crime figure, Joseph Scutelli. The organization began to specialize in complicated logistical planning in order to avoid leaving trails. A Peruvian connection was established, improving certainty of supply and reducing price.

In a typical instance, three different private planes were used by the smuggling team. A ring member pilot flew his own aircraft from Lima to Stella Maris in the Bahamas where "the vacationers" were about to leave for Pittsburgh on a charter. "The vacationers" were a retired Erie Police Department detective and his wife, who were used repeatedly because of their ability to blend in with Caribbean tourists. Arriving in Fort Lauderdale at midnight, the couple (and the "dope") boarded another of the organization's planes, which dropped them in Pittsburgh and delivered the cocaine to an unused, unlighted runway of the Morgantown, West Virginia airport.

At the South American end, drugs were usually packed in a pillow stuffed with llama hair. When transported by car in the United States, the drugs were wrapped in a shoe box and addressed for mailing. If challenged, the driver would report having found the box at a rest stop and say that he planned to mail it.

The Five Star attorney was versatile. At times he stored drugs or money at his home for the group. When an insurance arson was planned by the gang, this "corporate counsel" gave such advice as "put a dog and cat in the house, and you'll get paid easier." According to other defendants, it was he who arranged for and delivered monthly payments to "the Charlies" to give the gang protection from law enforcement. "The Charlies," Anderson and Dodd, were the county prosecutor and the sheriff, both convicted at later dates. The lawyer also was accused of acting as lookout while the brothers broke into the police garage seeking to recover cash and cocaine that they thought was hidden in an impounded car. (Somebody else got there first.)

A fellow barrister (actually a city judge) was hired to keep police occupied inside the station next door during the break-in. The young judge was seduced into drug dealing by Donnie's offer of a trip to South America to "run some errands." He was halfway to Peru when he learned that the only errand was to pick up drugs and that he would be paid $65,000 for doing so. The temptation was too great.

The information and evidence necessary to bring down the "stars" was developed over a period of four years by agents of the FBI, IRS, West Virginia State Police, and Fairmont Police Department under auspices of the Organized Crime Drug Enforcement Task Force. Faced with a possible life sentence in prison, the Spadafores all entered plea agreements. The mastermind, Donnie, pleaded guilty in the Northern District of West Virginia to charges of operating a continuing criminal enterprise, unlawful possession of an unregistered firearm, and filing a false income tax return. He was sentenced to 20 years without parole. John Spadafore's primary role in the organization had been providing the muscle; he pleaded guilty to RICO charges in connection with drugs and also received 20 years. Ralph's role was to provide financial services and present a legitimate front for the organization. He was the overseer of the gambling operation and was responsible for all hiring. Ralph pled guilty to violating the RICO statute in connection with gambling and was sentenced to six years. All but one of the 21 persons indicted have been convicted or have pleaded guilty. The last is a fugitive believed to be somewhere in South America.

One of those convicted was Carol Rae Olson, a key supplier to the Spadafore organization and a vice president of an oil company whose jet aircraft were used to move drugs. Her conviction was especially important because it severed a direct cocaine pipeline from Peru to the United States. Olson was apprehended in Hawaii with Donnie Spadafore's help and found guilty of six counts of racketeering, conspiracy, and cocaine importation. Others found guilty included Scutelli, the ring's lawyer, the city judge, two pilots, and "the vacationers."

Source: OCDETF, 1988.

The Drug Audit

One of the nine control mechanisms contained within the 1970 Controlled Substances Act is a recordkeeping requirement for all registrants. This provision requires that full records of quantities of all controlled substances, regardless of which schedule they are under, be kept by registrants. This requirement applies to drugs manufactured, purchased, sold, or inventoried. Limited exceptions to this requirement are available only to researchers and physicians. It is from these records that audits can be performed to trace the flow of any drug from the time it is first manufactured, through the wholesale level, though its final destination at a pharmacy, hospital or physician's office, and on to the patient. The mere existence of this requirement is often enough to discourage many types of diversion.

Under the recordkeeping requirement, one distinction is made. That is, all records for all Schedule I and II drugs must be maintained separately from all other records of the registrant. The purpose for this requirement is to allow investigators the ability to audit the more abusable drugs more expeditiously.

Summary

Although foreign traffickers make significant contributions to the drug problem in the United States, many domestic criminals also play a significant role. Domestic drug production primarily centers around three types of illicit activities: marijuana cultivation, clandestine laboratories that primarily manufacture methamphetamine and PCP, and pharmaceutical diversion.

The marijuana cultivator will produce one of two types of marijuana: commercial or sinsemilla. The commercial grade is the most common type of marijuana and is generally the easiest to grow. Sinsemilla, on the other hand, is the most potent type of marijuana and will bring twice the street price of the commercial strain. Sinsemilla is, however, a much more difficult strain to grow, as it requires more personal attention and time on the part of the cultivator. This explains why fewer marijuana growers are involved with sinsemilla farming than commercial.

The clandestine lab problem is one of growing proportions in the United States. Lab operators are the most active in the manufacturing of methamphetamine and PCP, both of which have achieved a growing popularity throughout the United States.

Finally, we examined the problem of pharmaceutical diversion by both scammers (also known as professional patients) and registrants. The diversion of addictive and dangerous drugs happens for many reasons. Some reasons include profit motive while others occur because of personal addictions developed by the registrants themselves. In either case, the problem results in the diversion of a significant amount of dangerous drugs that are eventually marketed on the street for exorbitant prices.

Do you recognize these terms?

cloning

commercial marijuana

flower tops

hash oil

hashish

hydroponics

Indian hemp

precursors

professional patients

scammers

sinsemilla

Discussion Questions

1. List the three most common types of marijuana grown in the United States.

2. How is sinsemilla grown, and why is its potency so much higher than that of commercial marijuana?

3. What are the two most common methods of indoor growing of marijuana?

4. List the primary drugs manufactured by domestic clandestine laboratories.

5. Why are illicit laboratories considered so dangerous for police investigators?

6. Who are the most likely candidates for the diversion of pharmaceutical drugs?

7. What factors explain why a registrant might become involved in the diversion of pharmaceutical drugs?

8. Discuss some ways in which controlled drugs can be diverted from legal channels of distribution.

9. Explain why the pharmaceutical drug case is usually so difficult to prosecute.

Drugs and Crime 6

This chapter will enable you to:

- Understand the relationship between various types of crime and drug abuse

- Comprehend the extent of the police corruption problem as it pertains to drug trafficking

- Understand the domestic and international problem of money laundering

- Realize who the money launderers are and how they operate

- Understand what legal tools are available to prosecutors to combat money laundering

In addition to the physiological effects and medical complications associated with drug abuse, one of the greatest public concerns is the rising spectrum of crime as it relates to the use of drugs. Clearly, a definitive but complex correlation exists between drug crimes and other types of crime, but the nature and extent of the link between drugs and crime are far from being understood. Therefore, the catch phrase "drug-related crime" remains somewhat general. Criminal justice researchers hope to clarify this category of crime in coming years in order to predict both drug trafficking patterns and nondrug criminal behavior.

The drugs and crime issue causes one to consider one fundamental question: To what extent does one perpetuate the other? For example, it is clear that abuse and trafficking and use of some substances are by their very nature illegal—users of heroin must possess the drug to do so, but possession of it is forbidden under law. Accordingly, stricter penalties on both the state and federal level exist for its transportation and sale. What's more, some forms of drug abuse are more likely than not to spur particular types of antisocial behavior. For instance, amphetamine use has been linked to the increase in one's level of aggression, which has been shown to lead to assaultive behavior in some cases. Frequency of drug use is another factor. One who uses drugs several times a day is at a greater risk of involvement in crime than one who is an occasional user. Finally, many crimes not normally associated with drug use or drug dealing result from drug-related behavior. For example, a user might steal to support his or her habit, or prostitution might finance one's drug usage. In fact, studies have shown that criminal activity is almost two to three times higher among frequent users of heroin or cocaine than among irregular users or nonusers of drugs (BJS, 1992). This is not to imply that if drugs were to be eliminated so would crime, but it does suggest that a causal link probably exists.

Evidence of the Drug-Crime Relationship:

- Drug users report greater involvement in crime and are more likely than nonusers to have criminal records.

- Persons with criminal records are much more likely than ones without criminal records to report being drug users.

- Crimes rise in number as drug use increases.

Source: Chaiken and Chaiken, 1990.

This chapter will identify and discuss three critical forms of drug-related crime: drug use and predatory crime, police corruption, and money laundering. Each of these plays a significant role in the overall drug problem and should be considered when seeking solutions to the nation's drug dilemma.

Drug Use and Predatory Crime

There has long been suspicion among some law enforcement officials and researchers that some link exists between addictive drugs and the propensity of drug users to commit crime. The available empirical research indicates that drug addicts, particularly heroin addicts, commit crimes more frequently than other population groups. Drug addiction appears to escalate the rate of criminal participation. But that does not mean that drug use causes crime. Almost all heroin addicts committed crimes, particularly property crimes, prior to their heroin use or addiction. The need for financial resources to insure a steady supply of the drug appears to escalate their already manifest criminal involvement. Several important sources of information about drugs and crime are currently available for study. For example, urine testing of arrested persons; surveys of offender populations; criminal justice system records of arrests, convictions, and incarcerations; and surveys of drug users who have entered drug treatment programs help us determine the extent of drug use.

One of the best tools for measuring drug use and crime is the **Drug Use Forecasting** (DUF) program which tests the urine of arrested persons in custody who voluntarily submit to testing. The program tests for the presence of 10 different drugs. In the majority of cities, more than half of those tested were found to have used drugs recently (BJS, 1992).

Jail inmate surveys also provide data regarding the link between drugs and crime. Such surveys have shown that three out of four inmates surveyed in 1989 reported some drug use in their lifetime. More than 40 percent had used drugs in the month before their offense with 27 percent under the influence of drugs at the time of their offense. Prison inmate surveys tell a similar story. More than one-third reported having used illegal drugs at the time of the current offense (BJS, 1988).

Finally, two national studies have shown that most people in treatment for drugs had been arrested or had admitted committing crimes for economic gain prior to entering treatment. The **Drug Abuse Reporting Program** (DARP) concluded that 71 percent had been in jail before entering treatment while the **Treatment Outcome Prospective Study** (TOPS) discovered that about 60 percent of people entering residential treatment programs reported that they had committed one or more crimes for economic gain during the year before treatment.

It is also logical to assume that people who buy or sell drugs, or who are under the influence of them will make likely targets for predatory attacks since they probably possess some cash or drugs on their person. Since these persons are involved in criminality themselves, other offenders may assume that they may be less likely to report robberies, assaults, or thefts to the police. This brings up another interesting point. Because a drug buyer or seller may choose not to report being victimized to the police they may choose to take the law into their own hands and settle disagreements in their own manner. This can often lead to violent encounters such as murder, assault, and drive-by shootings. Let's look closer at this problem.

Drugs and Violent Crime

Legal drugs such as alcohol as well as illicit drugs like cocaine, amphetamine, and PCP affect one's physiological functions, cognitive abilities, and moods. However, there is no existing evidence which shows a pharmacologically based drugs-violence relationship. It is the general impression of most experts in the field that the effects of drugs or alcohol do not directly precipitate violence, but a combination of factors such as the type of drug, the user's personality, and other situational factors may influence one's propensity towards aggressive behavior.

A recent study showing the relationship between certain drugs and violent criminality was conducted by Jeffery Roth for the National Institute of Justice (1994). In the study, several general observations were made. First, it was noted that violence is *diverse* with acts as different as drive-by shootings and those such as highly planned serial killings. Secondly, the report noted that causes of violence are *complex,* involving a wide variety of factors which were broken down into four levels for study:

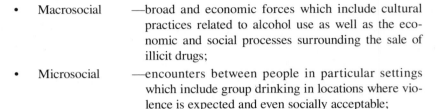

- Macrosocial   —broad and economic forces which include cultural practices related to alcohol use as well as the economic and social processes surrounding the sale of illicit drugs;

- Microsocial   —encounters between people in particular settings which include group drinking in locations where violence is expected and even socially acceptable;

- Psychosocial   —individual behavior development from childhood through adulthood. Examples include patterns of heavy drinking and aggression which develop during adolescence and continue into adulthood;

- Neuro-Behavioral—processes that underlie all human behavior which can include the effects of substance abuse during pregnancy on fetal development and the effects of chronic drug abuse on brain functioning.

These factors may operate long before the occurrence of violent events, but it is evident that the causal events for violence are often linked to alcohol or other drugs (Roth, 1994). Specific findings include:

- For the last several decades, alcohol drinking by either the perpetrator of a crime, the victim, or both has immediately preceded at least half of all violent crime;

- Chronic drinkers are more likely than others to have histories of violent behavior;

- Criminals who use illegal drugs commit robberies and assaults more frequently than do nonuser criminals, and they commit them especially frequently during periods of heavy drug usage;

- About 60 percent of arrestees booked for violent crimes were confirmed by laboratory tests to have used at least one illegal drug in the hours before arrest.

Interestingly, alcohol and drugs modify encounters between people in ways that make such substances a particular risk for violence. Specifically, in the case of alcohol, the risk of violence tends to be associated with the effects of the substance on the user, compared to illegal drugs where most violence is associated with the business of drug purchases and sales. This is illustrated by the fact that many therapists who treat violent sex offenders have reported that their patients have both histories of alcohol abuse and high levels of testosterone. This is further validated by animal studies which show that although alcohol tends to reduce levels of testosterone in some animals, in those with high-testosterone levels alcohol promotes aggression at greater levels (Roth, 1994).

In addition to the pharmacology of some drugs, the business of drug trafficking may also be linked to crime. Drug markets, which operate outside the
world of contract law as a means for arbitrating disputes, substitute illegal
mechanisms developed for handling "business-related" problems. Violence is
often used to protect or expand markets, intimidate competitors, and retaliate
against sellers and buyers who are thought to be cheating. In addition, violence
is focused against the police, witnesses, and informers who threaten to identify
and convict the trafficker. It has even been suggested that the illicit drug trade
even attracts persons who are prone to violence (Haller, 1989). Problematic situations are many in the drug trade and can include:

- protection of drug-producing crops during harvest season
- territorial disputes between rival drug organizations
- robberies of drug dealers and their subsequent retaliation
- interpersonal violence between buyers and sellers of drugs
- elimination of drug informers and witnesses
- punishment for selling poor quality or adulterated drugs
- failure to pay debts
- violence involving people other than buyers and sellers such as victims of
  robberies

Finally, it is important to mention that much violence is related *indirectly* to
the illicit drug trade. Examples include the robbery of a business by a person
who has spent the rent money on drugs or spousal assaults arising out of disputes over money.

Other Factors

Cities both large and small across the United States are now targeted by an
array of drug gangs claiming turf for drug sales. According to a report by the
Department of Justice, an estimated 80 percent of these individuals have
already been in jail or prison, with one of every five having six or more convictions on his or her record. Based on these figures, it seems apparent that a
more specifically defined public policy is needed in the many areas of drug
abuse, and a closer interaction between anti-drug programs and the criminal
justice system is necessary.

Police Corruption

In addition to the street crimes discussed above, there are other examples
of criminal activity that are directly related to the illicit drug trade. This activity may manifest itself in numerous ways, including the corruption of public

officials that taints governments and societies both domestically and abroad. Corruption, regardless of who perpetuates it, erodes communities and the governments that oversee them. That is, where official corruption exists, public service, confidence in government competency, and an overall lack of public trust and credibility result.

It is impossible to gauge exactly how much corruption there is in American policing today. However, despite the fact that police officers are reluctant to openly discuss the problem of corruption, a substantial body of literature is available to give a general understanding of the magnitude of the problem. .

As far back as 1930, the **Wickersham Commission** declared that in nearly all large cities, there existed an alliance between criminals and politicians. Throughout the decades since then, it has generally been the case that efforts to control corruption have proven to be ineffective at best. Even in cases where corruption was identified and successfully dealt with by police administrators, it was not uncommon to see its return.

James Inciardi (1992) writes that one of the more pervasive problems in the political arena is the wholesale corruption of both *individuals* and *institutions.* With regard to institutional corruption, money laundering has long tainted the banking industry. Official corruption also affects law enforcement and public safety. For example, it permits criminals to continue in their activities, it erodes the reputation of the department and the morale of officers, and it hampers the general effectiveness of community crime control efforts.

Corruption on the official level may take many forms. Specifically, one who has been compromised by criminal elements may take either a passive or active role in corruption. A good example of this was in 1988 when more than 75 Miami police officers were under investigation at one time for possible involvement in criminal activities. Allegations included drug dealing, robbery, theft, and even murder. One investigation in particular revealed several officers who had ambushed drug dealers bringing cocaine into Miami. This investigation revealed that officers stole $13 million in cocaine from a boat anchored in the Miami River and loaded it into marked police vehicles. Duffel bags full of cocaine were reportedly stacked to the ceilings of the patrol cars. Three of the suspects, in an effort to escape, jumped into the river and drowned.

Preconditions for Corruption

The problem of corruption has been exacerbated by the problem of drugs and drug abuse. Millions of dollars in seized currency create temptations for officers predisposed for wrongdoing. Some argue that police officers involved in proactive investigative efforts such as drug, gambling, and prostitution enforcement are more vulnerable to corruption than uniformed officers. This is primarily because crimes that the undercover officer discovers have not yet come to the official attention of the department. So, the vice officer can "easily agree to overlook offenses known only to him or to even participate in illegal transactions (e.g., buying and selling drugs) for his own gain rather than the organization's advantage" (Abadinsky, 1990:401).

A management dilemma relating to the drug abuse problem is the number of police officer applicants who have drug abuse in their past. Due to the pervasiveness of the drug problem, many police departments are now receiving applications from individuals who are former or even current drug abusers. In fact, a study by Peter Kraska and Victor Kappeler found that more than 20 percent of the police officers in a local police department used marijuana and non-prescription drugs while on duty (1988:1-10).

But corruption opportunities are not limited to vice or narcotics officers; they are also readily available to officers working in the patrol capacity as well. Money and drug seizures made by patrol officers may actually take place with much less supervision than those made by the drug enforcement division and, thus, create a greater opportunity for corruption.

The police **"socialization"** process also contributes to the corruption problem in that rookie officers are often advised to forget all they have learned in the police academy and learn the "rules of the street" in order to survive. The implication is that [some] rules need to be bent or even broken in order to literally survive on the streets as well as to climb the career ladder in police work. Sherman suggests that the socialization process also creates a situation where officers learn to "map out the environment." This means that as officers gain experience on the job and encounter various circumstances, they develop attitudes that rationalize their own deviant behavior.

Common rationalizations include, "the public is the enemy and doesn't want the law enforced"; "politicians are crooked and shouldn't be trusted"; "minorities are amoral, a drain on society's resources, and cop haters who are not to be believed or shown respect"; "everybody's on a hustle"; "judges are too lenient"; and "police administrators are the enemy" (Sherman, 1982:10-19). When such attitudes become a part of a police officer's view of police work, it is likely they also become part of that officer's attitude toward society as well.

Types of Police Corruption

As definitions of the term suggest, corruption is not limited to its most conspicuous form—the acceptance of cash in exchange for an official favor. Several experts have identified different varieties of police corruption. For example, Michael Johnston (1982:75) cites four major corruption categories:

1.   *Internal corruption.* These include acts among police officers themselves and involves behaviors from the bending of rules to the outright commission of illegal acts.
2.   *Selective enforcement.* Police officers exploit their officer discretion. For example, a detective who arrests and releases a drug trafficker in exchange for valuable information about the trafficker's organizations is not abusing his or her authority, but one who releases the same trafficker for money is in clear abuse of his or her discretion and authority.

3. *Active criminality.* Police officers participate in serious criminal activity using their positions of power and influence to commit the criminal acts they are entrusted to enforce.

4. *Bribery/extortion.* This occurs when police officers use their vested authority to generate a personal source of money. Bribery is initiated by the citizen while extortion is initiated by the officer.

Another researcher, Ellwin Stoddard (1968), has constructed a list of several specific forms of behavior that he considers corrupt in nature:

Bribery: The receipt of cash or a "gift" in exchange for past or future assistance in avoidance of prosecution, as by a claim that the officer is unable to make a positive identification of a criminal or by being in the wrong place at a time when a crime is to occur, or by any other action that may be excused as carelessness but not offered as proof of deliberate miscarriage of justice. It is distinguished from mooching (see below) by the higher value of the gift and by the mutual understanding in regard to services to be performed upon the acceptance of the gift.

Chiseling: The demand for price discounts or free admission to places of entertainment regardless of any connection with official police work. This differs from mooching (see below) as it is initiated by the officer, not the business proprietor. In this case, business owners and workers comply out of fear, fear that the police officer will be less than responsive when and if a crime is ever committed on the premises or fear that the officer will look closer for some kind of violations committed by the business or its employees if the favor is not granted.

Shakedown: The common practice of holding "street court" where minor traffic tickets can be avoided with a cash payment to the officer and no receipt given. Using the shakedown, police have also been known to extort money from tavern owners and other businesses by threatening to enforce city health and zoning codes.

Favoritism: The practice of issuing license tabs, window stickers, or courtesy cards that exempt users from arrest or citation from traffic offenses (frequently extended to family members of officers).

Mooching: The acceptance of free coffee, cigarettes, meals, liquor, groceries, justified by being in an underpaid profession or for future acts of favoritism performed for the donor. Many restaurant chains as well as doughnut and coffee shops have adopted policies of providing discount meals on a regular basis. This ensures that there will be a continued police presence at the establishment at virtually all times and is justified as being cheaper than hiring a full-time security guard for protection.

Perjury: A willingness to lie under oath to provide an alibi for fellow officers apprehended in unlawful activity.

Prejudice: Treatment of minority groups in a manner less than impartial, neutral, or objective, especially members of such groups who are unlikely to have "influence" in city hall which might cause trouble for the arresting officer.

Premeditated theft: Predatory criminal activity which includes planned burglary involving the use of tools, keys, or other devices to gain entry or any prearranged plan to acquire property unlawfully. This form of corruption, unlike some others, is rarely tolerated by police departments.

Shopping: Opportunistic theft such as picking up small items like cigarettes, candy bars, jewelry, money, etc., at a store which has accidentally been left unlocked at the close of business hours or at the scene of a fire or burglary.

Even seemingly benign actions such as accepting a free cup of coffee or free admittance to the local movie theater may constitute corruption—or at least a predisposition for such behavior. More (1992:251) suggests that although on the surface the acceptance of a free meal or cup of coffee may seem insignificant, there is every reason to believe it creates an atmosphere conducive to corruption. So, to ensure a police force who can function within the community while being free of compromises, all such behavior should be closely scrutinized. This will protect the citizenry from a police force who gives preferential treatment to businesses that offer gratuities.

Case in Point

A former sheriff in Pitkin County, Colorado, upon learning of a federal undercover investigation, placed an advertisement in the local newspaper warning residents of the investigation and advising them to leave the area if they had recently sold drugs to strangers.

Source: Drug Trafficking: A Report to the President of the United States (1989).

Police corruption is nothing new in America. Much official corruption in the areas of liquor and gambling was well documented during the early part of the century when prohibition was still in effect. In many such cases, a link was established between police and politicians which favored clients who would be protected while competitors would be harassed.

Corruption in New York City

Of the many examples of police corruption in America, perhaps the most highly publicized investigation in recent history stemmed from charges made in the 1970s by two New York City police officers: Frank Serpico and David Durk. The corruption problem began to surface when the officers began to protest to fellow officers about corrupt practices in their precinct. They were told to shut up and mind their own business or go along with the others and their corrupt practices. Out of frustration the officers then complained about corruption to top brass high up in the police department and were assured that their charges were being fully investigated—but nothing was ever done. Finally, Serpico and Durk took their story to *The New York Times*, and the paper ran a series of stories about the police corruption problem in the NYPD. As a result of widespread public concern, the **Knapp Commission** was appointed to investigate these allegations.

Detective Frank Serpico's testimony before the Knapp Commission provided revealing information about corruption within the New York Police Department. Although the commission's findings revealed that minor offenses were much more commonplace than serious ones, it still concluded that overall corruption was widespread in the New York City Police Department. The majority of officers who received outright bribes usually didn't vigorously seek cash payments but rather took advantage of offers that came their way from contractors, trucking operators, and criminals. Specific findings of the Commission included: 1) plainclothes officers received regular payoffs on a semiweekly or weekly basis; 2) detectives in some divisions were involved in shakedowns (discussed earlier); 3) undercover officers in the narcotics division were receiving payoffs; 4) mid-level managers such as sergeants and lieutenants had been taking bribes; and 5) uniformed officers were receiving payoffs from local businessmen and gamblers.

In addition, the Commission found that in five of the 17 plainclothes divisions, corruption followed the same basic pattern. That is, officers assigned to the vice divisions were receiving payoffs from criminals. Detectives collected payoffs ranging up to $3,500 per month from each gambling location. This amount represented a "nut" (the officer's share) which ranged anywhere from $300 to $1,500 of the "pad" (list of payoff money). As might be expected, those officers who were higher in rank would receive a higher payoff. Specifically, supervisors would receive a share-and-a-half, which ranged from $450 to $2,250. Plainclothes officers who were newly assigned were required to wait two months before they were eligible for payoff benefits (Knapp, 1972).

The Commission also reported that uniformed officers were receiving much smaller payoffs than their plainclothes counterparts—typically under $20. Such payoffs included shakedowns from small-time gamblers, payoffs for "fixing" traffic tickets, and bribes and payoffs from bars, grocery stores, and other places of business. Although these payoffs were small, they were plentiful enough to significantly enhance the officer's income.

Another form of corruption identified by the Commission was the incidence of *payoffs between officers on the force*. These consisted of bribes to receive more desirable assignments or to speed up certain police procedures. Other types of corruption included special "pads" for sergeants only, excluding participation by subordinate officers. The Knapp Commission was unable, however, to identify evidence of corruption by officers above the rank of lieutenant, although much circumstantial evidence supported this assumption. This was due, in part, to the fact that superiors would commonly use lower ranking officers to collect payoffs or serve as "bagmen," and as a result, it was extremely difficult to implicate supervisory personnel.

Thinking Critically #10

Suppose that large-scale corruption is discovered within the police department in your community. Moreover, you are a member of a citizens' group who has been asked by the city council to study the corruption problem and suggest means of correcting it and preventing future incidents. What suggestions will you make to the city council?

Arising out of the Knapp Commission's findings were two unique descriptive terms used to characterize corrupt officers: **grass eaters** and **meat eaters.** The grass eater is an officer who accepts payoffs as they are presented to him while performing normal police duties. In comparison, the meat eater is considerably more aggressive and contentious in his or her pursuit of illegal abuses of police power for personal gain. However, the Commission reported that, "Although meat eaters get huge payoffs, getting all of the headlines, they represent a small percentage of corrupt officers. The truth is the vast majority on the take don't deal in large amounts of graft" (Knapp, 1972). In fact, the Commission felt that grass eaters were at the center of the problem and that those who were involved were looked upon by other officers as respectable.

The specter of police corruption in New York City fell into the public spotlight once again in September 1993, when a special commission was appointed by Mayor David Dinkins to investigate police corruption in the 30,000-member police force. The commission, headed by former appeals judge Milton Mollen, made new inquiries into the problem. The **Mollen Commission's** star witness was 32-year-old police officer Michael Dowd, who described his indoctrination by superiors into petty crime and brutality and an evolution of behavior which resulted in his own drug dealing. Ultimately, more than 25 police officers were implicated in organized corrupt activities.

Dowd shocked listeners in describing how he would do lines of cocaine off the dashboard of his patrol car while his partner looked on. His testimony revealed that his weekly "take" rose from $200 per week to an $8,000 payoff from a drug dealer. In his statement he said that he became a "hero" to rookie cops who wanted to know how he acquired his red Corvette, expensive wardrobe, and his many vacations. Probably the most troubling testimony provided by Dowd was regarding his education into corruption, which began at the police academy. He claimed that officers at the academy promoted an "us against them" mentality—"Us is the police officers and them is the public." Dowd's testimony also revealed how drinking on the job sealed a social pact of illegal activity by officers. In doing so, officers comprising literally the entire patrol force in Brooklyn's 75th Precinct would "regularly rendezvous at a hidden location for drinks, laughs, shooting off guns and other 'immature stuff'" (Frankel, 1993).

In addition to Dowd's testimony, the Commission focused on issues of brutality by officers. One such officer was Bernie Cawley. Also known as "the Mechanic," Cawley gave statements about how he would "tune [beat up] people up with night sticks and lead-lined gloves." According to his testimony, it was nothing to kick "johns" out of bed and force prostitutes to have sex with him. . . and nothing to lie before grand juries as well as steal drugs and money from drug dealers (Frankel, 1993).

Perhaps one of the more disturbing aspects to the Mollen Commission's findings was the involvement of upper echelon police managers and administrators in corrupt activities. In fact, one of the common denominators in the inquiry was the specter of widespread corruption coupled with a total disregard for the police department's system of internal scrutiny. During the inquiry, internal affairs detective Sergeant Joseph Trimboli testified how the five-year investigation was systematically stymied by top police supervisors working within the internal affairs division itself. In fact, after presenting a Brooklyn police commander with the identities of corrupt officers in the 75th precinct, the commander advised his officers to cover it up.

Corruption in Philadelphia

The quality of law enforcement was studied in Philadelphia by the **Pennsylvania Crime Commission,** which found that corruption was continuing, prevalent, and organized at all levels of the police department. In fact, the corruption problem was almost identical to that found in New York City. During the course of the investigation, virtually all districts within the department had some degree of corruption which involved officers holding ranks up to the position of inspector. As in New York City, Philadelphia corruption included the use of "bagmen" who made periodic rounds to illegal gambling operations, nightclubs, prostitutes, and businessmen to collect payoff money which was later distributed to participating officers. More than 400 officers were identified by name or badge number as the recipient of cash monies, merchandise, sexual favors, meals, or services. As with the New York investigation, the Commission reported that officers viewed drug money to be the dirtiest kind of graft, but that attitude didn't deter some officers from "scoring" suspected drug dealers for sizable payoffs. The Commission also heard reports that in an estimated 65 to 75 percent of all drug arrests, at least part of the drugs were not turned in as evidence. Instead, these drugs were used by officers as "plants" to frame suspected drug dealers or to sell on the black market for cash profits.

More writes that the police department in Philadelphia had endured corruption since its inception (1992:260). During the twentieth century alone, three grand jury investigations have revealed the existence of widespread corruption in the Pennsylvania Police Department. "Numerous interacting factors" were cited by the Pennsylvania Crime Commission during the mid-1970s as reasons for corruption. These factors included the department's general attitude toward the problem of corruption. Other reasons included perceived pressures on law enforcement officers and the reaction to corruption by other parts of the criminal justice system. The specific types of corruption identified by the Pennsylvania Crime Commission (1974:677-801) included the following:

1. Payments to overlook liquor law violations.
2. Payments from after-hours clubs that operate beyond the legal closing time.
3. Payoffs from illegal nightclubs.
4. Payments for allowing illegal gambling, including numbers, horse bets, and sports wagering.
5. Payoffs for allowing gamblers to use illegal gambling machines.
6. Cash payments for allowing prostitution.
7. Promises to prostitutes that charges would be dropped in exchange for sexual favors.
8. Extortion of money and drugs from drug offenders.
9. Illegal cash payments from businesses, in exchange for services such as providing escorts to banks and guarding business premises.
10. Cash payments from motorists for traffic violations.
11. Theft of unprotected valuables from premises.
12. The stripping of impounded cars.
13. The filing of false reports and committing perjury in court.

Problems of police corruption in both New York and Philadelphia touched off calls by the public for reform. These cases have been underscored in the 1980s and 1990s by recent accounts of corruption in other cities such as Miami, Boston, and San Francisco. It should be noted that although there appear to be areas of widespread corruption within some police departments, other forms of corruption also exist in other parts of the criminal justice system as well. For example, prosecutors enjoy considerable discretion in filing cases, dismissing cases, and plea bargaining, and judges are vested with powers which can mold the trial process and make determinations regarding sentencing of offenders; both have considerable influence to offer the corruptors in our society.

Institutional Corruption

Lawrence Sherman (1974) suggests that **institutional corruption** can also exist in police departments themselves. Such organizations can be categorized on the basis of the level and type of corruption existing within them. He identifies three types:

- *Type I—Rotten pockets and rotten apples.* This category consists of a few scattered corrupt police officers using their position for personal gain (rotten apples). When these officers get together they form a rotten pocket. Rotten pockets help institutionalize corruption because they expect newcomers to conform to their corrupt practices and to a code of secrecy.

- *Type II—Pervasive unorganized corruption.* A Type II police department employs a majority of officers who are corrupt but who have little relationship to one another. Although each officer may be involved in a variety of styles of corruption, most are not working in collusion with others on the police force for personal gain.

- *Type III—Pervasive organized corruption.* The Type III police department represents a police force in which almost all of the officers are involved in organized and systematic corruption for personal gain. Such a situation was identified in New York by the Knapp Commission where a group of corrupt officers working out of the vice division would regularly extort money from local criminals and businesses. Such behavior was accepted by the officers as part of the job.

In addition to the blatant acceptance of currency for official services rendered, corruption may also include subtle arrangements in which an agreement is implied. Sometimes termed *conflicts of interest,* such agreements as with those discussed above often encompass situations where the officer becomes the beneficiary of favors or gifts from persons with whom the officer conducts his or her duties.

Case in Point

In Tennessee, a marijuana and cocaine distribution ring operated with the assistance of the county sheriff and his chief investigator. The organization imported marijuana as well as cultivated it in rural areas of the county. The sheriff and his assistant also sold drugs confiscated from other dealers to members of the distribution ring.

Source: Drug Trafficking: A Report to the President of the United States (1989).

Fighting Police Corruption

It is difficult to offer a simple and comprehensive explanation for some of the abuses of police power and authority. Clearly, however, better formal training and socialization may be the key to reducing deviant behavior among police officers. Policy changes are necessary to address those officers who are borderline or who have already become tainted by corruption.

Why, then, do some police officers become corrupt and others don't? Several explanations can be considered. For example, some argue that *the type of individual who becomes a police officer* is at the root of the problem. Studies show that most police personnel have been recruited from lower-class neighborhoods and many lack the financial where-with-all to adopt a much desired middle-class lifestyle. As the cynical, authoritarian police personality develops, the acceptance of graft seems to be a logical method of attaining financial security (Johnston, 1982:82).

Corruption can also be viewed as *a function of police institutions and practices* (Sherman, 1974:40-41), for example, the degree of discretion enjoyed by police officers. The police officer's ability to intervene or not, coupled with low visibility and lack of supervision in the communities and within the agencies may create an atmosphere conducive to corruption. Institutionalization of corruption is also evident when corrupt officers are protected by the code of secrecy within their ranks as well as by their own supervisors who have risen up through the ranks and may be less than willing to report any wrongdoing.

A third explanation holds that corruption is a product of *society's reservations toward the enforcement of many types of vice-related crimes.* Because vice crime is so difficult to control and because a large segment of society wants it to persist, officers who are charged with enforcing vice laws might feel they are justified in accepting money from criminals involved in these types of crimes.

Corruption in Foreign Countries

When considering the problem of official corruption in the drug trade, it is often difficult to determine whether complicity in criminal actions is on an individual basis by officials seeking their own financial enhancement or whether it is systematic and under the sanction of an entire government or official unit of that government. The corrupt official is the *sine qua non* (essential element) of drug trafficking, and it is his or her participation through the corruption of an official office that protects and aids sophisticated criminals in the manufacturing, smuggling, and distribution of illicit drugs. We have briefly discussed how corruption affects law enforcement domestically; let us now examine how corruption affects drug control in illicit drug source countries.

Cuba

The United States government first suspected the Cuban government's complicity in the drug trade during the early 1960s, but many of the allegations were unsubstantiated. Finally, in the early 1980s, many of these accusations were verified. In particular, in November 1982, the United States District Court indicted four major Cuban officials on charges of conspiring to traffic drugs. Among those four were the Vice Admiral of the Cuban Navy and the former Cuban Ambassador to Colombia. According to the indictment, the officials were allowing Cuba to be used as a transshipment center for drug shipments destined for the United States. On one occasion, in exchange for its participation in this scheme, the Cuban government was to receive $800,000 for the sale of 10 million methaqualone tablets (Quaaludes) and 23,000 pounds of marijuana.

Other reports of official corruption have surfaced, alleging Cuban cooperation with drug smugglers who flew smuggling aircraft through Cuban airspace. According to the President's Commission on Organized Crime (America's Habit, 1986), this was accomplished by assigning the smuggling pilots a corridor or "window" through which they could pass without any interference from the Cuban government. Recently, the Cuban government tried and convicted several high-ranking military and government officials for participating in drug trafficking.

Mexico

United States government officials have always been hesitant to make public accusations of Mexican involvement in criminal activity and in particular the drug trade. Reasons for this are that Mexico is not only one of our closest neighbors but a staunch ally and trading partner as well (see Chapter 4).

Since the early 1980s, however, evidence has surfaced to support the assertion of official corruption in both the Mexican Directorate of Security and the Mexican Judicial Police. Probably one of the most widely publicized and tragic events that illustrated the complicity of several governmental officials in the Mexican drug trade was the 1985 abduction and murder of United States Drug Enforcement Agent Enrique Camarena Salazar and his pilot Alfredo Zavala Avelar in the city of Guadalajara. As a result of the subsequent investigation into this incident, six Mexican police officials were indicted on related charges, including protection of personnel and goods, custody of drugs while in transit, and providing information. The officers cited in this investigation were reportedly receiving payoffs for official protection that ranged from $200 to $6,250 a month.

One of these six officials, the First Commandante Jorge Armando Pavon Reyes of the Mexican Judicial Police (who also headed the Camarena investigation in Mexico), accepted a bribe from drug suspect Rafael Caro Quintero in exchange for Caro's freedom.

Subsequent to the Camarena incident, Mexican President Miguel de la Madrid announced a major reorganization and consolidation of police forces. Under the reorganization, one governor dismissed an entire judicial system, including the state attorney general and more than 100 security agents (see Chapter 9).

Foreign Corruption Allegations in the Drug Trade

Panama. General Manuel Antonio Noriega, the country's former military dictator, was indicted February 4, 1988 by two federal grand juries in the United States for allegedly accepting $4.6 million in bribes concerning drug trafficking activities. Noriega allegedly provided cocaine traffickers in the Medellin Cartel, which is thought to account for most of the cocaine that lands in the United States, with secure airstrips for transport. He is also charged with turning Panama into a money-laundering center and a safe haven for fugitives.

Haiti. Colonel Jean-Claude Paul, a senior military leader is suspected of aiding the flow of cocaine into the United States. His wife was indicted on drug charges in March 1987.

Honduras. Juan Ramon Matta Ballesteros, allegedly a major dealer in the Medellin Cartel, now lives in the Honduran capital and is a friend of senior officers and politicians. Matta is wanted in the United States for murdering a Drug Enforcement Agent in Mexico; Honduras refuses to extradite him.

Also, Jorge Ochoa, another alleged Medellin dealer, was arrested in November 1987 in Colombia while driving a Porsche that belonged to the Honduran military attaché to Colombia. This raised questions about how Ochoa borrowed the car and how the attaché could afford it on his military salary.

Bahamas. In February 1988, a known marijuana trafficker testified in Jacksonville, Florida, that he had paid Prime Minister Lynden Pindling $400,000 to allow marijuana shipments to pass safely through the Bahamas. In 1984, an independent commission of inquiry cleared Mr. Pindling of drug-related crimes, with reservations. The commission linked two Bahamian cabinet ministers to drug trafficking.

Mexico. In 1985, Enrique Camarena Salazar, a U.S. DEA agent, was kidnapped and killed in Mexico, allegedly by drug traffickers. In May, 1987, a Los Angeles grand jury indicted two officers in Mexico's Federal Judicial Police with preventing the apprehension of the kidnappers.

Colombia. In June 1987, Colombia's Supreme Court declared its extradition treaty with the United States unconstitutional. On December 30, a judge let Jorge Ochoa, a Medellin Cartel dealer who is wanted for the murder of a DEA agent walk out of prison. DEA agents say that Colombian drug enforcement units are so infiltrated with Medellin informers that they are unwilling to share information with their Colombian counterparts. [The tide turned again on August 18, 1989 when former President Virgilio Barco declared a "state of siege," suspended the normal operations of criminal and civil law, and reinstated extradition. This set off a civil war between the democratically elected government and the cocaine traffickers.]

Turks and Caicos Islands. Norman Saunders, chief minister of these Caribbean islands, was indicted by a U.S. grand jury in 1985 on drug charges. He later was tried in his own country and sentenced to eight years in prison.

Suriname. Military commander Atienne Boerenveen was convicted in September, 1986, by a federal grand jury in Miami of conspiring to sell safe passage through Suriname for cocaine-laden planes.

Source: Bradley, B. (1988). "Drug Suspicions Follow Officials in High Places." Reprinted by permission from the Christian Science Monitor, copyright 1988. The Christian Science Publishing Society. All rights reserved.

The Bahamas

The Bahamas and other countries in the Caribbean basin are ideally located for transshipment and refueling for drug smugglers from Mexican and South American countries. In fact, many allegations about the role of smugglers transshipping drugs in this region have surfaced since the early 1980s. In 1986, U.S. government intelligence reports alleged that widespread corruption had reached high government offices in the Caicos Islands where in March 1985, the Bahamas' Chief Minister Norman Saunders was convicted of conspiracy in a drug-trafficking scheme. Witnesses in the Saunders' trial testified that he received a total of $50,000 for allowing drugs from Colombia to pass freely through his country.

In yet another case, Bahamian Prime Minister Lynden Pindling was suspected in 1984 of complicity with drug traffickers when an investigation revealed that his personal bank accounts reflected deposits of $3.5 million in excess of his salary during a six-year period. Convicted drug trafficker Carlos Lehder (see Chapters 4 and 9) also commonly used Norman's Cay as a refueling and transshipment point for his cocaine runs between 1978 and 1982. Subsequent to Lehder's arrest in 1987, it was learned that Lehder paid "substantial bribes" to police and customs officials to aid him in trafficking cocaine to the United States (PCOC, America's Habit, 1986).

Panama

In the late 1980s, Panama and its leader at the time, General Manuel Antonio Noriega, a longtime United States ally, emerged in a complicated web of corruption and drug trafficking. In February 1988, he was indicted by federal grand juries in Miami and Tampa, Florida, on charges of drug trafficking, racketeering, and money laundering. Drug enforcement officials had been aware of Noriega's involvement in the drug trade since the early 1970s, but until December 1989, concern for maintaining stability in Panama and the Canal Zone outweighed United States concern for illicit drug activity there.

Noriega had previously worked as an informer for the Central Intelligence Agency (CIA) and allowed the agency to operate a listening post in Panama monitoring Central and South America. Lieutenant Colonel Oliver North, then a junior member of the National Security Council, and General Richard Secord also used Panama as a base for training soldiers and a place for setting up "dummy" corporations to help fund Nicaraguan contras.

In 1988, DEA reports disclosed that Noriega did provide information to the United States regarding certain drug smuggling operations. During that same time, he was accepting large bribes from Colombia's Medellin Cartel for his assistance in drug-trafficking operations and for offering cartel members a safe haven in Panama to avoid prosecution. In 1985, Senator Jesse Helms of North Carolina proposed legislation cutting off aid to Panama, only to be persuaded to withdraw it later because of Noriega's assistance to the contras.

In the summer of 1987, the second-in-command of Panama's defense forces, Colonel Roberto Diaz Herrera, went public with several charges aimed at Noriega. Diaz first accused Noriega of fraud in the 1984 presidential election. He also implicated Noriega in the 1981 death of Panama's President General Omar Torrijos, which at the time it occurred was thought to be accidental.

In the late 1980s, it became increasingly clear that Noriega had no intention of restoring democracy to Panama, in particular in the aftermath of national elections in 1989, in which "goon squads" were dispatched by Noriega to intimidate his opposition and the voters of Panama. Political corruption of the caliber seen in Panama, Mexico, and the Bahamas is slow in development but once entrenched, difficult to purge (see the following section on cocaine money and Panama).

Finally, Noriega's reign as leader of Panama ended on December 20, 1989, as President Bush authorized "Operation Just Cause," a surprise overnight invasion in which 2,000 U.S. troops invaded Panama. Although the initiative resulted in 23 U.S. soldiers being killed and more than 200 being injured, it was successful in restoring the democratically elected government to power.

The target of the invasion, Noriega, escaped during the attack, and remained on-the-run for about 48 hours. The deposed dictator then turned himself over to the Vatican Embassy on Christmas Eve, seeking political sanctuary and asylum. This sparked international diplomatic concern over the legality and appropriateness of using embassies to shelter suspected international drug traffickers who are wanted by the governments of other countries. On January 3 1990, Noriega turned himself into authorities of the DEA outside the Vatican Embassy. He was then transported to Miami to face federal drug trafficking charges.

Money Laundering

The illicit drug business is a *cash* business. At virtually every point along the distribution chain, each and every transaction is conducted with cash. With the rare exception of bartering with stolen goods bearing price tags, cash is the one commodity with a known value and which does not leave a paper trail for police to follow.

In the summer of 1991, news stories proliferated about how regulators in several foreign countries shut down the Bank of Commerce and Credit International (BCCI). Top executives of BCCI were convicted of money laundering charges in Tampa, Florida, New York, and Washington DC. BCCI was termed "the most pervasive money-laundering operation and financial supermarket ever created" and a steering service for Colombian drug traffickers to deposit hundreds of millions of dollars outside the country (Webster and McCampbell, 1992). As pervasive as it is, BCCI is still only one example of money-laundering operations that exists today. It is probably impossible to accurately determine how much money is laundered either domestically or in foreign countries annually. However, some perspective can be gained when considering that the total amount of money estimated to be spent on illicit drugs worldwide each year is $500 billion with $200 billion of that figure being spent in the United States (ONDCP, 1993:11).

While the benefits of dealing in cash are apparent, three serious problems present themselves to the drug trafficker. Cash is bulky and often heavy ($1 million in $20 bills weighs more than 100 pounds). Many trafficking organizations produce millions of dollars of profit per month, which must be regularly transported. Secondly, large amounts of cash laying around present an attractive target for rival criminals who might wish to steal it. After all, stolen drug money is usually not traceable and is easy to liquidate. Finally, drug cash can only be worth face value compared to legitimate business profits, which are available for reinvestment in stocks, bonds, money markets, or other potentially profitable investments.

The supreme paradox in the drug trade is that although many drug organizations produce considerable profits, persons in such organizations must struggle with how to enjoy those profits without getting caught. The trafficker's goal, of course, is to spend profits on ways to build the business as well as to enjoy a lavish lifestyle with expensive homes, clothing, nightlife, and luxury vehicles. However, the profits are syphoned off into salaries for employees, equipment, attorneys' fees, travel costs, and clandestine investments. In time, the drug money works its way into various aspects of the legitimate economy where it is all but impossible to detect.

The success enjoyed by drug traffickers poses somewhat of a dilemma for them: how to reduce the likelihood of detection and subsequent asset seizure by law enforcement officials. This is accomplished by a criminal technique known as money laundering, in which illegal cash proceeds are made to appear legitimate or in which the sources of illegal proceeds are disguised. As money laundering laws become more and more effective against the leaders of drug organizations, the risk of detection of such leaders is more likely. The money laundering process can take many forms, including: 1) simply merging illicit money with a legitimate cash source, which usually utilizes a business that generates large amounts of cash and 2) using sophisticated international money laundering techniques (discussed next). The goal of the financial investigation is to reduce the rewards achieved through drug trafficking and, therefore, immobilize drug trafficking organizations.

The term *money laundering* is defined as "the process of converting illegally earned assets, originating as cash, to one or more alternative forms to conceal incriminating factors such as illegal origin and true ownership" (NIJ, 1992:1). The practice of money laundering began in Switzerland during the 1930s as concerned Europeans began funnelling their capital beyond the clutches of Hitler's Third Reich. In time, Switzerland's well-known numbered accounts became an enormously profitable business. Today, Swiss bank secrecy laws have been relaxed due to numerous criminal cases involving money laundering. Criminals, therefore, are seeking other financial havens in which to deposit their ill-gotten gains.

The flooding of entire regions with drug money is one of the more sinister and surreptitious types of drug-related crime. The term "flooding," tracked by the regional Federal Reserve Banks, seems to describe this phenomenon with great precision. For example, every year since 1980, the Miami branch of the Federal Reserve Bank of Atlanta has reported a cash surplus in the $5 to $6 billion range. In the late 1980s, the Los Angeles Federal Reserve reported a great increase in its surplus; in 1988, the surplus was approximately $4 billion. Despite these surpluses and others like them, investigators have a difficult time pinpointing their exact origin.

It is ironic that the very institutions that could do the most to stop money laundering seem to have the least incentive to do so. For example, the basic fee for recycling money of a suspicious origin averages 4 percent while the rate for drug cash and other "hot" money may range from 7 percent to 10 percent.

Perhaps one should inquire why the investment of drug money in legitimate businesses should be a cause for concern. Considered very narrowly, the influx of large amounts of cash has provided some short-term financial benefits for Latin American debtor nations as well as for domestic beneficiaries of illegal drug money. It cannot be overemphasized, however, that this flood of money is not only a consequence of the drug problem but a major problem in its own right. The money that enters the local economy is a primary cause of inflation. Even the banks that stand to gain from accommodating drug traffickers ultimately bear the costs of any losses that drug-related transactions generate.

Part of the problem the United States has with regard to money-laundering activities is that American drug users are primarily consumers rather than producers of drugs. Additionally, the United States is used as a repository for large amounts of drug proceeds. Most drug profits are funneled to upper-echelon members of drug cartels rather than the low-level producers and growers. Therefore, it is because of the tremendous profits of drug trafficking organizations that new members are constantly being lured into this illicit business. Unfortunately, profits are also so large that any losses due to forfeitures by the government can usually be easily absorbed through future illicit dealings, making it unlikely that a drug organization will actually be put out of business.

Presumably, large-scale dealers consider that the risk of imprisonment or loss of assets is a mere risk of conducting business. Therefore, if we assume that the motivation behind the illicit drug trade is profit, then we should conclude that government action against such a lucrative class of crime must include an attack against the proceeds of that criminal act.

Operation Polar Cap

In March 1989, federal agents with search warrants seized three boxes of documents from the New York City branch of Continental Illinois Bank. This seizure was the culmination of a two-year investigation that broke up a Colombian Medellin cartel money laundering organization operating in Europe, South America, and the United States. Colombian cocaine manufactured by the Medellin Cartel was sold on the streets of New York. The cash from these sales was packed in boxes, labeled as jewelry, and delivered by armored car to La Guardia Airport for shipment to Los Angeles. The money was then delivered to nearby banks and deposited as if it were the proceeds of jewelry sales. Then it was transferred by wire back to New York banks. These unsuspecting banks wired the money to accounts in other New York banks. The money was then transferred by wire to banks in Colombia. During the first phase of the investigation, 127 persons were arrested. A federal grand jury in Atlanta returned indictments against two South American banks, charging involvement in laundering more than $300 million in drug proceeds in the United States. In the most recent phase, as of November 21, 1991, more than $10 million in cash and bank accounts has been seized.

Source: Webster and McCampbell, (1992). *International Money Laundering: Research and Investigation Join Forces.* National Institute of Justice. September: 1-7.

Between 1987 and 1990, both the FBI and the DEA have been actively involved in the investigation of this type of drug-related crime. In such investigations as Operation CASHWEB (FBI), Operation PISCES (DEA), and Operation C-CHASE (U.S. Customs), undercover agents infiltrated sophisticated money-laundering operations in the United States, Canada, Mexico, Panama, Colombia, the Bahamas, Aruba, and the Cayman Islands.

The Laundering Specialists

Technology and modern conveniences of the 1990s make it possible for modern-day money launderers to ply their craft. However, because most criminals fear detection by police agents, many have chosen to employ specialists to aid them. For a fee, laundering specialists sell their services to criminals, often in the form of multiservice packages but sometimes in a simple one or two step laundering process. Three types of laundering specialists can be identified for this purpose.

1. *Couriers* arrange for the movement of currency to a site designated for laundering, where the cash is converted to another method of payment such as money orders. In the event the courier is employed by a foreign trafficker, cash may be smuggled out of the country to a "safe" foreign jurisdiction with strict bank secrecy laws. The value of the courier rests in apparent legitimacy and lack of any obvious connection with the criminal who actually owns the money. In many cases, couriers don't even know the identity of the true owner of the currency.

2. *Currency exchange specialists* operate both formal and informal businesses that can either be a front for laundering operations or dedicated to illegal clientele. Of the most common formal exchanges is the *casa de cambio*, which exchanges dollars for pesos. As a rule, the exchanges are legitimate foreign currency exchange houses used by criminals seeking quasi-banking services.

3. *Business professionals* include attorneys, accountants, and even bankers who provide investment counseling, create nominee trust accounts, handle international funds transfers, and take advantage of tax avoidance schemes in foreign countries. The goal is to conceal the true origin of the assets under their control.

Those specialists who launder cash for large criminal organizations may create informal organizations to facilitate their services. Many laundering organizations are loose confederations united by a common criminal objective—profit. On only the rarest occasion does a laundering organization operate as part of a larger organization. Instead, specialists operate as part of a loose-knit network of entrepreneurs who sell their services on a piecemeal basis. Such organizations might work for more than one criminal organization at a time in addition to working for individuals who manage large criminal organizations at high levels.

Concealment

The first and foremost objective of the money laundering process is *concealment* of cash, the source of ownership, and the future destination of the illegal funds. If money launderers are not successful in hiding their cash and the ownership of it, then they run the risk of exposure to police, subsequent forfeiture of those assets, and possible imprisonment. To this end, launderers must consider a second objective—*anonymity*. This option becomes more practical with the threat of detection by police. So, the backup strategy becomes obvious: even if the illegal cash is discovered, its connection to the owner becomes obscure. One of the most typical ways of deterring investigation is through layers of false ownership and sales documents.

Figure 6.1
Money Laundering

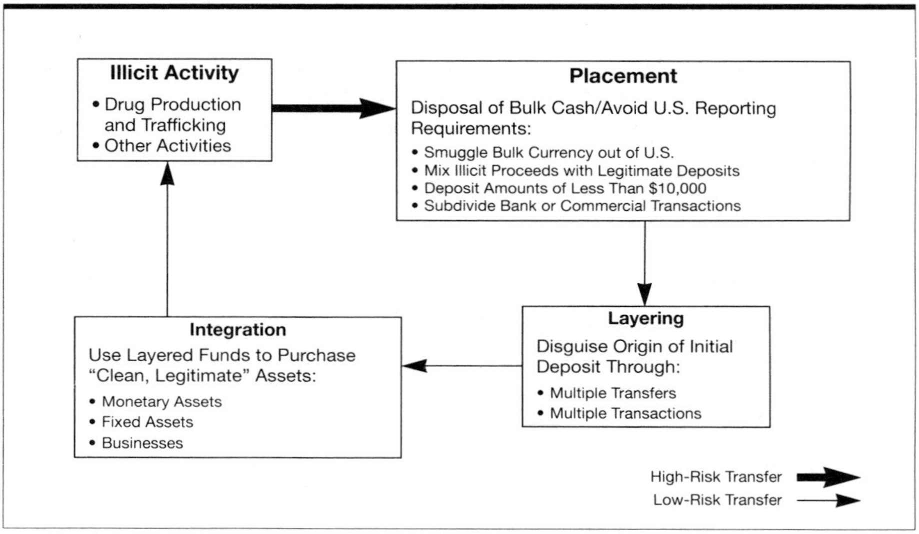

Source: ONDCP, 1989.

Money-Laundering Techniques

Illegal drug transactions are usually cash transactions using large amounts of currency to pay off the different actors in each drug deal and to purchase sophisticated equipment. It is important for the trafficker to legitimize cash proceeds in a fashion that permits the trafficker to spend it wherever and whenever he or she desires without attracting suspicion. Obviously, the trafficker could choose to store the cash in a strongbox or wall safe, but such methods would not be plausible for the trafficker who generates hundreds of thousands or even millions of dollars in illegal cash each year.

The many different techniques for laundering illicit proceeds are limited only by a trafficker's imagination and cunning. An entire wash cycle to transform small denominations of currency to legitimate business accounts, money market deposits, or real estate may take as little as 48 hours. The chosen method used by any given trafficker will no doubt reflect his or her own situation and any unique circumstances involved. The following six money-laundering techniques illustrate the ingenuity of the drug trafficker in hiding millions (and even billions) of dollars of illicitly gained revenues.

Technique 1—Bank Methods

The most common method for laundering money is one called "bank methods." In this basic technique, the trafficker takes cash to a bank and conducts a number of transactions that usually involve trading currency of small denominations for larger ones. This is done for obvious portability purposes. It is also common for cash to be exchanged for treasury bills, bank drafts, letters of credit, traveler's checks, or other monetary instruments.

In Miami (considered the hub of the cocaine banking business in the United States), large daily shipments of currency arrive and are deposited in numerous accounts, but they are then immediately disbursed through the writing of checks payable to true or nominee names. Ultimately, these funds will be deposited in other domestic accounts in the same or different banks or wire-transferred to offshore bank accounts in foreign countries with strict bank secrecy laws. Ironically, there is no requirement to report these transactions because the Bank Secrecy Act's reporting requirements do not pertain to interbank transfers. Therefore, the biggest problem posed to the traffickers is the initial depositing of the currency into the banks. Once funds are deposited, a trafficker can communicate with the bank through a fax machine or personal computer and literally route funds all over the world without ever coming face-to-face or even speaking with a banker. One method of conducting mass deposits, called "smurfing," first appeared during the mid-1980s and is discussed next.

Technique 2—Smurfing

A trafficker provides several individuals (or "smurfs") with cash from drug sales. Each smurf goes to different banks and purchases cashier's checks in denominations of less than $10,000, thus bypassing the reporting requirement. The smurfs then turn the checks over to a second individual, who facilitates the subsequent deposits into domestic banks or physically transports the checks to banks in Panama or Colombia. In some instances, the monetary instruments are premarked "for deposit only," making them nonnegotiable to the courier.

Figure 6.2
Smurfing

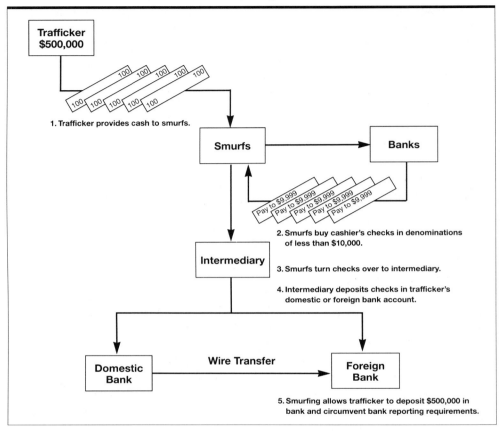

Source: DEA, 1987.

Steps in Smurfing Operations

1. Trafficker provides cash to smurfs.

2. Smurfs buy cashier's checks in denominations of $10,000 or
    less.

3. Smurfs turn checks over to an intermediary.

4. Intermediary deposits checks in trafficker's domestic or foreign
    bank account.

5. Smurfing allows trafficker to deposit $500,000 in bank and cir-
    cumvent bank reporting requirements.

When transporting monetary instruments out of the country, such as those described above, the trafficker is also able to circumvent the Bank Secrecy Act's guidelines which requires reporting the international transportation of currency in amounts of $10,000 or more. This is also a technique commonly adopted by money launderers.

Technique 3—Currency Exchanges

Traffickers may also use either money exchanges or brokerage houses for facilitating the movement of their money. Foreign currency exchanges are frequently set up as store fronts that deal in large cash transactions regularly. In using the exchange, the trafficker can avoid using traditional banking institutions and, therefore, avoid risky reporting requirements. Banks traditionally deal with exchange companies and customarily will not question large transactions from these businesses.

The currency exchange business can also move money in other ways for the trafficker. In particular, money sent to other jurisdictions in payment for foreign drug shipments is common. Using a "dummy" corporation, a trafficker will sometimes contact his lawyer and request that the lawyer accept a huge deposit into his foreign account. The lawyer will then wire the money directly into the dummy account, where it remains undetected.

Technique 4—Double Invoicing

Double invoicing is yet another popular method of hiding illicit financial gains. In this technique, a company orders merchandise from a foreign subsidiary at an inflated price. The difference between the inflated price and the actual price is deposited by the subsidiary in a special offshore account. Occasionally, the same technique in reverse is also employed. This occurs when the company sells merchandise at an artificially low price and the difference between the two prices is deposited in a secret foreign bank account maintained by the company.

Technique 5—Acquisition of Financial and other Legitimate Business Institutions

The fifth money-laundering method is possibly the most difficult of all to detect. It simply involves acquiring a domestic or international financial institution or other legitimate business. After all, by controlling an entire institution, traffickers can go far beyond the immediate aim of concealing illicit earnings. They effectively take over part of the local banking system or use an established business to either hide or divert funds for their own needs. In the case of banking institutions, traffickers are able to manipulate correspondent banking relations, make overnight deposits, arrange Eurodollar loans, and use the so-called abuse list (those customers exempted from cash reporting requirements). The use of legitimate businesses provides the criminal a legitimate source of employment and helps to cultivate a public image of respectability. Further, acquired legitimate businesses allow criminals a source of reportable income for tax purposes, which is especially useful when those businesses have a high cash turnover business. Examples of these businesses are bars, restaurants, entertainment establishments, and vending machines.

Technique 6—Wire Transfers

The wire transfer is one of the most commonly used methods for moving large amounts of money from one point to another. Its use depends on finding a United States-based financial institution willing to accept large cash deposits. One method used to accomplish this is for traffickers to bribe key bank personnel. For example, in 1980 and 1981, drug traffickers bribed a head teller, a loan officer, and the vice president of the Great American Bank in Miami. The bank processed large amounts of cash for a fee, which was divided among the three individuals and the bank. In exchange, the three employees agreed not to file CTRs. Instead, they issued the traffickers cashier's checks disguised as loan proceeds that were used to make wire transfers.

Thinking Critically #11

Write a letter to one of your U.S. Senators or Representatives asking that stricter laws be enacted to combat money laundering by drug traffickers. Be specific in your suggestions.

Fighting Money Laundering

One principal tool utilized to detect, measure, and punish money laundering is the *Bank Secrecy Act (BSA)*, originally passed into law in 1970. The BSA can help authorities flag the movement of illegally acquired cash moving through banking institutions and across international borders. However, the very inclusion of a minimum dollar amount has given traffickers a way to skirt around the law. Criminals can simply deposit less than the $10,000 amount which triggers banking records of a deposit. In any case, the current regulations under this act, issued by the Secretary of the Treasury, provide law enforcement with several basic tools to investigate money laundering:

1. A *paper trail* of bank records must be maintained up to five years.
2. A *Currency Transaction Report (CTR)* must be filed with the Internal Revenue Service within 15 days when a currency transaction is more than $10,000. Notably omitted from the reporting requirements, however, are wire transfers, bank checks, bank drafts, or other written orders of transfer. In 1989, the U.S. government processed an estimated seven million CTRs, compared to an estimated 100,000 ten years earlier. Traffickers quickly circumvented this requirement by bribing bank employees.
3. A *Currency or Monetary Instrument Report (CMIR)* must be filed whenever currency or monetary instruments of more than $10,000 are taken into or out of the United States. CMIRs are filed with the Customs Service. Cashier's checks and bearer bonds made out to cash (rather than to an individual) are not covered by the reporting requirements.

Another powerful tool to combat money laundering is the Currency and Foreign Transactions Reporting Act, which empowers the United States government to compel other countries to maintain certain records similar to those used under the BSA. Finally, one the greatest prosecutorial and investigative aids in years was the enactment of the Money Laundering Control Act. Prior to its passage by Congress in 1986, money laundering, per se, was not a crime, although various federal statutes were used to prosecute different stages of the money laundering process. Under the new act, money laundering was made a separate violation of federal law punishable by a fine of $500,000 or twice the value of the property involved, whichever is greater, and twenty years imprisonment. Powerful forfeiture clauses were also added to federal law in 1988, which provide for the seizure of any property associated with a money-laundering scheme.

Money Laundering: How It Works

An American "businessman" approaches a banking officer of the Curacao branch of the French-owned Credit Lyonnais Nederland with an offer to deposit a six-figure cash windfall from a successful "business venture." After assuring the banker that the money is not tainted, the trafficker persuades the banker to facilitate the transaction, referring to the banking arrangement as a "Dutch Sandwich."

Under this plan, the Paris bank sets up a corporation for the customer in Rotterdam, where he deposits his cash in the bank's local branch. The American controls the newly created Dutch corporation through an Antilles trust company, but his identity as the owner is protected by the island group's impenetrable secrecy laws. The Caribbean branch then "lends" the American his own money held in Rotterdam. If the American is questioned by the Internal Revenue Service or other authorities about the source of his wealth, he can point to his loan from a respected international bank.

Source: Beaty, J. and R. Hornik (1989). "A Torrent of Dirty Dollars." *Time* (December 18):50-56.

The Money Laundering Prosecution Improvement Act of 1988 included a provision authorizing the U.S. Department of Treasury to require financial institutions to verify the identity of persons who purchase bank checks or money orders in amounts of $3,000 or more. The law also authorized the Secretary of the Treasury to target certain types of institutions or geographic areas for special reporting requirements.

These techniques represent only a few of the ways traffickers hide their illicit revenues from drug sales. It is generally thought that traffickers, regardless of their national origin, make regular use of these techniques. The fact that so many different mechanisms exist for money laundering makes investigation of these crimes difficult and presents many unique challenges to the investigator.

Financial Havens

Because of the sophistication of the international financial community, there exists a custom-made mechanism for the laundering of illegally made currency. The financial tax haven is, therefore, an attractive and effective mechanism for money laundering. Countries whose laws provide little or no tax on certain sources of income and in some cases where strict bank secrecy laws play an important role in international banking are popular places for the trafficker to seek a tax haven. The use of an international tax haven allows the trafficker not only to achieve a tax benefit but also to effectively move money easily while insuring anonymity.

Let us examine the specific reasons why traffickers may choose a particular tax haven. Several factors might contribute to this decision, in particular, ease of access and proximity to established trafficking routes. This explains why North and South American traffickers alike frequently choose havens in the Caribbean. The Cayman Islands, for example, offer secrecy to traffickers and can easily be reached by air from both continents. Certain features are generally favored by drug traffickers in their selection of financial havens:

- little or no tax on foreign earnings of foreign-owned corporations
- lax corporation laws
- commercial and/or bank secrecy
- attractive transportation and communications facilities
- minimal restrictions on foreign currency exchange of foreign corporations or individuals
- location near established trafficking routes
- relatively stable political climate
- availability of professional and/or business advice and assistance

One of the first obstacles that the trafficker must overcome is convincing the financial institution with access to international transfer facilities to accommodate deposits of large amounts of cash on a regular basis. The trafficker realizes that once the money is introduced into the financial system, it then becomes virtually indistinguishable from legitimate monies and can easily be moved, both quickly and confidentially, through the system. Indeed, the very aspects of this system which are designed to protect legitimate confidential business dealings are the ones that conceal the proceeds of the illegal drug trade and inhibit law enforcement efforts.

Cocaine Money and Panama

For years Panama has served the cocaine trafficking community of South America as a money laundering hub. In Panama, the Banco Nacional de Panama acts much like the Federal Reserve Bank in the United States in that it is a clearinghouse for cash. In 1982, the U.S. Department of the Treasury examined Federal Reserve receipts of Banco Nacional de Panama to determine the amount of cocaine money accumulated in Panama. In the audit, it was determined that there was a four-fold increase in reported cash flow between 1980 and 1983. This cash flow, as it was concluded, was probably the most significant recorded flow of currency and was most likely illegal drug money. The Treasury Department during this inquiry estimated that more than $2.2 billion in unreported cash was transported to Panama through a variety of methods.

Heroin Money and Hong Kong

In 1984, the President's Commission on Organized Crime began to evaluate the heroin trafficking networks operating in southeast Asia. It was determined that southeast Asia's share of the opium and heroin business increased by 10 percent in 1981, 14 percent in 1982, and 19 percent in 1983. In fact, in 1983 the heroin originating in southeast Asia accounted for an estimated 41 percent of the heroin seized or detected in the United States.

Hong Kong's role in laundering money from the heroin trade in Southeast Asia parallels that of Panama in the South American cocaine trade. Hong Kong's specific role has been defined by the President's Commission on Organized Crime as follows:

> Hong Kong is the major financial center for Southeast Asia's drug trafficking. Hong Kong-based trafficking organizations operate throughout the world. Longstanding ties between Hong Kong traffickers and sources of supply in Thailand allow Hong Kong organizations to operate on a very large scale. Large numbers of heroin trafficking ventures throughout the world are financed and controlled from Hong Kong. There is evidence that Hong Kong-based groups are involved in directing the smuggling of heroin into Europe and North America.

Specific information regarding the extent of Hong Kong's involvement in laundering money in southeast Asia has been difficult to acquire. This is primarily due to two factors: (1) inordinately strict bank secrecy laws there preclude foreign law enforcement agencies from obtaining required information during criminal investigations and (2) the country lacks currency exchange controls and a central bank, which makes it difficult to trace the flow of funds to and from Hong Kong.

> Responsible for moving most heroin money in Southeast Asia, it operates through gold shops, trading companies, and money changers, many of which are operated in various countries by members of the same Chinese family. Record keeping susceptible to standard audit rarely exists in this underground banking system, and coded messages, "chits," and simple telephone calls are used to transfer money from one country to another. Nonetheless, the system has the ability to transfer funds from one country to another in a matter of hours, provide complete anonymity and total security for the customer, convert gold or other items into currency, and convert one currency into that of the customer's choice.

Source: PCOC, 1986.

Detecting the Money Launderer

Money laundering is a sophisticated white-collar crime requiring the use of several investigative techniques. Generally, the circumstances of any particular case will dictate a specific investigative technique.

- *The financial audit.* It is essential for law enforcement agencies and responsible banking authorities to maintain a degree of expertise in tracking records and accounting techniques. Such audits have aided authorities in locating discrepancies between the amounts of income and other assets accumulated by suspects and their reported "legitimate" income. This technique relies upon the IRS technique commonly called the "net worth" method.

- *Undercover operations.* Another powerful money laundering detection technique is the use of undercover agents in **sting operations**. Such investigations involve undercover agents posing as either criminals who are in search of laundering services or the launderers themselves who are offering their services to traffickers.

- *Electronic surveillance.* Through the use of hidden "bugs" and wiretaps, police are able to document conversations between launderers and traffickers who discuss specifics about the movement of drug money into hidden assets. This technique, stemming from authorized court orders, is one of the most effective but presents a labor-intensive operation for police—one that is cost-prohibitive, time consuming, and requires considerable training for officers.

As police pressure traffickers in any given geographical area, distribution operations will most likely move to other locations. Accordingly, so will their money-laundering operations, extending into more communities across the nation. As a result, police are continuing the struggle to meet the fast pace of the illicit business, the changing distribution operations, and the innovative schemes that permit criminals to make, hide, and spend their ill-gotten gains.

Summary

When the so-called drug problem is discussed, the subject of drug-related crime is also deliberated. The very term "drug-related crime" means different things to different people because it represents many types of criminal activity. Although many consider drug crimes to be street crimes, for example, robbery, assault, burglary, and murder, other crimes also accompany drug abuse.

Studies of the behavior of drug users have revealed that the crime rate (street-type crimes) for users may be anywhere from four to six times as high as for nondrug users. In addition to street crimes associated with drug use, ancillary crimes such as corruption and money laundering accompany drug use.

Official corruption in the United States poses a major problem for drug control strategists and enforcement officials. Corruption is pervasive and may take any of several forms, from bribery, extortion, favoritism, and mooching to more serious types of corruption, such as perjury, premeditated theft, and shakedowns of suspects.

Both the Knapp and the Mollen Commissions' inquiries into police corruption in New York have shed light on the city's corruption within the police department. In addition, many cases of police and official corruption have surfaced around the country, making it clear that the drug trade can penetrate even the most reputable of professions.

The problem of foreign corruption parallels that experienced in the United States with even greater repercussions. Many drug-source countries, such as Colombia, Peru, and Myanmar, are experiencing criminal forces that threaten to rival the legitimate government because of political influence gained through payoffs. Unscrupulous links have been documented between Panama's former dictator Manuel Noriega and Fidel Castro (see Chapter 9), between Colombian traffickers and Honduran officials, and between high-ranking Mexican Federal Judicial Police officials and known heroin traffickers in Mexico.

For decades, the laundering of illegally obtained currency has been a logistical problem for many organized crime organizations. The trafficker's basic concern is how to transform illegally obtained money to currency appearing to be legitimate.

The 1970 Bank Secrecy Act has provided investigators with much-needed legal tools with which to combat this type of crime. These tools consist of specific reporting requirements for banking institutions and individuals alike.

These reporting requirements enable investigators to follow the path of illicitly gained currency to its source.

Money-laundering techniques are sophisticated and represent considerable ingenuity on the part of the criminal. Such techniques include bank methods, "smurfing," the use of currency exchanges, and a technique called double invoicing. Laundered money is typically routed to financial institutions in foreign countries whose bank secrecy laws are much stricter than those of the United States. This gives traffickers considerable flexibility in the movement and storage of illicitly gained currency.

Do you recognize these terms?

Drug Abuse Reporting Program	Mollen Commission
Drug Use Forecasting	Pennsylvania Crime Commission
grass eaters	smurfing
institutional corruption	socialization
Knapp Commission	Treatment Outcome Perspective Study
meat eaters	Wickersham Commission

Discussion Questions

1. List three reasons why corruption is considered a threat to public safety.

2. Discuss the different types of corruption commonly practiced by corrupt police officers.

3. List the sequence of events that occur during the practice of "smurfing" in a money-laundering operation.

4. What roles do Panama and Hong Kong play in global drug trafficking?

5. Discuss the use of currency exchanges in money-laundering operations.

6. Discuss the Bank Secrecy Act (1970) and the use of the CTR, and the CMIR, as each pertains to money laundering investigations.

7. What is the difference between corrupt officials who are termed "grass eaters" and those called "meat eaters?"

8. List the four basic legal tools to investigate money laundering as provided for under the Bank Secrecy Act.

9. List and discuss the six most common techniques used by traffickers to launder illicitly gained currency.

Part II

Gangs and Drugs

Organized crime has historically played an important role in American society. The drug problem specifically has afforded many organized criminals increased sources of revenue with which to expand their operations and influence throughout the nation's communities. Accordingly, conflicts between these organizations have also escalated resulting in gangs warring with each other over territory and gangs recruiting new members from our schools. Furthermore, larger crime organizations have developed the resources and capabilities to insulate themselves from detection by infiltrating legitimate businesses and corrupting public officials. This section will examine the concept of organized crime, its origins and growth, and its growing alliance with the illicit drug trade.

Organized Crime and the Drug Trade   *7*

This chapter will enable you to:

- Understand the term *organized crime*
- Differentiate between traditional and nontraditional organized crime
- Understand the alien conspiracy theory
- Understand the factors that contribute to the growth of nontraditional organized crime

---

Reminiscent of Prohibition-era gangs, today's drug trafficking organizations are varied and have become increasingly organized and powerful. With an array of ethnically and geographically based groups, today's illicit drug trafficking organizations have surpassed the sophistication and influence of many of their early twentieth-century counterparts.

Crime in America has undergone many significant changes since the Roaring Twenties but today has become more pernicious due to two interrelated developments: drug abuse and organized crime. For decades, the **Mafia** was thought to have monopolized the drug trade, but today many different criminal groups compete for territory and the tax-free profits offered by illicit drugs.

For many years the term organized crime was synonymous with **La Cosa Nostra,** or the *Mafia*. This term, discussed later in this chapter, generally refers to the popular public view of Italian and Sicilian criminal groups. Although both Sicilian and Italian-American criminal organizations are involved in the lucrative drug trade, so are many other criminal groups. All of these groups have their sights set on the immense profits to be earned in drugs. Indeed, such profits can be considerable. For example, in 1989 the FBI reported that the Sicilian criminal organizations alone netted an estimated $40 billion in heroin revenues. Today's groups whose criminal enterprises focus on the illegal drug trade include outlaw motorcycle gangs, Jamaican posses, African-American organized crime groups, and California-based youth gangs, to name a few.

Organized crime has not only demonstrated an alarming degree of violence but also an ability to corrupt public officials at the highest levels. The pervasiveness of such activity threatens businesses and neighborhoods. To operate both efficiently and effectively, large-scale drug trafficking operations require superb organization. These abilities are essential in order to avoid police detection while maintaining their ability to compete with other criminal groups. To this end, these organizations can be characterized by a number of common activities. These include:

- obtaining the illicit substances (or the raw materials with which to manufacture them);
- making "connections" to acquire the illicit substances;
- arranging for the processing of drugs (either through overseas or domestic sources);
- developing smuggling networks with which to transport illicit materials;
- arranging for protection of the operation through corruption of public officials or the hiring of enforcers;
- locating distributors on both the wholesale and retail levels;
- developing a process whereby illegal money can be laundered or otherwise concealed from detection by law enforcement authorities.

In the coming chapters we will consider some of the significant actors on the criminal side of the "war on drugs." The following segment, however, is intended to acquaint the reader with various gang characteristics so rational conclusions can be drawn regarding the role of organized crime in the American drug scene.

The Nature of Drug Trafficking

As we observed in Chapter 6, there is no single drug problem in America, but rather myriad separate drug problems, each of which interact with one another. Likewise, there is no single, predictable pattern for drug trafficking organizations. They vary widely in size, sophistication, area of operation, clientele, and product. They also have varying degrees of vertical and horizontal integration, different proclivities for the use of violence, and distinct patterns of interaction with one another.

Obviously, drug trafficking organizations share the distinct characteristic of being engaged in the same illegal business, but because of that they do not have access to and are not subject to the normal channels of production, distribution, sales, finance, taxation, regulation, and contract enforcement that shape the legitimate business arena. Ironically, a dichotomy presents itself as this illicit "business" is still subject to many of the same dynamics as the laws of supply and demand, the need for efficiency in operation, and the necessity for a set of rules by which to operate. Traffickers must operate outside of the normal financial and legal structures of commerce while at the same time remaining subject to all of the market pressures which that structure normally accommodates. Recognizing this dichotomy is one of the keys to understanding the nature of drug trafficking organizations.

To best understand the nature of drug trafficking organizations, we must realize that such organizations re-create the structures of legitimate commerce. Experience shows us that many of these organizations do so with astonishing precision, yet they are skewed by the limitations of the illicit nature of their activities.

As we will discuss in the upcoming chapters, some of the more well-established organizations may have a board of directors, a CEO (chief executive officer), and a bureaucracy which is disciplined and whose functions and benefits mirror those of executives and middle management in modern corporations. To that extent, many enjoy amenities such as expense accounts, bonuses, and even company cars. On the other hand, the normal commercial concept of contracts, in which disputes are adjudicated by an impartial judiciary, and restitution, which is almost always of a financial nature, is skewed in the world of drug trafficking. Here, a system exists where the rule of law has been replaced by the threat of violence and retribution.

Although there is no single type of organizational structure that describes major drug trafficking organizations, a few well-defined patterns have been identified. First, there are major international, vertically integrated trafficking organizations which are best exemplified by the Colombian cartels (see Chapter 9). In addition, other groups, such as outlaw motorcycle gangs, operate domestically and tend to have smaller, less sophisticated operations. For example, their lines of supply are shorter, bank accounts are fewer, and the quantities of drugs transported are not as great. Next, there are city-based groups, such as youth gangs, which operate in many of our large, inner-city areas. These groups tend to have minimal organization in the management end of their operations but still have extensive distribution networks run by low-level operatives, many of whom work directly on the street and concentrate primarily on local distribution and retail aspects of drug distribution (see Chapter 8).

Two features common to many of the larger trafficking organizations are their ability to tap into alternate sources of supply and to adapt to readily changing conditions. For example, the Cali Cartel can buy its coca leaves or paste in either Peru, Bolivia, Ecuador, or Colombia itself. This flexibility enables the major traffickers to regroup and redirect a segment of their operations without disrupting the entire organization. In many respects, Colombian trafficking organizations are on the cutting edge of international technology. They easily operate across international borders, and the flexibility of their organizational structure enables them to form partnerships with other groups.

Like large legitimate corporations, major traffickers are immense because they are good at what they do. Careless errors are few as are unnecessary risks. Leaders of these organizations are keenly aware of the importance of being insulated from street-level drug sales. One of the characteristics that prevails in the world of drug trafficking is the predilection for dealing in cash and the incentive to transfer that cash into the legitimate economy so it can be converted into goods and services from the legitimate business community. This alone represents one of the biggest problems for trafficking organizations. In fact, so much cash is involved in the drug trade that it is often more advantageous for police to track cash proceeds than the drugs themselves. Indeed, it is the money from which even the most cautious drug manager can not be totally isolated. Accordingly, tracking this money, as we discussed in the previous chapter, remains one of the most challenging investigative endeavors for drug control agents.

Defining "Organized Crime"

Organized crime is a complex criminal phenomenon which conjures up the image of gangsters with broad-rimmed hats, dark pin-striped suits, and Thompson submachine guns. Over the years, this popular image has been perpetuated by movies, television, and novels and tends to leave the average person with a limited concept of the term. Contributing to the enigma of organized crime is the absence of a codified "legal" definition of it. Ironically, despite the lack of an official definition of the term, many federal statutes address types of criminal activity which typically involves organized crime. For example, statutes exist dealing with criminal conspiracies, continuing criminal enterprise (CCE), and racketeer-influenced and corrupt organizations (RICO), but all of these are separate from and more specific than the general term "organized crime."

The very words "organized crime" imply criminal involvement by a group of individuals operating in an organized fashion. But, does this broad definition include a group of three youths involved with a shoplifting scheme, or should it be applied to larger, more sophisticated criminal organizations? The general term itself fails to give adequate guidelines to criminal justice professionals, who are in need of a more precise distinction between the high-level organized drug trafficking organization and a group of two or three low-level "street-corner" drug dealers. In 1968, Congress passed into law the first major organized crime bill, the Omnibus Crime Control and Safe Streets Act, which is the only federal statute that refers to the term organized crime. As part of the act, the term is loosely described as follows:

> [Organized crime includes] the unlawful activities of members of a highly organized, disciplined association engaged in supplying illegal goods or services, including but not limited to gambling, prostitution, loansharking, narcotics, labor racketeering, and other unlawful activities. . . .

Clarity was given to the term when the President's Commission on Organized Crime concluded in 1986 that several variables can be identified that make up an organized crime unit (PCOC, The Edge, 1986). These include: 1) the **criminal group,** which is made up of core persons who share certain bonds; 2) the **protectors,** who protect the group's interests; and 3) **specialized support,** which consists of persons who knowingly render services on an ad hoc basis. We will now examine each of these.

The Criminal Group. The criminal group is composed of individuals who are usually bound by ethnic, racial, geographic, or lingual ties. The individuals display a willingness to engage in criminal activity for profit while using violence and intimidation to protect their criminal interests and to avoid detection. Organized crime (hereinafter referred to as "OC") groups are characterized by the longevity of the group itself, which outlasts the lives of individual members. Such a group maintains rules and a code of conduct while its management is structured in a hierarchical or pyramid-style chain of command.

Membership in the OC group is restricted and is usually based on a common trait, talent, or need of the group. Acceptance into the criminal group is closely scrutinized by the existing members, and typically an initiation is required for all recruits. Motivation for individual membership is based on the premise that the successful recruit will enjoy economic gain, protection by the group, and a certain prestige within the organization.

The Protectors. The protectors are usually associates of the criminal group that appear (at least on the surface) to be law-abiding members of the community. In fact, this group may include prominent members of the community such as corrupt politicians, bankers, attorneys, or accountants. They work to insulate the criminal group from government interference and to protect the assets of the organization.

Specialized Support. The larger the criminal group, the more it is in need of specialized support. Those individuals offering specialized support for the OC unit make up a component that possesses talent enabling the group to attain its goals and objectives. Unlike the seemingly lawful existence of the protectors, specialists include laboratory chemists, smuggling pilots, and enforcers ("hit men") for the OC unit. Most OC specialists are overtly involved in illicit aspects of criminality.

In addition to the specialists discussed above, the organized crime group relies on outside individuals, that is, members of the general public for financial and other support:

A. *User Support.* User support includes those individuals that purchase the OC group's illegal goods and services. These individuals include drug users, patrons of prostitutes, bookmakers, and those that willfully purchase stolen goods.

B. *Social Support.* Social support includes individuals and organizations that grant power and an air of legitimacy to organized crime generally and to certain groups and their members specifically. Social support includes public officials that solicit the support of organized crime figures, business leaders that do business with organized crime figures, and those that portray the criminal group or organized crime in a favorable or glamorous light.

When considering organized crime organizations in both the United States and in foreign countries, several operative characteristics can be recognized. One such characteristic is the attempt by the group to compete with the functions of legitimate government. Examples include the following:

- *In Colombia:* cocaine cartels such as the Medellin and Cali Cartels are competing with the legitimate government in attempting to control segments of the society, offering to pay off the country's national debt and generally acting like an alternative government.

- *In Italy:* the Sicilian Mafia has been responsible for the assassinations of many investigators and federal police that were assigned to anti-Mafia investigations. In addition, judges, mayors, union leaders, and representatives of government have been killed by organized crime members because they opposed the political or criminal activities of the Mafia.

- *In Myanmar:* the Shan United Army has used force to control the Shan State since 1948 when Myanmar became independent from the British.

In the United States, such displays of violence against the government are not quite as blatant, but many of the same principles are still at work. In one case, for example, organized crime members in Chicago attempted to levy a "street tax" on bookmakers and pornographers. Although these activities are illicit, the function of taxing is one rightfully belonging to legitimate government. Additionally, many cities that have experienced the influx of youth gangs have recognized that these groups have attempted to take control of neighborhoods for crack distribution. In many cases, witnesses who have offered to testify against criminal organizations have been intimidated because of the organization's reputation and encouraged not to cooperate with the government through threat of violence. Clearly, this characteristic of the organized crime unit threatens many of the fundamentals of a free, civilized society.

Thinking Critically #12

Hollywood occasionally produces films about organized crime (*The Godfather, Goodfellas, Scarface*). Evaluate the role the movie industry plays in supporting organized crime.

According to the U.S. Department of Justice, for a criminal group to be considered an organized crime group, several variables must be present. It must have an organizational structure, it has to engage in a continuing criminal conspiracy, its underlying goal must be the generation of profits, and it must have sufficient continuity to carry out its purpose over a long period of time. Groups which fit into this category include both foreign and domestic organizations and will be discussed later in this chapter.

Numerous similarities are evident between the groups discussed in this and the following two chapters. They all have taken advantage of the burgeoning market for illegal drugs and the numerous international sources for those drugs. Other similarities include a common disrespect for the law, a willingness to use violence to further their individual group goals, and the use of corruption to aid them in achieving their criminal intentions. Individually, each organized crime group poses an individual threat to society and public order, but collectively they make up what we consider the true scope of organized crime in the 1990s.

The Alien Conspiracy Theory

The very term *organized crime* tends to invoke images of men of foreign descent, steeped in feudal traditions and sharing a blind allegiance to the organization to which they belong. These images are what some criminologists have dubbed the **alien conspiracy theory** of organized crime. This theory holds that organized crime is a direct spin-off of a secret criminal society—the Mafia, a criminal organization dating back to Sicily during the mid-1800s. The basic premise of the theory is that the Mafia is a single organization that is centrally coordinated through a national commission which arbitrates disputes and mandates policy (Cressey, 1969).

There is considerable debate among scholars as to whether such a multinational organization actually exists, although some local, state, and federal law enforcement agencies are convinced of its authentication and base the formation of public organized crime policy on that premise. Disbelievers in the alien conspiracy theory argue that the Mafia is a figment of both the media's and law enforcement's imagination. They insist that organized crime consists of numerous ethnically diverse groups who compete for profits in the providing of illegal goods and services. Furthermore, they claim that these groups are not bound by a single, national organizational leadership but act independently on their own.

Thinking Critically #13

Do you believe the Mafia exists or is it merely a myth—an exaggerated stereotype? Support or refute your belief in the Alien Conspiracy Theory.

Supporters of the alien conspiracy theory conceive two organized crime contingencies: traditional organized crime (the Mafia) and nontraditional organized crime. The latter represents organized criminal groups which have emerged during the last two decades and who have focused on the illegal drug trade as their major source of illegal revenue. They are made up of ethnic groups that include blacks, Hispanics, and Asians. The next section will briefly discuss the alleged role of the Mafia as traditional organized crime participants in the drug trade followed by a discussion of some emerging nontraditional drug trafficking groups.

The Mafia

At the core of the alien conspiracy is the traditional crime group known as the La Cosa Nostra (this thing of ours), or more commonly, the Mafia. Operating in different factions in both Sicily and the United States, the Mafia is thought to have "**families**" in 24 or so major U.S. cities. It is estimated that although total membership is around 1,700 "**made men**" or "**wise guys**," the influence of the organization is much greater due to a vast network of associates who are not actual members (PCOC, The Edge, 1986). In 1986 the President's Commission on Organized Crime estimated that as many as 17,000 associates are criminally involved in the businesses of the "mob."

Mafia crime families are believed to operate in geographically assigned areas around the United States. In New York City, for example, five families—the Gambino, Colombo, Lucchese, Bonnano and Genovese—operate, each named after their founding godfathers and heavily involved in both illicit and legitimate businesses.

Most traditional crime families got their start during Prohibition (1920-1933) in the illegal liquor business. This created a multimillion-dollar bootlegging business following violent wars over territory and the control of illegal rackets. Today, believers of the alien conspiracy theory argue that the Mafia represents a highly sophisticated criminal network with a complex structure and chain of command that is emulated by many other new and emerging crime groups. Although not every Mafia family participates in the illicit drug trade, many do. For decades the primary illicit drug sold by alleged Mafia members was heroin. Today heroin is still worth an estimated $40 million per year to the organization, but trafficking in cocaine and marijuana has also been documented. In addition to drugs, Mafia families deal in loan-sharking, illegal gambling operations, public corruption, money-laundering operations, and an array of legal business enterprises designed to cloak their criminal rackets.

In many cities, the nontraditional crime organizations, such as the Colombian cartels and the youth gangs, have rivaled the Mafia for territory. In some cases, drug territory has even been surrendered to the newer gangs with drugs being viewed as too risky or competitive. In the 1990s, advocates of the Mafia theory argue that the Mafia is still a strong criminal organization with criminal interests all over the world. However, they assert that a new breed of mafioso is beginning to emerge. The new mafiosi are more willing to inform on fellow mafiosi and seem to be more oriented to individual gain than family organization. For example, in 1992, New York mob boss John Gotti was convicted after his underboss turned federal witness and offered damaging testimony as to his role in the murder of former mob boss Paul Castellano.

Drug Gangs as Organized Crime

Those criminal organizations concerned solely with drug trafficking share many of the same characteristics as more established organized crime. In the early 1970s a new kind of drug trafficking organization began to emerge. Four fundamental factors can be seen as contributing to the genesis of this new configuration of organized crime:

1. Profound social, political, and economic changes in the drug-producing and drug-consuming nations combined to accelerate and intensify the spread of drugs.
2. There was vastly increased mobility within and between consuming and producing nations, and this was aided by cheap, readily available, international transportation. Also immigration greatly increased from South America and the Far East to the United States.
3. In the opium-producing countries, many peasants and urban workers had surplus time for the kinds of work needed to sustain the drug traffic.
4. In the consuming nations, old restrictions against many types of behavior, including the taking of drugs, had declined sharply. All of these factors made possible a new kind of trafficking.

When attempting to understand these organizations as a whole, we should first recognize that no one drug trafficking organization is "typical." Rather, a multiplicity of trafficking organizations follow a few well-defined patterns. Thus, as mentioned above, several conditions exist that seem to lend cohesiveness to the modern-day drug trafficking organization: vertical integration, alternate sources of supply, exploitation of social and political conditions, and insulation of leaders from the distribution network.

1. *Vertical Integration.* **Vertical integration** is illustrated by the major international trafficking groups such as the Colombian cartels and some domestic criminal groups like outlaw motorcycle gangs that control both the manufacturing and wholesale distribution of drugs. Also, city-based operations such as the California street gangs, which concentrate on domestic distribution and retail sales, represent an organization with operations that are more directly linked to the end user than are the Colombian cartels or the motorcycle gangs.

2. *Alternate Sources of Supply.* Among the various types of organizational structures and operational types, most have common distribution channels and operating methods. Many cocaine and heroin trafficking groups acquire illicit drugs outside of the United States and from any of a number of sources. This principle was illustrated when the Turkish government clamped down on the illicit cultivation of opium poppies, drug organizations shifted their production to regions in the Golden Triangle in southeast Asia and the Golden Crescent in southwest Asia. Exceptions are marijuana and certain drugs made in domestic clandestine labs. Consequently, distribution channels are long and complicated. For instance, there are numerous links between the coca leaves grown and harvested in the Huallaga Valley of Peru and the destination of the finished product—an American city.

3. *Exploitation of Social and Political Conditions.* Drug trafficking organizations today demonstrate a willingness to capitalize on vulnerable social and national milieus. This occurs, for instance, in inner-city areas and even countries where labor markets are willing to take risks to partake of the huge profit potential offered in drug trafficking operations. Generally, most players drawn into drug trafficking are expendable, provided that the leaders remain untouched. The leaders can then choose individuals from a large pool of unskilled labor. These individuals must be willing to take personal risks and be able to learn one or two menial duties in the trafficking system.

    Traffickers have even demonstrated that they can manipulate market conditions to make trafficking more profitable. In particular, the introduction of black tar heroin in the mid-1980s was a response to heroin shortages while the change from cocaine HCl to crack in the mid-1980s was also an effort to offer the nonaffluent drug user affordable cocaine.

4. *Insulation of Leaders.* The organizational structure of a drug trafficking group can be described as a solar system with the leaders at the center. It is only these leaders (or kingpins) that see the organization as a whole. Trafficking leaders minimize any contact with drug buyers or the drugs themselves as a strategic effort to insulate themselves from governmental detection.

Although the four preceding operational variables help explain how drug trafficking organizations function, they fail to adequately explain the tremendous growth of such groups. The growth of a particular organization can partially be attributed to highly addictive qualities of some drugs such as heroin. This accounts, at least in part, for a certain degree of "return business" for many trafficking organizations. Here, the drug users themselves effectively become salesmen or "ambassadors" who work in behalf of the drug trafficking organization by introducing drugs to new users. Additionally, powdered drugs such as heroin can be much more easily transported (smuggled) than a bulkier commodity such as marijuana.

Applying your personal code of ethics, do you believe that the benefits of participating in organized crime outweigh the risks, or is the reverse true? Do you think you would ever be tempted to participate in organized crime?

The political climate in foreign source countries also contributes to the growth of trafficking organizations. In many countries the cultivation of raw materials for drugs is actually encouraged. Five of the most significant source countries—Mexico, Colombia, Ecuador, Peru, and Myanmar—are currently experiencing serious economic and political problems reflective of their move from conventional crops to coca, opium poppies, and marijuana; legitimate crops simply fail to provide parallel incomes realized by the illicit harvest.

As one can observe, the very structure of today's drug trafficking organizations poses serious tactical and investigative challenges to law enforcement officials. Additionally, serious public policy issues with regard to the law, personal freedoms, and priorities addressing the social order also arise from investigations of drug trafficking organizations. The volume of drugs entering the United States, the great number of trafficking organizations in existence, and the fact that methods of operation used by these groups can change so quickly dictate that unconventional approaches to detecting and prosecuting drug-related organized crime be considered by public officials.

Summary

In order to understand the many problems associated with the illicit drug trade, one must first comprehend what constitutes organized crime. Defining organized crime is no easy task as there is no "official" definition of the term. According to researchers, certain characteristics are unique to the "criminal group" or members of the organized crime unit. Such characteristics include the provision of illicit goods or services, the arbitrary use of violence, the establishment of a code of conduct for members, the ability to corrupt public officials, and a recruitment strategy based on ethnic, racial, geographical, or kinship factors.

Those that belong to the criminal group are usually supported by individuals belonging to two other categories of criminals, the protectors and specialized support. The protectors are not full-fledged members but still work on behalf of the organization while appearing to be legitimate parts of society. Protectors include accountants, attorneys, and government officials. The specialized support group also consists of individuals that are not official members but possess certain talents necessary for the success of the organization. Professionals with such traits are pilots, enforcers, and chemists.

Case Study: Droznek/Rosa Case

During the course of the *Droznek/Rosa* case, two dozen defendants pled guilty, individually and in small groups, leaving only two to be tried in this four-year-long OCDETF investigation by the FBI, DEA, IRS, ATF, and the Pennsylvania Bureau of Narcotics. Among those entering agreements with the government were Marvin "Babe" Droznek and Joseph Rosa, both are self-proclaimed members in the LaRocca/Genovese LCN family of western Pennsylvania.

Having confessed to participating in a continuing criminal enterprise, Droznek made consensually recorded phone calls and "wore a wire" while pursuing business as usual—dealing cocaine. This risky activity made Droznek a devastating witness in a case noteworthy for the lack of physical evidence. There were plenty of guns but no cocaine. Droznek eventually testified against Rosa and most of the other defendants.

The prime target of Droznek's testimony was a friend that he never quite trusted, Joe Rosa. When Rosa invited him to bring $200,000 along and join him on a buying trip to Florida, Droznek set up a unique "death insurance" policy. A third party was to hold $20,000 to pay for Rosa's murder if anything happened to Droznek. Fortunately for both, the trip was canceled. When Droznek later told Rosa of his "insurance," Rosa admitted he that had indeed considered a rip-off. Droznek lived his adult life in a violent world. He admitted using threats and violence as an enforcer. He owned many guns, including submachine guns, and on occasion would fire one into the ground as a "demonstration."

Close associates of Droznek that met untimely deaths included Robert George and Mark Puzas. George was a hotel operator, drug addict, and cocaine dealer. On a Tuesday, he told Droznek that he was suspicious that a man with whom he had been dealing might be "a dirty cop." The man was, in fact, an undercover county detective. The next day, George confronted the detective with a loaded shotgun. The brave officer slapped the gun away and killed George with one shot from his .357 Magnum. Mark Puzas became a confidential informant who was used by county narcotics detectives when they searched Droznek's home for marked cash after Puzas had purchased a kilogram of cocaine from him. A county grand jury recommended prosecution of Puzas during its separate investigation of Droznek. Two days after a visit from Droznek, Puzas hanged himself in jail.

Droznek worked his way up through the gambling ranks: first, as a numbers writer, then as a bookie, then as a collector and loan shark, and then as a "beard," a lay off man paid a commission to keep big bookmakers from recognizing the real source of a bet. In 1984, having lost a Las Vegas sports informer that had enabled him to make some sure-thing bets, Droznek made his first "coke" deal. In the next three years, he and his associates distributed more than 200 kilos of cocaine in the Pittsburgh area.

During early 1985, Droznek was introduced, by a mutual customer, to a drug dealer and vending machine entrepreneur, William Kostrick. This customer had been a part of Kostrick's prior operation, in which Kostrick and Rosa had obtained cocaine in south Florida and utilized couriers to transport the drug to Pennsylvania. The cocaine was cut, stashed, and redistributed to various dealers. In a process that continued throughout the conspiracy, Kostrick and/or Rosa would travel to Florida to purchase quantities of cocaine. Couriers would fly to Miami or Fort Lauderdale and rent cars for transportation back to Pittsburgh and redelivery to Kostrick, Rosa, or Droznek.

Throughout 1985 and 1986, each of the three principals developed separate sources and systems of delivery, and each would supply the others according to their needs. Kostrick, for example, developed contacts with a family from western Pennsylvania that had relocated to the west coast of Florida. This family had developed its own contacts with various Colombian and Cuban suppliers. The family members would transport cocaine in multi-kilogram lots to Kostrick in Pittsburgh. Rosa had developed contacts through his LCN connections. The three partners each maintained various stash houses that concealed both the cocaine and the money generated from the sale thereof. As a sideline, Droznek and Rosa, together with various other members of the conspiracy, also trafficked extensively in automatic and silenced weapons.

Each of the principals generated large amounts of cash during the operation of the enterprise. Droznek purchased a restaurant in Pittsburgh and a comfortable home in the suburbs. He also invested in certificates of deposit and utilized a number of safe deposit boxes to store his cash. Through his gambling and cocaine operations, Droznek established associations with a number of racketeers that owned and operated semi-legitimate businesses. Droznek used these associates to purchase fictitious W-2 wage statements to shelter him from income tax evasion charges. One such business operated as a pollution spill cleanup business. Droznek purchased his W-2 by paying the owner, a compulsive gambler and fraud artist, a 10 percent commission for each check.

Kostrick lived relatively modestly, investing his money in the vending business, possibly stashing some of his profits with family members. Most of the locations where Kostrick's machines were placed were owned by cocaine customers or loan shark victims. Rosa spent large amounts of income for automobiles, jewelry, and entertainment. He made a number of expensive real estate purchases, which he attempted to conceal through the use of nominees. Rosa also formulated a construction and landscaping business in an attempt to generate a legitimate income in response to an extensive IRS investigation. Much of Rosa's ill-gotten gains, including $175,000 worth of jewelry Rosa had stolen from his own store in an insurance scam, were passed on to the LCN underboss.

The membership of this criminal organization included a number of past and present law enforcement officers. Robert George, a hotel owner and a major dealer for all three of the principals, had been the chief of police for a small township in the northern suburbs of Pittsburgh. George had been fired from that position in the early 1980s as a result of various acts of administrative misconduct. Kostrick and two of his convicted associates had been former North Versailles Borough police officers. Michael Monaco, who provided Droznek with gun permits, had been an Allegheny County Deputy Sheriff prior to his arrest for cocaine trafficking in 1985. Perry Perrino, convicted and sentenced to 10 years incarceration, had been an Allegheny County Assistant District Attorney during the course of the conspiracy. At Perrino's sentencing, it was alleged that he had accepted both money and cocaine from Droznek while employed as a District Attorney and that Perrino had discussed with Droznek the status of an informant in an investigation then pending against Droznek. According to Charles Sheehy, the Acting U.S. Attorney, many of the persons contacted during this investigation have abandoned their jobs, careers, or professions as a result of cocaine addiction. Almost without exception, each individual that became involved in heavy cocaine use turned to criminal activity in order to support the habit. The lure of cocaine and the wealth that can be generated from its sale were shown to have corrupted numerous public officials entrusted with the responsibility of law enforcement.

Source: Organized Crime Drug Enforcement Task Force, 1988.

Modern-day gangs are, in part, distinguished from traditional organized crime organizations by their recent vintage. For instance, the genesis of groups such as the Jamaican posses, the California youth gangs, and the Colombian cocaine cartels occurred around 1970 when drug abuse began to flourish in the United States. Four characteristics unique to the emerging groups are vertical integration, the use of alternate sources of supply, a propensity to exploit social conditions to further the organization, and the insulation of leaders from street-level dealers.

Do you recognize these terms?

alien conspiracy theory
criminal group
families
La Cosa Nostra
made men/wise guys

Mafia
protectors
specialized support
vertical integration

Discussion Questions

1. Define the term "traditional organized crime," and discuss how it pertains to the illicit drug trade.

2. Compare and contrast the differences and similarities between legitimate and illegal business enterprises.

3. Discuss the three variables that make up an organized crime unit, according to the President's Commission on Organized Crime.

4. Having examined the organized crime "criminal" and "protector" groups, discuss and compare them to the players in an organized crime "support group."

5. What factors created the spawning of the new drug trafficking groups during the early 1970s?

6. Discuss some of the more successful drug trafficking organizations and how they have been able to manipulate the drug-user market to improve profits.

7. List and discuss the four conditions that lend a cohesiveness to the "modern-day" drug trafficking organization.

8. Give examples of criminal drug trafficking groups that may be considered vertically integrated.

9. List some examples of individuals that may act as "protectors" for the or-ganized crime unit.

Class Projects

1. Go to the library and research the historical roots of old-time organized crime organizations in the United States, and compare their emergence to the emergence of today's drug trafficking organizations.

Domestic Drug Trafficking Organizations *8*

This chapter will enable you to:

- Distinguish between traditional and nontraditional organized crime

- Learn about the origins of the criminal group known as the Mafia

- Understand the role of outlaw motorcycle gangs in the illegal drug trade

- Appreciate the role of Jamaican posses and youth gangs in the drug trade

- Learn the origins of prison gangs and their involvement in the illicit drug trade

---

The problem of organized crime (OC) in America is nothing new. In fact, it has been an American phenomenon for close to 100 years. The drug trade, however, has reshaped organized crime by creating new, violent, and more sophisticated criminal groups. Although these groups frequently clash with one another, more and more are learning to work together, as they did during Prohibition, to maximize profits and minimize their risk of detection. This chapter will examine some of the largest and most active OC groups in the domestic illicit drug trade.

Traditional Organized Crime: The Mafia

In 1988, the FBI estimated that approximately 25 percent of the alleged crime families making up the Mafia are involved in drug trafficking. The Mafia or La Cosa Nostra has been a source of controversy in criminology and law enforcement in the United States for more than 70 years. Because it had its genesis in Italy and Sicily during the mid-1800s, this group could very well be discussed under the following chapter dealing with foreign trafficking organizations; however, because some argue it plays such a significant role in criminality in the United States and because a great number of its alleged members are naturalized United States citizens, the Mafia is commonly referred to as a "domestic" criminal organization.

Today, two factions of traditional organized crime operate in the United States: the alleged American Mafia (also called the Italian Mafia or Italian-American Syndicates) and the Sicilian Mafia. To better understand their alleged role in drug trafficking, perhaps we should first consider the history of the organization itself. Because the roots of the Sicilian Mafia go back further than those of its American compatriots, that organization will be examined first.

The Mafia's History

Through corruption, assassination, extortion, and manipulation, the Sicilian Mafia has established itself as Italy's premier criminal group. Its criminal influence reaches around the globe with particular strength in Western Europe, and North and South America. Sicily is an island located off the southwestern coast of Italy and is the main region of influence of the Sicilian Mafia. This area, known as the "mezzogiorno," is a territory claimed by also another powerful Italian organized crime group, the *Camorra*.

The Camorra has a lengthy history as a prison gang originating in Italy. Spanish kings had ruled Naples and Sicily between the years 1504 and 1707 and again between 1738 and 1860. The Camorra was organized during the first Spanish reign, and the Sicilian Mafia, which was considered the most powerful criminal organization during the eighteenth and nineteenth centuries, was formed during the second reign. Both the Camorra and the Sicilian Mafia shared similar traits:

- each existed by selling criminal services to either individuals or corrupt members of the government;
- each had a formal organizational structure: the Camorra was organized into brigades or "brigata" while the Sicilian Mafia was organized into "families;"
- each had a strict code of silence or "omerta," which 1) dictated that family members never cooperate with government officials and 2) instituted the "vendetta," the code of retribution against anyone that in any way attacked or insulted a member of the "family."

The word "Mafia" appeared for the first time in the newspaper in November 1860, when it was acknowledged that a Camorra group had established itself in the general area of Palermo, Sicily. In 1878, Giuseppe Esposito, a Sicilian mafioso, was credited as being the first Sicilian Mafia member to relocate, along with six others, to the United States. Upon arrival in New York, Esposito and his men not only found America hostile to non-English speaking immigrants but also witnessed a criminal underworld dominated by the Irish and the Jews. Consequently, he moved to New Orleans with his Sicilian entourage, where he organized and headed the flourishing Sicilian Mafia. After being arrested in 1881 by Police Chief David Hennessey on an outstanding Italian fugitive warrant, Esposito was first transported to New York and was then extradited back to Italy.

Joseph Macheca, an American-born member of the organization, succeeded Esposito as crime boss of New Orleans. He soon began reinforcing the numbers of the New Orleans Mafia with new immigrants from Sicily, a practice commonly used by the American Mafia over the years. In 1890, Police Chief David Hennessey was assassinated by the Macheca crime family, of which 10 members were charged with murder. After a lengthy trial, all were acquitted amidst claims of jury tampering.

The acquittals created public outrage, and an angry crowd stormed Parish Prison where 19 Sicilian prisoners were housed. The ensuing carnage resulted in the largest lynching in history—16 prisoners were murdered. Some were shot and many were hung from the city's lamp posts. However, this failed to prevent the rise of the Mafia in New Orleans. Indeed, as the turn of the century approached, other Sicilian Mafia families formed around the United States in cities like San Francisco, St. Louis, Chicago, New York, and Boston.

Lasting between 1920 and 1933, the Prohibition era was probably the single most influential factor in providing up-and-coming Mafia families with what they needed most, enough money to infiltrate legitimate business. Such capital would make their illicit enterprises more difficult to detect and would give the mafiosos an aura of public respectability. During this time, some of the more notorious Mafiosi were arriving in the United States. Carlo Gambino, Joe Profaci, Joe Magliocco, Mike Coppola, and Salvatore Maranzano joined the likes of Joe (Joe Bananas) Bonanno and Charles (Lucky) Luciano. During the 1930s, Luciano and other Italian organized crime bosses solidified their base of operation, which some believe grew into a national organization that now occupies 24 American cities with close to 2,000 actual members.

The World of the "Made Man"

During January 1986, the President's Commission on Organized Crime solicited testimony from Martin Light, an attorney with close ties to La Cosa Nostra. Light, formerly a government witness, was sentenced to 15 years in prison for a drug conviction. He testified that prospective members are watched closely from childhood on, judged on their toughness and ability, and on their respect for superiors. Their willingness to "do the right thing" may be to share criminal profits with family leaders, to risk jail terms for refusal to cooperate with a grand jury, or to plead guilty to a crime actually committed by more important members in the family. It is to follow unquestioningly the self-perpetuating practices of a most secret exclusive criminal society.

Source: PCOC, *The Impact,* 1986.

One of the most important developments during the 1930s was the formation of a national Mafia alliance or "commission" whereby heads of some of the most influential Mafia families would meet to divide territory, choose rackets, approve new members, and arbitrate disputes between families.

La Cosa Nostra Organizational Structure

Boss. The head of the family. He does not participate in the day-to-day activities of the organization but is supposed to receive a cut from every income source. He usually has his own legitimate and illegitimate businesses.

Underboss. Assistant to the boss. Usually he is being groomed to succeed the boss, but succession is not automatic. There is only one underboss per family.

Consiglieri. Literally, "counselor." He assists the boss but has no leadership authority. He is generally an older, experienced member that can advise family members. There is usually only one Consiglieri per family.

Capo. Caporegima, or captain; supervisors of the family's day-to-day criminal operations; represents the family among the soldiers, whom the capos oversee. A capo gains his position by proving his ability as an "earner"—one that earns a great deal of profit for the family. Capos may have their own legitimate and illegitimate ventures and retain a part of the income paid by their soldiers before passing it on to the leadership. The number of capos in a family depends on the size of the family.

Soldier. The basic rank in the family. Sometimes known as a "wise guy," "buttonman," or "made man"; the last term refers to any formal member of the LCN, one that has undergone the initiation ritual. To be "made," a man must be of Italian ancestry.

Associates. An informal position, yet one that is crucial to the family. An associate need not be of Italian descent; he is someone whose skills or position make him of value to the organization. Some are used as soldiers while others are more distantly connected. The FBI has estimated that for every formal member of La Cosa Nostra there are 10 criminal associates that cooperate with members and share their enterprises.

Protectors. Among any family's associates is a support network of "protectors." These are corrupt public officials, bankers, lawyers, accountants, and other professionals that protect the criminal group from governmental intervention, both civil and criminal.

Source: PCOC, April 1986.

The Mafia and the Drug Trade

During the late 1960s and early 1970s, France became well known as a distribution point for an estimated 80 percent of the world's heroin. Marseilles became the center of heroin laboratories that processed raw opium brought in from Turkey. Heroin was then smuggled into the United States by French Corsicans as well as Sicilian Mafia members (the "French Connection"). In the early 1970s, the French Connection was broken up as a result of a joint investigative effort by U.S. and French authorities. Today, France is no longer considered a major producer of heroin sold on the American market.

In 1986, the President's Commission on Organized Crime stated that "heroin is the biggest money maker for the Mafia." It is thought that since the collapse of the French Connection, Italy and Sicily have assumed the role of distribution points for heroin. Intelligence sources have also indicated that French chemists have assumed their traditional role of converting raw opium into heroin. The opium is transported from sources in the eastern Mediterranean countries of Syria, Lebanon, Pakistan, and Jordan.

The FBI reports that the Sicilian Mafia controls the transshipment of heroin through Italy to the United States from both southwest Asia (SWA) and southeast Asia (SEA) (see Chapter 8). According to the DEA, the proportion of SWA heroin to SEA heroin entering Italy is 70 percent to 30 percent, with indicators showing SWA heroin on the decrease. Methods of smuggling by the Sicilian Mafia have included:

- members or associates traveling by air and wearing body packs of 2 to 3 kilograms of heroin, and
- heroin secreted in toys, statues, wheels of provolone cheese, film canisters, coffee machines, drycell batteries, cans of baby powder, electronic appliances, mail, and clothing.

Figure 8.1
Location of American Mafia Families in the Continental United States

The Pizza Connection

The investigation that revealed the extent to which the Sicilian Mafia operated in the United States is popularly known as **the Pizza Connection.** The Pizza Connection was a massive operation involving heroin smuggling and money laundering by Sicilian Mafia members operating in the United States, an operation headed by Sicilian crime boss Gaetano Badalamente. Through the aid of crime boss turned witness, Tommaso Buscetta, arrests stemming from the Pizza Connection were made possible.

The operation ultimately led to the 1984 indictments in New York of 35 alleged members of the Sicilian Mafia. The investigation revealed that, between 1982 and 1983, the Sicilian Mafia had scheduled 1.5 tons of heroin with an estimated wholesale value of $333 million for importation to New York. In addition, between 1980 and 1983, the New York Sicilian Mafia was reported to have shipped in excess of $40 million in cash from New York to Sicily via Switzerland.

The breadth of the investigation expanded worldwide with Mafia members identified in such countries as Brazil, Canada, Spain, Switzerland, Italy, and the United States. So vast was the investigation that it took federal prosecutors one full year to try. Ultimately, the trial turned out to be the most costly and lengthy criminal proceeding in United States history but proved rewarding by the securing of convictions for all but two of the defendants. Those convicted received lengthy sentences.

As a result of the information produced at this trial, some argue that not enough is being done to fight drug trafficking. Columnist Shana Alexander stated "[the case] did not make the slightest dent in the nation's desperate drug problem. More heroin and cocaine are on the streets today than before 'Pizza' began. The trial severely overtaxed every branch of our legal system—law enforcement, bench, and bar—and taxed unfortunate jurors worst of all" (1988:B-11).

Testimony revealed that one member of the Sicilian Mafia operating in the United States, Salvatore Salamone, was entrusted with the job of changing small denomination bills to large denomination bills and transporting the money in suitcases overseas (see Chapter 6). Once the money arrived in Switzerland, several other individuals converted the bills into Swiss francs and then to Italian lira for delivery to Sicily.

The Pizza Connection illustrates a working relationship between the Sicilian and American-based Mafia operatives and their "common interests" in drug trafficking and money laundering. Each organization needed the other, and the relationship was established on a basis of mutual trust and respect. In 1987, the FBI observed the following:

1. The Sicilian Mafia operates in the United States as a separate criminal organization that specializes in heroin smuggling. The first allegiance of its members is to the "family" in Sicily.

2. Before initiating a major heroin smuggling operation, the Sicilian Mafia obtains the sanction of certain American Mafia families.

3.   As payment for the American Mafia family granting its sanction for the operation, the Sicilian Mafia pays the American Mafia family up to $5,000 per kilogram of heroin brought into the United States.

The number of Sicilian mafiosi operating in the United States is hard to predict. They are, however, thought to concentrate in the northeastern United States, principally in New York City and New Jersey, and are thought to operate without geographical jurisdictions.

The Mafia Wars

Over the decades Italy's Mafia has undergone several periods of severe repression by police authorities. For example, in the 1920s, Mussolini attempted to purge La Cosa Nostra from the island, which resulted in many members migrating to the United States seeking safe havens in American-based families. Many of these refugees later became formidable bosses of the most influential crime families in the nation.

During the early 1980s, Italy experienced an increase in violence between members of the estimated 20 Mafia families operating in and around Palermo. The violence resulted in the murders of mobsters, policemen, judges, and politicians in what was dubbed the "heroin wars." The central government of Italy has since taken initiatives toward controlling Mafia-related criminal activity. These initiatives include anti-Mafia legislation enacted on September 11, 1982. It features these measures:

- "association" with known Mafia types is illegal, whether a crime is committed or not;
- "association" also applies to the Camorra and other "Mafia-type" groups;
- "exile" locations for convicted "Mafiosi" have been established in towns with populations of less than 10,000, and an unauthorized exit of the location shall result in imprisonment;
- property and other assets are subject to confiscation;
- telephone wiretaps are authorized on persons suspected of belonging to "Mafia-type" organizations; and
- the term "omerta" is defined in its most negative connotation as a "conduct of noncooperation with public safety officials due to fear."

The implementation of this law resulted in the 1984 arrests of more than 450 suspected Mafiosi and the subsequent trial that has become known as the "Maxi-Processo," or maxi-trial. The arrests, which are considered the greatest Mafia crackdown since Mussolini's 1920s Mafia purge, resulted from a 40-volume, 8,632 page indictment that outlined more than 90 murders, countless kidnappings, and even the use of torture chambers. Additionally, the indictment included charges of heroin smuggling and money laundering for Mafia members. In spite of all of the media fanfare over the Mafia trials, in the mid-1990s it appears that they were little more than just show-trials for the Mafia continues to operate with virtual impunity in Italy and Sicily.

Jury Convicts Italy's Top Mafia Bosses of Murders, Drugs

ROME—A Sicilian jury convicted top Mafia bosses of murder and drug trafficking yesterday, and judges sentenced 19 of them to life in jail to climax Italy's most serious attempt in modern times to cripple the mob. Verdicts and sentencing of 452 defendants came in a bunker-like Palermo courtroom last night, 20 months after the historic Mafia trial began and 36 days after jurors and two judges began their deliberations inside an armored room. The mass trial, which was estimated to have cost at least $100 million, including $19 million for construction of the courtroom, is seen as the most severe blow against the Mafia in postwar republican Italy. Still, nobody was claiming total victory last night. "This is not the end of a repressive epoch, but the beginning of a new legality," said Assistant Judge Pietro Grasso after the findings were reported.

Giovanni Falcone, an examining magistrate who was instrumental in assembling the 8,636-page indictment, called the court's action "an important starting point—not the end, but the beginning." In all, the six jurors and two judges, who also weigh evidence under Italian law, convicted and sentenced 338 defendants, more than 100 of whom are still at large. Another 114 were acquitted.

With an army of police on guard outside, more than 1,300 witnesses depicted the Mafia's growth from a Sicily-centered syndicate to an international organization that made billions trafficking heroin, principally to the United States. In addition to the drug charges, prosecutors accused the defendants of 90 murders, racketeering, money laundering and other crimes, including participation in a criminal organization.

Inside the courtroom, which is connected by tunnel to Palermo's Ucciar-done Prison, defendants lounged in barred, bulletproof cages as chief judge Alfonso Geordano read the court's findings, answered by scattered protests and the sobbing of relatives. During the trial, the most damning evidence came from about 30 repentant Mafia members, called "pentiti," that broke the gang's historic vow of silence and testified for the government in exchange for more lenient sentences.

In a nation that has no death penalty, prosecutors had asked for 28 life sentences and more than 5,000 years in prison. Michele "The Pope" Greco, undisputed "boss of bosses" in Palermo and chairman of the 12-man commission of Mafia Bosses that oversaw assassinations and heroin trade, was sentenced to life in prison.

As the jury began deliberating last month, the 64-year-old Greco wished the members "peace and tranquility." He was among those accused in the 1982 assassination of Italy's most respected anti-Mafia hunter, Gen. Carlo Alberto della Chiesa, and his young wife. Greco's brother, Salvatore "The Senator" Greco, got 18 years. Giuseppe "Pippo" Calo, a Mafia financial wizard and money launderer, got 23 years.

Ignazio Salvo, a millionaire businessman and one-time tax collector for the government, got seven years for criminal association. The same charge brought four years and six months for Salvatore Chiaracane, a prominent lawyer. The jury rejected the prosecution's call for 15 years for bespectacled Luciano Liggio, Mafia boss of the hill town named Corleone, which figured prominently in Mario Puzo's novel "The Godfather." He has been serving a life term since 1974, but the jury acquitted him of four murders that prosecutors charged he had masterminded from his jail cell in Sardinia.

A key prosecution witness, Tommaso Buscetta, was sentenced to three years and six months. Extradited from Brazil on drug charges in 1984, Buscetta gave investigators detailed insights on the Mafia's internal structure and decisionmaking. A Mafia member that "turned" after six members of his family were murdered in gang warfare, Buscetta proved as credible to the Sicilian jury as he did to one in New York, which convicted 18 of 19 defendants on heroin charges following his testimony.

Montalbano, W.D. (1987). "19 Get Life Terms in Sicilian Mafia Trial." Copyright 1987, *Los Angeles Times*. Reprinted by permission.

The Mafia Controversy

While, as we have seen in the preceding discussion, there is a substantial body of opinion that argues that La Cosa Nostra, or Mafia, is the dominant organized crime group in the United States and plays a major role in drug trafficking, considerable controversy surrounds what this organization actually is and what it actually does. Many scholars and law enforcement officials have come to doubt the view of a hegemonic Italian organized crime syndicate that is presented by the FBI and other federal agencies. They argue that the evidence in support of the existence of such a group is weak and open to other interpretations and that empirical research has failed to confirm the existence of such a dominant, complex, hierarchically organized criminal group.

Criticisms of the Mafia model fall into two distinct categories: (1) the historical evidence is sometimes weak and contradictory, and (2) empirical research conducted on organized crime fails to demonstrate the existence of the Mafia as a single criminal conspiracy, and there are alternative models of organized crime that explain the reality of criminal entrepreneurship. To this list we will add a third—the evidence of LCN or Mafia "domination" of the drug trade is fragmentary and debatable.

Historical Controversies

Anthropological, historical, and social studies of the Sicilian Mafia, such as those conducted by Henner Hess and Anton Blok, have failed to turn up evidence of a single criminal organization (Hess, 1973; Blok, 1974). Rather, the studies point strongly to a series of localized village-based organizations, which were primarily created to protect the interests of absentee landlords and foreign invaders. These organizations formed a kind of "shadow government" in Sicily, meting out justice, controlling jobs, and providing for social control in an unstable society. While the "Mafia" may have had its origins in such a rural ruling class, it is not the same "Mafia" proposed by conspiracy theorists.

In addition, evidence relating to the importation of organized crime by Italians to the United States is open to similar questions. For example, proponents of the Mafia theory cannot tell us how it is that Italian immigration brought this criminal organization to the United States, but similar waves of Italian immigration did not bring the same organization to England, Australia, and other nations.

Supporters of the Mafia model have failed to account for organized crime's existence in the United States long before the inception of Italian immigration. Further, proponents of the Mafia model must engage in considerable factual acrobatics to account for non-Italian figures that appear to have been dominant forces in the history of American organized crime, men like Arnold Rothstein, Meyer Lansky, Longie Zwillman, Bugsy Siegel, Bugs Moran, Dutch Schultz, Owney Madden, and dozens of others.

Finally, specific historical "facts" presented by proponents of the Mafia model appear weak against close scrutiny. The Hennessey assassination is a prime example. Was the police chief of New Orleans killed by the "Mafia?" Or was the "Mafia" created, as Dwight Smith Jr. suggested, to justify the lynching of innocent immigrants? The fact is that the New Orleans grand jury failed to turn up any evidence of an Italian conspiracy, and the courts failed to convict any of the defendants. Similarly, questions have been raised about other "proofs" offered for the Mafia model.

Contemporary Research on Organized Crime

But far more significant to our discussion is the failure of empirical research on alleged LCN families to substantiate the model proposed by the federal government. For example, Francis A.J. Ianni's study of an LCN family in New York suggested that the only organizational arrangement was one of an extended family (Ianni, 1972). For Ianni, kinship became the prime variable in explaining how and why Italian-Americans worked together in both legal and illegal businesses. He found no evidence of an interconnected, national Italian-American crime syndicate. Joseph Albini's study of organized crime in Detroit also failed to confirm the existence of a monolithic crime structure (Albini, 1972). Albini reviewed historical documents and journalistic accounts and interviewed both law enforcement officials and participants in organized crime operations and concluded that organized crime was based on a series of loosely constructed "patron-client relations," not on a massive criminal conspiracy.

Yet other studies, such as the one conducted by William Chambliss (1971), focused on organized crime in Seattle and found a syndicate composed of local political and business leaders, leading Chambliss to argue that "organized crime" was a misnomer and that the study of official corruption would be more revealing in describing criminal syndicates. Mark Haller's study (1989) of organized crime operations in Chicago, New York, and Florida concluded that, rather than being dominated by a tightly organized criminal conspiracy, organized crime was a series of complex and often overlapping business partnerships in illicit enterprise.

Peter Reuter's exhaustive study (1983) of the gambling and loan sharking industries in New York City failed to turn up either LCN domination or even widespread participation in those industries. Reuter argued that if the Mafia existed at all, it "was a paper tiger" living off its popular reputation, which was fueled by journalistic and law enforcement speculation. And finally, a study of organized crime in Philadelphia revealed that not only did the Mafia not dominate organized crime in the past (at best its alleged members were functionaires of other, very large, criminal syndicates), but that the alleged Cosa Nostra family of Angelo Bruno was only one of several dozen major organized crime syndicates operating in that city. Additional studies by Alan Block, John Gardiner, Virgil Peterson, Jay Albanese, and many others have served to dispute the theory of any dominant role of the Cosa Nostra (Albanese, 1996; Block, 1983; Peterson, 1983).

The Mafia and Drugs

While the views of some law enforcement officials tenaciously cling to the view of La Cosa Nostra as a single, massive criminal conspiracy, others have moved away from that position. The Pennsylvania Crime Commission, for example, has been quite active in exploring the role of other organized crime groups, particularly black crime groups and motorcycle gangs, in drug trafficking and other illicit business ventures. Potter and Jenkins, in their study of organized crime in Philadelphia, identified black gangs, Greek gangs, the K & A Gang, and motorcycle gangs as more important in drug trafficking.

There is little doubt that some individuals linked with Italian-dominated criminal organizations both in the United States and Sicily have been involved in large-scale drug trafficking, as we have seen in the case of the Pizza Connection. But perhaps one should be cautious in attributing any degree of hegemony to these groups in the drug market. Drug trafficking is conducted by thousands of different criminal organizations, many of which are complex and quite large when compared to LCN groups. Despite many successful Mafia-related drug investigations, the focus on the Mafia or La Cosa Nostra has tended to distort the perception of organized crime's role in drugs. For example, it ignores the vital role played by organizations headed by Frank Matthews, Nicky Barnes, Jeff Fort, and other crime figures. It also ignores the role of non-Italians, such as Meyer Lansky and Nig Rosen, who played the major coordinating role in the infamous "French Connection." And it ignores the major role in the organization of drug trafficking played by truly pioneering organized crime figures like Arnold Rothstein, Happy Meltzer, "Dopey" Bennie Fein, and others. The role of the Mafia must be kept in perspective, and the roles of other major drug trafficking groups must be given appropriate attention.

Outlaw Motorcycle Gangs

Outlaw motorcycle gangs have etched an historic role in organized crime and the drug trade. Outlaw motorcycle gangs, according to the U.S. Treasury's Bureau of Alcohol, Tobacco, and Firearms (ATF), have evolved into one of the most "reprehensible" types of criminal organizations, consisting of "killers, psychotics, panderers, and social misfits (ATF, 1988)."

Hunter S. Thompson, an authority on the Hell's Angels, traced the origin of outlaw motorcycle gangs back to 1947, when the POBOB or the "Pissed Off Bastards of Bloomington" (later known as the Hell's Angels), transformed an American Motorcycle Association (AMA)-sponsored hill climb in Holister, California, to a week-long brawl. Later that same year in Riverside, California, thousands attended a motorcycle run that resulted in riot, destruction, and even two deaths. The following year, a similar motorcycle event in Riverside ended up as a riot. The police chief then blamed the outcome of the event on the visiting "outlaws," which is a term now commonly associated with members of some motorcycle gangs.

The outlaw motorcycle phenomenon continued during the 1950s and 1960s and soon became a symbol of lawlessness and rebellion. That is to say, for the most part, the bikers were more concerned with uninhibited good times than organized criminal endeavors. The entertainment industry portrayed these outlaw gangs in the popular films *The Wild Ones*, *Easy Rider*, and *Angels on Wheels*.

In the late 1960s, the former president of the AMA, William Berry, became irritated over the bad publicity outlaw bikers gave to law-abiding motorcycle riders. He declared that only one percent of the motorcyclists in the United States functioned outside the spirit and intent of the law. The statement, of course, was a public relations effort on the part of the AMA to explain that only a small number of motorcycle riders represented a criminal element. The term "one percenter," however, was immediately adopted by the larger outlaw motorcycle gangs as a public affirmation of their criminal intent, and the "1%" patch is now commonly worn by gang members.

Thinking Critically #15

Suggest creative methods by which society can protect itself from organized crime, both traditional and nontraditional.

The years between 1947 and 1967 were formative ones for the early gangs like the POBOBs. Imitators soon began to appear. In addition, larger gangs absorbed smaller ones or just muscled them out of existence. Roaming members calling themselves "nomads" traveled throughout the United States and formed alliances with other gangs. Formal organizational structures were formed, and leaders were placed in charge of the various gangs or "chapters." Still, gangs in this period lacked focus and were rarely considered to be more than troublemakers by local law enforcement.

By 1970, however, outlaw motorcycle gangs were viewed differently. The gangs contributed to a monumental social change underway in the United States. This change was characterized to some degree by an explosion of drug use. First as drug users and then as dealers, motorcycle gangs were drawn into the phenomenon. As the Treasury Department proclaimed in 1988, "whatever else the 1960s changed in America, it changed outlaw motorcycle gangs" (ATF, 1988).

Today, outlaw motorcycle gangs have emerged into sophisticated criminal groups that, according to the DEA, number about 850 with a membership exceeding 8,000 in the United States alone. Their criminal activities are many and varied but include drug trafficking, contract killings, extortion, arson, fraud, embezzlement, and money laundering.

The philosophy of the outlaw motorcycle gang is of particular significance to law enforcement as it illustrates the sociopathic nature of the organization. "Fuck the World" (FTW) is the motto and attitude of outlaw motorcycle members, and the phrase is frequently embroidered on patches or even tattooed on the members themselves. They choose not to live as normal citizens and delight in sporting their own dress code, which is one that many people would consider filthy and repulsive. Acts typically considered outrageous and shocking only serve to enhance the biker's image within his own environment.

With the obvious exception of minority or ethnically dominated gangs, most outlaw motorcycle gangs embrace racist beliefs that closely parallel those of the Ku Klux Klan and the neo-Nazis. This "white supremacist" philosophy is evidenced by the wearing of Nazi swastikas, white-power fists, and other symbols of white supremacy.

In addition to their racist values, bikers also practice a chauvinistic attitude toward female associates of the organization. In fact, in most clubs females fall into one of two categories: mamas/sheep or old ladies. Because females are not permitted to be "members" of the gang, their roles in the organization are limited. For example, the mamas are considered "property" of the gang at large and must consent to the sexual desires of anyone at any time. In addition, they

Figure 8.2

Similarities of Organizational Structure

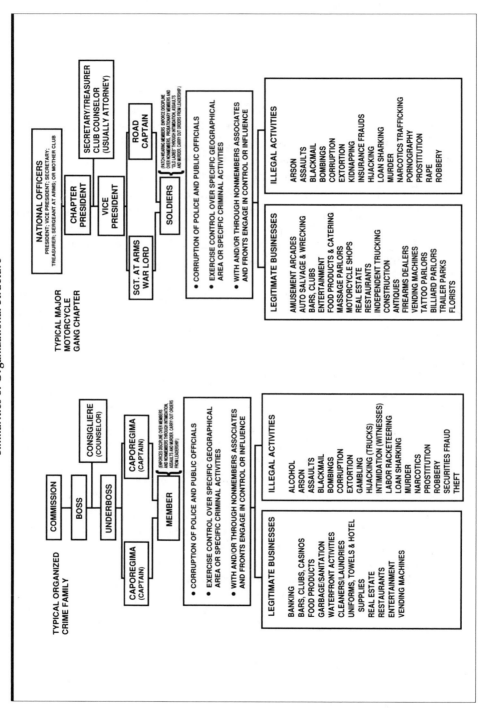

also perform menial tasks around the clubhouse. Old ladies, on the other hand, are wives or steady girlfriends of members and, therefore, belong to only one member of the club. Old ladies proudly wear colors similar to those of male members, with the difference being the words "property of . . .," which are displayed on the bottom "rocker" of the club patch.

As indicated, outlaw motorcycle gang members place a great deal of importance on respect for the club's colors, which are basically the uniform of the gang. A gang's colors are typically a sleeveless denim or leather jacket with the club name and claimed territory affixed to the back. The colors consist of a top rocker with the name of the gang and a bottom rocker that usually claims territory, states, or cities occupied by the gang. The gang colors are the proudest possession of a biker, and members are expected to protect their colors at all costs.

The biker's motorcycle also plays a major role in his life. So esteemed is the motorcycle that its destruction or loss to a rival gang member not only results in loss of face but also could be grounds for expulsion from the club. The motorcycle is not just a means of transportation for the biker but a requirement for club membership and a status symbol in its own right. The motorcycle, along with the dress of the gang members, perpetuates the image of a disciplined and paramilitary organization and has a certain "shock" value in dealing with members of the general public or other gangs.

There are two prerequisites for motorcycles that outlaw motorcycle gangs frequently enforce: they must be a certain size (usually a 900 cc minimum), and they must be American made. Bikers will commonly spend more time with their motorcycles than with anything else, and it is not uncommon for a biker to park his motorcycle inside his home.

Finally, the club's bylaws or charter, which most clubs enforce, are of particular importance in the role that bikers play. The charter outlines accepted standards of conduct for gang members and administrative procedures for the gang's operations. Charter rules include the following:

- no member will strike another member
- all members must attend funerals of fellow bikers in the same chapter
- chapters must have one organized meeting per week
- chapter meetings may be attended by chapter members only
- members must respect their colors
- a club prospect must be sponsored by one member who has known the prospect for at least a year.

As mentioned, hundreds of outlaw motorcycle gangs operate in the United States today, but four of them have emerged as the largest and most criminally sophisticated. These are the Hell's Angels, the Outlaws, the Pagans, and the Bandidos.

Outlaw Motorcycle Gang Organizational Structure

National President. The national president is often the founder of the club. He will usually be located at or near the national headquarters. In many cases, he will be surrounded by a select group of individuals who answer only to him and who serve as bodyguards and organizational enforcers. Quite often, the national president will possess the authority to make final decisions.

Territorial or Regional Representative. The individual in this position is also called the vice president and is in charge of whatever region or district to which he is assigned. His duties usually include decisionmaking on all problems that local chapters are unable to solve. Any problems that involve the club as a whole will usually be dealt with through the national headquarters.

National Secretary-Treasurer. The responsibility for handling the club's money, including collecting dues from local chapters, is that of the national secretary-treasurer. He makes changes in existing club bylaws and drafts new ones. He records the minutes and maintains the records on all headquarters or regional office meetings.

National Enforcer. The national enforcer answers directly to the national president. He ensures that the president's orders are carried out. He may act as the president's bodyguard, and he may also handle all special situations, such as retrieving the colors from a member that has left the club. He has also been known to locate ex-members and remove club tattoos from them.

Chapter President. Usually the chapter president, through a combination of personal strength, leadership, personality, and skills, has either claimed the position or has been voted in. He has final authority over all chapter business and members. Usually his word is law within that chapter.

Vice President. Second in command and "right hand" of the chapter president is the vice president. He presides over club affairs in the absence of the president. Normally, he is hand-picked by the president and is heir apparent to the club's leadership.

Secretary-Treasurer. Usually the chapter member possessing the best writing skills serves as secretary-treasurer. He will keep the chapter roster and maintain a crude accounting system. He records the minutes at all chapter meetings and collects the dues and/or fines. He is responsible for paying the chapter's bills.

Sergeant at Arms. Due to the unruly and violent nature of outlaw motorcycle gangs, each chapter has an individual whose principal duty is to maintain order at club meetings and functions. The sergeant at arms is normally the strongest member physically and is completely loyal to the president. He may administer beatings to fellow members for violation of club rules and is the club enforcer for that chapter.

Road Captain. The road captain fulfills the role of gang logistician and security chief for the club-sponsored "runs." The road captain maps out routes to be taken during runs and arranges for refueling, food, and maintenance stops. He will also carry the club's funds and use them for bail if necessary.

Members. The rank-and-file, dues-paying members of the gang are the individuals that carry out the decisions of the club's leadership. Limiting membership affords the president greater control over the affairs of the gang. At the same time, it helps to ensure that the gang's criminal efforts are not compromised to law enforcement. When a gang becomes too large,—it tends to divide the membership into various chapters, based on geographic location.

Probate or Prospective Members. These are the club hopefuls that spend from one month to one year in probationary status and must prove during that time that they are worthy of becoming members. Many clubs require the probate to commit a felony with fellow members observing, so as to weed out weak individuals and infiltration by law enforcement. Probates must be nominated by a regular member and receive a unanimous vote for acceptance. They carry out all menial jobs at the clubhouse and for other members. They are known to carry weapons for other club members and stand guard during club parties. The probates will not wear the club's colors; instead, they wear jackets with the bottom rocker of the club patch showing the location from which they come. Until he is voted in, completes his initiation, and is awarded his colors, a probate has no voting rights.

Associate or Honorary Members. An individual that has proved his value to the gang is known as an associate or honorary member. The associate may be a professional that has in a manner commensurate to his profession been supportive of the gang, or he may be a proven criminal with whom the gang has had a profitable, illicit relationship (see Chapter 7). Some of the more noted associates are attorneys, bail bondsmen, motorcycle shop owners, and auto wrecking yard owners. These individuals are allowed to party with the gang, either in town or on runs; they do not, however, have voting status, attend club meetings, or wear club colors.

Source: United States Marshals Service, U.S. Department of Justice, 1986.

The Hell's Angels

In 1950, the POBOB'S leader, Otto Friedli, formed a new gang, the Hell's Angels, named after a World War II bomber. The Angels' "mother chapter" was originally established in San Bernardino, California, where it remained until the mid-1960s. During that time, Ralph Hubert (Sonny) Barger, then-president of the Oakland chapter, became National President and moved the mother chapter to Oakland, where it currently remains.

The Hell's Angels (HA) are distinctive because they are considered the most professional and the wealthiest of the outlaw motorcycle gangs. They are also an international organization that, according to the U.S. Drug Enforcement Administration, has 33 U.S. chapters, 18 foreign chapters, and an estimated 900 members (450 to 600 are active members). Because of its lengthy and colorful history, the HA have evolved into a model gang that other gangs, both large and small, have continually emulated.

The FBI reports that, during the mid-1960s, the HA began drug trafficking in the San Francisco area with LSD as the main commodity. Later, their inventory expanded to cocaine, PCP, marijuana, and methamphetamines. Today, they are still active in methamphetamine manufacturing and trafficking, and it is estimated that most of the methamphetamine trafficked in California is directly or indirectly tied to the HA organization.

Figure 8.3
Location of Hell's Angels Chapters in the Continental United States

Figure 8.4
Location of Outlaws Chapters in the Continental United States

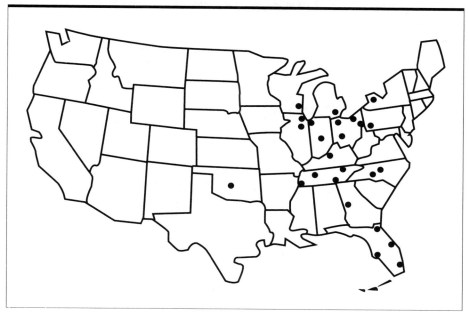

The Outlaws

The Outlaws motorcycle gang was founded in 1959 by John Davis in Chicago, Illinois. The Outlaws quickly expanded across the country and with the absorption of the Canadian "Satan's Choice" gang became an international organization. Under the current leadership of Harry Joseph Bowman, the Outlaws are considered the largest motorcycle gang in the United States with an estimated membership between 1,200 and 1,500 members located in 25 U.S. cities and six Canadian chapters. The Outlaws are engaged in trafficking of cocaine as well as Valium tablets manufactured by Canadian laboratories and distributed from Chicago to locations throughout the United States.

The Pagans

The Pagans originated in Prince George's County, Maryland, under the presidency of Lou Dolkin. The Pagans are concentrated on the east coast and differ from the other major four gangs because they do not have a geographically fixed "mother chapter." It is, therefore, directed by a "mother club," which is made up of 13 to 18 members who are in charge of other chapters.

Figure 8.5
Locations of Pagans Chapters in the Continental United States

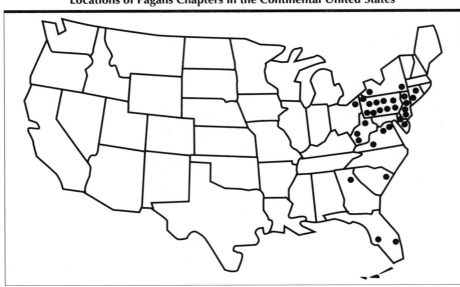

The Pagans, currently led by Kirby Keller, have a particular presence in the Philadelphia area. Between New York and Florida, there are 44 chapters, with an estimated 700 to 900 members. The Pagans have earned the reputation of being one of the most ruthless and organized motorcycle gangs. The Pagans have also become commonly associated with other, more traditional organized crime groups, frequently acting as killers and enforcers. In addition, the Pagans play a major role in the illicit sex industry, as they have considerable business interests in massage parlors and other prostitution outlets and often work closely with local pornography syndicates to provide protection, models, and the like.

Figure 8.6
Location of Bandidos Chapters in the Continental United States

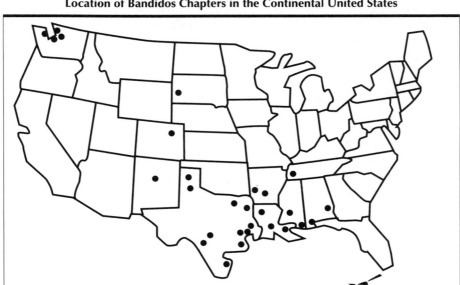

The Bandidos

The Bandidos were formed in 1966 by Donald Chambers in Houston, Texas, and are currently headquartered in Corpus Christi. It is estimated that the Bandidos have 26 chapters and 500 members. They concentrate in both the southern and northern regions of the country and are generally considered less sophisticated than the three outlaw motorcycle gangs previously discussed. The Bandidos are heavily involved in the manufacturing and distributing of methamphetamines.

Youth Gangs

Reports of violent youth gang activity are not merely media hype but often an actual social phenomenon in many U.S. communities. The youth gang violence, inspired by the drug trade, poses real problems for certain neighborhoods. In many cases, residents are either fearful of leaving their homes or afraid to let their children play in the public parks taken over by gangs. Neighborhood businesses suffer economically because residents are hesitant to leave their homes to shop. The cost of dealing with gangs via community efforts, law enforcement efforts, and the court system is escalating.

A powerful mystique has evolved around gang activity over the years with many of today's movie and television programs focusing on gang-related themes. It is difficult to estimate exactly how many gangs exist today in the United States, but according to the Los Angeles Police Gang Control Manual (1991), in Los Angeles alone youth gang numbers exceed 650 with more than 50,000 members. Although many other cities experience such problems, Los Angeles has become well-known for its exceedingly sizable gang problem. The major difficulty in predicting gang numbers is the secrecy and the everchanging nature of most juvenile gangs, making it burdensome for authorities to determine identities of both members and associates.

Thinking Critically #16

Place yourself in the position of a youth gang member. Describe what would have to happen to induce you to leave the gang.

The origin of youth gangs dates back to the early 1900s, but as late as 1990 they were for the most part localized into an estimated 10 cities which were thought to have a "gang problem." However, in 1994, that number has grown to 125 U.S. cities with the most serious problems in the Midwest and western states (Klein, 1991). One of the most compelling reasons for gang expansion is the expansion of the drug trade, particularly with regard to crack cocaine. The crack trade is a relatively easy entry business generating thousands, if not millions, of dollars each year. Because cocaine can be easily cooked by make-shift chemists and because it is easy to conceal, crack provides a considerable financial incentive for gangs members in poverty-stricken, jobless neighborhoods. Furthermore, since crack is obviously addictive, the entrepreneurial crack dealer can look forward to a substantial return business.

In addition to profits generated from drug sales, illegal firearm sales, which include AK-47s and Uzi machine guns, are also escalating. Accordingly, not only are youth gangs of today more heavily armed, but they are increasingly violent as well. Disputes over gang turf and drug deals often result in murder. As a result, the widespread notoriety of gang violence spreads throughout neighborhoods, serving to intimidate law abiding citizens who live in gang-infested communities. Sadly, police reports reveal that most gang-related murders are not a result of soured drug deals but rather spontaneous shootings (e.g., drive-by shootings) where innocent people who are not even associated with gangs are killed.

Special Youth Gang Problems

Police experience great difficulty in monitoring and controlling youth gangs. Undercover agents are more effective when targeting adult gangs than youth gangs because most youth gang recruiters know their recruit from the neighborhood. Additionally, a youthful gang member is dealt with considerably more leniently by the juvenile justice system than is his or her adult counterpart in the adult justice system. One factor making it hard for police to estimate the number of gang members is difficulty determining the status of a possible member. For example, a hard-core leader is commonly called an "original gangster" while part-timers and would-be members are called "wannabees." Confusing the matter is the varied ethnic composition of youth gangs. In 1989, a U.S. Justice Department survey estimated that about 50 percent of the nation's youth gang members are black, 35 percent are Hispanic, and the rest white or Asian (NIJ, 1989). Another problem with most youth gangs is difficulty in determining whether a particular assault, robbery, or murder was committed by an individual who happened to belong to a gang, or by a gang member furthering the objectives of the gang.

Asians, one of the fastest growing segments of ethnic gangs, are posing special problems for authorities. Language and cultural barriers in particular, make investigation of gangs difficult. In addition, gangs such as Chinese, Vietnamese, Laotian, and Cambodians have a fluid membership and are highly mobile. A new trend of the Asian gangs in the 1990s is the home invasion. Home invasions against Asian nationals have resulted in countless rapes, robberies, beatings, and shootings of innocent women and children. Most of the violence occurs when valuables are not readily surrendered. Victims of home invasions are often distrustful of the criminal justice system and many times are reluctant to report the crimes for fear of retaliation.

Police departments respond in different ways to the gang problem and have adopted various approaches. In Chicago, special gang units exist with as many as 400 officers, compared to other large cities such as New York and Philadelphia that designate less than 10 officers as gang specialists. The creation of such units can cause controversy within the community. For example, some critics argue that a police department that recognizes a gang problem in the community may do so in order to justify a greater operational budget. Accordingly, members of the community may become unrealistically fearful of the gang problem. On the other hand, police departments that fail to recognize a gang problem in light of mounting evidence may not be adequately serving the needs and best interests of the community.

In the 1950s and 1960s, the typical police approach to gangs was intervention. That is, officers encouraged youths not to join gangs or employed social service agencies to work with gang members themselves. During the 1970s and 1980s, most police departments used a suppression policy that focused on identifying gangs and arresting their members. It is unclear which, if either, method worked. Today, debate still exists about which approach is more effective.

Defining the Youth Gang

A major problem in the study of youth gangs is the lack of consensus as to what defines a youth gang. Is it correct to refer to any congregation of youths as a gang? Many law enforcement agencies use the term narrowly to refer to a group of delinquents that hold and defend self-claimed territory or "turf." Frederick Thrasher, a sociologist in a pioneering study, attempted to define a youth gang:

> A gang is an interstitial group originally formed spontaneously and then integrated through conflict. It is characterized by the following types of behavior: meeting face to face, milling, movement through space as a unit, conflict, and planning. The result of this collective behavior is the development of tradition, unreflective internal structure, esprit de corps, solidarity, morale, group awareness, and attachment to local territory.

This definition, first appearing in 1927, still seems to capture the essence of group cohesiveness that remains the prevailing characteristic of many gangs. Yet another behavioral scientist, Malcolm Klein, offered a more recent description of a youth gang, which includes the element of danger:

> Any denotable group of youngsters who (a) are generally perceived as a distinct aggregation by others in their neighborhood; (b) recognize themselves as a denotable group (almost invariably with a group

name); and (c) have been involved in a sufficient number of delinquent incidents to call forth a consistent negative response from
neighborhood residents and/or law enforcement agencies (1971:13).

Sociologist Lewis Yablonsky (1966) made an important contribution to the
understanding of the youth gang with his definition of a "near group." According to Yablonsky, human collectives tend to range from highly cohesive, tight-
knit organizations to mobs with anonymous members that are motivated by
their emotions and led by disturbed membership (p. 109). Teenage gangs fall
somewhere in between and are, therefore, categorized as near groups. Near
groups have the following traits:

1. Diffuse role definition
2. Limited cohesion
3. Impermanence
4. Minimal consensus norms
5. Shifting membership
6. Disturbed leadership
7. Limited definition of membership expectations

Gang Formation

Unlike legitimate business, organized crime groups like youth gangs do not
have employment recruiting drives. In places like Watts, Little League is nonexistent, leaving gangs as the only membership option for many. Typically, social
scientists have suggested that gangs appeal to kids in low-income, inner-city
areas, marked by poverty, racial strife, broken families, and limited job and
educational opportunities. In fact, that premise is widely supported by media
accounts and scholars alike. Experts have suggested that when minority youth
don't have jobs or an education, they attempt to demonstrate their power in
other ways. The gang represents a means whereby members can feel they are a
part of something. This is not to suggest, however, that gangs in middle-class
America don't exist, as they do.

Historically, gang formation has been closely linked with surges in immigration. With many such groups, especially those with strong language and cultural barriers, good-paying jobs were non-existent. In other cases, social prejudice made it difficult for immigrants to secure jobs and earn a respectable living. Essentially, however, ethnic groups who found themselves at the bottom of
the social ladder were more likely to end up in gang activity.

Youth gangs of many ethnic origins have been a perennial nuisance
throughout American history. In fact, Benjamin Franklin lamented the trouble
caused by youth gangs in pre-Revolutionary War Philadelphia. However, only
since the early- to mid-1980s have youth gangs become violent and well established in most major American cities. Perhaps the most threatening develop-

ment of gangs in the late 1980s was the expansion of two black California-based youth gangs, the *Crips* and the *Bloods*.

The Crips and Bloods

Black youth gangs in California have roots tracing back to the early 1920s when they first organized as loose-knit, opportunistic street gangs in the south-central Los Angeles area. The early gangs consisted primarily of family members and close friends that generated income from small-time criminal activity while perpetuating a "tough-guy" street image.

By 1965, police authorities in the Los Angeles and Compton areas observed a comparatively higher number of gangs with an increasing degree of criminal sophistication. Gangs would form as protection organizations from rival gangs in other neighborhoods. Examples of gangs during the 1960s include:

• Farmers	• Businessmen
• 135s	• Swamps
• Slausons	• Sir Valiants
• Roman 20s	• Treetops
• Huns	• Gladiators
• Pueblos	• Valiants

By 1969, the first Crips gangs were organized. Some theories about the origin of their enigmatic name are as follows:

- The name Crips might stand for "Central Revolution In Progress," reflecting the antiestablishment atmosphere of the era.

- The name Crips may have evolved from the title of the 1950s Vincent Price movie *Tales from the Crypt.*

- The name Crips might have been derived from the street gang called the Cribs, which was reportedly one of the largest street gangs in the L.A. area during the early 1960s.

- One theory is that the original members of the Crips were crippled and they were called "Crips" because of their handicap. It is also maintained that most early Crips carried walking canes as a means of identification.

- The term Crips may have evolved from a desire on the part of gang members to find a gang name that represented the toughest, strongest thing in existence, and that substance was "kryptonite," the only substance that could kill Superman.

Crips gang activity originated on the campus of Washington High School in Los Angeles, where the color blue was adopted as the gang color. It was from here that the reputation of the Crips spread rapidly as a violent street gang committing robberies, assaults, and extortion. Crips members would travel to other neighborhoods to prey on unsuspecting youths there. Other youths also formed gangs to protect themselves from the violence of the Crips, and the per-petuation of the youth gang phenomenon was well under way.

One of the gangs formed in response to the Crips is the *Compton Pirus*, originating on Piru Street in Compton, California. It was the Compton Pirus that evolved into the first *Bloods* gang in the Los Angeles area. As of the prepa-ration of this text, Compton-based gangs, adopting red as their gang color, are referred to as Pirus while gangs from other areas of Los Angeles also using red as a gang color are called Bloods. Although membership numbers are difficult to ascertain, estimates place the total number of black youth gang members at a conservative 15,000 members total, with the Crips outnumbering the Bloods three-to-one (LA Police Gang Control Manual, 1991).

Case in Point

In the summer of 1987, the Crips sent representatives to Kansas City, Missouri to exploit the cocaine distribution market, which at the time had a gap due to the successful neutralization of the Jamaican Posses by police. Gangs took up residence in the outlying areas of the city but targeted the inner city for cocaine distribution. Initially the gangs were identifiable by their dress, language, and habits but they now tend to avoid such dead giveaways to prevent unwanted attention from law enforcement.

As the Los Angeles-based youth gangs evolved, drugs became the chosen moneymaker for them, and gang rivalries and accompanying warfare became more and more intense. Fully automatic firearms are now used with more fre-quency than ever before, and since the mid-1980s, the "drive-by shooting" is a common retaliatory gang tactic used in the Los Angeles area.

According to the Los Angeles Police Department, in 1988, Los Angeles-based youth gangs consisted of as many as 192 Crips gangs and an estimated 65 Bloods gangs, and each was composed of numerous smaller gangs or "sets" within the organization. Each set is comprised of several members numbering up to 30, 40, or even 50 individuals. The age group of each set will generally range from 12 to 14 years of age (called gang-bangers or "gangsters"), but some members may be as old as the mid- to late-20s (called "OGs" or "origi-nal gangsters").

In recent years, crack cocaine has become the biggest money-generating commodity for the black youth gangs originating in Los Angeles. Older gang members commonly use younger members as street dealers, and it is these older members that may realize as much as $400 per day. Much of these drug profits are usually kept within the gang.

Because the price of cocaine in the Los Angeles area has declined so dra-matically since the mid-1980s (from $100 to approximately $20 to $30 per gram), gang members are finding that great profits can be realized by purchasing the drug in Los Angeles and smuggling it to other cities in the United States, where it can be converted to crack and sold for exorbitant profits ranging from $100 to $150 per gram.

Figure 8.7
Location of Crips and Bloods in the Continental United States

Of the many unique characteristics of the black Los Angeles gangs is the use of graffiti on public buildings and structures to identify claimed turf. The use of graffiti sends a message to rival gangs that the particular area around the graffiti has been claimed as territory for drug sales and that other gangs should not interfere. Although many strategies are being considered in dealing with the youth gang problem, the consensus still focuses on two fundamental goals: reform the juvenile justice system so that it holds juveniles more accountable for their actions and intensify efforts to keep youths from joining gangs.

Jamaican Posses

Jamaican organized crime gangs, known as posses, emerged in the United States during the mid-1980s. The approximately 40 posses operating in the United States, Canada, Great Britain, and the Caribbean are conservatively estimated to have 10,000 members. The majority of them are convicted felons or illegal aliens. Almost all posses have connections in Miami and New York, which have large Jamaican populations.

The volatile political history of Jamaica was discussed in detail in Chapter 4 and explains the basis for the creation of dangerous politically motivated gangs. Because of the political segregation of neighborhoods in Jamaica, posses were formed to rally support for their chosen political party. Many posses name themselves after the neighborhoods from which they hail (as do many youth gangs).

In the mid-1970s, two large and violent groups emerged in Jamaica: the Reatown Boys and the Dunkirk Boys. The Reatown Boys consisted of members from the Reatown area of Jamaica and were loyalists to the People's National Party (PNP). They soon became known by the community as the *Untouchables* because of the number of murders perpetrated by PNP members. Today they have evolved into the *Shower Posse*. The Dunkirk Boys became known as the *Magentas* and aligned themselves with the Jamaican Labor Party (JLP). They have now evolved into the *Spangler Posse*. Both the Shower and the Spangler Posses are considered the largest of the Jamaican organized crime groups.

Drug wars between the Spanglers and rival gangs were responsible for an estimated 350 to 500 murders in the U.S. between 1985 and 1987. The Spanglers operate primarily in larger cities and because of their large size, assess a "tax" on drug sales by other smaller groups. It is this tax that is the basis for much of the intergang violence in many American cities.

The posses have distinctive operating methods. Compared to the Colombians, they are more vertically integrated, as they are involved as importers, wholesalers, distributors, and even retailers. The posses normally purchase cocaine in small quantities (usually 4 to 5 kilograms) from Colombians or Cubans in Jamaica, the Bahamas, southern California, and South Florida. By excluding the middleman, the posses can substantially raise the profit margins to the point that, for example, one posse controlling 50 crack houses realized $9 million per month.

Figure 8.8
Location of Jamaican Posses in the Continental United States

Posse Violence

The Jamaican posse has clearly demonstrated a proclivity for violence seldom displayed by other organized crime groups. In 1988, the Justice Department stated that Jamaican posses have been directly responsible for hundreds of murders in the United States and cited their increasing level of violence throughout the country as a major public safety threat.

Thinking Critically #17

Support or refute this statement: Because of the violence associated with Jamaican posses, immigration from Jamaica to the U.S. should be strictly limited.

As previously mentioned, most of the violence perpetrated by the posses is attributed to the crack cocaine "glut" in many urban areas of the United States. This deluge has caused a decrease in the retail price of the cocaine market nationwide and has created territorial feuds between crack house operators. The violence used by Jamaican posses is, therefore, one of their most notable characteristics.

The violence committed by the posses frequently includes torture. Cases in Washington D.C. and New York have involved victims being shot in the ankles, knees, and hips prior to being shot in the head. In addition, some cases have documented victims being tortured in bathtubs through the use of scalding hot water.

The potential violence and arrogance of the posses are also illustrated by their willingness to issue contracts on police and federal agents that the posses feel are disrupting their operation. In one Virginia case, a $25,000 reward was offered to anyone that killed a police officer. Some Jamaican criminals have even attempted to entrap police by identifying their telephone and beeper numbers and then luring them to prearranged shootouts.

Violence by the posses is directed at virtually anyone that creates problems for them in their crack cocaine business, including members of their own posse and rival posses alike. Violence against posse enemies is strategically performed to intimidate others that may pose a threat to the organization; the violence is directed to both civilians and law enforcement officials.

Investigations have revealed that posse members have been caught with dangerous explosives such as MK-II grenades, which were once seized from a posse in a 1987 incident. In addition, the following explosives have also been recovered from posse residences: one-quarter pound of TNT, numerous cans of smokeless powder, hundreds of firearms, and clandestine publications on how to produce plastic explosives.

> **The Case of Lester Lloyd Coke**
>
> The case of Jim Brown, who became the "top ranking gunman" of Tivoli Gardens, is an example of Jamaican gang operations. In October, 1984, Brown came to Miami on a visitor's visa in the name of Lester Lloyd Coke (ironically enough). Ten months later, when Coke was arrested for marijuana trafficking, his true identity was learned, which revealed that he was wanted for at least 12 murders in Jamaica. In spite of repeated attempts to extradite Coke to Jamaica, Jamaican government officials refused to accept Coke back or to initiate extradition proceedings. Coke wasn't returned to Jamaica until March 1986; he was deported after an investigation of Jamaican gangs revealed that he was the leader of Miami's Shower Posse. Coke (or Brown) ultimately was released from custody in Kingston after being acquitted of one of the 12 murders. He also has been hailed as a hero in Jamaica after thousands of supporters paraded in Kingston following his release.

Source: Ronald A. Pincomb, New Mexico State University. Published in the *International Association for the Study of Organized Crime Newsletter,* 1989, volume 4, number 2.

A treaty ratified by the Jamaican Parliament in December 1987 broadened the category of those wanted in the United States and apprehended in Jamaica that could be returned to the United States. Under the terms of the treaty, Jamaica must extradite fugitives wanted in the United States for any crime that would be an offense in Jamaica. The treaty also covers fugitives wanted in the United States for conspiring to traffic narcotics, a charge that was not extraditable before the treaty was ratified. The new treaty and related legislation also permit the extradition of offenders wanted in the United States for the unlawful possession or use of firearms, another crime that was not previously covered.

As of the preparation of this book, Jamaican posse activity in America has abated. This is largely attributable to the completion of the 1989 elections there, by which Michael Manley was once again elected into office. However, if history is to serve as a predictor for posse violence, then perhaps yet another wave of violent gang activity can be anticipated in American streets as elections draw near in Jamaica.

Prison Gangs

When studying the evolution of many major organized crime groups, it becomes clear that inmate associations in both state and federal prisons often help sow the seeds of criminal activity. The existence of prison gangs is nothing new, as the Italian Camorra had its beginnings in the Spanish prisons of Naples back in the 1860s.

Figure 8.9
Crack Profit Margin

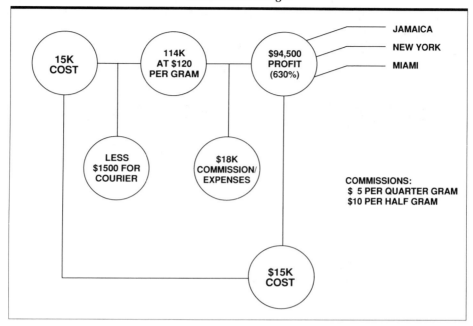

Indeed, a similar criminal phenomenon has taken place in the United States and has produced many violence-prone criminal organizations. In 1987, the U.S. Bureau of Prisons estimated that 114 prison gangs operated in state and federal prisons across the country. Of these, five have emerged as the largest, most violent, and most sophisticated. These are the Mexican Mafia (EME), the Nuestra Familia (NF), the Aryan Brotherhood (AB), the Texas Syndicate (E Ts E), and the Black Guerrilla Family (BGF).

The more sophisticated of the prison gangs share similar traits, as we have previously discussed, with regard to their dedication to the organization and members. Other traits are also prevalent:

- Prison gangs commonly have a "blood in—blood out" policy, which requires prospective members to injure or kill a designated target individual in the prison system
- Prison gangs operate both inside and outside the prison walls
- Prison gangs commonly form alliances within the prisons in order to build presence, strength, and clout within the prison walls.

Most gangs are typically formed as protection organizations for members, but once accepted, the recruit enjoys the power, prestige, influence, and protection that the organization offers.

Prison gangs in the United States became widely known in 1957 when the EME first organized at the Deuel Vocational Institute in Tracy, California. The gang originally formed as a protection organization for gang members, but the membership grew rapidly. After gaining considerable size and influence in the prison system, gang members acquired control over such activities as homosexual prostitution, drug trafficking, debt collection (extortion), and gambling. The group, now numbering an estimated 600 members, focuses most of its aggression against white and black inmates, while leaving Mexican inmates alone.

Thinking Critically #18

If prison gangs in fact operate within the walls of prisons, then do they pose a threat to public safety? Defend your answer.

The EME established a goal for itself to control drug trafficking in all areas where it had become established. The gang gained a reputation for violence after the 1967 stabbing death of a suspected police informer operating within the ranks of the gang. As violence grew, even some members of the gang felt uneasy. It was the same year that a group of EME members formed its own gang, called Nuestra Familia (NF), meaning "our family." The NF waged war with the EME and over the years has caused numerous deaths.

Because of the ongoing war with the EME, the NF has formed an alliance with the Black Guerrilla Family as well as other ethnic prison gangs. The NF has surpassed the EME in organizational capabilities, and its size, now estimated at around 700 to 800 strong, makes the NF one of the largest prison gangs in the United States.

Another prison gang that has achieved considerable notoriety is the Nazi-oriented Aryan Brotherhood. A characteristic of particular significance is the association between outlaw motorcycle gang members and the AB. Frequently, when members of outlaw motorcycle gangs are convicted and sent to prison, they no longer have the protection of their gang. The AB, being a white-supremacist organization, has commonly accepted bikers into the gang, who also share a racist philosophy. The hierarchy of the AB consists of a commission and a governing council. Members are promoted through the ranks based on individual acts of violence committed on behalf of the gang's organizational goals.

The Black Guerrilla Family (BGF) was founded in 1966 by the late George Jackson in San Quentin Prison. The BGF is a politically motivated organization following a Maoist philosophy and operates on a command structure that incorporates a Supreme Commander, Central Committee, Field Generals, and Captains of Security. As with the adoption of bikers by the Aryan Brotherhood, the BGF recruits members of black street gangs in prison. Members of the Crips and Bloods have been known to become instant members of the BGF once they are in the prison system.

The last of the five major prison gangs is the Texas Syndicate (E Ts E), which organized in Folsom Prison in 1974. Although considered the smallest gang in membership (an estimated 175 strong), the Texas Syndicate is also considered the most violent of the five major gangs. The gang consists of Mexican-American inmates that originally hailed from the areas of El Paso and San Antonio, Texas. One particular characteristic of Mexican-oriented prison gangs is an intense loyalty between members, which contributes to their reputation for violence. The gang is active in assaults and extortion and has targeted drug trafficking as its primary criminal enterprise both inside and outside the prison.

Case Study: Ray Ray and the BGF

The Black Guerrilla Family is a close-knit gang that originated in the 1970s in California prisons. BGF members and affiliates are engaged in many types of crime and are best characterized as "simply prone to violence."

This OCDETF case involved an investigation by a Task Force team consisting of the DEA, IRS, ATF, Los Angeles County Sheriff's Office, California Department of Justice, and local police officers from four jurisdictions. Their goal was to uncover and prosecute the narcotics, strong-arming, and homicide activities of the Elrader "Ray Ray" Browning organization. After two years of investigation, working undercover and using informants; six months of intensive surveillance; and three months of wiretaps on residences, automobiles, and portable phones, 28 defendants were indicted on a variety of cocaine, heroin, and firearms charges. Browning's drug couriers, whose consignment of cocaine was seized by the DEA in Detroit, were also indicted.

Browning was released from prison in 1979 after serving part of a state term for a murder that he committed as a juvenile. In August of that year, a man identified as Browning walked into a cafe and shot two men to death. The attack was to avenge a drug robbery of James "Doc" Holiday, Ray Ray Browning's associate. Ray Ray's conviction was overturned when a California Supreme Court decision rendered inadmissible the testimony of a witness that had been hypnotized in an attempt to refresh her memory.

In 1983, Browning was found guilty of firebombing and shooting into a Pasadena home in an incident related to drug territories. Again, his conviction was overturned, and he was released in September 1985. Browning then began organizing his major drug ring.

Like a corporation's chief executive officer, Ray Ray headed a broad narcotics empire with senior executives in at least four cities. Gross sales were estimated at $1 million to $3 million per month! Profits were funneled into a pricey lifestyle for Browning, his girlfriend and second-in-command, Nei Marie Wells, and a very small group of top confederates such as "Doc" Holiday. The rest were mainly small-time drug dealers ordered by Ray Ray to work for him or close up shop.

At home in Pasadena, everyone knew Ray Ray. Seeing him being driven in his white limousine or smiling behind the wheel of his Rolls-Royce, young boys watched in reverence and adults spoke in hushed tones. To those that knew him, Browning always seemed to beat the system. Folklore produced a man larger than life. Tales of drug rivalries, intimidation, and murder abounded.

The turning point was an incident in Detroit. Big John Milan, a Browning operative, arrived by bus with 18 kilos of cocaine in two suitcases. Observing two men and a dog examining his luggage, Big John refused to claim it. The agents had been alerted to his arrival by their Los Angeles counterparts, who were tapping Ray Ray's phone. They later testified that they did not detain Milan in order to protect the integrity of the wiretap.

Milan called Nei Wells to ask permission to abandon the bags but was told that he might as well get arrested because Ray Ray wouldn't believe his story. He then approached the baggage clerk, who gratuitously told Milan not to claim the bags because the police had discovered the "bricks" inside. At that, John departed without the bags and checked into a Detroit hotel that the gang customarily used. Within a few hours, he changed hotels at Ray Ray's direction. The next evening, two men fired several .45 caliber slugs into Big John's room, wounding him seriously. At that point, Big John decided to cooperate with authorities in order to save his life. Nei's to-the-point comment registered on tape was: "We never heard of dogs sniffing buses before."

John Milan would make a zealous witness but not a particularly well-informed or reputable one. Nei Marie Wells, however, was all of these things. Nei functioned at the center of the web and knew more of the details than anyone but Ray Ray himself. Facing CCE charges and sentencing possibilities of up to 80 years, Nei decided to cooperate, provided she and her children could be protected from Ray Ray's wrath. Nei Wells became "the most diligent, conscientious, cooperating witness" that the prosecutor had ever seen. She is presently out on bond awaiting sentencing, and she and her family are secure in the U.S. Marshal's Witness Security Program.

The raid that closed down the Ray Ray Browning operation involved several hundred officers and agents, who went to 17 locations simultaneously and seized 15 pounds of cocaine, $300,000 in cash, four homes, an apartment building, and 10 cars. They arrested 21 persons, and seven more were later detained on additional federal warrants. The Browning case and several immediate spin-offs resulted in seizures totaling almost a million dollars in cash and several million dollars worth of real estate, jewelry, and vehicles.

Twenty of the 28 charged defendants were prosecuted in federal court. Of those 20, 18 pled guilty and received sentences of up to 20 years in prison without parole; the only defendants to go on trial in federal court were Browning and Holiday. After a three-week trial in which they chose to handle their own defense, both were convicted. While awaiting sentencing, Browning tried to escape from Terminal Island Federal Prison by posing as an attorney, complete with wig, mustache, briefcase, and law book, but was foiled by an alert guard that recognized Ray Ray's "swagger."

Ray Ray is presently serving two life sentences plus 120 years in Leavenworth. He was among the nation's first defendants to be prosecuted under the 1986 statute mandating a life term for a conviction as the chief of a continuing criminal enterprise involving drugs. He was ordered to pay $2 million in fines (just in case anything should be left after forfeitures and the collection of unpaid taxes on the drug income). "Doc" Holiday was sentenced to life without possibility of parole.

The judge remarked at sentencing on August 29, 1988, "When Congress passed the [statute] it had a certain individual in mind. Well, Mr. Browning, you are it." Under the newest drug law, which took effect November 21, 1988, a defendant in Browning's position that is proven to have committed or ordered a drug-related murder faces the death penalty. Perhaps Ray Ray lucked out once again.

Source: Organized Crime Drug Enforcement Task Force, 1988.

Ancillary Trafficking Organizations

Other than those organizations already discussed, there are many other smaller organizations operating throughout the United States. These organizations do business in both urban and rural settings and account for a significant segment of the domestic drug trafficking picture.

The urban trafficking organizations make up a significant category of drug dealers. These organizations are frequently well-organized, highly structured, and are usually composed of extremely violent career criminals. In many cases, these organizations consist of younger criminals that, as they age, assume a leadership role. Many are later convicted and sent to prison, or they are killed. This places the urban trafficking organizations in a constant state of metamorphosis.

Urban drug gangs exist throughout the country but have been particularly active in such cities as Chicago, Detroit, St. Louis, and East St. Louis, Illinois. It is common for members to be heavily armed with fully automatic weapons and to be especially violence-prone. Violence by these organizations frequently occurs because of rivalries between trafficking groups over "turf," but the violence may manifest itself as aggression toward police, prosecutors, and witnesses in drug prosecutions.

As discussed earlier in this text, most drug sources are either Mexican or Latin American nationals. Females are also commonly used as couriers from the source city to the ultimate destination, and profits for drugs acquired are usually considerably high. For example, a kilogram of cocaine purchased in a source city may cost $12,000 to $15,000 but can be resold for $30,000. Because of this enormous profit margin, control of the industry is a primary goal of the urban trafficking organization.

There are also other "small-time" trafficking organizations operating in rural America. In some cases, drug trafficking may be a variation of another type of criminal activity that has been going on for some time. For example, in some parts of the Southeast, rural people that once produced moonshine have discovered that marijuana is more profitable. The isolation of many rural areas enables traffickers to conduct operations such as marijuana farming and clandestine laboratories and, in doing so, remain relatively free of detection from law enforcement authorities. In many cases, such locations are also good areas for use as "drop zones" or secluded landing strips for smuggling pilots.

Summary

Because of the profit potential for drug trafficking, criminal organizations with both foreign and domestic origins compete for the market share. This chapter deals with domestic drug trafficking organizations; many of these have their roots in foreign countries or are relatively new to the illegal drug trade.

The term traditional organized crime is most commonly associated with Italian criminal groups or La Cosa Nostra (LCN or Mafia). The LCN originated in Italy and Sicily during the 1800s and is now considered the premier criminal group in Italy and a major criminal phenomenon in the United States. The origin of Italian organized crime in prisons parallels that of many domestic prison gangs in the United States.

The first Mafioso arrived in the United States in the late 1800s and gained a foothold in New York and New Orleans. Prohibition (1920-1933) was conducive to Mafiosi criminal activities, which spread to other large cities throughout the United States. Today there are an estimated 25 LCN families, and according to the FBI, 19 of those are involved, in one way or another, with drug trafficking.

Outlaw motorcycle gangs represent yet another domestic criminal group actively involved in the drug trade. Originating in the late 1940s, gangs with names like the Hell's Angels, the Pagans, Bandidos, and the Outlaws have now cornered much of the methamphetamine market and frequently dwell in cities outside the continental United States. These gangs have also gained a reputation for violence and on many occasions have worked in collusion with other criminal groups such as LCN. The DEA estimates that approximately 850 outlaw motorcycle gangs currently operate in the United States. Some of these organizations have demonstrated considerable sophistication and pose a very real threat to many major U.S. cities.

In the early 1970s, California youth gangs such as the Crips and Bloods organized in the east Los Angeles area. Today, they have grown to about 60,000 to 70,000 strong and occupy an estimated 30 American cities. Youth gangs have concentrated on the crack/cocaine trade and, like outlaw motorcycle gangs, are vertically integrated so that they produce and distribute drugs on both the wholesale and retail level.

Youth gang members are customarily a very young age (between 14 and 18 years old) and have become very willing to engage in violent turf battles with other gangs. This type of criminal group has made it necessary to consider the restructuring of laws dealing with juvenile offenders to make youthful offenders more accountable for their actions.

Other groups have also recently emerged that parallel the organizations of the youth gangs. Political unrest in the late 1970s and early 1980s created one such violent gang in the area of the Caribbean basin, the Jamaican Posse. The posses began their drug dealing ventures with the smuggling of high-grade marijuana known as "ganja" but have now also identified the crack/cocaine trade as their primary source of revenue. It is thought that posses have formed alliances with other criminal organizations such as the Colombian cartels.

Jamaican posses may account for an estimated 10,000 members with connections to Jamaican neighborhoods in both New York and Miami. In addition to dealing drugs, the posses are very active in firearms trafficking from the United States to Jamaica, where weapons are used to gain unlawful political influence in the Jamaican society.

Prison gangs also represent a unique domestic brand of organized crime. Of the estimated 114 prison gangs operating in the United States, five have emerged as the most sophisticated: the Mexican Mafia, Nuestra Familia, Aryan Brotherhood, Black Guerilla Family and the Texas Syndicate. All of these organizations possess a particularly violent nature, and they have all identified drug trafficking as a primary criminal goal.

Do you recognize these terms?

blood in—blood out
ganja

home invasions
the Pizza Connection

Discussion Questions

1. Discuss the hierarchical structure of La Cosa Nostra, and compare it to that of the Los Angeles-based youth gangs, the Bloods and the Crips.

2. Review some of the reasons why some researchers perceive La Cosa Nostra as a fragmented group of semi-organized criminals.

3. List those domestic criminal organizations most actively involved in cocaine/crack trafficking.

4. What is the relationship between the American and the Sicilian Mafia in the illicit drug trade?

5. Name and discuss the structure and other similarities of the four major outlaw motorcycle gangs that operate in the United States.

6. To what extent do Jamaican posses play a role in international drug trafficking, and in what other illicit operations are the posses involved?

Foreign Drug Trafficking Organizations *9*

This chapter will enable you to:

- Understand the role of Colombian drug criminals in global drug trafficking
- Learn about the role of Mexican and Cuban drug traffickers
- Understand the link between drug trafficking and terrorism
- See how Asian drug traffickers are gaining influence in U.S. illegal drug markets.

In Chapter 4 we discussed some general dynamics of foreign drug source countries, but in this chapter we will take a closer look at the criminal trafficking groups originating in those countries. Today it is clear that drug abuse in the United States has created a growing incentive for escalating foreign involvement in the drug trade for the allure of profits for traffickers is considerable. For example, in 1995, the Office of National Drug Control Policy estimated that in 1993 Americans spent $31 billion for cocaine, $7 billion for heroin, and $9 billion for marijuana. The degree to which various criminal organizations involve themselves depends greatly on factors such as the type of drug trafficked, the source country's proximity to the United States, established trafficking routes, and the ability to move money and personnel in and out of the country.

Interdiction efforts have shown that international boundaries pose little resistance to the flow of drugs into the country. Accordingly, criminal organizations whose purpose it is to traffic these substances are varied and widespread. For example, most people are aware of the Colombian cartels in South America who manufacture and traffic a majority of the world's cocaine and great deal of marijuana as well. Despite the widespread international notoriety of these groups, many other trafficking organizations play important roles in the illegal drug trade. Specifically, the Jamaican posses, originating in the Caribbean basin, have proven to be formidable players in the international drug scene, while Chinese triads and tongs (organized crime groups discussed later in the chapter) pose new threats to domestic law enforcement through their trafficking of high-quality heroin from Southeast and Southwest Asia. Additionally, the long-established Japanese Yakuza continue to diversify their international base of criminal operations which are cloaked by legitimate business and industry. We will now discuss some specifics about these groups and their contribution to global drug trafficking. We will also attempt to compare organizational dynamics of these groups to help us better understand their origin, structure, and purpose.

Colombian Organized Crime

The term **cartel** has been associated with many Colombian organized crime groups since the mid-1980s, but before we discuss the role and operations of the more significant Colombian cartels, we would first like to define the term "cartel." To do so we could begin by comparing the function of a cartel to that of a "legitimate" group of business entrepreneurs. An example of one such group is OPEC (the Organization of Petroleum Exporting Countries). The OPEC countries are well-known for practicing political and social manipulation in attempts to control the production of oil for maximum economic gain. The Colombian cartel is similar in that its goal is to control cocaine traffic through illegal means with profit as its principal intent.

Colombian cartels are structured in what can be described as an "onion-like" layering of organizational power. Kingpins and top managers are safely located in the center surrounded by layers of subordinates who are responsible for directing various aspects of the cartel's operations. Subordinates are those who are directly responsible for production, supply, and sale of the illegal product. Included in this group are growers, smugglers, and small-time distributors. As discussed in the last chapter, the providers of services are the next layer of the onion. These individuals consist of accountants, lawyers, bankers, corrupt politicians, and others who support and protect the organization and who benefit from it while never understanding its entire nature or scope. This organizational dynamic makes it easy for these persons to be replaced.

The power and influence of the drug cartels over Colombian society demonstrates the terrorizing impact of a criminal organization when it becomes a state within a state. One characteristic of these powerful cartels is their willingness to display their power and wealth. They have evolved in a country, Colombia, that by one estimate is home to 140 right-wing paramilitary squads and six Marxist guerrilla groups. According to the State Department, the murder rate in Colombia is two-and-one-half times that of New York City (Bagely, 1988).

By 1989, four principal Colombian cartels emerged as the most active in cocaine trafficking: the *Cali Cartel*, the *Bogota Cartel*, the *North Atlantic Coast Cartel*, and the *Medellin Cartel* (whose future is uncertain). These cartels act as true cartels in the classic sense that they attempt, through collaboration, to set prices and eliminate any effective competition.

The cartels originated during the late 1970s, and it is believed that at one time or another they have worked with one another. Today, Colombian cartels have grown to exercise considerable global influence, with the exception of the Medellin Cartel, whose influence has been greatly diminished with the death of cartel leader Pablo Escobar in 1993. The word cartel is somewhat misleading, however, because it suggests a greater degree of cohesion than exists among major drug trafficking countries. More accurately, cartels are communities with shared interests of greater or lesser duration; they are groups that pool their drug shipments, share methods of transportation, or exchange certain types of information vital to each organization's drug trafficking operations.

In one sense, the Colombian cartels do function like traditional cartels, except they attempt to set prices and eliminate any competition through violence and corruption. They have successfully fixed prices for cocaine on both the wholesale and retail levels and have diversified into other drug markets, such as marijuana and heroin. Most notably, they have accumulated the necessary funds (through corruption) to purchase the consent of major forces in Colombian society, for example, the police, the judiciary, and journalists that influence public opinion. The cartels also initiate threats, acts of violence, and intimidation against those that are not subject to the inducements of bribery.

Of the four major cartels, the largest is the Cali Cartel, which now controls an estimated 70 percent of the raw cocaine transported from Bolivia, Ecuador, and Peru for processing in Colombia (DEA, 1993). The Cali Cartel and the embattled Medellin Cartel were thought to have worked together up until 1987, pooled funds to defend their members, and even worked with the Basque ETA organization (a Spanish terrorist group), which is noted for its expertise in the use of car bombs. The cartels also have typically staked out territory for drug trafficking. New York, for example, was assigned to the Cali group because it had become well-established in its operations there. Other areas, however, such as Miami, are considered "open" territories for the cartels.

While Colombia has long been accustomed to unusually high degrees of violence, the rise of the cartels in the 1970s dictated a change in the tide of violence. In addition to fighting among themselves, the cartels have waged war against government authorities seeking their extradition to the United States. Much of this violence is perpetrated by paid assassins known as sicarios (see Chapter 4).

The membership and organizational structure of the Colombian cartels has remained consistently fluid, which contributes to their continual ability to avoid detection. That is, leadership varies with drug trends and power plays within the organization resulting in a continuing perpetuation of the organization. In addition, numerous smaller organizations constantly strive for power and pose competition for the major organizations. For years, the Medellin and Cali Cartels were at war with one another, and an estimated 100 lives were lost to the conflict. Because of the high visibility of the Medellin Cartel during the 1980s and because in the mid-1990s the Cali Cartel has emerged as the most powerful Colombian cartel, this chapter will examine both organizations in depth. The organizational structure of the cartel insures several distinct advantages for the organization. Specifically, these advantages are 1) control over the price and the quality of Colombian cocaine, 2) greater access to smuggling and processing equipment, and 3) mastery of a wide variety of methods to avoid detection by law enforcement.

In response to the drug and crime problem in Colombia, in November 1993, the Colombian Congress approved "middle-of-the-road" legislation which increases benefits for drug traffickers and other organized criminals who surrender to authorities, confess their crimes, and provide police information that leads to the arrest of other criminals. In response, cartel lawyers have argued that cartel members who have indictments against them should be given reduced sentences for surrendering even if they do not confess to crimes. As of the preparation of this text, these proposals are still under consideration by Colombian government officials.

Figure 9.1
Typical Colombian Cocaine Organization

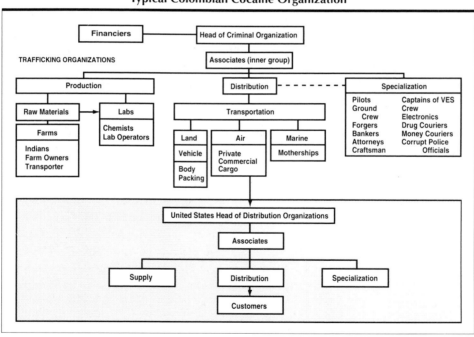

Source: U.S. Drug Enforcement Administration.

The Legacy of Medellin's Cartel

In 1988, the U.S. State Department publicly announced that Americans should stay away from the Colombian city of Medellin, the capital of Antioquia and headquarters of the once-infamous criminal organization known as the Medellin Cartel. This announcement was based on the fact that the Medellin Cartel, Colombia's premier organized crime group, had claimed the city as its international base of operation.

The Medellin Cartel was at one time reputed to earn $2 billion to $4 billion a year and to rival many Fortune 500 companies in terms of global influence. For over a decade the Medellin Cartel, known as *Los Grandes Mafiosos* by the Colombian press, was perceived as the most powerful of the Colombian cartels. With humble beginnings similar to other famous organized crime groups, the Medellin cartel was founded by four individuals: Pablo Emilio Escobar Gaviria, Jorge Luis Ochoa Vasques, Jose Gonzalo Rodriguez-Gacha, and Carlos Enrique Lehder-Rivas. During the height of their activities, the cartel's operations extended far beyond the production and transportation of cocaine. In fact, its influence greatly affected political, social, and cultural activities of people well beyond the drug trade.

The origins of the Colombian cocaine trade go back to the 1950s when traffickers produced small amounts of cocaine for shipment to Cuban criminals. After many Cubans moved to the United States in the 1960s, the Colombian cocaine trade followed. Slowly, the Cartel was organized during the mid-1970s by Escobar, who was until then a known car thief. After realizing the greater financial profit in the drug trade, Escobar converted his long-established stolen-car trafficking routes to drug trafficking pathways. Much of the Medellin Cartel's success in drug trafficking can be attributed to Carlos Lehder, who was also a small-time car thief and marijuana dealer. It was Lehder, who around 1976 conceptualized the use of small aircraft to smuggle cocaine into the United States. His idea made use of existing smuggling routes formerly used for trafficking marijuana. The difference was that cocaine was easier to transport, more easily concealed, and required fewer people than marijuana. More importantly, it was considerably more profitable. Escobar soon convinced Fabio Ochoa, then a smuggler of Scotch whisky and television sets, to work with him in the cocaine trade. Ochoa, a wealthy rancher, was never charged with drug trafficking.

Escobar's criminal influence gradually earned him the reputation as one of the world's most dangerous and wanted fugitives. His wealth stemmed from the cocaine trade and earned him a mansion in Miami and a Colombian ranch stocked with giraffes, camels, and kangaroos. Although he became known as a ruthless killer, he was nonetheless adored by Medellin's poor, who looked upon him as a rebel looking out for Colombia's peasants. Escobar could be credited with making cocaine the world's most popular drug of choice (in addition to the world's most profitable drug) by trafficking it to booming markets in the United States and Europe. To do so, he systematically organized small-time criminals into a large, almost bureaucratic, crime machine which operated with the efficiency of a multinational corporation.

Escobar was an innovator. He was quick to employ huge money laundering operations in major financial centers which were linked to his headquarters by telephones, fax machines, and computers, but his most notable contribution to the illicit drug trade was his propensity for violence. With an army estimated at 1,000 gunmen, he ordered the killing of rival cartel members, an attorney general, a justice minister, three presidential candidates, more than 200 judges, 30 kidnapping victims, dozens of journalists, and more than 1,000 police officers—virtually anyone who threatened the Cartel's operations (Fedarko, 1993). Also included in the carnage was the bombing of a Colombian airliner, which was blown out of the air with 107 people aboard. None survived. This incident alone helped Escobar earn the reputation as a so-called **narco-terrorist.**

The Rise of the Medellin Cartel

The Medellin Cartel gained prominence in global drug trafficking during the late 1970s and endured in that capacity during the following decade. One event that gave rise to the violence in which the Medellin Cartel became famous occurred in 1981. During that year leftist guerrillas known as the M-19 kidnapped Fabio Ochoa's 28-year-old daughter Marta and held her for ransom to help finance their insurgent movement. After being invited by Pablo Escobar, a meeting of some 223 cocaine traffickers was held in Medellin, out of which grew an organization calling itself "Death to Kidnappers." The group then systematically began to assassinate members of the leftist group regardless of the victims' involvement in the abduction of Fabio's daughter. Marta was soon released, and the Cartel surfaced as a powerful criminal organization with a reputation for violence.

Jose Gonzalo Rodriguez-Gacha, another original player in the cartel, had earned the reputation as one of the most vicious of the cartel's members. He lived an opulent life of extravagance and was constantly surrounded by bodyguards and beautiful women. One of his mansions was a mission-style ranch equipped with a gym and its own disco. His trademark was to inscribe his initials on his bullets. In December 1989, an extensive manhunt, consisting of more than 1,000 police and government troops supported by seven helicopters, was undertaken to locate Gacha through information given to authorities by farmers in the area. Ultimately, he was tracked to a farm owned by Escobar, located about 360 miles from Bogota; there Gacha, at age 42, was ultimately shot and killed during an exchange of gunfire with government troops. The manhunt resulted from a national government crackdown on drug traffickers, initiated shortly after presidential contender Luis Carlos Galan was assassinated by unknown gunmen in August of that year. During the early 1980s, Gacha had achieved prominence by organizing military squads made up of landowners to wage a campaign against the Revolutionary Armed Forces of Columbia (FARC) (discussed later in this chapter). The FARC had repeatedly tried to take control of the coca growing fields from the farmers in Colombia.

Important events contributing to the reputation of the cartel extend back to 1984, when Jorge Luis Ochoa was taken into custody in Spain. The DEA, at the time, told him that it would arrange for his release if he would implicate the Sandinistas in drug-smuggling operations. Ochoa refused, claiming that they were not involved. Several months later, Spain refused to extradite Ochoa to the United States because of the political nature of the request and sent him back to Colombia to face drug charges there. Once in Colombia, Ochoa was "mistakenly" released from custody.

Of all of the cartels, the Medellin Cartel was considered the most sophisticated, with managers that were dispatched to the United States for "tours of duty" as business representatives. Additionally, its headquarters received fax transmissions from operatives and had links to legitimate business interests. Each controlled a separate organization within the cartel, but each worked in harmony with the other. By not competing with each other, these traffickers learned that they could both maximize their profits and share resources at the same time.

The Medellin Cartel's Notable History

1960s	Cocaine returns to United States drug abuse scene
Late-1970s	Cocaine demand begins to explode in United States and is considered a drug of the rich. Cartel activity begins to become more active in South Florida.
	The Colombian "Cocaine Cowboys" wage cocaine war against competition in Dade County, Florida, where more than 250 murders are documented.
	Colombian cartel activity was first documented in Southern California.
	Roberto Suarez Sr., and ex-Nazi Klaus Barbie organized a 1,500-man army in Bolivia.
1980	Suarez organized 189th coup of the Bolivian government and takes control of the country for one year.
1981	As smuggling efforts spread through western United States, M-19 leftist guerrillas terrorize citizens in Colombia.
	Jorge Ochoa's daughter kidnapped by the M-19.
	In response to the Ochoa kidnapping, the traffickers form a massive meeting of all traffickers at the International Hotel, which parallels the 1957 meeting of Mafia Chiefs at Appalachia.
	The first judge is assassinated by a cartel.
1982	Suarez offers to pay off the $3 billion Bolivian foreign debt in exchange for immunity from prosecution.
1983	The Tranquilandia cocaine laboratory is discovered: 14 labs, 80-bed dormitory, air strip, 7,000 pounds of cocaine per month of production.
1984	Justice Minister Rodrigo Lara Bonilla is machine-gunned to death as extradition proceedings progress.
	Escobar, Ochoa, and Gacha are accused of masterminding Lara Bonilla murder.
	First extradition order is signed for Carlos Lehder.
	Ochoa is arrested in Spain on outstanding U.S. warrant.

1985	The judge in the Lara Bonilla case is murdered.
	First Colombian cartel members are extradited to U.S.
	The cartel joins forces with former enemies the M-19 to attack the Palace of Justice—extradition files are destroyed and 11 Supreme Court Justices are killed.
1986	U.S. government informant Barry Seal is machine-gunned to death in Louisiana by a cartel hit squad.
	Seventeen thousand peasants riot in Bolivia in protest of government interdiction in coca harvesting.
	During this year alone more than 1,700 people are killed in the city of Medellin, Colombia, as a result of cocaine-related violence.
	Spain extradites Ochoa to Colombia, where he is released and returns to control his cocaine empire.
	Former Chief of Anti-Narcotics Operation, Colonel Jamie Ramirez Gomez, is murdered.
	Editor Guillermo Cano of the *El Espectador* newspaper is murdered because of his anti-drug editorials.
1987	Enrique Parejo-Gonzalez, former Justice Minister, is located by cartel hit squad in Budapest, Hungary, and assassinated.
	Carlos Lehder is extradited to the United States.
	Colombian Supreme Court voids United States-Colombian extradition treaty after extreme pressure from the cartel.
1988	Attorney General Carlos Mauro Hoyos is kidnapped and murdered.
	Pablo Escobar and Panamanian Dictator Manuel Noriega are indicted in the United States.
	Pablo Escobar and Fabio Ochoa are indicted by the U.S. for the murder of Justice Minister Lara Bonilla, the murder of Barry Seal, and for a 15-year conspiracy to import cocaine into the U.S. through the Bahamas.
1989	Senator Luis Carlos Galan, a leading presidential candidate, is assassinated by five unknown gunmen during a campaign speech.
	President Barco enacts "summary extradition" and declares an all-out war against the traffickers after Galan's murder.
	Jose Gonzalo Rodriguez Gacha, former Medellin Cartel boss, is killed in a shoot-out with government troops.

Source: Post, M. (1990). "Colombian Crime and Cocaine Trafficking." *The Narc Officer,* (December):11. Reprinted by permission of the International Narcotics Enforcement Officers Association.

The Medellin Cartel espoused an ideology to legitimize and support their operations. It stemmed from the fact that they were businessmen and their power was a function of their wealth, which just happens to be derived from an activity that is considered illegal. It was this ideology that not only sought to protect them from prosecution but to give them legitimacy to ensure the continued operation of their business. Supportive of their ideology is a strong anti-American sentiment, which stems from the efforts of the U.S. to extradite cartel members to America for prosecution. Colombian politicians who support extradition are viewed by the cartels as unpatriotic sellouts to American imperialism. Extradition is especially hated by the traffickers because it brands them as criminals rather than businessmen, as they view themselves (Filippone, 1994). It has been said than there are thousands of Colombians who are sympathetic to many aspects of this ideology. Many have argued, however, that in actuality, Colombian cartels are motivated less by ideology than by greed and the tremoundous wealth of the drug trade.

Escobar's Demise

In 1991, Escobar surrendered to Colombian officials as part of a plea agreement. As a result, he served a short stint in a luxurious prison located in Envigado, which Escobar himself helped design. He was even placed in charge of the prison, which had luxuries that included cellular phones, computers, a waterbed, rugs and curtains, a king-sized bed, private bath and Jacuzzi, its own soccer field, a bar, a woodburning fireplace, a big-screen TV, and handpicked guards who served him as waiters at parties complete with prostitutes. Despite these luxuries, Escobar feared that his enemies with the Cali Cartel would try to kill him by bombing his jail. So, he demanded and received a bomb shelter along with authority from aviation officials to close the air space over the jail as a precaution. Finally, when accounts of his luxurious living surfaced in July 1992, the government ordered that he be moved to a regular prison. While in transport, Escobar managed to escape into the Colombian jungle, prompting a 16-month manhunt.

The hunt for Escobar was a true hare and hound parable. During the first year of his escape, he managed to elude the 1,500-man Search Block unit by moving secretly among his friends and supporters in Medellin and the surrounding countryside. His hiding placed proved to be secret rooms carved out between walls, under stairs, and underground. Often he cloaked himself in disguises, dressing as a woman or riding in coffins as a corpse. At least four times, moments before the trap sprang shut, the wily farmer's son with the double chin and potbelly slipped away and mysteriously vanished (Fedarko, 1993). Despite his slipperiness and his offer to pay $27,000 for any Search Block officer killed, 26 of Escobar's closest collaborators, including his brother-in-law and his children's teacher, were murdered. In addition, Escobar's prized collection of classic cars was bombed, including a Pontiac once owned by Al Capone,

one of his boyhood heroes. The culprits were rival criminals from the Cali Cartel who were also hunting for Don Pablo. The Cali Cartel's reputed leader, Gilberto Rodriguez Orejuela, and his brother Miguel secretly funded a vigilante organization known by its Spanish acronym **PEPES** (People Persecuted by Pablo Escobar). The group, whose members shared a $5 million stipend every two months, was made up of former colleagues whom Escobar had betrayed, rebel police officers, and members of the Cali Cartel.

Pablo Escobar: A Biography

Pablo Emilio Escobar Gaviria was born on December 1, 1949, in Rio Negro, 25 miles east of Medellin. His father was a farmer and his mother a teacher. One year later they moved to Envigado, a run-down suburb of Medellin, where he grew up, finished high school, and went to work for a smuggler of stereo equipment.

The teenaged entrepreneur began selling tombstones he had stolen from a cemetery and sanded flat. Escobar was first arrested in 1974 for stealing a car. Behind a soft spoken facade, he came to be known to associates and enemies as brilliant and ambitious, a quick learner with a talent for business and an unforgiving memory. By 1976 he was an established drug smuggler with a growing fleet of airplanes. Caught with 39 pounds of cocaine in a pickup truck, he walked out of jail three months later, his arrest mysteriously revoked. Both officers who arrested him were later murdered.

With his pot belly and greased-down hair, he never outgrew the appearance of a thug. But Escobar surrounded himself with luxury. In 1980 he bought a Miami Beach mansion; a year later he paid $8.3 million for an apartment complex in Florida and filled his Medellin condominium with paintings and Chinese porcelain. A 7,000-acre ranch in Colombia, said to cost $63 million, was his favorite estate. He imported hundreds of exotic animals, including giraffes, camels, bison, llamas, a kangaroo, and cockatoos. Hiding his drug dealing behind claims of legitimate business wealth and the image of a bene-factor, he had his own radio show and was often accompanied by Roman Catholic priests.

He built housing projects for the poor, soccer stadiums, and roller rinks, often naming them after himself. In 1982, he won an alternate representative's seat in Colombia's Congress. Two years later he was forced out of office when a Justice Minister exposed his criminal record. The Minister, Rodrigo Lara Bonilla, was later slain. As Escobar's empire grew, he was soon thought to be providing an estimated 80 percent of the U.S. cocaine market. In 1991, *Forbes* magazine listed him as being one of the world's richest people.

Indeed, what ultimately brought down Escobar and the Medellin Cartel was the Bloque de Busqueda (Search Unit), an elite police commando squad made up of officers who were handpicked and screened by the Central Intelligence Agency (CIA), and the U.S. Drug Enforcement Administration (DEA). The Bloque had only one assignment: to catch Escobar.

History proved that Escobar's true weakness was his family. Although he was the subject of a national manhunt, he feared for the safety of his 16 year-old son, Juan Pablo, 5-year-old daughter, Manuela, and wife, Victoria Eugenia Henao. In fact, in late 1992, Escobar flew them to Germany to seek political asylum prompting both the United States and Colombian goverments to urge Germany to refuse the Escobars—which it did. After being denied admittance by German officials, the Escobars were returned to Colombia where authorities located them in a secret apartment under the protection of the army.

The incident in Germany caused Escobar to make two fatal mistakes. First, out of anger, he telephoned a Medellin radio station to complain about the lack of solidarity by the German government. Next, he telephoned his family to tell them he was fine and told them to stay in Bogota for the time being. Both calls were traced by Colombian police with the use of specialized equipment provided by the U.S. The trace lead them to a two-story house in west Medellin.

Rather than conducting an all-out operation, a small 17-man squad was sent to surround the house. Telephones were disconnected so no neighbors could call Escobar and warn him of the presence of police. "I see a man talking on the phone," radioed an officer in a stakeout van. The wiretapper heard Escobar tell his son: "I see something strange. See you later." He then hung up the phone and ran upstairs as members of the Busqueda unit charged the house. Almost instantly, the 44-year-old Escobar was hit with a torrent of bullets, leaving him dead on the roof. Within moments, an officer proudly radioed to headquarters with the message—*viva Colombia* (Watson and Katel, 1993). The death of Escobar ended, at least symbolically, an era of terror in which the Medellin Cartel used the income of a multinational corporation to wage war against a modern nation.

Resulting from Escobar's death, Colombia's President Cesar Gaviria promised to crack down on other cartels. However, the Cali Cartel is considerably less violent than their rivals and is thought to be more skillful in bribery and public relations. Consequently, the campaign against it will most likely lack the intensity of that which focused on the Medellin Cartel. It has also been speculated that Escobar's family might seek revenge against both the Colombian government and their arch rivals in Cali. In either case it seems evident that the cocaine trade is still thriving even in the aftermath of Escobar's death.

The Medellin Cartel paved the way for an international cocaine market and similar trafficking mechanisms which are being exploited by the remaining cartels. Only time will tell which of these will wield the most global influence, but by all indications the Cali Cartel is the most likely successor to the Medellin cocaine machine.

Figure 9.2
A Cocaine Collaboration: The Ochoa/Escobar Joint Venture

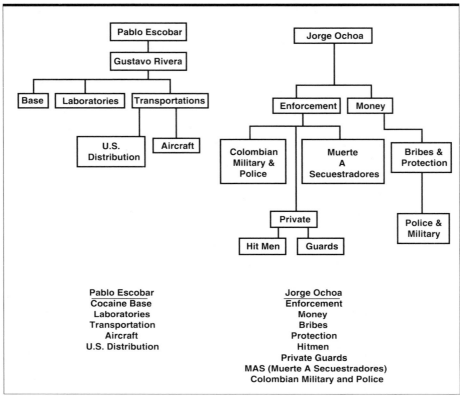

Source: PCOC, *The Impact,* 1986.

One of the events which shed light on the innerworkings of the Medellin Cartel during the early 1980s was the discovery of a chart detailing a temporary cooperative venture based in Medellin between the Pablo Escobar organization and the Jorge Ochoa organization. It was confiscated from a mid-level trafficker involved in the operation and was later provided by the DEA to the President's Commission on Organized Crime in 1986. As diagrammed in Figure 9.2, the Escobar and Ochoa organizations combined and divided the trafficking responsibilities typically completed by a single organization. The same component parts, such as labor, processing, transportation, finance, and enforcement, were carried over from the individual organizations with the Escobar group taking responsibility for production activities and the Ochoa group handling enforcement and finances (PCOC, 1986).

For more than a decade, the Medellin Cartel was thought by the DEA to be one of the world's best-organized criminal organizations. The financial division, for example, was not only responsible for collecting revenues and making investments but also for money laundering. The enforcement division was charged with corruption in the form of bribes as well as with hiring guards and assassins. The Cartel employed a decentralized type of management structure, where certain decisions were made on an individual basis by specific family members.

The Conversion Process

When coca leaves are steeped in kerosene, sulfuric acid, and an alkali, coca base is formed. This is a rather crude conglomerate of coca alkaloids and oils and has a cocaine content of 70 to 85 percent. Addition of hydrochloric acid will provide the salt, cocaine hydrochloride, with a purity of 90 to 100 percent, depending on the sophistication of the extraction process. It looks like fine white flakes or rocks and feels powdery when crushed.

It is either crude paste or cocaine hydrochloride that is brought from Peru and Bolivia to Colombia for transshipment to Miami and other large American cities by air and sea. From the point of entry, the cocaine product is redistributed through a dealer network that is generally separate from the heroin distribution system. Before arriving at the ultimate consumer, it is ordinarily cut (diluted) four to eight times, so that pure cocaine is essentially unknown at present and is not available except to major distributors that have access to it. In fact, some "cocaine" sold on the street turns out to have no cocaine at all in the product.

Note: 500 kilograms of coca leaves are required to produce one kilogram of cocaine paste.

Source: DEA, Fall 1986.

In many areas of South America, the cartels have actually achieved a degree of popularity. Many poor Latin Americans view themselves as likely candidates for someday becoming cartel members. In other cases, the wealth of the cartels has actually reshaped the Colombian economy, and many citizens on both ends of the financial spectrum enjoy short-term financial benefits. For example, Colombia has recently enjoyed one of the highest economic growth rates in South America. Some prominent Colombians have even openly defended the presence of drug traffickers. For example, in an interview published in the January 8, 1989 *Washington Post*, a Colombian attorney named Mario Arango claimed that narcotics trafficking has led to an egalitarian "social revolution." Arango further stated,

> [W]ith narcotics, the mestizos, mulattoes, and blacks . . . have had the opportunities to enter consumer society and gain substantial wealth. The best vehicles that are driven in the city of Medellin are in the hands of people who have black or dark skins. . . . I consider

the drug trade to be the support for a country in crisis. This explains the contradictions in the establishment, which on the one hand denounces it and on the other hand lives with it and benefits from it.

These phenomenon could be attributed to the presence of illicit drug revenues, but in a practical sense, the poor in Colombia have been devastated by the illegal drug trade primarily because of an exceedingly high rate of addiction.

Figure 9.3
Cocaine: Production to Sales

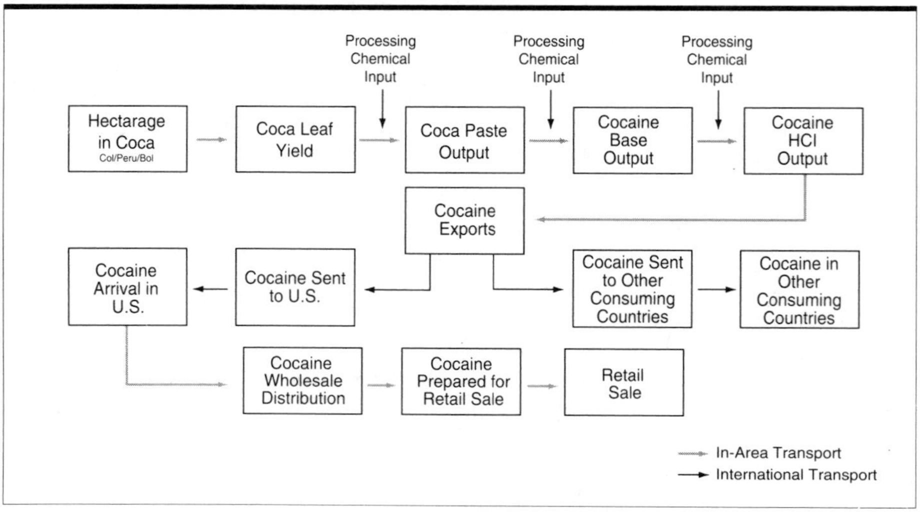

Source: ONDCP, 1989.

The Cali Cartel

With 1.6 million people, Cali is Colombia's third largest city, and one whose economy appears to be booming. It is a city which is only two hours from the port of Buenaventura on the Pacific coast, the fastest route to Asia and many South American markets. In addition to the standard sugar, fruit, and coffee industries, an estimated 40 multinational companies are based in the area. Augmenting the positive economic effects of legitimate industry, the illegal drug trade has served to boost the city's financial status. In fact, many experts fear that with the elimination of the Medellin Cartel, a so-called "Medellinization" of the city is currently underway, that is, an increased wave of violence provoked by drug lords against both the people and government of Colombia who oppose and hinder the drug rackets of local cartels. Recent statistics seem to support this supposition. For example, In January 1994, *Economist Magazine* reported that during the first nine months in 1993, 1,268 murders were recorded in Cali. This figure is reflective, in part, of overcrowding and poverty in the city. But it also suggests that the lucrative drug trade is spawning unprecedented new levels of violence.

So strong is the fear of a "**narco-democracy**" developing in Colombia, that as of this writing, U.S. officials in the State Department and DEA have ceased sharing criminal intelligence with the Colombian government.

Because for years law enforcement agencies had a tendency to focus their efforts on the best-known of the cartels, the Medellin Cartel, the Cali was given more freedom in which to operate. The Cali Cartel is not thought to be an actual cartel but rather a consortium of loosely affiliated and cooperating trafficking groups. The Cali organization, led primarily by Gilberto Rodriguez Orejuela (also known as the Chess Player), operates primarily out of Cali and Buenaventura and is closely tied to another organization in the town of Pereira. The Cali organization has demonstrated an ability to expand its operations through the use of alliances with other groups, such as the North Atlantic Coast Cartel. One of the major reasons for the success of the Cali Cartel is its high degree of integration into the Colombian economy. Unlike the larger Medellin Cartel, the Cali Cartel has been careful to cultivate popular support and strong economic, political, and social ties and to conduct its operations in a discreet, businesslike manner.

Thinking Critically #19

Support or refute this statement: The United States should expand the role that American DEA agents play in South America.

While other drug trafficking organizations have engaged in disruptive acts of violence and have attained a high degree of notoriety, the Cali Cartel has been careful to be as unobtrusive as possible, thereby avoiding the crackdown directed against the Medellin Cartel. As a result, it appears to be expanding its base of operation in the United States from cities such as Miami, New York, and Los Angeles to other American markets.

The Cali Cartel's Innerworkings

It has been said that the structure and organization of the Cali Cartel can be described in one word: precise. The ruling managers of the Cali Cartel are Jose Santacruz Londono, otherwise known as Don Chepe or "El Gordo"; Gilberto Rodriguez Orejuela, or "the Chess Player"; and his brother Miguel. Santacruz is the hands-on designer of worldwide trafficking efforts while Rodriguez is in charge of financing transactions and laundering money (Shannon, 1991). During the mid-1970s while the Medellin Cartel's gunmen were attempting to control drug territory in Miami, Santacruz was doing the same in

New York City. It was estimated that in 1991 four out of every five grams of cocaine sold in New York had its origin with Santacruz, the Orejuela Caballero brothers (partners in the Santacruz operation), and the Pancho Herrera organization (cousins of the Caballero brothers). There is additional evidence that the Cali families are attempting to monopolize the market in Europe and Japan, even to the extent that criminal alliances were forged between Cali managers and higher-ups in the Japanese Yakuza. European and Asian markets are attractive for Colombian traffickers because of the potential profits to be realized there. For example, it is estimated that the average wholesale price of a kilogram (2.2 pounds) in Japan is as high as $65,000 (DEA, 1993).

Despite several significant government seizures of cocaine, the growth of Cali's cartel seems to not have been impeded. Leaders of the Cartel have carefully compartmentalized the organization so individual losses do not threaten the entire enterprise. In the tradition of the great Mediterranean trading dynasties, the major families have a patriarchal, authoritarian structure demanding absolute discipline and loyalty, yet leaving some room for creativity on the part of Cartel operatives. Smuggling techniques differ greatly from those of the former Medellin Cartel. For example, Medellin operatives would brazenly ship cocaine across international borders in fast boats or specially outfitted planes, compared to the Cali Cartel's method of using much slower merchant marine vessels. Accordingly, the Cartel has perfected ways to hide drugs in virtually all types of legitimate-appearing cargo. For instance, in 1988, 3,270 kilograms of cocaine were found hidden in a load of Brazilian cedar boards; later that same year customs agents found 2,270 kilograms of cocaine encased in 1,200 blocks of chocolate shipped from Ecuador. Large shipments of cocaine have even been discovered buried in toxic waste. In one such case in 1989, over 5,000 kilograms of cocaine marked with the logo "Baby I" were concealed in 252 drums of powdered lye. The same logo was found on an 18,000 kilogram seizure of cocaine in Los Angeles two months earlier. In spite of such innovative concealment methods, whenever U.S. agents locate a shipment, the cartel responds by adopting a new shipper, using different routes, and employing more clever deceptions.

In 1991, Elaine Shannon observed that like big corporate CEOs, Cali Cartel leaders are also thought to be conservative managers. At the home office is the chief executive officer and his senior vice presidents for acquisition, production, transportation, sales, finance, and enforcement. Dozens of overseas branches, or cells, handle the logistics of importing, storing, and delivering the product. These decisions are overseen by the corporate office which keeps tabs through daily or sometimes hourly telephone calls.

Each cell (or workgroup) is directed by a manager called a Caleno, and is staffed by relatives and neighbors whose salaries are based on an account system in Cali. When they make minor mistakes, their accounts are debited. A strict code of conduct is also rigidly enforced. For example, the use of nondescript clothing is required along with four-door "family-type" cars. In addition, drunkenness is not permitted nor are loud parties. Each arouses public suspicion and encourages police intervention. There are no excuses, no failures, and no second chances. This unforgiving system permits few defections as the penalty for dissension is death—not only for cell members but for their entire family as well (Shannon, 1991).

One of the many reasons why federal agents have such difficulty infiltrating or detecting Cali operations is that Calenos sell only to people they know, in particular to other Colombians. Prospective buyers must establish their credentials directly with top management in Cali. If approved, the buyer is not required to pay cash up front. Rather, payment is made after the drug is resold to middlemen. However, wholesale buyers must put up collateral in the form of cash or deeds to real estate as insurance in the event of an arrest. Family members in Colombia are also used as collateral in case the buyer ever turns informer against the cartel. Under this policy, a cartel member's faithfulness is guaranteed under the threat of his or her family members being murdered for acts of disloyalty.

Cali Cartel trafficking operations are extremely complicated but highly effective. When a shipment of drugs is shipped to the United States, the home office faxes a list to the cell of the prospective buyers, detailing the amount of their purchases and their pager numbers. The head cell contacts the buyers via pager to arrange the delivery—typically in a parking lot or on a street corner. Deals usually take less than two minutes to consummate. After the customer sells the drug, he or she at a later time arranges a second meeting to make payment. After each meeting the driver alerts the head cell via cellular phone or fax, and detailed ledgers are maintained in both countries. If seized, such ledgers provide investigators an abundance of information useful in investigation and prosecution. In the event anyone in the transaction fails to call in or suspects that the police are catching on to the transaction, the cell is shut down.

The Cartel's need for goods and services has produced thriving ancillary industries. "Front" companies purchase cellular telephones by the dozen and "sublet" them to cell operators. Traffickers are aware that it takes law enforcement four or five days to acquire a court-ordered wire tap for the phones, and by that time the phone has been discarded. In the event a phone call is traced, the lead stops at the front company. In addition to phones, document specialists obtain clean drivers' licenses and car registrations for the cells. In 1989, the FBI and the New York City Police Department uncovered a scheme whereby State Department of Motor Vehicles employees accepted bribes of $100 each to prepare phony registration papers for hundreds of falsely documented cartel vehicles.

Next to drugs, the Cali Cartel's biggest industry is money laundering. The monthly gross for some New York cells is estimated at $7 to $12 million all in $10, $20, and $50 bills. This translates to 1,000 to 3,000 pounds of cash per month. Most of the cash is shipped to Cali, where some is invested, some is converted into pesos, and some wired back to banks in the United States or Europe under a relative's name.

The Bogota Cartel

Although little is known about the Bogota Cartel, its evolution parallels that of many of the other Colombian groups. Specifically, the Bogota Cartel began as a smuggling group dealing with contraband emeralds and later marijuana. It was through close association with American criminal contacts that trafficking networks were established for cocaine. Among these contacts were Miami and Caribbean associates of the late Meyer Lansky and his associates. Once the group gained access to Colombian political power, cocaine processing and later trafficking became its primary focus due to the high profit margin of the drug.

The Bogota Cartel has kept a much lower profile than the Cali (or Medellin) Cartel. It is known for buying police protection in Colombia. In fact, according to a 1989 DEA intelligence report, the Bogota organization has possibly purchased more police and governmental protection than the other cartels. In addition to corruption, its leaders have striven to become "well-connected" in Colombian politics. They have used their wealth to purchase land near processing plants in growing areas of eastern Colombia, which has made them more vertically integrated in recent years.

The North Atlantic Coast Cartel

Generally considered the smallest and least cohesive of the major cartels, the North Atlantic Coast Cartel occupies the cities of Cartagena, Barranquilla, Santa Marta, and Rio Hacha. Originating as a smuggling organization, the North Atlantic Coast Cartel is made up of a loosely knit set of transient associations that formed a short-term cooperative arrangement. The North Atlantic Coast Cartel is less vertically integrated than the other three cartels and still offers a smuggling service for the other organizations. As with the other cartels, the North Atlantic Coast Cartel began in the marijuana business and graduated to the cocaine trade in which it now concentrates. Federal sources report that in one case the North Atlantic Coast group accepted a proposition from the Medellin and Bogota Cartels to smuggle large amounts of cocaine to pre-arranged points off the American coasts for a fee. To oversee this operation, the cartel established members on the east coast in Florida cities of Miami, Jacksonville, and Gainesville as well as Atlanta, New York, and Boston. In the west Los Angeles and San Diego were centers for the operation.

The Colombian cartels have proven to be much more than just criminal organizations in their native land. Their influence has spread to the point where they are considered as a state within a state operating openly and with impunity.

Mexican Drug Traffickers

As discussed in Chapter 6, Mexico has long played an important role in international drug trafficking. In fact, Mexican nationals operating in the United States represent one of the oldest groups of foreign nationals involved in drug trafficking. Operating especially in the west and southwest, they traffic mainly in heroin and marijuana. However, in recent years, Mexican drug dealers have been known to transship cocaine from South America in collusion with Colombian trafficking groups. Several factors can be cited to explain this partnership. First, the Mexican-U.S. border is long and difficult to patrol. Secondly, the extensive rural Mexican countryside is ideal for the cultivation, processing, and manufacturing of drugs. Thirdly, a tradition of corruption in elements of the Mexican government and its law enforcement agencies exists. Finally, the expanding drug market in the United States provides Mexican drug traffickers with endless financial incentives.

A number of different, and sometimes competing, Mexican trafficking organizations exist. Examples are the well-known prison gang *The Mexican Mafia* (discussed in the previous chapter), loosely knit cartels such as the *Guadalajara Cartel*, and smaller, less organized trafficking groups. The structure of Mexican trafficking groups is thought to be much more family oriented than those of other foreign cartels. They are often vertically integrated, using family members for each stage of the operation. One such trafficking group located in central California was the *Sanchez-Carranza organization,* which relied upon family members living in mountainous regions of Durango, Mexico. They would be employed to cultivate their opium poppy fields and send the crop to other family members in Mexico who would process it into heroin. The heroin was then smuggled into the United States by couriers, many of whom were family members, where it would be delivered to yet another set of family members residing in the United States. To illustrate the capabilities of Mexican drug traffickers, two of the most notable Mexican drug barons during the 1980s, Rafael Caro Quintero and Jamie Herrera will be discussed next.

Rafael Caro Quintero

Like many Latin-American criminals in the drug trade, Rafael Caro Quintero entered the drug trade early-on in the 1980s. Raised as an illiterate peasant in the Sierra Madre uplands, he became the head of what has been called the *Guadalajara Drug Cartel*. To the people of Sinaloa, he achieved the reputation of a protector of the people who built a vast drug empire (as was the case with Pablo Escobar). Caro Quintero's two uncles, Emilio and Juan Jose Quintero Payan, had been smuggling heroin and marijuana into the United States for many years. Rafa, as he was called, enlarged the family business by offering an expensive grade of marijuana at below market prices. Imitating the growing techniques pioneered by U.S. marijuana cultivators, Caro Quintero began producing sinsemilla, a seedless, potent form of marijuana that sold for $2,500 a pound in the U.S. markets (see Chapter 5). During the early 1980s, he converted acres of irrigated desert into flourishing sinsemilla fields. Soon Caro Quintero and his partner, Ernesto Fonseca Carrillo, were trucking tons of marijuana into the United States over routes formerly used by produce growers.

By 1985, Caro Quintero headed a drug empire unrivaled anywhere in Mexico. He and his associates controlled all traffic and distribution through systematic payoffs to the Mexican Federal Judicial Police (MFJP) and the Federal Bureau of Social and Political Investigations (IPS). MFJP officers were said to have delivered bags of drug money to the traffickers operating near the Mexican border.

In Guadalajara, U.S. Drug Enforcement Administration (DEA) agent Enrique Camarena had been gaining ground against the Mexican drug rackets. His efforts ultimately led to the seizure of large quantities of marijuana ready for shipment. Annoyed by the persistence of this Mexican-American operative, Caro Quintero had Camarena abducted and killed outside Guadalajara on February 7, 1985. The U.S. State Department pressured the Mexican government to crackdown on the Cartel, resulting in Caro Quintero being forced into hiding (see Chapter 6).

In March, DEA agents in Costa Rica received reports that Colombia's Pablo Escobar had paid $500,000 cash for a villa outside San Jose, Mexico. It was in this villa that Caro Quintero sought refuge. The free-spending Mexicans in Costa Rica soon aroused the suspicion of the DEA. On April 4, 1985, after many days of aerial reconnaissance and undercover surveillance, an expert U.S.-trained anti-terrorist team, known as the Departmento Inteligencia Seguridad (DIS), attacked the former coffee plantation and captured Caro Quintero. Then the MFJP sent in a plane the following day to bring him back to Mexico City. While awaiting trial, Caro Quintero admitted bribing hundreds of politicians, judges, and police officials, including Comandante Jorge Armando Pavon Reyes, and financing a large marijuana plantation in Chihuahua. Ernesto Fonseca Carrillo told police that Camarena had been abducted to avenge the Cartel's loss of revenue in the DEA raids at Chihuahua and Zacatecas. Quintero was convicted of arms smuggling and impressing local peasants into forced labor on his marijuana plantations. He was finally sentenced in 1988 to 34 years in prison.

Jamie Herrera

One of the largest Mexican trafficking organizations is that headed by Jamie Herrera, which has been in operation since the early 1970s. Herrera's organization is best described as a confederation of families mostly related by blood and kinship. Older family members are thought to be involved in processing opium while younger ones are involved in its transportation and wholesale sales in both Mexico and the United States. Some of the group's 3,000 to 5,000 members are thought to be naturalized citizens in the United States (PCOC, America's Habit, 1986).

In 1978, Jamie Herrera was arrested and convicted on drug charges along with many other family members. In July 1985, 135 persons in the United States, making up eight separate Herrera-related distribution groups, were indicted in Chicago on drug trafficking charges. These groups were convicted of trafficking heroin and marijuana from Mexico thru El Paso to middlemen in Texas where the drugs were then shipped to Chicago. Once in Chicago, the drugs were distributed nationwide. This particular Herrera enterprise, which is thought to be only one of many, is estimated to have gross annual profits of more than $200 million. Although this case did not completely shut down the Herrera organization, it is believed to have greatly affected its effectiveness in the United States.

Narco-terrorism

By definition, a distinction exists between the motivations of organized crime groups and the motives of terrorist groups. Organized crime is generally associated with a profit motive opposed to terrorist groups who share more political motives. However, even for terrorists some degree of financial gain is necessary to achieve political ends. Since the early 1970s, the drug trade has fostered a marriage of these two diverse groups, evidenced by events in such countries as Jamaica, Colombia, and Myanmar. Some examples of this criminal activity will be discussed in greater detail in this section.

Terrorism and the drug trade are parallel "businesses" that tend to interact in a synergistic fashion. That is, both rely on international infrastructures that extend largely underground and can be shared to achieve mutual benefit. For the terrorist, the drug business provides the cash with which to purchase weapons and finance clandestine operations. The drug trafficker, on the other hand, uses terrorist methods to protect sources of supply and the internal discipline and integrity of his organization. In either case, the result is the disruption of an organized and lawful society through methods of violence that are used outside the norms of international diplomacy and war.

In the 1970s, many terrorist groups began, either directly or indirectly, to generate funds through drug-related activities. This trend is especially prevalent in drug source countries (see Chapter 4). As of the preparation of this text, however, no domestic drug/terrorist groups per se have been identified.

The Colombia/Panama/Cuba Connection

The use of terrorist tactics in the drug trade is becoming more and more evident in Colombia. In an attempt to halt the extradition of traffickers, many Colombian traffickers have resorted to threats against the government of Colombia and the presence of the DEA there. Many of these threats come from members of Colombia's cartels, who produce most of the world's cocaine. In

1985, former Medellin Cartel member Carlos Lehder, now imprisoned in the United States, stated that if the extradition of Colombians was not stopped, he would have 500 Americans killed. Lehder boasted of his contacts with the M-19 guerrillas as well as with elements of the police and army. In addition, Lehder maintained long-standing connections with international right-wing and neo-Nazi terrorist organizations.

History has shown that traffickers have not hesitated to follow up on their threats with violence. In November 1984, a car bomb exploded outside the fence of the American Embassy in Bogota, killing one Colombian woman. In January 1985, a bomb exploded at the Meyer Institute, a language school in Bogota owned by a U.S. citizen; three Colombians were injured. Other examples include the following:

- on March 16, 1985, six men traveling in a jeep fired on the Spanish Chancery in Bogota. This was reportedly in retaliation for the incarceration in Spain of major Colombian cocaine violators whom the United States was seeking to extradite.
- In late April 1985, an influential Colombian judge was gunned down, the eighth killed that year.
- By January 1988, the total had grown to 57 judges and two cabinet members that had been assassinated by suspected drug traffickers in Colombia (DEA, 1985).

Examples of terrorist links to the drug trade in countries such as Colombia, Cuba, Panama, and Myanmar illustrate the magnitude of the terrorist situation in Central and South America. As a case in point, Jose Blandon Castillo, a former intelligence aide to Panama's now-deposed dictator Manuel Noriega, provided testimony before the U.S. Senate Foreign Relations Subcommittee in January 1988. This testimony enabled U.S. prosecutors in Miami to indict Noriega for his involvement in the drug trade. In addition, Blandon's testimony also shed light on previous evidence of Cuba's role in the trafficking of drugs to the United States. Specifically, Blandon testified that Fidel Castro had orchestrated a system whereby drugs and arms were trafficked between Central/South America and the United States. His testimony asserted that Castro had a theory: "If you want to have influence in Colombia's political world, then you need influence in the drug trafficking world too" (PCOC, America's Habit, 1986).

Blandon's testimony further described the joint ventures of Noriega, Castro, the Colombian M-19 (discussed next), and the Medellin Cartel in overseeing drug shipments from Colombia to Cuba and on to the United States, as well as in the laundering of drug money in Panama and the providing of arms to insurgents in Central America. This scheme, according to Blandon, also included participation by Nicaraguan rebels that were supposedly paid in cash for their role in the drug trafficking scheme.

Case Study: Los Diamantes

This Houston, Texas, OCDETF investigation offers a quick glimpse of the "Colombian invasion"—following cartel cocaine, cartel employees move into U.S. assignments as wholesalers, money launderers, and street dealers. This conspiracy came to the attention of federal authorities when two Special Agents of an IRS Money Laundering Task Force observed Mario Restrepo in an area frequented by known traffickers and money launderers. The agents followed Restrepo and discovered two residences in southwest Houston that were the hub of a great deal of vehicular and pedestrian activity. The agents stopped an approaching trash truck and arranged with the driver to pick up the garbage outside the houses and give it to them. They quickly set up a 24-hour surveillance and headed for the office with the trash.

In the bags was perfect evidence of a large-scale cocaine distribution and money laundering operation: money wrappers and rubber bands, a duffel bag, and ledger pages recording multi-kilo cocaine transactions. A "drug detection dog" from U.S. Customs responded positively to cocaine residue on the papers. Over the next few days, the surveillance identified additional suspects. By the end of the week, based on the "garbage," officers obtained search warrants for the two homes and for four other locations. The searches produced more than $1.3 million in United States currency, 55 kilograms of cocaine, cellular phones and digital pagers, and the current books and records of the drug distribution/money laundering operation. Seven persons were arrested, including Carlos Mancado-Rua, who was wanted by Houston police on a murder charge. A federal grand jury originally indicted seven persons for these offenses; all but one were Colombian citizens. Two teenage boys were later dismissed from the indictment as required by law, and federal juvenile proceedings were commenced against them. Ultimately, the boys were adjudicated delinquents and deported to Colombia. Four of the five remaining defendants entered guilty pleas to drug or money laundering offenses.

During the course of the trial for the remaining defendant, Mario Restrepo, one cooperating defendant testified for the government and gave the jury a rare insight into that portion of the Pablo Escobar cocaine cartel operating on American soil. The defendant testified how large quantities of cocaine were stored in local stash houses for eventual distribution in Houston as well as New York. He explained that some members of the conspiracy would distribute the cocaine, while others were responsible for the receipt of cash and maintenance of the accounts receivable books.

Witnesses testified that the local boss of this operation was a Colombian named Samuel Posada Rios Lemonada, who returned to Colombia in August 1988, when his picture appeared on Houston television in the context of a murder investigation. In Lemonada's absence, a 400-kilogram load of cocaine was delivered by a group of traffickers formerly employed by him. The group consisted of the five indicted adults and the 15- and the 17-year-old juveniles.

Between August 9 and September 9, 1988, the group distributed 260 kilograms of cocaine around Houston and drove 140 kilos to New York City. Each kilo package bore the name "DIAMANTE," the trademark of Pablo Escobar of Medellin, Colombia. During the same time period, the group collected more than a million dollars in payment for the cocaine.

In the course of this brief investigation, OCDETF mobilized agents of Customs, INS, DEA, and the Houston Police Department, in addition to the originating IRS team.

An FBI expert in illicit business records and documents testified that the drug records seized from the conspirators evidenced over $5 million in cocaine transactions; $1.5 million was still owed for parts of the last 400-kilo consignment. In addition to more than $1.3 million in cash, two houses, six vehicles, and a submachine gun were seized.

The jury convicted Mario Restrepo on all counts. All defendants forfeited their interest in the houses, cars, money, and electronic communications equipment. Restrepo and his four co-conspirators were sentenced on April 14, 1989. From his safe retreat in Medellin, Lemonada presumably continues to command markets in Houston through Colombian contacts living there.

Source: Organized Crime Drug Enforcement Task Force, 1988.

Colombia, with one of the most skewed patterns of income distribution in Latin America, has been plagued for decades by increasingly violent guerrilla warfare. All in all, some 12,000 to 15,000 guerrilla combatants currently are active there (DEA, 1991). Two such groups most commonly associated with the cocaine and marijuana trade in Colombia during the last 15 years are the *Revolutionary Armed Forces of Colombia* (FARC) and the *19th of April Movement* (M-19), named after the date on which they were organized. The FARC, the oldest Marxist guerrilla organization in the hemisphere, is also the largest and best-equipped insurgent group in Colombia and is the armed wing of the Colombian Communist Party. The DEA estimated in 1985 that FARC operated through approximately 25 fronts, most of which are in coca- and cannabis-growing regions in Colombia. FARC has some involvement in the cultivation of the coca leaf but primarily acts as a protection organization guarding hidden airstrips and growing areas for drug traffickers.

According to an article published in the *Miami Herald* in 1983, the DEA had documented the use of a Colombian drug ring to funnel arms and funds to the non-Marxist M-19 guerrillas since 1980. The drug ring referred to in the report was led by the now-deceased Jamie Guillot-Lara. The M-19 has gained a reputation for extorting money from drug growers and traffickers in cultivation areas. Investigations have revealed that the M-19 has been the recipient of arms from Cuba through the smuggling network of Colombian trafficker Jamie Guillot-Lara.

The Medellin Cartel M-19 Connection

The drug-running Medellin Cartel bought the services of Colombia's most infamous guerrilla group to do the Cartel's dirty work. According to U.S. intelligence reports, the revolutionary group called the "April 19 Movement" or "M-19" has acted as a hired gun for the multibillion-dollar Cartel.

The M-19 and the Medellin Cartel have not always been so tight. M-19 was formed in 1970 and was named after the date that year when a populist ex-president favored by the rebels lost an allegedly fraudulent election. At its greatest strength, M-19 numbered approximately 8,000 guerrillas, but today it may have fewer than 1,000.

In 1979, M-19 tunneled into an army arsenal in Bogota and made off with 5,000 guns. In 1980, the group stormed the embassy of the Dominion Republic in Bogota and took 52 hostages, including 15 ambassadors. The American Ambassador, Diego Asencio, was one of those held for 61 days, after which the hostages were freed as the guerrillas escaped into Cuba. M-19 took over the embassy to call attention to human rights violations in Colombia and to guarantee fair treatment of guerrillas that were in jail there. The M-19's normal method of operation was to pay its way by kidnapping members of wealthy families and collecting ransoms.

In late 1981, the M-19 kidnapped the wrong person. They snatched the daughter of Colombia's alleged first family of cocaine, the Fabio Ochoa family of Medellin. The Ochoas reasoned that they or anyone that was prospering in the drug trade would be safe from kidnappings. The Ochoas banded together with over 200 other narcotics traffickers, which included Pablo Escobar, to form the Medellin Cartel. Its original purpose was to wage war against the M-19.

M-19 released Ochoa's daughter after the Cartel murdered dozens of guerrillas. It was the beginning of a strange friendship. M-19 began a hands-off policy toward the Cartel, and the Cartel put M-19 on the payroll. On November 6, 1985, M-19 took over the five-story, marble Colombian Palace of Justice in downtown Bogota. It was just one block from the Colombian Congress and two blocks from the presidential mansion. Colombian soldiers besieged the building for 27 hours, then stormed it with grenades and gunfire. All 35 rebels died, along with 12 of the 24 supreme court justices.

The sum paid to M-19 for its services, $5 million, was pocket change for the Cartel, which makes as much as $7 billion a year supplying the United States and Europe with cocaine. The Cartel still hires M-19 for other assassinations of government officials, judges, policy officers, and journalists. Some "sicarios," as the hit-men are called, will kill for as little as $50.

The Cartel appears to be befriending one leftist group, but evidence indicates that it also has been killing other leftists by the hundreds, particularly the supporters of Colombian Revolutionary Armed Forces (FARC). FARC was the oldest and largest leftist guerrilla group in Colombia until it struck a deal with the Colombian government in 1984 and became a legitimate political party, the Patrioc Union. Since then, FARC has become the most successful leftist party in Colombian history. For over a decade the former leaders of the Medellin Cartel used their drug profits to become the largest landholders in Colombia out of fear that the growing power of the leftist party would lead to land reform. They didn't want to see their valuable land holdings divided up among the peasants.

Source: Anderson, J. and D. Van Atta (1988). "The Medellin Cartel/M-19 Gang." *The Washington Post* (August 28):87.

Guillot had an arrangement with several high-level officials of the Cuban government. The Cubans provided a safe haven for Guillot's drug smuggling vessels from Colombia destined for the United States. In return, Guillot agreed to pay the Cubans for this facilitation. Guillot also assisted the Cubans by using his ships to smuggle arms to the M-19 in Colombia. In November 1981, a large quantity of weapons was off-loaded from one of Guillot's ships, the *Karina*, onto another Guillot ship, the *Monarca*. Shortly thereafter, the Colombian navy sank the *Karina*; the ship went down with an estimated 100 tons of weapons on board. Ten days later, Colombian authorities seized the *Monarca* after it had successfully delivered its weapons cargo to the M-19 (DEA, 1985).

Figure 9.4
Cocaine Transportation

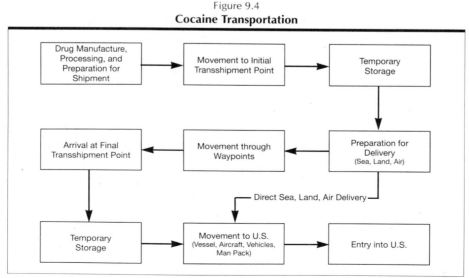

Source: ONDCP, 1989.

The Nicaraguan Connection

In some cases, local authorities have used the drug trade for more than just personal wealth. Such is the case with Cuba where Castro used the drug trade to further his own ideological interests. During the late 1970s, Castro saw a link between drug trafficking and revolution. He sought to use the power and money of drug trafficking to launch a revolution in Central America and, at the same time, align himself with traffickers following the example set by Panama's General Manuel Noriega (Filippone, 1994). This connection led to the involvement of the Sandinista government of Nicaragua.

According to the Justice Department, abundant evidence indicates that Castro lost little time after the consolidation of the Sandinista regime in Managua to harness his Nicaraguan allies to drug trafficking operations. Antonio Farach, a former minister in the post-revolutionary Nicaraguan government, testified that he first learned of Nicaragua's involvement in the illicit drug trade during a visit by Raul Castro to Managua in 1981. According to Farach, the purpose for the Cuban Defense Minister's visit was to establish a narcotics infrastructure "for the Nicaraguan revolution" with Cuba's help. When questioned about this, Farach was told by Nicaraguan officials of two moral and political justifications for their state-sponsored drug trafficking:

> In the first place, drugs did not remain in Nicaragua; the drugs were destined for the United States. Our youth would not be harmed, but rather the youth of our enemies. Therefore, the drugs were used as a political weapon because in that way we were delivering a blow to our principal enemy. In addition to a political weapon against the United States, the drug trafficking produced a very good economic benefit, which we needed for our revolution. We wanted to provide food to our people with the suffering and death of the youth of the United States.

Farach also testified to the personal involvement in the drug offensive of Humberto Ortega, Nicaraguan President Daniel Ortega's brother, as well as Tomas Borge, the veteran Sandinista and Minister of the Interior. On March 16, 1986, President Ronald Reagan, in his televised accusation of the Sandinista regime, displayed a photograph and asserted:

> The Sandinistas have been involved themselves in the international drug trade. This picture, secretly taken at a military airfield outside Managua, shows Frederico Vaughn, a top aide to one of the nine commandantes that rule Nicaragua, leaving an aircraft with illegal narcotics bound for the United States. No, there seems to be no crime to which the Sandinistas will not stoop—this is an outlaw regime.

But once again, we can see the confused nature of the politics/drug connection in the President's statement. Several days after Reagan accused the Sandinistas of involvement in cocaine trafficking, the DEA publicly repudiated the

charge, stating that no such evidence existed. This led to an embarrassing exposure of White House operatives to portray the Nicaraguan government of criminal involvement through the activities of well-known drug smuggler Barry
Seal. Seal, as discussed in Chapter 10, had been arrested for drug trafficking
and had negotiated a plea bargain with the Justice Department. As part of the
deal, Seal was to contract for a load of cocaine in Colombia, and then while
transshipping it to the United States, land in Nicaragua under the guise of having engine trouble, photograph the cocaine off-loaded and subsequently
reloaded on to his plane in Managua, and thereby provide "proof" of a Sandin-
ista-Colombia connection. Unfortunately, the camera provided to Seal by the
CIA failed to work, and the photographs he subsequently took, which were
hand-exposed, were of such a poor quality they were virtually useless.

Thinking Critically #20

   Considering the Nicaraguan Contra's involvement in the illegal
cocaine trade, should the United States have sponsored their attempts
to oust the Marxist-backed Sandinista government in Nicaragua?
Defend your answer.

   The Barry Seal incident was one of several events that led to congressional
inquires into the role of the United States-backed contras with the assistance of
United States intelligence agencies and the National Security Council in
cocaine trafficking. Subsequent testimony indicated that both the contras and
their intelligence community handlers were heavily involved in cocaine trafficking. For example:

- Several major cocaine seizures were made that directly tied the contras to
  cocaine smuggling, including the infamous "Frogman Case" in San Francisco (the largest West Coast cocaine bust up to that time).

- Colombian cocaine traffickers routinely used contra bases in Costa Rica
  for the refueling of planes and the transshipment of cocaine to the United
  States.

- Several pilots testified that they regularly flew loads of cocaine to the
  United States on behalf of the contras in a drugs-for-guns scheme.

- A U.S. Senate inquiry uncovered evidence of regular payoffs to the contras from Medellin Cartel members through El Salvador.

- Direct U.S. government payments to drug traffickers through the State
  Department's Nicaraguan Humanitarian Aid Organization were uncovered during congressional investigations.

Other Terrorist/Insurgent Groups

An array of other narco-terrorist groups have emerged over the years. Each has its own political agenda while taking advantage of available profits from the lucrative drug trade. Let's consider some of the more notable groups.

The Shining Path

The cocaine industry in Peru has produced a large and extremely influential drug trafficking terrorist group called *Sendero Luminoso*, or the *Shining Path*. The organization allegedly controls the upper Huallaga Valley, a region that produces more than 60 percent of the world's coca. The group was founded around 1970 by Abimael Guzma'n (known by followers as "Presidente Gonzalo"), a professor of Marxist philosophy at the University of Huamanga in Ayacucho who embraced Maoism during several visits to China.

From the beginning Guzma'n was known to his followers as the Fourth Sword of International Communism. The ideology of the Shining Path is "Marxism-Leninism-Maoism, Gonzalo Thought." The comma is important, as it says that Gonzalo's ideas are still in formation and that they are also the "fullest, most scientific, most modern development of Communist ideology." (Robbins, 1989). The President's Commission on Organized Crime (America's Habit, 1986) also discussed the significance and role of the Shining Path:

> The Shining Path seeks a rural-based revolution to rid the predominantly peasant population of the "imperialistic" influences of the United States and other foreign governments. While existing evidence is insufficient to link the Shining Path to the drug trade, the group has incited peasants, many of whom make their living from coca cultivation, to rebel against anti-coca projects in major growing areas. During 1984, several anti-coca projects, including a United States-supported crop substitution program, were attacked by armed mobs, resulting in many injuries.

Shining Path tactics have included converging on a town for the purpose of driving out or murdering local officials and imposing a puritanical new order. This is accomplished by holding "people's trials" and by redistributing livestock and land. Although many believe that the Sendero Luminoso's activities seem unorganized and random, many assert that they are systematically tearing down the structures of authority by removing influential and wealthy citizens from communities.

One of the authors has spoken with a DEA official based in Peru who has suggested that the Shining Path has been responsible for numerous violent murders of Peruvian police officers and high-ranking government officials in an effort to deter government interference in drug trafficking operations. An illustration of this goal is the January 1990 assassination of Peru's former defense minister, Enrique Lopez Albujar, which was attributed to the Shining Path. According to DEA sources, the guerrilla methods of operation used by the Shining Path are similar to those used by the North Vietnamese during the Vietnam conflict. Experts that have studied the Shining Path fear that the group's level of violence and number of victims will soar greatly in the near future.

The strength of the Shining Path was lessened by the 1992 arrest of Guzma'n in Peru. Although some experts have argued that his removal has seriously reduced the movement's prospects for seizing power, the Shining Path is thought to still carry out extensive operations, but most are terrorist rather than strictly military or paramilitary in nature (Rosenau, 1994).

Burmese Communist Party

Halfway around the world in Myanmar, the Burmese Communist Party (BCP) has been attempting to exert its control over the Shan State since 1948 when Myanmar became independent from the British. The Shan State is the primary opium poppy cultivation area in the Golden Triangle, adjoining Laos and Thailand. For years the BCP was involved, to some degree, in extorting tax money from opium farmers in the region. After expanding its operations in the late 1970s, the BCP now controls its own heroin refineries and controls most of the opium grown in the Northern Shan State.

Shan United Army

In the 1960s and 1970s, the Shan United Army (SUA) was an insurgent group fighting for the independence of the Shan State. The SUA now focuses on manufacturing heroin, heroin base, and morphine base, and from the smuggling of heroin generate profits to finance its insurgency. To illustrate the volatility of the SUA, members have threatened to kidnap three DEA agents and hold them for $3 million in ransom. Because of the immense profit potential of the heroin trade, the SUA represents a clear example of an insurgent group that has traded its political zeal for the allure of drug profits.

The head of the SUA is Kuhn Sa, originally named Chang Chifu after his Chinese father. He was born in 1933, and although he never progressed beyond elementary school, he formed his own army out of the remnants of a local militia originally organized by the Burmese government to fight communist insurgents. It is estimated that Khun Sa now commands an army exceeding some 15,000 soldiers whose primary mission is to protect the drug trafficking operations of Khun Sa. Khun Sa's SUA has been such a dominant force in Myanmar for so long that today it operates with virtual impunity (Lintner, 1994). In December 1993, thousands of Myanmar troops launched a massive attack against two important SUA camps north of the Thai border, but met surprisingly little resistance from Khun Sa's soldiers. The objective of the Myanmar

Army is to disrupt Kuhn Sa from his stronghold in the eastern mountains and if not eliminate him, then capture and turn him over to the United States where he is currently under federal indictment.

Illustrating the arrogance of Khun Sa was his request to the United States government to phase him out of the heroin business in exchange for $300 million annually over a period of eight years. Washington has rejected this offer since it originated in 1977, not just because drug enforcement officials are understandably skeptical about Khun Sa's sincerity, but also because of obvious moral and ethical reasons.

Cuban Drug Traffickers

Since 1959, more than one million Cuban refugees have arrived in the United States. Although many have come seeking political freedom, a significant percentage of Cuban immigrants has been documented as having close involvement in drug trafficking operations. Three periods of mass Cuban immigration to the United States occurred as follows:

1. Before and after the fall of the Batista regime until Fidel Castro halted emigration in 1959.
2. Between 1965 and 1972, during the Camarioca boatlift "freedom flotilla," prompting the family reunification program under which more than 250,000 Cubans migrated to the United States.
3. Between April 21 and November 10, 1980, during a boatlift from Mariel Harbor, bringing nearly 125,000 new Cuban refugees to the United States.

Unquestionably, the greatest concentration of criminals was in the Mariel Harbor exodus, with nearly 2 percent of those arriving in the United States having been classified as prostitutes, criminals, drug addicts, or vagrants. The minority of these Cuban immigrants were soon given the name **"marielito,"** meaning criminal or undesirable.

The sophistication and organizational structure of the criminals that immigrated during the first two boatlifts was greater than those that came over on the Mariel boatlift. In particular, many of the earlier Cuban immigrants had ties with more traditional and well-established criminal organizations in the United States, particularly gambling and drug operations associated with Meyer Lansky and Santo Trafficante, Jr. In addition, many of the early Cuban refugees participated in United States government-supported paramilitary and intelligence operations directed against the Castro government. As a result, they were given considerable training in intelligence techniques (including smuggling) by the CIA, and provided with financial and logistical support. When United States support for these activities ended in the 1960s, many of these immigrants had no lawful trade to fall back on and initiated organized crime activities to support themselves. The marielitos, on the other hand, demonstrated a great propensity for violence.

> The Mariel boatlift had its genesis on April 1, 1980, when a small band of Cubans in a city bus attempted to gain political asylum by crashing the gates of the Peruvian Embassy. One Cuban guard at the gate accidently killed another guard while trying to stop the bus. Fidel Castro was enraged and publicly announced the removal of all guards from the gates. Within days over 10,000 people had crowded into the embassy grounds, requesting political asylum. Eventually Castro allowed them to be flown out of the country. This group and those that followed later included primarily decent and working-class people that genuinely sought liberty. Castro, however, proclaimed the refugees to be the scum of Cuban society. When the exodus continued, he tried to prove his description by forcibly including convicts, hard-core criminals, prostitutes, and the mentally ill among those that left by boat from Mariel.

Source: PCOC, April 1986.

During the 1960s, two major Cuban groups became well established in the United States: *La Companía*, a well-known drug trafficking organization concentrating primarily on cocaine trafficking, and *The Corporation*, headed by Jose Miguel Battle. This group is also well established but concentrates primarily on gambling operations.

The marielitos have been documented as joining established crime organizations such as La Companía, working as collectors and enforcers. They have also been associated with Colombian cartels in the same capacity. Although some debate continues over the exact number of marielitos that were part of the Mariel boatlift, there have been widespread reports of violent marielito activity in such cities as Miami, New York, Las Vegas, and Los Angeles.

Asian Organized Crime

Yet another type of organized crime emerging in the drug trade is Asian gangs. Chinese gangs in particular have demonstrated considerable growth in drug trafficking activities. From 1970 to 1980, for example, the number of Chinese in the United States escalated from 435,062 to 806,027. This increase in population might also reflect the fact that Chinese traffickers are becoming more proficient in their smuggling of southeast Asian heroin to the United States. In 1988, the DEA reported that in New York, heroin from southeast Asia rose from 3 percent to 40 percent of the total supply in that city.

The Chinese Tongs and Triads

Chinese organized crime (**COC**) primarily involves two well-established organizations, the *tongs* and the *triads*. Although criminal activity by these two groups marks a relatively new presence in the United States, it represents a degeneration of several much older and secret societies in China. The Triads, predominantly based in Hong Kong, began in the seventeenth century as an opposing force to China's ruling Manchu government. The Tongs, on the other hand, originated in the nineteenth century as legitimate mutual aid societies that were in the United States to assist immigrant Chinese railroad workers.

Triads and Tongs are both characterized by devotion to members of the organization and by acts of violent retribution against those that reveal its secrets to outsiders. Since the mid-1960s, three incidents have had particular impact on the growth of Asian organized crime in America:

1. The liberalization of quotas of Asian immigrants in 1965.
2. The ending of the Vietnam conflict.
3. The agreement between the United Kingdom and the People's Republic of China which determined that Hong Kong will revert to the Chinese in 1997 after more than 150 years of colonial rule by the British.

The third event listed above may very well be the cause of Chinese organized crime groups moving to the United States in great numbers. It is estimated that there are as many as 100,000 Triad members belonging to more than 50 Triads in Hong Kong. The primary Triads are organized into five groups, of which the Wo group and the 14K are the largest. In Taiwan, the United Bamboo Gang claims 1,200 members, and the Four Seasons Gang has 3,000 members. Among the Triads known to have active U.S. connections are the Sun Yee On, 14K, Wo Hop To, Wo On Lok, and Leun Kung Lok.

A much greater threat than that of the Triads is represented by the highly structured Asian street gangs. The Wah Ching is the most sophisticated Chinese criminal organization that operates on the West Coast. It boasts some 600 to 700 members. Like the Triads, it also has a highly organized command structure. In New York, Chinese street gangs are affiliated with the Tongs and incorporate the positions of co-presidents, executive officers, and staff.

The Japanese Yakuza

Enduring through the centuries along with the Chinese Triads is the Japanese Yakuza, which came into existence in the early 1600s. The structural makeup of the Yakuza closely resembles that of the Mafia and is centered from city to city around families in which the elder leader is the supreme boss and whose word is life and death to its members. In the beginning, Yakuza members were bandits who by the turn of the twentieth century expanded into all manner of rackets, particularly drug trafficking, prostitution, and gambling. Yakuza members were thought to number in the tens of thousands before World War II and were fervent nationalists in their political posture. The organization was even thought to have played a major role in Japan's decision to embark on World War II.

Thinking Critically #21

In the past several years, first the Medellin and currently the Cali Cartels have zealously exported illegal cocaine across the U.S. border. In light of the Cartels' determination to supply a vast American market, how do you believe the anti-drug budget should be divided? Should more federal dollars go to interdiction efforts, or should more emphasis be placed on gang prevention and treatment programs? Defend your viewpoint.

One of its members, Toyama Mitsuru, leader of an offshoot Yakuza gang, the Kyoshisha, founded the Black Dragon Society in the 1880s. This criminal organization grew so powerful that it literally controlled all commerce and business in Japan for the next 70 years. Toyama and the Black Dragons actually dictated Japan's foreign policy and were the influencing factor that led Japan into World War II. Following the war, the Yakuza modernized, replaced traditional swords with guns, and moved into the import-export business. The group took control of all goods flowing in and out of Japan's ports and collected private taxes for these goods, enriching the organization by billions.

By the late 1950s, the Yakuza numbered around 184,000 members, and its strongest boss was Taoko Kazuo, who became known as the Al Capone of Kobe, Japan. In Yokohama, Inagawa Kakuji bossed thousands of Yakuza in running the rackets of that town. During the 1970s, Japan's most powerful Yakuza mastermind, Kodamo Yoshio, organized all the Yakuza gangs, spreading their influence to Thailand, Malaysia, Hong Kong, and Taiwan, where they aligned with the Chinese Triads and established one of the most powerful drug trafficking organizations in the world, one that is thought to produce billions in illegal profits each year. The Yakuza now vies for world domination of organized crime with the Mafia in the U.S. and the drug cartels in South America.

Vietnamese Gangs

A growing threat to the Vietnamese communities throughout the United States is the expansion of Vietnamese youth gangs. Preying mostly on members of their own community, their crimes include extortion, rape, assault, auto theft, murder, and a new brand of robbery—the home invasion. Members typically range from 14 to 23. Gambling is also popular with Vietnamese gangs. Gambling houses are often operated in the homes of gang members and their associates, making it difficult for police to conduct surprise raids.

Drug trafficking by COC does not yet parallel that of the cartels, but the scope of their influence is noteworthy nonetheless. Working with Asian nationals, Chinese-American criminals are the largest importers of southeast Asian heroin, which originates in the Golden Triangle. This was evidenced by a 1989 seizure of more than 800 pounds of processed heroin in New York's Chinatown. Most Golden Triangle heroin is shipped to the West Coast of the United States via Hong Kong and through secondary transit points such as Singapore, Seoul, Tokyo, and Taipei. Chinese criminal organizations operate mainly as shippers and wholesalers; that is, they are active in buying the raw product, processing it, arranging for its transshipment, and finally, turning it over to retailers.

Summary

Illicit drugs in the United States finance drug trafficking organizations with both domestic and foreign origin. The Colombian cartels, one of the more visible modern-day drug trafficking organizations, have achieved a certain notoriety for their role in the cocaine business. Of the four major cartels discussed, the Medellin Cartel, now defunct, first emerged as one of the most powerful and influential in the drug trade. Today, the Cali cartel is thought to be the new leader in cocaine production and distribution worldwide. Over the years the Colombian cartels have gained a reputation for violence and are known for their ability to corrupt political and governmental authorities in pursuit of their goals.

Drugs have also attracted the participation of terrorist and insurgent groups in the cocaine trade, such as the Colombia's M-19 and Peru's Sendero Luminoso organization. Such groups have been documented as operating in Latin American countries and exerting influence over significant portions of the drug trade. The existence of these groups is fueled by unstable governments and economies of many source countries. The influence of these types of terrorist organizations reaches other Latin American countries as well, such as Bolivia, Panama, and Cuba.

Similarly motivated groups exist in southeast and southwest Asian drug-producing countries. For example, in Myanmar, the Shan United Army (SUA) exerts influence through terrorist activities and is able to control a significant portion of the heroin trade in the Golden Triangle. The SUA is headed by Khun Sa and reportedly has more than 15,000 soldiers that are charged with protecting the trafficking operations of the organization.

Other Asian criminal organizations, such as the Chinese Triads and Tongs and the Japanese Yakuza, operate both in the United States and Hong Kong and also are very active in the illicit drug trade. With the increase in Asian nationals in the United States, the ranks of the Chinese Tongs are growing in Los Angeles, New York, and other cities.

Do you recognize these terms?

COC	narco-democracy
cartel	narco-terrorist
marielito	PEPES
Medellinization	

Discussion Questions

1. List the various foreign organized crime groups that are considered the greatest contributors to the U.S. drug abuse problem. Specify the dangerous drugs with which each organization is most likely to be involved.

2. What role does the Cali Cartel play in the illicit global drug trade?

3. Identify and discuss the link between FARC and the M-19 (insurgent groups in Colombia) and drug traffickers.

4. Discuss the interplay between drug trafficking and insurgent terrorists.

5. Discuss the roles that former Panamanian leader Manuel Noriega and Cuba's Fidel Castro allegedly played in international drug trafficking.

6. Peru's Shining Path is another terrorist-related drug trafficking organization. Discuss its connection with the cocaine trade and global drug trafficking.

7. Historically, what events have played the most significant roles in Cuban immigration into the United States?

8. Explain the expanding role of Asian organized crime groups in the illicit drug trade.

Part III

Fighting Back

Because drug abuse is so diverse and because it touches so many different lives, many concerned people throughout our communities have strong commitments to combating the problem. These people include police officers, social workers, educators, church officials, and concerned parents to name only a few. Each of these persons seeks new and innovative ways to control drug abuse and crime in their neighborhoods. To this end, some important questions can be asked: In addition to relying on the police, what other community resources can be used to confront drug abuse? Should drug control policy focus on controlling the supply or the demand side of the drug abuse problem? What role should churches and schools play in ensuring a drug-free community? To what extent can the average person make a difference in society's fight against drugs? The remaining five chapters of this book deal with these questions and more, by addressing both the government's and the public's responses to the nation's drug abuse dilemma.

The Drug Control Initiative

10

This chapter will enable you to:

- Understand the different goals of drug control
- Learn the different categories of drug laws
- Learn the strategies of drug enforcement agencies
- Understand the role of federal interdiction efforts
- Gain insight regarding the assorted efforts and coordination agencies involved in drug control

Many controversial and vital issues must be considered when designing drug control strategies. A paradox of sorts becomes evident when we see, for instance, one interest group demand that law enforcement officers be given more police authority with which to perform their drug control duties, while at the same time, others protest that expanding the roles of government authority decreases the constitutional and personal freedoms of individuals.

Controlling dangerous drugs involves a profusion of tasks that are sometimes contradictory; these include reducing the overall demand for drugs, reducing both the international and domestic supply of drugs, controlling organized crime, minimizing the spreading of dangerous diseases (such as AIDS) through intravenous drug use, using nontraditional drug enforcement tactics such as reverse stings and criminal profiling, and minimizing the use of dangerous drugs in professional and amateur sports. These issues will be discussed later in this section, but first we will examine the role of the federal government in illicit drug suppression.

The response to the nation's drug problem by the government on both state and federal levels has been shaped by a number of important variables. For example, both levels of government must consider their statutory and constitutional authority to intervene. In addition, the jurisdiction of each law enforcement agency must be considered along with the realization that the extent of drug use across the country varies according to cities and communities. For instance, crack cocaine and heroin are predominantly a big city problem with marijuana and methamphetamine primarily plaguing rural areas.

Strategies to combat the drug problem also vary widely depending on community public opinion, the resources and jurisdiction of the law enforcement agencies in those communities, and the type of drugs most commonly abused and sold on the streets. Common community strategies include drug education, drug testing of workers, and police intervention on both the supply and demand side of abuse and trafficking. It is the latter strategy which we will discuss in this chapter.

The Goals of Drug Control

In addition to controlling drug use and crime associated with drug use, it is the goal of drug enforcement agencies to disrupt criminal organizations which infiltrate neighborhoods and communities. As we discussed in Chapter 4, many business-related facets exist in the drug trade, which include production, manufacturing, transportation, and sale of drugs. It is these various components to the drug trade that drug law enforcement attempts to upset. Therefore, each level of the drug business remains as a viable enforcement target. These are 1) the *source* of the drugs, which concern cultivation and production of opium poppies, coca leaves, and marijuana; 2) *smuggling* operations, which transport drugs into the country and across state lines; 3) *wholesale* distribution of drugs; and 4) *retail* sales.

It could be argued that the enforcement of drug laws makes selling drugs all that much more enticing and exciting for criminals. In addition, it increases the cost of the drugs while making the drug business more dangerous for those involved in it. Risks incurred by law enforcement officials at each stage of the drug trade increase from one level to another. The philosophy behind enforcement efforts is that if police seize drugs belonging to traffickers along with other assets and arrest and imprison the traffickers and their associates, others considering entering the trade will be sufficiently deterred from doing so. For those not deterred, incarceration prevents their continued participation in the drug trade.

Drug Laws

An illegal sale of drugs violates both state and federal laws. Depending on which law enforcement agency is able to document the violation, either state or federal charges are brought against the offender. In any case, it is those laws that provide the essence of reducing the supply and demand of drugs. Drug laws are specific about what constitutes a criminal violation, and although specific features of those laws vary across jurisdictions and levels of government, three categories of law can be identified.

Possession or use. This category of law prohibits people from possessing controlled drugs on their person, in their car, or in their home. The only notable exception is possession of drugs pursuant to a lawful prescription. Some states even go so far as to prohibit persons from being under the influence of drugs or using them. The specific levels of proof, like the amount of the drug that constitutes "simple" possession from possession "with intent to sell," vary from one state to another.

Manufacturing. These laws generally include any activity related to the production of controlled drugs. The term "manufacturing" is broadly used in some legal language and can include cultivation, conversion of certain chemicals to other forms, and preparation and packaging of drugs for retail sales.

Distribution. This category of laws generally refers to the sale and delivery of drugs on both the wholesale and retail levels. Also included are provisions for transportation, importation, and storage of drugs. Generally, the type of drug involved will dictate the specific charge to be filed against the offender.

Other prohibited activity. In addition to the three categories of laws discussed above, many other types of laws are available for the prosecution of drug offenses. These include:

- drug paraphernalia laws
- drug precursor laws
- money laundering laws
- conspiracy laws
- forfeiture laws
- racketeering laws (RICO)
- drug diversion laws

A virtual alphabet soup of federal law enforcement agencies are charged in one fashion or another with the task of domestic and/or international drug enforcement. These agencies include the Drug Enforcement Administration (DEA), the Federal Bureau of Investigation (FBI), the Customs Service, the Coast Guard, and the Immigration and Naturalization Service (the Border Patrol). In addition, a wide variety of other federal agencies, totaling 32, have been organized to coordinate certain aspects of drug enforcement activities.

Drug Enforcement Goals

- to control drug use
- to control drug-related crime and violence
- to disrupt the development and growth of criminal organizations
- to protect neighborhoods

Because of the bureaucratic fragmentation of federal law enforcement agencies charged with drug enforcement, the exchange of information as well as coordination and cooperation between agencies is often problematic and difficult to achieve. Discussed next is a broad characterization of the primary drug enforcement agencies and the specific roles that they play in the overall federal drug-control strategy.

The History of Federal Drug Enforcement

Alcohol prohibition marked the first legal recognition of problems emanating from substance abuse. The enforcement mechanism for the National Prohibition Act was placed under the Commissioner of Internal Revenue. "Because it seemed logical to place responsibility for enforcement of the Harrison Act within this prohibition unit, a narcotics unit was created" (PCOC). The narcotics unit originally employed 170 agents and had an appropriation of $250,000. The Narcotics Unit operated between 1919 and 1927. By 1927, all powers of drug enforcement were transferred to the Secretary of the Treasury.

During the years of the Narcotics Unit's operation, the general public associated narcotics enforcement with the none-too-popular liquor enforcement efforts of the era. Additionally, scandals tarnished the image of narcotics agents when some agents were found to be falsifying arrest records and accepting payoffs from drug dealers. In response, Congress moved the responsibility of narcotics enforcement to the newly created Federal Bureau of Narcotics (FBN) in 1930. It was after the creation of the FBN that the term "narcotics agent" was generally adopted to refer to FBN drug enforcement personnel.

For the next 35 years, the mission of federal drug enforcement remained somewhat consistent. Through the mid-1960s, the federal government's drug suppression efforts were primarily directed toward the illegal importation of drugs into the country. The authority of the FBN was expanded in 1956 with the passing of the Narcotics Control Act, which, among other things, authorized narcotics agents to carry firearms and granted them authority to serve both search and arrest warrants.

In 1965, the Drug Abuse Control Amendments (to the 1956 NCA) were passed. These addressed the problem of drugs in the depressant and stimulant category being diverted from legal channels. In 1966, another agency was created to enforce the Amendments: the Bureau of Drug Abuse Control (BDAC) within the Health, Education, and Welfare Department's Food and Drug Administration (FDA). Another advance in drug enforcement occurred in the late 1960s as a result of a study conducted by the Katzenbach Commission. The study concluded with the following recommendations to reduce both the supply and demand of drugs:

1. Substantially increase the enforcement staffs of the FBN and the Bureau of Customs;

2. Permit courts and correctional authorities to deal flexibly with violators of the drug laws;

3. Undertake research to develop a sound and effective framework of regulatory and criminal laws relating to dangerous drugs;

4. Develop within the National Institute of Mental Health a core of educational and informational materials relating to drugs.

In 1968, for the first time in history, the Department of Justice was given authority for the enforcement of federal drug laws. With this authority, the FBN and the BDAC were abolished and enforcement responsibility was passed to the newly created Bureau of Narcotics and Dangerous Drugs (BNDD). This was done to eliminate friction between enforcement agencies and to minimize bureaucratic fragmentation within the federal government's drug enforcement effort.

To assist state and local drug enforcement agencies, the Office for Drug Abuse and Law Enforcement (ODALE) was established in 1972. Several months after ODALE was created, the Office of National Narcotic Intelligence (ONNI) was created. This was to serve as a clearinghouse for any information considered useful in the Administration's anti-drug initiative. ONNI was also charged with disseminating information to state and local law enforcement agencies for which there was a demonstrated "legitimate official need."

In 1973, President Richard Nixon implemented a drug enforcement reorganization plan that addressed the supply side of drug abuse as well as the demand component of the problem. One of the most important directives of the plan was the creation of the Drug Enforcement Administration (DEA) within the Department of Justice. Under the plan, the Administrator of the DEA would report directly to the Attorney General and would assume all manpower and budgets of the BNDD, ODALE, and ONNI.

As of the writing of this text, the drug enforcement agencies discussed below are those agencies responsible for drug control on the national level.

The Drug Enforcement Administration (DEA)

As previously mentioned, the DEA, established in 1973, was declared the lead agency in the federal government's efforts to suppress the illicit drug trade. Acting under the Justice Department, the DEA is the only federal law enforcement agency that has drug enforcement as its only responsibility. The DEA has primary responsibility for investigating drug-related events as well as collecting and disseminating drug-related intelligence information. In addition, they try to coordinate efforts between federal, state, and local law enforcement agencies which also involved in drug suppression.

The dominant philosophy of the DEA is to eliminate drugs as close as possible to their source and to disrupt the drug trafficking system by identifying, arresting, and prosecuting traffickers. In furtherance of this philosophy, drug shipments are sometimes permitted to enter the United States while under close surveillance by agents. Once the shipment is delivered, agents can arrest traffickers and, hopefully, leaders of the drug smuggling organizations. The DEA philosophy, focusing on investigation and conviction, conflicts with the mission of other agencies, such as the U.S. Customs Service, that are charged with interdiction of drugs as soon as they enter the United States. Interagency rivalries are therefore created that tend to hamper the overall effectiveness of the federal drug enforcement initiative.

Figure 10.1
A Genealogy of DEA's Predecessor Organizations

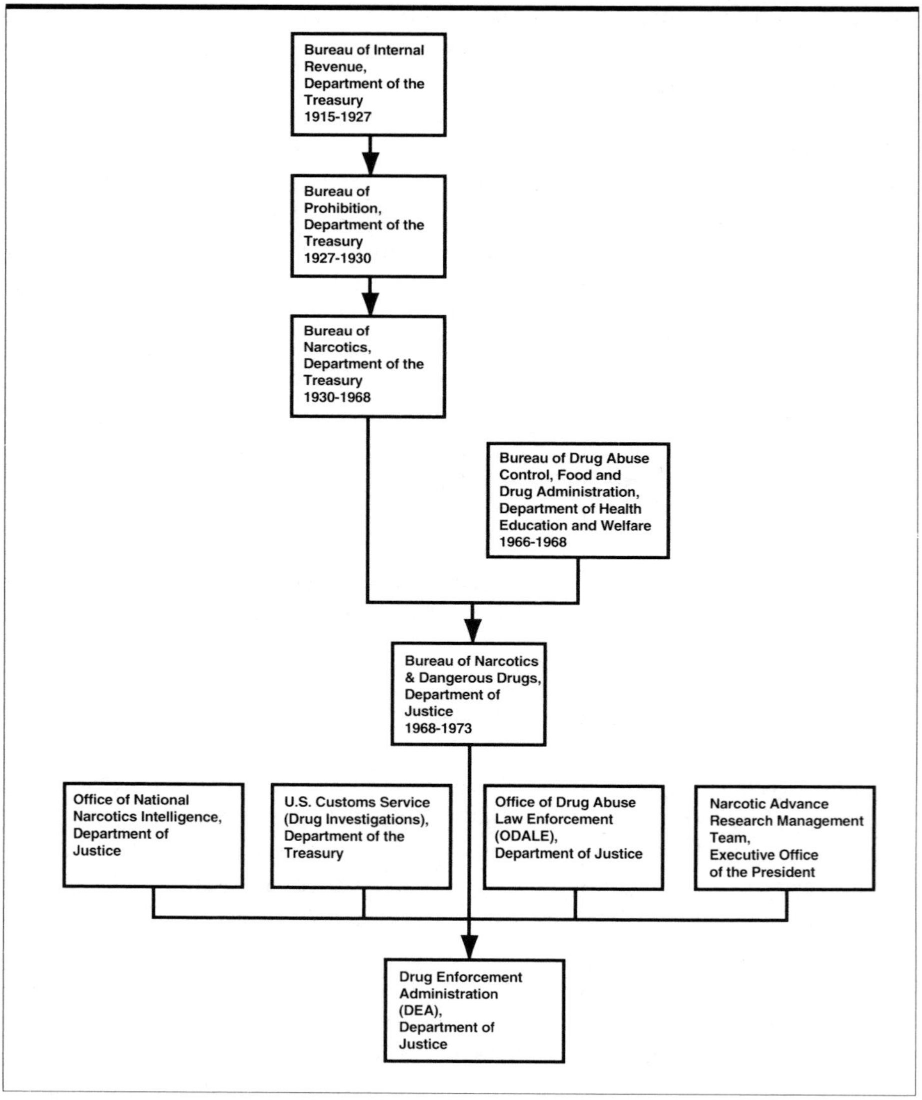

The DEA's mission is both domestic and foreign with a total of more than 2,400 special agents and intelligence analysts located throughout the United States and in 42 other countries. Agents stationed in foreign countries possess no arrest powers and act primarily as liaisons with the host law enforcement agencies.

DEA agents and analysts provide information about general trends in drug trafficking as well as specific information regarding the actions of drug criminals. The information collection process begins in drug source countries and includes analysis of drug production (illicit farming operations and laboratories) and transportation methods (smuggling) used by traffickers.

Intelligence collected by the DEA is a major source of information about drugs in transit and is also shared with other law enforcement agencies. Through the DEA's El Paso Intelligence Center (EPIC), intelligence is collected, analyzed, and disseminated from all enforcement agencies. During recent years, the DEA's budget and work force have burgeoned. For example, in 1982 the DEA employed 1,849 agents with a budget of $242 million. In 1990, the number of agent personnel ascended to 2,958 with an increased budget of $549 million. Although supporters of the federal drug enforcement initiative claim that the greater numbers of agent personnel account for the rising number of arrests and seizures, detractors of federal drug policy claim that hiring more enforcement agents is not the best way to approach the drug problem. In 1990, John Lawn expressed his frustration with drug enforcement initiatives by resigning his post as DEA administrator and by conceding that the DEA is unable to keep pace with many of today's drug trafficking organizations. Many analysts agree and suggest that the best way to confront the drug problem is to systematically analyze every aspect of how major drug trafficking organizations operate and then attack the "choke points" of distribution as opposed to mounting an all-out effort on "every front." In short, the suggestion is to make better use of raw intelligence information by drug enforcement personnel who are already in place.

The Federal Bureau of Investigation (FBI)

The FBI is the chief law enforcement arm of the federal government and a division of the Justice Department. In 1982, Attorney General William French Smith delegated to the FBI concurrent jurisdiction with the DEA for the overall drug law enforcement effort. This was a major change in the FBI's normal jurisdiction, which had traditionally included all federal laws not specifically assigned to other enforcement agencies.

Since assuming these new drug enforcement responsibilities, the FBI has assigned more than 1,000 Special Agents to drug investigations. The primary impetus of the FBI's role in drug enforcement is the investigation of organized crime activity in the drug trade. These activities include probing into specific trafficking organizations as well as scrutinizing illegal financial transactions pertaining to drug trafficking.

Both the DEA and FBI are responsible for enforcement of the Controlled Substances Act of 1970. The FBI, however, is more concerned with drug-related violations of such laws as the Continuing Criminal Enterprise (CCE) statute and the Racketeer-Influenced and Corrupt Organizations (RICO) law. Although the participation of the FBI in domestic drug enforcement benefits the overall goals and objectives of the federal effort, some degree of conflict, overlapping responsibilities, and confusion about jurisdiction between the DEA and the FBI still exists.

As an offshoot of the FBI's involvement in drug enforcement, the OCDETF task force concept was adopted in 1983. Through this joint law enforcement initiative, many high-level cases have been culminated (see section on OCDETF).

Drug Interdiction

The process of interdicting drug smugglers is one of the primary focuses of United States drug control policy. **Interdiction** prevents illegal drugs from entering the United States from foreign sources by intercepting and seizing contraband. As we have learned, drugs enter the country in a variety of different ways, and smugglers of drugs regularly vary their methods to counter enforcement actions. Basically, interdiction consists of five rather broad categories of activity: intelligence, command and control, surveillance, pursuit, and capture. The interdiction process addresses areas off the shore and within the 12-mile "**Customs search**" radius surrounding the United States, as well as all ports of entry.

In April, 1990, the U.S. Air Force introduced a new long-range radar system that was originally designed to provide early warning of a Soviet attack. Its new application is to detect airborne drug smugglers. The system, located in Maine, consists of two gigantic antennas, each spreading more than two thirds of a mile and forming the first "over-the-horizon" capable of seeing 10 times farther than conventional systems—up to 1,800 miles.

The system is operated by bouncing signals off of the ionosphere, and a series of computer screens maps every plane flying over a 4-million-square-mile area of the Atlantic from Iceland to South America. In theory, the system will match the aircraft against known flight plans and air traffic control information, identifying suspected drug flights and scrambling U.S. Customs or Coast Guard pursuit planes.

Figure 10.2
Roles of Drug Interdiction Agencies

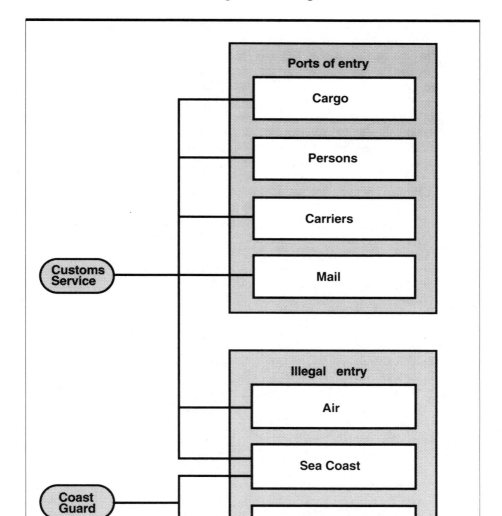

Source: Office of Technology Assessment, 1987.

Case Study: Devoe Airlines

Devoe Airlines was a scheduled commuter air service operating between Miami and smaller Florida cities during the early 1980s. Owned by Miami pilot Jack Devoe, the business was essentially a front for a Colombian drug trafficking operation, which included regular, large-quantity marijuana and cocaine smuggling. In total, 8 to 10 contract pilots employed by Devoe were involved in more than 100 trafficking flights over a five-year period and carried roughly 7,000 pounds of cocaine from South America to the United States. Jack Devoe estimates that his flying organization grossed millions of dollars each month during peak smuggling periods.

Devoe's trafficking pilots initially travelled nonstop routes between the United States and Colombia, but in the 1980s, they developed a transshipment point on Little Darby Island in the Bahamas for purposes of "security and police protection." Devoe hired six to eight employees to work as needed at the island base to unload and repackage drug shipments. There was no interference from Bahamian law enforcement at the Little Darby Island "as long as payments [to officials] were on time."

Typically operating midsize turbo-prop aircraft, Devoe pilots departed for Colombia either from the base at Little Darby Island or from Florida airports. Their route generally took them through the Windward Passage (see Chapter 4) to Colombian locations about 60 miles south of the equator. In the early stages of the operation, landings were made at official Colombian airports, including the airfields at Santa Marta and Riohacha. In at least one instance, cocaine was openly loaded onto the smuggling aircraft at Riohacha airport. In the early 1980s, Devoe shifted landings to clandestine jungle airstrips maintained by the organization's cocaine supplier, Pepe Cabrera. This system streamlined the trafficking process by eliminating transport of the cocaine to an airport. The cocaine shipment was loaded directly onto the aircraft near the strip while the plane was simultaneously prepared for the return flight.

Generally, Devoe pilots returned to the United States within one day. Their preferred return route extended along the Colombia/Venezuela border, over Haiti, and to the Bahamian base on Little Darby Island. There, cocaine was sealed into the wing fuel tanks of a small aircraft and flown directly into South Florida for delivery to the cartel's representative there.

The Devoe organization's methods for avoiding interdiction between South America and the United States were relatively simple and typical of such smuggling operations. A Devoe pilot learned the frequencies of DEA surveillance aircraft on one occasion by "acting like a helicopter buff" inspecting a DEA Cobra pursuit helicopter parked near the Devoe hangar. Inside the helicopter the pilot copied the frequencies from a clipboard hanging in the instrument panel. As the pilot explained to the President's Commission on Organized Crime:

> By [subsequently] using our scanner and our knowledge of
> the frequencies in use, we could monitor the activities of
> DEA planes . . . we could learn not only the activities of the
> planes, but also go up and check the plane out. By learning
> what types of aircraft the DEA was using we could plan our
> own strategy more effectively. . . .

Devoe also regularly sent "cover-flight" aircraft ahead of the
smuggling planes along the trafficking route to monitor DEA and
Customs Service surveillance patrols by radio. These planes, which
carried no drug cargo, were also used to decoy pursuit aircraft. Once
in the United States, Devoe's strategy for clearing Customs was to:

> . . . act normally and file a flight plan, come in and land,
> and let them inspect the airplane . . . Customs inspectors
> were far less interested in a lengthy examination of my
> plane if I came in on a Sunday afternoon in the middle of
> the televised football game. If the Dolphins were playing,
> that was even better.

Using these tactics, Devoe Airlines was able to complete more
than 100 trafficking flights from Colombia without interference from
law enforcement authorities.

Source: PCOC, 1986.

The Coast Guard

The Coast Guard focuses on identification and interdiction of maritime
smuggling, principally by private, seagoing vessels. The Coast Guard concentrates on larger cases in the open ocean, although it also conducts patrols and
makes seizures in near-shore areas, where it has concurrent jurisdiction with
the U.S. Customs Service. Primarily, the Coast Guard concentrates on the areas
in and around the Gulf of Mexico, the Caribbean, and around south Florida.
Coast Guard seizures are of three distinct types:

1. *Incidental seizures.* These occur while carrying out other more standard
   missions. Many incidental seizures occur when conducting search and
   rescue missions where the vessel in trouble turns out to be involved in
   smuggling activity.

2. *Intelligence-based seizures.* The second most common type of Coast
   Guard seizure is the seizure that results from hard criminal intelligence.
   Such intelligence pinpoints the specific location and time of the smuggling operation. This type accounts for a large percentage of seizures
   conducted by the Coast Guard.

3. *Interdiction patrol operations.* The third and *predominant* type of seizure
   results from drug interdiction patrol operations. Coast Guard cutters, usually accompanied by Coast Guard interdiction aircraft, search for, identify, visually inspect, and board suspect target vessels.

Designated "**choke points**" are heavily patrolled by Coast Guard cutters in four Caribbean and Gulf of Mexico areas. The primary goal of this operation is to identify, through a system of profiling, "mother ships," which meet contact boats near the coast that deliver drugs into the United States. The ability of the Coast Guard to interdict illicit drug shipments is restricted in several ways. Although the Coast Guard will focus on choke points, these areas frequently are expanses of ocean 100 miles wide and patrolled by a single cutter. The quantity of vessels through the choke points is large, and only a small number of the vessels traveling through them can be searched. The Coast Guard can only conduct choke point coverage part of the time because it not only has limited equipment and personnel resources, but also their cutters must escort seized vessels to a port, which could tie the cutter up for several days at a time and leave the choke point unpatrolled. Finally, the mission of the Coast Guard, interdiction and search and rescue, will always take precedence over investigating a suspected smuggling operation.

Coastal Interdiction is Difficult Because Smugglers

- easily conceal drugs
- use small fast boats to travel short distances requiring fast response time
- blend in easily with ordinary marine traffic
- are unlikely to be inspected upon arrival to the U.S. if they declare what cargo they are bringing into the country

---

The U.S. Customs Service

The Customs Service has primary interdiction responsibilities for land border smuggling through official ports of entry as well as concurrent jurisdiction with Coast Guard vessels in coastal waters of the United States up to 12 miles offshore, also known as the "**Customs zone.**" As of late 1986, the Customs Service had about 4,200 full-time inspectors (500 of which were assigned to special contraband enforcement teams), located at 290 ports of entry. It is their responsibility to process all individuals that enter the United States, totaling close to 300 million persons annually.

Cargo, vessels, and passengers from foreign locations are regularly inspected by customs officials to ensure the payment of required duty as well as to stop the flow of contraband. Each of these is a formidable task. For example, in 1990 the U.S. Customs Service seized 7,952 vehicles, 229 vessels, and 144 aircraft (BJS, 1992). Dogs trained to smell illicit drugs are also used at ports of entry and are an important tool in interdiction. Developed in 1970, the U.S. Customs Canine Enforcement Program has resulted in more than 75,000 drug seizures with a street value of more than $10 billion (BJS, 1992).

Case Study: Barry Seal

Adler Barriman Seal, a former TWA 747 Captain, flew cocaine from Colombia to the United States for over seven years during the late 1970s and early 1980s. Seal was recruited as a trafficking pilot by a personal friend who worked for the Colombian cocaine trafficking organization headed by Jorge Ochoa. Seal eventually worked directly with that organization's leadership.

Initially, Seal flew direct trafficking flights between Louisiana and Colombia. He piloted a number of different smuggling aircraft, the largest of which was a Vietnam-vintage C-123 capable of holding tons of packaged cocaine. Seal always departed and returned to his Louisiana base late at night to reduce chances of interdiction. His typical route took him over the Yucatan Peninsula (not over the more heavily patrolled Yucatan Channel) and directly over Central America to the eastern tip of Honduras, then south to any one of a number of airstrips and airports in north Colombia.

According to Seal, the Ochoa organization paid Colombian officials bribes of $10,000 to $25,000 per flight for a "window," i.e., a specific time, position, and altitude designated for the smuggling flight's penetration of Colombian airspace. If this payment was not made, the aircraft was susceptible to interception by Colombian authorities. Seal generally arrived in Colombia at dawn. His aircraft was loaded with cocaine and refueled within an hour, sometimes within fifteen minutes, and he returned immediately to the United States.

Seal used two fairly simple techniques to avoid interdiction on his return trip to the United States; both were effective because of the heavy helicopter traffic running between the Gulf Coast states and the hundreds of oil rigs located offshore. First, when he reached the middle of the Gulf on his return trip, Seal slowed his aircraft to 110 to 120 knots, which caused monitoring to mistake it for a helicopter. Secondly, at a distance of about 50 miles off the United States coast, he dropped the aircraft to an altitude of 500 to 1,000 feet in order to commingle with helicopter traffic and thereby arouse even less suspicion.

Once in United States airspace, Seal proceeded to prearranged points 40 to 50 miles inland. The points were mapped out in advance with Loran C, a long-range navigational instrument. Further inland, he was generally joined by a helicopter. The two aircraft continued to a drop zone, where the helicopter hovered close to the ground. Seal then dropped the load of cocaine from the airplane on a parachute; the helicopter picked up the load from the drop zone and delivered it to waiting automobiles, which eventually moved the cocaine to Miami. Seal then landed his drug-free aircraft at any nearby airport.

> Seal was paid well for his services. He claims his top fee for smuggling a kilogram of cocaine was $5,000; an average load was 300 kilograms. His most profitable single load netted him $1.5 million. He was never apprehended in connection with this operation.
>
> _____
>
> Author's note: Subsequent to testifying before the President's Commission on Organized Crime, Seal was killed in Louisiana by gunmen believed to be contracted by the Medellin Cartel.

Source: PCOC, *The Edge,* 1986.

Figure 10.3
Interdiction Functions

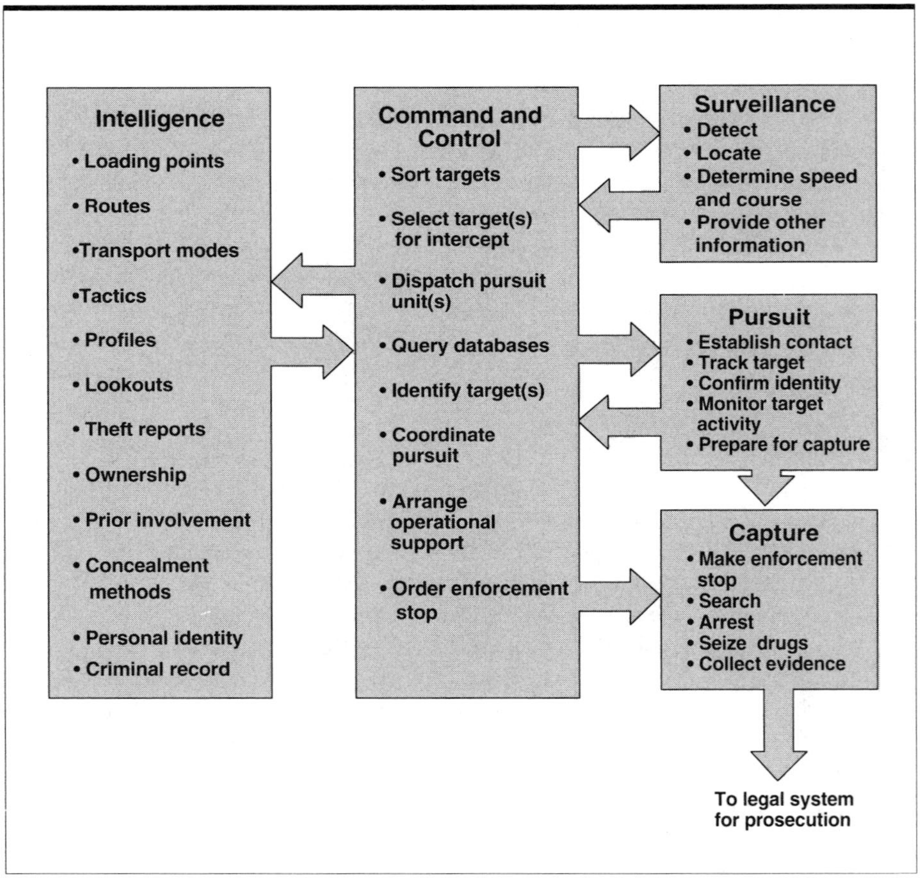

Intelligence
- Loading points
- Routes
- Transport modes
- Tactics
- Profiles
- Lookouts
- Theft reports
- Ownership
- Prior involvement
- Concealment methods
- Personal identity
- Criminal record

Command and Control
- Sort targets
- Select target(s) for intercept
- Dispatch pursuit unit(s)
- Query databases
- Identify target(s)
- Coordinate pursuit
- Arrange operational support
- Order enforcement stop

Surveillance
- Detect
- Locate
- Determine speed and course
- Provide other information

Pursuit
- Establish contact
- Track target
- Confirm identity
- Monitor target activity
- Prepare for capture

Capture
- Make enforcement stop
- Search
- Arrest
- Seize drugs
- Collect evidence

To legal system for prosecution

Source: Office of Technology Assessment, 1987.

It is also the responsibility of the Customs inspectors to inspect all international cargo, all vessels entering sea ports from foreign countries, all aircraft entering the United States from foreign countries (including general and commercial aircraft), all land vehicles such as trucks, automobiles, trains, and busses, and all international mail. The Service's interdiction strategy at ports of entry has several components:

- It operates most effectively when it has prior reliable intelligence. Intelligence sources include informants, private citizens, transportation companies, and intelligence agencies.
- Profiles of people, vehicles, and cargo are used to initiate searches. Profiles include data such as the origin of the individual or cargo and the sex, age, or citizenship of the individual (see Chapter 11).
- Inspectors conduct periodic blitz-type inspections of passengers and cargo.
- Officials use dogs to sniff out hidden drugs as well as metal detection devices and a variety of support and detection technologies to track suspect aircraft.

One primary responsibility of the Customs Service is to interdict drugs in the nation's near-shore waters. This initiative utilizes the Marine Branch of the Service, which uses a system of stopping and searching incoming vessels that behave suspiciously (especially small boats referred to as "go-fast" boats).

A Smuggler's View

Well, it used to be easy. However, now it has become a little less attractive for some of the younger pilots. Some of the older pilots, as myself, have been indicted.

We've been cognizant of law enforcement techniques and the improvements in it, and the younger pilots are seeing the newspaper reports of the older pilots and the amount of time they are being convicted on and serving, and it's not as attractive a proposition as it used to be.

I think that the more flights that are interdicted, the word gets around. For instance, I have absolutely—or had in my capacity—no desire whatsoever to go into and would do anything to stay out of the south Florida area simply due to the fact that is where the concentrated interdiction efforts are being made due to the Vice Presidential Task Force, which has been highly publicized and which has taken its toll on the paranoia of the drug smuggler.

Source: PCOC, *America's Habit*, 1986 (testimony from Barry Seal, drug smuggler).

The best-developed marine interdiction capabilities appear to be in the Miami area where the Blue Lightning Operations Center (BLOC) operates. This initiative was implemented in February 1986, and is a joint operation between

Customs and the Coast Guard, designed to collect and coordinate information from air and marine centers. The BLOC tracks suspicious vessels, plots the course and speed of the suspect target, and directs interceptors toward it.

The Customs Air Branch is responsible for interdicting airborne drug smuggling. In 1985, general aviation aircraft were suspected in being responsible for more than 50 percent of the cocaine and 10 percent of the marijuana entering the United States. Drug smugglers prefer light, twin-engine general aviation aircraft and will usually fly at a low altitude, placing them under the line-of-sight coverage of coastal scanners. These smugglers will typically operate at night to minimize their chance of detection by law enforcement.

Once suspicious aircraft have been sighted, they are normally tracked both by cutters and/or by high-speed chase planes. The interdiction process will usually involve Customs strike teams that are transported to the landing site by helicopters.

A Typical Interdiction Scenario

Following a plane from Colombia to a landing site in Tennessee, for example, may involve not only a team of aircraft and helicopters but coordination with the FAA, the North American Air Defense Command (NORAD), and a variety of federal, state, and local police organizations. The problem is made more difficult because smugglers may not have the drugs on board when they land the airplane. In some instances smugglers fly in, air drop, or land their cargo at prearranged sites and then fly on to landing sites elsewhere in the United States.

As will be discussed further in Chapter 11, a 1988 study by the RAND Corporation revealed some disturbing conclusions regarding the ability of the military to successfully affect drug demand through interdiction. The study, commissioned by the Defense Department and directed by Peter Reuter, concluded that it was more costly for the government to attempt to interdict drugs than it was for traffickers to replace seized shipments.

In the study, Reuter found that the assets of the drug traffickers are so vast that the losses caused by interdiction go unnoticed. Dealers have to spend more on transporting shipments than police can on stopping them. He claims that this is because raw materials and highly skilled labor are surprisingly cheap in the markets utilized by drug traffickers.

To facilitate the study, Reuter developed a computer model called SOAR to estimate more exactly how smugglers would adapt if interdiction efforts were increased. In an all-out drug war, assuming that the interdiction rate on 10 of 11 routes could be more than doubled, SOAR estimated that the cost of smuggling would increase 70 percent, but the retail price of drugs would increase only 10 percent. The increase would, therefore, only affect the street crack user by $2 per purchase.

The Border Patrol

The federal agency most actively involved in interdiction on land between ports-of-entry is the Border Patrol. The Border Patrol operates under the Department of Immigration and Naturalization Service (INS), which is within the Department of Justice. The Border Patrol, as of late 1986, employed approximately 3,700 officers, most of which were stationed along the United States-Mexico border.

The primary function of the Border Patrol is the enforcing of laws related to admission, exclusion, and expulsion of aliens, but while performing this function, Border Patrol agents frequently interdict drugs. This is because some drug smugglers enter the United States through the same routes used by illegal aliens, and some individuals that smuggle aliens also smuggle drugs.

As is typical with many drug interdiction law enforcement agencies, the Border Patrol is grossly lacking in resources—particularly manpower. For example, a recent interdiction problem is the smugglers' use of commercial containers on cargo ships and in trucks. Cocaine has been found in such containers in shipments of cement mix, honey, fruit pulp, caustic lye, and pumpkins. Due to manpower constraints, agents can only inspect 4 percent of the estimated 8 million containers arriving yearly.

Interdiction Support Agencies

In addition to the interdiction efforts by the Coast Guard and the Customs Service, other support agencies share certain responsibilities. Such support services share intelligence, equipment, and other resources. The primary support groups used in the interdiction effort are the Department of Defense, the Federal Aviation Administration (FAA), and various state and local law enforcement agencies.

> *The Department of Defense (DOD).* The historical separation of powers between the police and the military is defined under a law known as the Posse Comitatus Act. It was refined in 1981, resulting in a relaxation of the provisions for using military equipment and personnel for domestic law enforcement. While DOD personnel cannot make arrests, the new provisions of the law allow sharing of intelligence equipment and assisting in certain operations that lead to arrests.

The Federal Aviation Administration (FAA). The FAA supports the drug interdiction effort with its flight information systems. The FAA requires all flights by private aircraft that originate in foreign countries to file flight plans 24 hours in advance and to land at the airport nearest to its point of entry that has a customs officer. Those aircraft crossing the border without having filed a flight plan are automatically considered suspicious and are subsequently investigated.

Other agencies sharing certain drug enforcement responsibilities include the Internal Revenue Service (IRS), the United States Marshals Service, and the Bureau of Alcohol, Tobacco, and Firearms. Most of this cooperation is done on a case-by-case basis.

Thinking Critically #22

Refute or defend a need for additional drug enforcement agencies in the United States. What, if any, changes would you support in the jurisdiction of existing agencies?

Coordination Organizations

Drug traffickers are mobile and respect neither political boundaries nor the division of jurisdictions between law enforcement agencies. Therefore, police have responded to the drug problem by joining their efforts. Coordination efforts can be either horizontal, involving efforts between agencies operating in a particular region, or vertical, involving agencies at various levels of government. Several agencies offer services to the primary drug enforcement agencies in the federal and state governments. These agencies will be discussed next.

Operation Alliance

Operating as a multiagency effort to prevent drug smuggling across the Mexican border, Operation Alliance was developed. It essentially serves as a task force under the direction of the INS's Border Patrol and includes officers from DEA, INS, persons from the United States Attorney's Office, as well officers from state and local law enforcement agencies. The philosophy of Operation Alliance is to share resources while seeking to interdict the flow of drugs coming from Mexico.

The National Drug Policy Board

The National Narcotics Drug Policy Board (NDPB) was created by the 1984 National Narcotics Act. The Board originated as a Cabinet-level agency consisting of the Attorney General as chairman and the Secretaries of State, Treasury, Defense, Transportation, and Health and Human Services, as well as the Directors of Central Intelligence and the Office of Management and Budget as members. Despite the diversity of federal agencies involved, it was the Board's objective to coordinate and focus strategies in the fight against drug abuse. Specifically, the statutory language outlining the mission of the National Drug Policy Board was as follows:

1. Maintain a national and international effort against illegal drugs;
2. Coordinate fully the activities of the federal agencies involved; and
3. Charge a single, competent, and responsible high-level Board of the United States Government, chaired by the Attorney General, with responsibility for coordinating United States policy with respect to national and international drug law enforcement.

In 1988, the NDPB was dissolved to make way for the Office of National Drug Control Policy.

Office of National Drug Control Policy (ONDCP)

In 1988, the Office of National Drug Control Policy (ONDCP) was created to assume control of the federal drug policy effort and was to be directed by a high-level "**Drug Czar.**" Director William Bennett, the former U.S. Secretary of Education, assumed this office in 1989 and was charged with formulating a workable plan for drug control on a nationwide basis. As of the preparation of this book, the ONDCP has released several reports detailing the national drug control strategy. Each of the reports specifies goals and objectives of both domestic and foreign drug control initiatives.

In 1990, ONDCP designated five areas as **High Intensity Drug Trafficking Areas:** New York, Miami, Los Angeles, Houston, and along the southwest border. The program's goals are to identify and disrupt drug trafficking organizations operating in these areas and who are thought to be major contributors to the drug problem in the nation. Funding for this program is provided to federal and state local law enforcement projects that can not be funded on individual agency budgets.

The Regional Information Sharing System (RISS)

The Regional Information Sharing System program is an innovative, federally-funded program that was created to support law enforcement efforts and to combat organized crime activity, drug trafficking, and white-collar crime. The

RISS project began with funding by the LEAA (Law Enforcement Assistance Administration) discretionary grant program. Since 1980, the U.S. Congress has made a yearly appropriation of funds to the RISS projects as a line item in the Department of Justice budget.

The primary impetus of the projects is to augment existing law enforcement agencies with intelligence information on criminal activities in their jurisdictions. Additionally, the RISS project provides services to member agencies regarding assistance in asset seizures, funds for covert operations, analysis of investigative data on organized criminals, loans of investigative equipment, and training in the use of such equipment in criminal investigations. The RISS program operates within seven Regional Information Sharing Projects:

1. Mid-State Organized Crime Information Center (MOCIC). Missouri, Kansas, Illinois, Iowa, Nebraska, South Dakota, North Dakota, Minnesota, and Wisconsin.

2. Western States Information Network (WSIN). California, Oregon, Washington, Hawaii, and Alaska.

3. Rocky Mountain Information Network (RMIN). Colorado, New Mexico, Arizona, Nevada, Wyoming, Idaho, and Montana.

4. Regional Organized Crime Information Center (ROCIC). Texas, Oklahoma, Arkansas, Louisiana, Tennessee, Mississippi, Alabama, Georgia, Florida, Kentucky, South Carolina, North Carolina, Virginia, and West Virginia.

5. Middle Atlantic Great Lakes Organized Crime Law Enforcement Network (MAGLOCLEN). Indiana, Ohio, Pennsylvania, New York, Michigan, Rhode Island, New Jersey, Maryland, and Delaware.

6. New England State Police Information Network (NESPIN). Massachusetts, Maine, Vermont, Connecticut, New Hampshire, and Rhode Island.

7. LEVITICUS. Alabama, Georgia, Indiana, Kentucky, New York, Pennsylvania, and Virginia. The LEVITICUS Project provides coordination to agencies investigating crimes related to the coal, oil, and natural gas industries.

The National Narcotics Border Interdiction System (NNBIS)

The NNBIS system was created to provide guidance for interdiction systems and is under the chairmanship of the Vice President. Regional NNBIS units are established at six locations throughout the country. These regional components are chaired by the heads of various regional enforcement agencies that have responsibility for that particular geographical area. For example, three of these regional directors are admirals in the Coast Guard.

The Organized Crime Drug Enforcement Task Force (OCDETF)

In 1981, the effects of drug trafficking and drug abuse in South Florida had so greatly affected the quality of life there that several particularly vocal public groups demanded immediate attention be given to the problem. In 1982, President Reagan established a cabinet-level South Florida Task Force known as "Operation Florida" to address the problem. The primary focus of Operation Florida was interdiction, arrest, and prosecution of drug smugglers. The task force was staffed with officers from federal agencies such as the DEA, FBI, Customs, ATF, the Marshals Service, the DOD, and the Coast Guard.

The establishment of the Operation Florida task force led to the creation of the Organized Crime Drug Enforcement Task Force (OCDETF) in 1983. The objectives of OCDETF are, however, quite different. While the primary focus of the South Florida program is interdiction, the focus of the OCDETF program is the detection and prosecution of leaders of large criminal organizations that control illicit drug importation and distribution. As of the preparation of this text, the OCDETF has proven to be one of the most effective enforcement initiatives in the nation's drug control effort. The participating federal agencies include: the United States Attorney's office, DEA, FBI, Customs, ATF, IRS, Marshals Service, and the Coast Guard.

Figure 10.4
The Organized Crime and Drug Enforcement Task Force (OCDETF) Agencies

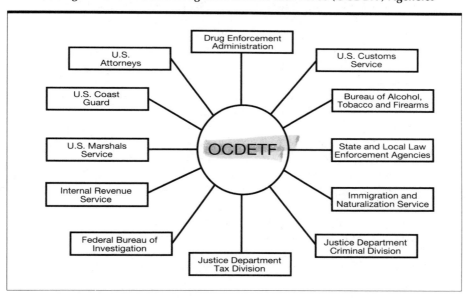

Source: Organized Crime Drug Enforcement Task Force Program, U.S. Justice Department, 1989.

Particularly supportive of the OCDETF program is the sustained use of the investigative grand jury (see Chapter 11). Prosecutors have employed the grand jury as an investigative technique in more than 60 percent of all task force cases. Additionally, investigators make extensive use of undercover techniques in the development of cases that result in indictments. This technique is particularly suited to the OCDETF mission, in which there is a need for a long-term, complicated investigation that requires agents to follow all leads in pursuit of major dealers, be they manufacturers, suppliers, or money launderers.

The success of the OCDETF program is evidenced in part by the statistics on net prison terms. In 1988, for example, the percentage of defendants sentenced to terms of five or more years of confinement increased to 54.2 percent, compared to the six-year cumulative rate of 50.9 percent. Of greater significance is the fact that in fiscal year (FY) 1988, top leaders, major suppliers, and mid-level suppliers were sentenced to average prison sentences of 16.4, 7.0, and 8.3 years, respectively. This represents an increase in years sentenced, over all the years of task force operation, of more than 20 percent for top leaders, 6 percent for major suppliers, and 27 percent for mid-level leaders. Today, the OCDETF concept has become the principal federal weapon in investigation and prosecution of drug traffickers and their organizations.

Good Guys As Bad Guys: The Temptations of the Undercover Cop

In the movie *Rush*, the female undercover narcotics agent sits curled up in a corner so strung out on heroin, she can't tell what's real or hallucination. She's a police officer doing her job, she tells herself. Or is she what she looks like—a wasted drug addict? When did she cross the thin line that distinguishes the good guys from the bad?

That fine line—and what makes an undercover cop cross over it—is territory Michael Girodo has explored in a 15-year study of more than 200 undercover agents. A professor of psychology at the University of Ottawa, Canada, during July 1993 he was a visiting professor at the FBI Academy in Quantico, Virginia. Using interviews, psychological tests, and agents' responses to role-playing situations, Girodo concludes that the personality traits making a good undercover officer are often the same ones predisposing him or her to corruption and psychological distress.

Girodo found that officers best suited for undercover work are fast-talking, risk-taking, and assertive. The job description also involves manipulation, deception, and lying—characteristics hardly considered virtues by most people. Yet the person enjoys it—indeed, is selected by the agencies because people who enjoy these risks make the best undercover officers. It's up to the cop's style and wits to get him or herself in with the criminals and stay in. People adaptable to a wide range of roles seem to have "a native talent for misrepresentation and guise," he says. "For this small but noteworthy percentage of agents, the undercover field offers rich opportunities to indulge natural inclinations to con."

The agent gathers information before the criminal activity takes place, seeing it unfold before his eyes. While other cops come in after the act, the undercover officer has a hand in making the crime happen. "He becomes one of them," Girodo continues. "But the criminals get caught, while he gets away with buying and selling drugs, say, and the government sanctions it."

After these situations happen over and over again, the agent may start believing his own lines, thinking the criminals are his friends, confusing right and wrong. "To sustain the insults he gets, maintain his motivation, he often has lots of money, clothes, liberty. He's reimbursed for his alcoholic expenses. It's a heady experience, especially if he's rewarded for it," says Girodo. Paradoxically, he needs that arrogance and self-confidence to be convincing. As he commands increasing influence, he dreams of appearing on *60 Minutes* and having a movie made of his adventures. He feels entitled to special favors, treatment, and dispensations. There are outbursts with bosses, abuses in relationships.

Psychologists might say this character has a personality disorder, but these components are nurtured and developed in undercover work. The work predicts misconduct. "The longer you're on the job, the greater the odds that you're going to get into trouble," Girodo says. "At the same time, no vice commander is going to let some skilled, valuable resource go. The agent is the asset they need." So the personality continues to change.

After the cowboy comes the prima donna. Then, less visibly, he begins to develop his own laws. The exception becomes the norm. Since he's scamming all the time, he begins to think everyone has a scam. So enamored of a role, he may refuse to abandon it. Girodo recounts a classic case: "An undercover officer about to retire was to go into a counterfeit money operation, flash a roll of $80,000, and 20 minutes later get back out. He went in without a wire and was to signal his support team. The guy stayed in the room two-and-a-half hours. The bosses were frantic. When he finally came out, he explained, 'This was my last job. I didn't want to give up my role. They enjoyed me. They really liked me!'"

There are no precise figures on how many undercover agents are corrupted, says Girodo, "but I do know the number is far greater than what police and the public are willing to accept. And it's increasing all the time." How can an agent avoid the temptations? "Best is a solid home life, of course," says Girodo, who is creating programs to train agents to become more aware of psychological risks inherent in their personalities and work. "We get them to slow down, take greater cognitive responsibility for their actions." They also make "public confessions" in front of other agents. "No one wants to do something stupid in front of his or her peers," he adds.

Source: Bladow, Janel (1994). "Good Guys as Bad Guys: The Temptations of the Undercover Cop." *Omni Magazine*. v. 16, May. p. 12. Reproduced by permission of Omni, © 1994, Omni Publications International, Ltd.

Other Task Forces

In addition to OCDETF, 44 formal and 12 provisional DEA-funded state and local task forces operate throughout the country. Augmenting this effort, another 700 multi-jurisdictional drug enforcement task forces operate with funding provided by the Anti-Drug Abuse Acts of 1986 and 1988.

The Task of Agency Coordination

A formidable task in the nation's drug war is the coordination of enforcement efforts between agencies located within both the state and federal governments. As mentioned above, both NNBIS and OCDETF were designed to pool resources in the enforcement effort, but many organizational problems still prevail.

Figure 10.5
Organized Crime Drug Enforcement Task Forces

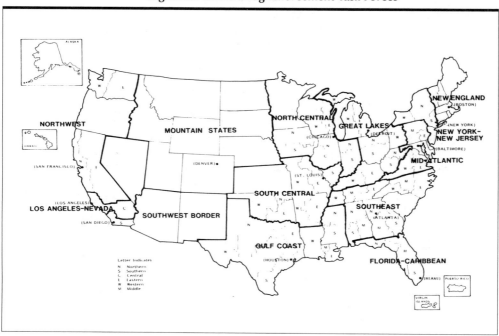

Source: Organized Crime Drug Enforcement Task Force Program Annual Report.

On the federal level, "turf" wars and inner-agency bickering often result in a reluctance to share information or coordinate enforcement efforts. For example, confusion often results when many different departments play some role in the drug suppression effort. The U.S. Department of Agriculture, for example, handles crop eradication, Customs is responsible for interdiction, yet the armed services also monitor the military's role in interdiction. The FBI and DEA have similar roles in investigating federal violations of the Controlled Substances Act.

The primary responsibility for coordination on the federal level rests with the Director of the Office of National Drug Control Policy. Former Director William Bennett, appointed by President George Bush in 1989, assumed a hard-line attitude on this problem and stated: "If they're not in line, we'll get them in line." To partially illustrate the problem, examples are given below:

- The Drug Enforcement Administration (DEA), Federal Bureau of Investigation (FBI), the U.S. Customs Service, the State Department, the Central Intelligence Agency (CIA), and the Defense Department all gather intelligence information separately.
- Customs and DEA have been involved in feuds over who keeps assets and money seized during drug investigations.
- An FBI-DEA National Intelligence Center, proposed in William Bennett's 1989 National Drug Strategy, was rejected after officials at the Justice Department claimed that it would infringe upon Attorney General William Thornburgh's power.

Federal Drug Control Agencies

The Justice Department
Drug Enforcement Administration
Federal Bureau of Investigation
Criminal Division
Tax Division
U.S. Attorneys Offices
U.S. Marshals Service
U.S. Bureau of Prisons
Immigration and Naturalization
 Service

Department of the Interior
Office of Justice Programs
Interpol
Inspector General
Fish and Wildlife Service
Bureau of Land Management
National Park Service
Bureau of Indian Affairs

The Department of Treasury
U.S. Customs Service
Internal Revenue Service
Bureau of Alcohol, Tobacco,
 and Firearms

Transportation Department
U.S. Coast Guard
Federal Aviation Administration
National Highway Traffic
 Safety Administration

U.S. Information Agency

The State Department
International Narcotics Matters

Department of Agriculture
Agriculture Research Service
U.S. Forest Service

Health and Human Services
Alcohol, Drug Abuse, and
 Mental Health Administration
Indian Health Service
Food and Drug Administration

Department of Defense

Department of Labor

Department of Education

Veterans Affairs

**Agency for International
 Development**

Cannabis Eradication

Each year during the summer months, marijuana cultivation becomes big business. To counter the growers who cultivate marijuana, an alliance between DEA and state and local law enforcement agencies has been formed. Initiated in 1979 by the DEA, the Cannabis Eradication Suppression Program gives state and local police such resources as technical assistance, training, and special equipment for this task. To date, every state participates in the program, which also operates in conjunction with other federal agencies. Included is the U.S. Forest Service, the Bureau of Land Management, the Bureau of Indian Affairs, and the Department of Defense. In many states, the National Guard has also provided manpower and equipment for this undertaking.

In addition to outdoor marijuana cultivation operations, the task of cannabis eradication extends to indoor operations as well. As discussed in Chapter 5, indoor growing operations pose special problems to police. In 1987, these operations emerged in great numbers throughout the nation, and government statistics indicate that the amount of indoor operations is increasing. One initiative designed to identify such operations is DEA's Operation Green Merchant, which targets suppliers of cannabis seeds, growing equipment, cultivation information, and the growers themselves. In 1989, the operation resulted in 441 arrests and the seizure of 356 indoor growing operations which produced more than one ton of processed sinsemilla (BJS, 1992).

Investigating Illicit Laboratories

As with marijuana cultivation, illegal drug laboratories also pose serious problems for drug control officials. During the 1980s the number of such labs soared, and in addition to their being illegal in nature, they pose specific dangers for investigators. The federal government estimated that one in five illicit laboratories discovered are noticed as a result of fire or explosion. As discussed in Chapter 5, drug labs are volatile and unstable, posing dangers to both lab operators and police alike. Adding to the dangers of investigating drug labs are counter surveillance measures such as cameras, automatic weapons, and booby traps, all commonly associated with these operations.

Because of the nature of the illicit drug laboratory, many pose an environmental hazard when dangerous chemicals are indiscriminately disposed of by lab operators. In one case, a California drug lab operator dumped chemicals into the sewer system in a remote rural area. Consequently, the lab's chemicals killed the bacteria which was used to treat sewage, resulting in the raw sewage being returned to the environment.

Another problem associated with investigating the drug lab is disposal of the chemicals used in the lab process once they are seized. Most chemicals used in LSD, methamphetamine, and PCP labs are corrosive, explosive, and unstable, and when they are seized by police, they must be properly disposed of.

One of the challenges police face is the identification and tracking of precursor chemicals used in the laboratory process. Aiding police was the passing of the 1988 Chemical Diversion and Trafficking Act, which is designed to prevent legal chemicals from being used to process illicit drugs. According to the provisions of the law, domestic distributors of precursor and essential chemicals must meet specific reporting and records requirements. The law requires distributors to:

- identify their regular customers
- maintain records of sales for a specified period of time
- declare the import of such chemicals
- report questionable orders to the DEA

Under the law, it is the seller who makes the decision as to whether a specific purchase is shady. A classic example is an order for a large quantity of chemicals which is under the minimum amount of chemicals required for reporting purposes from a buyer who is not involved in the type of business in which that chemical is normally used.

Strategies for Street-Level Enforcement

Although the problem of foreign drug traffickers smuggling dangerous drugs into the country is a high priority of the federal government, the coexisting problem of controlling local street-level dealers prevails. Adopting a policy that effectively deals with the street-level dealer is a major priority.

Discreet and Nondiscreet Markets

Primary responsibility for this task has typically rested with the local law enforcement agency and has been associated with two distinct illegal street markets, discreet and nondiscreet markets. *Discreet drug market*s are those in which the drug seller and the drug buyer are well-acquainted. Drug transactions taking place under these circumstances typically involve exchanges of drugs for money in the work place or within a social environment such as a bar or nightclub. These operations are frequently difficult to discover by police because of the private nature of the transactions and may, therefore, go undetected for long periods of time. In comparison, *nondiscreet drug markets* differ from the discreet drug trade in that the drug seller is rarely acquainted with the drug buyer. The nondiscreet market accounts for the so-called *open-air* trade that flourishes in public places. This type of drug market is attractive for the drug dealer because it will generate greater profits because of a greater number of customers available to the dealer. The nondiscreet market is also an easy target for police intervention and control, as its whereabouts are easily learned through police surveillance operations and informants.

The Kingpin Strategy

Enforcement strategies differ from one jurisdiction to another. Some are aimed at the heads or "kingpins" of the organizations. Under this strategy, police believe that once the top manager of a drug trafficking organization has been eliminated from the organization then the rest of the organization will shut down. Thus, the amount of drugs on the streets will be reduced and the price of drugs available to buyers will rise, making them less attractive to consumers. Recent research, however, has shown that there were no documented cases where these drug-reduction strategies had actually resulted in a reduction in drug consumption (Kleiman and Smith, 1990). Experts also disagreed with the assumption that no new management figures would assume control of the organization once the "kingpin" was removed.

However, another expert in the field, Mark Moore (1990), suggests that strategies such as undercover operations targeting drug kingpins tend to make the organization more cautious, which results in some transactions being restricted out of fear of discovery by police. In addition, Moore argues that enforcement successes against organizations result in a loss of inventory and the future capacity to supply drugs.

Marijuana Citations

One original approach by many municipalities in dealing with offenders caught with small amounts of marijuana is the issuing of citations by uniformed patrol officers. For example, when a small amount of marijuana is seized as a result of a vehicle stop, in lieu of taking the violator into custody, a citation is written and signed by the violator. This process basically works like a traffic citation, as it requires the offender to appear in court on a later date.

This procedure has generally been considered a successful street-level enforcement tactic because it reduces the commitments of time and money by the police, the prosecutor, and the courts through streamlining the adjudicatory process. At the same time, the practice enables law enforcement to identify and convict drug users in the community that might otherwise escape detection by the criminal justice system.

Undercover Operations

Due to the secret nature of drug trafficking organizations, information on their activities is difficult to obtain. We have discussed in Chapter 5 that the number of people involved in drug trafficking organizations is limited in order to ensure control by managers. So one method of learning the inner workings of such operations is through the use of undercover operatives. The typical undercover operation involves an undercover officer buying drugs and then arresting the seller, a "buy-and-bust."

Both police officers and informants are used in the undercover capacity, which typically focuses on street-level dealers who are easily persuaded to exchange information for leniency. Undercover operations also depend heavily on surveillance, which sometimes includes wire taps, examination of financial records, and the use of other electric monitoring devices. In 1989, 62 percent of the 763 state and federal court orders for the interception of wire, oral, or electronic communications resulted from investigations in which a drug violation was the most serious offense (BJS, 1992).

Other Concerns

It is clear that law enforcement initiatives alone are not successful in adequately containing the existing problem of street drug trafficking. Modern-day strategies must include tactics such as the enlistment of the support of community groups, seizing assets of both sellers and users, and cracking down on all street sales operations.

Drug dealing, a fragmented and broadly generalized term, addresses all levels of illicit drug distribution and many different types of drugs. Although different types of drugs, such as marijuana, methamphetamine, heroin, and so forth, are prevalent in different geographical areas of the country, the problem of crack cocaine sales has been identified by many larger departments as an enforcement priority. The popularity of crack cocaine among dealers is closely related to its popularity by the drug-using public; that is, crack is a highly addictive drug that consequently creates much repeat business for the seller and generates a correspondingly high profit margin. Street sales of crack cocaine and powdered (HCl) cocaine seem to follow two distinct patterns: the use of the *crack house* and the *nondiscreet market*.

> ### Thinking Critically #23
>
> Suggest guidelines by which law enforcement agencies may better monitor the activities of undercover drug agents and, thus, reduce police corruption.

The crack house is the most common means of street distribution of crack cocaine by dealers. Frequently, the crack house is an abandoned house that has been commandeered by street dealers for use as a base of operation. These houses are structurally fortified with steel bars on windows and metal door jambs to prevent easy access by police. The crack house may operate in an "open" fashion, which enables the drug buyer or user to enter the house, purchase the crack, and ingest it on the premises.

Street corner sales have also contributed greatly to the proliferation of the crack cocaine problem. Although primarily an inner-city phenomenon, this nondiscreet method for retail crack sales has, in some cases, created vehicular traffic congestion because of dealers that literally approach any passing automobile and inquire of the driver if he or she is interested in purchasing any crack. This system of illicit drug trafficking illustrates the arrogance and lackadaisical attitude that many street dealers share with regard to the criminal justice system.

Specific tactics used to reduce street sales largely depend on the scope of the problem in each community. The task force concept (previously discussed) is one such tactic and has proven to be one of the more effective enforcement tools in the fight against street trafficking and for use in interdiction. Other traditional strategies to tackle the problem include the use of the "buy-bust," where undercover police officers posing as drug buyers target the street dealer.

New, nontraditional strategies of street enforcement are being considered by many law enforcement agencies. One such tactic is the use of the *reverse-sting*. This innovative approach to controlling street drug sales involves undercover police officers that pose as drug "dealers" rather than buyers. The focus of the strategy is to arrest those that purchase crack or attempt to engage in an illicit drug transaction. The reverse-sting concept has three primary advantages: the ability to identify and seize personal assets of the drug dealer (discussed later in this chapter), the ability to arrest large numbers of street dealers and thus deter criminal activity, and the ability to generate positive media coverage of police department activities.

A common problem for police crackdowns on street-level drug operations is *displacement*. For decades, traditional vice units have dealt with the problem of displacement of offenders in attempting to control such operations as prostitution. Typically, once a strong police presence is detected by potential violators, alternative markets for the criminal activity are identified and pursued.

Displacement in retail drug enforcement operations is a common problem. If law enforcement efforts are not as concentrated in outlying areas as in the area of the crackdown, then drug dealers will almost assuredly set up their operations in these outlying areas (also see Chapter 8).

Police-Community Drug Control Efforts

In neighborhoods infested with drugs and drug traffickers, people who are law-abiding are sometimes aware of who the drug dealers and users are. Granted, the specific names and addresses of those involved with illicit drugs may not be known, but drug transactions are routinely witnessed as dealers come and go from crack houses and as acts of violence are committed. As discussed in Chapter 6, the practice of community and problem-oriented policing is designed to tap into this crucial source of information by cultivating community-police partnerships. The premise of this philosophy rests on two realities: first, the police need public assistance in pinpointing locations of drug production and sales, as

Reno Scores a Victory in War on Drugs: COP-Plus Targets Open Dealing

When Capt. Tom Robinson of the Reno (NV) Police Department first tried to organize a Neighborhood Advisory Group in his North-Stead area, he held open meetings in Pat Baker Park in the heart of the black community. The park, nicknamed "Instant Park" because it had literally been put in over a weekend, had been the site of disturbing clashes between local residents and drug dealers, particularly the crack dealers that began to appear in ever larger numbers about two years ago. At one of the first meetings, the officers put up 75 chairs, but only 25 people actually sat in them—an equal number of young toughs stood behind, looking ominous. "One brave resident stood up at that meeting and told us that if we got rid of the drug dealers and troublemakers, they would fill all the chairs," says Chief Robert V. Bradshaw.

Inspired by that challenge, the department put together a plan to drive the dealers from the park, using a Community Policing approach. In addition to traditional undercover operations, the COP-Plus approach included high-visibility patrols, deployment of officers in walking beats, and development of liaisons with the area's black ministers.

Within a two-month period, the police made 40 arrests for drug law violations—and all of the arrestees were black. "In the past, whenever we tried to deal with the problems in the park, the headlines in the local paper talked about how the police were the problem," said Bradshaw. Traditional police action often triggered mini-riots—people threw bottles and rocks at the police.

"This time, we held a news conference at the end of the 60-day period, with the involvement of the black ministers, and we didn't have a single complaint about race," says Bradshaw. Bradshaw says that their COP-Plus approach has improved race relations, regardless of the race of the officer.

"Just recently, when we arrested a drug dealer in the park, the people stood up and cheered," said Robinson. He attributes the change to their Community Policing focus. COP-Plus has succeeded in generating information about drug dealing beyond what dangerous and expensive undercover operations produced. "People call their officer and then the officer shares the information with narcotics," says Bradshaw. "We now get calls every day and, within two sunsets, we get them (the dealers)."

Drug Gangs and Gang Violence

Though Reno is typically conservative and low-key, two years ago, an influx of drug gang members from California threatened to rip the city wide open. Notorious gangs, including California's Crips and Bloods, appeared in Reno seeking recruits for their burgeoning crack franchise.

"At that time, we were averaging two drive-by shootings a week," says Bradshaw. One of the most unnerving incidents involved two Los Angeles Crips and three locals that they had recruited into their gang. "Their basic plan was simple—rob someone and then rape someone," says Bradshaw.

First, the quintet stole a vehicle and sprayed it with graffiti, then they robbed and severely beat a college student. Next they snatched a 13-year-old girl from her bicycle and gang-raped her. The police succeeded in catching the perpetrators, and two were sentenced to prison for life.

"We have a Gang Task Force, but it's really been the COP-Plus focus that has driven most of the gangs away," says Bradshaw. He says that the community cohesion fostered by a Community Policing approach persuaded the gangs that there are other places that are more hospitable than Reno for them to ply their trade.

Bradshaw doesn't claim that Reno is drug-free—no city is. But gangs are now a minor problem, and places like Pat Baker Park are no longer plagued by open dealing. He says that communication is what shut the drug gangs down and that COP-Plus was the catalyst. "And I can't really remember when we had our last call about a drive-by shooting," he says.

"The difference is that people used to stand up and bash the police at meetings, and now they go on TV telling everyone what a great job we're doing," says Bradshaw. "Now they want to know why everyone in city government isn't doing as well as the police."

Under this plan, suspects may be arrested on the spot or during a larger scale "round-up" occurring at a later time. This strategy, however, is not as common as others because of legal and operational considerations (with regard to officer safety) that are inherent in the operation.

Source: *Footprints—The Community Newsletter,* Spring 1990.

well as learning the identities of those responsible and secondly, the community relies on the police to eradicate drugs and drug dealers from neighborhoods within the community.

Many studies have been conducted where such partnerships have been tried, and it is clear that closer ties between the police and the community result in safer neighborhoods. For example, experience has shown that the implementation of foot patrol programs in some cities has raised citizen satisfaction with the police as well as the quality of life for residents.

Community Policing

Apprehending and incarcerating retail drug dealers is not the only way to intercept street-level drug sales. As discussed in Chapter 4, maintaining a high police profile in the community can often deter street dealers from initially entering a neighborhood. The community policing concept integrates the police into the community so that its citizens will be more receptive and willing to exchange information with the police. Patrols on foot are thought to be one of the most important aspects to community policing because citizens are apt to feel that the police are greater contributors to the overall safety of the community.

Figure 10.6
Local Law Enforcement Strategies Against Drugs

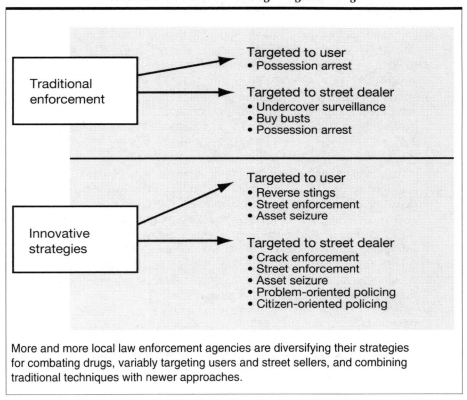

More and more local law enforcement agencies are diversifying their strategies for combating drugs, variably targeting users and street sellers, and combining traditional techniques with newer approaches.

Source: National Institute of Justice, U.S. Department of Justice, 1989.

Some communities have even found that the presence of police officers who stand in the vicinity of open-air drug markets (blatant street drug dealing) or conspicuously take pictures of dealers and prospective drug buyers tended to deter potential customers and forced drug dealers to leave the area. In one case, patrol officers in Charleston, South Carolina, kept drug dealers moving from block to block, preventing them from establishing a foothold in the neighborhood. Officers also knock on the doors of suspected crack houses, which often frightens the dealers into flushing their illegal drug inventory down the drain. In another case, officers in both Yakama, Washington, and Ft. Lauderdale, Florida, deterred drug dealers by sending owners of cars seen cruising near drug markets notices that their vehicles were observed in an area known to be filled with drug dealers.

**Case Study: Hill Street Crime Watch Committee,
Boston, Massachusetts**

The Hill Street Crime Watch Committee was formed by residents of a troubled Boston neighborhood to help police crack down on the drug trade that was instilling fear and creating disorder there. The area, which one narcotics officer called "the worst section in the whole city," was well-known to police as a major center for drug dealing.

Frustrated by conditions in her neighborhood, Hill Street resident Carmen Peralta called Christopher Hayes for help. Hayes, a civilian employee of the Boston Police Department who ran its Neighborhood Crime Watch Program, had already organized crime watch groups in about 100 Boston neighborhoods. After meeting with Peralta and other Hill Street residents and recognizing the extreme fear and danger present in the community, Hayes asked then Police Commissioner Francis (Mickey) Roache to meet with the group. The meeting between Roache and the Hill Street residents convinced the commissioner that drastic measures were needed.

To give the Hill Street neighborhood high priority, the police department established a special drug task force for that area. The Hill Street Crime Watch members were asked to participate in the drug reduction efforts by acting as informants, providing police with information that could lead to arrests and abatement of the problem.

However, after an intensive effort in the area, the cooperation began to break down. The task force was transferred from the local police district to the department's citywide Drug Control Unit. The Hill Street Crime Watch Committee members felt abandoned, as they perceived that police efforts in the neighborhood waned while drug trafficking and related threats of violence continued. Intimidated relentlessly by drug dealers, the Crime Watch leader left the group and moved his family out of the country. Fear escalated among group members, and the effort fell apart.

Source: Weingart, Saul N. et al. (1994). *Case Studies of Community Anti-Drug Efforts.* National Institute of Justice. October.

Problem-Oriented Policing

Although immediate action is important in many criminal incidents, research has shown that so-called "incident-driven" policing does not prevent many of the problems that citizens want solved. Problem-oriented policing (POP) gained popularity during the 1980s. We should note that although POP was not developed with drug control as its initial focus, its principles can be applied in approaching numerous drug problems in many communities. Originally developed by Herman Goldstein, the concept of problem-oriented policing is based on three concepts:

- Police effectiveness can be achieved by attacking the underlying problems that contribute to a particular criminal incident.
- The expertise of line officers should be tapped into more often to develop solutions to problems.
- Police should work more closely with the public to ensure that police are addressing their needs.

One of the first problem-oriented policing programs was conducted several years ago in Newport News, Virginia. It employed four phases:

1. *The Problem Identification Phase:* Rather than focusing on broad, legal concepts of crime, such as robbery and burglary, officers group individual incidents which come to their attention as "problems" and then define those problems in more specific and practical terms. For example, an incident that would typically be classified as an "assault" might be seen as part of a pattern of drug-related assaults in center city parks.
2. *The Analysis Phase:* Once a "problem" is defined, then officers work on collecting information from a variety of public and private sources in addition to police information. Then the underlying nature of the problem is illuminated with the use of the information, a cause is identified, and options for resolution are pinpointed.
3. *The Response Phase.* Next officers work with members of the community (public organizations and private businesses) to address the problem. Often, solutions to problems go beyond standard police practices and may incorporate nontraditional remedies from service organizations or private industry.
4. *The Assessment Phase.* Finally, officers evaluate their efforts to see if the problems have been adequately solved.

The result of problem-oriented policing has shown that in most cases crime-related incidents have decreased in cities which have adopted the program. Experience with problem-oriented policing has also shown the public is generally willing to work with the police and that such partnerships are possible. But the creation of police-public partnerships cannot be assumed and is generally achieved in different ways, depending on local conditions and the nature of the drug problem in each area. One innovative program to achieve such a partnership is the **weed and seed** approach.

Weed and Seed

Originating under the Bush Administration, Operation Weed and Seed is a national initiative designed to link law enforcement efforts with social services in an effort to revitalize crime and drug-ridden neighborhoods. Essentially the focus of the program is to use a multiagency approach to 1) eliminate crime, gang activity, and drug trafficking from selected neighborhoods, and 2) to pro-

Case Study: Whittier Block Watch, Denver, Colorado

Shortly after Jan Johnson and her family moved into the Denver neighborhood of Whittier, they discovered that it was rapidly deteriorating into a haven for drug trafficking. Because she felt the police were not responding as effectively as they might, Johnson and her neighbors mounted a persistent effort to document and report suspicious activity in the neighborhood and to hold police and other agencies accountable for the condition of the neighborhood.

When the extent of the drug trade grew intolerable, Johnson organized a meeting of an existing neighborhood block group and other concerned residents. The new group, which members simply called Block Watch, had a two-pronged agenda. First, residents wanted to convince the police to intensify the law enforcement response to the drugs. Second, Johnson and her fellow Block Watchers pressed zoning officials to implement a new nuisance ordinance that permitted the eviction of drug-dealing tenants.

Drug-related activity soon began to abate. Several months after Block Watch began, Johnson and her neighbors held their last meeting, convinced that they had accomplished much of what they set out to do by improving the quality of police enforcement in the area and reducing the level of drug trafficking. (The police, on the other hand, felt that the role of the neighborhood group had not been as large as the community believed.) Jan Johnson and her neighbors then began to play a more active leadership role in a larger, existing neighborhood association.

Source: Weingart, Saul N. et al. (1994). *Case Studies of Community Anti-Drug Efforts.* National Institute of Justice.

vide a safe environment for all law-abiding citizens in which to live, work, and raise their families. The program is divided into three basic phases: 1) weeding, 2) community policing, and 3) seeding.

Weeding: Removing Violent Criminals from the Community. It is well-known that after many drug dealers are arrested and arraigned, they return to the street to resume their criminal activity. This problem is addressed by the first phase of the program under the supervision of the local U.S. Attorney, whereby such individuals are subject to pretrial detention, a speedy trial, and mandatory minimum sentences. Under this program, the offender is immediately removed from the streets, and the public instantly sees the result of enforcement efforts. In addition, the offender receives swift justice and, if convicted, will serve longer prison sentences which are mandated under federal law.

Community Policing: Maintaining Law and Order. Serving as an important link between the weed and seed phase of the program, community policing focuses on increasing the public perception of police presence as well as encouraging a working relationship between the police and the citizens they serve. Community policing incorporates techniques such as foot patrol, citizen neighborhood watches, targeted mobile units, and various community relations activities which promote interaction between the police and the community. As a result of the "weed" component to the program, community policing helps to ensure the maintenance of reduced levels of drug trafficking and crime. It also reduces the general sense of fear by the community at large so that economic development projects can take root.

Seeding: *Revitalizing Neighborhoods.* When drug traffickers take hold in communities, especially urban neighborhoods, those areas begin to deteriorate. So, unless existing social and economic problems are addressed along with the removal of violent criminals, they remain prime areas for new drug traffickers. After the weeding phase is completed, new recreational, educational, and health programs will be established. Examples of seeding programs include 1) prevention, intervention, and treatment programs designed to foster individual responsibility among youth and to curb drug abuse and 2) neighborhood restoration programs which promote police and community partnerships designed to organize and train citizens to recognize and resist drug behavior in the community.

Operation Weed and Seed was originally funded by the U.S. Bureau of Justice Statistics and was first tested in cities such as Kansas City, Missouri; Trenton, New Jersey; and Omaha, Nebraska. Specifics in the administration of each program varied from one city to the next. For example, in Kansas City the program was launched in August 1991, and was administered by the U.S. Attorney and the Kansas City Police Department. The KC Police employed a data system known as the Data, Research, and Analysis for Geographic Narcotics Enforcement Targets (DRAGNET). With the aid of additional patrol resources, the following activities were employed:

- *Door-to-door Policing.* This involves brief visits to residents to encourage citizen participation in reporting suspected drug dealers in the neighborhood and to demonstrate the officer's personal involvement in the effort.

- *Gun Tips and Busts.* This component encourages citizens to use the 911 telephone system to report people who are suspected of carrying concealed weapons. It also includes the implementation of a hand-held metal detector program to search the person of alleged gun carriers as well as their handbags or other gear.

- *Hot Spot Patrols.* These include the increased use of police patrols during specific times and locations, such as street corners, businesses, drug houses, or other locations identified by the DRAGNET data system.

- *Drug House Raids and Cleanups.* This initiative includes serving search warrants on suspected drug houses, towing abandoned vehicles, boarding up burnt-out houses, and removing trash from yards of vacant houses or vacant lots.

After drug dealers have been removed from the area, abandoned houses formerly used for drug trafficking are converted into affordable housing suitable for raising families. Another important component to Kansas City's program is the "Hub House." This is a location where citizens can go for information on drug abuse treatment programs, family therapy, education, child development programs, and youth services to name a few. Jobs are made available through the Corrections Options Program, designed to place first-time drug offenders in the construction field where training and practical work skills can be developed. Participants are often used in the renovation of confiscated drug houses.

It appears that the greatest impact of community-police programs is their influence on citizen perceptions of crime, the fear of crime, and the quality of police service. But actually reducing the level of drug consumption and drug trafficking remains a constant challenge for law enforcement agencies.

Summary

When one studies the extensive history of United States federal drug control policy, many interesting occurrences can be observed in drug abuse trends and in the formation of public policy relating to drug abuse. Prohibition created the need for enforcement of the federal anti-liquor laws. From the first narcotics unit operating under the Commissioner of Internal Revenue in 1919 to the current Drug Enforcement Administration, which was formed in 1973, many policies and agencies have been implemented. Some of these were more successful than others.

To date, the primary thrust of drug enforcement is carried out by the Drug Enforcement Administration, the Federal Bureau of Investigation, and the U.S. Customs Service. Many other federal agencies also share different degrees of enforcement responsibility in drug control.

A priority of the federal drug enforcement initiative is interdiction, which is the interception of drugs coming into the country. The United States Customs Service, the Border Patrol, and the Coast Guard play major roles in this effort.

Other organizations exist that act as task forces for drug trafficking in the United States. The Office of National Drug Control Policy serves as the coordinating agency for the federal drug control effort. The ONDCP is charged with coordinating efforts with all federal agencies to reduce drug abuse and trafficking.

The federal Organized Crime Drug Enforcement Task Force (OCDETF) also plays a major role in detecting and prosecuting domestic drug traffickers. The OCDETF is made up of agents representing DEA, FBI, IRS, Customs, ATF, Marshals Service, and Coast Guard.

On the local level, many different drug enforcement/suppression organizations and strategies exist. Strategies include ways to reduce or eliminate both discreet and nondiscreet drug markets operating in communities. This is accomplished by the use of problem- and citizen-oriented policing by the patrol function of local police departments. These initiatives are designed to more closely unite the police with the general public as well as to empower police to make certain managerial enforcement decisions in their own beats.

Do you recognize these terms?

choke points	high intensity drug trafficking areas
community policing	interdiction
Customs search	nondiscreet drug markets
Customs zone	problem-oriented policing
discreet drug markets	undercover
drug czar	weed and seed

Discussion Questions

1. Explain the evolution of the Drug Enforcement Administration (DEA) and its current role in federal drug control policy.

2. What was considered the first drug enforcement agency that operated in the federal government?

3. When the investigation of drug offenses is considered, name the primary federal drug enforcement agency in the United States and discuss its emergence.

4. Under what circumstances was OCDETF developed, and what purpose does it serve in the overall federal drug suppression effort?

5. Explain why there was so much bureaucracy in the development of so many different drug enforcement agencies during and after Prohibition.

6. Why was the DEA created, and what is its goal?

7. Explain the role of the RISS project in drug enforcement.

8. Describe the concepts of problem-oriented and citizen-oriented policing and how these relate to drug control in communities.

9. List some traditional drug enforcement strategies that deal with reducing the supply of illicit drugs.

10. Discuss some new innovative strategies currently being used in drug enforcement to reduce both retail and wholesale illicit drug supplies.

11. Characterize and discuss the differences between discreet and nondiscreet illicit drug markets.

Critical Issues in Drug Control *11*

This chapter will enable you to:

- Discover contemporary policy options in drug control
- Understand how the reverse sting tactic is used by police
- Understand the utility of electronic surveillance and its legal implications
- Learn the issues surrounding drug testing policies
- See how officials attempt to control drug use in sports

Accepting responsibility is often a first step in problem solving on any scale. Just as an alcoholic must first acknowledge his or her condition to be able to overcome it, the United States must acknowledge the extent to which it provides a market for drugs in order to combat the entire drug menace. This leads to several critical issues facing actors in the war on drugs: Are U.S. strategies properly balanced? Are U.S. strategies aimed at both domestic and international criminals? Are U.S. strategies tackling both ends of the supply/demand cycle? Are U.S. strategies sufficiently flexible to protect civil liberties for the general public while giving adequate authority to drug enforcement officials? These are just a few of the issues facing drug enforcement policymakers.

In the early 1990s, drug control has expanded its scope and ingenuity to include such tactics as eviction, curfew, random searches, and forfeiture of property. Although many of these techniques have drawn political and social fire from civil libertarians, they have generally been supported by state legislatures, state and federal courts, and the United States Congress. To illustrate the trend toward harsher punitive measures for drug offenders, in October 1989, the Justice Department asked President Bush to consider expanding the application of the death penalty to leaders of drug trafficking organizations. Commenting on the demand for drugs in the United States, Colombian President Belisario Bentancur said in 1985:

> In the world war against narcotics, we need the commitment of the consumer nations to attack the demand with the same vigor we have shown. We can make all the sacrifices possible, but if there is enormous demand, production will never be completely eradicated.
>
> Source: *Los Angeles Times*, Dec. 1, 1985.

Many strategies for drug control are controversial. In many cases, conventional methods offer little hope for controlling the problem. As mentioned, unconventional methods frequently create some controversy because they usually rely on expanded police powers. Some citizens, therefore, fear an erosion of personal freedom. On the other hand, many unconventional methods of drug enforcement have proven more effective and innovative than the traditional approaches.

Drug Lord Abductions

One example of unconventional drug control tactics is the controversial police practice of kidnapping or abducting drug lords in foreign countries. Such a practice is favored by some partly due to the degree of official corruption observed in many foreign countries, which commonly protect drug lords from prosecution or extradition. As a case in point, Dr. Humberto Alvarez-Machain, a Mexican citizen, was abducted in April 1990, from his office in Guadalajara, Mexico, by a group of Mexican mercenaries working for the DEA. Alvarez was one of 19 persons wanted by the federal government in connection with the 1985 kidnapping/murder of DEA agent Enrique Camarena in that city (see Chapter 6). Although this practice usually occurs on foreign soil, many detractors claim that it is an erosion of police authority. The issue was resolved in 1992 when the U.S Supreme Court reviewed the Alvarez-Machain abduction case (*United States v. Alvarez-Machain*, 112 S. Ct. 2188, 1992). In court, Alvarez-Machain moved to dismiss the indictment against him, claiming that the federal court system had no jurisdiction to try him because he was abducted in violation of an extradition treaty between the U.S. and Mexico. After reviewing the case, the Court decided that Alvarez-Machain's abduction was not in violation of the extradition treaty; therefore, such abductions did not deprive the U.S. District Court of jurisdiction in a criminal trial.

The practice of abducting criminal suspects in foreign countries and bringing them to United States soil for trial is nothing new. In fact, it is more than a century old, and in numerous cases the United States courts have found it perfectly legal. Other official abductions include:

- The April 1988, drug kingpin Juan Ramon Matta Ballesteros was abducted from Honduras. He was ultimately found guilty of drug trafficking and sentenced to life in prison.

- Mexican trafficker Rene Verdugo-Urquidez, also accused of involvement in the Camarena murder, was shoved through a border fence by Mexican authorities in 1986. He was ultimately convicted in United States courts.
- Roberto Suarez Levy, the son of Bolivian trafficker Roberto Suarez Gomez, was arrested in Switzerland in 1980 on drug charges. After nine months of waiting, federal agents arranged with local police to have Suarez smuggled out of the country and into Miami.

The precedents addressing abductions clearly show that judges need not consider how a defendant got into their courtroom. Such morality judgments have generally been left to law enforcement agencies. In deciding the Alvarez-Machain case, the courts recognized that the practice of abducting criminals from foreign countries began over a century ago and cited the case of Frederick Ker. Ker was an embezzler who absconded to Peru (*Ker v. Illinois,* 119 S. 436, 1886) but was hunted down and brought within the court's jurisdiction by reason of a "forcible abduction." Although Ker's lawyer argued that he was kidnapped, the Supreme Court ruled in 1886 that Ker had no right to due process while abroad and that how he was brought to the courtroom in Chicago had nothing to do with the charges he was facing there.

In another abduction case, however, an exception was delineated by the courts. In 1974, Francisco Toscanino was abducted in Uruguay and transported to the United States. Toscanino's attorney claimed that he was tortured en route to the United States. In that case, the court held that it is appropriate for judges to consider the apprehension of defendants if there is a suggestion that the behavior of apprehending officers might "shock the conscience of the court." The Toscanino case also recognized that a United States judge may throw out an arrest if another country objects to the manner in which an arrest was made within its borders.

We will now examine several enforcement alternatives currently in effect or under consideration by drug enforcement authorities in the United States.

Drug Courier Profiling

The practice of profiling suspected drug couriers by law enforcement officers is yet another innovative method of apprehending drug traffickers. The technique, originally developed in the 1970s by the DEA for use in detecting drug smugglers in airports, has now been extended to the highways for identifying automobiles driven by drug couriers.

The practice involves trained officers watching vehicles on highways and looking for certain characteristics unique to drug traffickers. The practice gained national attention in 1987 after a segment on *60 Minutes*, a CBS newsmagazine television show, that featured an interview with a Florida state trooper who had achieved a certain reputation for his ability to spot or "profile" such vehicles. To make the stop, the officer must watch cars on those traveled routes that are most likely to be used by smugglers. If the officer identifies any traffic violation, such as speeding, the car can be stopped. The officer then looks for other telltale signs of a typical "drug runner." These include inappropriate dress, a large roll of cash, nervousness around police, the use of a rental car with no car rental papers available for inspection, and the lack of any travel gear such as luggage. Finally, the officer asks the driver for permission (consent) to search the vehicle.

Thinking Critically #24

Profile the "typical" drug dealer in your community; that is, how would you recognize this individual?

Although **drug courier profiling** has resulted in numerous drug seizures and arrests, it has been criticized by the American Civil Liberties Union (ACLU), which views it as a violation of one's personal freedoms and an unfair infringement of one's Fourth Amendment search-and-seizure rights. The critical issue in drug courier profiling is the constitutionality of the technique and whether it violates one's Fourth Amendment freedom from unreasonable searches and seizures. Critics of the technique argue that a vague profile is not enough to create "reasonable suspicion" in the officers' minds.

The significance of the *Sokolow* decision, discussed later in the chapter, addresses the issue of whether or not the use of drug courier profiles is valid under the Fourth Amendment. The Supreme Court said that there is nothing wrong with such use in this case because the facts, taken in totality, amounted to a reasonable suspicion that criminal conduct was taking place. The court suggested that whether or not the facts in the case fit a "profile" was less significant than the fact that, taken together, they establish a reasonable suspicion. So, in essence, the court was saying that while a drug courier profile might be helpful, the totality of the circumstances is more important in establishing the legality of the stop and the subsequent search (del Carmen and Walker, 1995).

Lawyers for the DEA's criminal law division claimed in 1989 that agents do not make stops on the basis of profiles. Defense attorneys, on the other hand, maintain that suspicion triggered by a profile will often lead to an arrest on the pretext of a traffic violation. They also assert "voluntary" questioning and searches by police can, in fact, be highly coercive. Yet another unanswered question is by what standard should one's behavior be analyzed to determine whether it is suspicious? To some officers, the first person getting off a plane may be suspicious, while to other officers, the last person getting off a plane may seem suspicious.

Drug "Profile" Tactic Upheld

The Supreme Court ruled on April 3, 1989, that the Constitution permits the police to stop and question airline passengers that display behavior patterns that may have an innocent explanation but that parallel the actions of drug couriers. While the 7 to 2 decision made little new law, it marked the Court's clearest validation to date of the techniques that the federal Drug Enforcement Administration (DEA) has developed for surveillance and detection of drug traffic through airports and railroad depots.

Over the last 15 years, the agency has what it calls a "drug courier profile," based on patterns of behavior that agents' observations have shown are typical of those individuals that use commercial airline flights to transport drugs. The profile includes paying for tickets with cash, using an alias, boarding a long flight without checking luggage, and staying briefly in distant cities known to be sources of drugs.

Because these actions can be entirely innocent, the profile has long been under attack as an unconstitutional shortcut to establishing the level of suspicion that the Constitution requires before the police can interfere with a person's liberty. Most lower courts have rejected these challenges on the basis of earlier Supreme Court decisions permitting the use of a "totality of the circumstances" approach to brief detentions by the police.

Source: Greenhouse, L. (1989). "High Court Backs Airport Detention Based on 'Profile'." *The New York Times* (April 4):A1. Copyright © 1989 by the New York Times Company. Reprinted by permission.

Some previous high court decisions have upheld informal questioning of suspects fitting a suspect profile but have prohibited coercive searches and formal arrests unless the police have additional evidence upon which to base a decision. Until terms such as "coercive," "profile," and "voluntary" have been further defined, the United States Supreme Court may have to continually fine-tune its conclusion as to the constitutionality of this drug enforcement technique.

The Reverse Drug Sting

The reverse undercover operation is one in which the officer poses as a drug dealer and places buyers under arrest after certain necessary conversations and actions have been documented. Controversy about the appropriateness of the **reverse sting** as a police tactic centers around the legal question of **entrapment**. Since the initiation of this covert police tactic, some courts have excluded all but the most compelling evidence obtained in the operation. Other courts, however, have accepted this practice as lawful and appropriate.

Other dangers are also inherent in this type of operation. For example, an undercover officer working in this capacity must maintain constant contact

Case Study: *U.S. v. Sokolow*

On April 3, 1989, a decision (*United States v. Sokolow* 109 S. Ct. 1581, 1989) written by Chief Justice William H. Rehnquist summarized the overturning of a previous ruling by the United States Court of Appeals for the Ninth Circuit in California. That court had ruled that the brief detention by federal drug agents of a passenger at the Honolulu International Airport was unconstitutional.

The agents detained the man long enough to get a trained dog to sniff his luggage, and then they found several pounds of cocaine in his shoulder bag. When agents stopped the man, they knew little about him except that he had paid $2,100 for tickets from a role of $20 bills, he had just made a round-trip flight from Honolulu to Miami, he stayed in Miami less than 48 hours with no checked luggage, he looked nervous, and he used a name that did not match the name under which his telephone number was listed.

The man, Andrew Sokolow, was eventually convicted on federal drug charges. The appeals court overturned the conviction on the ground that the agents lacked the "reasonable suspicion" required by the Fourth Amendment for brief detentions.

While the Fourth Amendment requires the police to have "probable cause" for a formal arrest, the Supreme Court for the last 20 years has applied a lower standard, "reasonable suspicion," for brief "investigatory stops" that can turn up additional evidence needed for probable cause. The question whenever such a detention is challenged is whether the police had enough evidence for the threshold determination of reasonable suspicion.

In the opinion for the Court, Chief Justice Rehnquist described in some detail the evidence available to the agents in what he described as "a typical attempt to smuggle drugs through one of the nation's airports." He noted Sokolow's attire: a black jumpsuit with gold jewelry. The role of $20 bills "appeared to contain a total of $4,000." The Chief Justice said: "While a trip from Honolulu to Miami standing alone is not a cause for any sort of suspicion, here there was more: Surely few residents of Honolulu travel from that city for 20 hours to spend 48 hours in Miami during the month of July."

He added: "Any one of these factors is not by itself proof of any illegal conduct and is quite consistent with innocent travel. But we think taken together they amount to reasonable suspicion."

with street dealers that will soon become familiar with the physical description of the officer and spread the description to other drug dealers. On the other hand, an advantage of the reverse sting operation is that it requires little funding for "buy money," which is often needed in greater amounts in long-term drug investigations. In many instances, law enforcement agencies may actually generate revenue to help compensate for future drug investigations. In Washington, D.C., for example, undercover officers sold inert substances to would-be drug buyers, who were penalized by the loss of their cash (through forfeiture) rather than by arrest.

Entrapment and Reverse Stings

In a related case, *Jacobson v. United States* (1992), the U.S. Supreme Court limited the authority of police in reverse sting-type operations. The Jacobson case involved a 1984 reverse sting operation conducted by the United States Postal Service. In February of that year, Jacobson ordered two magazines from an adult book store, *Bare Boys I* and *Bare Boys II,* each containing photographs of nude preteen and teenage boys. Although Jacobson's purchase was not illegal at that time, the Child Protection Act of 1984 was passed which criminalized the receipt through the mail of a "visual depiction that involves the use of a minor engaging in sexually explicit conduct . . ." After finding Jacobson's name on a mailing list, Postal Inspectors sent him a letter and application for membership from a fictitious organization associated with pornographic material. Over the following 26 months, Jacobson was contacted by five different organizations. In one contact, Jacobson was sent a brochure advertising photographs of young boys engaging in sex. Finally, from a brochure Jacobson ordered the magazine *Boys who Love Boys*. The magazine was delivered, and Jacobson was arrested.

The question in the *Jacobson* case was did the government's operation, which lasted over two years, offer enough inducement to cause the "unwary innocent" to commit a crime, constituting entrapment? The U.S. Supreme Court said yes. The court stated that "in their zeal to enforce the law . . . government agents may not originate a criminal design, implant in an innocent person's mind the disposition to commit a criminal act, and then induce commission of the crime so that the government may prosecute." This case is important because the court reversed Jacobson's conviction on the basis that the government agents used entrapment to make their case by implanting in the defendant's mind the desire to commit a criminal act.

In drug cases where reverse stings are used, similar principles apply. As a rule, these operations will target the novice drug user rather than one that has spent more time on the street. Experienced users usually patronize a specific dealer, thereby reducing their need to purchase drugs from a stranger on the street corner who might be a police officer or informant.

Zero Tolerance

Under the Reagan administration, the **zero tolerance** enforcement initiative was implemented in March 1988, with the support of Customs Commissioner William von Raab. Essentially, the policy directs the Coast Guard, Customs Service, and other arms of the federal government to enforce existing law to the utmost degree, thereby addressing the demand side of the drug abuse problem. The plan focuses on the seizing of vehicles, boats, and planes if even a tiny amount of any controlled substance is found on board.

Zero tolerance has its roots in the seizure sanctions of federal law where "administrative seizures" are possible without the owner necessarily being convicted of any crime. Police in cities such as New York and Miami have used this method to impound automobiles of drug buyers whose drug purchases themselves would only result in a misdemeanor charge. Customs Commissioner von Raab said in 1988 that the purpose of the zero tolerance program is to "put pressure on drug users who ordinarily are not reached by criminal penalties."

In May 1988, Customs seized the Atlantis II, an $80 million research vessel once used to explore the wreck of the Titanic, after a routine search netted traces of marijuana and two marijuana pipes in a crew member's shaving kit. The ship was returned but only after its owner, the Woods Hole Oceanographic Institution, agreed to send Customs a letter supporting the anti-drug campaign and promising to tighten security.

Controversy about this policy has arisen over the argument that many owners of such vessels and vehicles may risk the loss of their property without personal knowledge of any controlled substance being aboard. Members of the American Civil Liberties Union (ACLU) have stated that this is an unconstitutional practice because of the traditional premise in American jurisprudence that the punishment fit the crime.

Mandatory Minimum Sentencing

One of the more controversial issues in drug control of the 1990s is the mandatory minimum sentencing policy of the federal court system. At the core of the issue is the realization by police and prosecutors that drug dealers are innovative and cunning and will employ many measures to avoid detection. Because one of the drug dealer's greatest fears is a prison sentence, experts have suggested that the best deterrent to drug crime is the threat of mandatory incarceration. So under mandatory minimum sentencing laws, an arrested offender has but two choices: to go to prison if convicted or to become a government witness against his or her supplier. This is the basis and hallmark of mandatory minimum sentencing. This gives prosecutors the option to not file a drug charge provided the offender agrees to work with police in collecting evidence on others in the drug trafficking operation. As experience has shown, the informant "working a beef" has proved to be one of the most powerfully motivated players in the criminal investigation process.

How They Work

Under federal law, sentences take into consideration the type and amount of drugs involved. In addition, aggravating and mitigating circumstances are considered as well as the criminal history of the offender. Judges are also permitted to impose longer sentences than the mandatory minimums. For example, a first-time offender facing a 10-year minimum sentence could receive anything including and up to life imprisonment; or a person facing a five-year sentence could be sentenced up to 40 years.

In addition to other drugs, federal law also specifies mandatory minimum sentences for possession of crack cocaine. Those convicted will be sentenced to a minimum of five years and a maximum of 20 years for possession of:

- 5 grams of crack for a first conviction
- 3 grams for a second conviction
- 1 gram for a third conviction

In some circumstances, harsher penalties can be assessed. For example, for first-time offenders in which death or bodily injury results from using the drug, the mandatory minimum sentence is 20 years, regardless of the amount of drug involved. A second conviction where death or bodily injury results carries a sentence of life imprisonment.

Thinking Critically #25

Support or refute the federal court system's policy of mandatory minimum sentencing for the possession of crack cocaine.

Another interesting feature of mandatory minimum sentencing is the establishment of minimum periods of supervised release after the "full" prison sentence has been served. These periods range from one to 10 years and depend on the drug involved and the criminal history of the offender. The reason for supervised release is surveillance of the offender to ensure they are abiding by the conditions of the court, rather than an effort to reintegrate him or her back into the community.

Electronic Surveillance

The past 25 years have seen a virtual revolution in technology relevant to electronic surveillance. Advances in electronics, semiconductors, computers, imaging, data bases, and related technologies have greatly increased technological options for police surveillance activities. Although the use of electronic surveillance in drug control is nothing new, techniques such as the wiretap have raised renewed concerns over the protection of one's right to privacy.

The major law addressing electronic surveillance, Title III of the Omnibus Crime Control and Safe Streets Act of 1968, was designed to protect the privacy of wire and oral communications. At the time this act was passed, electronic surveillance was primarily limited to telephone taps and hidden microphones (bugs). Since then, however, basic communications have undergone rapid technological changes with the advent of such technologies as cellular telephones, personal pagers, personal computers, cordless telephones, electronic mail, and electronic bulletin boards. Many of these devices are now commonly used by drug traffickers to assist them in communicating with drug suppliers and customers.

As there are new and increasingly mobile drug gangs evident throughout the country, law enforcement agencies at both the state and federal level are making more frequent use of electronic surveillance technology to combat drug trafficking. Public concerns arise with regard to the circumstances under which these technologies are applied and how they might infringe on First, Fourth, and Fifth Amendment rights. But at the same time, the public is also concerned about crime (especially violent crime) and generally supports the use of electronic technology in criminal investigations. So, the balancing of these concerns remains a critical issue in drug control.

Categories of Behavior Subject to Electronic Surveillance

1. *Movements.* Where someone is. Individuals can be tracked electronically via beepers as well as by monitoring computerized transactional accounts.

2. *Actions.* What someone is doing or has done. Electronic devices to monitor action include keystrokes on computer terminals, telephone numbers called with pen registers, cable TV monitoring, financial and computerized accounts, and computerized law enforcement or investigatory systems.

3. *Communications.* What someone is saying, writing, hearing or receiving. Two-way electronic communications can be intercepted (whether the means be analog or digital communication) via wired telephones, cordless or cellular telephones, or digital electronic mail. Two-way non-electronic communication can be intercepted via a variety of microphone devices and other transmitters.

4. *Actions and communications.* The details of what someone is doing or saying. Electronic visual surveillance, generally accompanied by audio surveillance, can monitor the actions and communications of individuals in both public and private places and in daylight or darkness.

5. *Emotions.* The psychological and physiological reactions to circumstances. Polygraph testing, voice stress analyzers, and brain wave analyzers attempt to determine an individual's reactions.

Source: U.S. Congress (1985). *Electronic Surveillance.* Office of Technology Assessment.

The primary purpose of electronic surveillance is to monitor the behavior of individuals, including individual movements, actions, communications, emotions, and/or various combinations of these. From a law enforcement and investigative standpoint, the potential benefits offered through new technologies may be substantial: for example, the development of more accurate and complete information on suspects, the possible reduction in time and manpower required for case investigation, and the expansion of the options for preventing and deterring crimes. From a societal perspective, the possible benefits are also important—including the potential for increasing one's physical security in the home and on the streets, strengthening efforts to prevent drug trafficking, and enhancing the protection of citizens and government officials from terrorist actions.

In general, electronic surveillance is used primarily in gambling and narcotics cases. In 1974 gambling was the most common object of electronic surveillance, and narcotics was second most common; in 1984 the order was reversed. According to the U.S. Office of Technology Assessment, an average of about 25 percent of intercepted communications in 1984 were incriminating in nature, 2,393 persons were arrested as a result of electronic surveillance, and about 27 percent of those arrested were convicted.

The difficulty in using intrusion as a principle by which to evaluate a "reasonable expectation of privacy" and the appropriateness of using a particular surveillance device is that no criteria have yet been explicitly formulated to determine intrusiveness. Instead, the facts of individual cases seem to determine individual courses of action.

Still, based on court rulings, congressional statutes, and executive orders, it is possible to isolate five dimensions that are important in determining whether the situation warrants violation or protection of ordinary civil liberties. The five dimensions are the nature of the information, the nature of the area or communication to be placed under surveillance, the scope of the surveillance, the surreptitiousness of the surveillance, and pre-electronic analysis. In evaluating the legitimacy of the government's use of surveillance devices, three dimensions are considered: the purpose of the investigation, the degree of individualized suspicion, and the relative effectiveness of the surveillance.

It is clear that the use of higher technology in surveillance activities by law enforcement agencies will prevail. In particular, with the more frequent use of detection devices and readily available electronic equipment by drug traffickers, the more sophisticated surveillance equipment will become. Implementing such technology will no doubt continue to fall under close scrutiny by courts and public groups in the coming years. Its use, however, is clearly an important factor in the detection and documentation of covert criminal activity in the drug trade.

Drug Testing

Hardly a day goes by without more news detailing the extent of drug abuse in our society. The staggering statistics are clear evidence that something must

Dimensions for Balancing Civil Liberty Interest Against Government Investigative Interest

Civil liberty interest:

1. Nature of information: The more personal or intimate the information that is to be gathered about a target, the more intrusive is the surveillance technique and the greater the intrusion to civil liberties.

2. Nature of the place or communication: The more "private" the area or type of communication to be placed under surveillance, the more intrusive is the surveillance and the greater the threat to civil liberties.

3. Scope of the surveillance: The more people and activities that are subject to surveillance, the more intrusive is the surveillance and the greater the threat to civil liberties.

4. Surreptitiousness of surveillance: The less likely it is for the individual to be aware of the surveillance and the harder it is for the individual to detect it, the greater the threat to civil liberties.

Government's investigative interest:

1. Purpose of investigation: Importance is ranked as follows: national security, domestic security, law enforcement, and the proper administration of government programs.

2. Degree of individualized suspicion: The lower the level of suspicion is, the harder it is to justify the use of surveillance devices.

3. Relative effectiveness: More traditional investigative techniques should be used and proven ineffective before using technologically sophisticated techniques.

Source: U.S. Congress (1985). *Electronic Surveillance.* Office of Technology Assessment.

be done to curtail the problem. For example, in 1988 the National Institute of Justice (NIJ) reported that 25 percent of all hospital admissions stemmed from drug abuse. In addition, 40 percent of admissions from accidents are drug-related while cocaine overdose deaths are running at a rate of 25 per week (which is up 25 percent from 1986). Drug addiction of newborn babies is also a growing health concern for the 1990s. The dollar figure of drug-related accidents is staggering: the national figure has been calculated at $81 billion per year, half of which is attributed to drug abuse. Naturally, since most drug abuse is done in private, it is difficult to detect.

Studies in recent years have shown that drug testing may play an important part in deterring drug usage. For example, experts have discovered that drug testing by the government during the Vietnam War played a significant role in deterring soldiers from using drugs, especially when testing was linked to punishment. In the early 1970s, when the Department of Defense began testing troops returning from Vietnam, about 5 percent tested positive for drugs even though the troops were aware that they would be tested and that their departure for home would be delayed. After the first six months of testing, the number dropped to 2 percent. Today, the criminal justice system regularly tests criminal defendants during different stages of the criminal process: arrest, incarceration, and supervised release. The idea is to deter continued drug use by defendants by detecting it through drug tests.

Testing employees in the workplace has also been suggested by some as an effective way to identify, treat, and control drug abuse. The goal of workplace testing is to enhance on-the-job performance and safety by identifying people who are impaired on the job. Armed security guards and transportation workers, for example, may pose a public threat if impaired while on the job. Testing also helps employers identify drug users so they can be referred to treatment as well as promotes public trust in companies who have established drug testing policies.

Despite cries by critics of invasion of privacy and unreasonable search in violation of federal and state constitutions, drug testing in various forms is either legal or in the process of becoming legal. For example, in 1988 the Congress passed the Drug-free Workplace Act. A Gallup Poll taken that year found that 11 states had passed laws regulating the confidentiality and accuracy of drug testing programs, 7 states regulate who can be tested and under what circumstances, and 14 more states have introduced legislation for drug testing, most of it regulating testing procedures but not the circumstances under which testing can be performed. Additionally, federal and state executive departments and agencies have promulgated drug testing rules. For example, a 1990 survey of state and local police agencies found that 23 percent of local police agencies had adopted policies authorizing testing of applicants, and 14 percent of those authorized drug testing of officers working in drug-related positions.

Because the workplace offers of a captive pool of subjects, proponents of the drug testing control strategy have advocated that drug testing be accomplished in that forum. The Supreme Court has legitimized some kinds of drug testing. Accordingly, testing in the workplace is generally concerned with the following five areas:

- who to test,
- when to test,
- what procedure to follow,
- what to test for, and
- what sanctions to impose on employees with positive test results.

Federal and state courts have generally held that an employer may test an applicant for drugs if the applicant is told of the testing beforehand. An employer may, therefore, withhold an employment offer based on a confirmed test result. The issue of testing employees raises other concerns. Arguments in favor of drug testing for employees generally focus on concerns for employee safety and employer liability. Other pro-testing arguments address issues such as decreased job performance and productivity, rising absenteeism, and rising health care costs.

Most of the controversy over drug testing stems from the arbitrary, random, or unannounced testing of the worker on the job, as mentioned above. Civil libertarians argue that this is a classic invasion of one's privacy and drug testing in the workplace is a violation of one's Fourth and Fifth Amendment rights.

Despite the above assertions, most courts have held that employees may indeed be tested under certain circumstances. Specifically, if the employee is on notice of being tested for drugs, an employer may test upon reasonable suspicion of drug use after a reportable injury or after a chargeable accident. In addition, legal trends indicate that employee testing as part of a physical examination or random testing if the employee is in a safety-sensitive position will become more customary.

The Department of Transportation's extensive drug testing program delineates many specific procedures for administrators to follow. In particular, the program addresses the confidentiality of records and employee identity, specimen tampering, control over the transfer of collected specimens (the chain of custody), certification of laboratories, testing methods (including confirmation of an initial positive test result by MS and GC technology [discussed below]), medical evaluation of test results, and sanctions for confirmed test results of employees. At the time of this writing, current law does not uniformly identify the drugs for which an employee may be tested. Many companies and agencies have chosen to follow the lead of the Department of Transportation and test only for the NIDA-5 (National Institute on Drug Abuse): marijuana, cocaine, opiates, phencyclidine, and amphetamines. Most drug testing programs have adopted one of three ways of screening for drugs. These are as follows:

1. *Pre-employment Screening.* This method tests all or selected applicants for employment, usually in conjunction with a pre-employment physical. A positive result will usually be followed up by a second or confirmatory test. In some cases, the applicants are informed ahead of time of the drug test and are questioned about any medication they are on, including reasons for the medication. This is because both prescription and non-prescription drugs can be abused as readily as illicit drugs and presence of these drugs should be investigated.

2. *For Cause.* Supervisors or employers can request this test if they suspect that an employee is unfit for work or is impaired by drugs or alcohol. A specimen may be requested to determine if the employee has indeed been under the influence of drugs or alcohol. Typically, this method occurs after an accident or an observable change in behavior of the employee.

3. *Random Urinalysis.* This method involves the selection of an appropriately significant number as well as a scientifically drawn, random sample of employees for screening. Screening is usually performed several times a year, each time on a different random sample. Basically, this means that all employees in a particular job category are eligible at any time for screening.

The testing cycle usually involves the initial screening of a urine sample, followed by a confirmatory test for samples suspected of containing drugs. These procedures are discussed in greater detail below:

Drug Screening. The methods used to screen urine samples are designed to be an accurate and reliable means to distinguish negative specimens from those that may contain drugs or drug metabolites. Drug screening techniques should be precise so that operator technique cannot adversely affect performance. Examples of the major immunoassay technologies are given below.

Abbott-Fluorescence Polarization Immunoassay (AFPI). This system is an extremely sensitive, rapid, precise, and reliable screening technique that is also fully automated. The system functions on an inverse relationship between signal to drug concentration, which provides excellent sensitivity at low drug concentrations. The system also uses a reagent (chemical) bar-coding technology that virtually eliminates the possibility of operator error.

Roche-Radioimmunoassay (RIA). RIA technology is also an extremely sensitive and reliable screening system. It has even been chosen by the United States Armed Forces as the screening method of choice. Drawbacks to the system are that it requires expensive ancillary equipment for operation and that it uses radioactive reagents to detect the presence of drugs. This requires operators to wear special protective clothing and to be specially trained in handling discarded materials, all of which add to the cost of the testing procedure.

Syva-Enzyme Multiplied Immunoassay Technique (EMIT). The EMIT system functions on a direct relationship between signal to drug concentration; it is less sensitive than FPIA and RIA and less precise at low drug concentrations. The disadvantage of the EMIT system is that there are significant variations in test results between technologies and a high rate of poor performance when challenged by blind testing (EMIT has a 40 percent false negative rate in that it will miss 40 percent of individuals that have smoked marijuana in the previous 48 hours).

Confirmation Tests. As mentioned, when drug tests may affect an individual's personal rights, a positive drug screening must be followed by a secondary or confirmatory test. The second test must be based on different chemical principles with an equal or lower threshold value than the screening test and must specifically identify the drug present in the sample using a different portion of the original sample.

The technology most commonly used for the confirmatory test is **Gas-Liquid Chromatography** (GC) or **Mass Spectrometry** (MS). Of these two technologies, the MS is considered the more reliable, but it is also more expensive to purchase and operate. Recently,

Hewlett-Packard Corporation developed a detector, called a mass selective detector (MSD), that is less expensive than a full mass spectrometer and provides the same high quality data.

Chain of Custody. This is the method of documenting which urine sample belongs to which testee, and who handled the sample from the time that it was originally collected. Without strict procedures for establishing the chain of custody of the urine sample, even the most technologically advanced drug testing method will be of no value. The issue of chain of custody involves several critical phases of the testing procedure. These are as follows:

- Collecting the sample
- Labeling the sample
- Limiting the number of individuals that handle the sample
- Ensuring that samples are stored properly
- Limiting access to information about test results to individuals with a legitimate need to know

Other important issues that should be considered in drug testing are:

(1) the passive inhalation of marijuana when an individual is present in a room where it is being smoked;

(2) the ingestion of certain foods that may result in false positive drug readings (poppy seed bagels may test positive for opiates, for instance);

(3) the lack of standards directing drug testing laboratories to operate under the same set of criteria;

(4) the cause-and-effect relationship between the presence of drugs and one's behavior, which is usually an issue in "probable cause" testing;

(5) the distinction between the different drug testing arenas, such as hospitals, treatment centers, sports testing (discussed later in this chapter), the military, schools, probation and parole programs, and so on; and

(6) the adulterations of specimens, such as when urine substitution or dilution takes place.

If it is true that a substantial group of drug abusers utilize them only on weekends, at parties, and for purposes of relaxation and diversion, drug testing may alter drug use patterns. For example, marijuana users will test positive for drug use for a far longer period of time than cocaine users will. A user that wants to get high on a Friday night is relatively safe from a positive drug test on Monday morning if he or she uses cocaine, but the same person can be almost certain of a positive test if he or she uses marijuana. The same relationship occurs with regard to amphetamines. As a result, some theorize that for those drug users that are hell-bent on getting high, drug testing may cause many of them to switch to harder drugs, which last a shorter period of time in their systems.

As technology progresses, drug testing may someday be done by the analysis of human hair follicles. A 1987 study by Dr. Gideon Koren of the Hospital for Sick Children in Toronto compared urine and hair samples for evidence of drug abuse. Dr. Koren contended that once traces of drugs enter the hair, they are permanently registered there. Testing hair follicles, he asserted, would eliminate the problem of employees avoiding detection of drug use by abstaining from drug use just before being tested by employers.

In 1990, however, the American Medical Association reported on Koren's findings and argued that although there is some credence to the testing of hair follicles for drugs, urine provides the most reliable data to date. According to the AMA, dyeing or bleaching hair, in addition to exposure to other substances such as automobile exhaust fumes, can contaminate test results.

These issues and others pose important questions and considerations that must be addressed in this critical area of drug control. Because existing technology is generally considered reliable by professionals in the area, the "ironing-out" of other ancillary issues may result in effective alternatives to traditional drug control methods.

Needle Exchange Programs

To date, the problem of AIDS (Acquired Immune Deficiency Syndrome) dominates much of the medical profession's public health and policy concerns. Although the transmission of the disease is often accomplished through sexual activity, an estimated 20 percent of AIDS cases were reported to have been transmitted through the sharing of needles by intravenous drug users.

Needle-sharing has become a major problem in inner cities, where heroin addiction prevails. The heroin addict, for example, typically injects himself with the drug several times a day. Because sterile needles are not always available, the sharing of needles between one person and another sometimes occurs. According to testimony before the U.S. House of Representatives in April 1989, one HIV-infected drug user can conceivably expose up to 100 other users over the course of a few months. (Other communicable diseases such as hepatitis are also transmitted in this fashion.)

In an effort to curb the spread of the disease, both researchers and medical professionals have considered the controversial idea of exchanging dirty needles belonging to drug addicts for clean needles. Most needle exchange programs consist of three basic functions:

1.   To dispense sterile needles to current IV (intravenous) users.

2.   To promote and accept returns of used needles to control how needles are discarded.

3.   To change the behavior of IV drug users through health education and counseling.

Controversy exists with this program because many feel that such a program encourages drug use, that needles will not be used, and that the program will only create more drug addicts and, accordingly, more AIDS carriers. The assertion that the needles will not be used is based on the view that needle sharing is a ritualistic practice, deeply embedded into the subculture of IV drug users. Another argument against the exchange programs is that giving away needles is illegal. The question of legality may be a valid one, at least in certain jurisdictions, and is constantly being addressed at the state and local government levels.

Exchanging Needles in New York City

After operating seven months, New York City's program to give intravenous drug addicts new hypodermic needles to help the city stem the spread of AIDS has finally begun to attract more participants but remains under attack.

On one hand, city health officials running the program say drug addicts are learning to clean needles after using them, but on the other hand, it is difficult to determine whether addicts have actually stopped sharing needles. Health officials are having trouble attracting participants for the year-long experiment—160 have enrolled in a program intended for 400. And detractors, calling it a failure, are demanding that it be ended soon.

Reynaldo H., with a small Bible and a pack of Kool cigarettes stuffed in the breast pocket of his Hawaiian-style shirt, said he never imagined being part of the experiment, in which intravenous drug users are given clean needles in exchange for their used ones. But a year ago, the 32-year-old heroin addict and dealer was stricken with AIDS-related infections. "I was sick," he said, describing the open lesions in his scalp and mouth that kept him from eating for days. "The program took me in, got me in a clinic, got my health back, and put me in drug treatment."

More than half of the city's estimated 200,000 intravenous drug users are believed to be infected with the deadly virus that causes Acquired Immune Deficiency Syndrome, according to the City Health Department, which operates the program. The purpose of the program is to learn whether intravenous drug users can change their behavior and not share hypodermic syringes when injecting illegal drugs. The program, which is to cost $230,000 for a year, also counsels addicts and tests them for AIDS and other diseases.

Source: Marriott, M. (1989). "Drug Needle Exchange is Gaining but Still Under Fire." *The New York Times* (June 7):B1. Copyright © 1989 by The New York Times Company. Reprinted by permission.

When considering the appropriateness of such a program, perhaps we should consider the success or failure of similar programs in England, the Netherlands, Sweden, and Australia, where needle sharing programs have been operational since 1984. The results are extremely consistent. In Amsterdam, for example, researchers noted that 80 percent of needle-exchange users in the program stopped sharing equipment since the program began, as compared to 50 percent of nonexchangers. When considering the question of rising addiction among IV drug users, 71 percent of Amsterdam's exchangers reported a decrease or no change in the rate of IV drug users.

In addition to the previously listed countries, Switzerland has also attempted to deal with its addiction problem through the use of a needle exchange program. In Zurich, community leaders created a ghetto of sorts known as "needle park," where addicts can use heroin or cocaine without fear of arrest from police. Addicts in the needle park are estimated to require an average of $400 to $500 daily to support their habits. Many of these addicts consequently turn to stealing, drug dealing, or prostitution as a means of income. The government in Zurich exchanges an estimated 7,000 clean needles daily for used ones in the needle park.

Forfeiture of Attorney's Fees

It is logical to assume that, considering the enormous cash flow of many drug traffickers, much of the money earned through illicit drug transactions ends up in the bank accounts of lawyers that represent drug traffickers. Through the use of carefully sculpted laws such as the 1984 Federal Comprehensive Forfeiture Act (CFA), the instances of lawyers knowingly accepting "dirty" money or assets for legal fees have greatly decreased. The most conspicuous legal precedents addressing the issue were handed down by the Supreme Court in 1989 in *United States v. Monsanto, United States v. Caplin and Drysdale*, and *Chartered v. United States*. These decisions basically held that the government's ability to enforce forfeiture extends to drug assets needed to pay attorney's fees.

In reviewing these cases, the Monsanto decision involved a defendant that was facing charges under the federal CCE statute of creating a continuing criminal enterprise. The indictment asserted that the defendant had acquired an apartment, a home, and a sum of $35,000 in cash as a result of drug trafficking activities. The government subsequently sought to freeze all assets of the defendant until the trial was over. In response to this, the defendant claimed that those assets were necessary to retain a competent lawyer for his defense. His claim was rejected by the district court.

As the trial progressed, an appellate court reviewed the district court's ruling and found that the frozen assets should, indeed, be used to pay attorney's fees. The defendant, however, declined because of the advanced stage of the trial. He was ultimately convicted of the trafficking charges and was required to forfeit his assets. At a later stage in the appeals process, the Supreme Court agreed to hear the case involving forfeiture of attorney's fees. The Supreme Court ruled that the sale or transfer of potentially forfeitable assets is forbidden.

The issue of lawyers accepting drug assets in lieu of payment for services rendered raises several legal and ethical questions. Such legal questions include whether defendant's Fifth or Sixth Amendment rights are violated through the use of such a tactic. Those opposed to the forfeiture practice point out that the Sixth Amendment provides the accused the right to counsel and the Fifth Amendment protects the right to due process under law. On both issues, however, the Supreme Court has upheld forfeiture sanctions against attorney's fees.

The ethical concerns of forfeiture have centered around three issues. First, in the two cases above, opponents to forfeiture argued that the CFA actually encouraged attorneys to be less than thorough in investigating a client's case so that any fees they might have received would be protected from forfeiture. Additionally, some argue that when faced with losing legal fees under the CFA, an attorney may compromise his client's position during plea bargaining if a longer prison sentence were suggested in lieu of forfeiture of legal fees. In a third scenario, an attorney may be tempted to manipulate the justice system by representing a client on a contingency basis. Although the practice is considered unethical by the American Bar Association, the attorney could conceivably make an agreement with his client that only after *acquittal* of the client would the attorney be paid his designated fee. Thus, the unscrupulous attorney could avoid losing his fee under the CFA.

On the same day that the government argued its case in *Monsanto*, the Supreme Court heard oral arguments in the *Caplin* case. In this case, illicit-drug importer Christopher Reckmeyer paid the law firm of Caplin and Drysdale $25,000 for preindictment legal services. Before the case could go to trial, Reckmeyer pled guilty to the charges, and virtually all of his assets were declared forfeitable by the court—including fees paid to the law firm. After an extended legal process whereby the firm's lawyers attempted to secure a release of the fees already paid to them, the Supreme Court ultimately ruled that the forfeiture was lawful, and that there are no statutory, ethical, or constitutional impediments to the forfeiture of attorney's fees under the Federal Comprehensive Forfeiture Act.

Drug Control and Sports

Perhaps no segment of society has received more glaring publicity for its use of illicit drugs than America's athletes. The use of drugs by competing athletes dates back more than 100 years. During that time, caffeine and alcohol were the drugs predominantly abused. Drug abuse by athletes today has developed to the point where an array of dangerous drugs are commonly used, including amphetamines, steroids, and cocaine. The drug abuse problem among athletes is not limited to professional athletes, but extends to amateur sports at both the college and high school levels.

Drug abuse awareness in sports was heightened in 1985 with the untimely deaths of athletes Len Bias and Don Rogers, both of whom died from cocaine overdoses. With regard to drug use in the NFL, former St. Louis Cardinal Carl Birdsong (1986) states, "I don't think drug abuse in the NFL is any greater than in any other segment of society. I think the media has sensationalized drug abuse in the NFL. . . . I'd say 90 percent to 95 percent of them [the players] don't use drugs; they're productive and hard working, devoting a good deal of their time to charities" (p. 43).

Reports, however, of athletes possessing, using, and distributing illicit drugs have now become commonplace in newspapers, magazines, and on television. One popular illicit drug, cocaine, is used by many athletes both for recreation and enhancement of performance. In addition, the non-medical use of steroids is becoming more commonplace among athletes and non-athletes as well.

The high visibility of athletes, especially the successful ones, seems to make their drug problems more newsworthy than those of the average citizen. Most of the media accounts of drug abuse involving athletes report the use of illicit recreational drugs. Such activities have created a public outcry for control and have prompted athletic organizations to initiate anti-drug programs. What is it that attracts athletes to drug abuse? Three different reasons can be identified to help explain their involvement with illicit drugs:

1. Drugs taken at the time of competition immediately enhance performance.
2. Drugs taken during training or well before competition enhance performance.
3. Athletes use recreational drugs for the same reasons that nonathletes do.

Steroids and Athletes

Athletes around the world began using steroids more than 30 years ago, after East European and Soviet athletes dominated an international sporting event. It was later discovered that these athletes had used testosterone to strengthen themselves. Despite the dangers steroids present to users, athletes are often attracted to them because of their ability to build strength. In the mid-1980s the *American Pharmacy Journal* reported: "[H]ad the medical profession been honest with athletes 20 years ago in answering their question, 'what do these drugs do?', and said 'we don't know what they do but they probably work,' we would not have lost face with the athletes" (1986, p. 41).

The allure of steroids to the athlete is one of promise for a stronger body in a shorter period of time. Mirkin and Hoffman state, "Since the stress of prolonged exercise results in tissue damage, quicker healing means quicker recovery time and ultimately more time for training and muscle building, anabolic steroids have a reputation for this" (1978, p. 89).

Defining Steroids

Anabolic steroids, originally developed in the 1930s to help maintain strength in aging males, are synthetic forms of the male sex hormone testosterone. The many functions of testosterone include stimulating the development of bone, muscle, skin, and hair growth as well as lowering the voice and emotional responses. Because women produce so little testosterone, they develop masculine characteristics when they take anabolic steroids.

Because steroids are a controlled substance in the United States, a prescription is necessary to acquire them. Consequently, physicians have been inundated over the years with requests for prescriptions from athletes in all disciplines; these athletes all hope to improve their performance. A 1986 study of steroid use conducted by Dr. Robert Voy, Chief Medical Officer for the U.S. Olympic team, found that up to 40 percent of the steroids used by athletes were obtained by prescriptions from physicians. The rest were thought to be diverted from legal distribution channels or manufactured clandestinely.

As mentioned, athletic organizations, especially amateur ones, are concerned with this type of drug activity and may restrict such drugs in an effort to maintain a degree of competitive fairness. Let us now examine the drug control programs.

Drug Control in Amateur Sports

The two major governing bodies for amateur athletics in the United States are the United States Olympic Committee (USOC) and the National Collegiate Athletic Association (NCAA). Each organization bans the use of certain substances by competitors.

> *USOC.* The USOC has developed a list of banned drugs. The list consists of five categories of drugs, including psychomotor stimulants, sympathomimetic amines, narcotic analgesics, anabolic steroids, and miscellaneous central nervous system stimulants. Drugs in these categories are banned to discourage use of them to improve an athlete's performance during competition.
>
> Drug testing is conducted by one of numerous methods for testing urine. The USOC tests athletes in events such as the Olympic

and Pan American trials and games. Athletes are disqualified if they test positive for drugs or refuse to be tested. In the event that an athlete withdraws from a competition, no penalty is imposed.

NCAA. During the 1986 NCAA convention in New Orleans, drug testing legislation was passed. The list of banned drugs is similar to that of the USOC but includes substances banned for specific sports, diuretics, and street drugs. Unfortunately, the NCAA does not include narcotic analgesics, which are on the IOC list.

Drug testing is done at 73 NCAA championships and football postseason bowl games. Drug testing during the regular season remains the responsibility of each school. If any player tests positive for any of the banned drugs, the NCAA can render the player ineligible for that particular postseason competition as well as for post-season play for a minimum of 90 days after the test date.

Drug Control in Professional Sports

The trend to pursue drug testing for professional athletes has fallen somewhat behind that of amateur sports events. Many opponents of drug testing in professional sports claim violations of privacy and civil liberties. Resulting from the problem of drugs in professional sports, a variety of programs have been developed:

Tennis. In 1985, the Men's International Professional Tennis Council approved mandatory drug testing, which had been endorsed by the Association of Tennis Professionals. This is the first (and only) professional player's association to sponsor mandatory testing. Random testing for street drugs is also conducted at two of the top five tournaments each year (Australian Open, French Open, Wimbledon, U.S. Open, and Lipton International Players Championship).

Baseball. Peter Ueberroth, former Major League Baseball (MLB) Commissioner, placed emphasis on the removal of substance abuse from professional baseball. As a result, mandatory testing of all baseball management personnel was introduced in May 1985. Although MLB was hopeful that the MLB Players Association would follow its lead, proposals for drug testing were met with opposition from the association, which warned that any drug testing would be challenged in court. Currently, drug testing is the responsibility of each individual team, and any team player that is convicted of a criminal drug charge is subject to disciplinary action by the commissioner.

Basketball. In September, 1983, the National Basketball Association (NBA), along with the NBA Players Association (NBAPA), instituted an anti-drug program. Under the program, the NBA is permitted to administer drug tests that consist of four tests in a six-week period without prior notice. The program provides that any player found guilty of criminal charges involving drugs be immediately dismissed from the league. Ousted players may seek reinstatement after a two-year period, but such action requires approval of both the commissioner and the NBAPA. If reinstated and later convicted of a second drug offense, the player is permanently dismissed from the league.

The NBA program is unique in that it focuses on drug education. This is accomplished through a series of seminars on drugs, with emphasis placed on helping rookies adapt to a new lifestyle.

Football. In 1986, National Football League (NFL) Commissioner Pete Rozelle announced a drug-testing program that included mandatory drug testing. Under the program, two unscheduled drug tests during the regular season would be required of each player. The program also required that any player convicted of a criminal drug violation or requiring hospitalization for substance abuse be removed from the team's roster for 30 days and receive only 50 percent of his pay during that time. A second such infraction would result in another 30-day suspension, but this time the player would not be paid. A third violation would suspend the player from the league but would still provide a means for reinstatement after one year.

Other Public Policy Issues

Reduce Aid to Source Countries

Hardliners that advocate reducing aid to foreign countries usually argue that the only way to disrupt drug trafficking is to eliminate the source of supply. One possible means to use leverage against source countries is to cease trade practices and/or eliminate aid to them. The prevailing theory is that if drugs are made less available, the price of them will rise, reducing the number of users. This theory may not be a valid one, however, because past increases in drug prices have proven to have little effect on the demand for drugs.

Opponents of this measure argue that it is not the supply but the demand that fuels the drug business and that cutting off one source will just force traffickers to find another. Additionally, many feel that forcing source countries to eradicate crops and extradite their citizens would jeopardize already fragile economies and create political instability. Both of these possibilities would, of course, damage relations with the United States.

Increase Aid to Source Countries

Many feel that, instead, a concerted effort to revive economies and promote economic development in source countries is necessary to persuade these countries to stop trafficking drugs. Under this strategy, all countries affected by drug abuse would contribute some form of aid. The opposition to this proposal contends that such an action would, in effect, reward the drug traffickers and would encourage other countries to participate in the drug trade in order to qualify for aid.

Expand the Role of the Military

While some drug enforcement strategists debate the merits of economic strategies, still others have considered the use of force. The Reagan Administration declared that drug trafficking poses a threat to national security. It has been suggested, therefore, that the United States military is better equipped to deal with such a threat than are civilian law enforcement agencies. This is supported by arguments that the military has at its disposal advanced intelligence capabilities, training, equipment, and other resources to launch a successful, full-scale drug control initiative.

Case Study: Buddies

Alan Greenwald began life as the privileged youngest son of a prominent Hagerstown, Maryland family. By age 29, however, he had become the fugitive former ringleader of the state's largest and longest-standing cocaine smuggling ring. Having had casual customer contact with local drug dealers, young Greenwald and his hometown buddy Marshall Jones, a physician's son, reached the fateful decision that made them rich but notorious—to become narcotics kingpins. The two moved to Miami and on Collins Avenue quickly found a major Colombian supplier, Jorge Torres. With Torres' help, they proceeded to supply Maryland with an estimated $100 million worth of dope over a period of 10 years.

Of course, there were glitches. First, an effort to sell 700 pounds of marijuana in Florida failed. The customers were state drug agents. The buddies were to be locked up for a year, but Jones found a great work-release program, Silver Touch Talent Consultants, which put him right to work—dealing drugs. During their "imprisonment," a boat that they had hired to move marijuana from Jamaica strayed into Cuban waters, its cargo was confiscated, and its three-man crew was imprisoned, requiring congressional intervention to get them freed. By the time of their release, the two buddies had acquired a staff: Steven Silver (of Silver Touch), who served as a money launderer, and the other two Jones brothers, Nathan and Frank, who, along with one Carl Martin, handled the Hagerstown end of things and also worked as couriers.

On his first trip on Amtrak, young Frank Jones chickened out and threw two kilos of cocaine off the train in Georgia. Both the

Maryland and Florida ends of the conspiracy rushed to Savannah and walked the track for days, but to no avail. The package was never found. Other Greenwald/Jones couriers were arrested with cocaine from time to time, such as Dale Blevins at O'Hare Airport and Charles "Billy" Hoffman in Florida, but the organization bought them good defenses. Blevins was acquitted, based on an illegal luggage search; Hoffman served a few months. More recently, Jeffrey Sollenberg, a Maryland friend whom Greenwald asked to store money in a basement safe, gave information to Washington County, Maryland detectives, resulting in invaluable evidence against the partners.

Notwithstanding these setbacks, the enterprise was profitable for almost 10 years and, although a full accounting can never be made, some evidence of its level of cash flow is provided by the following:

- During his prison stay, Marshall Jones received $200,000 from Silver and a known $200,000 to $250,000 from Maryland dealers. Jones later invested $325,000 in Silver Touch, and when arrested he was relieved of $136,000 and his $61,000 Maserati.

- Silver is known to have purchased $1.8 million worth of cashier's checks.

- More than $100,000 passed through Sollenberg's safe, including $18,000 seized by the arresting officers.

- In 1986, Guy Varron, a Hagerstown distributor, stored $100,000 for Greenwald and Jones.

- By 1987, federal authorities had seized $1.9 million of the ring's assets, including Silver's Miami recording studio, several houses, a racing boat, three luxury cars, and $135,000 in cash.

- Federal prosecutors confidently estimated that more than 1,600 pounds of cocaine flowed through just the avenues known to be controlled by Greenwald and Jones at purchase prices from $12,000 to $25,000 per pound.

Early on, Jones became the marketing expert, building teams of distributors in Virginia and West Virginia, as well as Maryland, that would sell all the drugs that Greenwald could buy. Raymond Carnahan was Jones' distributor in Alexandria, Virginia. An OCDETF team there, composed of IRS and DEA agents, made undercover purchases from Carnahan and eventually arrested him with a pound of cocaine.

At about the same time, "Billy" Hoffman again was arrested, this time by narcotics detectives in Florida, with a kilo of cocaine and a one-way ticket to Baltimore. After five more months in jail, Hoffman pled to a reduced charge and began to cooperate with authorities. An assistant state's attorney in Hagerstown made the connection between Hoffman and Greenwald, and through Hoffman's information, a Washington County, Maryland grand jury returned an indictment against Greenwald. The case and the county prosecutor moved to Maryland's U.S. Attorney's office as the evidence grew. Washington County and Maryland state police investigators worked alongside the DEA, IRS, ATF, and others to expose the organization's tentacles. The long series of investigations that retrospectively uncovered the Greenwald, Jones, and Silver partnership provides a fine example of coordinated enforcement effort by local, state, and federal agencies.

To date, more than 125 persons having criminal culpability have been identified in the investigation, and more than 40 have been convicted in Maryland, Virginia, and Florida. Several million dollars worth of drugs have been seized in the three states. Silver and Martin were sentenced to 35 years each; Torres, the supplier, 25. Nate Jones was sentenced to 10 years, and his younger brother, Frank, of Amtrak fame, awaits sentencing.

Greenwald was the first to fall, and Marshall Jones was the last. Faced with indictments in Hagerstown, Greenwald made arrangements to surrender but instead disappeared. He left behind several thousand dollars, his Mercedes, and his wife, Deborah, eight months pregnant (who was later convicted on state drug charges). In December, 1988, Greenwald was indicted in Baltimore for operating a continuing criminal enterprise. Marshall Jones decided to cooperate with federal prosecutors and has continued to do so throughout the many trials. Nonetheless, in January, 1989, Jones was sentenced to 18 years in federal prison, closing Maryland's biggest narco-business.

Source: Organized Crime Drug Enforcement Task Force Program, U.S. Department of Justice, 1988.

Some jurisdictions have implemented the National Guard to assist drug control officers in raids. The primary use of National Guardsmen is to augment staff in nonthreatening functions in certain operations. These duties include transporting and booking prisoners, facilitating certain paperwork, and other tasks.

Predictably, this school of thought has its critics, who hold that drug trafficking is not a military problem and to empower the military with civilian police powers opposes the country's foundation of democracy, which is based, in part, on the separation of powers. Recent studies have even cast doubts on the ability of the military to make an impact on drug consumption through interdiction.

In 1988 the Pentagon sponsored a study directed by Peter Reuter of the RAND Corporation. The report dealt with the suggestion that the military become more involved with drug interdiction and protecting national borders. The study, reflecting some bias on the part of the sponsor, examined the presumption that the armed forces would be able to construct an impenetrable electronic net around the country through the use of advanced surveillance aircraft.

Reuter devised a mathematical model to estimate the impact that increased spending on interdiction would have on domestic drug consumption. He concluded that a key factor in the issue is that at least 75 percent of the money spent to buy cocaine goes to the bottom level of the market—the street dealers. Only 10 percent of the final price allegedly goes to the production and smuggling sector. The study cited the Coast Guard, an able player at the job of interdiction, which found drugs on only one out of every eight boats that it boarded in 1986, even when acting on intelligence information. Therefore, doubling the number of patrols by adding Navy vessels will not double the success rate unless intelligence is vastly improved.

Reuter concluded with the assertion that seizures of big shipments have little impact on buyers and little to no impact on demand. At best, according to the results of the study, the use of the military would only reduce cocaine shipments from 120 metric tons to 90 metric tons per year.

Legalize Drugs

While the previous strategies are aimed at reducing drug trafficking, another strategy is based on the assumption that drug abuse will never be eliminated. The strategy that accepts drug abuse calls for legalization of drugs and is aimed instead at reducing the control that criminals have over the drug trade.

The prospect of legalizing drugs has attracted considerable attention from the media, civil libertarians, some public officials, and some members of Congress. The arguments for and against the legalization of illicit drugs are many and should be carefully weighed with such considerations as public safety and personal freedoms. In addition, other considerations include the rights of the people as a free society versus the rights of innocent victims of the drug trade (see Chapter 12).

Increase Spending for Drug Education Programs

A final strategy focuses on the demand side of the drug cycle. One traditional school of thought is for the government to continue to spend more and more on public education and treatment programs, although it is conceded that this strategy will take many years to be considered successful. In theory, once demand is under control, the supply will dry up. Of course, the response to this argument is that to stop drug trafficking, sources must be cut off at the supply rather than the demand side.

Summary

Controversy is nothing new in considering the fate of the drug abuse problem in the United States. Much of the controversy in drug control stems from the tactics that are adopted by law enforcement officials. On one hand, many traditional police tactics have proven less than effective, but on the other hand, the use of more unconventional enforcement techniques, such as the forfeiting of ill-gotten attorneys' fees and needle exchange programs, raise concerns for civil liberties and expanded police authority.

One controversial technique that has proven effective in identifying drug traffickers is the criminal profile. Although police tend to shy away from the word "profile," the use of this tactic has resulted in many major seizures. The profiling procedure focuses on drug couriers in transit. The 1989 Sokolow decision gave legitimacy to this procedure, which basically enables agents to stop and question individuals that look or act like a typical drug dealer. The court in this decision has recognized that certain traits are unique to drug dealers and typically are not practiced by the general population.

The reverse sting is another enforcement technique that has proven effective in identifying drug buyers (or users) rather than sellers. This technique requires the undercover officer to pose as a drug seller. The officer is authorized to sell a quantity of drugs to a prospective buyer, but the buyer is immediately arrested and the drugs are seized as evidence. Those that criticize this technique claim that an atmosphere of entrapment prevails and that police are enticing people to commit crimes. The proper use of this technique, however, requires police to show a defendant's "criminal intent" and his or her predisposition to purchase the drugs.

With so many different enforcement techniques, the practice of surveillance is common. Because covert observation by the police has always generated a certain degree of skepticism by the public, the police must take great care in initiating certain surveillance operations. Officers must be careful that the activities for which the suspect is under investigation are authorized (for investigation) under federal guidelines. In addition, the concerns of both the government and civil libertarians must be observed throughout the operation.

Drug testing is not a new concern for drug control strategists, but the issue is far from being resolved. Most of the concern revolves around the questions of who should be tested, where, and under what set of circumstances. Drug testing of federal transportation and law enforcement employees has been authorized, but what about drug testing in the general work place? Some claim that the examination of a blood or urine sample violates one's Fourth and Fifth Amendment rights.

The subject of drug testing leads us into the discussion of the problem of drugs and sports. This issue deals with several aspects, including nonaddictive and recreational drug use, and the use of drugs such as steroids, which are designed to aid the athlete in his or her particular sport. Regulatory agencies governing drug use in sports have created punitive provisions for those that use dangerous drugs. Such provisions may include fines, suspension, or expulsion from professional athletics and even criminal prosecution.

Do you recognize these terms?

drug courier profiling

entrapment

gas-liquid chromatography

mass spectrometry

reverse sting

zero tolerance

Discussion Questions

1. Discuss some of the more valid concerns in the practice of "officially" abducting drug traffickers wanted in the United States.

2. List some possible options that the United States government could consider to eliminate international drug trafficking.

3. What fears do civil libertarians have regarding the practice of drug courier profiling by police?

4. What is meant by the term "zero tolerance," and why has the term become so controversial?

5. Discuss some of the legal and moral ramifications of the practice of seizing attorney fees.

6. Discuss why needle exchange programs are controversial throughout the world.

7. Discuss the different circumstances under which one may be tested for drugs in the workplace. What are the pros and cons of drug testing in such a manner?

8. Discuss the physiological effects of steroids on the human body.

9. Should the military be considered for the drug enforcement effort? Explain your answer.

Class Projects

1. Study the controversies surrounding drug control in your community, and discuss both their strong and weak attributes.

The Issue of Legalizing Drugs   *12*

This chapter will enable you to:

- Understand the basis for the drug legalization argument
- Understand the distinctions between decriminalization and legalization
- Appreciate public policy concerns with regard to the legalization issue
- Compare pros and cons of the drug legalization debate
- Learn why legalization hasn't worked in other countries
- Discover alternative solutions for the reduction of drug abuse

---

As an alternative to the growing problem of drug abuse in America, some politicians and social scientists have suggested that the laws governing drug control be repealed or at least modified ("decriminalized"). Glaring questions about the social responsibility of such a policy surface when a radical shift is considered. We have learned thus far that because attitudes about drugs are complicated and contradictory, resolution of the drug issue is enigmatic at best. For example, cigarettes and alcohol are both thought to be harmful, yet both are legal and readily available. On the other hand, cocaine and heroin are generally considered as dangerous drugs, and they both are controlled under federal and state laws. When we add in the factor of addiction, which is ever present in both controlled and legal drugs, the stage is set for combat between conservatives and liberals.

Most people agree that the problem of drug abuse cannot be ignored. Crimes to which some addicts resort to finance their habits and in which suppliers of drugs regularly engage exact their price both financially and in victims' lives. Illegal drugs are the financial cornerstone for organized crime the world over. Drug abuse draws users into a world of syringes, dirty needles, poisoned doses, disease, deceit, and drug dealers bent on selling more and more addicting and potent drugs. However, the manner in which government might undermine such effects has basically focused on tough law enforcement. We know that cigarettes are considered to be one of the most affordable causes of death in the world second only to alcohol, which not only deprives drinkers of their health but causes many deaths along the highways as well. Yet, here the notion of dissuasion within the law is broadly accepted.

To address the problem, some have suggested that drug **legalization** or its lesser form, **decriminalization**, be considered. Concurrent with this proposition is the fear that changing the laws would increase drug consumption and addiction. An important question in the legalization issue is: how will legalization affect the crime rate and public health? This chapter will examine this and related issues.

Much of today's legalization debate began in April 1988, when Baltimore's Mayor Kurt Schmoke publicly proclaimed that legalization of illicit substances should be considered by lawmakers. Then in December 1993, Surgeon General Joycelyn Elders publicly proclaimed that the Clinton administration should consider studying the effects of the legalization of drugs. Elders' statement prompted calls from conservatives for Elders to resign while President Clinton quickly distanced himself from both her and the issue. Such episodes have proven how politically taboo it is to even approach the subject of legalizing drugs despite support from several other public figures like former Secretary of State George Shultz, economist Milton Friedman, columnist William F. Buckley, and American University Professor Arnold Trebach, who is also the president of the Drug Policy Foundation in Washington D.C. Perhaps most surprisingly, the legalization issue has been raised in recent years by some law enforcement officials, such as organized crime expert Ralph Salerno, former New York City Police Commissioner Patrick Murphy, now head of the Police Foundation, and Metro-Dade's Wesley C. Pomeroy. Still other police executives, such as Joseph Mac-Namera, Police Chief of San Jose, and former Minneapolis Police Chief Anthony Bouza, have raised questions about the damage resulting from law enforcement efforts to suppress drug use.

Some reformers argue that drug use is a personal moral decision and that it is not the responsibility of government to police social morality. Additionally, many of those that want to legalize drugs claim that crime rates soar as high as they do because drugs are treated as a criminal problem rather than a medical problem. Opponents of legalization argue that, while regulation of public morality may conflict with some personal freedoms, the government has a legitimate responsibility to insure order and public safety in our society.

Public Opinion

As of the preparation of this text, the Clinton administration rejects the notion of drug legalization as a public policy alternative that is unrealistic, risky, and socially irresponsible. This view is shared by Congress and, according to most opinion surveys to date, a high majority of Americans. With regard to the latter, the National Opinion Research Center, through its studies, has concluded that the public rejects the idea of legalization by five to one. Additionally, five-sixths of those surveyed said marijuana should not be legalized. In 1990, a Gallup poll asked respondents to react to the question:

> "Some people feel that current drug laws haven't worked and drugs like marijuana, cocaine, and heroin should be legalized and subject to government taxation and regulation like tobacco and alcohol. Do you think legalization is a good or a bad idea?"

In response, 80 percent said legalization was a bad idea while only 14 percent said it was a good idea. A majority of those questioned feared that if drugs were legalized, drug abuse in the public schools would increase along with the number of drug addicts, drug overdoses, and drug-related crime. High school students have also been polled for their reaction to the legalization question. In 1989 the High School Senior Survey showed that only 17 percent of high school seniors favored making marijuana completely legal while 19 percent felt that it should be considered as a minor violation like a parking ticket but not a criminal offense (decriminalized). In comparison, 50 percent felt that it should be a crime with 15 percent unsure. Not since 1977 has a large number of high school seniors favored making marijuana completely legal. During that year, 34 percent favored legalization, but in recent years that number has fallen sharply.

As an alternative to legalization or decriminalization, polls have shown that restricting the supply of drugs is the most favorable method of decreasing drug abuse. Interdiction, along with increasing penalties for drug abusers was also cited as a popular public opinion in a 1989 Gallup Poll. Results of recent surveys are as follows:

What is the most important thing that can be done to help reduce crime?	Percent of respondents	
	1981	1989
Cut drug supply	3%	25%
Harsher punishment	38	24
Teach values/respect for the law	13	12
Reduce unemployment	22	10
More police	11	5
Try cases faster	6	2
Other	13	21
No Opinion	11	14

Source: The Gallup Report (Princeton, NJ: The Gallup Poll, June 1989). 285 as presented in *BJS, Sourcebook of Criminal Justice Statistics 1989*. NCJ-124224, 1990, table 2.28, 175.

Some argue, however, that such statements of public and political opinion are subject to rapid change as more information becomes available or as social conditions change. Perhaps one should consider how at one time public opinions also strongly supported segregation, the Vietnam War, and slavery in America.

Much research has addressed the various issues of drug control. The research trend, however, seems to focus on the issue of legalization rather than the more pressing problem of drug abuse suppression and on how existing drug control policy can be enhanced. In December 1989, former Drug Control Policy Director William J. Bennett remarked in a speech at Harvard University that, generally, academics have not been supportive of drug control initiatives. Bennett added, "[I]n the great public policy debate over drugs, the academic and intellectual communities have, by and large, had little to contribute, and little of that has been genuinely useful or for that matter mentally distinguished." (Jaschik, 1990). In his speech, Bennett urged academics to focus their research into the improving of drug control methods rather than trying to discredit them.

Bennett has publicly claimed that many academics have attempted to identify the root of drug abuse in society not as the drugs themselves, but as poverty, racism, or "some equally large and intractable social phenomenon." Supportive of Bennett's stance on the issue is Harvard Professor Mark Moore, who stated: "[W]e in academe have been ill-prepared to offer help, because the problem has changed so quickly that researchers have not been able to accumulate experience-based knowledge fast enough to keep up with the need to take action" (Moore, 1989). Let us now consider both sides of the legalization argument.

The Pros: Arguments for Legalization

Many of those who advocate the legalization of drugs base their arguments on assertions of the historical practice of the policing of "victimless" crimes. In particular, the experience of Prohibition is singled out. Reformers allege that the passage of the 1920 Volstead Act outlawing the production, possession, and use of alcohol created more problems than it resolved and that the end of Prohibition in 1933 saw bootlegging gangsters, along with their violence and corruption, fade away. This argument is now put forth to support legalization as a means of disbanding modern-day drug gangs in the same fashion.

Many scholars that are supportive of legalization assert that Prohibition was responsible for the transformation of organized crime from small, isolated vice peddlers serving urban political machines to major crime syndicates. This occurred as a result of the profits realized from Prohibition, the political and law enforcement contacts that they made, the respectability that came from serving the drinking public, and the logistical and structural reorganization of organized crime that bootlegging required (see Chapter 13 for a more comprehensive look at prohibition and public policy).

Proponents of drug legalization base their argument on a number of points. One such point is the traditionally liberal argument stating that a free society allows its people to do as they wish so long as they harm no one. The state, therefore, should be reluctant to use criminal law to constrict personal freedoms. In addition, drug reformers argue that drug laws fail to impact the availability of illicit drugs and may even make the situation worse. For example, a study of the Marijuana Interdiction Program by Mark A.R. Kleiman of Harvard's Kennedy School of Government concluded that the interdiction campaign stimulated domestic production, increased the supply of marijuana in the United States, and raised the potency of marijuana available from 1 percent to 18 percent. A similar study of marijuana eradication campaigns in Kentucky also concluded that the result of the campaigns was increased supply, increased potency, introduction of new dangerous drugs to the market, and the creation of marijuana syndicates in place of the usually small, disorganized growers that had dominated the market before the eradication effort.

Of course, skeptics question the specific correlations between the eradication program and the advances in the marijuana production trade. For example, since the late 1960s, trends toward the rising potency of marijuana and trends toward indoor hydroponics growing methods had been well-documented prior to the implementation of the eradication program. Additionally, research has concluded that one fundamental reason why traditional organized crime (La Cosa Nostra) has been unable to dominate the domestic marijuana trade is because it represents an easy-entry market for entrepreneurs. According to a 1984 DEA Special Intelligence Report on Domestic Marijuana Trafficking, "efforts to organize certain dispersed [marijuana trafficking] elements of society would prove futile and too costly." This illustrates how difficult and impractical (if not impossible) it would be for the government to attempt to control and tax the marijuana market after legalization.

Reformers also point to the connection between illegal drugs and crime, arguing that addicts are lured to other crimes such as prostitution, burglary, and robbery as ways to help finance their expensive habits. In addition, it is argued that the illegality of drugs forces consumers to enter a criminal underworld to purchase them, thereby having contact with criminal actors with whom they would ordinarily never interact, creating conditions for both victimization and subsequent criminality.

Proponents of drug legalization argue that those crimes traditionally associated with drug dealing would be greatly reduced if the context of drug control were changed from a law enforcement to a **medical model**. In addition, the organized crime groups formed around the drug trade would find the illicit market constricted under a medical model and would leave the black market in drugs for other criminal opportunities. Lastly, legalization opponents argue that law enforcement and political corruption associated with drug trafficking, abuse of due process and procedural rights sometimes associated with drug enforcement, and the problem of selective drug enforcement would also be mitigated under a medical model.

According to remarks by Mayor Schmoke in 1988:

> If you take the profit out of drug trafficking, you won't have young children selling drugs on behalf of pushers for $100 a night or wearing beepers to school because it makes more sense to run drugs for someone than to take some of the jobs that are available. I don't know any kid who is making money by running booze.

In Favor of . . .

America's failed national drug strategy is responsible for much of the violence in Baltimore and other urban communities. The enormous profits available from the sale of drugs create crime. Drug traffickers kill to protect or seize drug turf, and addicts commit crimes to get money for drugs. Almost half the murders in Baltimore in 1993 were drug related. . . .

The war on drugs is endangering young people in another way. In Baltimore, AIDS is the No. 1 killer of both young men and young women. Most of these deaths are attributable to intravenous drug use. . . . That is why I advocate a policy called medicalization. Other advocates for changing national drug policy support setting up a private market like the ones we now have for alcohol and cigarettes. My approach to the problem is health regulatory rather than free market.

Medicalization means giving the public-health system the leading role in preventing and treating substance abuse. Under medicalization, the government would set up a regulatory regime to pull addicts into the public health system. The government, not criminal traffickers, would control the price, distribution, purity and access to addictive substances—as it already does with prescription drugs. Public-health professionals would have the authority to maintain addicts, using currently illegal drugs, as part of an overall treatment and detoxification program. Addicts would get counseling, health services and AIDS-prevention information to help break the cycle of addiction, crime and prison. Our communities, in turn, would get relief from the fear and despair that comes from having unremitting violence, addiction, and open-air drug markets in their midst. . . .

But changes in Baltimore's drug policy are not enough. We must have a new national drug strategy—a strategy that will reduce crime by taking the profit out of drug trafficking, make our criminal justice system more effective and increase the availability of treatment. As a first step toward achieving those same goals, we should set up a new national commission to study how all drugs—legal and illegal—should be regulated. Hundreds of prominent Americans have already signed a resolution calling for the establishment of this kind of commission.

A similar commission was set up in 1929 by President Herbert Hoover to study the prohibition of alcohol. Hoover asked the commission to recommend ways in which Prohibition could be more strictly enforced. But the commissioners came to the conclusion that alcohol prohibition was, in the words of Walter Lippman, a "helpless failure." A similar objective study will likely come to the same conclusion about drug prohibition.

Source: Schmoke, Kurt (1994)."Side Effects." *Rolling Stone,* May 5.

Let's now take a closer look at some of the most commonly advanced arguments for the legalization of drugs:

The Tax Revenue. Another common argument in favor of legalization is that it would save billions of tax dollars currently spent on law enforcement efforts. This includes the $8 billion spent on law enforcement and other monies spent on prison facilities to house drug violators every year. In addition, some drug-law reformers envision taxing legalized drugs such as marijuana and generating additional revenues. Of course, these savings may be illusory in that the adoption of a legalization model would require a massive additional investment in drug education programs, drug rehabilitation facilities, and licensing personnel.

The Futility of Enforcement. As we discussed above, drug law enforcement has also come under considerable critical scrutiny. Some researchers claim that there has been no reduction in supply from enforcement efforts and have also pointed to an alarming fall in the retail price of drugs and an increase in their potency. Adding support to this claim are the findings of the federally-funded study of intensive street-level drug enforcement in Lynn, Massachusetts, which pointed to "temporary" and "transitory" successes. This is considered by some to indicate not much more than a marginal success.

In addition, it is argued that fully suppressing the demand for drugs would require the jailing of a large proportion of the nation's population. Fully 70 million Americans admit to having used drugs. Federal studies estimate that, despite constantly escalating numbers of drug arrests, we are still reaching less than 1 percent of users with law enforcement efforts. This is particularly disturbing in view of the notion that the United States ranks number one in the world in the percentage of its population presently behind bars (Associated Press, January 5, 1991).

The Restriction of the Drug Market. Reformers also argue that legalization of some drugs, particularly the so-called **recreational drugs** or "drugs of choice," would serve to restrict the drug market. Since most drug experts agree that marijuana, cocaine, and heroin are the preferred substances for most drug users, their availability might reduce demand for more dangerous substances such as Ice and Angel Dust. This would reduce the economic incentive for the production and distribution of these more dangerous substances.

The Hypocrisy of Drug Laws. It is also argued that it is hypocritical to ban drugs when our society has already legalized two exceedingly dangerous drugs, tobacco and alcohol. The argument is that a much larger percentage of the population is threatened through health risks, automobile collisions, assaults, and associated family problems attributed to these drugs than from many of the drugs presently proscribed by law. One should recognize, however, that such a comparison is difficult to make because legalized recreational drugs are not a reality and no existing scientific or empirical data is available to support this assertion. The hypocrisy of drug laws is also apparent when comparing differ-

ent state laws and offenses for drug offenses. For example, charges for possession of some drugs is based on the amount of the drug in the defendant's control. This not only varies from one state to another but sentences for those convicted differ greatly from one state (or jurisdiction) to another.

International Relations. Some drug reformers have also pointed to problems
created by drug enforcement efforts, specifically, our strained relationships with
some foreign countries. These reformers argue that foreign relations with countries such as Mexico, Peru, and Colombia are being hampered by the intensity
of enforcement efforts and the political rhetoric attached to the drug war.

More compellingly, some critics argue that foreign policy considerations
have resulted in a double standard in drug enforcement in the United States.
These critics point to the lack of intense criticism (or even, as was the case in
Panama military action) directed to countries such as the Bahamas (a major
transshipment site for cocaine made safe by massive political corruption), Chile
(where the DINA, Chile's secret police, has been actively engaged in cocaine
trafficking for over two decades), Thailand (a major heroin refining center), and
Taiwan (source of much of the financial backing and logistical support for the
southeast Asian heroin trade). Critics are also disturbed by the relations between
United States intelligence agencies and drug traffickers: the CIA's role in Australia's drug money-laundering Nugan-Hand bank and in Caribbean drug
money-laundering enterprises; support for fundamentalist Moslem Afghan
groups actively engaged in heroin trafficking; and the National Security Council's alleged relationships with General Manuel Noriega and certain members of
the Medellin Cartel in support of the Contra's war against Nicaragua.

Personal Freedoms. To some critics of present drug enforcement policies,
the possibility of severe threats to personal freedoms posed by tougher drug
laws creates concern. New and expanded search-and-seizure powers granted to
law enforcement officers, random drug testing by employers, and the use of the
military in domestic law enforcement raise major concerns about potential due
process abuses, further erosion of constitutional protections, and the potential
for serious systematic corruption.

The Crime Rate. As mentioned above, reformers also claim that legalization would cut down on street crimes because addicts could acquire their drugs
inexpensively rather than by committing burglary, robbery, and murder for
money. Drug reformers also argue that legalization would reduce the drug turf
wars that have driven urban homicide rates to record levels in recent years.

Public Health. Proponents of drug legalization argue that the drug laws
themselves create many of the severe health problems normally associated with
drug use. Obviously, the spread of AIDS, closely associated with the sharing of
needles by intravenous drug users, is one such concern. Reformers also point to
the problem of pregnant drug addicts, who, out of fear of legal repercussions,
may not seek prenatal care.

> **Thinking Critically #27**
>
> Explain your own view of marijuana usage. Defend or refute arguments in favor of decriminalizing the possession, consumption, and sale of marijuana.

Finally, some have argued, at least in the case of heroin, that illegality of heroin means that there is no control over the quality of the drug being purchased. Heroin and other drugs are commonly adulterated with dangerous substances by retail dealers, and users are unsure of the potency or quality of the drugs they have purchased. From a pharmacological point of view, unadulterated heroin causes little physical damage to the human body (this of course excludes such health threats as AIDS and brutal physical addiction). It is the uncontrolled nature of street heroin that causes poisoning and overdose.

Despite these arguments for the legalization of drugs, drug reformers have yet to come up with a comprehensive plan that delineates any practical program for legalization. Some reformers have complained that they have not had equal access to federal research monies with which to formulate their approach. Those monies have been exclusively reserved for research on drug abuse pathologies and drug repression strategies.

In 1988, Democratic Congressman Charles Rangel, who represents the drug-infested Harlem district in New York City and who strongly opposes legalization, posed questions that drug policy reformers will have to answer in coming years:

1. Which drugs should be legalized—marijuana or the harder drugs such as heroin and cocaine?
2. How would the legalized drugs be sold: By prescription or over-the-counter, by hospitals or pharmacies?
3. Would there be an age limit and, if so, how would it be enforced?
4. As addictions and dependencies developed, would any limit be placed on the amount of drugs that users could purchase?
5. Who would manufacture the drugs? Private companies or the federal government?
6. Would the drugs be provided to the public at cost? If not, how much profit margin would be allowed? Would they be taxed?
7. Who would assume the responsibility of allowing a drug user to take so much of a particular drug? The government or physician?
8. Should recreational use of drugs be authorized or just drug use for treatment?

In response to these questions, some reformers have offered the argument that drugs could be sold in the same fashion as alcohol. That is, sold to only licensed dealers, who would be taxed and held under close government scrutiny. Regulations would include prohibiting the sale of drugs to anyone under 21 years of age. Another proposal is a lesser form of legalization called decriminalization. This vague concept generally calls for the reduction of criminal penalties for drug use or possession while retaining a degree of social disapproval. Regardless of which approach seems most popular, it seems increasingly clear, at least to some, that a serious fault does exist in the current public policy that addresses drug control. The fault is that current policy has failed to cut drastically the supply of drugs through the use of police action alone.

KNOW

Arguments for Reform

- It is not the responsibility of government to regulate the private morality of its citizens.

- Legalization of drugs would provide new revenue to be used in drug education and rehabilitation efforts.

- Drug laws are unenforceable and result in selective and discriminatory enforcement practices.

- Drug laws are hypocritical.

- Drug laws create criminals out of otherwise law-abiding citizens.

- Drug laws strengthen and expand organized crime.

- Drug laws create an environment where police officials are tempted to use unscrupulous enforcement tactics, and they increase the danger of corruption.

The Cons: Arguments against Legalization

The prevailing opposition against drug legalization is voiced by many politicians, law enforcement officials, and concerned citizens alike. Opponents of legalization contend that the problems created by Prohibition were minuscule compared to today's situation. Specifically, children of the 1920s were not the victims of alcohol consumption, at least in an addictive sense.

Additionally, users would possibly face a greater risk of debilitating dependencies from cocaine and narcotics if those drugs were legalized. Today, more than a half of a century after the repeal of Prohibition, alcoholism is considered, more so now than ever, one of America's most lethal killers. Indeed, the legalization of drugs would very likely provide drug lords, both foreign and domestic, the vehicle to success that they have been waiting for: the conversion of the black market to an open market.

Figure 12.1

Most people do not favor the legalization of drugs

In 1990, the Gallup Poll asked respondents to react to the following: "Some people feel that current drug laws haven't worked and that drugs like marijuana, cocaine, and heroin should be legalized and subject to government taxation and regulation like alcohol and tobacco. Do you think legalization is a good idea or a bad idea?"

In response—
- 80% said it was a bad idea
- 14% said it was a good idea
- 2% said some legalized, some not
- 4% had no opinion.

Most of the population felt that if drugs were legalized, drug use in the public schools would increase, and the number of drug addicts and drug overdoses would increase; about half felt that the amount of drug-related crime would increase.

In 1989, the High School Senior Survey showed that 17% of high school seniors favored making marijuana use entirely legal; 19% felt that it should be a minor violation like a parking ticket but not a crime; (15% were unsure). The percentage of high school seniors favoring making marijuana use entirely legal peaked at about 34% in 1977. In recent years, the percentage of high school seniors favoring legalization of drug use has fallen.

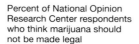
Percent of National Opinion Research Center respondents who think marijuana should not be made legal

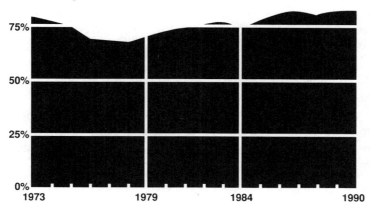

Note: This line was constructed from interpolated data. Between 2% and 5% responded "don't know," depending on the year.
Sources: Graphic: Data from the National Opinion Research Center are made available through the Roper Public Opinion Research Center as presented in BJS. *Sourcebook of Criminal Justice Statistics, 1990.* NCJ-130580. 1991, table 2.87, 228.
Text: Diane Colasanto. "Widespread Public Opposition to Drug Legalization."
The Gallup Poll Monthly (Princeton, NJ: The Gallup Poll, January 1990). 292:6 and NIDA, Lloyd D. Johnston, Patrick M. O'Malley, and Jerald G. Bachman, *Drug Use Among American High School Seniors, College Students and Young Adults, 1975-1990,* Volume 1, High School Seniors. DHHS Publication No. (ADM) 91-1813, 1991, table 21, 142.

A primary concern about the reform of drug laws is the erosion of public morals. Specifically, many feel that the simple act of legalizing drugs would send a public message about society's lack of social responsibility and its unwillingness to deal with such a major health and public safety issue: a kind of surrender to the drug dealers of the world. Opponents, therefore, predict that adoption of such a public policy would increase drug abuse enormously and would multiply the ancillary problems of poor health, violence, and disjoined families.

Certainly, legalization would serve as a "quick fix." How responsible is it, some might argue, to take a crime against society and legalize it for the sole purpose of eliminating it as a criminal problem and as a threat to public safety? This is a complex question that has been raised with regard to the legalization of prostitution, gambling, abortion, and pornography, as well as drugs. In the case of violent crimes and property crimes, of course, the answer is obvious. It is not always as clear with morality crimes.

According to some treatment officials, the rate of addiction to alcohol is only 10 percent of those that use it. The addiction rate of crack cocaine, however, would probably exceed 75 percent of those that use it; these are statistics that reformers strategically avoid.

The Alcohol Argument. Opponents to drug reform turn around the alcohol argument by acknowledging alcohol as a dangerous and addictive drug, but the fact that it is so harmful to society is the very reason that additional dangerous substances of abuse should not be added to the list of legal drugs. The toll of alcohol consumption is well-documented in broken homes, violence, ruined careers, accidents, and loss of productivity on the job and in the schools. So the question is whether legalized alcohol and drugs would create a worse situation than has legalized alcohol alone.

The Crime Rate. Although proponents of reform argue that legalized drugs would cause a decrease in the crime rate, opponents claim just the opposite—that is, although some drug-type crimes would be reduced (i.e., smuggling), a black market would always exist. This is particularly significant in considering that many addicts would be unable to hold down jobs because of their addictions to even the cheapest of "government-made" drugs.

Many people involved in drug enforcement have suggested that numerous drug-related felonies are committed by people who were involved in crime before they started taking drugs. The drugs, so routinely available in criminal circles, make the criminals more violent and unpredictable. Certainly there are some kill-for-a-fix crimes, but how logical is it to assume that a cut-rate price for drugs at a government outlet will stop such psychopathic behavior? It is a simple fact that under the influence of drugs, normal people do not behave normally, and abnormal people function in chilling and horrible ways. This argument extends to children who are among the most frequent victims of violent, drug-related crimes that have nothing to do with the cost of acquiring the drugs (Bennett, 1990). In Philadelphia in 1987, more than half the child-abuse fatalities involved at least one parent who was a heavy drug user. Seventy-three per-cent of the child abuse deaths in New York City in 1987 involved parental drug use (Bennett, 1990).

New Revenues. In response to those who claim that legalizing drugs would save the public billions in taxes, opponents are convinced that the black market would actually be broadened because of the lack of taxes on illicit drugs. After all, cigarette bootlegging is still one of organized crime's varied enterprises because of high tax-rate differentials. Additionally, it can be argued that stepped-up enforcement in conjunction with powerful forfeiture laws that pro-vide for government seizure of drug money, property, and assets will substan-tially reduce the costs of drug enforcement. Furthermore, it is maintained that what the government might save in law enforcement costs would be spent many times over as a result of traffic deaths, lost productivity, and medical costs. In fact, the Select Committee on Narcotics Abuse and Control estimated that Americans spent $140 billion on illegal drugs in 1987 alone.

The Addicts. Another opposing view of reform is the argument that money would still be required even in the event of legalized drugs. Specifically, it is believed that many addicts would not hold regular jobs and, therefore, would continue to commit ancillary crimes such as robbery, prostitution, and theft in order to acquire money. Even though some studies have indicated that heroin addicts are able to lead fairly normal lives if their drug needs are met, there is no evidence to convince us that all addicts would choose to leave the drug-crimes subculture. Additionally, drug-related crimes that result from intoxicated drug users would no doubt rise, including assault, spouse/child abuse, and drug-related traffic accidents.

Additionally, perhaps we should remember that when pornography was legalized de facto by the Supreme Court, it did not just go away as some antici-pated. In fact, it gradually became more obscene because of public boredom with the product. For example, *Playboy* magazine was superseded by *Penthouse*, which was then outdone by *Hustler*. Then came the sadistic "snuff" films which depicted gang rapes, sadism, and ultimately murder.

Organized Crime. The legalization of drugs would have three profound effects with regard to the black market: (1) it would give drugs a social sanc-tion, creating a broader use of drugs (as was the case with legalized gambling, which created more gamblers rather than reducing the influence of organized crime in the market); (2) it would make drugs available without risk of arrest and prosecution; and (3) if the legal price of drugs did not undercut the price on the illicit market, users would continue to purchase drugs from drug dealers on the street and organized crime would continue to reap its drug-related profits.

After all, as pointed out above, legal lotteries have not dismantled the ille-gal numbers racket. Also, the end of Prohibition did not devastate organized crime—it merely led to diversification and new areas of criminal enterprise.

Many legalizers are willing to admit that drugs such as crack and PCP are simply too dangerous to allow the shelter of the law. Thus, as former Drug Czar William Bennett has suggested, criminals will provide what the government will not (1990). "As long as drugs that people very much want remain illegal, a black market will exist," says legalization advocate David Boaz of the Liberation Cato Institute. Crack is a good example. In powdered form, cocaine was an expensive indulgence. But street chemists found that a better, far less expensive (and far more dangerous) high could be achieved by mixing cocaine with baking soda and heating it. So, crack was born, and "cheap" coke invaded low-income communities with furious speed. It could be argued that if government drugstores do not stock crack, addicts will find it in the clandestine market or simply bake it themselves from their legally purchased cocaine.

Finally, there exists the issue of children and teenagers. Certainly, under the legalization model they would be barred from drug purchases, just as they are now prohibited from buying beer and liquor. But drug dealers will no doubt continue to cater to these young customers with the old, time-honored come-on—a couple of free fixes to get them hooked. And what good will anti-drug education be when these children observe their older brothers and sisters, parents, and friends smoking and shooting up with government permission? Legalization will give us the worst of both worlds: millions of new drug users and a thriving criminal black market (Bennett, 1990).

Personal Freedoms. Proponents of legalization contend that drug laws increasingly deprive the people of their personal freedoms and that drug users should be permitted to consume drugs in their own home if they desire. While this argument entails a rather lofty debate over political philosophy, it should be pointed out that an equally strong argument can be made that whenever one person's personal freedoms are safeguarded, someone else's may be restricted. In a nation with more than 250 million people, carte blanche cannot be given to everyone desiring to live his or her own way without regard to rights and needs of others.

The Cost of Legalization. While legalization proponents argue that taxes from legal drugs and reduced expenditures related to drug enforcement would result in reductions in government spending, that argument fails to provide for the unacceptable and exorbitant social costs of such a program. For instance, a 1983 study by the Research Triangle Institute found that drug abuse costs the American economy more than $60 billion annually. The specific costs identified by the study are discussed below:

> $24 billion of the total figure was from drug-related crimes: the police, the courts, the jails, victims, and so forth.

> $36 billion of the total was the cost of lost productivity, injuries, and other harm caused by heavy drug users.

In Opposition to . . .

It is astonishing that Mayor Kurt Schmoke of Baltimore has aligned himself with the drug culture and a small group of elitists and Ivy League intelligentsia (who loves social experimentation without regard to the cost in dollars or human tragedy) that promote legalization of an unhealthy, illegal lifestyle.

They simply refuse to learn from the experiences of England and Switzerland. They tried decriminalization/legalization and paid a dear price. Use increased by multiples, as did crime rates and health consequences/costs for the adventure. Switzerland is taking a second run at harm reduction, and the Netherlands have informally decriminalized hashish. In a few years, we'll have two more spectacular failures to provide us with the evidence that all drug use outside legitimate medical use is, in fact, abuse. The pseudo public-health, responsible-use, harm-reduction alternative is simply a recipe for a national disaster. . . .

It has been proven that marijuana can cause low birth weights and developmental problems in infants born to users. Some scientists believe that, when all the science is in, it will be proven that there is a Fetal Marijuana Syndrome and Effect, similar to that of alcohol. Yet, Mr. Schmoke and his band of users, elitists and theorists advocate making this dreadful, toxic substance legally available and, thus, more easily accessible and acceptable. What toll in human tragedy must accrue before they deem their drug of choice unacceptable?

The increase in drug use that would accompany decriminalization/legalization would cause a dramatic rise in health damage and the associated health costs. . . . increased random and family violence committed by persons on drugs, accidents caused by drug-impaired drivers/equipment operators, loss of productivity and increased related costs by workers, higher infant mortality and drug-damaged children to care for and to try to educate. The never-to-be-realized mental and physical potential of young and future generations is simply a price too dear to pay for surrender.

The drug culture seeks to confuse, divide and, thus, conquer the so-called straight society. We must act to stop this schizophrenic behavior and work to break the cycle of use, damage, and addiction. We need to commit ourselves to expend as much money, time, and effort on prevention and treatment as we do on law enforcement. When we mount such a three-pronged attack with the full support of the care providers and all levels and agencies of government, then we will make the inroads and strides necessary to excise the cancer of drug use from our society.

Source: Roques, Wayne J. (1993). *The Washington Times,* December 17. Copyright © 1993 The Washington Times. Reprinted with permission.

Given that more than half of this enormous figure was attributed to work-related accidents and lost productivity, is it not logical to assume that legalized drugs, selling for a fraction of the price of illicit drugs and, therefore, being more widely used, would increase that cost figure by five, six, seven times, or even higher? Many experts in the field believe so.

Arguments against Legalization

- Legalization of drugs would allow organized crime groups to continue in the drug trade but on a legal basis, using established drug distribution networks.

- The governing of morality through enforcing "victimless" crimes upholds the moral viability of our nation.

- Just because a law seems unenforceable is no reason to abolish it. For example, laws against murder or robbery have not eliminated such criminal acts; however the states continue to make murder illegal.

- Legalizing drugs would create much regulation and licensing and would, therefore, create many new opportunities for official corruption.

- Just because the criminal justice system seems to be overburdened, laws should not be eliminated. The answer is to dedicate more resources to the system, thus making it a more effective one.

Even those who oppose legalization recognize that drug enforcement places a critical financial burden on the nation's resources, but they argue that the price of not doing so would be too costly for society. After all, all civilized societies have seen fit to exert some form of control over mind-altering substances. Even the few experiments in legalization have shown that when the drugs are more widely available, addiction increases. For example, in 1975, Italy liberalized its drug laws and now has one of the highest heroin-related death rates in western Europe. As we will discuss later in this chapter, in Alaska, where marijuana was decriminalized in 1975, the relaxed atmosphere increased usage of the drug, particularly among children. After 15 years Alaskans have successfully won a petition to "recriminalize" marijuana. Let's now look at some examples of legalization around the world.

Drugs in Amsterdam: The "Dutch Way"

Other countries, such as the Netherlands, have legalized drugs as a remedy for their drug problems. Let us now consider Amsterdam and its experience with decriminalizing drugs. Although drugs are not totally legal in Amsterdam, they are, at least, tolerated.

Over the years, Amsterdam, a city of 700,000, has earned the reputation of being a drug mecca in western Europe because of the widespread availability of marijuana. Indeed, marijuana and hashish alike are imported from many different source countries and are sold openly in coffee shops and ice cream parlors. Only a few blocks from Amsterdam's business district, cocaine and heroin dealers operate without fear of being arrested because the government has adopted a strategy in which these dealers are quarantined to this designated area of town called the "red light district."

This selling is tolerated because Dutch police authorities feel that drug trafficking can be more closely monitored if it is confined to a small area, thereby providing controls not only over drug retailing but over all ancillary criminal behaviors. Throughout the rest of town, marijuana and hash are treated much like alcohol and tobacco are treated in America.

The Dutch policy separates marijuana and hashish from the harder drugs. It is generally felt that if young people can purchase their marijuana in coffee shops rather than from criminal drug dealers that also sell harder drugs, it is less likely that the customer will be tempted by the seller to try other more potent and addictive substances.

In addition, the Dutch have adopted a policy that they feel makes drug use "boring" and less glamorous. The ease with which cannabis products can be obtained removes the mystique often attached to acts of rebellion and nonconformity that many young people engage in as part of the maturing process. Marijuana reformers claim that there is much to be said for this argument in that available data indicate strikingly lower patterns of drug use in Amsterdam than in the United States (Trebach, 1982):

- Following the decriminalization of cannabis in the Netherlands, consumption declined significantly. In 1976, before decriminalization, 3 percent of 15-and 16 year-olds and 10 percent of 17-and 18-year-olds used cannabis occasionally; by 1985, after decriminalization, the percentages had declined to 2 percent and 6 percent respectively.
- Heroin use in Amsterdam is estimated at 0.4 percent, and cocaine use has stabilized at 0.6 percent.
- Only 8 percent of Dutch AIDS patients are intravenous drug users, compared to 26 percent in the United States.
- Drug experimentation among high school students has dropped from 12 percent in 1976, before legalization, to 1 percent today.

Ancillary to the liberal law enforcement approach in Amsterdam is a concomitant medical model used to treat addiction and abuse. In Amsterdam, a widespread methadone maintenance program, targeting heroin addicts, makes use of mobile units that travel around the city bringing methadone treatment to addicts. Of course, the methadone program in Amsterdam is beset by many of the same problems as United States experiments with the heroin substitute. In particular, methadone, which is also an addicting drug, has failed to divert users from heroin, so that some addicts have adopted a style of use combining both heroin and methadone.

In 1988, the Amsterdam health department estimated that there were 7,000 addicts in the city, 20 percent of whom were foreigners. Additionally, police estimate that 60 percent of petty crimes are committed by members of the addict population in Amsterdam. It should also be noted, however, that drug-related homicides in Amsterdam are very rare events. Washington, D.C. has 15 times as many drug-related murders than does Amsterdam. On the other hand, it is likely that the Dutch have considerably more control over street crime than we do in the United States.

Unlike many American cities, Amsterdam has a well-funded and a more-than-adequate police department. Amsterdam's police strength is 3,500, of which 2,900 are uniformed officers assigned to street beats. An estimated 400 of these officers, however, are assigned to the diminutive four-block area of the "**red light district**" to contain the high rate of crime there. In contrast, the same number of officers (400) is adequate to serve the entire city of El Paso, Texas, a city of about 500,000.

Some Dutch police officials are concerned with the overall rise in the crime rate that has occurred since the tolerance policy towards drugs went into effect. This increase in crime cannot be blamed entirely on Dutch drug users. As with many countries that experience a flourishing drug abuse problem, blame is conveniently placed on other countries whose stringent drug control policies have succeeded in ridding the country of many drug abusers and related criminals. It makes sense to assume that someone that steals to support a drug habit in Germany would not pass up an opportunity to steal just because he or she is in Amsterdam, where there is greater availability and affordability of drugs.

One unfortunate and unforeseen side effect of the Amsterdam project is the emergence of droves of porno shops and houses of prostitution in the drug district. Dutch officials are quick to admit that the crime rate has dramatically risen since the so-called "Dutch Way" was adopted.

Those who lend support for the Amsterdam experiment, however, claim that the relationship between sexual trafficking and drugs is difficult to establish because of several perceived factors. For example, some of the prostitution and pornography enterprises in Amsterdam preceded the legalization of drugs in that country. In addition, such "red light districts" exist in European cities where drug retailing is not tolerated, although history has shown that the sex and drug industries are very closely correlated.

In the United States, one need only travel through Boston's "Combat Zone," San Francisco's "Tenderloin," or Philadelphia's "Arch Street" districts to find evidence of close links between the sex and drug industries.

The British Experiment

Britain passed legal controls regarding dangerous substances at about the same time that the United States passed similar laws; the first such measure was passed in 1916. The early drug control efforts in both countries were aimed at controlling drug addiction and abuse by outlawing cocaine and opium and their derivatives. Much confusion surrounded the application of drug control laws in both Britain and the United States.

A second piece of anti-drug legislation, known as the Dangerous Drug Act, was passed by Parliament in 1920. Basically, the law prohibited possession of opiates or cocaine except with a lawful prescription. Paralleling problems with the Harrison Act in the United States, confusion over the specifics of the new British legislation led to difficulty in its interpretation and enforcement.

In 1924, a committee of British physicians was formed to determine whether drug abuse should be approached as a criminal justice or a medical problem. The committee was inclined toward the latter and instituted the so-called "**British system**," which prevailed well into the late 1960s.

The "British system" gave opiate addicts, most of whom were older persons, legal access to heroin and morphine. The goal of the program was to wean addicts from their addiction to heroin. This was done through medical supervision of addicts by physicians, who would prescribe just enough heroin for the addicts to stay "well" but not enough to get high.

By the late 1950s, the number of heroin addicts began to grow. By the mid-1960s, England became a major market for smokable heroin, similar to the opium traditionally smoked by Chinese addicts. The availability of this type of heroin was thought to contribute to the increasing numbers of addicts. Compounding the problem was the diversion of heroin from legitimate sources (e.g., doctors' offices) to the streets.

The British system of drug maintenance by prescription is still in operation, although several factors have made it a less effective practice than it had been in the past. First, a sizable increase in illegal heroin supplies was noted in the 1970s, offering a realistic alternative to visiting doctor's offices. This was accompanied by a general economic downturn with high unemployment, declining wages, and racial tensions in most large British cities. Some students of the British system suggest that the real crisis came when British economic policies under the former Thatcher government resulted in declining buying power and an increase in the cost of alcohol, thereby making heroin a cheaper high than booze.

Thinking Critically #28

Say that legalization of drugs is adopted as a public policy in the United States. Suggest guidelines to implement this policy.

No matter which of the many problems actually resulted in the increase in heroin use in Britain, the fact remains that the system is not as effective as it used to be. Nonetheless, it is interesting to note that recent legislation has relaxed some of the restrictions imposed on heroin maintenance by the Thatcher government, making it once again a more viable option. Some leading physicians and law enforcement officials, such as H.B. Spear, head of Scotland Yard's drug enforcement wing, have been actively campaigning for an expansion of both heroin and cocaine maintenance programs in Britain.

The Alaskan "Pot" Legalization Experience

Although now illegal, possession of marijuana for personal use was considered lawful in Alaska between 1975 and 1990. During that time, Alaska state law allowed people over 19 years of age to possess up to four ounces of marijuana in private without penalty, though it could not be sold or bartered. In addition to other public concerns, the Alaskan law conflicted with federal law prohibiting the drug.

The "legalized pot" experiment has since given researchers and policy makers a model to study. In this section we will consider the history and repercussions of their social experiment with this controversial public policy. Ironically, Alaska's 1975 legalization of marijuana was not a result of a public movement or one anchored by elected representatives of the people. In fact, it resulted from a decision by the Alaska Supreme Court. The landmark decision was *Ravin v. State*, 537 p. 2d 494. *Ravin* was based on Article I, Section 22 of the Alaska Constitution, which stated that "the right of the people to privacy is recognized and shall not be infringed." In deciding this case, the court held that the state had no authority to exert control over the activities of an individual unless their activities affected the public health and safety of others (or the public at large).

As mentioned, the *Ravin* decision was based on two basic premises: 1) that marijuana was a "harmless substance," and 2) that a 1972 state constitutional amendment guaranteeing Alaskans the right to privacy extended to marijuana use in one's home.

Indeed, the court had declared that the effects of marijuana were not serious enough to justify widespread concern . . . "at least as compared with the far more dangerous effects of alcohol, barbiturates and amphetamines." The court

A Synopsis of the *Ravin* Case

Irwin Ravin—a Homer, Alaska lawyer—had deliberately set out to be stopped while driving and had purposely possessed a small amount of marijuana in his pocket. Later, in his defense, Ravin filed a motion to dismiss the criminal complaint in district court. During the court hearings, several experts testified, and numerous books and written articles were introduced into evidence. The district court denied the motion to dismiss, so Ravin appealed to the superior court, which also denied the motion.

Finally, the Alaskan Supreme Court agreed to review the case. The court noted at the time that "most marijuana available in the United States contained THC content of less than one percent." After considering both long- and short-term effects of the drug on users, the court overturned the lower courts' decisions and protected an adult's right to possess marijuana in his own home for personal use. In coming to this decision, the court placed more importance on an individual's right to privacy than on the state's responsibility to preserve public health and safety. The court, however, failed to define an "adult," how much marijuana could be "possessed," and what constituted a person's "own home."

further held that until conclusive evidence was available to show that marijuana is a dangerous drug, the state could not prohibit its possession and use in the home by adults.*

With regard to the use of marijuana by minors, the *Ravin* court also contended that "adolescents may not be equipped with the maturity to handle the experience prudently. . . ." Therefore, it still made it illegal for anyone under 18 years of age in Alaska to use or possess marijuana.

Despite the fact that marijuana possession by minors was outlawed, law enforcement officials in Alaska had a difficult time keeping it out of the hands of school-aged children. For example, in 1982, seven years after the *Ravin* decision, the National Institute of Drug Abuse disclosed that approximately 72 percent of high school students in Alaska had used marijuana at least once. The corresponding figure nationwide was 59 percent. Young people are aware of the hypocrisy of a government that restricts the use of a substance by one age group but authorizes its use by persons only two to three years older.

Yet another study of school-aged children was conducted in 1988 by Bernard Segal, a Professor of Health and Sciences at the University of Alaska. Segal reported that marijuana had "become well incorporated into the lifestyle on many adolescents" and for them, could no longer be considered an experimental drug. The study revealed that overall use of marijuana rose between

---

* Note: As of the 1990 recriminalization of marijuana in Alaska, the average THC content of "commercial" marijuana ranged between 5 and 7 percent, which is considerably higher than the 1 percent cited by the Alaska court in 1975. Additionally, the popular sinsemilla strain typically averages twice the THC content of commercial marijuana.

1983 and 1988 and that its popularity was 16 percentage points above the national average.

Between 1975 and 1990, interest groups opposed to the legalization measure lobbied in the state legislature to re-outlaw the drug. Large oil companies, for example, made substantial contributions in support of a recriminalization proposal while groups such as "Alaskans for Privacy" (a citizen group consisting of local professionals) and members of "NORML" (the National Organization for the Reform of Marijuana Laws) maintained their support for decriminalization.

In 1989, another citizens group, frustrated by inaction in the legislature, began circulating petitions for a recriminalization measure. The result was the required 42,000 signatures that were obtained for the acclaimed "Proposition Two," which was then placed on the ballot.

In examining the former state drug policy of Alaska, three distinct problems should be noted:

> *Problem #1.* Because possession or distribution of marijuana was a violation of federal law in Alaska, any person using the drug in his or her own home was still in violation of the law. So, one could argue that the state of Alaska had basically sanctioned the use of a substance that the federal law prohibits.

> *Problem #2.* While federal agents, through interdiction efforts, were attempting to curb the flow of drugs into the country, a simultaneous signal was also sent to the traffickers in foreign source countries such as Colombia and Mexico. The message was that the United States does not want foreign-made drugs brought into the country yet, at the same time, certain jurisdictions in the United States condone drug use.

> *Problem #3.* Although the state of Alaska permitted the personal use of marijuana in the home, it refused to allow the drug to be sold in the state. So, in order to support the marijuana appetite for drug users, a vast illicit pot growing network was created to meet the demands of the consumer. This developed drug manufacturing problems for not just Alaska but for neighboring states such as Washington and Oregon.

In addition, when drug dealers were arrested in Alaska, the moral stigma was removed as they were seen as merely trying to furnish a product that was already legalized by the state government. Additionally, the penalty for an individual over 18 years of age found in possession of marijuana in a public place was a civil fine of only $100.

In summation, after considerable public outcry over the rise of adolescent drug abuse in Alaska, a voter proposition was passed in November 1990 to "recriminalize" possession of any amount of marijuana. As a result, even small quantities of marijuana are punishable by up to 90 days in jail and a $1,000 fine.

A Proposed Solution

Unquestionably, the issue of legalizing drugs should be debated, as should any other strategy for solving the nation's drug woes. It would seem, however, that legalization is an option whose time has not yet come. To date, the best strategies for fighting the "drug war" are through the use of education, prevention, rehabilitation, and innovative law enforcement strategies.

The appropriateness of some law enforcement tactics remains the topic of a vigorous debate, even among police executives. It is doubtful, however, that interdiction, eradication, and intensive street-level enforcement strategies alone will yield a "quick fix" to the drug problem. It should be remembered that America's perceptions of its drug problem have emerged from more than a century of changing attitudes, morals, and standards of living. Because drug use is a complex social problem, we must expect the solutions to be equally complex.

Perhaps when considering a solution to the problem, we should be aware of the successes that have been achieved over the years in reducing tobacco consumption. The positive image of the cigarette smoker has been greatly minimized over the last ten years due to public campaigns deglamorizing tobacco. This began with a government anti-smoking campaign, which was later embraced by Hollywood and segments of the media. For example, in a report from the Surgeon General, the nation's nicotine addiction rate was at 40 percent in 1964; today, it stands at 30 percent, not a great difference but a significant one that is considered by public health officials to be a notable victory. As parts of a proposed solution, there are several possibilities that opponents of drug legalization are considering as viable although sometimes contradictory alternatives. Let's look at each of these.

1. *Deglamorize Drugs.* This might be the single most important component of drug control in the 1990s. As mentioned earlier, the success of the deglamorization of tobacco became evident in the decrease in tobacco use and cigarette smoking over a 25-year period. In the deglamorizing process, massive drug education programs in the schools combined with anti-drug advertising in the media should convince would-be drug users not to use illegal substances.

   All available evidence suggests that drug education is the most effective means of drug control. However, such a strategy would require either a massive infusion of new money into educational programs or a major diversion of present funds from other drug control efforts in order to be successful. Present drug education efforts are woefully underfunded.

2. *Boycott Drugs.* It could be argued that if people can successfully boycott grapes, fur and leather clothing, and the killing of baby seals, then why not organize an embargo on illicit drugs. In addition to the deterrent effect of arrest and prosecution, education and prevention programs are our best ways to encourage a national initiative to boycott the illicit drug trade and dry up demand.

3. *Rehabilitate and Counsel*. Once again, considerable research points to great successes in drug rehabilitation and drug counseling. The problem is that these programs are simply not available where they are needed (particularly the inner city) nor are they available in sufficient numbers (most drug rehabilitation programs targeted at lower income groups have long waiting lists). To make use of this promising strategy, new revenues would have to be created or present allocations would have to be diverted from other sources.

4. *Target the Drug User*. A fact of drug enforcement is that to quell the drug problem, either the supply or demand (or both) of the drugs has to be reduced. Obviously, in focusing resources on interdiction of drugs (i.e., reducing the supply), international and political problems are encountered. These pose serious questions regarding the legality and appropriateness of international law enforcement. An alternative is, of course, to focus our law enforcement resources on the drug user here in our own country. This would send the message that even idle drug use is not tolerated.

5. *Break Down the Trafficking Infrastructure*. This solution is in precise contradiction to the idea of targeting the user. Experts in organized crime have long argued that criminal organizations cannot be controlled by either a "headhunting" strategy (arresting as many illicit entrepreneurs as possible) or by attacking consumers. They argue that the way to control organized drug trafficking is to make the business of drugs very difficult to conduct.

   Essential to successful criminal organizations are money laundering mechanisms and corruption, as these make up the infrastructure of the drug organizations. It is argued that the United States facilitates organized crime of all types and drug trafficking in particular in that, unlike almost any other western nation, we exercise little regulatory control over the activities of corporations, banks, holding companies, trusts, and the like. Stepped-up reporting requirements, stiff penalties, and the reallocation of law enforcement resources from users to the business community allies of drug organizations, it is argued, would strangle the cartels in their own money. In addition, it is axiomatic in the organized crime literature that corruption is necessary for success. Similar targeting of law enforcement and political corruption would make the logistics of drug trafficking very difficult indeed. This strategy would shift the aim of enforcement strategies from users and small-time dealers to their "upperworld" partners, who have much more to lose and are more easily deterred.

6. *Broaden Forfeiture Sanctions*. The use of forfeiture sanctions against drug offenders has proven to be a valuable asset to law enforcement in the drug war. As an alternative to incarceration, perhaps imposing stricter forfeiture sanctions against dealers would deter some drug crimes and would supply law enforcement with additional financial resources. Additionally, there is a strong argument to be made for the expansion of forfeiture laws to include money laundering activities by legitimate business allies of drug traffickers. An investment house faced with the seizure of its depositors' assets might be less likely to handle dirty money.

7. *Impose Harsh Fines*. This is yet another alternative to incarceration of drug dealers and users. The use of strict and harsh fines might serve as a deterrent to criminal activity and would aid in financing drug education, rehabilitation, and law enforcement efforts.

A Word from the Authors

Debating a controversial public issue such as this and adequately deliberating all important considerations of the issue is not an easy task. Headway in arriving at a viable solution is frequently stifled by fragmented (mis)information promulgated by people that are merely trying to "muddy the waters" or promote their own personal interests. Clearly, drug dealers and consumers represent one such interest group, but so do some government bureaucracies that do not want to give up funding, private hospitals that profit from drug abuse and related problems, and politicians that often seek votes through emotion and fear rather than reason.

Perhaps one can argue that our country has slowly evolved into a passive society that is becoming both drug and violence-tolerant. The drug problem for many is merely one that is seen on television or read about in the local newspaper. Unfortunately, many people have an "ostrich type" mind set in that just because they are not victims of drug abuse or because they do not personally know a victim, they believe the drug problem is somebody else's concern.

Additionally, drug users frequently consider themselves victims of governmental and societal repression rather than victims of drug abuse. Accordingly, many people view a "victim" of drug abuse as one that suffers an overdose or experiences some negative physical manifestation created by the use of a particular substance. When this occurs, little consideration is given to the drug user's employer and coworkers that are affected by the user's inability to function on the job; the taxpayer that foots the bill for drug enforcement; and the costs of expensive and often lengthy drug trials, incarceration, and treatment programs for drug dependent people.

In addition, the unsuspecting victims of drug crimes suffer from fatal accidents, assaults, robberies, or murders. In cases of drive-by shootings, the murderers are often intoxicated, under the influence of drugs, or consciously operating on behalf of drug-dealing groups.

For others, the drug problem is one that needs a "quick fix" and, therefore, should be easily remedied through either ill-conceived legalization policies or, on the other extreme, the introduction of repressive law enforcement measures. Our country's drug problems are the product of more than 100 years of social change and evolution, touch-and-go drug control policy, and a myriad of other factors, such as the media and the entertainment industry. Additionally, a passive reluctance seems to exist on the part of our present-day society to learn from past historical experience in dealing with drug abuse.

It is clear that solutions, whatever they are, will be time consuming and will no doubt require equal yet positive participation on the part of law enforcement, schools, colleges and universities, researchers, and social treatment programs. In addition, an effective drug control policy must include unified participation from a general public that is both willing, informed, and ready to make constructive choices about controlling drug use and related criminal activity.

Do you recognize these terms?

British system   medical model
decriminalization   recreational drugs
legalization   red light district

Discussion Questions

1. What are the arguments for the legalization of drugs, and how realistic are those arguments?

2. Discuss the possible consequences of drug legalization with regard to public health.

3. List the arguments for not legalizing drugs.

4. If drugs are never legalized in the United States, then what other measures could be considered to insure public safety and health?

5. What would be the possible effects of drug legalization on drug gangs and organized crime groups?

6. How would legalizing drugs in the United States affect international relations or efforts to control "black market" drugs entering the country from foreign sources?

7. What are the social consequences of Amsterdam's drug policies?

8. How would legalizing drugs affect domestic production of "black market" drugs in the United States?

9. Discuss the 1975 Alaska *Ravin* case and how it has affected issues such as personal freedom, public safety, and public health in Alaska.

10. Discuss Britain's experiment with legalizing heroin.

11. Discuss your interpretation of the social changes over the last 20 years that have affected public attitudes either for or against legalization of drugs.

Class Projects

1. In considering the question of legalization of drugs, what patterns of criminality or addiction do you feel would evolve if drugs were legalized?

2. Survey classmates or friends to see what their position is on the legalization issue. Take note of the reasons given to support their position; are these realistic or rational?

Understanding Drug Control Policy

13

This chapter will enable you to:

- Understand social and political philosophies of drug policy
- Learn which government and private agencies share responsibility for drug control
- Appreciate the contribution of private industry in drug control
- Compare and contrast federal drug control strategies
- Consider both supply- and demand-oriented drug policies
- Understand the utility of federal drug control legislation

Perhaps one of the greatest ironies in the search for a modern, workable drug control policy is that most people, despite their political preferences or social differences, desire basically the same thing: a safe society. As simplistic as that may sound, the truth is that most of us want to live in our neighborhoods without fear of drive-by shootings and crack houses. We want our schools and places of employment drug free. And we want to have the peace of mind of knowing that the lives of our loved ones are not ruined by drug abuse. So then, what should be done? What approaches are best?

Over the decades, local and national drug control initiatives have resulted in the hiring and training of more law enforcement officers, a more expanded interdiction campaign, the development of more education programs, and the establishment of more treatment and prevention programs than ever before in history. Yet, the drug problem persists.

To begin our discussion on drug control policy, let's first consider one of the absurdities in modern drug control policy thinking which might serve to illustrate the philosophy of today's failed drug policy. During the mid-1980s, it was surprising and even horrifying when the House passed an amendment requiring the military to "seal the borders" against drugs within 45 days. Although the amendment was defeated by the Senate, the nature of our dysfunctional national drug control policy became glaringly apparent. After all, how could such a mandate be fulfilled with over 88,000 miles of U.S. coastline, 7,500 miles of borders with Mexico and Canada, and 300 ports of entry?

Today, the so-called drug war has mostly resulted in more than two-thirds of the federal drug budget being diverted to law enforcement, interdiction, and foreign initiatives. This budgetary scenario was nearly the opposite when President Nixon launched the war on drugs more than 20 years ago. Under Nixon's administration, two initiatives were pursued: *enforcement* through interdiction and *treatment* through the recently developed methadone maintenance program, which focused on treating hard-core heroin addicts. The Carter Administration quickly sought to downplay the drug problem and to scale back enforcement initiatives. Instead, a program of **eradication** was implemented in which the herbicide Paraquat was used to eliminate marijuana fields in Mexico. Next, the Reagan Administration took a hard stance against drug offenders by supporting the passage of several powerful drug control measures and initiating the Pentagon into the national drug control effort. George Bush, followed through by expanding Reagan's initiatives, spending more on the drug effort than all previous presidents combined (Wilkinson, 1994).

But establishing a workable drug control policy is a strange and complicated social undertaking. As we observed earlier in this book, many countries, such as China and Babylonia, were early victims of drug use and also may have been among the first to recognize a fundamental correlation between drug use and crime. Lawmakers during that period recognized that a large percentage of people were unable to make judgments about their own ability to safely use mind-altering and addicting substances and, therefore, posed a threat to public order and safety. Furthermore, these early laws characterized the necessity of government to attempt to control drug-related crime by making it unlawful to use, possess, or traffic in dangerous substances.

In the United States, the federal response to the nation's drug problem is dynamic with both successes *and* failures. Critics of current federal drug policy and proponents of drug legalization claim that laws designed to control drug use and related activity violate personal freedoms and the spirit of the Constitution and as a result are too repressive in nature (see Chapter 12). They maintain that the government has no business regulating and criminalizing public morals. However, if the history of global drug use offers any yardstick as to the dangers of drugs and related activity, as many feel it does, then the option of decriminalization or legalization is not a viable one. So, if we reject decriminalization/legalization, the remaining alternative is to outlaw dangerous drugs, prosecute offenders, and attempt through numerous public programs and policies to deter individual involvement with substances that are thought to be dangerous.

In addition to physical and psychological harm done by drug abuse, one of the most threatening components to the illicit drug problem is the paralleling issue of organized crime. As we discussed in Chapter 7, the term means many things to many people, but a significant number of groups that comprise organized crime provide a perfect mechanism for the manufacturing, trafficking, and managing of criminal drug operations. Ways to dismantle these groups should also be a part of today's drug policy approach.

Typically, the nation's drug control policy cycle shows how the government assumes a particular method of dealing with drug use and trafficking, and drug users and traffickers then take defensive measures to counter those policies. The government then assumes yet a different strategy, which causes the traffickers to again take defensive actions, and so the cycle goes. This reactive response has characterized the federal drug control strategy for decades but especially since the 1960s. As we will see in the upcoming discussion, federal controls in the last 80 years have generally focused on the supply of illicit drugs rather than attacked the public demand for them. In 1986, the President's Commission on Organized Crime (America's Habit, 1986) made the following remarks regarding supply and demand policies:

> Although the supply and demand of drugs have often been considered separate issues, by both the public and private sectors, they are in fact inseparable parts of a single problem. The success of supply efforts is related to commitments made to reduce the demand for drugs through drug abuse education, treatment, research, vigorous enforcement of drug laws, and effective sentencing. Drug supply and demand operate in an interrelated and dynamic manner. The strategies employed to limit each should be similarly connected.

Today, politicians continue to support measures designed to control drug use. These measures have been in response to growing public demands for increased use of drug testing in the work force, stricter laws dealing with both drug users and dealers, and renewed attempts by government to curtail drug-related corruption.

On one hand, it may seem that today's national focus on drug control is so intense that faulty drug control initiatives go unchecked, immunized from critical examination. On the other hand, widespread community concern and a tendency toward making the public more aware of domestic drug policy may provide an adequate check against misuse of governmental power.

Shared Responsibility

Over the years efforts in drug control have involved a fusion of agencies operating at virtually all levels of government. Essentially, they call on the functions of local, state, and federal government. At the federal level, international relations are concerned with regard to the manufacture, smuggling, and sale of drugs in the United States. The primary responsibility for drug control, however, rests with state and local agencies as they are closest to the drug problem in our communities. For example, as we will discuss in the following chapter, education, prevention, and treatment programs exist almost exclusively at the local and state level and are administered in our school districts and state and regional health organizations. Local schools provide prevention drug abuse information to children while treatment services are administered in residential and outpatient facilities in most every community. The role of the federal government in these areas is essentially to provide funding and technical assistance through the Departments of Education, and Health and Human Services.

Justice system responses to the drug problem are primarily the function of state and local agencies. It is safe to say, however, that with drug trafficking being such a significant international problem, federal law enforcement organizations are more heavily involved in drug control than in almost any other type of federal criminal offense. Still, it is state and local law enforcement agencies that are faced with the harsh realities of the nation's drug war.

Development of Federal Drug Control Efforts

Although states have always had police authority, under the Constitution the federal government was originally granted power to raise taxes and handle international relations, not police its citizens. As we learned in Chapter 1, at the turn of the century federal control over drug abuse and prescription practices was considered unconstitutional. Thus, federal drug control efforts were restricted to tactics within federal authority, in particular, the ability to tax the people and develop international treaties. Again, we explained how during the late 1800s state laws, specifically those aimed at cocaine and morphine, required that drugs be obtainable only by a doctor's prescription. These laws were generally ineffective because controlled drugs could be transported from other states which didn't have such restrictions. At the turn of the century the federal government became active in drug control efforts through the State Department's participation in international initiatives. The majority of these were in the form of international conferences such as the 1909 Shanghai Opium Convention, the 1911 International Conference on Opium (The Hague), and the 1913 International Opium Convention. The result was congressional approval of the Harrison Narcotics Act in 1914, which used the federal government's authority to raise taxes and regulate the manufacture and sale of certain drugs. The broad enforcement powers of the Harrison Narcotics Act were upheld in two crucial U.S. Supreme Court decisions: *U.S. v. Doremus* and *Webb v. U.S.* For the following 50 years, the Harrison Narcotics Act remained the basis for federal narcotics regulation.

In 1970 the myriad regulations and amendments to the Harrison Narcotics Act were consolidated into a new piece of federal legislation, which became known as the Controlled Substances Act (officially titled the Comprehensive Drug Abuse Prevention and Control Act). Under the new legislation, courts interpreted powers of commerce as the new basis for drug control, supplanting the need for the government to portray the police function of drug control as a tax measure.

Policy-Related Factors

Although the federal government has adopted its own drug control policy and enforcement initiatives, for the most part such efforts are a local option. This means that drug laws, policing policies, and prosecution philosophies are all driven by local governmental initiatives. For example, in the case of drug enforcement options, a drug dealer facing state criminal charges may be given the choice to cooperate with police, testify against other drug dealers, or risk going to jail. Local authorities have full authority to make such an offer and do so every day. Police can also choose any number of enforcement methods and techniques, which include gang sweeps, undercover operations, wire taps, and reverse stings.

Regardless of the enforcement options chosen, these tactics have a significant impact on the criminal justice system in the community, especially in the adjudicatory process, which includes the courts, prosecution, and public defense. For example, operations such as street sweeps result in a high number of people being arrested and ultimately being convicted and receiving prison sentences. On the other hand, so-called kingpin strategies, where upper-level traffickers are targeted by police, often result in lengthy trials and related criminal proceedings which also place financial and logistical burdens on the justice system. Even the investigation phase of drug kingpins poses special concerns to police in that these investigations are costly and lengthy, and the only outcome may be the arrest of a handful of people. Although those arrested may be primary managers in crime organizations, members of the public are sometimes slow in realizing the importance of such investigations as opposed to street sweeps of low-level dealers whose arrests make attractive media headlines but in actuality are easily replaced by the kingpins whom they serve.

Complicating drug control policy is the problem of variances in drug use from one area to another. Crack cocaine seems to be the predominant problem in many major metropolitan cities while in rural areas drugs like methamphetamine and marijuana are more widely abused. In addition to the different drugs of abuse, consequences of the drug trade also differ from one area to another. In particular, with regard to drug-related violence, trends vary from one city to another. For example, drug-related homicides in Washington D.C. increased dramatically from 1989 to 1990 while other cities, such as Los Angeles and San Francisco, did not experience similar increases in violence (BJS, 1992).

Private Sector Responses

Organizations and agencies not affiliated with government have also risen to combat the nation's drug abuse problem. Many companies have developed extensive drug prevention programs for their communities. As we will discuss in the following chapter, the Drug Abuse Resistance Education (DARE) program frequently has corporate sponsorship. Furthermore, the media provide free air time for public service drug abuse prevention announcements, and many companies require prospective employees to undergo drug testing. In recent years, private companies whose employees have developed drug problems offer employee assistance programs whereby referral services offer treatment options. Accordingly, many treatment facilities are privately owned, and benefits are usually covered by private insurance companies as well.

The Role of the Military

We learned how thousands of military veterans during the Civil War became hopelessly addicted to morphine. With the exception of that war, the military has had little experience with controlling drug abuse and trafficking. It was in 1967, during the Vietnam War, that a special Department of Defense (DOD) task force was established to study the extent of drug abuse by American troops assigned to Vietnam and other areas in Europe. In 1972 a key policy directive, born out of the "drug scare" of the 1960s, recommended preventive drug and alcohol abuse education along with strict enforcement procedures and the establishment of treatment policies.

In 1980, a new DOD directive was established to replace the 1972 initiative. The new policy reflected a stricter, less tolerant attitude toward drug abuse and was a drastic departure from the military's previous treatment-oriented attitude. 1980 was also an important year due to a major incident—the "under-the-influence" crash of a jet airplane on the aircraft carrier USS Nimitz with 14 Navy personnel killed and 44 seriously injured. This incident illustrated the extent of the military's drug problem and resulted in the establishment of urine testing for drugs by 1981. The DOD's drug testing policy is still firmly in place today.

Development of American Drug Policy

American drug control policy has evolved over a period of time and has undergone a number of distinctive phases. As we discussed in Chapter 1, the earliest drug control efforts focused on regulation, (1906 Food and Drug Act), taxation (1914 Harrison Narcotics Act), and prohibition (1970 Controlled Substances Act). **Regulation** of drugs specifies the circumstances under which they can be lawfully distributed and used. Prescription medications and alcohol are the most commonly regulated drugs. **Taxation** requires those who legally produce, distribute, or possess drugs to pay a fee based on the quantity or value of the drugs. Criminal penalties result for failure to pay taxes rather than for specific drug violations themselves.

Next, international efforts attempted to establish cooperation between the U.S. and foreign countries sharing similar drug abuse problems. Afterward, policies moved toward **prohibition** efforts with a focus on enforcement of criminal sanctions and, more recently, civil penalties. The essence of prohibition is the ban on manufacturing, distribution, and use of drugs which are designated as illegal under state and federal law. Violators face prosecution and an array of penalties from the imposition of fines to imprisonment.

Today, criminal penalties for drug violations have become firmly imbedded in drug control public policy. Although it is unlikely that there will be much support for the abandonment of criminal sanctions, a few scholars and legal practitioners have suggested that the "crime control" model of drug control be abandoned and that drug legalization be considered under a new "medical model" of drug control. Suggestions have ranged from totally removing criminal penalties to a system of regulation similar to that used in the manufacture and distribution of cigarettes and alcohol. Instead of total legalization, some have even suggested a system of decriminalization whereby penalties for possession or distribution of certain drugs would be reduced. During the 1970s several states attempted to do just that. Complicating the drug policy question is the fact that drug abuse trends change over time. For example, at the turn of the century heroin and opium products were the main drugs of concern. Through the years other drugs such as marijuana, barbiturates, LSD, PCP, and more recently crack cocaine became popular.

Because of the complexity of today's drug problem, control initiatives are varied and widely utilized. Each policy incorporates its own tactics and strategies to further its successful implementation. For example, drug prohibition is the predominant control policy in today's local and national arena. Strategies for accomplishing drug prohibition include both demand and supply reduction, and each of these are supported by law enforcement and drug treatment programs. Let's now consider some particulars of demand and supply since these strategies are the cornerstone of our national drug control policy.

Demand Reduction

Those who believe that the market for illicit drugs is the reason for the country's drug problem also believe that users of drugs should be targeted by police. In theory, once users are sufficiently afraid to purchase drugs for fear of being arrested, fewer customers mean higher prices for drugs. If prices can be raised high enough, the profit margin for dealers will be too low to make it worth their while. Another demand reduction philosophy focuses on changing the behavior of drug users or potential users. This is accomplished by programs such as DARE, which are aimed at resisting peer pressure and informing people about the dangers of drug abuse. The power of such programs is their ability to thwart the onset of drug use by potential first-time users.

Zero tolerance was discussed in Chapter 11 as a demand reduction policy option. This policy holds drug users, sellers, and buyers fully accountable for their offenses under law. The philosophy behind zero tolerance is that violators

Figure 13.1

A wide variety of policies, strategies, and tactics have been used to control the illegal drug problem

■ Policies

Prohibition is the ban on the distribution, possesion, and use of specified substances made illegal by legislative or administrative order and the application of criminal penalties to violators.

Regulation is control over the distribution, possession, and use of specified substances. Regulations specify the circumstances under which substances can be legally distributed and used. Prescription medications and alcohol are the substances most commonly regulated in the U.S.

■ Strategies

Demand reduction strategies attempt to decrease individuals' tendency to use drugs. Efforts provide information and education to potential and casual users about the risks and adverse consequences of drug use, and treatment to drug users who have developed problems from using drugs.

Supply reduction focuses diplomatic, law enforcement, military, and other resources on eliminating or reducing the supply of drugs. Efforts focus on foreign countries, smuggling routes outside the country, border interdiction, and distribution within the U.S.

User accountability emphasizes that all users of illegal substances, regardless of the type of drug they use or the frequency of that use, are violating criminal laws and should be subject to penalties. It is closely associated with zero tolerance.

Zero tolerance holds that drug distributors, buyers, and users should be held fully accountable for their offenses under the law. This is an alternative to policies that focus only on some violators such as sellers of drugs or users of cocaine and heroin while ignoring other violators.

■ Tactics

Criminal justice activities include enforcement, prosecution, and sentencing activities to apprehend, convict, and punish drug offenders. Although thought of primarily as having supply reduction goals, criminal sanctions also have demand reduction effects by discouraging drug use.

Prevention activities are educational efforts to inform potential drug users about the health, legal, and other risks associated with drug use. Their goal is to limit the number of new drug users and dissuade casual users from continuing drug use as part of a demand reduction strategy.

Taxation requires those who produce, distribute, or possess drugs to pay a fee based on the volume or value of the drugs. Failure to pay subjects violators to penalties for this violation, not for the drug activities themselves.

Testing individuals for the presence of drugs is a tool in drug control that is used for safety and monitoring purposes and as an adjunct to therapeutic interventions. It is in widespread use for employees in certain jobs such as those in the transportation industry and criminal justice agencies. New arrestees and convicted offenders may be tested. Individuals in treatment are often tested to monitor their progress and provide them an incentive to remain drug free.

Treatment (therapeutic interventions) focus on individuals whose drug use has caused medical, psychological, economic, and social problems for them. The interventions may include medication, counseling, and other support services delivered in an inpatient setting or on an outpatient basis. These are demand reduction activities to eliminate or reduce individuals' drug use.

of drug laws, even for the smallest amounts of drugs, should be held criminally responsible for their actions (see Chapter 11).

Supply Reduction

Enforcement initiatives typically focus on reducing supply of drugs through arrest and prosecution of those responsible for their manufacture, distribution, and sales. The availability of drugs can also be reduced through special approaches such as crop eradication programs, investigation of smuggling routes, and interdiction of drugs at U.S. borders. For the most part, supply reduction programs rely on domestic law enforcement and criminal justice system responses.

Other Variables

Although the above policies have shared some successes in controlling drug use and trafficking, other factors which also have an impact on supply and demand should also be considered. For example, intense *police initiatives* such as gang sweeps, undercover operations, and reverse stings also tend to (at least temporarily) disrupt supplies in local drug markets and make drug buyers themselves fearful of being arrested. In other cases, courts have imposed *mandatory drug treatment* of addicts, resulting in many of them reducing their drug usage and consequently reducing their frequency of drug purchases.

Strategies in National Drug Control

Since the early 1970s, the U.S. government has devised a series of strategies designed to combat the nation's drug problem. Strategies are the ways and means in which drug policy can be set in motion and typically include an array of programs and tactics. During 1973, 1974, and 1975, documents titled *Federal Strategy for Drug Abuse and Drug Traffic Prevention* were published. Each was designed to identify problems and possible solutions to drug abuse trends in the nation. Similar publications were produced in 1976, 1979, and again in 1982, all focusing on similar drug-related issues. In 1984 the first federal effort referring to itself as a "national strategy" was published by the White House Drug Abuse Policy Office, followed in 1987 and 1988 by publications from the White House Conference for a Drug-Free America.

Essentially, the 1973 strategies focused on the reduction of drug abuse and identification of those drugs that cause the greatest harm to society. The focus shifted somewhat by 1976 when the federal strategy initiated the "lead agency concept" by making the Justice Department responsible for enforcement of federal drug laws. In 1988, the Office of National Drug Control Policy (ONDCP) was developed. As part of its charge, comprehensive plans are required to be published each year on federal drug control policy issues. Statistics are also offered regarding issues such as:

- current overall drug use
- cocaine use
- adolescent drug use
- drug availability
- marijuana production
- student attitudes toward drugs

In addition, each National Drug Control Strategy identifies national priorities in the areas of drug enforcement, prevention, treatment, international initiatives, and drug education.

Drug Control in the Reagan-Bush Era

In 1980, when Ronald Reagan was elected president, the general consensus within the federal drug control community was positive. Many drug enforcement practitioners "were soon disappointed—Reagan talked a good game, but despite his speeches bemoaning the threat of violent crime, when it came to more money for fighting crime, including drug traffickers, Reagan was as parsimonious as Carter" (Shannon, 1988).

In 1981, Reagan, under the prodding of his legal adviser David Stockman, declared a 12 percent across-the-board cut for all federal agencies except the Pentagon. Drug enforcement was not spared, and certain effects were felt immediately. DEA and Customs airplanes and cars were grounded; money to make undercover drug transactions ran out. Things changed, however, during the years following the recession of the early 1980s as the Reagan administration's spending on drug law enforcement more than tripled, from $800 million in fiscal year (FY) 1981 to $2.5 billion for FY 1988. The administration soon emphasized the supply side in its war on drugs: More than 70 percent of 1988 federal anti-drug spending was earmarked for law enforcement programs such as crop eradication in foreign source countries and the interdiction of drugs entering the United States from foreign countries (see Chapter 4).

Reagan-era drug control initiatives included the passing of the Department of Defense Authorization Act of 1982. This act contained a provision called "Military Cooperation with Civilian Law Enforcement Authorities," which permitted military personnel to operate military equipment that had been loaned to civilian drug law enforcement agencies. The act otherwise broadened the authority of the military in national drug control efforts.

The years between 1984 and 1990 proved to be prolific for drug control legislation. An example of some of the most important laws passed during this period include:

- *The Comprehensive Crime Control Act of 1984.* This act increased many existing penalties for drug offenses. In addition, it expanded criminal and civil asset forfeiture laws, established a determinate federal sentencing system, and provided for pre-trial detention of defendants accused of serious drug offenses.

- *The Comprehensive Forfeiture Act of 1984.* Extensive revisions of federal, civil, and criminal forfeiture laws were made in the passing of this act. In part, the act streamlined the process in which personal assets could be seized by federal and state officers.

- *The Anti-Drug Abuse Act of 1986.* Among other things this act provided special funding for prevention and treatment programs, restored mandatory prison sentences for large-scale marijuana violators, provided new penalties for money laundering, and added controlled substances' analogs (for making designer drugs) to the drug schedule.

- *The Anti-Drug Abuse Act of 1988* was yet another, more comprehensive drug bill designed to shift drug control policy priorities from the supply to the demand side. In this legislation, a set of strict penalties focused on the recreational drug user rather than the drug dealer. Another controversial provision of the bill allowed for, but did not require, the death penalty for anyone that kills a policeman during the commission of a drug-related crime and for murderers that have been involved in at least two drug-related crimes.

- The *Crime Control Act of 1990* further defined sanctions for drug violations. It expanded regulation of precursor chemicals used in drug laboratories; outlawed anabolic steroids under the Controlled Substances Act; and provided for increased penalties for international money laundering, additional funding for rural drug enforcement, and drug-free school zones.

The U.S. Build-Up in Latin America

Generally speaking, the international thrust of the drug war is led by the State Department's Bureau of International Narcotics Matters. The Bureau controls an interregional air wing of more than 50 aircraft, which include fixed-wing, C-123 cargo transports and Vietnam-era helicopters. The aircraft are used to ferry troops, move supplies, and most important, to spray crops (Massing, 1990). Eradication initiatives by the State Department include the spraying of coca, marijuana, and poppy fields in Colombia, Guatemala, Belize, Jamaica, and Mexico.

While the Bureau monitors the skies, the Drug Enforcement Administration (DEA) focuses on ground smuggling. Traditionally assigned to domestic drug enforcement, the DEA is strengthening its presence in Latin America. Today, more than 150 agents work in 17 countries. Agency personnel are also

Figure 13.2

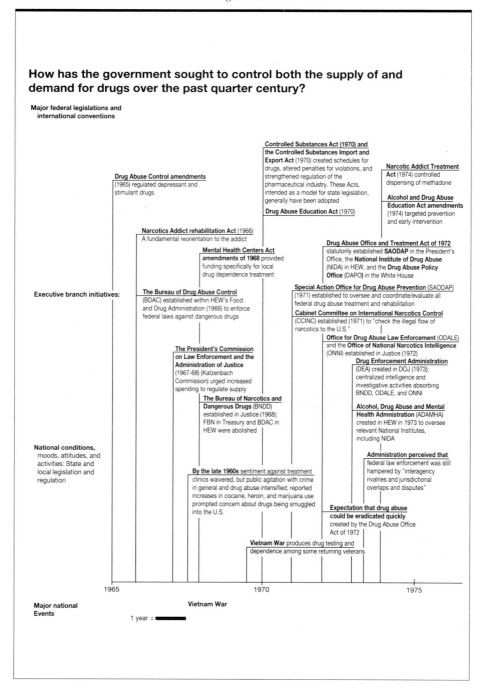

How has the government sought to control both the supply of and demand for drugs over the past quarter century?

Major federal legislations and international conventions

Controlled Substances Act (1970) and the Controlled Substances Import and Export Act (1970) created schedules for drugs, altered penalties for violations, and strengthened regulation of the pharmaceutical industry. These Acts, intended as a model for state legislation, generally have been adopted

Narcotic Addict Treatment Act (1974) controlled dispensing of methadone

Alcohol and Drug Abuse Education Act amendments (1974) targeted prevention and early intervention

Drug Abuse Control amendments (1965) regulated depressant and stimulant drugs

Drug Abuse Education Act (1970)

Narcotics Addict rehabilitation Act (1966) A fundamental reorientation to the addict

Drug Abuse Office and Treatment Act of 1972 statutorily established **SAODAP** in the President's Office, the **National Institute of Drug Abuse** (NIDA) in HEW, and the **Drug Abuse Policy Office** (DAPO) in the White House

Mental Health Centers Act amendments of 1968 provided funding specifically for local drug dependence treatment

Special Action Office for Drug Abuse Prevention (SAODAP) (1971) established to oversee and coordinate/evaluate all federal drug abuse treatment and rehabilitation

Executive branch initiatives:

The Bureau of Drug Abuse Control (BDAC) established within HEW's Food and Drug Administration (1966) to enforce federal laws against dangerous drugs

Cabinet Committee on International Narcotics Control (CCINC) established (1971) to "check the illegal flow of narcotics to the U.S."

Office for Drug Abuse Law Enforcement (ODALE) and the **Office of National Narcotics Intelligence** (ONNI) established in Justice (1972)

The President's Commission on Law Enforcement and the Administration of Justice (1967-68) (Katzenbach Commission) urged increased spending to regulate supply

Drug Enforcement Administration (DEA) created in DOJ (1973); centralized intelligence and investigative activities absorbing BNDD, ODALE, and ONNI

The Bureau of Narcotics and Dangerous Drugs (BNDD) established in Justice (1968); FBN in Treasury and BDAC in HEW were abolished

Alcohol, Drug Abuse and Mental Health Admistration (ADAMHA) created in HEW in 1973 to oversee relevant National Institutes, including NIDA

Administration perceived that federal law enforcement was still hampered by "interagency rivalries and jurisdictional overlaps and disputes"

National conditions, moods, attitudes, and activities: State and local legislation and regulation

By the late 1960s sentiment against treatment clinics waivered, but public agitation with crime in general and drug abuse intensified; reported increases in cocaine, heroin, and marijuana use prompted concern about drugs being smuggled into the U.S.

Expectation that drug abuse could be eradicated quickly created by the Drug Abuse Office Act of 1972

Vietnam War produces drug testing and dependence among some returning veterans

1965   1970   1975

Major national Events

Vietnam War

1 year = ▰▰▰

Figure 13.2, *continued*

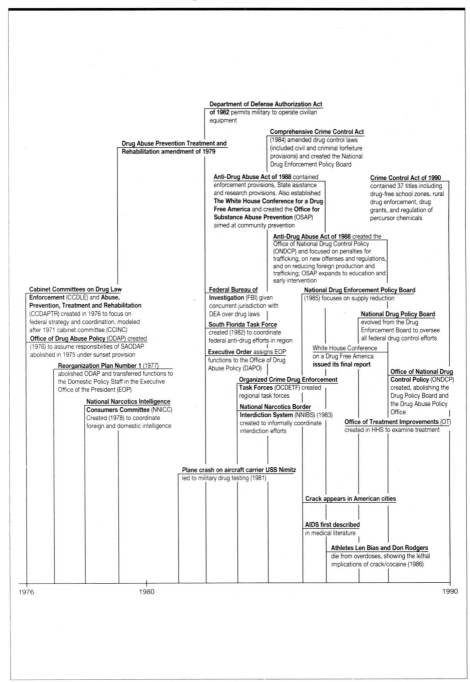

Source: Bureau of Justice Statistics, 1992.

more and more involved in paramilitary actions in the coca-growing regions of South America, where, armed with machine guns and jungle knives, they conduct helicopter raids on processing labs and clandestine air strips.

The Central Intelligence Agency (CIA) has also expanded its presence in Latin America in recent years, with new agents assigned to Colombia, Peru, and Bolivia, just to name a few. At CIA headquarters in Langley, Virginia, the agency's Counter-Narcotics Center collates the steady stream of data coming from agents, informants, wiretaps, radar, and satellites.

The Pentagon is yet another player in United States-Latin American drug control. The U.S. Southern Command in Panama is stepping up activities in Latin America. To this end, the situations in Andean nations are regularly assessed to determine the needs of the local military and police. For example, in 1988 Colombia, Peru, and Bolivia received a total of $3 million in military aid, compared to the estimated 1990 total of $170 million (Massing, 1990). During the latter part of the 1980s, the U.S. Customs Service also extended its services to Latin America to assist drug source countries in sealing their borders. In addition, the Coast Guard has commissioned mobile training teams to instruct local police officers in river interdiction.

Drug Control and the Clinton Administration

Reminiscent of President Jimmy Carter's lackluster drug policy of the late 1970s, national drug control policy has shown little promise or initiative since Bill Clinton was elected President in 1992. Although before the election Clinton sharply criticized Bush's policy of locking up drug offenders, once elected, his passion for the issue faded. Clinton's election platform promised federal assistance for community-based drug treatment programs and expanded drug education programs in schools. At the same time, he emphasized that strong innovative drug enforcement is also an important component to dealing with the nation's drug problem—all seemingly legitimate public concerns.

However, these promises turned out to be little more than campaign rhetoric. Once in office, Clinton had little to say about drug policy. In addition to inaction and indecisiveness, he was criticized for massive staff cutbacks at the Office of National Drug Control Policy as well as lengthy delays in appointing its director. There were also delays in the submission of the administration's annual drug control strategy. Furthermore, critics complained about Clinton's efforts in cutting funding for national drug interdiction programs to the tune of $94 million from the budgeted $1.3 billion allocated for that purpose. Though the policy says otherwise, the administration claims to be replacing interdiction, a failed policy of the 1980s, with a renewed emphasis in source reduction, a failed policy of the 1970s (Wilkinson, 1994).

One of the few times President Clinton spoke out against drugs, however, was in December 1993, when then-Surgeon General Joycelyn Elders publicly suggested that the effects of drug legalization should be studied. Clinton's response was characterized as both knee-jerk and anti-intellectual when he proclaimed "no way, no how, not now, not ever." Possibly more troublesome was the abandonment of his pledge to reverse the ratio of spending on drug interdiction versus treatment, a split that continues to allocate $13.1 billion of federal anti-drug money in favor of law enforcement by more than two to one (Kramer, 1993). Although Clinton has supported efforts to increase drug treatment in prisons, his commitment has lacked conviction in the area of community-based treatment efforts. In 1993, there were an estimated 12,000 long-term, residential treatment beds available in the U.S. Clinton's critics have argued that without an increase in drug treatment funding outside the criminal justice system, most addicts will be forced to commit crimes before being treated. They have further suggested that the $18,000 per year (per patient) cost for treatment is still lower than what it would be to house an offender in prison. Although, Clinton did indeed allocate more funding for national treatment efforts, his efforts were less than promising. In 1994, the Clinton Administration proposed a 14 percent increase in drug treatment funding, which, according to the Drug Policy Foundation, would only serve a mere 5 percent of the nation's 2.7 million addicts (Wilkinson, 1994).

Politics and the ONDCP

One of the perennial hindrances to a workable drug control policy is the political arena. This is apparent in virtually all political campaigns, but it can be best illustrated by the role and function of the Office of National Drug Control Policy. The ONDCP was created in 1988 at the behest of a Democratic Congress who forced reluctant Republican bureaucrats to make the concept a reality. As originally envisioned, the drug czar was to study the fragmented drug war effort and better organize, coordinate, and consolidate the troops (Witkin, 1993). In actuality, during its early phases, the office had no real power and soon gained the reputation of being little more than a ministry of propaganda.

The first drug czar was former Education Secretary William Bennett, who brought respectability to the office by his zeal for media coverage and his willingness to take on difficult policy questions in many different public forums. Next, defeated Florida Governor Bob Martinez was appointed drug czar by President Bush. Interestingly, none of the low-profile Martinez's top 11 aides had ever worked for any of the nation's lead drug enforcement agencies, and in addition another 40 percent of the office's jobs went to political appointees, a figure that dwarfed other federal departments (Witkin, 1993). Finally, with the election of President Clinton, the staff of the ONDCP was cut from 146 people to 25, which forced many policy experts to question the sincerity of Clinton's drug policy intentions. Clinton's budget cuts also jeopardized many meaningful drug-control programs, including the Counter-Drug Technology Assessment Center, which drug experts had touted as being an effective program.

Clinton's drug czar appointee, former New York City Police Commissioner Lee P. Brown, holds the position as of the preparation of this text. The director's position has now been elevated to cabinet status, which supposedly gives it more authority over federal drug control spending. However, in the aftermath of drastic cuts in staff, the question could be asked: How effective is a general with no troops? In addition, it would be an almost impossible task for any person holding the position of drug czar to command respect from both treatment and drug enforcement officials across the nation. Indeed there are many such agencies. For example, in addition to multitudes of local and state drug enforcement agencies, more than 40 federal agencies currently retain a piece of the drug-fighting pie from the Bureau of Indian Affairs to the Centers for Disease Control (Witkin, 1993).

Prohibition Then and Now

As we discussed in Chapter 1, many social scientists have characterized prohibition as a dismal failure to control human behavior. Although this premise is supported by many elements of the era, let us pose the question: Could any aspects of the experiment be termed a success? Surprisingly, the answer is yes. For decades many experts have suggested that alcohol abuse actually increased during the Prohibition years. In actuality and contrary to popular myth, alcohol consumption was fairly well controlled during the Prohibition era as records reveal that levels of alcohol consumption declined significantly during the era and rose again sharply after its repeal (Goode, 1993). However, since alcohol consumption was a clandestine practice during Prohibition, no hard and fast data is available which can be scrutinized. In a thought provoking discussion on the matter, Goode has suggested that rates of cirrhosis of the liver (which are closely related to alcoholism) be considered before, during, and subsequent to Prohibition to determine the extent of alcohol abstinence. He points out that the rate of death from cirrhosis of the liver remained between 12 and 17 per 100,000 people each year between 1900 and 1919, but it dropped to between seven and nine per 100,000 in the 1920s and early 1930s, a reduction of almost half (1993:170). After 1933, however, (the end of Prohibition) it began to escalate again.

So why is it generally believed that excessive alcoholism during the period was common? One explanation could be the popular belief that speakeasies, jazz clubs, and the like existed around every street corner and that opportunistic gangsters like Al Capone had bootleg beer and whiskey all but flowing in the streets. Movies, books, and other popular literature tend to foster the notion that everyone was drinking, partying, and living the high life. The truth about Prohibition is just the opposite. It was a drab, unexciting period in which most Americans did not drink, and those who did drank considerably less than they did before or after the passing of the 18th Amendment.

Despite the "successes" of Prohibition as we have discussed, several important lessons were also learned about the era and the notion of Prohibition as a public policy option. First, the illegal alcohol made available by criminal entrepreneurs during the era was considerably stronger than that which was obtainable before the Prohibition period. Before Prohibition, low-alcohol beer made up almost half of the alcohol consumed, compared to the rise in availability of distilled spirits during the era. Secondly, much of the available alcohol was adulterated with toxins, which were used as substitutes for ethyl alcohol (Morgan, 1991). In fact, in one case a medicinal tonic known as "Jake," a Jamaican ginger extract containing 75 percent alcohol, resulted in over 50,000 people becoming permanently paralyzed. Finally, as we have learned, bootlegged alcohol products provided organized crime groups the financial boost they needed to become more integrated into society. This resulted in their increased power on the street and into the ranks of politics. It has been said that Prohibition actually increased the number and types of people involved in the production and distribution of alcohol (Levine and Reinarman, 1992).

Comparative Lessons from Prohibition

So what exactly have we learned from all of this? To begin, we have learned that Prohibition of the 1920s and 1930s did what it was intended to do—make people stop or reduce their alcohol intake. But we have also learned that along with the medical successes of this policy, other unforseen social problems resulted, which have probably overshadowed the original social concern of alcohol.

We must also be careful when comparing Prohibition of alcohol during the 1920s to the prohibition of drugs, as many of today's social and political variables are considerably different. For example, alcohol Prohibition gave rise to looseknit gangs and transformed them into powerful crime organizations. Today, however, these organizations are already in place—well-funded, highly organized, and interlaced throughout both the criminal and legitimate business world. So if drug legalization is being considered as a policy option, we must carefully consider its intent, especially if it is designed for doing away with these immense criminal empires. Would this be a realistic outcome in the 1990s? Secondly, at the time of its passing, Prohibition had the general support of the American people, compared to today's drug prohibition which, according to national polls, also enjoys considerable support by the American people. Assuming a democracy represents a government by and for the people, then if for no other reason, how socially responsible is it for our elected officials to pursue a public policy which lacks public support—for example, legalization?

Next we should consider how decriminalization or legalization has worked in other states. Our discussion in Chapter 12 about Alaska's 15-year experiment with marijuana decriminalization shows how such policies appear on the surface to be a workable solution but in practice create problems of their own.

A fourth point is that we have also learned that alcohol prohibition did work in reducing alcohol consumption. Accordingly, we see current trends of reduced drug abuse in recent years under our current prohibition policy. We also see the positive effects of innovative drug laws such as RICO, CCE, and forfeiture statutes, which in many cases have resulted in the successful arrest, prosecution, and conviction of dangerous drug lords and organized crime figures.

Finally, while many experts have suggested the abolition of drug prohibition in place of a policy of regulation, we must remember that we have already been there. Our current policy of drug prohibition originated from a time when drugs were perfectly legal in this nation and readily available over-the-counter. Slowly, as the dangers of drug abuse were realized, taxation and regulation were imposed to "reduce and control" drug abuse without arbitrarily outlawing drugs. So, after 75 years of legally obtainable drugs (before 1878) and regulation (e.g., the 1906 Federal Food and Drug Act, the 1914 Harrison Narcotics Act, and the 1937 Marijuana Tax Act), we as a society willfully adopted our current system of prohibition as our chosen public policy regarding drug control. After all, even inexpensive, highly regulated pharmaceutical drugs such as cocaine have not deterred Colombian criminals from producing tons of it on the black market at exorbitant prices.

This discussion illustrates how the solution to formulating a successful drug control policy is unclear. Contradictions in facts, opinions, and impressions of prohibition both then and now have only served to muddy the waters. Although it's hard to recommend one policy option without condemning another, responsible social policy must consider not just what the people need but what they want as well.

Legal Tools in Drug Control

As we discussed earlier, the use of innovative anti-drug laws has proven to be one of the most powerful weapons against drug trafficking and a strong ally in the development of drug control policy. Although some of the most effective laws have been in place for some time, many new laws have been written to address the many unique aspects of the drug trade and the constantly changing structure of drug organizations. We now know that most drug prosecutions occur at the state and local levels, and those laws are discussed in previous chapters in this book. However, due to the influence and mobility of organized crime groups in the drug trade, several significant federal laws have become widely used over the last two decades.

Our current system of justice is predicated on crimes which, for the most part, affect individual behavior and specific, unrelated incidents. For example, the burglar, the armed robber, the rapist, and the drug dealer are all persons whose behavior violates specific criminal codes. Because courts have traditionally viewed guilt as being individual in nature, organized crime now represents group criminal behavior, which presents a new and more complicated way of viewing drug-related crime. In the past prosecutors have been forced to approach organized crime with a narrow and shortsighted focus, convicting criminals either one at a time or in a single conspiracy. For example, over the past 60 years, federal prosecutors have attempted to prosecute the heads of the Genovese crime family, beginning with Charles "Lucky" Luciano, who was convicted of operating a prostitution ring in Manhattan. His successor, Frank Costello, was convicted of federal tax evasion followed by the conviction of Vito Genovese, who was found guilty of running a drug conspiracy, and so on. For years federal prosecutors were able to temporarily incapacitate the heads of a crime organization for various crimes but were never able to adequately weaken the organization's power. When the head of an organization was finally removed, he was easily and quickly replaced, and the organization continued to flourish. As a result, in 1970 Congress passed legislation which incorporated antiracketeering elements that targeted the criminal organization instead of the individual. Such laws are today's primary weapon against organizations and the persons who control them. This section will look at some of the most effective federal drug control tools.

The Racketeer-Influenced and Corrupt Organizations Act (RICO)

The 1970 Racketeer-Influenced and Corrupt Organizations Act (RICO) is yet another invaluable tool in the fight against organized crime in the drug trade. The purpose of RICO is to broaden the power of the prosecutor by allowing one prosecution of a multi-defendant crime organization for all of the criminal enterprises in which it is involved. In addition to imprisonment of members of the crime group, RICO allows for seizure of assets and proceeds from illegal enterprises. Successful application of the RICO statute in recent years has resulted in the conviction of top-level La Cosa Nostra members in Kansas City, St. Louis, Philadelphia, and Cleveland. Cases such as these help illustrate to the general public the magnitude of organized crime organizations and the extent to which they operate.

Although the act has been law since 1970, it was not widely used until the early 1980s. Before that time, prosecutors tended to apply the RICO statute to criminals who were not members of large crime organizations or who were not management-level OC players. RICO is a statute that criminalizes a pattern of conduct characteristic of organized crime. Specifically outlined in the RICO statute are the criminal acts that constitute a **"pattern of racketeering,"** two of which must have occurred during the last ten years. Under RICO, racketeering is defined as "any act or threat involving murder, kidnapping, gambling, arson, robbery, bribery, extortion, or trafficking in narcotics or dangerous drugs."

Close-Up: How RICO Works

To help illustrate how RICO works, consider the ABC drug cartel, which is a criminal group controlling the "South Shore Bank" through known criminals or their associates that hold key positions. Through this control, the cartel is able to launder money from the sales of illegal drugs conducted throughout the country and in South America.

Assume that 1) a bank president and several members are criminally prosecuted under RICO and identified as a "criminal enterprise"; 2) the RICO predicate acts include drug trafficking; 3) members of the cartel are shown to have received profits from drug sales and to have acquired personal assets as a result; and 4) with drug money, the drug cartel assumed legitimate control over other businesses such as the Oasis Restaurant, Oyster Bar, and the Hungry Man Catering Service. At the time of the criminal indictment, all such assets (equivalent to their illicit proceeds) are frozen to prevent liquidation of them prior to seizure. After conviction, these assets are then seized.

At this point, the investigation is not yet over because some members of the drug cartel will no doubt remain in control of the bank. The civil provisions of RICO are now placed into motion, as members of the cartel can be permanently enjoined from controlling the bank. A lesser standard of proof than is required in a criminal case is needed to accomplish this (the criminal case standard is "beyond a reasonable doubt"). The prosecutor must establish the cartel's control over the bank and request "injunctive relief." The bank may then be placed under a government trustee, and cartel members are then prohibited from assuming control over it. From here on out, if the government can demonstrate that an ABC drug cartel member is assuming control, that member will then be held in contempt of the civil order under RICO and prosecuted.

Source: Lyman, M. (1989). *Gangland: Drug Trafficking by Organized Criminals.* Springfield, IL: Charles Thomas Publishing Co.

The Continuing Criminal Enterprise Statute (CCE)

The Federal Continuing Criminal Enterprise Statute (Section 848 of Title 21, United States Code), enacted as part of the Comprehensive Drug Abuse Prevention and Control Act of 1970, is one of the strongest statutory weapons against drug trafficking. This statute, like RICO, gives prosecutors the means to reach the organizers, managers, and supervisors of major drug trafficking organizations. Prosecution under this statute requires proof of five elements to sustain prosecution:

1. The defendant's conduct must constitute a felony violation of federal narcotics laws.
2. The conduct must take place as part of a continuing series of violations.

3. The defendant must undertake this activity in concert with at least five other individuals.

4. The defendant must act as the organizer, manager, or supervisor of this criminal enterprise.

5. The defendant must obtain income or resources from this enterprise.

CCE provides for some of the most severe criminal penalties for illicit drug trafficking. These include imprisonment for a minimum of ten years with no possibility of parole. In addition, the court may impose a life sentence with no provision for parole and fines totaling $100,000. Moreover, under CCE, all profits and assets that have afforded the defendant a source of influence over the illegal enterprise are subject to forfeiture.

Conspiracy

The use of conspiracy laws in drug enforcement has proven to be one of the most beneficial tactics of the last decade. Although conspiracy laws have existed for quite some time, their use is now common among federal, state, and local authorities alike. Although state law in this area may differ from one jurisdiction to another, the basic principles of conspiracy are the same. Conspiracy is defined as an agreement between two or more persons that have the specific intent either to commit a crime or to engage in dishonest, fraudulent, or immoral conduct injurious to public health or morals. In studying this definition, one can easily see the benefits of such a law in the area of drug control.

Drug trafficking is a criminal endeavor that usually requires more than one player, for example, a grower sells drugs to a manufacturer that contracts with a smuggler for transportation. The smuggler then transports the drugs to a wholesale buyer, who in turn sells them to a retail distributor. The retail distributor then sells the drugs to numerous dealers and users on the street. Given the required documentation by investigators, conspiracy charges can be brought against all such players in a drug operation. Because most conspiracy cases involve numerous defendants, a degree of confusion may result. Generally, three types of conspiracy cases are most commonly used in prosecutions of drug traffickers. These are the chain, the wheel, and the enterprise conspiracy.

> *The Chain.* **Chain conspiracies** occur when a criminal endeavor is dependent on the participation of each member of the criminal organization. Each member represents a "link" in the chain, and the success of the criminal goal requires all participants. If one link in the chain is broken (i.e., the member fails to accomplish his or her particular task), the criminal act will be incomplete. To successfully prosecute a chain conspiracy, each member must be shown to be aware of the intended goal of the operation.

The Wheel. **Wheel conspiracies** are comprised of one member of a criminal organization that is the "hub" or organizer of the criminal plan and members that make up the "spokes." Wheel conspiracies must show that all members that are spokes are aware of each other and agree with each other to achieve a common illegal goal. For this reason, the wheel conspiracy is a difficult one to prosecute, as it is difficult to show a common agreement between the spokes.

The Enterprise. As discussed under the RICO section, a person that has been shown to participate in two or more patterns of racketeering may be prosecuted. The definition of **enterprise conspiracy** makes it a separate crime to conspire to commit any of the substantive offenses under RICO. Basically, RICO defines the term as an agreement to enter into an enterprise by engaging in a pattern of racketeering. The enterprise conspiracy recognizes that in some criminal organizations not all members have one common goal. Therefore, all that must be shown is a member's willingness to join a criminal organization (an "enterprise") by committing two or more acts of racketeering.

Thinking Critically #29

Create a scenario in which you are a prosecutor attempting to bring several organized crime racketeers to trial. Describe and illustrate the type of conspiracy involved and your methods of proving the racketeer's complicity.

Forfeiture Sanctions in Drug Control

Forfeiture is the ancient legal practice of government seizure of property used in criminal acts. Such an enforcement strategy has proven to be one of the most effective legal tools in the fight against illegal drugs. The federal government's momentum was somewhat slow in the area of forfeiture until recent years. For example, in 1983 more than $100 million in cash and property was seized and forfeited to the government by convicted criminals. The figures in 1989 are more than double that of 1983.

The 1984 Federal Comprehensive Forfeiture Act increased existing forfeiture powers under federal law. This was accomplished in part by lessening the degree of proof necessary for officials to seize property from the traditional "beyond a reasonable doubt" standard to "probable cause." The Act reads:

> [A]ny property of a person convicted of a drug felony is subject to forfeiture if the government establishes probable cause that the defendant acquired the property during the period of violation, or within a reasonably short period thereafter, and there was no likely source for the property other than the violation.

The Comprehensive Forfeiture Act, in addition to many state laws addressing forfeiture of assets, enables officers to seize automobiles, aircraft, vessels, bank accounts, and securities, as well as real estate holdings and privately owned businesses. In addition, it enhances penalty provisions of the 1970 Controlled Substances Act to include a 20-year prison term and/or fines of up to $250,000. Basically, the act works in this fashion:

> If a drug dealer uses his automobile to drive to a location to sell a quantity of drugs, his car then becomes the conveyance which the dealer used to facilitate the crime. The car, therefore, is permitted to be seized under law. Along the same lines, if investigators can show that an automobile was purchased with drug money, it is also allowed to be seized under the law.

Federal law also contains a sharing provision whereby an equitable transfer of the property can be facilitated. This provision basically divides property and distributes it among participating law enforcement agencies. After the seizure, a determination is made to determine the degree of involvement of each participating agency, and a proportionate distribution of the assets is then made between the agencies.

Drug Tax Laws

A recent innovative approach to drug enforcement is drug tax laws. During the 1980s, such laws were enacted in 21 states, with provisions similar to the 80-year-old Harrison Narcotics Act. Most drug tax laws are covered under state tax codes, and failure to pay the required taxes on illicit drugs results in both civil and criminal penalties—in addition to any penalties the offender faces regarding the drug violation itself. State drug tax codes include stamp, sales, and excise taxes on specified criminal activities which include the manufacture, sale, acquisition, and possession of drugs in the state—virtually all types of drug-related activities. Typically, the tax is $3.50 for each gram of marijuana and $200 for each gram of other illegal substances. In addition, there is a specified amount for drugs sold in a manufactured form of dosage units.

Here's how the drug taxes work. When someone comes into possession of drugs, he or she is required to buy a state drug stamp—a procedure which is usually performed anonymously. Law enforcement officials are aware that in most cases, drug traffickers will be hesitant to do so because they don't want to inform the police about being in possession of illicit drugs (this in and of itself would certainly warrant an investigation). So, if a person is found to be in illegal possession of dangerous drugs for which tax has not been paid, they are subject to a financial penalty and a prison sentence for *tax evasion* (not drug possession). Prosecution for possession of drugs is a separate criminal matter carrying additional penalties.

The primary reason for the drug tax is to give investigators a powerful tool for investigating large-scale drug traffickers opposed to small-time dealers.

Such offenders can be found guilty of a civil violation of the state tax code providing the state can show they have not paid the tax. As a result, violators can be required to pay back taxes and fines which can be substantial. For example, a trafficker caught with one kilogram (2.2 pounds) of cocaine would be subject to taxes of $200,000 as well as a civil fine of $200,000. Additionally, he or she would also be required to pay a criminal fine of up to $10,000 as well as serve a prison term. Revenues resulting from drug taxes are often used for drug enforcement efforts, treatment, and prevention programs such as DARE.

Grand Juries and Immunity

The use of the grand jury has proven effective in drug suppression efforts because of the broad range of power that it enjoys. The roots of the grand jury go back to the twelfth century, when it served as a safeguard against governmental abuse. The grand jury sought citizen approval for prosecutorial actions. Some of the more powerful rights granted the grand jury are represented by its authority to subpoena persons and documents, to punish, to grant immunity, to issue indictments, and to maintain secrecy of the proceedings.

The grand jury has been successfully used on both the federal and state levels, and in the case of the latter, the authority to call a grand jury may rest with the governor, the state attorney general, or the local prosecutor. As indicated, the ability of the grand jury to grant immunity broadens the powers of this investigative body. This ability is particularly useful because many witnesses are criminals that have intimate knowledge of criminal operation.

Most criminals are aware that, under the Fifth Amendment, they cannot be compelled to give testimony against themselves. When this occurs, prosecutors may pursue one of several options:

1. The prosecutor can compel the testimony by seeking a contempt citation if prosecutors can prove that the testimony would not incriminate the witness.
2. The prosecutor can release the witness and continue the proceedings without the benefit of the witness' testimony.
3. A plea bargaining agreement can be sought, whereby the witness' testimony would be given with the understanding that a lesser charge could be levied against the witness than if he or she did not give the testimony.
4. Total immunity from prosecution can be given by the prosecutor in exchange for the witness' testimony. In this case, once the witness is given total immunity, he or she can then be compelled to testify. Refusal under these circumstances can result in punishment of the witness.

Two kinds of immunity may be granted to witnesses in organized crime prosecutions:

1. *Transactional Immunity*. A witness given **transactional immunity** for testimony about a specific criminal act is literally immune from ever

being prosecuted for that particular crime in the future. Some witnesses have in the past attempted to blurt out additional crimes connected with the primary offense in an attempt to take an "immunity bath" and be free from all responsibility of those crimes. In fact, immunity is not attached when the witness purposely mentions additional crimes. It is extended to other crimes, however, when the prosecutor chooses to mention them during the examination of the witness in court.

2. *Derivative Use Immunity.* When **derivative use immunity** is granted to a witness, the witness is only immune from having his or her own testimony later used against them. If evidence of an independent nature is uncovered, however, the witness may be prosecuted on the basis of that evidence.

As one can see, use immunity has considerable advantages over transactional immunity. When using transactional immunity, a witness may give broad-sweeping and vague testimony referring to specific criminal acts, thus bringing them under the "umbrella" of the immunity grant, but being ambiguous enough so that specifics essential to prosecution are not provided (Kenney and Finckenhaur, 1995). On the other hand, a grant of use immunity will not bar prosecution.

The Witness Security Program

Before the inception of the Federal Witness Security Program, those witnesses that testified on behalf of the government were sometimes brutally tortured or even murdered. Until 1970 the protection of government witnesses was left up to each individual law enforcement agency. Because of limited resources and inconsistent services, the need arose for a single unified federal program.

The Witness Security Program (**WITSEC**) was implemented in 1970, and since then, more than 5,300 witnesses have entered the program and have been protected, relocated, and given new identities by the U.S. Marshals Service (U.S. Department of Justice, 1989). The WITSEC plan provides persons with psychological counseling and training along with employment assistance, and new identities for both witnesses and their families. The program is the first of its kind in the United States and has served as a prototype for similar programs in other countries.

The WITSEC program, operating under the United States Marshals Service, has now been proven to be one of the most significant prosecution tools in cases involving large-scale organized crime figures. The program is one that basically offers witnesses lifelong protection if they testify against organized crime figures. The program is necessary because of criminal conspiracies, secretive and clandestine drug operations, and the general covert nature of organized crime. The WITSEC program is considered a successful program, as more than eight out of every 10 defendants are convicted and receive substantial prison sentences.

The Federal Witness

Life is closing in on him. He has been an insider to all kinds of criminal activity, such as drug trafficking, money laundering, and bribery. But he's been offered a chance to turn his life around and to start all over again.

This man has been targeted as a potential witness for the case that the government is developing against his criminal associates. If he agrees to testify against others in the organization, the government will protect him under the Witness Security Program.

He knows that the information he brings to the witness stand will be devastating to his associates. His testimony will put them in prison for years and destroy a sophisticated criminal network, but he's afraid. These guys believe in retribution—an eye for an eye.

He is told that a lifetime of protection is available to him and his family as long as they follow the established security guidelines of the program. The man agrees to testify, and as he does, he closes the door to his former life. The person that he was no longer exists. He and his family are given new names and a new place to live, and they will never again publicly refer to their former lives.

Source: *The Pentacle,* 1988 (U.S. Marshals Service).

Thinking Critically #30

Evaluate the federal WITSEC program in terms of its success or failure to contribute to a reduction of drug-related crime in the United States. Do you believe that tax dollars are well-spent in allowing drug criminals to evade prosecution to begin new lives?

Summary

Modern drug control policy is earmarked by a number of policy strategies, each designed to address a specific aspect of the nation's drug problem. These strategies include demand reduction, supply reduction, eradication, education, and treatment. However, despite many notable successes, none of these policies has proven to be successful in reducing drug abuse to what could be termed an acceptable level. The implementation of control strategies involves a concerted effort by many organizations and agencies. Those in both the public and private sector share responsibility for fighting the drug abuse problem in our communities and schools. These include law enforcement agencies on the federal, state, and local levels as well as the military, local schools, and private businesses which offer support for prevention and treatment programs.

Today's drug control policy originated with a series of federal laws designed to regulate the manufacture, sale, and use of dangerous drugs. Drug control efforts in the United States, however, date back to the late 1800s when opium and its extracts were first recognized as dangerous. Momentum on the federal level began in 1906 with the passing of the Pure Food and Drug Act, which required medications containing opium or coca derivatives to say so on their label. In 1914, the Harrison Narcotics Act further controlled opiates by restricting the dispensing of them to medical purposes and pursuant to a written authorization. Ambiguities in the law, however, prevented this act from being fairly enforced.

In 1937, marijuana was controlled under the Marijuana Tax Act in much the same way as opiates were under the Harrison Narcotics Act. Taxes were imposed for those growing marijuana in an effort to deter growers from involvement with this plant. Finally, in 1970 the Controlled Substances Act was passed as an effort to update all preexisting federal drug laws. This comprehensive act placed all supposed dangerous drugs in one of five schedules. Each drug was categorized according to danger. The law also set forth new criminal and civil penalties for possession and distribution of drugs.

The year 1970 also marked the enactment of several new and innovative drug control laws that are still being used today. One such law, RICO (Racketeer-Influenced and Corrupt Organizations Act), enables law enforcement to prosecute leaders of large trafficking organizations and to seize assets associated with the organizations. A similar law, the Continuing Criminal Enterprise Act (CCE), also affords authorities special powers in arrest and forfeiture of assets of drug kingpins. To provide further aid in the drug enforcement initiative, conspiracy and forfeiture legislation have greatly enhanced the ability of law enforcement officers to arrest dealers and their associates. These laws also provide the legal basis to seize assets acquired by drug offenders.

Drug control, by virtue of its economical, political, and social implications, is extremely complicated. Not everyone agrees on the most effective and efficient manner in which to contain the nation's drug abuse problem, but the strategies and policies discussed in this chapter demonstrate the breadth and complicity of control efforts regardless of how successful they are or have been.

Do you recognize these terms?

chain conspiracy	regulation
derivative use immunity	taxation
enterprise conspiracy	transactional immunity
eradication	wheel conspiracy
pattern of racketeering	WITSEC
prohibition	

Discussion Questions

1. What major drug control legislation was passed during the Reagan administration?

2. The RICO statute requires that a pattern of racketeering be established. What are the predicate offenses that constitute a pattern of racketeering?

3. How do the CCE and RICO statutes differ?

4. Discuss the elements of a conspiracy.

5. How do the forfeiture sanctions under federal law help in the national drug control effort?

6. Discuss why the grand jury is considered a valuable asset in the prosecution of drug offenders?

7. List and discuss the two types of immunity most commonly used in federal drug prosecutions.

8. Discuss how the Federal Witness Security program (WITSEC) aids in the prosecution of high-level organized crime figures.

Control through Treatment and Prevention   *14*

This chapter will enable you to:

- Understand public opinion as it relates to drug treatment
- Understand the drug user
- Appreciate the plight of the drug addict
- Compare and contrast drug treatment programs
- Learn differences in treatment philosophies
- Discover what works in drug treatment and what doesn't

Although many drug enforcement and community efforts are designed to deter drug abuse, there will always be those that develop dependencies on addictive substances or that seek escape through the use of drugs and alcohol. Although casual use of drugs has been declining in the United States, the National Drug Control Strategy of 1994 shows little change among heavy users of heroin and crack cocaine. This was supported by a recent RAND Corporation study which estimated that only 13 percent of heavy cocaine users have been successful in avoiding use after treatment (Rydell and Everingham, 1994). However, it is the hard-core drug abusers, typically at the bottom of the socioeconomic ladder, who have had the least amount of success with drug treatment programs. Those who advocate more treatment centers have argued that the new programs will more than pay for themselves in areas such as reduced crime and more cohesive family life. In fact, some have even suggested that despite the high rate of relapse for treatment centers, treating drug users is still more cost effective than incarceration. On the other side of the argument are people who oppose the addition of more treatment programs, claiming that no one is sure as to which approach is the most effective.

The task of increasing the number of treatment centers is complicated by an almost universal lack of funding for them. Since 1989, Republicans and Democrats alike have failed to seek sufficient funding for treatment. In 1993 the Clinton administration proposed an initiative aimed at 74,000 hard-core drug addicts, but funding for the proposal was not approved by Congress. Indeed, a political atmosphere seems to exist in which treatment initiatives are viewed by politicians with a degree of moral indignation in that drug addicts brought on their troubles themselves and, therefore, deserve what they get. Thus, despite the considerable amount of crime and disease that drug abuse generates, treatment remains an unpopular item on the nation's political agenda.

The drug abuse predicament is complicated because there are so many different drugs in America and a vast number of people using them. Furthermore, America's addiction problem is not limited to illegal drugs. According to the National Institute on Alcohol Abuse and Alcoholism, about 9 percent of the adult population (an estimated 15 million people) abuse alcohol (1993). The same problem which plagues abusers of hard-core drugs also haunts alcohol abusers: relapse. In fact, an estimated 50 to 90 percent of alcoholics will drink again after completing treatment. We will look closer at relapse later in this chapter. For this reason, both alcohol and drug treatment experts refer to addiction as a "**chronic relapsing disorder.**" Many of these people simply fail to respond to prevention, education, or treatment programs, and their lives are committed to the acquisition of illegal drugs.

There is some encouragement, however, in that drug use has dropped sharply since the 1980s. Cocaine use, for example, dropped from 5.8 million users in 1988 to 3.4 million in 1992 (Office of National Drug Control Policy, 1994). Unfortunately, crime and health-related problems have failed to decline accordingly. These topics are the essence of this chapter. But before we examine drug treatment and prevention, let's first take a look at the primary player in America's drug abuse dilemma—the drug user.

Understanding the Drug User

Many illusions exist about drugs and those that use them. Therefore, this section will attempt to uncloud perceptions of the role of the drug user in society. The statistics about the typical drug user are provided by the National Household Survey of Drug Abuse (1991) and reveal some interesting findings. For example, males are more likely than females to use drugs and the most active drug abusing age group are 18- to 25-year-olds. Furthermore, both the National Household Survey (1991) and the High School Senior Survey (1990) suggest that whites are more likely than blacks to use drugs.

Drug dependent people present not only a danger to themselves but to those around them. Users lie to friends and family. They take advantage of those that attempt to help them. They steal from loved ones to support their habit and are frequently involved in a lifestyle that includes predatory criminal acts such as robbery, assault, and murder. This is why society's response to the drug problem involves not only the medical and health care industries, but also the criminal justice system.

Today, society bears most of the burden for offering treatment to those that have fallen victim to drug abuse. Failure to provide a means for addicts to "get well" not only endangers the lives of the addicts, but also threatens the well-being of those that become victims of drug crimes, communicable diseases such as AIDS, and other related drug abuse problems. Unfortunately, the tendency to believe that drug treatment is a supple, nurturing, and easy way out of drug dependency is quite far from the truth. Indeed, to the drug addict, the successful drug treatment program is one that imposes stringent physical and emotional demands and is, therefore, an unappealing experience.

It is also a misconception that all drug users develop a dependency and, therefore, require drug treatment. Indeed, most people that use drugs do not become addicted the first time that they use them. For example, the casual drug user, one that uses drugs no more than once a month, does not usually need drug treatment in order to stop using drugs. But a social (which includes governmental) climate of intolerance of drug use is an important ingredient in building a drug-free community.

The heroin or cocaine user that uses the drug once a week is a different story. This person may be able to ward off dependency alone but is more likely to require a treatment program than those users that fall in the once-a-month category. Still, there are others that are only persuaded by arrest and adjudication through the criminal justice system. Finally, there are those addicts that are physically and psychologically addicted to drugs and that genuinely require a formalized treatment program such as Narcotics Anonymous (NA).

Studies have been conducted over the past 25 years in hopes of identifying biological or personality factors to connect drug use to potential drug users. To date, no empirical evidence exists to show what type of person is the most likely candidate for drug use or addiction, nor is there evidence as to which user can control drug use and which cannot. In reality, many drug users make poor assessments about their ability to tolerate the effects of drugs. In fact, they are often the last to realize that they are addicted.

The use-to-abuse cycle is one that slowly engulfs the drug user. For example, many addicts experience what could be termed a "honeymoon" of drug use early in their abuse cycle. Typically, this begins with the use of alcohol, cigarettes, and sometimes marijuana at a young age. The use-to-abuse cycle then expands over time to the use of harder, more effective drugs. The honeymoon stage may last several years and is usually a manageable period for the drug user. Once the potency of drugs and the instances of use increase, the honeymoon is over, and the user is well on his or her way to physical dependency. Addressing the problem of treatment of drug abusers, former drug czar William Bennett stated in his 1989 National Drug Control Strategy:

> If our treatment system is to do the job required of it, the system
> must be expanded and improved. We need more treatment 'slots,'
> located where the needs are, in programs designed to meet those
> needs. We must improve the effectiveness and the efficiency of treat-

ment programs by holding them accountable for their performance. We must find ways to get more drug dependent people into treatment programs, through voluntary and, when necessary, involuntary means. And we need much better information about who is seeking treatment, who is not, and why.

Adding to the list of drug abuse misconceptions is the premise that addicts will eventually come to their senses and seek treatment. Several reasons can be identified to explain why addicts avoid treatment. First, addicts by nature have chosen to seek out the euphoric effects of drugs; they can logically be expected to prefer such effects to the demands of a formal treatment setting. Second, treatment by its very nature denies addicts their only real form of pleasure—drugs. Finally, because abuse usually involves ingesting illicit drugs, many addicts fear that confidentiality will not be maintained and that local police may learn their identities.

Many addicts that begin treatment programs eventually drop out of them and return to their drug abuse lifestyle on the street. Sometimes this is because addicts are lured back into drug abuse circles by associates. Additionally, they may hope to "stay clean" for a period of time so that their drug tolerance goes down; smaller and cheaper amounts of drugs will then produce better "highs."

As mentioned, the drug addiction cycle is compounded by the common, use of addicting drugs such as caffeine, alcohol, and nicotine. Regardless of the type of drug on which one becomes dependent, a treatment program must be identified. The immediate objectives of most treatment and rehabilitation programs can be generally characterized in three ways:

1. To control or eliminate drug abuse;
2. To give the drug users alternatives to their (drug-using) lifestyle;
3. To treat medical complications (both physical and psychological) associated with drug use.

Problems of drug abuse and addiction also prevail, in part, because such activity is covert in nature. Accordingly, drug use usually comes to the attention of the family and the community only when it has developed into either a personal or public problem. At this juncture, the drug dependent person must pursue any of a number of treatment options, which we will discuss in this chapter.

The Rise in Addiction

Chapter 1 discussed our nation's gradual acceptance of drug use over many decades, but the problem of addiction has not always been clearly understood. Historically, Americans have alternated between viewing addiction as a medical problem and a social ill. Accordingly, the public's response to addiction has vacillated between treatment of offenders and aggressive police crackdowns.

During the 19th century, medications such as opiates were essential for use by medical practitioners. By the late 1800s, thousands of middle-class women whose doctors had prescribed powdered morphine became hopelessly addicted. Even then, asylums were established by physicians to treat those who had become addicted. By the early 1900s, however, synthetic, injectable forms of morphine had been developed, and public concern grew about so-called "plea-sure users" of the drug.

In 1914, the Harrison Narcotics Act was passed as a measure to control the distribution of narcotics, followed by Prohibition in 1920, which was designed to curb alcohol consumption. During this period, the government also cracked down on drugs by closing the remaining municipal clinics which had provided low-cost morphine, heroin, and cocaine to registered addicts. As a result, virtu-ally no treatment facilities remained in existence throughout the country. Soon, the jails filled with addicts. To ease the overcrowding problem, Congress authorized the building of two massive prisons for narcotic addicts—one in Lexington, Kentucky, which opened in 1935, and the other in Fort Worth, Texas, opening in 1938. Both institutions offered a mixture of a penal and psy-chotherapeutic environment.

As the 1940s approached, heroin use was growing in major U.S. cities, fol-lowed by what was later called a heroin epidemic in the 1950s. In 1964, Vin-cent Dole, a physician, and Marie Nyswander, a psychiatrist, published an arti-cle in the *Journal of the American Medical Association* about methadone. In the article they reported that addicts taking methadone orally experienced neither withdrawal symptoms nor euphoria from the drug. As a result, they were able to return to reasonably productive lives. Hence, the so-called medical model of addiction was born. As a result, the Nixon-era war on crime helped finance the expansion of methadone maintenance clinics with the hope that addicts would no longer have to commit crimes to finance their drug habits.

Philosophies of addiction were reconsidered during the 1980s with the rise in cocaine use and the arrival of crack on the American drug scene. Until then, cocaine was so expensive that it was only affordable by the rich and affluent. Almost overnight, crack was available in most major cities at a price anyone, especially adolescents, could afford: $5 to $10 per rock. Soon, crack had replaced heroin as the inner city drug of choice. This phenomenon forced drug treatment professionals to refocus their efforts from heroin and opiate addiction to cocaine dependency. Accordingly, special problems arose because cocaine use altered the brain's dopamine receptors, which govern the user's sense of pleasure, making users not want to stop. This factor alone has presented new and special treatment concerns for clinicians in the 1980s and through the mid-1990s.

Treatment Programs

We have thus far learned that there exist many different types of drugs of abuse, drug users, and explanations for involvement in drug abusing behavior. Just as there is no single typology of drug abuser, programs for drug treatment are diverse, as there is no single treatment for what we know as "drug abuse." It might be tempting to think of drug abuse under a simple medical model of acute illness, but it is far more complex than that. Symptoms of this chronic disorder and those interventions employed to treat the symptoms range well beyond the physiological and psychological and may even include explanations which are social, legal, and economic. A treatment program that works well for one user may not for another due to the dynamics of what motivates drug abuse in the first place.

Treatment programs incorporate psychological and pharmacological components but also rely upon efforts to teach communication skills, interpersonal skills, and the ability to deal with one's involvement in criminal behavior. As we learned in Chapter 6, many types of criminal activity are associated with the drug user. Included are drug crimes, such as dealing and possessing controlled drugs; property crimes, such as burglary and larceny; and acts of interpersonal violence. These depend on the type of drug being used and the extent of one's dependency. Experts believe that a small number of drug users are responsible for the majority of drug-related crime. In general, treatment programs serve both alcohol and drug dependent clients, and most of the nation's 5,000 treatment programs fall in one of two settings: 1) nonresidential, where the client receives treatment at a specific location but lives elsewhere; 2) residential, where clients receive treatment and reside at the treatment facility. Typically, residential facilities include hospitals or halfway houses.

In addition to the two types of settings, treatment programs can be divided into one of five categories: 1) detoxification programs, usually inpatient, which have the short-range goal of ending a user's physical addiction to substances; 2) chemical dependency units, primarily private inpatient or residential three- to four-week programs; 3) outpatient clinics, offering counseling and support for those that want to stop using drugs while they continue to work in the community; 4) methadone maintenance programs, which treat addicts by coupling counseling with the administration of methadone, a prescription medicine that blocks the craving for heroin while eliminating the usual pain of withdrawal; and 5) residential therapeutic communities, where users may spend up to 18 months in a highly structured program.

Detoxification

When treatment alternatives are considered, the term "**detoxification**" is frequently used. Detoxification, is usually the first step of the treatment process and is designed to withdraw patients slowly from their dependence on a particular drug. Its aim is to stabilize heavy drug users until their bodies are relatively free of drugs. This process generally takes from 21 to 45 days and is best performed on an inpatient basis. "Detox," in and of itself, is not considered a form of treatment. The distinction is that detoxification helps users get off drugs while treatment helps them to stay off. Therefore, experts generally agree that the detoxification process does little good unless it is followed up by a sound treatment program.

Subsequent to the detoxification process, the patient is no longer physically addicted to the drug and, theoretically, is able to abstain from future use of the drug. Research suggests that there is no single method of detoxification that is considered effective in the treatment of all drug abusers. Detoxification procedures are, therefore, individualized to meet the needs of each patient.

A patient's susceptibility to this form of treatment depends on several variables. These include the type of drug to which the patient is addicted, the degree of tolerance that has developed, and how long the patient has been dependent on the particular drug. Let us now look at some typical detoxification scenarios.

>*Heroin Detoxification.* The detoxification process is often a futile one due to the instances of relapse by many addicts. For example, opiate drug addicts tend to have a high relapse rate because they return to their peer and social groups that are still involved in drug abuse. Methadone maintenance, discussed later in this chapter, is considered one of the more successful ways to accomplish the goal of detoxification.

>*Self-treatment*, or the "cold turkey" approach, is fairly common among heroin addicts and is usually attempted at the addict's home. In some cases, this approach is undertaken in therapeutic communities or with the support of friends. In almost all cases, this type of detoxification is not successful.

>*Alcohol and Barbiturate Detoxification.* Detoxification or withdrawal from either alcohol or barbiturates is considered extremely dangerous and should be performed only under medical supervision. In this situation, withdrawal may not occur until several days after the last dose. With these two drugs, detoxification is usually accomplished by a physician administering increasingly smaller doses of the drug to the patient to ward off withdrawal symptoms.

>*Marijuana and Other Hallucinogens.* Because these two categories of drugs are not physically addicting and there are no withdrawal symptoms, detoxification can usually be accomplished with little or no hospitalization.

>*Cocaine and Amphetamine Detoxification.* Of the two, cocaine poses the greatest challenge in treatment, primarily due to the addict's craving for the drug. So far, there are no proven successful treatment strategies comparable to those that have been developed for heroin addiction. Depression is common in patients experiencing withdrawal from these drugs, and suicide attempts may become prevalent. Treatment for cocaine and amphetamines is not usually life threatening but can cause great discomfort for the patient.

Narcotic Antagonists

The term "**narcotic antagonists**" refers to a category of drugs that was developed as a treatment for heroin addiction but that does not produce physical dependence. These drugs, as the name implies, block or reverse the effects of drugs in the narcotic category.

Naloxone (Narcan), having no morphine-like effects, was removed from the CSA when it was introduced in 1971 as a specific antidote for narcotic poisoning. Nalorphine (Nalline), introduced into clinical medicine in 1951 and now under Schedule III, is termed a narcotic agonist-antagonist. In a drug-free individual, Nalorphine produces morphine-like effects, whereas in an individual under the influence of narcotics, it counteracts these effects. Another agonist-antagonist is pentazocine (Talwin). Introduced as an analgesic in 1967, it was determined to be an abusable drug and was placed under Schedule IV in 1979.

Maintenance (Substitute Therapy)

The term **maintenance** refers literally to maintaining a drug abuser on a particular type of drug for the purpose of helping him or her avoid the withdrawal syndrome. Opiate drug addiction, for example, is a common problem for many treatment programs because it is so widespread. Because a cross-tolerance and cross-dependence exists between all opiates, any of them can be used to eliminate withdrawal symptoms and to detoxify the addicted patient.

Methadone maintenance is the most common type of maintenance program. Methadone, a synthetic narcotic analgesic, was first introduced during World War II because of a shortage of morphine. It is an odorless, white crystalline powder that shares many of the same effects as morphine, but the two are structurally dissimilar. Methadone is best known for its use in the controversial methadone maintenance program that was introduced in 1964.

The use of methadone in treatment of persons addicted to opiates has always been a controversial practice. The drug does have one distinct advantage over heroin—methadone is a longer-acting drug, requiring less frequent administering. Additionally, the effects of methadone differ from those of heroin. In particular, methadone has a longer duration of action, lasting up to 24 hours, thereby permitting the administration of the drug once a day as treatment for heroin addiction. Time-tested results of methadone maintenance reveal that those addicts that went through the program had much less criminal involvement and were better able to function within their communities.

As mentioned, the effects of methadone closely resemble the effects of morphine and heroin but fail to provide the user the euphoric effects caused by those two drugs. Methadone is also an extremely physically addicting drug—a fact that has created much of the controversy surrounding its use. The program is structured so that the patient leaves a urine sample at the clinic, where the urine is tested for signs of morphine (heroin is excreted as morphine) and other drugs. Once patients have demonstrated they are responsible and is committed to rehabilitation, they are permitted to take a one-day supply of methadone. Later, the take-home dosage is increased to a three-day supply.

Detoxification is achieved through slowly reducing the amount of methadone mixture administered to the patient. Frequently, however, addicts find that their psychological dependence is more difficult to overcome than their physical dependence, and, therefore, many addicts remain in the program for most of their lives.

The Psychological Approach

As with most psychoanalytic types of treatment, a lengthy commitment is generally required on the part of the patient. The role of the psychoanalyst in drug treatment is to identify repressed feelings in the patient that were experienced early in life and that may contribute to drug abuse. Once the feelings or thoughts are uncovered, they can be dealt with through traditional psychoanalytic methods. Studies have shown that the length of treatment ranges from a few weeks to several years and that the success rate for recovery is marginal at best.

Group Treatment

Group therapy in drug treatment has demonstrated one of the highest success rates of any type of drug treatment program. Group treatment programs use an approach that creates an environment of personal interaction between peers. In theory, group interaction is more successful than the one-on-one interaction between the psychoanalyst and the patient. This is because the analyst often lacks a basic understanding of the drug abuse process and other variables that contribute to addiction. The analyst, therefore, often acts as a facilitator for the group. The treatment group may be formed during different phases of addiction and treatment and may involve not just the patients but their family and friends as well.

The Therapeutic Community

Therapeutic Communities (TCs) view drug use as symptomatic of the user's personality and social problems and, therefore, employ a mixture of psychological and behavior therapies. They are designed to force patients to face their addiction to drugs and to promote change in their personalities so that they can live without drugs. More importantly, TCs are designed to provide a secure environment where recovering addicts remain drug-free and also develop the social skills necessary to function in society. TCs have been established in many communities and were originally modeled after the Maxwell Jones communities for psychiatric patients. The program relies on the equal participation by TC residents in decisionmaking and program organization.

Types of Treatment Programs

Outpatient Programs. Outpatient programs range from completely unstructured drop-in or teen rap centers located in store fronts to highly structured programs offering individual, group, and family therapy. Most outpatient programs provide basic individual counseling and require that patients be self-motivated. Generally, the programs are small in size and serve between 20 and 30 clients.

Inpatient Programs. The inpatient programs for drug abusers are growing but are still relatively small in number. These programs provide more intensive service for patients that require a controlled setting. Unlike some other drug treatment centers, some inpatient programs have lock-up wards, where patients cannot leave. Services provided include diagnostic testing and evaluation, psychotherapy, group therapy, and counseling. The inpatient treatment program is generally the most expensive of the drug treatment plans and because of this is usually a shorter program in length.

The Halfway House. This is offered as an alternative for those that need to be housed in a location away from their own homes but cannot afford an inpatient program. Clients attend school or work during the day and return to the halfway house in the afternoon or evening, where they eat and sleep. The halfway house is frequently used as a transition from a therapeutic community to the outside community or in conjunction with outpatient therapy.

One of the first TCs was founded in California in 1958 and was called Synanon. By the late 1970s, Synanon had become controversial and was no longer regarded as a treatment program. Still, some components of the original program were thought to be successful; therefore, the Synanon model remains the foundation of hundreds of TCs throughout the United States. TCs, staffed by both former addicts and professionals, range in organization from the structured to the democratic. Each model usually attracts a particular type of drug abuser. For instance, a person that is suffering from the use of hallucinogens and that is searching for "a new identity" usually desires a more democratic treatment environment. On the other hand, an opiate drug addict that suffers severe social and personal problems and has an addiction fueled by attempts to avoid depression, usually requires a more structured treatment environment.

The majority of TCs are structured in a hierarchical manner and closely resemble concepts adopted by Phoenix House or Daytop Village in New York.

The largest, Phoenix House, with roughly 15 percent of the nation's 12,000 beds for addicts, uses what *Rolling Stone* describes as a "military-style, in-your-face, group-encounter approach" (Atkins, 1994). New residents scrub toilets before being allowed to graduate to chores of a higher status. Although about one-third of the clients leave the program during the first six weeks, an estimated 80 percent of those who complete it remain drug free (Atkins, 1994).

These types of treatment centers, however, are more easily adapted to the intravenous drug user. The historic success of the TC is evidenced by fewer relapses into drug use, higher rates of abstinence, and a higher incidence of good self-image and job satisfaction.

Thinking Critically #31

Assume your community has committed local funds to building and maintaining a drug treatment center and you have been asked to serve on the center's board of directors. After studying various kinds of treatment centers, you decide which one would best fits the needs of the city. Defend your choice to the rest of the board.

Each member of the TC is given responsibilities and is expected to carry his or her own weight. House rules are imposed and are rigidly enforced. The TC staff uses a reward system, in which good behavior is reinforced through the assigning of more responsible duties at the TC. Bad behavior is dealt with through "learning experiences," such as the suspension of privileges. The typical length of stay at a TC is anywhere from 6 to 24 months and may cost from $1,200 to $2,500 per month. As a result, TCs experience an extremely high attrition rate, with four out of five patients dropping out or being expelled from the program. For those completing the program, however, the success rate is high. Generally, four out of five of those successfully completing the program remain drug-free for several years after treatment.

Narcotics Anonymous

Narcotics Anonymous (NA) is a drug treatment program that started in California in 1953. Since then NA has spread to all parts of the United States (and some foreign countries) and supports a World Service Office in Los Angeles that unifies its global efforts. The NA program was adapted from Alcoholics Anonymous (AA), from which NA borrowed its 12-step program for recovering addicts. The philosophy of NA basically says: if you want what we have to offer and are willing to make the effort to get it, then you are ready to take certain steps. The NA group operates in a relatively structured manner;

that is, it has regular meetings at specified places and times. The group members are required to follow the 12 steps and are duly registered with the World Service Office in Los Angeles.

The goal of the organization is to carry the wellness message to the addict as well as to provide group members a chance to express themselves and hear the experiences of others. NA offers two types of meetings: open (to the general public) and closed (for addicts only). The meetings vary in format from group to group, as some are participation meetings, some are question-and-answer sessions, some are meetings for the discussion of special problems, and some are a combination of some or all of these formats.

The Twelve Steps of Narcotics Anonymous

1. We admitted that we were powerless over our addiction, that our lives had become unmanageable.

2. We came to believe that power greater than ourselves could restore us to sanity.

3. We made a decision to turn our will and our lives over to the care of God as we understood him.

4. We made a searching and a fearless moral inventory of ourselves.

5. We admitted to God, to ourselves, and to another human being the exact nature of our wrongs.

6. We were entirely ready to have God remove all these defects of character.

7. We humbly asked him to remove our shortcomings.

8. We made a list of all persons we had harmed and became willing to make amends to them all.

9. We made direct amends to such people wherever possible, except when to do so would injure others.

10. We continued to take personal inventory and when we were wrong, promptly admitted it.

11. We sought through prayer and meditation to improve our conscious contact with God as we understood him, praying only for knowledge of his will for us and the power to carry that out.

12. Having had spiritual awakening as a result of these steps, we tried to carry this message to addicts, and to practice these principles in all of our affairs.

Source: Narcotics Anonymous, (1987). *Narcotics Anonymous*, 4th ed. Van Nuys, CA: World Service Office Publisher.

Does Drug Treatment Work?

Occasionally, newspaper articles about recovered addicts surface, giving the impression that another addicted life has been spared through successful treatment. However, one of the hard truths about drug treatment is that experts know very little about the effectiveness of such programs. The assumption that drug treatment works is based on reports from clinicians and recovered drug addicts. Most research is so poorly conducted that it's hard to know whether treatment cures any more people than would have stopped using drugs on their own (Apsler, 1994). For example, studies have shown that between 45 and 70 percent of alcoholics are known to recover, but little empirical information is available for the rate of recovery for illegal drug users.

To assess the effectiveness of drug treatment programs, we should first consider the goals of treatment. Although total abstinence may seem like a likely goal of treatment, experts have suggested that lifelong abstinence from drugs or alcohol on the first try should not be the measure of success. Indeed, treatment goals are not restricted to simply reducing the consumption of drugs but also to reducing the demand for drugs, cutting down on related street crime, and improving the user's overall physical and mental health. Furthermore, clinicians have argued that the ultimate goal is to allow people to return to a normal, productive life—however that can be accomplished. Once again, this leads us back to the issue of gauging the "effectiveness" of treatment. But as we discussed earlier, a full recovery from drug dependency is not only unlikely but unrealistic. Complicating factors include the length of time which may be required for detoxification, as well as one's inclination for relapse.

We do know, however, that some treatment programs seem to have more positive outcomes than others. For example, the methadone maintenance program, which has been intensely studied since it originated in 1964, has the best documented success record. In the program, addicts are given a daily dose of methadone, which is designed to block the craving for heroin and other opiates. More than three decades of experience with methadone maintenance programs show that drug users tend to be less prone to drug consumption and criminal activity when maintained on the drug. Some controversy exists as to whether methadone simply substitutes one addicting drug for another (Apsler, 1994:52). Furthermore, drug addicts graduating from both therapeutic communities and non-methadone programs seem to perform better than addicts who fail to complete these treatment programs. Length of stay seems to have a high correlation with better patient outcomes.

Most people who enter drug treatment do so reluctantly, often under pressure from family or friends. One of the most important observations regarding drug treatment is the positive effects of court-imposed treatment. From time to time, judges will impose treatment as a condition of probation. In addition, corrections institutions will sometimes offer treatment programs for inmates. Studies have shown, however, that legal pressure from the criminal justice system tends to keep people in treatment longer. One such study is the Treatment Outcome Prospective Study (TOPS), a 1989 comprehensive study conducted at the Research Triangle Institute. The study showed that one of every two addicts seeking treatment did so because of an encounter with the criminal justice system and not because of his or her personal desire to kick the habit. Ironically, another 1988 TOPS study supports a different conclusion—that those addicts required to undergo treatment by court order do as well as those that do so under their own volition. Such studies, therefore, support the role of the criminal justice system in drug treatment and control.

Social Reintegration

This is the process whereby the benefits gained from treatment and rehabilitation are sustained and drug users adapt to a drug-free, productive existence within the community. This can happen in several ways: they can return to their family; they can complete or further their education; they can learn new skills; they can become employed on a full-time or part-time basis; they can continue participation in self-help groups; or they can develop friendships in non-drug-using environments.

Statistics show that most drug addicts lack a formal education. In many cases, they drop out of high school, and when they attempt to get jobs, they find themselves at a serious disadvantage. For those that do get jobs, frequently they are fired because of absenteeism due to drug abuse. Unemployment contributes to the drug-using cycle, and social reintegration then becomes difficult and sometimes impossible. We mentioned earlier that halfway houses were developed, in part, to help bridge the transition between drug abuse and reintegration back into the community. In these houses, residents have responsibility for their own lives—preparing food, cleaning their rooms, and managing their own money matters. In the houses, other members as well as therapeutic staff members offer the residents support and assistance in coping with the stress of learning to live independently.

Relapse

Over a period of years, drug misuse may be somewhat cyclical, and many people grow out of their drug dependence over time. Studies have revealed that even during the course of abusing drugs, periods of abstinence occur. Thus it is not uncommon for drug users to drop out of the program before its completion. Programs, therefore, must be prepared to readmit patients that have dropped out so that those patients have an opportunity to achieve control over their own drug use.

Research has shown that many drug users experience a temporary **relapse** at the end of treatment and rehabilitation. In many cases, however, after a period of a few weeks or months, these same users often achieve long-term stability and, eventually, abstinence. This finding strongly suggests that treatment opportunities offered by rehabilitation and social reintegration can be an important means of reducing the demand for drugs at early stages of abuse.

Problems with Drug Treatment

Factors that complicate the treatment process are attributed to drug addiction's both psychological and physiological characteristics. Addiction differs from diseases that are considered treatable through conventional medical methods. One major logistical problem to overcome is the lack of treatment capacity. Many publicly-funded programs, particularly those in large cities, maintain long waiting lists. Obviously, if addicts realize they may not get treatment for several months, their drive to seek help may greatly diminish.

Unfortunately, many treatment centers are not located in towns, cities, or neighborhoods where the need for treatment is greatest. Because of this, some programs have vacancies and others have waiting lists. Moreover, new drug treatment programs are difficult to begin, as funding is sometimes hard to secure and residents are frequently opposed to treatment centers being located in their neighborhoods.

Another problem in the drug treatment process is the soaring cost of health care. Drug treatment in the United States is a big business and accounts for millions of dollars in private, corporate, and insurance monies. For some employers, for example, costs of inpatient treatment may run as high as $1,000 a day for a 28-day treatment program.

Today, trends indicate that fewer patients are referred to inpatient care in lieu of the readily available, lower-cost outpatient programs. The dilemma becomes manifest when one tries to balance the cost of treatment with the quality of treatment—a frustrating and difficult task. Studies show that many people gravitate toward "brand-name" hospitals or rehabilitation services, regardless of their recovery rate.

When searching for a treatment solution, drug counselors tend to look for variables such as whether the hospital is approved by the Joint Commission on Accreditation of Hospitals, the availability of extended outpatient aftercare, the quality of the staff, and the recovery rate of the institution.

As we have seen, many treatment programs exist for the drug dependent person. The best programs insist on a sound code of conduct, individual responsibility, personal sacrifice, and sanctions for misbehavior. The evidence is mounting to support the contention that when these elements exist, the best results are attained.

The Cost of Drug Treatment

When considering the great need for drug treatment programs, one should first consider that the largest proportion of drug addicts are white males between the ages of 18 and 40. Many such individuals have the financial means or health insurance with which to pay for treatment. However, many do not. At private institutions, where these addicts most commonly seek treatment, it is not uncommon to have vacancy rates of up to 45 percent.

Publicly supported facilities, however, were financially strapped during the 1970s and 1980s, and they were unprepared for the great influx of addicts generated by the crack epidemic. Federal funding increased in the late 1980s and early 1990s to compensate for this rise.

If a single variable were identified that most greatly impedes the improvement and expansion of treatment, it would be the lack of trained, qualified personnel. In many cities, salaries are often too low to attract or retain those with proper training. Indeed, many starting salaries for drug treatment counselors begin at or below $14,000 per year, a figure that is unrealistically low for a professional position. Although improvements are slowly being made in this area, it will be some time before the competency and responsibility of treatment meets the needs of most communities.

Drug Prevention

Although as a rule most drug abuse begins during one's teenage years, many young people start using drugs much sooner. Because of this, most prevention programs focus on younger people. As former federal drug czar William Bennett stated in his 1989 National Drug Control Strategy: "[I]n the war against illegal drug use, the real heroes are not those who use drugs and quit; they are those who never use them in the first place." Thus, the goal of prevention is to insure that Americans, especially children, never begin the cycle of drug abuse, even through experimentation.

Unquestionably, drug prevention should begin in the home, with the parents of the potential drug user as the primary facilitators. After parents, school is probably the most effective place for the drug-education process to take place. School is where children spend a majority of their time and where they are subjected to peer groups. Additionally, it is school where first-time drug users frequently acquire their drugs.

Drug prevention through education is designed to reach those not yet personally affected by drug abuse to inform people about the hazards of drugs, and to reduce curiosity about drugs. Prevention strategists have identified two ways to influence young people against taking drugs. The first is to make people not want to use them, and the second is to warn of severe penalties to convince potential users that the consequences of drug abuse outweigh the advantages.

One of the more disturbing trends revealed by surveys on drug abuse is the decline in the average age of first-time substance abusers. In numerous studies, substantial numbers of school-aged children have reported initiating the use of alcohol, tobacco, and marijuana by the time they reach junior high school.

Schools are also primary sources of drug prevention programs and are well-equipped for such an undertaking. In addition to many community resources being housed within local schools, young people are required to spend much of their time there and are thus more accessible to prevention programs than are other people. As a rule, students in their final year of elementary school are targeted for prevention programs because the junior high school years are thought to be the time in which many students begin their drug experimentation. In addition to drug education classes, many schools have sponsored other types of prevention programs as well. For example, schools employ counseling and guidance for students in addition to sponsoring substance-free, extracurricular activities and peer support groups. Each is thought to show promise in enhancing the quality and effectiveness of drug prevention.

Communities and neighborhoods also play a role in developing drug-related prevention programs. Many of these are sponsored by churches, civic organizations, or parents groups; and their content, educational focus, and financial backing may differ greatly. An example of a community-based prevention program is SMART Move, which is associated with Boys and Girls Clubs of America. Trained staff involve youth in addressing problems of drug abuse, alcohol, and teen pregnancy. Other community-based prevention programs include a school-based program called the Midwestern Prevention Project, which interfaces with community groups and parents and Fighting Back. Fighting Back requires all participating communities to establish a task force of community representatives to join forces in drug prevention activities.

Various prevention efforts have also been implemented by law enforcement agencies to address the drug abuse problem. Conventional wisdom in recent years has held that the most effective initiatives should focus on building the self-esteem of young people, improving their decision-making skills, and enhancing their ability to resist peer pressure to use drugs. Two prevention approaches that are thought to have met with considerable success in this area are **DARE** (Drug Abuse Resistance Education), which originated in Los Angeles, and **SPECDA** (School Program to Educate and Control Drug Abuse), which began in New York City.

Project DARE

One of the main points of this chapter is that many different organizations and agencies, both private and public, are involved in drug prevention efforts. Project DARE (Drug Abuse Resistance Education) is one such example. It began as a joint project between the Los Angeles Police Department and the

Los Angeles Unified School District. Its purpose is to equip fifth-, sixth-, and seventh-grade children with the skills and motivation to resist peer pressure to use drugs, alcohol, and tobacco. A particularly innovative aspect of the program is the use of full-time, uniformed police officers as instructors, selected by DARE's supervisory staff. The project uses a variety of educational techniques which include lectures, video tapes, and exercises to teach students how to resist drugs. The community policing philosophy is also used in that attempts are made to develop positive attitudes toward police officers, who are carefully selected and trained to present the lessons.

Study: DARE Fails to Keep Kids Off of Drugs

Since its creation in 1983, DARE has become a darling of the United States' drug war. Parents who swear by DARE hold garage sales to raise money for the program—which teaches fifth- and sixth-graders about the dangers of drug use—and plaster the familiar red-and-black bumper stickers on their cars. Politicians, who know a strong applause line, praise DARE on the stump. And police departments, which have struck upon a public relations bonanza with the program, emblazon the DARE logo on their squad cars and dispatch officers to classrooms.

DARE has spread from Los Angeles into more than half the nation's schools, and with it has come a mix of federal grants, private donations, and local tax dollars that now total at least $155 million annually. But in the midst of DARE's rising popularity, a fundamental question has gone largely unasked: Does it work? According to a recently published study, the answer is no. The study, financed by the U.S. Department of Justice but rejected by that agency once the results were in, has touched off a political firestorm by concluding that the DARE program fails to accomplish its central goal: to keep kids off drugs. With egos on the line and money at stake, the study's conclusion has put DARE officials and the Justice Department on the defensive while the researchers find themselves fending off attacks on their methodology. "I don't get it. It's like kicking Santa Claus to me," DARE America executive director Glenn Levant said. "We're pure as the driven snow."

Indeed, no one disputes that the DARE program helps educate kids about drugs. But, the study found, it doesn't actually seem to stop kids from using them. That leads critics to wonder: Could the money and police power be better spent somewhere else? DARE's core curriculum, aimed at fifth- and sixth-graders with optional programs for students from kindergarten through high school, is taught by police officers in 45-minute to hour-long sessions over 17 weeks. DARE, which stands for Drug Abuse Resistance Education, teaches students not only about drug use, but also about self esteem and ways to resist peer pressure.

More than 5.5 million kids across the country will take the DARE course this year. But the recent study, conducted by the Research Triangle Institute in North Carolina, concluded that "DARE's limited influence on adolescent drug-use behavior contrasts with the program's popularity and prevalence." It also said that smaller, more interactive programs taught by teachers, not police officers, were more effective.

The Research Triangle Institute found Dare's effect on reducing or preventing drug use to be "statistically insignificant." Researcher Susan Ennett roughly translated the study's statistical analysis to mean that DARE "worked" for 3 percent of the 9,300 kids studied, compared with a 9 percent result for the alternative programs. RTI did not conduct original research but analyzed the data collected in eight previous studies of DARE's core curriculum for fifth- and sixth-graders. Those studies surveyed students' drug use, attitudes, and knowledge before and after taking DARE classes.

DARE did have a significant impact on students' knowledge about drugs and on students' social skills, Ennett said, "but we also know that knowledge has very little to do with behavior." DARE officials are vigorously attacking the RTI study, arguing that the sample size was too small; that the study examined DARE's old curriculum, not a more effective, interactive program that was introduced this fall; and that the study unfairly compared DARE to dissimilar programs.

Researchers acknowledge one more criticism: that it is difficult to measure changes in the behavior of DARE's target age group—fifth- and sixth-graders because they have not usually begun to use drugs. And both sides agree little research has been done on the long-term effects of the DARE program on students' drug use. "There's just not enough attention given to the need for well-done evaluation, and I think that is ultimately what the problem is," said William DeJong, a lecturer at the Harvard School of Public Health and a member of the Justice Department panel that reviewed the RTI study.

The $300,000 study originally was supported by DARE and was financed by the National Institute of Justice, an arm of the Justice Department. Once the findings came out, however, the Justice Department decided not to publish the report, although the department now has made it available. "We don't publish things when we don't agree with the results" or don't "think the research is good," Justice Department spokeswoman Anne Voigt said.

Source: *Chicago Tribune,* November 6, 1994.

The core curriculum consists of a 17-lesson program, each of which consists of a 45-to 60-minute lesson that teaches children various self-management skills and techniques for resisting peer pressure. The focus of the training rests on the premise that children who feel positive about themselves will be more successful in resisting peer pressure. Other lessons emphasize the physical, mental, and social consequences of drug abuse, and still others identify the different methods of coping with stress and having fun.

The scope of the 17-lesson DARE program core curriculum is as follows:

1. *Practices for Personal Safety.* Students are acquainted with the role of the police officer and methods to protect themselves from harm. The thrust of the lesson is to explain to the students the need for rules and laws designed to protect people from harm. The instructor and the students review a list of students' rights, which is contained in a notebook provided to each student. Finally, teachers instruct students in using the 911 emergency system to summon help.

2. *Drug Use and Misuse.* This segment explains the definition of drugs and the positive and negative effects of drugs on the body and mind. Each student then takes a true/false test that tests understanding of the lesson. The teacher defines the word "consequences" and the class considers the consequences of various actions. The students then discuss the consequences of using and not using drugs.

3. *Consequences.* The class discusses both negative and positive consequences of using drugs during this lesson. The students fill out a work sheet that asks them to list positive and negative consequences of using marijuana and alcohol. The officer points out that those who try to persuade others to use drugs will emphasize positive consequences, leaving the many negative consequences unstated.

4. *Resisting Pressure to Use Drugs.* A key component to this lesson introduces the students to the different types of peer pressure to take drugs that they may face. It teaches them to say no to such offers by considering the negative consequences of drug use. DARE instructors introduce four different sources of influence on people's behavior: personal preferences, family expectations, peer expectations, and the mass media. After defining "peer pressure," the DARE instructor explains different types of pressure that friends use to get others to use alcohol or drugs. These methods include threats and intimidation.

5. *Resistance Techniques: Ways to Say No.* This lesson reinforces the previous lesson by teaching students different ways to respond to peer pressure. Instructors write various techniques of resisting pressure on the chalkboard and discuss them with the class. These include giving a reason or excuse, changing the subject, walking away, and ignoring the person. The instructor also stresses that people can consciously avoid such confrontations by choosing to avoid hanging out with drug users. Because

long-term consequences for not taking drugs are usually not as effective as citing short-term consequences an emphasis is placed on explaining short-term consequences such as: "I don't like the taste."

6. *Building Self-Esteem*. In this lesson, DARE instructors explain that self-esteem is created out of positive and negative feelings and experiences. Students learn to identify their own positive qualities. They discover that drug use stems from poor self-esteem and that those with high self-esteem think for themselves and have accepted their limitations as human beings. In short, when people feel good about themselves, they can exert control over their behavior.

7. *Assertiveness: A Response Style*. Instructors teach assertiveness as a technique to refuse offers of drugs. The lesson begins with the DARE officer asking the class what occurrences happened during the previous week to heighten their self-esteem. They then emphasize that once people achieve self-esteem, they can more easily think for themselves without being pressured to do what they believe is wrong. The instructor defines the word "assertive" and stresses that people should learn how to assert their rights confidently without interfering with the rights of others. Role playing occurs in which each student and his or her partner practice (good posture, strong voice, eye contact, calm manner, etc.).

8. *Managing Stress Without Taking Drugs*. This step helps students recognize stress in their lives and how to relieve it without taking drugs. The teacher presents the "fight or flight" response to danger along with the physiological changes that accompany that response. The instructor notes that modern-day stressors, such as taking a test, fail to provide the individual with a means to "flee" or "fight," and alternative ways of coping with stress must be learned. Students then work in groups and devise ways of dealing with two types of stressors (from a class list) in their lives. The then share their strategies with the rest of the class and discuss them. Many such methods include ways to relax and exercise, talk out problems with a family member or a friend, and so on.

9. *Media Influences on Drug Use*. This lesson focuses on ways to resist media influences to use alcohol and drugs. The class discussed various advertising strategies to promote certain products, and the DARE instructor explains how to see through the strategies. For example, by showing a product being used by people that are enjoying themselves, the advertiser suggests that people that actually use the product will indeed have more fun.

    The students then work in groups to create an anti-alcohol or anti-drug commercial while using the techniques employed by professional advertisers. Next, each group performs their own commercial before the class.

10. *Decisionmaking and Risk Taking*. The objective of this lesson is to teach students to apply decision-making skills in evaluating the results of various kinds of risk-taking behavior, including drug use. First, the class gen-

erates a list of risk-taking behaviors, including the many everyday types of risks commonly encountered. Although many risks are worth taking (e.g., making new friends, trying out for a play, etc.), many are not and can result in harm (e.g., swallowing an unknown substance, riding with a drunk driver, etc.). The students learn that any assumption of risk involves a choice. The choices that we make are influenced by several factors, including family, friends, the mass media, and personal values. The key to intelligent decisionmaking is to think through the likely outcomes of various alternative actions.

11. *Alternatives to Drug Abuse*. This lesson examines rewarding alternative activities that do not involve taking drugs. Students recount the reasons why people take drugs and what basic needs people have. They also learn that these needs can be met in healthier ways than taking drugs (such as playing games or exercising). The students then fill out a work sheet titled "What I like to do." They write down their favorite activities and explain to the class why these are better than taking drugs.

12. *Role Modeling*. This phase involves older students who have resisted peer pressure to use drugs. The younger students ask the older students questions that they previously prepared.

13. *Forming a Support System*. Students discover that positive relationships with different people create a support system for the student. In this lesson, two fundamental questions are posed: Why do people need other people? What do other people do for us? The DARE instructor explains that everyone has needs that can only be met through positive relationships with other people.

    The students then complete a work sheet titled "Choosing Friends," which requires them to indicate what qualities they look for in friends (e.g., people that are honest with me, people that won't get me into trouble, etc.). When they are finished, students share their responses and discuss barriers to friendship and how to overcome them.

14. *Ways to Deal with Pressure from Gangs*. In this lesson, students learn how to deal with pressure put on them from gangs and how to evaluate choices available to them. The students begin with naming the social activities that they most enjoy and with whom they like to share these activities. These relationships help satisfy needs for recognition, acceptance, and affection. It is also recognized that people join gangs to satisfy these same needs. Students see that gangs use strong-arm tactics to get what they want. The students then learn to cope with bullying and intimidation by first avoiding places where gangs hang out and by leaving money or other valuables at home. Other techniques include keeping busy with constructive activities that meet the needs for friendship and love.

15. *Project DARE Summary*. This lesson is a summary of what the student should have learned through Project DARE. The class divides into competing teams, and the officer reads a series of questions about DARE,

giving each team an opportunity to earn points for each correct answer. Scores are then computed, and a winner is announced. Each student then individually completes a true/false questionnaire titled "What do you know about drugs?" The officer reviews the answers.

16. *Taking a Stand.* As homework, students must complete a work sheet, "Taking a stand," which asks them to articulate how they will (1) keep their body healthy, (2) control their feelings when angry or under stress, (3) decide whether to take a risk, (4) respond when a friend pressures them to use drugs or alcohol, and (5) respond when they see people on television using drugs or alcohol. This document represents the student's DARE Pledge.

17. *DARE Culmination.* The author of the winning DARE pledge reads his or her pledge in front of a school assembly. Each student that completed the DARE curriculum receives a certificate of achievement signed by the Chief of Police and the Superintendent of Schools.

Thinking Critically #32

Assume you are a DARE officer working in a sixth-grade classroom. Create a role-playing skit by which children may learn methods of resisting peer pressure to experiment with illicit drugs. The characters and dialogue in your skit must be realistic yet suited for the age group.

Project SPECDA

Project SPECDA originated in New York and parallels Project DARE in principle. A collaborative project by the city's Police Department and Board of Education, it offers students a 16-session curriculum with the units split between fifth and sixth grade. Like DARE, SPECDA makes students aware of the social pressures that cause drug abuse and teaches acceptable methods of resisting peer pressure to experiment with drugs.

The program involves weekly 45-minute classes taught by SPECDA instructional teams, which are composed of a full-time police officer and a drug counselor employed by the schools. SPECDA is described as a two-track program that includes the participation of the Police Department's Narcotics Division. In the program, detectives within the Narcotics Division intensify efforts to increase drug arrests and concurrently attempt to close "smoke shops" located within a two-block area of each school.

Close-Up: The SPECDA Program

Police officer Ronald Cato of New York City's SPECDA unit greets the sixth grade class at Our Lady of Miracles School with a big grin. Cato is a large man, powerfully built, but the students sense immediately that he is warm and accessible and that he genuinely cares about what happens to them.

The children, a New York mix of black, brown, yellow, and white, are primly dressed in clean school uniforms. The teacher, a middle-aged nun with spectacles, stands in the back, watching approvingly.

"How many of you know someone who uses drugs?" Officer Cato asks the class.

Several students raise their hands.

"And how many of you have been offered drugs?" he continues. He counts the outstretched arms.

Out of 25 students, eight—nearly one-third—say that they already have had to make a choice about whether to use drugs. No hint of surprise crosses Officer Cato's face. He pauses a moment and then begins his lesson. He wants to reach these children and hopes to arrest the demand for drugs.

Source: The National Institute of Justice, Arresting the Demand for Drugs, November 1987.

A SPECDA pilot program was evaluated in April 1985 by the Criminal Justice Center of the John Jay College of Criminal Justice. Researchers in the study obtained information from classroom observations, interviews, and pre- and post-test questionnaires. The findings of this study include the following:

1. SPECDA students showed significant gains in factual knowledge about drugs and the nature and scope of drug abuse. Most important, SPECDA students expressed a greater awareness of the risks of drug use, including one-time or occasional use, and of the role that peer pressure plays in drug abuse.

2. At the conclusion of the pilot program, SPECDA students showed strong positive attitudes toward SPECDA police officers and drug counselors, though not toward police officers in general.

3. On both the pre- and post-test questionnaires, students asserted that they were unlikely to use drugs within the next year. A majority of the students that were interviewed volunteered that SPECDA had strengthened their resolve to become or remain drug-free.

Prevention programs such as DARE and SPECDA have clearly demonstrat-ed the need for drug abuse education in the early years of a child's development. As of the preparation of this text, educators are constructing programs in which children at all levels of schooling will experience drug sensitivity education.

Summary

We have discussed the many ways in which to deal with drug abuse in our society, and because of the social dangers of drug abuse, more and more attention is being given to this critical issue. In addition to education and law enforcement initiatives, treatment remains one of the most viable options. The immediate objectives of most treatment programs are to control or eliminate drug abuse, give the drug user alternatives for his or her lifestyle, and treat medical complications associated with drug use.

Treatment programs are varied in nature because of the personality type of the drug dependent person as well as the specific drug of abuse for which the person is being treated. Options include detoxification, chemical dependency units, outpatient clinics, methadone maintenance programs, and residential therapeutic communities. After treatment, social reintegration is an important step in making the patient a productive member of the community. The halfway house is often used for this purpose; it permits members to assume some responsibilities in maintaining the operation of the house.

Drug prevention is another essential component to fighting drug abuse. The two ways most likely to achieve the drug prevention goal are to make potential first-time users not want to use drugs and to impose severe criminal penalties to deter first-time drug abuse. Prevention projects DARE and SPECDA are both prevention programs focused on children to teach them fundamental basics of individual thinking, decisionmaking, and personal choices when faced with the prospect of using illicit drugs. Many experts believe that treatment and prevention programs offer the most hope for successfully dealing with the nation's drug problem.

Do you recognize these terms?

chronic relapsing disorder	narcotic antagonists
DARE	relapse
detoxification	SPECDA
maintenance	therapeutic communities

Discussion Questions

1. List three characteristics of treatment and rehabilitation programs.

2. Compare and contrast the five categories of drug treatment.

3. Describe the detoxification process and its role in drug treatment.

4. Explain how the methadone maintenance program operates in treating opiate addicts.

5. Explain how the therapeutic community program treats drug addicts.

6. What are some problems with drug treatment in our communities?

7. Discuss some of the factors that drug treatment counselors look for when recommending a treatment facility for an addicted person.

8. List and discuss the two goals of drug prevention.

References

Abadinsky, H. (1985). *Organized Crime*, 2d ed. Chicago: Nelson Hall.

_____ (1989). *Drug Abuse: An Introduction*. Chicago: Nelson Hall.

_____ (1990). *Organized Crime*. 3rd ed. Chicago: Nelson Hall.

Adler, P. A. (1985). *Wheeling and Dealing: An Ethnography of an Upper Level Drug-Dealing and Smuggling Community*. New York: Columbia University Press.

Albanese, J. (1996). *Organized Crime in America,* 3d ed. Cincinnati: Anderson Publishing Co.

Albini, J.L. (1971). *The American Mafia: Genesis of a Legend*. New York: Appleton-Century-Crofts.

Alexander, S. (1988). *The Pizza Connection: Lawyers, Money, Drugs and Mafia*. New York: Weidenfeld and Nicolson.

Allen, H. & R. Kaiser (1987). "The Age of Aquarius Grows Up." *The Columbia Daily Tribune.* (November): 16.

Anderson, J. (1989). "Narcs Risk their Lives Daily to Battle Drug Scourge." *The Columbia Daily Tribune.* (May 23): 6.

Anderson, J. & D. Van Atta (1988). "The Medellin Cartel/M-19 Gang." *The Washington Post.* (August 28): 87.

Anderson, K. (1982). *The Pocket Guide to Coffees and Teas.* Clarke, R.J. & R. Macrae, eds. Random House.

Apsler, R. (1994). *Is Drug Abuse Treatment Effective?* The American Enterprise. (March/April): 48.

Arlachhi, P. (1986). *Mafia Business: The Mafia and the Spirit of Capitalism*. London: Verso.

Ashley, R. (1975). *Cocaine: Its History, Use, and Effects*. New York: St. Martin's Press.

Atkins, N. (1994). "The Cost of Living Clean." *Rolling Stone.* (May 5): 41.

Backer, T.E. (1987). *Planning for Workplace Drug Abuse Programs*. Washington, DC: National Institute on Drug Abuse.

Bagley, B. M. (1988). "Colombia and the War on Drugs." *Foreign Affairs* (Fall).

Bakalar, J.B. & L. Grinspoon (1988). *Drug Control in a Free Society*. Cambridge, MA: Cambridge University Press.

Barrett, R.E. (1987). "Curing the Drug-Law Addiction: The Harmful Side Effects of Legal Prohibition." In *Dealing with Drugs: Consequences of Government Control*, edited by Ronald Hamowy, pp. 73-102. Lexington, MA: D.C. Heath.

Beaty, J. & R. Hornik (1989). "A Torrent of Dirty Dollars." *Time Magazine.* (December 18): 56.

Bell, R. (1987). "Toward a Drug Free America." *Challenge News Letter*. National Drug Policy Board (March).

Bellizzi, J. (1989). "On the Legalization of Drugs." *International Drug Report*. (January): 6.

Bennett, W. (1990). "A Plea to Legalize Drugs is a Siren Call to Surrender." *Reader's Digest*. (March).

Birdsong, C. (1986). "Why Athletes Use Drugs." *American Pharmacy* NS26, 11. (November).

Block, A. (1983). *East Side-West Side: Organizing Crime in New York, 1930-1950*. New Brunswick, NJ: Transaction.

Blok, A. (1974). *The Mafia of Sicilian Village, 1860-1960*. New York: Harper and Row.

Bonnie, R.J. (1980). *Marijuana Use and Criminal Sanctions*. Charlottesville, VA: Michie Co.

Bonnie, R.J. & C.H. Whitebread II (1980). "The Forbidden Fruit and the Tree of Knowledge: An Inquiry into the Legal History of American Marijuana Prohibition." *Virginia Law Review* 56 (October): 971-1,203.

Bower, B. (1988). "Intoxicating Habits." *Science News*. (August 6): 88-89.

Boyle, J.D. & T. Pham (1988). "The Indochinese Community: A Police Perspective." *Law and Order*. (September): 69-2.

Bradley, B. (1988). "Drug Suspicions Follow Officials in High Places." *The Christian Science Monitor*. (February 26): 17.

Brecher, E.M. & the Editors of *Consumer Reports* (1972). *Licit and Illicit Drugs*. Boston, MA: Little Brown.

Bureau of Alcohol, Tobacco and Firearms (1988). *Special Report: Outlaw Motorcycle Gangs*. Department of Justice. U.S. Government Printing Office.

Bureau of International Narcotics Matters (1990). *International Narcotics Control Strategy Report*. Department of State

_____ (1991). *International Narcotics Control Strategy Report*. Department of State.

Bureau of Justice Assistance (1987). *Report on Drug Control*. Washington, DC: U.S. Department of Justice, Office of Justice Programs.

Bureau of Justice Statistics (1983). *Prisoners and Drugs*. Washington, DC: U.S. Department of Justice.

_____ (1986). *Drug Use and Crime: State Prison Inmate Survey*. Washington, DC: U.S. Department of Justice.

_____ (1987). *Drug Use Forecasting*. Washington, DC: U.S. Department of Justice.

_____ (1987). *Report on Drug Control*. Washington, DC: U.S. Department of Justice.

_____ (1989). *BJS Data Report*. Washington, DC: U.S. Department of Justice.

_____ (1991). *Sourcebook of Criminal Justice Statistics*. Washington, DC: U.S. Department of Justice.

_____ (1992). *Drugs, Crime and the Criminal Justice System*. Washington, DC: U.S. Department of Justice.

Carver, J. (1986). *Drugs and Crime: Controlling Use and Reducing Risk Through Testing*. Washington, DC: National Institute of Justice, U.S. Government Printing Office.

Centers for Disease Control (1992). *The HIV/AIDs Epidemic: The First Ten Years.* Morbidity and Morality Weekly Report, v. 40(8) Supplement. (January).

——————— (1992). Surveillance Report. (November).

Chaiken, J.M. & M.R. Chaiken (1990). *Drugs and Predatory Crime.* In Michael Tonry & James Q. Wilson (eds.), *Drugs and Crime* Volume 13, *Crime and Justice.* Chicago: University of Chicago Press, pp. 203-239.

Chambliss, W.J. (1971). "Vice, Corruption, Bureaucracy, and Power." *Wisconsin Law Review* 4.

Cloward, R.A. & L.E. Ohlin (1960). *Delinquency and Opportunity.* New York: Free Press.

Cockburn, L. (1987). *Out of Control: The Story of the Reagan Administration's Secret War in Nicaragua, the Illegal Arms Pipeline, and the Contra Drug Connection.* New York: Entrekin/Atlantic Monthly Press.

Corcoran, D. (1989). "Legalizing Drugs: Failures Spur Debate." *The New York Times* (November 27): A15.

Cressey, D. (1969). *Theft of the Nation.* New York: Harper and Row.

del Carmen, R.V. & J.T. Walker (1995). *Briefs of Leading Cases in Law Enforcement,* 2d ed. Cincinnati: Anderson Publishing Co.

Department of Health and Human Services (1988). "Mandatory Guidelines for Federal Workplace Testing Programs, Final Guidelines Notice." *Federal Register* 53, 69 (April 11).

——————— (1991). *Cocaine Trafficking.* Special Intelligence Report. Office of Intelligence. Washington, DC: U.S. Department of Justice.

——————— (1993). *Special Report: Drug Trafficking.* U.S. Department of Justice.

Drug Enforcement Administration (1984). *Domestic Marijuana Trafficking.* Special Intelligence Report, Office of Intelligence. Washington, DC: U.S. Department of Justice.

——————— (1985). *Drug Enforcement Administration Booklet.* (Summer) Washington, DC: U.S. Department of Justice.

——————— (1986). *Drugs of Abuse.* U.S. Government Printing Office.

——————— (1987). *Drug Enforcement Administration Booklet* (Summer) Washington, DC: U.S. Department of Justice.

——————— (1988). *Drugs of Abuse.* U.S. Government Printing Office.

——————— (1989). *Drugs of Abuse.* U.S. Government Printing Office.

——————— (1992). *Drugs, Crime, and the Criminal Justice System.* Washington, DC: U.S. Department of Justice.

Duster T. (1970). *The Legislation of Morality: Law, Drugs, and Moral Judgement.* New York: Free Press.

Engelberg, S. (1988). "Nicaraguan Rebels Tell of Drug Deal." *The New York Times* (April 8): L6.

Epstein, E.J. (1977). *Agency of Fear: Opiates and Political Power in America.* New York: Putnam's.

Fagan, J. (1989). "The Social Organization of Drug Use and Drug Dealing Among Urban Gangs." *Criminology.* (November 27): 633-667.

Fedarko, K. (1993). "Escobar's Dead End." *Time Magazine.* (December 13): 46.

Federal Government Information Technology (1985). *Electronic Surveillance and Civil Liberties.* Washington, DC: Congress of the United States, Office of Technology Assessment.

Filippone, R. (1994). "The Medellin Cartel: Why We Can't Win the Drug War." *Journal of Studies in Conflict and Terrorism*. Volume 17, pp. 323-344.

Fogarty, K. (1986). "Parents Who Use Drugs." *The Columbia Missourian*. (October 26): C1.

Frankel, B. (1993). "Ex-NYC Officer Tells Stark Tale of Cops Gone Bad." *USA Today*. (September 28): 3A.

Gardiner, J.A. (1970). *The Politics of Corruption: Organized Crime in an American City*. New York: Russell Sage Foundation.

Gilbert, R. (1984). "Caffeine Labeling." *Journal of the American Medical Association*. (August 10).

Goldstein, H. (1975). *Police Corruption: A Perspective on its Nature and Control*. Washington DC: Police Foundation.

Goldstein, P. (1985). "The Drugs/Violence Nexus: A Tripartite Conceptual Framework." *Journal of Drug Issues* 15. (Fall): 493-506.

Goode, E. (1972). *Drugs in American Society*. New York: Knopf.

——————— (1993). *Drugs in American Society*. 4th ed. New York: McGraw Hill Inc.

Greenhouse, L. (1989). "High Court Backs Airport Detention Based on 'Profile.'" *The New York Times* (April 4): A1.

Grimes, C. (1990). "Details Given on Noriega's Surrender." *St. Louis Post-Dispatch* (January 5): A14.

Grinspoon, L. (1987). "Cancer Patients Should Get Marijuana." *The New York Times* (July 18): 23.

——————— & J.B. Bakalar (1985). *Cocaine: A Drug and its Social Evolution*, rev. ed. New York: Basic Books.

——————— & J. Laszlo (1988). "Should Cancer Patients Smoke Marijuana to Limit Nausea?" *Physicians Weekly*. (June).

Gropper, B. (1985). *Probing the Links Between Drugs and Crime*. Washington, DC: National Institute of Justice, U.S. Government Printing Office.

Gugliotta, G. & J. Leen (1989). *Kings of Cocaine*. New York: Simon and Schuster.

Gusfield, J.R. (1963). *Symbolic Crusade: Status Politics and the American Temperance Movement*. Urbana, IL: University of Illinois Press.

Haller, M.H. (1989). "Bootlegging: The Business and Politics of Violence." In Ted Robert Garr (ed.), *Violence in America*. Newbury Park, CA: Sage Publishers, pp. 146-152.

Hamowy, R., ed. (1987). *Dealing With Drugs: Consequences of Government Control*. Lexington, MA: D.C. Heath.

Hayslip, D.W. Jr. (1989). *Local-Level Drug Enforcement: New Strategies*. Washington, DC: National Institute of Justice.

Helmer, J. (1975). *Drugs and Minority Oppression*. New York: Seabury Press.

Henningfield, J.E. (1989). *Insight Magazine* (May 9): 53.

Hess, H. (1973). *Mafia and the Mafioso: The Structure of Power*.

Hyman, T. (1986). "The World of Smoking and Tobacco." *Journal of the American Medical Association*. (February 28).

Ianni, F. (1972). *A Family Business: Kinship and Social Control in Organized Crime*. New York: Russell Sage Foundation.

_____ (1974). *Black Mafia: Ethnic Succession in Organized Crime*. New York: Simon and Schuster.

Inciardi, J.A. (1986). *The War on Drugs: Heroin, Cocaine, Crime and Public Policy*. Palo Alto, CA: Mayfield Publishing Co.

_____ (1992). *The War on Drugs II*. Mountain View, CA: Mayfield Publishing.

Innes, C.A. (1986). *Drug Use and Crime*. Washington, DC: Bureau of Justice Statistics, Department of Justice: U.S. Government Printing Office.

International Association for the Study of Organized Crime (1989). *Criminal Organizations*, 4,2.

Isikoff, M. (1988). "'Zero Tolerance' Held in Low Regard." *The Washington Post*. (July 13): A18.

Jaschik, S. (1990). "Scholars Are Irked by Bennett Speech Criticizing Their Approaches to Nation's Drug Problems." *Chronicle of Higher Education*. (January 3): 1.

Johnson, B.D. et al (1985). *Taking Care of Business; The Economics of Crime by Heroin Abusers*. Lexington, MA: Lexington Books.

Johnston, M. (1982). *Political Corruption and Public Policy in America*. Monterey, CA: Brooks Cole Publishing.

Jones, H.B. (1985). *What the Practicing Physician Should Know About Marijuana*. Narcotic Educational Foundation of America. Washington, DC: U.S. Department of Justice/Drug Enforcement Administration.

Karchmer, C.L. (1989). *Illegal Money Laundering: A Strategy and Resource Guide for Law Enforcement Agencies*. Washington, DC: Police Executive Research Forum.

Karchmer, C. & D. Ruch (1992). *State and Local Money Laundering Control Strategies*. National Institute of Justice. (October): 1.

Kaut, S. (1989). "Addicts Drawn to Life of Crime to Support Drug Habits." *The Kansas City Star*. (February 5): A14.

Kazman, S. (1991). "The FDA's Deadly Approval Process." *Consumer's Research*. (April): 31-36.

Kenney, D. & J. Finckenauer (1995). *Organized Crime in America*. Wadsworth Publishers.

Kleiman, M. (1985). "Drug Enforcement and Organized Crime." In *Politics and Economics of Organized Crime*, pp. 67-87. Lexington, MA: D.C. Heath.

Kleiman, M. & K.D. Smith (1990). "State and Local Drug Enforcement: In Search of a Strategy." In Michael Tonry and James Q. Wilson (eds.) *Drugs and Crime*, Volume 13, *Crime and Justice*. Chicago: The University of Chicago Press.

Klein, M. (1971). "Violence in American Juvenile Gangs." In Donald Mulvihill and Melvin Tumin (eds.), with Lynn Curtis, *Crimes of Violence*, Volume 13. National Commission on the Causes and Prevention of Violence. Washington: D.C.: U.S. Government Printing Office.

Klein, M. (1991). "Youth Gangs." *Congressional Quarterly*. (October 11): 755.

Knapp, W. (1972). *Commission Report: New York Commission to Investigate Allegations of Police Corruption and the City's Anti-Corruption Procedures*. (September 15).

Kramer, M. (1993). "Clinton's Drug Policy is a Bust." *Time Magazine*. (December 20): 35.

Kraska, P. & V. Kappeler (1988). "Police On-Duty Drug Use: A Theoritical and Descriptive Examination." *American Journal of Police* 7.

Krogh, D. (1992). "Smoking: Why is it so Hard to Quit?" *Priorities.* (Spring): 29-31.

Lamar, J. (1988). "Kids Who Sell Crack." *Time Magazine.* (May): 20.

Lender, M.E. & J.K. Martin (1987). *Drinking in America: A History.* New York: Free Press.

Levine, H. G. & C. Reinarman (1992). "From Prohibition to Regulation: Lessons from Alcohol Policy for Drug Policy." *The Milbank Quarterly.* 69 (3): 1-34.

Levins, H. (1980). "The Kabul Connection." *Philadelphia.* (August): 114-120; 192-203.

Levy, D. (1994). "46 Million Smoke: 70% Want to Quit." *USA Today.* (December 23): 1-A.

Lintner, B. (1994). "Hunt for a Heroin King." *World Press Review.* (March): 330.

Los Angeles Police Department (1991). *Gang Control Manual.* City of Los Angeles.

Lyman, M.D. (1987). *Narcotics and Crime Control.* Springfield, IL: Charles Thomas Publishing Co.

_____ (1989). *Gangland: Drug Trafficking by Organized Criminals.* Springfield, IL: Charles Thomas Publishing Co.

_____ (1989). *Practical Drug Enforcement: Procedure and Administration.* New York: Elsevier Publishing Co., Inc.

_____ & G.W. Potter (1995). *Organized Crime.* Englewood Cliffs: Prentice Hall.

Marriott, M. (1989). "Drug Needle Exchange Is Gaining But Still Under Fire." *The New York Times* (June 7): B1.

Marshall, J. (1987). "Drugs and United States Foreign Policy." In Ronald Hamowy (ed.), *Dealing with Drugs: Consequences of Government Control.* Lexington, MA: D.C. Heath.

Massing, M. (1990). "U.S. On Full Drug-War Footing." *The Kansas City Star.* (January 28): G3.

Mastrofski, S. & G. Potter (1987). "Controlling Organized Crime: A Critique of Law Enforcement Policy." *Criminal Justice Policy Review.* 2, 3: 269-301.

McCoy, A. W. (1972). *The Politics of Heroin in Southeast Asia.* New York: Harper and Row.

McGarrell, E.F. & T. Flanagan (1986). *Sourcebook of Criminal Justice Stastistics.* Washington DC: Bureau of Justice Statistics.

Mieczkowski, T. (1986). "Geeking Up and Throwing Down: Heroin Street Life in Detroit." *Criminology* 24. (November): 645-666.

Miller, N. (1988). *Toward a Drug Free America.* The National Drug Policy Board (March).

Mills, J. (1986). *The Underground Empire.* New York: Dell.

Mintz, J. & V. Churchville (1987). "Vice Officers Walk the Line Between Crime and the Law, In Drug World Integrity Easily Eroded." *The Washington Post.*

Mirkin, G. & M. Hoffman (1978). "Drugs: Is the Prize Worth the Price?" *The Sportsmedicine Book.* Canada: Little Brown: 90.

Moody J. (1989). "Noble Battle, Terrible Toll." *Time Magazine.* (December 18): 33.

Moore, M.H. (1990). "Supply Reduction and Drug Law Enforcement." In Michael Tonry & James Q. Wilson (eds.), *Drugs and Crime,* Volume 13, *Crime and Justice.* Chicago: The University of Chicago Press: 109-157.

More, H.W. (1992). *Special Topics in Policing.* Cincinnati: Anderson Publishing Co.

Morgan, J.P. (1991). "Prohibition is Perverse Policy: What was True in 1933 is True Now." In K. Melvin & E. Lazear (eds), *Searching for Alternatives: Drug Control Policy in the United States.* Standford, CA: Hoover Institution Press: 405-423.

Musto, D. (1973). *The American Disease: Origins of Narcotic Control.* New Haven, CT: Yale University Press.

—————— (1991). "Opium, Cocaine, and Marijuana in American History." *Scientific American.* (July): 40-47.

Nadelmann, E.A. (1988). "U.S. Drug Policy: A Bad Export." *Foreign Policy* 70 (Spring): 83-108.

—————— (1989). "Drug Prohibition in the United States: Cost, Consequences, and Alternatives." *Science* 245 (Sept. 1): 939-947.

Narcotics Anonymous (1987). *Narcotics Anonymous,* 4th ed. Van Nuys, CA: World Service Office Publisher.

Narcotics Control and Technical Assistance Program (1991). *Narcotics Enforcement and Organized Gangs.* Department of Justice, Bureau of Justice Statistics.

National Criminal Justice Association Newsletter (1988). Washington, DC: National Criminal Justice Association (January).

National Drug Policy Board (1988). *Toward a Drug Free America.* Washington, DC: U.S. Government Printing Office.

National Institute on Drug Abuse (1985). National Household Survey on Drug Abuse: Main Findings 1984, DHHS publication No. (ADM) 91-1788.

—————— (1991). National Household Survey on Drug Abuse: Main Findings 1990, DHHS.

—————— (1992). *Annual Emergency Room Data, 1991.* Data from Drug Abuse Warning Network, Series I, Number 10-B.

National Institute of Justice (1987). *Drug Testing, Crime File Study Guide.* Washington, DC: National Institute of Justice.

—————— (1987). *Issues and Practices: AIDS and the Law Enforcement Officer: Concerns and Policy Responses.* Washington, DC: U.S. Department of Justice, Office of Communication and Research Utilization.

—————— (1987). *Issues and Practices: Arresting the Demand for Drugs: Police and School Partnerships to Prevent Drug Abuse.* Washington, DC: National Institute of Justice.

—————— (1987). *Major Issues in Organized Crime: A Compendium of Papers Presented by Experts in the Field.* Washington, DC: National Institute of Justice.

—————— (1988). *Attorney General Announces NIJ Drug Use Forecasting System.* Washington, DC: U.S. Department of Justice, U.S. Government Printing Office.

—————— (1989). *Drug Trafficking: A Report to the President of the United States.* (August 3).

—————— (1992). *State and Local Money Laundering Strategies.* Research in Brief, U.S. Department of Justice. (October).

National Institute on Drug Abuse (1982). "Drug Taking Among the Elderly." *Treatment Research Report.* Washington, DC: U.S. Department of Health and Human Services.

—————— (1983). "Women and Drugs." *Research Issues 31.* Washington, DC: U.S. Department of Health and Human Services.

_____ (1985). "Effects of Drugs on Driving, Driver Simulator Tests of Secobarbital, Diazepam, Marijuana, and Alcohol." *Clinical and Behavioral Pharmacology Research Report*. Washington, DC: U.S. Department of Health and Human Services.

_____ (1985). *Treatment Services for Adolescent Substance Abusers*. Washington, DC: U.S. Department of Health and Human Services.

_____ (1986). *National Trends in Drug Use and Related Factors among American High School Students and Young Adults, 1975-1986*. Washington, DC: U.S. Department of Health and Human Services.

_____ (1986). *Urine Testing for Drugs of Abuse*, Research 73, Monograph Series. Washington, DC: U.S Department of Health and Human Services.

_____ (1988). "Marijuana." *NIDA Capsules*. (August).

Nelli, H. (1976). *The Business of Crime: Italian and Syndicate Crime in the United States*. New York: Oxford University Press.

O'Brien, R. & S. Cohen (1984). *The Encyclopedia of Drug Abuse*. Facts on File.

Office of National Drug Control Policy (1994). *National Drug Control Strategy, Executive Summary*. Washington, DC: U.S. Government Printing Office.

_____ . *Pulse Report*. Washington, DC: U.S. Government Printing Office.

_____ (1995). *What America's Users Spend on Illegal Drugs 1988-1993*. (Spring). Washington, DC: U.S. Government Printing Office.

Organized Crime Drug Enforcement Task Force (1990). *Annual Report*. U.S. Justice Department.

Pennsylvania Crime Commission (1974). *Commission Report*. Harrisburg, PA.

_____ (1980). *A Decade of Organized Crime, 1980 Report*. St. David's, PA: The Commonwealth of Pennsylvania.

Permanent Subcommittee on Investigations, Committee on Governmental Affairs (1983). *Crime and Secrecy: The Use of Offshore Banks and Companies*. Washington, DC: 98th Congress, First Session, U.S. Senate.

Peterson, V.W. (1983). *The Mob: Two Hundred Years of Organized Crime in New York*. Ottawa, IL: Green Hill Publishers.

Post, M. (1990). "Colombian Crime and Cocaine Trafficking." *The Narc Officer*. (December): 11.

Potter, G., L. Gaines & B. Holbrook (1990). "Blowing Smoke: An Evaluation of Marijuana Eradication in Kentucky." *American Journal of Police*. IX, 1: 97-116.

Potter, G. & P. Jenkins (1985). *The City and the Syndicate: Organizing Crime in Philadelphia*. Lexington, MA: Ginn Press.

President's Commission on Organized Crime (1984). *The Cash Connection: Organized Crime, Financial Institutions and Money Laundering*. Washington, DC: U.S. Government Printing Office.

_____ (1984). *Organized Crime and Cocaine Trafficking*. Washington, DC: U.S. Government Printing Office.

_____ (1985). *Organized Crime and Heroin Trafficking*. Washington, DC: U.S. Government Printing Office.

_____ (1986). *America's Habit: Drug Abuse, Drug Trafficking and Organized Crime*. Washington, DC: U.S. Government Printing Office.

_____ (1986). *The Edge: Organized Crime, Business and Labor Unions*. Washington, DC: U.S. Government Printing Office.

Pryor, D. (1994). "Prescription Drug Industry Must be Reformed." *USA Today.* (March): 74-75.

Rangel, C. (1986). *The Crack Cocaine Crisis.* Committee on Narcotics Abuse and Control, 99th Congress, Joint Hearing.

Raspberry, W. (1988). "Living and Dying Like Animals." *The Washington Post.* (November 2): A21.

Reuter, P. (1983). *Disorganized Crime: The Economics of the Visible Hand*. Cambridge, MA: MIT Press.

Reuter, P., G. Crawford & J. Cace (1988). *Sealing the Borders: The Effects of Increased Military Participation in Drug Interdiction*. (January) (R-3594-USDP) Santa Monica, CA: The RAND Corporation.

Reuter, P., R. MacCoun & P. Murphy (1990). *Money from Crime: A Study of the Economics of Drug Dealing in Washington DC.* Santa Monica: The RAND Corporation, (June): 66.

Riding, A. (1988). "Intimidated Colombian Courts Yield to Drug Barons." *The New York Times.* (January 11): A3

Rinehart, R., *et al*. (1981). *Thailand: A Country Study*. Washington, DC: U.S. Government Printing Office.

Robbins, C.A. (1989). "Bloody Footprints on Peru's Shining Path." *U.S. News and World Report.* (September 18): 49.

Rorabaugh, W.J. (1991). "Alcohol in America." *OAH Magazine of History.* (Fall): 17-19.

Rosenau, W. (1994). "Is the Shining Path the 'New Khmer Rouge'"? *Journal of Studies on Conflict and Terrorism*, Volume 17: 305-322.

Roth, J. (1994). *Understanding and Preventing Violence*. National Institute of Justice, Research in Brief. (February): 10.

Rovner, J. (1992). "Prescription Drug Prices." *Congressional Quarterly.* (July): 599.

Rydell, C.P. & S.E. Everingham (1994). *Controlling Cocaine: Supply Versus Demand Programs.* RAND Corporation: xv.

Schmetzer, U. (1991). "The Chinese Connection." *The Chicago Tribune.* (May 12): D1.

Schmoke, K.L. (1988). "Get Your Heads Out of the Sand." *USA Today* (May).

Select Committee on Narcotics Abuse and Control (1986). *The Crack Crisis*. Joint Hearing, 99th Congress, Second Edition, (July).

_____ (1987). *Strategic Report*. U.S. Congress.

Shannon, E. (1988). *Desperados: Latin Drug Lords, U.S. Lawmen, and the War America Can't Win*. New York: Viking Penguin, Inc.

_____ (1991). "New Kings of Coke." *Time Magazine.* (July 1): 29-36.

Sherman, L. (1974). *Police Corruption: A Sociological Perspective*. Garden City, NY: Doubleday.

Sherman, L. (1982). "Learning Police Ethics." *Criminal Justice Ethics.* (Spring-Winter).

Smith, D.C. Jr. (1975). *The Mafia Mystique*. New York: Basic Books.

Smith, R.N. (1986). "The Plague Among Us." *Newsweek* (June 16): 15.

Stein, B. (1988). "The Lure of Drugs: They Organize an Addict's Life." *Newsday,* (December 4): 6.

Stellwagen, L.D. (1985). *Use of Forfeiture Sanctions in Drug Cases.* Washington, DC: National Institute of Justice, U.S. Government Printing Office.

Stoddard, E.L. (1983). "Blue Coat Crime." In Carl Klockars (ed.) *Thinking About Police.* New York: McGraw-Hill.

_____ (1968). "The Informal Code of Police Deviancy: A Group Approach to Blue-Coat Crime." *Journal of Criminal Law, Criminology, and Police Science.*

Sutherland, E.H. (1973). *Edwin H. Sutherland: On Analyzing Crime.* Karl Schuessler (ed.). Chicago: University of Chicago Press.

Szasz, T. (1974). *Ceremonial Justice: The Ritual Persecution of Drug Addicts and Pushers.* Garden City, NY: Doubleday.

Toborg, M.A. & Michael P. Kirby (1984). "Drug Use and Pretrial Crime in the District of Columbia." *Research in Brief.* Washington, DC: National Institute of Justice.

Thrasher, F.M. (1927). *The Gang.* Chicago, IL: University of Chicago Press.

Toufexis, A. (1994). "A Health Debate that Won't Die." *Time Magazine.* (April 18): 61.

Trebach, A. (1982). *The Heroin Solution.* New Haven, CT: Yale University Press.

_____ (1987). *The Great Drug War: Radical Proposals that could Make America Safe Again.* New York: Macmillan.

United States Department of Justice (1978). "The Investigation of Nicky Barnes." *Drug Enforcement Magazine* (July).

_____ (1983). "Investigation and Prosecution of Illegal Money Laundering. Narcotic and Dangerous Drug Section Monograph," *A Guide to the Bank Secrecy Act:* Washington, DC: U.S. Government Printing Office.

_____ (1984). *Domestic Marijuana Trafficking, Special Intelligance Report.* Drug Enforcement Administration. Washington, DC: U.S. Government Printing Office.

_____ (1986). *Black Tar Heroin.* Special Report. Washington, DC: U.S. Department of Justice, Office of Intelligence.

_____ (1988). *Intelligence Trends Special Report: From the Source to the Street.* Volume 1. Washington, DC: U.S. Department of Justice.

_____ (1988). *Drugs of Abuse.* Washington, DC: U.S. Department of Justice.

_____ (1989). *Drug Trafficking: A Report to the President of the United States.* Office of the Attorney General. Washington, DC: U.S. Government Printing Office.

_____ (1989). *Drugs and Jail Inmates.* Special Report. NCJ-130 836 (August).

United States Department of the Treasury (1987). *Anti-Drug Law Enforcement Efforts and their Impact.* (August) Washington, DC: U.S. Customs Service.

Wagner, J.C. (1987). Substance-Abuse Policies and Guidelines in Amateur and Professional Atheltics. *American Journal of Hospital Pharmacy* 44 (February).

Watson, R. & P. Katel (1993). "Death on the Spot: The End of a Drug King." *Newsweek.* (December 13): 18-21.

Webster, B. & M. McCampbell (1992). *International Money Laundering: Research and Investigation Join Forces.* National Institute of Justice. (September): 1-7.

Weingart, S.N., et al (1994). *Case Studies of Community Anti-Drug Efforts.* National Institute of Justice. (October).

White, P.T. (1989). "Coca: An Ancient Indian Herb Turns Deadly." *National Geographic Magazine* 175: 1 (January).

Whitehouse, The (1989). *National Drug Control Strategy* (September). Washington, DC: U.S. Government Printing Office.

Wilkinson, F. (1994). "A Separate Peace." *Rolling Stone,* (May 5): 26-29.

Winick, C. (1965). *Epidemology of Narcotics Use.* Narcotics. New York: McGraw Hill.

Witkin, G. (1993). "How Politics Ruined Drug-War Planning." *U.S. News and World Report,* (Feburary 22): 29.

Wisotsky, S. (1987). *Breaking the Impasse in the War on Drugs.* Westport, CT: Greenwood.

Yablonsky, L. (1966). *The Violent Gang.* Baltimore, MD: Penguin Books.

Zinberg, N.E. (1984). *Drug, Set, and Setting: The Basis for Controlled Intoxicant Use.* New Haven, CT: Yale University Press.

Zwerling, C., J. Ryan & J. Endel (1990). "The Efficacy of Preemployment Drug Screening for Marijuana and Cocaine in Predicting Employment Outcome." *Journal of the American Medical Association.* (November): 264.

Index

AA. *See* Alcoholics Anonymous

AARP. *See* American Association of Retired Persons

Abbott-Fluorescence Polarization Immunoassay (AFPI) test, 349

Abductions, of drug lords, 336-337

Abstinence, 3

Abuse, dependence and, 34-35

Acquisitions, for money laundering, 193-194

Adams, Edgar H., 52n

Addiction, 12, 35n
  of babies, 81-83
  medical model of, 425
  rate of, 13
  rise in, 21, 424-425

Addictive personality, 73

Addicts. *See also* Addiction; Drug abuse; Scams
  British system and, 383-384
  legalization and, 377

Afghanistan, 130, 133. *See also* Golden Crescent

AFPI. *See* Abbott-Fluorescence Polarization Immunoassay test

Africa, 5

African-American youth gangs, 203, 240. *See also* Black Guerrilla Family; Bloods; Crips
  Crips and Bloods, 243-245

Agencies. *See also* agencies by name
  federal drug control, 319
  law enforcement, 297

Age of Aquarius, 21

AIDS (Acquired Immune Deficiency Syndrome), 27, 68, 84
  drug price crisis and, 143
  legalization and, 373
  needle exchange programs and, 351

Airborne drug detection, 302

Air Branch, of Customs Service, 310

Alaska
  marijuana legalization experiment in, 384-386
  recriminalization of marijuana in, 380

Albanese, Jay, 229

Albini, Joseph, 228-229

Albujar, Enrique Lopez, 286

Alcohol, 4. *See also* Prohibition era
  abuse of, 422
  benefits of moderate consumption, 49
  consumption limits on, 75
  as depressant, 47-51
  detoxification and, 427
  happy hour and, 75
  legalization of drugs and, 376
  metabolization of, 48-49
  Prohibition era and, 408
  in the Roaring Twenties, 15
  violence and, 170

Alcoholics Anonymous (AA), 431

Alexander, Shana, 224

Al-Hassan-ibn-al Sabbah, 5

Alien conspiracy theory, of organized crime, 209-210

Alkaloid ephedrine, 4

Alpert, Richard, 20

AMA. *See* American Motorcycle Association

Amateur sports, drug control in, 356-357

Amendments
  Drug Abuse Control, 23
  18th, 14
  Fifth, 416
  21st, 14

American Association of Retired Persons (AARP), 142-143

American Civil Liberties Union (ACLU)
  on drug courier profiling, 338
  on zero tolerance, 342

American Disease, The: Origins of Narcotic Control, 78-79

American Indians. *See* Native Americans

American Motorcycle Association (AMA), 230
American Opium Commission, 12
American Psychiatric Association, substance dependence defined by, 34-35
American Temperance Society, 13
Amphetamines, 20, 45
    detoxification and, 427
Amsterdam, drug legalization in, 381-383
Anabolic steroids, 26, 356
Anderson, J., 282n
Anesthetics, 7
Angel Dust. *See* PCP
Anger, 3
Anglo-French War, opium and, 6
Anomie theory, 88-89
Anslinger, Harry, 15
Anti-Drug Abuse Act (1986, 1988), 403
Anti-drug efforts, in U.S., 13-15
Anti-saloon League of America, 14
Aryan Brotherhood, 249
Ascencio, Diego, 281
Asia. *See also* China; Golden Crescent; Golden Triangle; Hong Kong; Japanese Yakuza
    drug trade in, 103
    money laundering in, 197-198
    organized crime in, 288-291
Assassin, origins of term, 5
Athletes
    and anabolic steroids, 26
    drugs and, 355-358
Atlantis II, seizure of, 342
Attorney's fees, forfeiture of, 353-354. *See also* Forfeiture
Audit, money laundering detection by, 198
Avery, Gordon B., 83
AZT, 143
Aztec Indians, 4

Babies, addicted, 81-83
Babylonia, 4
Backstabbing, 68
Badalamente, Gaetano, 224
Bad trip, 53
Bahamas, corruption in, 183, 184
Bandidos motorcycle gang, 239
Banking, money laundering and, 187, 191
Bank of Commerce and Credit International (BCCI), 186
Bank Secrecy Act, 194
    money laundering and, 191
Barbie, Klaus, 113

Barbiturates, 10, 51
    detoxification and, 427
Barco Vargas, Virgilio, 110, 111, 184
Barger, Ralph Hubert (Sonny), 236
Barnes, Nicky, 230
Baseball, drug control in, 357
Basketball, drug control in, 357-358
Basque ETA organization, 259
Bayer Company, 9
BCCI. *See* Bank of Commerce and Credit International
BDAC. *See* Bureau of Drug Abuse Control
Beacon group, 122-124
Beat Generation, 25
Beaty, J., 196n
Behavior. *See also* Drug abuse
    deviant, 88
    electronically surveyed, 344
    learned, 90
Belize, 102
Bell, R., 45n
Belushi, John, 26
Bennett, William, 313, 319, 407
    on drug abuser treatment, 423-424
    on legalization, 368, 378
    on prevention, 436
Bentancur, Belisario, 335-336
Benzedrine, 10
Berry, William, 230
Beverages, alcoholic, 48
Bias, Len, 26, 355
Biker gangs. *See* Motorcycle gangs
Birdsong, Carl, 355
Black Dragon Society, 290
Black Guerrilla Family, 249, 250, 251-253
Black market, legalization and, 378
Blacks, drugs and, 8. *See also* African-American youth gangs
"Black tar" heroin, 58
Bladow, Janel, 317n
Blandon Castillo, Jose, 278
Block, Alan, 229
Block Watch, Denver, CO, 330
Blok, Anton, 228n
Blood-alcohol concentration, 48-49
Bloods, x, 243-245, 250. *See also* African-American youth gangs; Gangs
Bloque de Busqueda, Escobar and, 267
Blotter acid (LSD), 100
Blue Lightning Operations Center (BLOC), 309-310
BNDD. *See* Bureau of Narcotics and Dangerous Drugs

Boaz, David, 378
Boerenveen, Atienne, 184
Boggs Act, 20
Bogota Cartel, 274
Bolivia, 102, 103, 113-115, 259
    trafficking trends in, 117
Bonanno, Joe (Joe Bananas), 221
Bonilla, Rodrigo Lara, 109-110, 266
Border controls, 393-394
Border Patrol, 104-105, 297, 311
Borge, Tomas, 283
Boston, MA, Hill Street Crime Watch Committee in, 328
Bouza, Anthony, 366
Bowman, Harry Joseph, 237
Boycotts, 387
Bradley, B., 184n
Bradshaw, Robert V., 325
Brain, drugs and, 32-33
Brazil, 102. *See also* Latin America
    trafficking trends in, 117
Bribery, police corruption and, 174
Britain, 5, 15
    drug control in, 383-384
    opium wars and, 6
British system, 383
Brown, Elrader (Ray Ray), 251-253
Brown, Jim, 248
Brown, Lee P., 408
Bruce, Lenny, 77
BSA. *See* Bank Secrecy Act
Buckley, William F., 366
Bugging devices, money laundering detection by, 198
Bureau of Alcohol and Drug Abuse Control, 23
Bureau of Alcohol, Tobacco, and Firearms (ATF), 230, 312
Bureau of Customs, 15
Bureau of Drug Abuse Control (BDAC), 298
Bureau of International Narcotics Matters, 403
Bureau of Justice Statistics, School Crime Survey, 69
Bureau of Narcotics and Dangerous Drugs (BNDD), 23, 299
Burmese Communist Party, 286
Buscetta, Tommaso, 224, 227
Bush, George, 185
    drug control policy of, 394, 402-406
Business. *See also* Drug trade; Money laundering
    acquisition for money laundering, 193-194
    drug trade as, 94-95
    U.S. marijuana growth as, 146-149
Business professionals, as money launderers, 189
Buttons, peyote, 55
Buying, drug-related consumerism and, 85-86

Caffeine, 37
Caicos Islands, 184
Cali Cartel, 205, 208, 259, 267, 270-273. *See also* Colombia; Latin America
    Escobar and, 266-267
    organization of, 272-273
    workings of, 271-273
California. *See also* Organizations; Prisons
    Project DARE in, 437-443
    Synanon in, 430
    youth gangs in, 203, 211, 243-245
Calo, Giuseppe (Pippo), 227
Camarena Salazar, Enrique, 108, 182, 183, 276
Cambodian youth gangs, 240
Camorra, 220
Cancer, tobacco and, 39, 41
Cannabis, 4, 5, 59-62. *See also* Marijuana
Cannabis Eradication Suppression Program, 320
Capone, Al, 93, 408
Carcinogen, tobacco smoke as, 40-41
Caribbean, and drug distribution, 102, 118
Caro Quintero, Rafael, 182, 275-276
Cartels, in Colombia, 205, 208, 258-274. *See also* Bogota Cartel; Cali Cartel; Medellin Cartel; North Atlantic Coast Cartel
Carter, Jimmy, 406
    drug policy of, 394
Casa de cambio, 189
Castellano, Paul, 211
Castro, Fidel, 109. *See also* Cuba; Latin America
    drug trafficking and, 287
    Nicaragua and, 283
Castro, Raul, 283
Cawley, Bernie, 178
CCE. *See* Continuing Criminal Enterprise Statute
Central America, drug trade and, 68. *See also* Cartels; Latin America; South America
Central Intelligence Agency (CIA), 109, 185, 406
    LSD testing by, 20
    role of, 372
Certification system, for new prescription drugs, 145

CFA. *See* Federal Comprehensive Forfeiture Act
Chain conspiracies, 413
Chain of custody, in drug testing, 350
Chambers, Donald, 239
Chambliss, William, 229
Chang Chifu, 286
Chartered v. United States, 353
Chasnoff, Ira, 82
Chemical Diversion and Trafficking Act, 155, 321
Chess Player. *See* Rodriguez Orejuela, Gilberto
Chiaracane, Salvatore, 227
Chicago, IL
  crime control in, 208
  police gang units in, 241
Child Protection Act (1984), 341
Chile, 372. *See also* Latin America
China, 125
  drugs in ancient, 4
  opium in, 6-7
  organized crime from, 288
  Tongs of, 257-258, 289
  Triads of, 257-258, 289
China white, 59
Chinese people
  opium among immigrants, 8
  triads and tongs, 257-258
  youth gangs, 240
Chiseling, police corruption and, 174
Chitwood, Dale D., 52n
Chloral hydrate, 8
Chloroform, 7
Choke points, 306
Chronic relapsing disorder, 422
CIA. *See* Central Intelligence Agency
Cigarettes, filter-tipped, 39. *See also* Nicotine; Smoking
Cities, urban drug gangs in, 253-254. *See also* Community policing
Civil liberties, drug testing and, 345-351
Civil War, drugs and, 7-8
Clandestine drug laboratories, 151-154
  seizures of, 154
Clinton, Bill, 80, 366
  drug policy of, 406-408, 421-422
  drug war budget of, iii
Cloning, 148
Cloward, Richard A., 89-90
Coast Guard, 297, 305-306
Coca-Cola, cocaine base of, 9

Cocaine, 4, 8-9, 21, 42-44. *See also* Cartels; Colombia
  babies addicted to, 83
  in Bolivia, 113
  in Colombia, 109-111
  conversion process for, 269
  crack, 25-26
  cycle of use, 43
  damaging effects of, 45
  declining use of, 82
  detoxification and, 427
  dopamine release by, 44
  importation of, 102
  Jamaican trade in, 119
  Ochoa/Escobar venture with, 268
  Panama and, 197
  in Peru, 115-116
  physical effects of, 44
  prices of, 114
  production to sales process, 270
  regulation of, 11
  transportation of, 282
  trends in, 117-118
  in U.S., 8
  U.S. intelligence agency involvement in, 284
  user of, 423
Coca plant, 102
  in Peru, 115
Codeine, 7
Code of Hammurabi, 4
Coffee, 5, 37-38
Coke, Lester Lloyd, 248
Colasanto, Diane, 375n
Cold turkey approach, 427
Coley, Jim, 122-124
College students, drug abuse trends and, 80
Colombia, ix, 102, 103. *See also* Bogota Cartel; Cali Cartel; Latin America; Medellin Cartel
  cartels in, 109, 205, 208, 211
  corruption in, 184
  drug trade in, 108-112
  guerrilla warfare in, 280-282
  narco-terrorism in, 277
  North Atlantic Coast Cartel, 274
  organized crime in, 258-274
  Panama, Cuba, and, 277-282
  presidential campaign in, 111-112
  trafficking trends in, 117
"Colombia Gold" marijuana, 100
Commercial grade marijuana, 148

Communism
  Burmese Communist Party and, 286
  Shining Path and, 285
Communities
  police cooperation with, 324-329
  prevention in, 437
Community Epidemiology Workgroup, 79
Community Mental Health Centers Act, 22
Community policing, 326-328, 329, 330-331
Companía, La, 288
Comprehensive Crime Act (1984), 403
Comprehensive Drug Abuse Prevention and
  Control Act (1970), 24, 396, 412-413
Comprehensive Forfeiture Act (1984), 403
Compton Pirus street gang, 244
Confirmation drug tests, 349-350
Conflicts of interest, of police, 180
Conspiracy, 413-414
Consumerism, drug-related, 85-86
Continuing Criminal Enterprise (CCE), 23,
  206, 302, 412-413
Contras, congressional inquiries into, 284
Controlled Substances Act (CSA), 23, 24-25,
  156, 396
    drug audit and, 163
Control policy. See Drug control; Policy
Conversion labs, 152
Coordination, of law enforcement activities,
  312-319
Copping areas, 100-102
COP-Plus, 325
Coppola, Mike, 2121
Coptic Christianity, marijuana use by, 76
Corporation, The, 288
Corruption
  in foreign countries, 181-186
  institutional, 180
  police, 171-181
Cosa Nostra, La, 203, 210, 411
  organizational structure of, 222
Cost crisis, in prescription medicines, 140-
  143
Costello, Frank, 411
Costs. See also Prices
  of legalization, 378-380
  of treatment, 436
Counseling, 388
Counter-Drug Technology Asessment Center,
  407
Couriers, for money laundering, 189
Crack, 25-26, 42, 44-45
  freebasing, 44-45
  profit margin on, 249
  in rural America, 151

Crack house, 323
Creativity, drug use and, 76-77
Crime, ix. See also Drug abuse; Organiza-
  tions; Theories
  drug abuse and, 86-90
  drugs and, 167-200
  police corruption and, 171-181
  predatory, 168-171
  social disorganization theory and, 87
  violent, 169-171
Crime control, as drug control method, 399.
  See also Drug control
Crime Control Act (1990), 403
Crime families. See Mafia
Crime rate
  in Amsterdam, 382
  legalization and, 372, 376-377
Criminal group, 207
Criminal justice, and policy, 400
Criminals, in Roaring Twenties, 14-15
Crips, x, 243-245, 250. See also African-
  American youth gangs; Gangs
CSA. See Controlled Substances Act
Cuartas, Belisario Betancur, 109-110
Cuba. See also Castro, Fidel; Latin America
  corruption in, 182
  drug traffickers in, 287-288
  Panama, Colombia, and, 277-282
Cuban Mafia, 109
Cultural transmission theory, 88
Culture(s)
  ancient, drug use by, 4-5
  delinquent subculture and, 89-90
  drinking and, 50-51
Currency and Foreign Transactions Report-
  ing Act, 195
Currency exchanges
  money laundering and, 192-193
  specialists, for money laundering, 189
Currency or Monetary Instrument Report
  (CMIR), 195
Currency Transaction Report (CTR), 195
Customs search, radius of, 302
Customs Service, 297, 306-311. See also
  Bureau of Customs
  drug policy and, 406
Customs zone, 306

DARE. See Drug Abuse Resistance Education
  (DARE) program,
DARP. See Drug Abuse Reporting Program
Davis, John, 237
DAWN (Drug Abuse Warning Network), 71
Daytop Village, 430

DEA. *See* Drug Enforcement Administration
Decriminalization, 365-366. *See also*
   Legalization of marijuana, 23-24
Defense Department, 311
de la Madrid, Miguel, 183
Delinquent subcultures, 89-90
Delirium tremens, 50
Della Chiesa, Carlo Alberto, 227
Demand, elasticity of, 97
Demand reduction, as policy, 399-401
Demerol®, 10
Department of Defense (DOD), 311
   Authorization Act (1982), 402
   task force of, 398
Department of Narcotics (Mexico), 108
Departments, federal. *See* departments by
   name
Dependence, 423
   versus abuse, 34-35
   cocaine and, 43
   genetic theory of, 72-73
   physical, 33, 35
   psychological, 34, 35
Depressants, 20, 36, 46-56
   alcohol as, 47-51
   barbiturates, 51
   in combination with alcohol, 47
   hallucinogens, 51-56
   LSD, 53
   PCP, 53-54
   peyote and mescaline, 55
   Quaalude®, 21, 51
   tolerance to, 47
Derivative use immunity, 417
"Designer drugs," 59
Desperados, 108
Detection, of money laundering, 187
Detoxification, 426-427
   with methadone, 429
Detroit Police Department, 101
Deviant behavior, anomie and, 88. *See also*
   Behavior; Drug abuse
Devoe Airlines, smuggling by, 304-305
Dextroamphetamine, 45
Diagnostic and Statistical Manual, The (DSM
   IV), 34
Diamentes, Los, 279-280
Diaz Herrera, Roberto, 185
Dilaudid®, 58
Dinkins, David, 177
Dir, Kojo A., 99n
DIS (Departmento Inteligencia Seguridad),
   276
Discreet drug markets, 321

Displacement, 324
Distribution, 98, 99, 100-101
   control of, 296
   laws and, 297
Diversions, investigations of, 160-161
Doctors, as drug offenders, 158-159
DOD. *See* Department of Defense
Dole, Vincent, 425
Dolkin, Lou, 237
Domestic drug production, 139-165
   clandestine laboratories and, 151-154
   marijuana, 145-149
Dominican Republic, 281
Dopamine, 32
   cocaine and, 44
Double invoicing, money laundering and, 193
Dowd, Michael, 177-178
Downers, 20, 36
DRAGNET, 331-332
Drinking. *See also* Alcohol
   habits, culture, and, 50-51
   happy hour and, 75
Droznek/Rosa case, 214-216
Drug(s). *See also* Domestic drug production;
   Drug categories
   of abuse, 31-64
   in Amsterdam, 381-383
   attitudes about, 71
   audit of, 163
   boycotting, 387
   and brain, 32-33
   and crime, 167-200
   defined, 31-32
   deglamorizing, 387
   domestic production of, 139-165
   effects of illegal, 52
   and family, 68-69
   federal approval of, 143-145
   and HIV, 84
   Mafia and, 229-230
   money for, 85
   nature of problem with, 65-92
   pharmaceutical, 139-145
   precursor chemicals as, 155
   prices of, 95-97
   quality of, 100
   in rural America, 150-151
   and schools, 69
   side effects of, 33
   sources of, 68
   usefulness of, 73-74
Drug abuse, iv. *See also* Drug control
   ancient, 4-5
   anomie theory and, 88-89

consequences of, 66-71
and crime, 86-90
cultural transmission theory and, 88
defined, 32
differential association and, 90
geographical differences in, 79
health effects of, 67-68, 70-71
history of, 3-29
measuring, 77-78
natural high and, 74-75
in 1960s, 3, 21-23
opportunity theory and, 89-90
outcomes of, 33-34
post-Prohibition, 15-17
during Prohibition, 13-15
reasons for, 72-74
social costs of, 80
social disorganization theory and, 87
social explanations of, 73
surveys on, 77-78
trends in, 79-80
in twentieth century, 10-13
use of term, 65
and victimless crime, 86-87
after World War II, 20
Drug Abuse Control Amendments, 23, 298
Drug Abuse Reporting Program (DARP), 169
Drug Abuse Resistance Education (DARE)
program, 397-398, 399, 437-443
Drug categories, 35-63
cannabis, 59-62
depressants, 46-56
inhalants, 63
narcotics, 56-59
stimulants, 35-46
Drug consumerism, 85-86
Drug control, 295-333. *See also* Decriminalization; Drug abuse; Law enforcement;
Legalization; Policy
agencies for, 319
aid to source countries, 358-359
in amateur sports, 356-357
in Amsterdam, 381-383
in Britain, 383-384
Clinton and, 406-408
crime control method of, 399
critical issues in, 335-364
deglamorization and, 387
demand reduction as, 399-401
drug lord abductions as, 336-337
drug testing programs, 345-351
education for, 362
federal drug control agencies, 319

federal efforts, 396
forfeiture of attorney's fees, 353-354
goals of, 296
history of, 16-17
history of government control, 404-405
law enforcement and, 86-87
laws, 296-298
legalization, 362
legal tools in, 410-417
medical model of, 399
in Mexico, 105, 107-108
milestones in, 18-19
military role in, 359-362
national strategies in, 401-402
needle exchange programs, 351-353
police-community efforts, 324-329
policies, strategies, and tactics for, 71,
393-420. *See also* Policy
in professional sports, 357-358
profiling drug couriers, 337-339
Reagan, Bush, and, 402-406
in Reno, NV, 325-326
and sports, 355-358
treatment and prevention for, 421-446
Drug courier profiling, 337-339
Drug czars, 313, 407-408
Drug Enforcement Administration (DEA),
64, 297, 299-301, 403-406
FARC and, 280
Drug-free Workplace Act, 347
Drug gangs, as organized crime, 211-213. *See
also* Gangs
Drug industry, ix
Drug interdiction, 302, 303
Drug laws, enforcement of, 298-302
Drug lords, abductions of, 336-337
Drug markets, 321
restriction of, 371
Drug Policy Foundation, 62
Drug production, control of, 296
Drug sting, reverse, 339-341. *See also* Sting
operations
Drug testing, 345-351
hair follicles for, 351
types of programs, 348
Drug trade, x, 93-138. *See also* Domestic drug
production; Opium
in Bolivia, 113-115
business of, 94-95
Caribbean routes for, 118
case study in, 122-124
in Colombia, 108-112
demand elasticity in, 97

distribution in, 100-101
financing drug deals in, 97-98
foreign governmental corruption in, 181-186
in Golden Crescent, 130-135
in Golden Triangle, 125-129
heroin trafficking organization, 132
in Hong Kong
illicit, 93-138
international perspective on, 103
in Jamaica, 119-124
Kurds and, 134-135
marketing in, 100
merchandising and distribution in, 98, 99
in Mexico, 103-108
money laundering for 186-199
national security and, 68
organized crime and, 203-217
in Peru, 115-117
pricing in, 95-97
profit margin in, 101-102
trends in South America, 117-118
Drug trafficking. *See also* Smuggling
breaking down infrastructure, 388
crime and, 171
domestic organizations, 219-256
economics of, 95-98
fighting, 224
foreign organizations, 257-292
organized crime and, 204-206
problems due to, 80-81
social effects of, 67
Drug Use Forecasting (DUF) program, 169
Drug users, 422-424
accountability of, 400
support for organized crime, 207
characteristics of, 78-79
targeting, 388
Drug war, 394
DTs. *See* Delirium tremens
DUF program. *See* Drug Use Forecasting program
Dummy corporations, money laundering and, 193
Dunkirk Boys, in Jamaica, 246
Durk, David, 176
Durkheim, Emile, 88
Dutch. *See* Amsterdam

Ecstasy, 63. *See* also Hallucinogens; MDMA
Ecuador, 102, 259
drug trafficking in, 118
Education, for drug control, 362

Egypt, ancient, 4
18th Amendment, 14, 408
"80-20 rule," 134
Elders, Joycelyn, 366, 406-407
Electronic surveillance, 343-345
money laundering detection by, 198
El Paso Intelligence Center (EPIC), 201
EMIT. *See* Syva-Enzyme Multiplied Immunoassay Technique
Employees, drug testing of, 347-348
Endocrine-producing glands, 74
Endogenous chemicals, 74
Endorphins, 74-75
Enforcement
futility of, 371
local options and, 397
by Treasury Department, 12
England, opium in, 7. *See also* Britain
Entrapment, 339, 341
Environmental Protection Agency (EPA), on tobacco smoke as carcinogen, 40-41
Ephedra, 4
EPIC. *See* El Paso Intelligence Center
Eradication, 394
Escobar, Pablo, 259, 261-262
biography of, 266
cooperation with Jorge Ochoa, 268
demise of, 265-268
Diamante and, 280
Esposito, Giuseppe, 220
Ethyl alcohol, 48
Europe
heroin in, 130
opium in, 7
Exploration, drug spread by, 5
Extortion, police corruption and, 174
Extraction labs, 152
Extradition treaty, with Colombia, 109, 110

FAA. *See* Federal Aviation Administration
Families, in Mafia, 210
Family, drugs and, 68-69
Farach, Antonio, 283
FARC. *See* Revolutionary Armed Forces of Colombia
Favoritism, police corruption and, 174
FBI. *See* Federal Bureau of Investigation
FBN. *See* Federal Bureau of Narcotics
FDA. *See* Food and Drug Administration
Federal agencies. *See* Law enforcement; agencies by name
Federal Aviation Administration (FAA), 311, 312

Federal Bureau of Investigation (FBI), 297, 301-302

Federal Bureau of Narcotics (FBN), 15, 298

Federal Chemical Diversion and Trafficking Act, 118

Federal Comprehensive Forfeiture Act (CFA), 353, 354, 414-415

Federal drug control. *See* Drug control; Policy

Federal drug enforcement. *See* Enforcement; Law enforcement

Federal Strategy for Drug Abuse and Drug Traffic Prevention, 401

Federal Witness Security Program (WITSEC), 417-418

Fein, Bennie (Dopey), 230

Fetal alcohol syndrome, 50

Fetus. *See* Babies

Field training officer program (FTO), 87

Fifth Amendment, 416

Fighting Back, 437

Financial audit, money laundering detection by, 198

Financial havens, for money laundering, 195-197

Financing, of drug deals, 97-98

Fines, imposing, 389

Firearms, youth gangs and, 240

Five families, in Mafia, 210

Five Star Health Club, 161-163

Flashbacks, 53

Flooding, by drug money, 187

Flower tops, harvest of, 148

Fonseca Carrillo, Ernesto, 276

Food and Drug Act, 398

Food and Drug Administration (FDA), 298
    new drug approval by, 143-145

Food, Drug, and Cosmetic Act (FDCA), 141
    Kefauver-Harris Amendments to, 144

Football, drug testing in, 358

Foreign Assistance Act, 68

Foreign countries, 181-186. *See also* individual countries by name
    Cuban corruption, 182
    Mexican corruption, 182-183
    political climate and gangs in, 213
    Foreign drug trafficking organizations, 257-292

Foreign initiatives, 394

Forfeiture
    of attorney's fees, 353-354
    broadening, 388
    sanctions and, 414-416

Fort, Jeff, 230

Four Seasons Gang, 289

14K, 289

Freebase metamphetamine, ice as, 46

Freebasing cocaine, 44-45. *See also* Cocaine; Crack

Freedoms, legalization and, 372, 378

French Connection, 59, 106, 223, 230
    Turkey and, 133

Freud, Sigmund, 9

Friedli, Otto, 236

Friedman, Gary, 49

Friedman, Milton, 366

Frogman Case, 284

Functioning, drug use for, 73-74

Galan, Luis Carlos, 11, 262

Gambino, Carlo, 221

Gambling, as victimless crime, 86

Gang-bangers, 244

Gangs, x, 171. *See also* African-American youth gangs; Organizations; Youth gangs
    anomie and, 89
    drug wars and, 81
    motorcycle, 230-240
    as organized crime, 211-213
    prison, 248-253
    in Reno, NV, 325-326
    supply sources of, 212
    urban, 253-254
    Vietnamese, 290-291
    youth, 239-240

Gangsters, in Roaring Twenties, 14-15

Ganja (Jamaican marijuana), 121

Gannon, Mariono (Father), 117

Gardiner, John, 229

Gas-Liquid Chromatography (GC) test, 349

Gaviria, Cesar, 112, 267

Gaviria, Pablo Emilio Escobar. *See* Escobar, Pablo

Gay, G. R., 52n

Gaziano, J. Michael, 49

GC. *See* Gas-Liquid Chromatography test

Generic drugs, 141

Genetic theory of dependence, 72-73

Genovese crime family, 411

Geography, drug abuse by, 79

Girodo, Michael, 316-317

Golden Crescent, 130-135

Golden Triangle, 124-129, 286
    hill tribes in, 126-127

Goldstein, Herman, 328

Gomez, Alvaro, 112

Gotti, John, 211

Government. *See also* Drug control
  corruption in foreign, 181-186
  drug industry and, ix
  drug problem and, 65-66
  pharmaceutical drug approval by, 143-145
  role of, 71
  U.S.-Peruvian cooperation, 116-117
Grand juries, immunity and, 416-417
Grass eaters, corrupt police as, 177
Grassley, Charles, 150
Great American Bank (Miami), money
  laundering and, 194
Great Britain. *See* Britain
Greco, Michele (The Pope), 226-227
Greco, Salvatore (The Senator), 227
Greece, ancient, 4
Greenhouse, L., 339n
Greenwald, Alan, 359-361
Groups, criminal behavior and, 90
Group treatment, 429-432
Guadalajara Cartel, 275
Guerrilla warfare, in Colombia, 280-282. *See
  also* Shining Path
Guillot, Jamie, 280-282
Guzma'n, Abimael, 285

Hair follicles, drug testing with, 351
Haiti, corruption in, 183
Halfway house, for treatment, 430
Haller, Mark, 229
Hallucinogens, 4-5, 51-56
  clandestine production of, 151-153
  detoxification and, 427
Hammurabi's Code, 4
Happy hour, 75
Harrison Narcotics Act, 9, 12-13, 15, 17, 42,
  298, 396, 398, 415, 425
Hashish, 5, 62, 148
  importation of, 102
Hash oil, 148
Hayes, Christopher, 328
Health, 70-71
  and drug abuse, 67-68
  drugs and, 4
  legalization and, 372-373
Heart attacks, moderate drinking and, 49
Heath, Robert, 61
Hell's Angels motorcycle gang, 230, 236
Hemp, Indian, 147
Hennessey, David, 221, 228
Herbicides, 394

Heroin, 9, 57-58. *See also* Golden Triangle
  "black tar," 58
  Designer China white, 59
  detoxification and, 427
  escalation of use, 21
  history of, 6
  Hong Kong and, 197-198
  international perspective on, 103
  Mafia and, 223
  marketing of, 100
  Mexican trade in, 106-107
  narcotic antagonists and, 428
  prices for Southeast Asian, 128
  prices for Southwest Asian, 131
  public health and, 373
  selling price of Mexican, 107
  trafficking organization of, 132
  user of, 423
Herrera, Jamie, 276-277
Herrera, Pancho, 272
Hess, Henner, 228
Hewlett-Packard Corporation, MSD test of,
  350
High, natural, 74-75
High Intensity Drug Trafficking Areas, 313
High schools
  drug abuse trends in, 79-80
  increased use in, 79
  legalization attitudes in, 367
Hill Street Crime Watch Committee (Boston,
  MA), 328
Hill tribes, in Golden Triangle, 126-127
Hippocrates, 4
Hiroppon, 46
Hispanic youth gangs, 240
HIV, 84. *See also* AIDS
  needle exchange programs and, 351-353
Hmong, 127
Hoffman, Albert, 20
Hoffman, Charles "Billy," 359-360
Holiday, James "Doc," 251-253
Holmes, Oliver Wendell, 77
Homer, 4
Honduras, corruption in, 183
Hong Kong, 125, 135
Hornik, R., 196n
Hospitals, emergency room admissions to, 70-
  71
Household Survey on Drug Abuse, 84-85
Housing projects, in Jamaica, 120-121
Hub House program, in Kansas City, 332
Huffing, 63
Huxley, Aldous, 76-77

Hydromorphone, 58
Hydroponic marijuana growth, 149

Ianni, Francis A. J., 228
Ice, 46
Illicit drugs. *See* Drug(s); Drug abuse; Drug
    trade; Pharmaceutical drugs
Immigrants and immigration
    Cuban, 287
    Chinese, 8I
Immigration and Naturalization Service, 297,
    311
Immunity, grand juries and, 416-417
Importation, of drugs, 102
Incas, 4
Inciardi, James A., 52n, 172
Income, of drug sellers, 101-102
India, 5, 125
Indian hemp, 147
Indians. *See* Native Americans
Inhalants, 63, 85
Inpatient treatment programs, 430
Institutional corruption, 172
    of police force, 180
Intelligence agencies, and cocaine trafficking,
    284. *See also* agencies by name
Interdiction, 302, 303, 394
    agencies for, 303
    functions of, 308
    spending on, 361-362
    support agencies for, 311-312
Internal Revenue Service (IRS), 312
International Conference at The Hague, 11, 12
International Conference on Opium (The
    Hague), 396
International conferences, 396
International cooperation, 398-399
International Narcotics Control Strategy
    Report, 94, 103
International Opium Convention, 396
International relations, legalization and, 372
Intravenous drug users, injection methods of,
    56-57
Iran, 130-131. *See also* Golden Crescent;
    Kurds
IRS. *See* Internal Revenue Service
IRS Money Laundering Task Force, 279
Issues, in drug control, 335-364
Italy
    Mafia crackdown in, 225-227
    organized crime in, 208
IV drug users. *See* Needle exchange programs

Jackson, George, 250
Jacobson v. United States, 341
Jail. *See* Prisons
Jamaica, 102
    drug trade and, 119-124
    narco-terrorism in, 277
    political history of, 120-121
    Rastafarians in, 121-122
Jamaican posses, x, 203, 245-248, 257
Japanese Yakuza, 258, 272, 289-290
Jenkins, P., 229
Jobs, lost productivity in, 84-85
Johnson, Ben, 26
Johnson, Bruce D., 99n
Johnson, Jan, 330
Johnston, Michael, 173
Joint Commission on Accreditation of
    Hospitals, 435
Jones, Marshall, 359, 361
Justice Department, 299, 311
"Just Say No," 26
Juveniles. *See* African-American youth
    gangs; Youth gangs

Kakuji, Inagawa, 290
Kansas City Police Department, 331-332
Kappeler, Victor, 173
Karen, the, 127
Katzenbach Commission, 298
Kefauver, Estes, 141
Kefauver-Harris Amendments, 144
Keller, Kirby, 238
Kennedy, Edward, 71
Ker, Frederick, 337
Kingpin strategy, of enforcement, 322, 397
Klatsky, Arthur, 49
Kleiman, Mark A. R., 369
Klein, Malcolm, 241-242
Knapp Commission, 176-178
Koren, Gideon, 351
Kozel, Nicholas J., 52n
Kraska, Peter, 173
Kuhn Sa, 286
Kurds, 134-135
Kyoshisha, the, 290

Laboratories, investigating, 320-321. *See*
    Clandestine drug laboratories
La Cosa Nostra. *See* Cosa Nostra, La
Lansky, Meyer, 109, 228, 230, 274, 287
Laos, 125, 127
    youth gangs from, 240. *See also* Bolivia

Latin America. *See also* Cartels; Colombia; Mexico; Peru
  drug trade and, ix, 4, 68, 80, 102, 103
  money laundering in, 197
  U.S. build-up in, 403-406
Laughing gas, 7
Laundering. *See* Money laundering
Law enforcement, 298-302, 394. *See also* Drug control
  agencies for, 297, 319
  cannabis eradication and, 320
  coordination organizations for, 312-319
  corruption in, 86-87
  federal drug control agencies, 319
  illicit laboratories and, 320-321
  kingpin strategy for, 322
  local strategies in, 327
  strategies for street-level, 321-324
  by U.S. and Bolivian agencies, 114
  weed and seed, 329-332
Law Enforcement Assistance Administration (LEAA), 314
Lawn, John, 301
Laws, 22-23. *See also* Drug control; Law enforcement; laws by name
  drug control, 296-298
  in early twentieth century, 10-13
  enforcement of, x
  hypocrisy of, 371-372
  money laundering and, 195
  and organized crime, 206
LEAA. *See* Law Enforcement Assistance Administration
Leaders, of drug gangs, 212
Learned behavior
  criminal behavior as, 90
  drug abuse as, 73
Legal drugs. *See* Pharmaceutical drugs
Legalization, 362, 399. *See also* Policy
  addicts and, 377
  in Alaska, 380, 384-386
  arguments against, 374-380
  arguments for, 368-374
  Clinton on, 406-407
  cost of, 378-380
  crime rate and, 372, 376-377
  drug law hypocrisy and, 371-372
  drug market restriction through, 371
  enforcement futility and, 371
  international relations and, 372
  issue of, 365-391
  in Netherlands, 381-383
  organized crime and, 377-378

personal freedoms and, 372, 378
  proposed solution and, 387-389
  public health and, 372-373
  public opinion on, 366-368
  revenues and, 377
  Schmoke, Kurt, and, 369, 370, 379
  tax revenue from, 371
Legislation, for pharmaceutical drugs, 141-142
Lehder, Carlos, 184, 261, 278
Lemonada, Samuel Posada Rios, 279-280
Leun Kung Lok, 289
LEVITICUS, 314
Liberation Cato Institute, 378
Librium, 76
Liebreich, Oscar, 8
Liggio, Luciano, 227
Local option, drug control as, 397
Los Angeles, California, youth street gangs in, 243-245
  drug gang wars in, 81
  Project DARE in, 437-443
  youth gangs in, 239
Los Diamantes. *See* Diamentes, Los
Los Grandes Mafiosos, 261
Lotus eating, 4
LSD (lysergic acid diethylamide), 20, 53
  clandestine production of, 152
  domestic production of, 139
  history of, 22
  marketing of, 100
  Luciano, Charles (Lucky), 221, 411
  Lung cancer, cigarette smoking and, 39, 41

M-19. *See* 19th of April Movement
Macheca, Joseph, 221
MacNamera, Joseph, 366
Madden, Owney, 228
Made men, in Mafia, 210, 221
Mafia, x, 203, 208, 210-211, 411. *See also* Cosa Nostra, La
  alien conspiracy theory and, 209, 210
  controversies over, 227, 228
  domestic drug trafficking and, 219-230
  and drugs, 223, 229-230
  family locations in U.S., 223
  Florida Cuban, 109
  history of, 220-222
  Pizza Connection and, 224-225
  studies of, 228
  wars among, 225-226
Magellan, 5
Magentas, in Jamaica, 246

Magliocco, Joe, 221
MAGLOCLEN, 314
Maintenance, 428-429
Mandatory minimum sentencing, 342-343
Manley, Michael, 120, 121, 248
Manning, Peter K., 86-87
Manufacturing, laws and, 297
Maranzano, Salvatore, 221
Mariani, Angelo, 9
Mariel boatlift, 287, 288
Marielitos, 287, 288
    Marijuana, 17, 60-61, 62. *See also*
        Cannabis; Hashish
    abuse of, 77
    business considerations in U.S. growth of,
        146-149
    citations for carrying, 322
    from Colombia, 108, 111
    controversy over, 62
    declining use of, 82
    decriminalization of, 23-24
    detoxification and, 427
    domestic production of, 139, 145-149
    eradication of, 320
    harmful effects of, 61
    health and, 67-68
    history of, 11
    Jamaican trade in, 119
    legalization in Alaska, 380, 384-386
    marketing of, 100
    Mexican trade in, 103-106
    prices of, 112, 147
    types of domestic, 147-148
    in United States, 8
Marijuana Interdiction Program, study of,
    369
Marijuana Tax Act, 17
Marine Branch, of Customs Service, 309
Marketing, of illicit drugs, 100
Markets, discreet and nondiscreet, 321, 323-
    324
Marley, Bob, 122
Marriott, M., 352n
Marseilles, France, French Connection and,
    106
Mass selective detector (MSD) test, 350
Mass Spectrometry (MS) test, 349
Materialism, anomie and, 89
Matta Ballesteros, Juan Ramon, 183
Matthews, Frank, 230
Maxi-Processo, 225
McCoy, Alfred, 127
McFadden, Robert, 266n

McKay, Henry, 88
MDMA (Ecstacy), 55-56, 63
Meat eaters, corrupt police as, 177
Medellin Cartel, 109-110, 115, 183, 184, 208,
    259
    legacy of, 260-262
    M-19 and, 281-282
    rise of, 262-264
Medicaid, 143
Medically-used drugs, 140-145
Medical model
    of addiction, 425
    of drug control, 399
    legalization and, 369
Medical profession, and drug offenses, 158-
    159
Medicare, 143
Medicare Catastrophic Coverage Act, 141
Medication Price Control Act, 142
Medicines, drugs and, 4, 75. *See also* Phar-
    maceutical drugs
Meese, Edwin, 113
Meltzer, Happy, 230
Merchandising, of drugs, 98, 99
Merton, Robert, 88-89
Mescaline, 55
Metabolism, altering, 76
Methadone, 59, 425
    maintenance with, 428-429
Methamphetamine, 21, 26, 45
    clandestine production of, 153
    domestic production of, 139
Methaqualone, 51. *See also* Quaalude®
Mexican-American inmates, Texas Syndicate
    and, 251. *See also* Mexican Mafia
Mexican Federal Judicial Police (MFJP), 108
Mexican Mafia, 249, 275
Mexico, 102
    Camarena murder in, 108
    corruption in, 182-183
    drug enforcement in, 105, 107-108
    drugs and, 8, 103-108, 275-277
    heroin trade in, 106-107
    marijuana and, 17, 103-105
    Operation Alliance and, 312
    opium poppy and marijuana cultivation
        areas, 106
Meza, Garcia Luis, 113
Mezzogiorno, Mafia and, 220
Miami, FL
    money laundering and, 191, 194
    police corruption in, 172
"Mickey Finn," 8

Middle East. *See* Golden Crescent
Midwestern Prevention Project, 437
Military
    drug interdiction by, 310
    drug use in, 398
    expanding role of, 359-362
    role of, 398
Mill, John Stuart, 71
Miller, N., 54n
Mirkin, Gabe, 356
Misoprostol, 144-145
Mitsuru, Toyama, 290
MOCIC, 314
Mollen, Milton, 177
Mollen Commission, 177-178
Mona Passage trafficking route, 111
Money laundering, 186-199
    by Cali Cartel, 273
    cocaine in Panama and, 197
    concealment of, 190
    defined, 187
    detecting, 198-199
    fighting, 194-195
    financial havens for, 195-197
    heroin in Hong Kong and, 197-198
    Mafia and, 224
    specialists in, 189
    techniques of, 190-194
Money Laundering Control Act, 195
Money Laundering Prosecution Improvement
  Act, 195
Montalbano, W. D., 227n
Mooching, police corruption and, 174
Moods, altering, 76
Moore, Mark, 322, 368
Morals, legalization and, 376
Moran, Bugs, 228
More, H.W., 175, 179
Morning glory seeds, 5
Morphine, 7
    in Civil War, 8
    cure for addiction, 8
    medicinal use of, 75
    regulation of, 11
Moslems, 5
Motorcycle gangs, 211, 230-240. *See also*
  Gangs; Organizations
    Aryan Brotherhood and, 250
    Bandidos, 239
    Hell's Angels, 236
    organizational structure of, 234-235
    Outlaws, 237
    Pagans, 237-238
MS. *See* Mass Spectrometry test

MSD. *See* Mass selective detector test
Multiagency approach, 329
Munday, Mickie, 122-124
Murphy, Patrick, 366
Mushrooms, 4-5, 55
Musto, David, 3, 78-79
Myanmar, 125
    narco-terrorism in, 277
    organized crime in, 208
    Shan United Army in, 286-287

NA. *See* Narcotics Anonymous
Nalorphine (Nalline), 428
Naloxone (Narcan), 428
Narco-democracy, 271
Narco-terrorism, 262, 277-287
    Burmese Communist Party and, 286
    Colombia/Panama/Cuba connection and,
      277-282
    Nicaragua and, 283-284
    Shan United Army (SUA), 286-287
    Shining Path and, 285-286
Narcotic Addict Rehabilitation Act, 23
Narcotic antagonists, 428
Narcotics, 56-59. *See also* Drug(s); Drug
  abuse; Laws
    agent, 298
    restrictions on, 11
Narcotics Anonymous (NA), 423, 431-432
Narcotics Control Act, 20, 298
Narcotics Unit, 298
National Association for Parental Addiction
  Research and Education, 82
National Basketball Association (NBA), 357-
  358
National Collegiate Athletic Association
  (NCAA), 356, 357
National Drug Control Strategy, 401-402,
  404-405, 421
    of Bennett, 436
National Drug Policy Board (NDPB), 80, 313
National Football League (NFL), 358
National Guard, 361
National Household Survey of Drug Abuse,
  422
National Institute of Drug Abuse (NIDA), 56
National Institute of Justice (NIJ), 346
National Institute on Alcohol Abuse and
  Alcoholism, 422
National Institutes of Health, 143
National Narcotics Border Interdiction Sys-
  tem (NNBIS), 314
National Prohibition Act, 298
National Prohibition Party, 14

National security, drug abuse and, 68
National Security Council, and cocaine
    trafficking, 284
Native Americans, 4-5
    peyote and, 10, 76
NBA. *See* National Basketball Association
NCAA. *See* National Collegiate Athletic
    Association
NDPB. *See* National Drug Policy Board
Needle exchange programs, 351-353
Neighborhoods, revitalizing, 331. *See also*
    Communities
Neurotransmitters, 32
    cocaine and, 44
New Drug Application, 143-144
New York City
    needle exchanges in, 352
    police corruption in, 176-178
    Project SPECDA in, 443-444
    treatment programs in, 430, 431
NFL. *See* National Football League
Nicaragua, 283-284
Nicot, Jacques, 5
Nicot, Jean, 39
Nicotine, smoking and, 39-42
NIDA. *See* National Institute of Drug Abuse
NIDA-5, drug testing and, 348
19th of April Movement (M-19), 280, 281-
    282
Nitrous oxide, 7
Nixon, Richard, methadone clinics and, 425
NNBIS. *See* National Narcotics Border Inter-
    diction System
Noble Experiment, Prohibition as, 14
Nondiscreet drug markets, 321, 323-324
Noriega, Manuel Antonio, 183, 185-186, 278,
    283
Norms, anomie and, 88-89
North, Oliver, 185
North Africa, 4
North America, 4-5
Nuestra Familia, 249, 250
Nyswander, Marie, 425

OCDETF. *See* Organized Crime Drug
    Enforcement Task Force
Ochoa, Fabio, 261, 262, 281
Ochoa, Jorge, 183, 184, 261
    Escobar cooperation with, 268
ODALE. *See* Office for Drug Abuse and Law
    Enforcement
Odyssey, The, 4

Office for Drug Abuse and Law Enforcement
    (ODALE), 299
Office of National Drug Control Policy
    (ONDCP), 94, 313, 401-402, 406
    politics and, 407-408
Office of National Narcotic Intelligence
    (ONNI), 299
Ohlin, Lloyd, 89-90
Ololiuqui, 5
Olympic games, steroids and, 356
Omnibus Crime Control and Safe Streets Act,
    206, 344
ONDCP. *See* Office of National Drug Control
    Policy
ONNI. *See* Office of National Narcotic
    Intelligence
Open-air trade, 321
Operation Alliance, 312
Operation Beacon, 122-124
Operation Iron Eagle, 151
"Operation Just Cause," 185
Operation Polar Cap, 188
Operation Rum Punch, 81
Operations, cash-laundering, 188-189
Operation Snowcap, 116
Operation Stop Prop, 113
Operation Weed and Seed, 329-332
Opium, 4, 103. *See also* Golden Crescent;
    Golden Triangle; Heroin
    and Chinese immigrants, 8
    derivatives of, 57-58
    in 1800s, 6-7
    global production of, 129
    in Greece, ancient, 4
    regulation of, 11-12
    in Sumeria, 4
Opium poppy. *See* Opium; Poppy
Opium wars, 6
Opportunity theory, 89-90
Organizations, domestic drug trafficking, 219-
    256. *See also* Gangs; Mafia; Narco-terror-
    ism; countries by name
    African-American youth gangs, 243-245
    alien conspiracy theory of, 209-210
    American, 228
    ancillary trafficking organizations, 253-
        254
    Asian, 288-291
    Colombian, 258-274
    crime family vs. motorcycle gangs, 232
    defined, 206-209
    domestic drug trafficking organizations,
        219-256

Droznek/Rosa case, 214-216
  drug policy and, 394
  drug trade and, 203-217
  drug trafficking by, 204-205
  Jamaican posses, 245-248
  legalization and, 369, 377-378
  Mafia, 203, 208, 210-211, 219-230, 232
  motorcycle gangs, 211, 230-240
  prison gangs, 248-253
  research on, 228-229
Organized crime. *See* Organizations
Organized Crime Drug Enforcement Task
  Force (OCDETF), 123, 314-316
Organized gangs. *See* Gangs; Organizations
Orphan Drug Act, 141, 142
Ortega, Daniel, 283
Outlaw motorcycle gangs, 230-240. *See also*
  Gangs
  organizational structure of, 234-235
Outlaws motorcycle gang, 237
Outpatient treatment programs, 430

Pagans motorcycle gang, 154, 237-238
Pakistan, 130, 131-133. *See also* Golden
  Crescent
Palermo. *See* Mafia; Sicilian Mafia
Panama. *See also* Latin America
  Colombia, Cuba, and, 277-282
  corruption in, 183, 185-186
  government involvement in narcotics and,
    108
"Panama Red" marijuana, 100
Paper trail, money laundering and, 195
Paraguay, drug trafficking in, 118
Parke-Davis, 9
Passive smoke inhalation, 40
Pathological materialism, 89
Patient, professional, 156-157
Pattern of racketeering, 411
Patterson, P. J., 119
Paul, Jean-Claude, 183
Pavon Reyes, Jorge Armando, 182, 276
Payoffs, in New York City, 177
PCP (phencyclidine), 21, 53-54
  clandestine production of, 152
  domestic production of, 139
  history of, 26
  physical and psychological damage of, 54
Pemberton, John Styth, 9
Penalties, for drug violations, 399
Pennsylvania Crime Commission, 178-179
  Mafia and, 229

Pentagon, drug policy and, 406
Pentazocine (Talwin), 428
PEPES (People Persecuted by Pablo Escobar),
  266
Perjury, police corruption and, 175
Persia, 5
Personal freedoms, legalization and, 372, 378
Personality, addictive, 73
Peru, 102, 103, 259
  drug trade in, 115-117
  Shining Path in, 115, 116, 117, 285-286
Peterson, Virgil, 229
Peyote, 4, 10, 55
Pharmaceutical drugs. *See also* Drugs;
  Medically-used drugs; Medical model
  diversion of, 139, 155-163
  federal approval of, 143-145
  industry for, 140-145
  substitution of, 160
  theft of, 159
Philadelphia, PA, police corruption in, 178-
  179
Philip Morris, on cigarette smoking as addic-
  tion, 40
Phoenix House, 430, 431
Physical dependence, 33, 35
Physical reactions, 70-71
Physicians. *See* Doctors
Pincomb, Ronald A., 248n
Pindling, Lynden, 183, 184
Pizza Connection, 224-225
POBOBs, 230, 231
Poe, Edgar Allen, 76
Police
  community cooperation with, 324-329
  problem-oriented policing (POP) and,
    328-329
  undercover, 316-317, 322-323
  youth gangs and, 241
Police corruption, 86-87, 171-181
  fighting, 181
  institutional, 180
  in New York City, 176-178
  in Philadelphia, 178-179
  preconditions for, 172-173
  socialization and, 173
  types of, 173-175
Policy, 71, 393-420. *See also* Drug control;
  federal listings
  critics of, 394
  development of, 398-401
  eradication as, 394
  foreign intiatives as, 394

interdiction as, 394
    law enforcement as, 394
    local option and, 397
    military role in, 398
    private sector and, 397-398
    reactive, 395
    responsibility for, 395-396
    treatment as, 394
Politics, police corruption and, 172. *See also*
    individual countries
Politics of Heroin in Southeast Asia, The, 127
Polls, on legalization, 366-367. *See also*
    Public opinion
Poly-drug use, 20, 33, 76
Pomeroy, Wesley C., 366
POP. *See* Problem-oriented policing
Poppy, 4, 103, 106. *See also* Morphine;
    Opium
        in Golden Triangle, 125
        opium, 57
Poppy straw, 133-134
Pornography, in Amsterdam, 382
Posse Comitatus Act, 114
Posses. *See* Jamaican posses
Possession, laws and, 297
Post, M., 264n
Potter, G., 229
Poverty, 87
Precursor chemicals, 155
Predatory crime, 168-171
Preemployment drug screening, 348
Prejudice, police corruption and, 175
Prescription Drug Cost Containment Act, 142
Prescription drugs, control chronology, 141.
    See also Pharmaceutical drugs
President's Commission on Organized Crime
    (PCOC), 182, 395
        organized crime defined by, 207
Prettyman Commission, 22
Prevention, 400, 436-437
    treatment and, 421-446
Prices. *See also* Costs
    of cocaine, 114
    of drugs, 95-97
    of marijuana, 112, 147
    of pharmaceutical drugs, 140-143
    for Southeast Asian heroin, 128
Priestly, Joseph, 7
Prison gangs, 248-253
Prisons, for narcotic addicts, 425
Privacy, electronic surveillance and, 345
Problem-oriented policing (POP), 328-329
Production, control of, 296
Productivity, loss of, 84-85

Profaci, Joe, 221
Professional patient, 156
Professional sports, drug control in, 357-358
Profit margin
    on crack, 249
    in drug trade, 101-102
Prohibition(s), 296-297. *See also* Laws
    efforts toward, 398, 399
    history of, 408-410
    as policy, 400
Prohibition era, 13-15, 408, 425
    Mafia and, 221
Project DARE. *See* Drug Abuse Resistance
    Education program,
Project SPECDA, 443-444
Protectors, 207
Psilocybin mushrooms, 4-5, 55
Psychedelic drugs, 21
Psychoactive drugs, 66
Psychological dependence, 34, 35
Psychological treatment approach, 429
Public health, legalization and, 372-373
Public opinion, on legalization, 375
Public policy. *See* Law enforcement; Laws;
    Policy
Puerto Rico, 142
Pure Food and Drug Act (1906), 10, 141

Quaalude®, 21, 51

Racism, of biker gangers, 231-233. *See also*
    Motorcycle gangs
Racketeer-Influenced and Corrupt Organiza-
    tions Act (RICO), 23, 206, 302, 411, 412
Racketeering, pattern of, 411. *See also* Racke-
    teer-Influenced and Corrupt Organizations
    Act (RICO)
Raleigh, Walter, 5
Rangel, Charles, 71, 373
Ras Tafari, 121
Rastafarians, 121-122
    marijuana use by, 76
Ravin v. State, 384-385
Reagan, Nancy, 26
Reagan, Ronald
    drug control policy of, 394, 402-406
    Sandinistas and, 283-284
Reasonable suspicion, 340
Reatown Boys, in Jamaica, 246
Reckmeyer, Christopher, 354
Recreational drugs, 3, 4
    future of, 27
    restriction of, 371
Recriminalization, of marijuana, 380, 386

Red light district, in Amsterdam, 382
Redlinger, Lawrence John, 86-87
"Red Lion" heroin, 100
Reform, arguments for, 373. *See also*
  Legalization
Reggae, ganja and, 122
Regional Information Sharing System (RISS),
  313-314
Regulation, 10, 398. *See also* Drug control;
  Law enforcement; Policy
    as policy, 400
Rehabilitation, 388. *See also* Treatment
Rehnquist, William H., 340
Relapse, 434-435
Religion, and drug use, 75-76
Reno, NV, drug control in, 325-326
Responsibility, drug control and, 335, 395-396
Restrepo, 279
Retail sales, control of, 296
Reuter, Peter, 105, 229
    Pentagon study by, 361-362
    SOAR model and, 310-311
Revenues, legalization and, 377
Reverse drug sting, 324, 339-341
Revolutionary Armed Forces of Colombia
  (FARC), 280
RIA. *See* Roche-Radioimmunoassay technolo-
  gy
RICO. *See* Racketeer-Influenced and Corrupt
  Organizations Act
RISS. *See* Regional Information Sharing Sys-
  tem
RMIN, 314
Roache, Francis (Mickey), 328
Roaring Twenties, 14-15
Robinson, Tom, 325-326
Roca Suarez, Renato, 113
Roche-Radioimmunoassay (RIA) technology,
  349
ROCIC, 314
Rodriguez-Gacha, Jose Gonzalo, 261, 262
Rodriguez Orejuela, Gilberto, 266, 271
Rogers, Don, 26, 355
Roosevelt, Theodore, 11
Roques, Wayne J., 379n
Rosen, Nig, 230
Roth, Jeffrey, 169
Rothstein, Arnold, 228, 230
Rural America, drugs in, 150-151

Salamone, Salvatore, 224
Salerno, Ralph, 366
Sales, control of, 296

Salvo, Ignazio, 227
Sanabria, Harry, 99n
Sanchez-Carranza organization, 275
Sandinistas, drug trafficking and, 283-284
Santacruz Londono, Jose, 271-272
Satan Brothers, 151
"Satan's Choice" motorcycle gang, 237. *See
  also* Motorcycle gangs
Saunders, Norman, 184
Scams, and pharmaceutical drugs, 156-157
Schade, Charles, 52n
Schmoke, Kurt, 366, 369, 370
    legalization and, 379
Schober, Susan, 52n
School Crime Survey, 69
Schools, drugs and, 69. *See also* High schools
Schultz, Dutch, 228
Schultz, George, 80, 366
Screening, for drugs, 348, 349
Seaga, Edward, 120, 121
Seal, Alder Barriman (Barry), 284, 307-308,
  309n
"Search and destroy" missions, 146
Sedatives, 8
Seeding, 331
Segal, Bernard, 385-386
Selassie, Haile, 121
Select Committee on Narcotics Abuse and
  Control, 94
Self-esteem, 87
Self-treatment, 427
Sendero Luminoso. *See* Shining Path
Senior citizens, 142
Sentencing, mandatory minimum, 342-343
Serpico, Frank, 176
Serturner, F. W. A., 7
Sex, and drug industry, 382-383
Shabu, 46
Shah of Iran, 130
Shakedown, police corruption and, 174
Shanghai Opium Convention, 10, 11
Shannon, Elaine, 108, 272
Shan United Army (SUA), 208, 286-287
Shaw, Clifford, 88
Sherman, Lawrence, 180
Shining Path, 115, 116, 117, 285-286
Shipping, of Colombian marijuana, 111
Shower Posse
    in Jamaica, 121, 246
Sicilian Mafia, 208, 220. *See also* Mafia;
  Organizations
Side effects, 33
Siegel, Bugsy, 228

Single Convention on Narcotics Drugs, 22
Sinsemilla, 60, 148
Small towns, drug dealing in, 150-151
SMART Move, 437
Smith, Dwight, Jr., 228
Smoking, 39-42
    quitting, 41-42
    Surgeon General's report on, 38
Smuggling
    airborne detection of, 302, 304-305
    case study of, 307-308, 359-361
    control of, 296
    by Devoe Airlines, 304-305
    from Mexico, 104-105
    Operation Alliance and, 312
Smurfing, money laundering and, 191-192
SOAR computer model, 310-311
Social disorganization theory, 87
Social effects, x
    of drug abuse, 80-85
    of drug trafficking, 67
    HIV and, 84
    lost productivity, 84-85
    violence as, 80-81
Socialization, of police, 173
Social reintegration, 434-435
Social support, for organized crime, 208
Society, crime-related attitudes of, 181
Socioeconomic status, 87
Sokolow, Andrew, 340
Sollenberg, Jeffrey, 360
Source countries, aid to, 358-359
South America, 4. See also Bolivia; Cartels;
    Latin America; Peru
    and drug distribution, 102
    drug industry in, ix, 103
    trafficking trends in, 117-118
Southeast Asia, drug trade and, 68, 125-129
Southwest Asia
    drug trade in, 130-135
    heroin prices and, 131
Spadafore brothers, 161-163
Spangler Posse, in Jamaica, 246. See also
    Jamaican posses
SPECDA. See Project SPECDA
Special Agents, of FBI, 301
Specialized support, 207
Speed, 45
Sports
    amateur, 356-357
    drug control and, 355-358
    professional, 357-358
Steerers, 98, 101

Stein, Benjamin, 72-73
Steroids
    and athletes, 355-356
    defined, 356
Stimulants, 35-56
    amphetamines, 45-45
    caffeine, 37-38
    cocaine, 42-44
    nicotine, 38-42
    usage trends and, 79
Sting operations. See also Drug sting
    money laundering detection by, 198
    reverse, 324
Stockman, David, 402
Stoddard, Ellwin, 174
Stol, W. A., 20
Strategy, national, 400, 401-402. See also
    Drug control; Policy
Street gangs, 211. See also African-American
    youth gangs; Gangs; Organizations
    Asian, 289
Street-level enforcement, 321-324
Stroessner (General), 118
SUA. See Shan United Army
Suarez Gomez, Roberto, Sr. and Jr., 113
Subcultures, delinquent, 89-90
Substance abuse, 35
Substitute therapy, 428
Sumeria, 4
Sun Yee On, 289
Supply reduction, as policy, 400, 401
Surgeon General. See also Elders, Joycelyn
    addictive nature of smoking and, 40
    report on smoking, 38
Surinam, corruption in, 184
Surveillance, electronic. See Electronic sur-
    veillance
Surveys, on drug abuse, 77-78
Sutherland, Edwin, 90
Switzerland, needle exchange program in,
    353
Synanon, 430
Synthesis labs, 152
Syva-Enzyme Multiplied Immunoassay Tech-
    nique (EMIT), 349

Tafari, Ras. See Ras Tafari
Tagamet®, 141
Taiwan, 289
Talwin, 428
Task force
    in Boston, MA, 328
    law enforcement, 318

Taxation, 398, 400
    evasion of, 415
Tax havens, for money laundering, 195-197
Tax revenue, from legalized drugs, 371
TCs. *See* Therapeutic Communities
Technology. *See* Electronic surveillance
Temperance movements, 13-14, 50
Tennis, drug control in, 357
Terrorism. *See* Narco-terrorism
Testing, 400
Testosterone, 355
Texas Syndicate, 249, 251
Thailand, opium trade in, 125, 127-129
Thalidomide, 141, 144
THC content, of marijuana, 60, 62, 149, 385
Theft, 85
    of pharmaceutical drugs, 159
    police corruption and, 175
Theories, of drug abuse and crime, 86-90
Theories of Drug Abuse, 72
Therapeutic Communities (TCs), 429-431
Thompson, Hunter, 230
Thrasher, Frederick, 241
Tientsin Treaty (1858), 6-7
Tivoli Gardens housing project, in Jamaica,
    120-121
Tobacco, 5. *See also* Smoking
    advertising of, 41
    as carcinogen, 40-41
    nicotine and, 38
Tolerance, 34, 35
Tongs, 257-258, 289
Tonics, opium in, 7
Tonry, Michael, 99n
TOPS. *See* Treatment Outcome Prospective
    Study
Torres, Jorge, 359, 361
Torrijos, Omar, 185
Toscanino, Francisco, 337
Trafficante, Santo, Jr., 109, 287
Trafficking, iv. *See also* Drug trade
    drug consumerism and, 85
Tranquilizers, 20
Transactional immunity, 416-417
Transportation Department, drug testing by,
    348
Treasury Bureau, of Alcohol, Tobacco, and
    Firearms, 81
Treasury Department, 298
    enforcement by, 12
Treatment, iii, 394, 400, 401. *See also* Drug
    Abuse Resistance Education (DARE)
    program; Project SPECDA

    cost of, 436
    detoxification, 426-427
    effectiveness of, 433-434
    group, 429-432
    halfway house, 430
    inpatient programs, 430
    maintenance (substitute therapy), 428-429
    narcotic antagonists, 428
    Narcotics Anonymous (NA) and, 431-432
    outpatient programs, 430
    and prevention, 421-446
    problems with, 435
    programs of, 424, 425-429
    psychological approach to, 429
    self-, 427
    social reintegration and, 434-435
    users and, 423
Treatment Outcome Prospective Study
    (TOPS), 169, 434
Trebach, Arnold S., 62n, 366, 381n
Trends, in drug abuse, 79-80
Triads, 257-258, 289
Trimboli, Joseph, 178
Trip, 53
Turf wars, in agency coordination, 318-319
Turkey, 133-134
    Kurds and, 134-135
Turks Island, corruption in, 184
Twelve-step program, 432. *See also* Narcotics
    Anonymous (NA)
21st Amendment, 14
Two-parent household, 69

Undercover operations, money laundering
    detection by, 198
Undercover police, 316-317, 322
    operations of, 322-323
Unemployment, 69
Uniform Narcotic Drug Act, 15
Uniform State Narcotics Law, 17
United Bamboo Gang, 289
United Nations, Single Convention on
    Narcotics Drugs, 22. *See also* International
    conferences
United States
    Civil War and drugs in, 7-8
    clandestine laboratories in, 151-154
    demand for drugs in, 335-336
    drug control involvement by, 16-17
    drug control milestones in, 18-19
    drug production in, 139-165
    Jamaican posses in, 246
    marijuana production in, 145-149

money laundering and, 188
opium and morphine in, 7
pharmaceutical drug diversion in, 139,
    155-163
Southeast Asian heroin politics and, 127
United States Marshals Service, 312, 417
United States Olympic Committee (USOC),
    356-357
United States v. Caplin and Drysdale, 353-354
United States v. Doremus, 396
United States v. Monsanto, 353-354
United States v. Sokolow, 340
Untouchables, in Jamaica, 246
Uppers, 20, 36
Urban drug gangs, 253-254. *See also* Gangs
Urban environment, crime and, 88
Urinalysis, for drug use, 348-349
Uruguay, drug trafficking in, 118
Use, laws and, 297
Users. *See* Drug users
USOC. *See* United States Olympic Committee

Valium, 76
Van Atta, D., 282
Venezuela, 102
Vertical integration, in drug gangs, 211
Vice, and victimless crime, 86-87
Victimless crime, 86-87
    drug abuse and, 87
Vietnam, 127
    youth gangs from, 240, 290-291
Vietnam War, 21
    drug testing during, 346-347
Vin Mariani, 9
Violence, ix, 80-81, 169-171
    causes of, 170
    by Jamaican posses, 247
    narco-terrorism and, 277-287
    weapons and, 85
    youth gangs and, 240
Voigt, Anne, 439
Volstead Act, 368
von Raab, William, 341
Voy, Robert, 356

Wah Ching, 289
War on drugs, iii
WCTU. *See* Women's Christian Temperance
    Union

Weapons, 85
Webb v. U.S., 396
Weed and seed, 329-332
Weinberger, Casper, 114
Wells, Nei Marie, 251-252
White House Conference for a Drug Free
    America (WHCDFA), 65
White supremacists, 231
Whittier Block Watch, Denver, CO, 330
Wickersham Commission, 172
Williams, Terry, 99n
Wilson, James Q., 99n
Windward Passage trafficking route, 111
Wine, 4
Wire taps, money laundering detection by,
    198
Wire transfers, for money laundering, 194
Wise guys, in Mafia, 210
Withdrawal, 34, 35
Witness security program, 417-418
WITSEC. *See* Federal Witness Security
    Program
Wo Hop To, 289
Women's Christian Temperance Union
    (WCTU), 14
Wo On Lok, 289
Workplace, drug testing in, 347-348
World War II, drug control after, 20
Wright, Hamilton, 12
WSIN, 314

Yablonsky, Lewis, 242
Yakuza. *See* Japanese Yakuza
Yoshio, Kodamo, 290
Young, Francis L., 62
Youth gangs, 203, 239-240. *See also* African-
    American youth gangs; Gangs
        defining, 241-242
        formation of, 242-243
        special problems with, 240-41
Yucatan Channel trafficking route, 111

Zantac®, 142
Zavala Avelar, Alfredo, 182
Zero tolerance, 341-342, 399-401, 400
Zones of transition, 88
Zwillman, Longie, 228